INTERNATIONAL ECONOMIC LAW IN THE 21ST CENTURY

The state-centred 'Westphalian model' of international law has failed to protect human rights and other international public goods effectively. Most international trade, financial and environmental agreements do not even refer to human rights, consumer welfare, democratic citizen participation and transnational rule of law for the benefit of citizens. This book argues that these 'multilevel governance failures' are largely due to inadequate regulation of the 'collective action problems' in the supply of international public goods, such as inadequate legal, judicial and democratic accountability of governments vis-à-vis citizens. Rather than treating citizens as mere objects of intergovernmental economic and environmental regulation and leaving multilevel governance of international public goods to discretionary 'foreign policy', human rights and constitutional democracy call for 'civilizing' and 'constitutionalizing' international economic and environmental cooperation by stronger legal and judicial protection of citizens and their constitutional rights in international economic law.

Moreover intergovernmental regulation of transnational cooperation among citizens must be justified by 'principles of justice' and 'multilevel constitutional restraints' protecting rights of citizens and their 'public reason'. The reality of 'constitutional pluralism' requires respecting legitimately diverse conceptions of human rights and democratic constitutionalism. The obvious failures in the governance of interrelated trading, financial and environmental systems must be restrained by cosmopolitan, constitutional conceptions of international law protecting the transnational rule of law and participatory democracy for the benefit of citizens.

International Economic Law in the 21st Century

Constitutional Pluralism and Multilevel Governance of Interdependent Public Goods

Ernst-Ulrich Petersmann

·HART·
PUBLISHING
OXFORD AND PORTLAND, OREGON
2012

Published in the United Kingdom by Hart Publishing Ltd
16C Worcester Place, Oxford, OX1 2JW
Telephone: +44 (0)1865 517530
Fax: +44 (0)1865 510710
E-mail: mail@hartpub.co.uk
Website: http://www.hartpub.co.uk

Published in North America (US and Canada) by
Hart Publishing
c/o International Specialized Book Services
920 NE 58th Avenue, Suite 300
Portland, OR 97213-3786
USA
Tel: +1 503 287 3093 or toll-free: (1) 800 944 6190
Fax: +1 503 280 8832
E-mail: orders@isbs.com
Website: http://www.isbs.com

British Library Cataloguing in Publication Data
Data Available

ISBN: 978-1-84946-063-7

Typeset by Hope Services, Abingdon
Printed and bound in Great Britain by
MPG Books, Cornwall

This book is dedicated in gratitude to my wonderful spouse Myszka, our eight children and especially to our youngest son, Leonard-Justin, in admiration of their search for justice in discovering and walking our paths of life.

Table of Contents

Abbreviations

ACHR	American Convention on Human Rights
ACP	African, Caribbean and Pacific Developing Countries
ACTA	Anti-Counterfeiting Trade Agreement 2011
AJIL	American Journal of International Law
ASIL	American Society of International Law
BATNA	Best alternative to a negotiated agreement
BRICS	Brazil, Russia, India, China and South Africa
BIS	Bank for International Settlements
BISD	Basic Instruments and Selected Documents of GATT 1947
BIT	Bilateral Investment Treaty
CBD	Convention on Biodiversity
CEDAW	Convention on the Elimination of All Forms of Discrimination Against Women
CSR	Corporate Social Responsibility
DDR	Doha Development Round
DSB	Dispute Settlement Body of the WTO
DSU	Dispute Settlement Understanding of the WTO
EC	European Community
ECB	European Central Bank
ECHR	European Convention on Human Rights and Fundamental Freedoms
ECJ	European Court of Justice
ECR	EU Court of Justice Reports
ECT	Energy Charter Treaty
ECtHR	European Court of Human Rights
EEA	European Economic Area
EEC	European Economic Community
EFTA	European Free Trade Area
EJIL	European Journal of International Law
EU	European Union (Treaty)
EUI	European University Institute
FAO	Food and Agriculture Organization
FET	Fair and Equitable Treatment
FSB	Financial Stability Board
FTA	Free Trade Area Agreements
GAL	Global Administrative Law
GATT	General Agreement on Tariffs and Trade 1947
GATS	General Agreement on Trade in Services
GDP	Gross Domestic Product
GMOs	Genetically Modified Organisms
GSP	Generalized System of Tariff Preferences

G20	Group of 19 Countries (G7 plus 12 additional states) plus the EU
HRL	Human rights law
IBRD	International Bank for Reconstruction and Development 1944
ICANN	Internet Corporation for Assigned Names and Numbers
ICAO	International Civil Aviation Organization
ICAT	International Convention Against Torture 1984
ICERD	International Convention on the Elimination of All Forms of Racial Discrimination
ICC	International Chamber of Commerce
ICCPR	International Covenant on Civil and Political Rights
ICESCR	International Covenant on Economic, Social and Cultural Rights
ICJ	International Court of Justice
ICN	International Competition Network
ICRC	International Convention on the Rights of the Child 1989
ICSID	International Centre for the Settlement of Investment Disputes 1965
IDA	International Development Association 1960
IEL	International Economic Law
IFC	International Finance Corporation 1956
ILM	International Legal Materials
ILO	International Labour Organization
IMF	International Monetary Fund
ISO	International Organization for Standardization
ITLOS	International Tribunal for the Law of the Sea
ITO	International Trade Organization
JIEL	Journal of International Economic Law
LDCs	Less-developed Countries
LLDCs	Least-developed Countries
MEAs	Multilateral Environmental Agreements
MERCOSUR	Common Market of Southern Countries in Latin America
MIGA	Multilateral Investment Guarantee Agency
NAFTA	North American Free Trade Agreement
NAMA	Non-Agricultural Market Access
NFIDC	Net-Food Importing Developing Countries
NGOs	Non-Governmental Organizations
OECD	Organization for Economic Cooperation and Development
OJ	Official Journal
PCIJ	Permanent Court of International Justice
PIL	Public International Law
REDD	Reduction of emissions from deforestation and forest degradation
RTAs	Regional Trade Agreements
SADEC	Southern African Development and Economic Community
SDT	Special and Differential Treatment
SPS	Sanitary and Phytosanitary Measures (Agreement)
TBT	Technical Barriers to Trade (Agreement)
TCE	Treaty Establishing a Constitution for Europe
TEU	Lisbon Treaty on European Union 2007
TFEU	Lisbon Treaty on the Functioning of the EU 2007

TNCs	Transnational Corporations
TRIPS	Trade-Related Intellectual Property Rights (Agreement)
UDHR	Universal Declaration of Human Rights
UN	United Nations
UNCITRAL	United Nations Commission on International Trade Law
UNCLOS	United Nations Convention on the Law of the Sea
UNCTAD	United Nations Conference on Trade and Development
UNEP	United Nations Environmental Program
UNESCO	United Nations Educational, Scientific and Cultural Organization
UNFCCC	UN Framework Convention on Climate Change
UNGC	UN Global Compact
VCLT	Vienna Convention on the Law of Treaties
VER	Voluntary Export Restraints
WHO	World Health Organization
WIPO	World Intellectual Property Organization
WTO	World Trade Organization

Tables Summarizing 'Normative Premises' and Case Law Examples

Table of Cases

International/Regional

Arbikal

ECJ

ECtHR

EFTA Court

IACtHR

ICJ

ICSID Arbitration

International Criminal Tribunal for Yugoslavia

MERCOSUR

Permanent Court of Arbitration

UNCITRAL Arbitration

WTO/GATT

National

Germany

Constitutional Court

India

United Kingdom

United States

Table of Legal Instruments

International Agreements

Regional Agreements

European Union

Bilateral

National

Australia

France

Germany

India

Latvia

South Africa

Switzerland

United States

This is a government of the people, by the people and for the people no longer. It is a government of corporations, by corporations, and for corporations

US President Rutherford Hayes (1876)

Imagination is more important than knowledge . . . We can't solve problems by using the same kind of thinking we used when we created them.

A Einstein

The problem of international constitutionalism is the central challenge faced by international philosophers in the twenty-first century.

P Allot

The struggle for one's human rights is a duty of the person whose rights have been violated as well as a duty to society.

(variation of a citation from R Jhering)

If Socrates was right to insist that the practice of contestation he engaged in deserves the highest praise in a democratic polity, it is equally true that a well structured and appropriately embedded court engaged in rights-based proportionality review deserves to be embraced as a vital element of liberal constitutional democracy.

M Kumm

Introduction and Overview: The Crisis of International Economic Law

GLOBALIZATION, IE, 'THE closer integration of the countries and the peoples of the world which has been brought about by the enormous reduction of costs of transportation and communication, and the breaking down of artificial barriers to the flow of goods, services, capital, knowledge, and (to a lesser extent) people across borders', affects not only the daily lives of ever more people everywhere – 'their jobs, their food, their health, their education, their leisure time'[1] – it also leads to far-reaching structural changes of the world economy. For instance, increasing numbers of goods, including not only high-technology products (such as mobile phones) but also shoes and clothing, are manufactured in global networks of suppliers of raw materials and intermediate goods and producers of final goods located in many countries. The failure to conclude the Doha Round negotiations in the World Trade Organization (WTO) since 2001, like the failure to conclude a new 'Kyoto II Climate Change Agreement', illustrate that waiting for global consensus on new worldwide agreements risks being an unreasonable strategy; unilateral safeguard measures (like border tax adjustments), bilateral agreements (like the thousands of bilateral double taxation and investment agreements), regional agreements (like the hundreds of free trade agreements) and 'experimental governance' (eg, in constructing regional monetary unions and 'carbon emission trading systems') may be necessary 'building blocks' for consensus-building on reforms of worldwide trade, financial and environmental rules. Although tariff preferences matter less and less, the international production networks and the failures of worldwide economic negotiations foster ever more preferential 'deep economic integration' agreements regulating markets and government interventions far beyond existing worldwide rules, with the risk of increasing regulatory and market segmentation. Whereas national and regional legal systems dynamically change, the international economic law (IEL) system established since the Second World War faces an unprecedented crisis requiring 'new thinking'. Regulatory and legal responses to the transatlantic banking crisis, 'sovereign debt' crisis, economic growth, governance and social crises are hampered by the simultaneous legitimacy and rule of law crises in IEL and by 'democratic disagreement' on appropriate reforms, for example, of the 'moral hazards', lack of competitiveness and ineffective fiscal disciplines in some southern European member states of the European Monetary Union. Arguably, the options of 'exit, voice and loyalty'[2] explain the

[1] J Stiglitz, *Globalization and its Discontents* (London: Penguin, 2002) 9.

[2] On the dependence of constitutional and economic law reforms, and of their legitimacy, on a political equilibrium between 'voice, exit and loyalty' see: AOHirschman, *Exit, Voice and Loyalty – Responses to Decline in Firms, Organizations and States* (Cambridge: Harvard University Press, 1970); J Weiler, 'The Transformation of Europe' (1990) 100 *Yale Law Journal* 2403 ff. On older, *ordo*-liberal conceptions of 'interdependence of

decreasing loyalty to the postwar IEL system, the recourse to 'legal pluralism' as a means of decentralized legal reforms in order to 'move from the world of Hobbes to the world of Kant'[3] and the need to analyze IEL in an interdisciplinary context.

As illustrated by the picture on the book cover, this book analyzes the vast and dynamically changing field of IEL from the perspective of citizens, their human and constitutional rights and the increasing number of national and international court decisions reviewing multilevel economic governance with due regard to human rights. It argues that the regulatory challenges of the twenty-first century require a 'paradigm shift'[4] in IEL: the 'Westphalian conceptions' of 'international law among sovereign states' – which continue to prevail in worldwide agreements and diplomatic practices mainly on grounds of 'path-dependence', in spite of the obvious failures of diplomatic 'business as usual' – need to be limited in IEL through more cosmopolitan regulation of the global division of labour at regional, transnational and national levels to protect more effectively human rights, consumer welfare, the environment, democratic support of IEL by citizens and 'constitutional coherence' among diverse, national and international legal orders. Underlying this proposition is the claim – based on both empirical, comparative institutional analyses as well as on constitutional and economic theories – that legal limitations of market failures and governance failures can be rendered more effective – in the economy no less than in the polity – by judicially enforceable, cosmopolitan rights of citizens to equal market freedoms, non-discriminatory conditions of competition and judicial protection of constitutional rights and transnational rule of law for the benefit of citizens. Rights-based approaches to IEL are not only a requirement of morality and justice, but even more so of political 'realism' and democracy: IEL must take into account the need for limiting the ubiquity of abuses of public and private power by 'countervailing powers' of citizens as self-interested guardians of their constitutional rights and of their mutually beneficial, economic cooperation across frontiers; individual rights and judicial remedies require justification of all government restrictions and enhance participatory, deliberative and 'constitutionally accountable democracy'. The rights-based approach offers not only citizen-oriented and comparative law perspectives on the increasingly complex and existentially important field of IEL, which state-centred textbooks describing IEL often neglect; it also offers different perspectives on the 'principles of justice' underlying IEL and illustrates the diverse traditions of translating human rights into practical economic regulation for the benefit of citizens. Proceeding from the basic premise of modern economics and of Rawls' theory of justice that human welfare depends on institutionalizing reasonable rules and institutions protecting open markets, the book emphasizes the importance of 'cosmopolitan liberties' and of moral duties of citizens to 'struggle for justice' and for a more cosmopolitan IEL. As illustrated by Mohammed Bouazizi, the young Tunisian street vendor whose protests against arbitrary market restrictions triggered Tunisia's human rights revolution in 2011, the freedom to sell in the market place (as pictured by Diego Rivera on the book cover) may

legal, economic and political orders' see ch VII. On the risk of 'social dis-embedding' by globalization, and the need for 'democratic re-embedding of IEL' through stronger protection of human rights and 'struggles for individual rights', see ch IV.

[3] *cf* P Lamy, who – in his speech of 6 October 2011 on 'What Multilateral Trading System for the Future?' (accessible on the WTO website) – stated: 'we need to do for international monetary relations what we already did for trade: move from the world of Hobbes towards the world of Kant'.

[4] *cf* TS Kuhn, *The Structure of Scientific Revolutions* (Chicago: University of Chicago Press, 1962).

trigger and justify a human rights revolution against welfare-reducing, economic and political oppression.

According to Mohammed's younger brother, the identification of millions of disempowered Arab people during the 'Arab Revolutionary Spring 2011' with the self-immolation of Bouazizi reflected a common suffering: 'that the poor also have the right to buy and sell'.[5] Modern economics and theories of justice confirm that social welfare depends on reasonable rules and institutions protecting economic freedoms, property rights and non-discriminatory conditions of competition of citizens to engage in mutually beneficial division of labour, subject to legal constraints of 'market failures' as well as 'governance failures'. Just as the arbitrary confiscation of the merchandise and other means of trade owned by Bouazizi destroyed his private business and prospects of autonomous self-development, millions of protesters in the 'Arab Spring' are challenging authoritarian, welfare-reducing government restrictions impeding individual and democratic self-development and emancipation of the poor. This book discusses more than a hundred case studies of legal and judicial disputes regarding fundamental economic freedoms, property rights, labour and social rights, access to justice, judicial 'balancing' of economic and human rights, multilevel 'judicial governance' and transnational 'rule of law' in the broader context of regional and worldwide IEL and its legal implementation in domestic jurisdictions; it emphasizes the need for assessing the diverse comparative law experiences with due respect for legitimate 'legal pluralism' (eg, acknowledging that similar legal concepts may be differently interpreted due to diverse constitutional traditions and social contexts in different jurisdictions). Even though written by a law professor and practitioner – during more than 35 years – of IEL, the main research interest underlying this book is to contribute to clarifying the impact of 'constitutional pluralism' and of diverse 'theories of justice' on the interpretation and design of IEL by the 'legal actors' and on their under-supply of interdependent 'public goods'.[6] One major lesson from this multilevel, comparative law and practice-oriented perspective is to challenge the apparent 'universalism' of worldwide human rights and IEL treaties: their universal, open-ended legal terms and underlying principles are often construed and implemented in legitimately diverse ways based on different theories of justice and of human rights informing the interpretations. As legal and judicial cooperation among constitutional, human rights and IEL institutions is more developed in European law than in other international legal systems, many case studies are taken from economic and human rights adjudication in the European Union (EU), the European Economic Area (EEA), the European Convention on Human Rights (ECHR) and national jurisdictions across Europe. The fact that cases decided by European courts and their often innovative, legal methodologies (like 'balancing' of economic and human rights) are increasingly cited also in investor–state arbitration and regional human rights and economic

[5] Quoted from H de Soto, 'The free-market secret of the Arab revolutions' *Financial Times* (9 November 2011) 9.

[6] On the defining characteristics of 'public goods' (like their non-excludable and non-rival use benefiting all citizens) which, in contrast to private goods, must be collectively supplied by governments, see I Kaul, I Grunberg and MA Stern (eds) (1999). On the 'constitutional functions' of the Bretton Woods Agreements and GATT for empowering citizens to engage in mutually beneficial trade transactions and for regulating trade in conformity with constitutional principles like freedom, non-discrimination and rule of law across frontiers see EU Petersmann (1991). On comparative constitutional, legislative, administrative and judicial regulation of trade and the economy see M Hilf and EU Petersmann (eds) (1993); this book's comparative, legal and institutional case studies of trade regulation across Europe, North America and Asia illustrate the diversity of regulatory options and 'laboratory' of regulatory approaches applied by lawmakers.

courts outside Europe, confirms that 'experimental, multilevel governance' in Europe may be relevant across jurisdictions: not only in less-developed countries (LDCs) and Anglo-Saxon 'majoritarian democracies' reassessing their nationalist legal traditions but, as I have argued long since, also in other fields of IEL. One major thesis of this study is that, as inside the EU, 'constitutional tolerance' (Weiler), respect for constitutional pluralism, the 'centrality of conflict' resulting from competing constitutional claims and legitimate 'constitutional heterarchy'[7] are also constitutive of the legitimacy of IEL and limit the necessary, yet functionally limited 'constitutionalization' of IEL.

THE LACK OF A THEORY OF JUSTICE FOR IEL

The successful outcome of complex games (like chess) depends on understanding the logic of the rules of the game as well as the strategic options of the players. Similarly, individual and democratic self-governance in the world economy and 'globally integrated production' require understanding the rules, institutions and underlying principles governing the global division of labour. These rules are becoming increasingly complex and contested in view of their failures to prevent unnecessary international poverty, banking crises, financial and environmental crises. As explained in chapter I, the prevailing 'Westphalian conception' of IEL as an instrument for promoting national interests lacks a coherent theory for protecting international public goods in conformity with the human rights obligations of all UN member states. Most governments and participants in the global division of labour take economic decisions with only limited knowledge of the international 'rules of the game' and their systemic implications, eg, their incentives for abuses of economic power due to inadequate competition rules, consumer protection and surveillance (eg, of the persistent violations of the EU Treaty's fiscal and debt disciplines in some eurozone member states). For instance, as individual member countries of the Eurozone Monetary Union can no longer control by national policy instruments (like devaluation of the exchange rate, monetary expansion by interest rate changes) the currency in which their debt is issued, they are confronted with new regulatory challenges to protect monetary stability and economic growth without succumbing to 'moral hazards'. The less the interactions between national, bilateral, regional and worldwide government interventions are transparent and justifiable in terms of principles of justice and human rights, the more citizens contest the legitimacy of the often opaque redistribution of income through economic regulation (eg, of public bailouts of insolvent industries, banks and foreign sovereign debts).

This book is about the joint responsibility of citizens and governments to institutionalize a more legitimate 'public reason' for a more cosmopolitan IEL which citizens – as 'primary subjects' of the global division of labour and 'democratic owners' of all governance institutions – have reason to support. Just as private life has to be lived morally in respect of other people and ethically with regard to ourselves, so must law, governance and individual conduct – also in the global division of labour – remain justifiable on grounds of political morality and justice rather than only in terms of utilitarian

[7] *cf* D Halberstam, 'Constitutional Heterarchy: The Centrality of Conflict in the European Union and the United States' in JL Dunoff and JP Trachtman (eds) (2009) 326–55.

output.[8] The less people understand IEL and international economic institutions, the greater are the risks for democratic contestation of the rules (eg, by nationalist 'Tea Party protestations') and for their abuses (eg, by states joining international economic institutions like the eurozone without ever complying with the relevant rules). For instance, the worldwide and European banking, financial and 'sovereign debt' crises which have occurred since 2008 have destroyed private savings worth billions of dollars. Most of the adversely affected citizens lacked effective remedies (eg, against losses of jobs and pension funds) and feel exploited by systemic 'problems of high debt, corruption and clientelism'[9] cultivated even inside European constitutional democracies like Greece. As the EU Treaty's fiscal and debt disciplines continue to be violated by more than 20 out of the 27 EU member states and EU law prohibits 'monetary financing' of 'sovereign debts' (Articles 123–125 TFEU), the former chief economist of the ECB concluded: '(a)lmost all treaties promising European fiscal discipline have been broken time and again', and '(a)ny attempt to "save" monetary union via agreements which transfer sovereignty to a European level, where violations of fundamental treaties have become a regular event, lacks any logic'.[10] Just as EU law considers fiscal, debt and economic policies as primarily national responsibilities in conformity with the 'principle of subsidiarity' (Article 5 TEU), this study argues in favour of 'bottom-up reforms' of IEL in order to better protect rights of citizens and transnational rule of law based on the classical 'constitutional methods' of empowering citizens to challenge market failures as well as governance failures by stronger legal and judicial remedies promoting 'public reason' and decentralized 'piecemeal social engineering' (Popper). By showing that IEL rules (like the transparency disciplines and judicial remedies required by Article X GATT) can support human rights objectives, and that democratic resistance to 'top-down governance' has to be taken seriously, this study should also be of interest to interdisciplinary scholars working on human rights and multilevel economic governance.

The 'Westphalian international law among sovereign states' up to the First World War did not provide for permanent worldwide institutions. The institutions established after the First World War (like the League of Nations) and after the Second World War (like the UN) were inspired by ideals of worldwide 'social engineering' that failed to realize many

[8] *cf* R Dworkin, *Justice for Hedgehogs* (Cambridge: Harvard University Press, 2011) (explaining why what people achieve – the 'product value' of a human life – is less important than the manner in which they live their lives and treat other people – their 'performance value'. The diverse value dimensions of social life – eg, what truth is, life means, morality requires and justice demands – are interrelated).

[9] G Rachman, 'How to tame the Greek beast?' *Financial Times* (26 July 2011) 7. An increasing number of comments in the *Financial Times* during 2011 described the euro crisis measures as a 'Ponzi scheme' violating the 'bailout' prohibition, fiscal and debt disciplines prescribed in the EU Treaty and transferring taxpayers' money without adequate involvement of national parliaments – 'a clear violation of the fundamental democratic principle of "no taxation without representation"' (*cf* O Issing, 'Slithering to the wrong kind of union' *Financial Times* (9 August 2011) 9).

[10] Issing (n 9): 'In the end, it will only further alienate the people from Europe itself', 'the fact that a member country of the euro – even in the case of permanent violations of the rules – will be saved at any price causes moral hazard and creates an obvious potential for blackmail'. Proposals for a European common bond would 'relieve some countries of their burden of a record of fiscal irresponsibility' at the expense of those EU member countries which respected the fiscal disciplines. Most economists proposing transformation of the European Monetary Union into a fiscal union with permanent financial transfers to over-indebted EU member countries disregard the limited legal powers, democratic legitimacy and political capacity of EU institutions to impose top-down comprehensive local governance reforms: 'The solutions to these problems in every case can only be found locally' (J Kay, 'As Europe's élite is fighting reality and will lose' *Financial Times* (26 October 2011) 7), even though EU financial adjustment assistance for inducing the necessary reforms of domestic labour markets, unproductive public sectors and weak banking systems remains indispensable.

of the 'grand strategies'. Prior to the entry into force of the 'Bretton Woods Agreements' in 1945 and the 'provisional application' of the General Agreement on Tariffs and Trade (GATT 1947) as of 1 January 1948, there existed no coherent system of IEL helping citizens and governments to increase their welfare through mutually beneficial rules limiting governance failures at national levels (such as protectionism and colonialism with 'harmful externalities') and promoting collective supply of private and 'public goods' across frontiers. The non-ratification of the 1948 Havana Charter for an International Trade Organization and the only 'provisional application' of many GATT provisions until 1995, illustrated the limited willingness of states to adjust their national legal systems to the requirements of a mutually beneficial world trading system. The absence of a Legal Office in the GATT Secretariat until 1983 reflected the predominant conception of GATT rules as a power-oriented framework for trade policymaking; for instance, the 'GATT Rounds' of trade liberalization focused on the export interests of industrialized countries, and mutually agreed 'voluntary export restrictions' were used for circumventing GATT's legal disciplines and discriminating notably against imports of cotton and textiles from LDCs. Since 1995, more than 450 dispute settlement proceedings in the WTO over alleged violations of WTO rules, like the current judicial proceedings in national courts (such as the German Constitutional Court) as well as in the European Court of Justice (ECJ) over violations of the Lisbon Treaty's prohibitions of 'bailouts' (Articles 123-125 TFEU) and of 'excessive government deficits' (Article 126 TFEU), illustrate the increasing difficulties in constitutional democracies to comply with IEL disciplines ratified by national parliaments for the benefit of citizens. Why do citizens, governments and courts fail so often to protect transnational rule of law for the benefit of citizens and social justice in IEL? Why are some international public goods effectively protected (like postal services, telecommunications, air and shipping transports), whereas the collective supply of others remains impeded by 'market failures' as well as 'governance failures'? The main thesis of this book is that – in IEL – the 'animal spirits' and rational egoism of individuals need to be restrained by stronger constitutional and institutional protection of 'public reason' based on cosmopolitan freedoms and other 'principles of justice'. The national 'rights revolutions' since the seventeenth century often focused one-sidedly on particular national constitutional traditions and prevailing political conceptions for instance in England on parliamentary sovereignty and utilitarian 'sentiments' (eg, in the works of Smith and Hume), in the French Revolution on popular sovereignty and rationality (eg, in replacing the '*ancien régime*' by a 'revolutionary democracy' that degenerated quickly into terrorism) and in the American Revolution on institutionalizing a national 'public reason' prioritizing civil and political over economic and social rights (thereby privileging powerful producer interests in exploiting market power, slaves and indigenous people);[11] as illustrated by multilevel constitutional and judicial protection of the

[11] On the diverse 'constitutional foundations' of the British, American and French 'democratic revolutions' see, eg, Petersmann (1991 133 f) and the 'Introduction' by C Porset in G Gusdorf, *Les Révolutions de France et d'Amérique: La violence et la sagesse* (Paris: La Table Ronde, 2005). Conceptions of majoritarian, parliamentary democracy and of representative 'rational representation by political élites' often assume people to act as rational agents rather than as sensible maximizers of their self-interests and 'slaves of their passions' (*cf* DHume, *A Treatise of Human Nature*, 1740). Constitutional and cosmopolitan conceptions of democracy emphasize the limited reasonableness and bounded rationality and control of individuals over oneself; the conscious, human reasoning is often distorted by unconscious biases, passions and limited understanding of the social 'rules of the game', as illustrated by the financial crises since 2008. The 'multilevel constitutionalism' endorsed in this study criticizes the authoritarian 'Westphalian conception' of human beings and of their human nature as illegitimate and a 'pretence of knowledge' (*cf* FA Hayek, *New Studies in Philosophy, Politics,*

individual rights of 500 million EU citizens, multilevel regulation of IEL in the twenty-first century requires a new 'reflective equilibrium'[12] with due regard to the human rights obligations and constitutional restraints adopted by all UN member states. This book argues that more effective supply of interdependent public goods in the twenty-first century requires 'constitutionalizing IEL', notably by stronger legal and judicial protection of cosmopolitan rights in multilevel, economic governance in order to better protect human rights, democratic governance, transnational rule of law and consumer welfare. Human rights and economic cosmopolitan rights set incentives for reconciling the often selfish struggles characterizing the 'human condition' and global competition by institutionalizing 'public cosmopolitan reason' as defined by democratic legislation, participatory democracy and judicial review of governmental restrictions of individual rights at the request of citizens. Can the prevailing, mercantilist '*government/producer partnership model*' dominating multilevel trade, investment, financial and environmental governance be transformed into a constitutionally more limited, more decentralized and more legitimate '*cosmopolitan democracy model*' providing for more effective legal and judicial protection of all general citizen interests?

THE LEGITIMACY CRISIS OF IEL

UN human rights treaties and worldwide IEL treaties continue to evolve as separate legal regimes without explicit coordination, as illustrated by the lack of any references to human rights in the IMF, World Bank, GATT and WTO Agreements. The 'intuitive, unconscious fast thinking'[13] of most human rights lawyers, economic lawyers and diplomats remains that the complexity of IEL should not be further complicated by linking IEL to the complexities and different legal culture of human rights law (HRL). This book emphasizes the need for 'slow constitutional thinking' challenging 'legal fragmentation': market economies, democratic politics and IEL as ever more important instruments for reducing unnecessary poverty need to be justified and 'constitutionalized' in terms of human rights and other 'principles of justice'. The apparent 'governance crises' in international monetary, financial, trade and environmental relations are increasingly perceived by citizens as a 'legitimacy crisis' challenging the 'Westphalian conceptions' of IEL. Instead of responding to citizen demand for more jobs, higher salaries and prevention of climate change, international economic institutions increasingly alienate citizens by imposing economic austerity programmes and failing to protect international public goods demanded by citizens. Worse, due to the delegation of vast foreign policy powers to executive institutions and the inadequate transparency and parliamentary control of multilevel governance, parliamentary, participatory and deliberative democracy at local and national levels are increasingly undermined without 'compensatory citizens' rights' to transnational democratic participation (as provided for in Articles 9–12 TEU)

Economics and the History of Ideas (London: Routledge, 1978) chapter 2) and of 'social engineering' capacities that are politically naïve.

[12] *Cf* J Rawls (2001) 29–32.

[13] On the distinction – as two dialectic thinking processes characteristic of human rationality – of 'unconscious, intuitive fast thinking' from 'conscious slow thinking' based on deductive reasoning double-checking the cognitive biases of expert intuition, see D Kahneman, *Thinking, Fast and Slow* (New York: Allen Lane, 2011).

and to transnational 'cosmopolitan self-governance' (as protected in the EU Charter of Fundamental Rights). As discriminatory trade restrictions and subsidies tend to redistribute income among domestic groups, discretionary trade and financial policies are increasingly shaped by rent-seeking interest groups at the expense of general consumer welfare. In contrast to the 'community vision' of EU law protecting both national and 'EU citizenship' (Article 9 TEU) as well as democratic representation by national parliaments and by the European Parliament (*cf* Articles 10, 12 TEU), the 'intergovernmentalism' of worldwide institutions does not even aim at complementing individual and democratic self-governance of citizens. Government representatives and specialized interest groups often collude in functionally specialized, international organizations without adequate democratic accountability of diplomats vis-à-vis general citizen interests (eg, in terms of general consumer welfare and human rights) and members of national parliaments. From the perspective of most citizens focusing their democratic participation and attention on local and national politics, the social legitimacy of distant, intergovernmental organizations tends to be perceived as even weaker than their limited, *normative* democratic credentials (eg, based on parliamentary ratification of international treaties establishing international organizations).

Lawyers, economists and political scientists disagree on the appropriate legal, economic and political methodologies for interpreting, applying, developing and evaluating rules of IEL. The 'dual nature' of modern national and international law – as legal systems composed not only of positive legal rules and practices, but also of moral 'principles of justice' as explicitly recognized in human rights law, national constitutions, the UN Charter and general international law – is often neglected in multilevel economic governance and in the dispute settlement practices of international economic courts and arbitral tribunals. For instance, in Europe's current 'sovereign debt' crisis, many politicians and economists call for 'financial solidarity' without regard to the prohibition of 'bailouts' in Article 125 TFEU and the 'moral hazards' that contributed to the banking, financial and sovereign debt crises. Many 'constitutional problems' of IEL – such as the relations between 'rules' and 'principles', or between producer-driven economic regulation and 'courts of justice' reviewing the 'rules of recognition' of IEL and the legal consistency and 'proportionality' of regulation – remain 'under-theorized'. The more government representatives and 'rent-seeking' interest groups perceive IEL as a power-oriented instrument for income distribution by means of regulation, the more civil society challenges the democratic legitimacy and 'principles of justice' of economic regulation for the benefit of powerful industries, for example in case of subsidies for, and 'bailouts' of banks, automobile and aircraft industries.

Human rights and democracy require public justification of legal rules and governance institutions and their support by the 'public reason' of citizens. The competing legal, economic and political conceptions of IEL reflect diverse approaches to justifying economic rules and governance practices. The rules of the 1994 Agreement establishing the WTO affect the individual lives and welfare of billions of producers, workers, investors, traders and consumers all over the world. Yet, most government representatives, international civil servants, economists, lawyers and political scientists interpreting, applying and negotiating WTO rules inside the WTO headquarters at Geneva have never read the 30,000 pages of WTO treaty rules and more than 50,000 pages of WTO dispute settlement reports. Their views on what the WTO Preamble calls 'the basic principles and objectives underlying this multilateral trading system' tend to be diffuse and contested. For example, the main entrance to the WTO's Centre William Rappard at the Lake of Geneva is flanked by two statues representing 'peace' and 'justice', the two central objectives and justifications of legal systems since ancient times. Even though the sculptor positioned the statues on either side of the entrance door in order to remind all people entering the building of the human ideals of justice and peace,[14] I met only a few people – during my 30 years as legal advisor inside the Secretariat of the GATT 1947 and the WTO – interested in exploring the relationships between world trade law, peace and justice, a perennial problem already identified in the publications by Ambassador William Rappard during the 1930s as one of the major causes of the breakdown of the world trading system ushering in the Second World War.[15] Outside the WTO, for instance in the 2005 World Summit Outcome, world leaders 'acknowledge that peace and security, development and human rights are the pillars of the UN system and the foundations for collective security and well-being. We recognize that development, peace and security and human rights are interlinked and mutually reinforcing'.[16] European citizens likewise acknowledge the achievements of the 1957 Treaty establishing the European Economic Community (EEC) not only in terms of historically unprecedented economic welfare and multilevel constitutional protection of fundamental rights of citizens. They value the Treaty also for having evolved into the most effective 'peace treaty' of all times protecting rule of law and 'democratic peace' far beyond the 27 member states of the EU, thereby putting an end to the periodic wars in Europe up to the Second World War. EU law illustrates the systemic importance of mutually beneficial IEL for the collective supply also of *non-economic* 'public goods' like transnational rule of law and peaceful cooperation for the benefit of citizens and their human rights.

By committing itself to a 'competitive social market economy' based on respect for human rights, rule of law and democratic constitutionalism (*cf* Articles 2–3 TEU), European economic integration law contributed to empowering the now 500 million EU citizens as legal subjects of human rights, constitutional rights, cosmopolitan economic rights and 'democratic principals' of multilevel economic governance inside the EU. The right of citizens to justification of governmental restrictions of individual freedoms can

[14] *cf* the explanations of the statues by their sculptor: L Jaggi in *Centre William Rappard. Home of the World Trade Organization* (WTO: Geneva, 2011) 34. Instead of representing 'justice' in the traditional way as a blind-folded woman holding a scale and a sword, the artist sculptured 'justitia' holding a dove (representing truth) and checking a serpent (symbolizing lying and deceitfulness) with her feet. On the history of the iconography of justice see J Resnik and D Curtis (eds), *Representing Justice. Invention, Controversy and Rights in City-States and Democratic Courtrooms* (New Haven: Yale University Press, 2011).

[15] The International Chamber of Commerce (ICC) was founded in the wake of the First World War with the explicit task of promoting 'world peace through world trade', economic growth, job creation, prosperity and peaceful international economic cooperation, *cf* F Lehmann and JP Lehmann (eds), *Peace and Prosperity through World Trade* (Cambridge: CUP, 2010). Also the WTO publication '10 Benefits of the WTO Trading System' mentions as the first benefit: 'The system helps to keep the peace'. 'The WTO trading system plays a vital role in creating and reinforcing . . . confidence. Particularly important are negotiations that lead to agreement by consensus, and a focus on abiding by the rules' (WTO, 2009) 2. The conference book edited by P Ala'l, T Broude and C Picker, *Trade as Guarantor of Peace, Liberty and Security?* (ASIL, 2006) focuses on the effects of trade and economic integration on the emergence of wars and armed conflict and the development of international economic law as a positive tool in promoting peace. The role of commerce as a driver not only of 'sociability' and norm-structured interactions, but of colonialism and imperialism was already discussed by the founding fathers of the Westphalian system of 'international law among states' like Grotius, Hobbes and Pufendorf, *cf* B Kingsbury and B Straumann, 'State of Nature versus Commercial Sociability as the Basis of International Law' in S Besson and J Tasioulas (eds) (2010) 33–52. For interdisciplinary analyses of the historical, economic, political and legal foundations of modern IEL see Petersmann (1991).

[16] UN General Assembly Resolution A/Res/60/1, 2005 World Summit Outcome, para 9.

be seen as one of the most basic human rights of crucial importance for effective enjoyment of other human rights such as access to justice and democratic participation.[17] Many IEL treaties – also beyond EU law – offer more legal and judicial guarantees for transnational freedom and non-discriminatory treatment in international cooperation among citizens than non-economic agreements, including UN human rights conventions focusing on protection of human rights *inside* domestic jurisdictions without offering effective judicial remedies at international levels. Yet, in the Bretton Woods and WTO Agreements, rule of law, 'justice' and human rights are nowhere mentioned. The prevailing paradigms of 'member-driven governance' and economic 'utilitarianism' (ie, focusing on economic 'efficiency' and welfare-maximization) prompt WTO diplomats and economic lawyers to shun questions of justice and human rights in international economic regulation. Also, philosophy books rarely explore the 'justice dimensions' of IEL and the legal justifiability of moral claims that international law violates 'the human rights of the poor'.[18] Freedoms from hunger and from unnecessary poverty are recognized as human rights in ever more constitutional democracies and in a few international conventions (eg, on human rights and food aid). Yet, their effective protection in IEL and in many LDCs remains a cosmopolitan dream.[19] UN human rights law offers inadequate remedies for overcoming power-oriented 'Westphalian conceptions' of 'international law among sovereign states' in order to protect basic human needs more effectively. Do the legal impediments to enforcing obligations of justice at the global level justify the conclusion that there can be no such legal obligations?[20] Can IEL be an effective instrument of governance without offering convincing answers to the increasing challenges of its input and output-legitimacy?

Diplomats and lawyers involved in intergovernmental economic regulation often justify their pragmatic neglect for the 'justice dimensions' of IEL by the need to avoid complicating the negotiation, interpretation and application of economic rules by perennial controversies about justice. Can such 'rational ignorance' be justified by 'realist' claims that international economic relations remain in an anarchical 'Hobbesian state of nature' where morality and legal restraints of 'state sovereignty' risk endangering national interests in foreign policy discretion and maximizing national power?[21] Does the often arbitrary income redistribution by means of illegal trade protectionism, subsidies, restrictive business practices and selfish financial practices[22] refute pragmatic propositions that questions of morality should be left to individuals? Can international economic regula-

[17] *cf* R Forst (2007); J Neyer, 'Justice or Democracy? Power and Justification in the EU and other International Organizations' in R Nickel (ed), *Conflict of Laws and Laws of Conflict in Europe and Beyond* (Antwerp: Intersentia, 2010) 33–47.

[18] *cf* T Pogge, 'Recognized and Violated by International Law: the Human Rights of the Poor' (2005) 4 *Leiden Journal of International Law* 717–45. On Pogge's neglect of basic principles of international law in his morally justified criticism of IEL see: R Howse and R Teitel, 'Global Justice, Poverty and the International Economic Order' in Besson and Tasioulas (eds) (2010) 437–49; P Emerton, 'International Economic Justice: Is a Principled Liberalism Possible?' in S Joseph, D Kinley and J Waincymer (eds) (2009) 133 ff.

[19] *cf* T Pogge, *Freedom from Poverty as a Human Right: Who Owes What to Whom?* (New York: OUP, 2007); C Häberli and B Karapinar (eds), *Food Crisis and the WTO: World Trade Forum* (Cambridge: CUP, 2010).

[20] *cf* T Nagel, 'The Problem of Global Justice' (2005) 33 *Philosophy and Public Affairs* 113–47.

[21] For a description and convincing rejection of allegedly 'realist state of nature arguments' see A Buchanan (2004) 29–37.

[22] Examples of such practices include sales of complex financial derivatives with unjustified 'triple A ratings', fraudulent investment funds based on 'Ponzi/Madoff schemes', privatization of profits (eg, by means of excessive bonuses for excessive risk-taking) and 'socialization of losses' (eg, by means of public bailouts) by 'banks that are too big to fail' and elude effective regulation.

tion be justified in terms of human rights and democratic self-government?[23] Does the right to popular self-determination include responsibilities limiting cosmopolitan duties of international assistance, as suggested by Rawls' refusal to extend the 'principles of justice' inside constitutional democracies to international law and non-liberal people that do not struggle for defending their human rights against authoritarian traditions and abuses of power? Does international law adequately protect citizens against illegitimate rulers abusing the 'borrowing privilege' and 'resource privilege' of states by borrowing on behalf of the country and wasting its natural resources at the expense of the domestic population? Answering such questions about the legitimacy of IEL raises deeper questions concerning international law and its relationships to domestic legal systems, especially concerning the role of citizens as subjects of international law, their human, constitutional and cosmopolitan rights in IEL, and the role of 'peoples' (rather than only states) and individuals as subjects of 'international justice'.

This study argues that the human rights obligations of all UN member states require reinterpreting and redesigning IEL for the benefit of citizens and their reasonable self-interests in more effective protection of human rights and other, national and international public goods. The classical international law principle of 'sovereign equality of states' (Article 2 UN Charter) must be interpreted in conformity with the rights to 'popular sovereignty' and 'individual sovereignty' (eg, as defined by human rights) in order to empower citizens to assume their individual and democratic responsibilities to respect, protect and fulfil human rights more effectively in the worldwide division of labour among producers, workers, investors, traders and consumers. Yet, in contrast to Rawls' *Theory of Justice* for an international *Law of Peoples*,[24] the individual and democratic responsibilities of citizens for their individual and social welfare do not justify neglecting cosmopolitan rights and obligations in IEL. As illustrated by the unnecessary poverty of so many people in LDCs, the prevailing 'Westphalian conceptions' of 'international law among sovereign states' fail to protect citizens against widespread abuses of foreign policy powers and under-supply of international public goods. The increases in consumer welfare and transnational rule of law made possible by regional and worldwide trade rules – as illustrated by the peaceful creation of common markets among the 30 member states of the European Economic Area (EEA) and among the four Chinese customs territories (the People's Republic of China, Hong Kong, Macau and Taiwan) – illustrate the 'interdependence' of national and international public goods: had China, rather than withdrawing from its GATT membership in 1949, complied with GATT rules since 1948, the impoverishment of hundreds of millions of Chinese citizens could have been avoided. Similarly, stronger protection of the economic welfare and human rights of billions of citizens in today's globally integrated world economy depends on whether IEL will succeed in regulating the 'collective action problems' of a mutually beneficial world trading, financial, environment and development system more effectively. This introduction gives an overview of the main normative assumptions and conclusions of chapters I to VIII of this study.

[23] *cf* P Lamy, 'Crisis is opportunity to restore coherence in global economic governance', lecture at the UN Office in Geneva (8 December 2010) (http://www.wto.org) 3: 'The global governance that the world needs cannot be severed from local governance roots. There is no shortcut to global coherence via our international institutions, all too often perceived by citizens as remote or obscure, even if it is their governments that are running them'.

[24] *cf* J Rawls, *Law of Peoples* (1999).

METHODOLOGY AND NORMATIVE FOCUS ON THE DUAL NATURE OF LEGAL SYSTEMS

The term *legal methodology* is used here as referring to the respective conceptions of the sources and 'rules of recognition' of law, the methods of interpretation, the functions and systemic nature of legal systems like IEL, and of their relationships to other areas of law and politics. This study analyzes both the *normative dimensions* of IEL (eg, as an 'overlapping plurality' of diverse, national and international legal orders based on common principles) as well as the *social-political dimensions* of IEL as being based on law-creating practices of social and political institutions.[25] The normative dimensions are being discussed not only from *constitutional perspectives* (eg, of 'courts of justice') and *functional-instrumental perspectives* (eg, of political regulators) based on legal positivism and related 'theories of justice'; the economic objectives and social dimensions of IEL also require analyzing 'law in context', notably from *economic perspectives* (eg, focusing on economic efficiency and 'optimal policy instruments') and *social-political perspectives* (eg, focusing on 'public choices' and 'public reason'). As no single author can cover all the fields of IEL, modern textbooks of IEL tend to be co-authored by several lawyers who often avoid clarifying their diverse legal methodologies and conceptions of the normative legitimacy of international economic rules. Most textbooks of IEL focus on *describing* the increasingly complex transnational economic rules and institutions, *interpreting* these rules and *explaining* specific regulatory problems. For instance, as competition, trade and most other IEL rules aim at promoting economic efficiency, most textbooks of IEL focus on the consistency of IEL with the underlying theories of economics, state sovereignty and public international law. Even if justice is recognized as a central problem of IEL – for instance, in discussions on whether international arbitration should be legally conceived as (i) a component of a single national legal order (assimilating the arbitrator to a national judge exercising the judicial function within the national legal order of the seat of the arbitration), as (ii) being anchored in a plurality of national legal orders (eg, of those states recognizing and enforcing international arbitral awards) or (iii) as an autonomous 'transnational law merchant' and 'arbitral legal order' offering legal services and 'international justice' to the business community – legal problems should not be seen as a question of 'truth', but rather in terms of which legal conception helps to resolve the regulatory problems most efficiently, effectively and legitimately.[26] One major hypothesis of this study is that rights-based 'cosmopolitan conceptions' of IEL have proven – empirically as well as normatively – to protect human rights, consumer welfare and other 'public goods' more effectively and more legitimately than state-centred 'Westphalian conceptions' of IEL.

This study suggests that the obvious failures of UN law and of large parts of IEL to realize their agreed treaty objectives require more *normative*, *conceptual* and *contex-*

[25] This constant interaction between 'law as a legal order' and 'law as legal practices' is emphasized by 'critical legal positivism', according to which law and its legal changes should be examined on (1) the surface level of positive law, (2) the legal culture, and (3) the deep structures of law; *cf* K Tuori, *Critical Legal Positivism* (Aldershot, 2002).

[26] *cf* E Gaillard, *Legal Theory of International Arbitration* (Leiden: Nijhoff Publishers, 2010). As explained by R Alexy, 'The Reasonableness of Law', in G Bongiovanni, G Sartor and C Valantini (2009), 5–15, reasonable judgments and justice (eg, in the sense of reasonable justification) can be perceived as the equivalent in normative legal sciences to truth in the natural sciences.

tual analysis of IEL rather than mere *description*, *formalistic interpretation* and *economic* analysis of IEL rules. For instance, there is a need for reviewing the often implicit 'Westphalian preconceptions' of IEL, for example, of judges and courts as – in the famous words of Montesquieu – mere '*bouche de la loi*' limited by the consent and 'sovereignty' of states even if the latter are represented by non-democratic rulers and use their regulatory discretion in welfare-reducing, arbitrary ways. Many fields of IEL are perceived from competing *private* and *public law perspectives*, for instance either as 'dialectical Hegelian progress' from power-oriented nationalism and bilateral agreements (eg, on trade, investments and related payments) towards multilateral safeguards of common interests (eg, in WTO law and investment arbitration) or, alternatively, as ongoing 'Marxian struggles' of conflicting interests (eg, if bilateral trade and investment agreements are perceived as reciprocal concessions in order to seek competitive advantages vis-à-vis third countries). Depending on such often unstated preconceptions, the interpretation of IEL rules – for instance, of 'fair and equitable treatment' (FET) obligations in bilateral investment agreements (BITs) – may differ depending on whether BITs are perceived as emerging multilateral standards of customary international law or as reciprocal concessions deviating from customary international law standards.[27] The *private law* and *public law dimensions* of IEL and human rights law are often inseparable. For instance:

- human rights protect both private and public autonomy;
- most economic transactions among citizens take place from a *private law perspective* of traders, producers, investors and consumers and derive their value from respect for 'normative individualism';
- also investment law and investor–state arbitration have both *public* and *private law* dimensions, whose dialectic evolution may be viewed positively (eg, as provision of 'international justice' through private arbitration services based on progressive 'multilateralization' of bilaterally agreed standards) or negatively (eg, as power struggles for imposing conflicting interests by avoiding national and international public law courts as well as 'publicness', *amicus curiae* briefs, precedents, systemic consistency and appellate review in arbitrating particular investment disputes).[28]

Hence, in investor–state arbitration, the legal distinction between 'treaty breaches' (eg, of 'fair and equitable treatment' obligations) and 'contract breaches' (eg, of 'corporate social responsibilities' as recognized in the 2006 'Equator Principles' applied by the World Bank and IFC), or between 'public interests' (eg, as defined by human rights) and private 'legitimate expectations' of investors (eg, in case of privatization of essential water, health and electricity services), must go beyond dogmatic 'public-private law divides'. In commercial arbitration, for instance, the constitutional limits of private

[27] On the interrelationships between conceptions of IEL and legal methodology see, eg, A Mills, 'Antinomies of Public and Private at the Foundations of International Investment Law and Arbitration' (2011) 14 *JIEL* 469–03, citing (at 483) the NAFTA/UNCITRAL arbitration award of 8 June 2009 in *Glamis Gold Ltd v USA* : 'those treaties with fair and equitable treaty clauses that expand upon, or move beyond, customary international law, lead their reviewing tribunals into an analysis of the treaty language and its meaning, as guided by Article 31(1) of the Vienna Convention'; 'those treaties and free trade agreements, like the NAFTA, that are to be understood by reference to the customary international law minimum standard of treatment necessarily lead their tribunals to analyze custom' (para 606).

[28] *cf* S Wilske and M Raible, 'The Arbitrator as Guardian of International Public Policy? Should Arbitrators go beyond Solving Legal Issues?' in CA Rogers and RP Alford (eds), *The Future of Investment Arbitration* (Oxford: OUP, 2009) 249–72.

party autonomy and of the freedom of arbitrators must be determined in conformity with human rights and public order.

This study describes the *historical evolution* and ever more complex 'positive law thicket' of multilevel regulation of international movements of goods, services, persons, capital and payments often only by means of short surveys (eg, in the 25 tables). All eight chapters of this book focus on methodological, normative and regulatory problems of multilevel economic governance, for instance by analyzing the input-legitimacy and output-legitimacy of IEL in terms of human rights and other 'principles of justice'. IEL is conceptualized and justified primarily from a cosmopolitan citizen perspective as a system of norms and legal practices in order to promote not only economic efficiency and 'sustainable development', but also the fulfilment of the human rights obligations of UN member states and democratic self-government. The study aims at combining rights-based, communitarian and utilitarian conceptions of economic law and of *practical reason* in view of the 'reasonable disagreement' and only limited 'overlapping consensus' on the normative foundations of modern international economic regulation.

The methodological starting point of this study is legal positivism and a concept of IEL as being composed of private and public, national and international *systems* of legal norms, including 'primary rules of conduct' and 'secondary rules' of recognition, change and dispute settlement. This broad conception of IEL excludes the traditional, state-centric view of states as the only subjects of international law – an authoritarian view which often neglects the human rights of citizens, the dominant role of non-state actors in the worldwide division of labour and the role of civil society and courts in the 'recognition' and interpretation of rules of IEL. As explained by Hart, a conception of valid law is to be identified, inter alia, by the criteria provided in the rules of recognition and their interpretation by citizens, governments and courts demonstrating that a legal system is accepted as such. The recognition by social actors – and notably by dispute settlement bodies – of valid 'law' may also depend on conceptions of justice and other moral values justifying human rights.[29] Hence, IEL cannot be limited to treaties, customary and other general international law rules to which states have agreed. As discussed in chapter V, transnational commercial and investment law, and the modern content of the initially vaguely defined investor rights and investment protection standards, dynamically evolve in response to hundreds of national and international arbitral and other dispute settlement decisions 'recognizing', interpreting, clarifying and progressively developing rules and principles of IEL based on a de facto practice of judicial precedents.[30] The interpretation of WTO rules and of regional economic integration law is likewise often more determined by judicial jurisprudence than by guidance provided by the contracting states. The frequently systemic effect of economic adjudication is confirmed by the fact that states respond to arbitral jurisprudence by means of inter-

[29] *cf* HLA Hart (1994) 105–10, 128, 247, 250, 259.

[30] *cf* JP Commission, 'Precedent in Investment Treaty Arbitration – A Citation Analysis of a Developing Jurisprudence' (2007) 24 *Journal of International Arbitration* 129, 148. The following finding in the ICSID Award of 30 April 2004 in *Waste Management v Mexico* (Case No ARB/00/3) para 98, is illustrative of arbitral interpretations focusing on previous arbitral precedents rather than on the customary methods of treaty interpretation: 'Taken together, the *SD Myers*, *Mondev*, *ADF* and *Loewen* cases suggest that the minimum standard of fair and equitable treatment is infringed by conduct attributable to the State and harmful to the claimant if the conduct is arbitrary, grossly unfair, unjust or idiosyncratic, is discriminatory and exposes the claimant to sectional or racial prejudice, or involves a lack of due process leading to an outcome which offends judicial propriety – as might be the case with a manifest failure of natural justice in judicial proceedings or a complete lack of transparency and candour in an administrative process'.

governmental interpretations (eg, legally binding 'Notes of Interpretation' pursuant to Article 1131 NAFTA) or by amendments of international investment agreements (eg, by including footnotes into the recent US investment treaties with Columbia and Peru clarifying that the most-favoured-nation clause shall *not* apply to dispute resolution mechanisms). The fact that arbitral awards may be annulled by ICSID ad hoc Committees or – in the case of commercial arbitration (unlike ICSID arbitration)[31] – may *not* be enforced by national courts on grounds of 'public order', is another illustration of the complex nature and frequent 'dialectics' (in Hegelian terms of thesis, anti-thesis and synthesis) of law-making and 'system-building' in modern IEL. In spite of the absence of a worldwide investment treaty coordinating the thousands of bilateral trade, investment and double taxation agreements, the bilaterally agreed most-favoured-nation and national treatment requirements, judicial clarifications and dispute settlements promote legal certainty and progressive systemic uniformity.[32]

Due to the legitimate diversity of private and public, national and international legal systems, conceptions of IEL and the interpretation and delimitation of economic rules may legitimately differ depending on the particular legal and social context and social practices (eg, of 'rule-following' rather than judicial contestation). The UN Charter, UN human rights instruments and the customary law requirement of interpreting international treaties and settling international disputes 'in conformity with the principles of justice' and human rights obligations of all UN member states justify a normative conception of law as a social pursuit of 'justice' on the basis of principles and rules whose 'right interpretation and application' often remain deeply contested.[33] This dual nature of modern legal systems – ie, their legal distinction between factual dimensions of law (as represented by authoritative issuance and social efficacy of rules) and its ideal claims to justice and moral correctness which, in cases of extreme injustice, may affect the validity of positive rules – are of crucial importance for legal interpretation and dispute settlement, not only inside constitutional democracies,[34] but also in IEL regulating the transnational cooperation among citizens and their constitutionally limited governments and other agents. For instance, the transformation of human rights as moral rights (eg, as tacitly accepted in discourse and reasoning among human beings accepting one another as autonomous and equal 'discursive creatures') into positive rules of constitutional law, human rights law and IEL never obviates normative questions of how such positively agreed rules should be interpreted in order to actually realize and 'optimize' their objectives and agreed principles of administrating justice and protecting human

[31] According to Arts 54 and 55 of the ICSID Convention, the only exception to enforceability of ICSID awards is state immunity. For non-ICSID arbitral awards, Art V(2)(b) of the 1958 UN Convention on the Recognition and Enforcement of Foreign Arbitral Awards ('New York Convention') allows the enforcement state to invoke its public policy against recognition and enforcement of arbitral awards.

[32] *cf* SW Schill, 'System-Building in Investment Treaty Arbitration and Lawmaking' (2011) 12 *German Law Journal* 1083–110.

[33] *cf* EU Petersmann, 'International Trade Law, Human Rights and the Customary International Law Rules on Treaty Interpretation' in Joseph, Kinley and Waincymer (eds) (2009) 69–90. On the distinction between the existence of a legal rule (ie, its autonomous norm-meaning as a sentence) and its interpretation and 'right application' see HG Gadamer, *Wahrheit und Methode* (Tübingen: Mohr, 1986) 314 ('understanding always is applying').

[34] *cf* R Alexy, 'The Dual Nature of Law' (2010) 23 *Ratio Juris* 167–82, who concludes that 'legal positivism is an inadequate theory of the nature of law' (at 180). Arguably, the inclusion of human rights and principles of justice into modern international and constitutional law also permits accommodating the dual nature of law within a broader concept of positive law.

rights.[35] Modern constitutional theory explains why protection of justice, human rights and legal security requires institutionalizing respect for reasonable 'constitutional pluralism', deliberative democracy and legal and judicial 'balancing' of competing rights supported by 'public reason'.

The universal recognition of inalienable human rights, of collective rights to popular self-determination and the legitimate diversity of individual and democratic preferences (as reflected in the diversity of democratic constitutions) require mutual respect for legitimate 'legal pluralism' in private and public, national and international economic regulation. Both national constitutions as well as international law proceed from the presumption of 'good faith' implementation of international legal obligations in conformity with human rights and other principles of justice common to national and international law. Hence, respect for human rights and for self-determination of peoples requires also respect for the legitimate diversity of 'constitutional pluralism'. Non-hierarchical legal relationships between diverse national and international legal sub-systems must be coordinated and clarified on the basis of 'universalizable' principles of justice, human rights, deliberative democracy, transnational rule of law and other common constitutional principles like judicial comity.[36] The borderlines between legal and non-legal rules of conduct dynamically evolve in response to legal and dispute settlement practices and struggles for human rights. Hence, international and 'transnational' legal practices – such as *lex mercatoria*, internet regulation, commercial and investor–state arbitration, elaboration of product and production standards by non-governmental organizations, UN and company codes of conduct for 'social corporate responsibility' and guidelines by international organizations (such as ILO core labour standards, IMF guidelines for 'floating exchange rates', for 'sovereign debt restructuring' and 'sovereign wealth funds', OECD guidelines for transnational corporations) – may be relevant context for interpreting IEL even if they remain 'soft law rules' challenging traditional interpretations of national and international rules without having 'hardened' yet into new positive law.[37]

From a historical perspective, private and public, national, transnational and international economic regulation and 'legal pluralism' have existed in Europe for more than two thousand years, as illustrated by market and banking regulations in ancient Greece, the trade agreements among ancient city republics in the Mediterranean, the transnational law merchant (*lex mercatoria*) under Roman law, the 'reception' of the Roman *jus commune* by more and more European states and city republics since the Middle Ages and the legal and judicial cooperation in transnational organizations like the 'Holy Roman Empire of the German Nation' and its Imperial Court (*Reichskammergericht*) which rendered thousands of judicial decisions during the seventeenth and eighteenth centuries.[38] Ever since the English, American and French revolutions, the democratic challenges of the 'Hobbesian paradigm' of the absolute state and of its Westphalian paradigm of 'international law among sovereign states' have continued to lead to ever more new forms of international cooperation, international organizations, transnational

[35] On such 'discourse justification' and 'existential recognition' of human rights as moral rights, and on disagreement of whether human rights are correctly transformed into positive law, see Alexy, ibid.

[36] On 'constitutional pluralism' see, eg, M Poiares Maduro, 'Contrapunctual Law: Europe's Constitutional Pluralism in Action' in N Walker (ed) (2003) 501–37.

[37] On the controversial demarcation of 'law' and 'non-law' see, eg, GP Callies and M Renner, 'Between Law and Social Norms: The Evolution of Global Governance' (2009) 22 *Ratio Juris* 260–80.

[38] *cf* R Zimmermann, 'Savigny's Legacy: Legal History, Comparative Law and the Emergence of a European Legal Science' (1996) 112 *Law Quarterly Review* 576–605.

private regulation, arbitration and collaborative 'private–public partnerships' aimed at regulating market failures as well as governance failures.[39] The 'fragmentation' of private and public, national and international legal regimes is an inevitable consequence of respect for legitimate 'legal pluralism' rather than proof of irreconcilable, perennial conflicts as claimed by some lawyers. For instance:

- Kelsen's conception of national law (including 'private international law' based on national choice-of-law rules) and international law as hierarchical legal orders commanding obedience on the basis of different 'basic norms' (*Grundnormen*) prompts many international lawyers to perceive competition among sovereign states as inherently power-oriented conflicts of legal authority and of conflicting conceptions of national and international law.[40]
- Similarly, advocates of 'critical legal studies' (like Koskenniemi) and 'radical pluralists' justifying authoritarian decision-making in antagonistic relations among 'friends and foes' (like Schmitt) often focus on 'strategic conflicts' among competing legal regimes rather than on their legal commonalities.[41]
- Disciples of Luhmann's 'autopoietic systems theory' perceive transnational regulation outside international treaty systems – like the *lex mercatoria* governing international trade transactions, the *lex sportiva* regulating international sports, transnational internet regulation or the emerging *lex culturalis* in transnational adjudication of restitution claims concerning stolen art and other illicit transfers of cultural heritage – as autonomously operating, de-nationalized social sub-systems with separate legal rationalities and law-creating institutions that are bound to clash with state-centred, national and international principles and rules.[42]

Up until the First World War, the classical 'Westphalian conceptions' (eg, by Grotius) of international law among sovereign states did not envisage permanent international institutions. In response to the First and Second World Wars and the world economic and political crises during the interwar period, UN law, IEL and regional human rights and economic agreements continue to provide for ever more international institutions and multilevel governance mechanisms aimed at limiting abuses of public and private power. Chapters II to IV emphasize that the more different actors – like free citizens, democratic institutions, national or international courts of justice, regulatory agencies, authoritarian rulers and their diplomats – pursue different interests and diverse interpretations of national and international economic rules, the stronger becomes the need for protecting inclusive decision-making and 'public reason' by means of constitutional rights and restraints. Rather than perceiving the 'fragmentation' of international legal regimes and the emergence of new, transnational regulatory regimes as a 'paradise lost', legal fragmentation often reflects inevitable, dialectic adjustments of the Westphalian system of 'international law among states' to the human rights obligations of all UN member states and the needs of their citizens. Chapters II and III use Kantian legal

[39] *cf* F Cafaggi, 'New Foundations of Transnational Private Regulation' (2011) 38 *Journal of Law and Society* 20–49.

[40] *cf* H Kelsen, *The Pure Theory of Law* (Berkeley: California University Press, 1989). Even though Kelsen derives legal hierarchies from the basic norm of international law, the national lawmaker remains sovereign to decide on the normative content of national law.

[41] *cf* M Koskenniemi, *La politique de droit international* (Paris: Pedone, 2007).

[42] *cf* A Fischer-Lescano and G Teubner, 'Regime-Collisions: the Vain Search for Legal Unity in the Fragmentation of Global Law' (2004) 25 *Michigan Journal of International Law* 999–1046.

theory for explaining why the antagonistic nature of social relations calls for multilevel constitutional protection of equal freedoms in all human interactions at national, transnational and international levels, as acknowledged in UN human rights law. Also, the antagonistic evolution of national and international legal systems in the context of the Westphalian 'international law among sovereign states' – as illustrated by colonialism, the First World War, the breakdown of international economic, social, political and legal cooperation during the 1930s, the Second World War and decolonization – can be interpreted in conformity with Kantian legal and historical theory as having contributed to today's universal acceptance by all UN member states of obligations to protect human rights and democratic self-government. 'Legal fragmentation' and 'legal pluralism' can provide building blocks for constructing needed 'syntheses' through 'trial and error' in order to reconcile diverse interests of citizens, non-governmental organizations, states and international organizations through adjustments of private and public, national, international and transnational legal systems. Chapters II to IV plead for citizen-oriented 'cosmopolitan conceptions' of IEL to strengthen legal and judicial protection of economic and social rights (eg, in human rights law, international trade law, investment, labour and economic integration law) on grounds of 'principles of justice', human rights, constitutional theory and the customary rules of international treaty interpretation.

HUMAN RIGHTS AND 'CONSTITUTIONAL JUSTICE' REQUIRE STRONGER PROTECTION IN IEL OF EQUAL RIGHTS OF CITIZENS AND TRANSNATIONAL RULE OF LAW

Law as an instrument of governance needs justification. In Europe and North America, there are longstanding traditions of justifying law not only in terms of 'output legitimacy' (such as peace and consumer welfare), but also in terms of 'input legitimacy' as defined by principles of justice, human rights and democratic self-governance. Investor–state arbitral awards recognize, for example, that investment protection 'should not be granted to investments made in violation of the most fundamental rules of protection of human rights'.[43] In the EU and the EEA, the empowerment of citizens by individual rights and judicial remedies contributed to the decentralized enforcement of the common market rules on the basis of equal guarantees of fundamental rights against welfare-reducing, private and public, national and international restraints of competition and trade. Beyond EU and EEA law, however, international trade, financial, investment and environmental regulation remain dominated by government bureaucracies and their business advisors without adequate representation and legal protection of general citizen interests in consumer welfare and protection of fundamental rights. Diplomats in the International Monetary Fund (IMF) and the World Bank Group often justify their neglect for human rights and constitutional rights in intergovernmental economic regulation by the claim that the Bretton Woods Agreements focus on regulation of economic policy issues (such as monetary sovereignty over the issuance of money, the international regulation of exchange rates, conditional balance-of-payments and development assistance) that do not directly interfere with the private rights of citizens. The intergovernmental regulation of international movements of goods, services, persons, capital,

[43] *Phoenix Action Ltd v Czech Republic*, ICSID Arbitration Award of 15 April 2009 (Case No ARB/06/5), para 78. All investment arbitral awards cited are electronically available (eg, at: ita.law.uvic.ca/).

related payments and property rights, by contrast, often operates by imposing tariffs and other discriminatory taxes on transnational economic transactions and restricting liberty rights, private contracts and national regulations in more direct ways that may be legitimately challenged by citizens in domestic courts, regional economic courts or investor–state arbitration. This book argues that the universal human rights obligations of all UN member states call for stronger constitutional and judicial protection of individual rights of citizens in IEL whenever governments restrict or distort mutually beneficial cooperation among citizens across frontiers. Yet, just as equal civil, political, economic and social rights need to be mutually balanced and entail obligations also for individuals, the rights-based approach to IEL is not only aimed at promoting individual and democratic self-government; it is also perceived as the most effective constitutional restraint on abuses of public and private power and as an incentive for institutionalizing 'public reason' through 'participatory' and 'deliberative democracy' and legal and judicial clarification of 'public reason'

The more than 50 years of GATT/WTO rules discriminating against competitive imports of cotton, textiles, agricultural products and other allegedly 'unfair competition' from LDCs – like the absence of GATT/WTO competition rules protecting consumer welfare and the inadequate regulation of international finance, investments and environmental pollution – reflect systemic 'producer biases' in intergovernmental economic regulation. As explained by 'public choice' theory, organized industries and government bureaucracies often collude in granting 'protection rents' in exchange for business support by elaborating trade and investment rules that – de jure or de facto – prevent citizens from holding governments legally, judicially and democratically accountable for welfare-reducing protectionism and violations of international economic agreements ratified by parliaments for the benefit of citizens. Diplomats from adversely affected LDCs often criticize such 'protection biases' of power-oriented, intergovernmental trade and investment agreements. Yet, they often also collude in opposing stronger legal protection of general citizen interests, for instance by opposing WTO competition and environmental rules, more transparent decision-making in the WTO, more effective involvement of parliaments and civil society in intergovernmental rulemaking, 'human rights impact assessments' and judicial protection in domestic courts of compliance with WTO law for the benefit of citizens. Beyond the WTO, the failures of the self-appointed 'G20' (composed of the EU and 19 countries with 'systemic importance' for the world economy) – which French President Sarkozy has presented as 'the planetary governance of the 21st century'[44] – to predict, prevent and effectively regulate the world financial crisis since 2008, the crisis in the WTO's Doha Round negotiations and the climate change crisis, likewise elude effective democratic, legal and judicial accountability with regard to citizens.

In the Uruguay Round of multilateral trade negotiations (from 1986 to 1994) ushering in the WTO Agreement, diplomats deliberately avoided any reference in WTO law to 'rule of law', 'courts of justice', democratic governance and human rights. During my work as secretary, member or chairman of numerous GATT and WTO dispute settlement bodies, I likewise observed the eagerness of diplomats and GATT/WTO lawyers to avoid referring to the customary law requirement of settling disputes and interpreting treaties 'in conformity with principles of justice' and the human rights obligations of states

[44] *Financial Times* (9 November 2010) 11.

(*cf* the Preamble and Article 31 VCLT). Reasonable people – even if they agree on the need for defending 'justice' and human rights – often disagree on how to define 'principles of justice', the human rights dimensions of international disputes, the legitimate functions of international 'courts of justice' and the legitimacy of IEL. Yet, respect for such 'reasonable disagreement' justifies neither treating citizens as mere objects of 'international law among states' nor the lack of effective legal and judicial remedies of citizens against arbitrary violations of intergovernmental rules. International economic transactions take place mainly among citizens in order to satisfy consumer demand for more, cheaper and a better quality of goods and services by enhancing division of labour, competition and productivity among producers. In the economic relations among the 30 EEA member states, IEL has been successfully transformed into a cosmopolitan 'integration law' protecting rule of law and equal rights for private economic actors rather than only rights and obligation for governments. European economic law suggests not only that legal and judicial consistency of economic rules with fundamental rights and judicial remedies of citizens is often a precondition for transnational rule of law and its democratic legitimacy; empowering citizens to actively participate in the decentralized enforcement of European economic and human rights law has also enhanced non-economic values like 'access to justice', 'participatory democracy' and civilian responsibility.[45] Hence, this book argues for a 'cosmopolitan paradigm change' in IEL: in the twenty-first century, international law must recognize citizens not only as legal subjects of human rights, but also of cosmopolitan rights to mutually beneficial economic cooperation across frontiers protecting citizens against arbitrary violations of transnational rule of law and other governance failures. Yet, politicians and diplomats have self-interests in limiting their legal and judicial accountability for their frequent violations of international rules and object to transforming intergovernmental economic rulemaking and adjudication (eg, in the WTO) into 'cosmopolitan economic integration law'[46] protecting also rights of citizens that are enforceable in domestic courts. Civil society rightly criticizes secretive WTO negotiations, dispute settlement rulings and investment arbitration that disregard consumer welfare and privilege powerful producer interests. As intergovernmental 'litigation strategies' shaping the progressive development of IEL remain one-sidedly dominated by political and producer interests, protecting civil society by broader cosmopolitan rights could enable citizens and courts of justice to engage in 'lawyering for social change' and protect transnational rule of law for the benefit of citizens.[47]

All eight chapters of this book discuss IEL with due regard to the human rights obligations of states and the customary law requirement of interpreting international treaties

[45] On the 'emancipatory potential' of 'judicial activism' for the benefit of citizen rights in the EU, the EEA and the ECHR and its impact on democracy in Europe see: TA Börzel, 'Participation through Law Enforcement. The Case of the EU' (2010) 39 *Comparative Political Studies* 128 ff; RA Cichowski, *The European Court and Civil Society. Litigation, Mobilization and Governance* (Cambridge: CUP, 2007).

[46] My publications have characterized IEL long since as 'integration law' in view of its 'constitutional functions' to go beyond reciprocal rights and obligations of states by protecting 'trading rights', investor rights, property rights, labour and human rights, consumer welfare and judicial remedies for the benefit of citizens engaged in the worldwide division of labour, as most visible in European economic law, *cf* EU Petersmann, 'From the Hobbesian International Law of Coexistence to Modern Integration Law: The WTO Dispute Settlement System' (1998) 2 *JIEL* 175–98.

[47] On 'lawyering for social change' in the US – by developing litigation strategies with the aim of changing the legal order by generating precedents with systemic legal importance beyond the particular dispute – see M Galanter, 'Why the Haves Come out Ahead: Speculations on the Limits of Legal Change' (1974) 9 *Law & Society Review* 95 ff. Galanter also mentions the risk that organized 'repeat players' in the legal system have considerable strategic advantages over individuals who only occasionally appear before courts.

and settling related disputes 'in conformity with principles of justice' and human rights, as explicitly recalled in Article 1 of the UN Charter as well as in the Vienna Convention on the Law of Treaties (Preamble and Article 31 VCLT). The main 'thesis' of this study is that human rights require stronger legal and judicial protection of cosmopolitan rights against the abuses of public and private power in IEL. Yet, 'cosmopolitan conceptions' of IEL must respect the legitimate diversity of theories of justice as reflected in the reality of 'constitutional pluralism'. All comprehensive theories of justice are likely to remain contested among citizens and governments in view of their often conflicting self-interests and value preferences – in international relations no less than inside states. Hence, whenever citizens and governments invoke 'principles of justice' as relevant context for interpreting economic freedoms, property rights, preferential treatment of LDCs, 'public interest exceptions' in international economic treaties or the jurisdiction of economic courts, reasonable disagreement over 'principles of justice' must be respected. For instance:

- Regional 'market freedoms' (eg, in EU law), 'trading rights' (eg, in WTO law) and worldwide liberalization of market access may be justified not only on utilitarian grounds[48] but – as in this study – as imperfect, cosmopolitan extensions of Rawls' 'first principle of justice', defined in terms of equal rights of citizens to 'the most extensive total system of equal basic liberties compatible with a similar system of liberty for all'.[49]
- The worldwide and regional rules on preferential treatment of LDCs (eg, by means of non-reciprocal tariff preferences, financial and technical assistance, 'trade facilitation' and capacity-building) may be justified not only on grounds of morality, but as an international extension of Rawls' 'second principle of justice' calling for differential treatment of the poor.
- International labour and social rights (eg, of access to water and other essential goods and services) may be justified as human rights rather than only as legislative or administrative rights.
- The 'general exceptions' and numerous safeguard clauses in worldwide and regional economic agreements can be construed as reflecting the Rawlsian claim that – as national welfare depends more on a country's social institutions than on its natural resources – each people can and should agree on social and constitutional arrangements that provide its citizens with the natural and social goods essential for satisfying basic needs.[50] Arguably, this 'democratic responsibility principle' also supports the cosmopolitan claim made in this study that respect for human dignity (eg, in the sense of individual autonomy and responsibility) requires empowering citizens by rights-based regulation of international economic cooperation at national and international levels.
- The increasingly comprehensive compulsory jurisdiction of national and international courts for protecting rule of law in international economic cooperation, and the customary law requirement of interpreting international treaties and settling related disputes 'in conformity with principles of justice' and the human rights obligations of

[48] On utilitarian Anglo-Saxon theories of 'justice as efficiency' see R Posner, *Economic Analysis of Law*, 2nd edn (Boston: Little Brown, 1977) 10: 'Efficiency means exploiting resources in such a way that "value" – human satisfaction as measured by aggregate consumer willingness to pay – is maximized'.

[49] *cf* J Rawls (1971) 250 and ch VI, section 4.

[50] *cf* Rawls (1999) 37–38, 106–20 ('the crucial element in how a country fares is its political culture – its members' political and civic virtues – and not the level of its resources') 117) and ch VI, section 4.

states, can be seen as protecting 'constitutional justice' (eg, in the sense of access to independent 'courts of justice') as one of the oldest paradigms of legal systems.[51]

The International Court of Justice (ICJ) and the ECJ often refer to their judicial functions of 'administering justice' and justify judgments in conformity with 'principles of justice' as reflected, eg, in the guarantees of UN and European human rights law. Also domestic parliaments and civil society – for instance, during their democratic debates on whether intergovernmental economic agreements deserve parliamentary ratification – increasingly insist that intergovernmental rules must be legitimated through 'deliberative democracy'. Yet, Habermas' 'ideal speech paradigm' – according to which 'just those action norms are valid to which all possibly affected persons could agree as participants in rational discourses'[52] – differs fundamentally from the frequent 'protectionist collusion' among parliamentarians and organized interest groups in parliamentary decision-making on economic rules and policies. Rather than deriving values from 'deliberative democracy ideals' or from realities of intergovernmental power politics, this study analyses and evaluates IEL – as explained in chapters II to IV – in the light of multilevel human rights law, Kant's justification of multilevel constitutional protection of cosmopolitan rights, and Rawls' explanation of the need for institutionalizing 'public reason' by constitutional, legislative, administrative and judicial protection of 'principles of justice'.

IEL MUST REMAIN JUSTIFIABLE IN TERMS OF JUSTICE AND 'PUBLIC REASON' (RAWLS)

Citizens trying to understand the modern thicket of worldwide IEL find it increasingly difficult to evaluate its legitimacy, even if governments invoke 'principles of justice' for justifying claims to distribution, compensation and legal reciprocity. One purpose of this monograph is to explore 'the wood hidden behind the trees' by contributing to a more critical discussion of the basic economic, legal, political and philosophical principles governing the thousands of economic rules and regulations. Chapters II to VI discuss modern 'theories of justice' for IEL based on the insight of Rawls that the constitutional legitimacy and 'public reason' of democratic legal systems depend on constitutional, legislative, administrative and judicial rules and institutions protecting an 'overlapping consensus' on 'principles of justice' and rule of law among citizens and governments with often conflicting value preferences and self-interests.[53] Yet, in contrast to Rawls' *Law of Peoples* (1999), this study argues in favour of a cosmopolitan conception of IEL focusing on multilevel protection of cosmopolitan rights. This normative claim – based on the incorporation of human rights into *positive law* – reflects the dual nature of the positive and ideal dimensions of modern legal systems and of the dialectic tensions between intergovernmental rulemaking in IEL and the human rights of citizens in UN member states.

The human rights obligations of all UN member states are based on universally recognized 'principles of justice' that require respecting, protecting and promoting indi-

[51] *cf* EU Petersmann, 'Human Rights, International Economic Law and "Constitutional Justice"' (2008) 19 *EJIL* 769–98.

[52] J Habermas (1996) 107.

[53] On the 'four-stage sequence' of legitimate rulemaking inside constitutional democracies like the US, see Rawls (1971) 195 ff.

vidual and democratic autonomy and legitimate diversity of citizens and people all over the world. Arguably, 'human rights is an account of what is right, not an account of what is good';[54] the legal empowerment of individuals by universal, inalienable, indivisible and interdependent human rights as constitutional safeguards against the historical experiences of abuses of political power reflects the same values that underlie common market and competition rules limiting abuses of public and private economic power so as to enable individuals to protect themselves against welfare-reducing market restrictions and injustice in the economy no less than in the polity. Multilevel human rights constitute equal rights of citizens as 'democratic principals', limit the power of all governments as 'agents', coordinate national and international legal regimes and promote 'principled' conflict resolution, legal coherence and synergies among national and international government policies for the benefit of citizens. American theories of justice and of the organization of the basic structure of national and international societies – like Nozick's theory of historical entitlement and Rawls' two basic principles of justice as fairness – tend to prioritize civil and political over economic and social rights like those acknowledged in the 1948 Universal Declaration of Human Rights (eg, Articles 23–26 UDHR) and in the 1966 International Covenant on Economic, Social and Cultural Rights (eg, Articles 9–13 ICESCR), which has not been ratified by the United States. European constitutional law, by contrast, protects the 'indivisibility' of human rights based on the insight that economic and social rights may be of no less existential importance for people and for interpreting and designing IEL than civil and political human rights.

Legal theories of justice legitimately vary depending on the individual and democratic preferences of people and their nationally and internationally agreed legal systems. This study uses Hart's concept of legal systems as a union of 'primary rules of conduct' and 'secondary rules' of recognition, change and adjudication; but it rejects Hart's outdated claim that international law 'resembles, (. . .) in form though not at all in content, a simple regime of primary or customary law' and, due to its incomplete 'secondary rules', a 'primitive legal order'.[55] In contrast to areas of international law where third-party adjudication remains an exception to the rule of 'auto-interpretation', modern IEL is characterized by an ever stronger role of national and international courts in clarifying, progressively developing and enforcing IEL and transnational rule of law in international economic cooperation among citizens, thereby transforming IEL into a more developed legal system than many other areas of international law. This is especially true for the diverse 'European conceptions' of IEL inside the EU and in the EEA, whose multilevel constitutional protection of fundamental rights and of transnational rule of law is, arguably, more developed than the 'constitutional nationalism' practised by most states outside Europe. The state-centred specificities of international law – in comparison with national legal systems – can be accommodated by respect for 'constitutional pluralism' with due regard to new forms of multilevel economic governance. The relationships between theories of justice and IEL must be clarified by interpreting IEL in the light of the human rights obligations and diverse constitutional obligations of governments and states with due regard to economic and social rights of the poor. As competition and conflicts among rights are a central constitutional problem in a world of limited resources, chapters V and VIII emphasize the need for constitutional and judicial protection of transnational rule of law

[54] M Ignatitieff, *Human Rights as Politics and Idolatry* (Princeton: Princeton University Press, 2000) 48.
[55] Hart (1994) 214.

in the international division of labour among citizens based on 'proportionality balancing' of competing human, constitutional, economic and social rights.

As protection of human rights calls for a cosmopolitan conception of IEL, this study supports the 'New Haven Approach' advocating leadership by constitutional democracies and 'courts of justice' for a post-Westphalian conception of international law. The continued validity of much of the criticism of the legitimacy of international law in recent research – for instance, in Franck's treatise on *Fairness in International Law and Institutions* (1995), Garcia's research on *Trade, Inequality and Justice: Toward a Liberal Theory of Just Trade* (2003) and Buchanan's study of *Justice, Legitimacy and Self-Determination: Moral Foundations for International Law* (2004) – has been illustrated by the international financial and banking crisis that started in 2008. My focus on Kantian legal and constitutional theory, as well as on European experiences with multilevel judicial protection of constitutional rights and other constitutional restraints on multilevel economic governance, distinguishes this study from Anglo-American legal philosophies and practices. The 'human rights approach' to IEL advocated in this book aims at contributing to autonomous self-limitation of the 'internal freedom' of reasonable individuals as well as to the 'constitutionalization' of their 'external, legal freedom' by 'principles of justice' and other constitutional restraints promoting 'public reason'. Arguably, the lack of such restraints during the financial crisis – as illustrated by perverse incentives for risk-taking and outrageous financial bonuses of bankers at the expense of taxpayers, private investors and consumers – was largely due to inadequate regulation of 'market failures' and of legal accountability of bankers and regulators 'socializing losses', for instance because banks were 'too big to fail' and regulators neglected 'systemic risks'. Strengthening 'countervailing rights' for adversely affected citizens and other 'constitutional restraints' on abuses of public and private power is not only justifiable on grounds of justice. It offers also the most 'realistic' means for enhancing transparency and limiting governance failures by promoting legal, judicial and democratic accountability for selfish abuses of power. A major task of a cosmopolitan theory of IEL is to go beyond regulating 'national self-interests' and relations among state agents by extending constitutional safeguards to citizens for their transnational economic cooperation. Rather than remaining a matter of 'natural law' or of discovering 'natural morons'[56] in an ideal 'third world' (beyond the physical 'outside world' and the psychological 'inside world' of human beings), clarifying cosmopolitan 'principles of justice' has become a task of interpreting positive law in conformity with the existing legal guarantees of human rights, popular self-determination and other constitutional restraints of governments.

[56] *cf* R Dworkin, 'Objectivity and Truth: You'd Better Believe It' (1996) 25 *Philosophy and Public Affairs* 87, 104: Objective moral reasoning need not embrace Platonic claims that moral values exist independently of subjective minds like 'some special particles – morons – whose energy and momentum establish fields that at once constitute the morality or immorality, or virtue or vice, of particular human acts and institutions and also interact in some way with human nervous systems to make people aware of the morality or immorality or the virtue or vice'. Dworkin's constitutional theory aims at explaining the implications for American law and politics of an essentially contractarian theory of constitutional rights that precede and stand above all government institutions and require them to protect these rights, apart from realizing other, more utilitarian tasks of promoting welfare and happiness.

GLOBAL PUBLIC GOODS THEORY AND THE UNDER-SUPPLY OF 'INTERDEPENDENT PUBLIC GOODS'

This book, as emphasized in its sub-title, differs from other books on IEL by its focus on constitutional and 'public goods' theories proceeding from the methodological premise that economic regulation needs to be justified also in terms of moral, political, constitutional and economic theories. Economists define 'public goods' by their 'non-excludable' and 'non-rival' use benefiting all citizens and preventing their commercial supply in private markets. As rules and institutions for public goods shape the infrastructure and welfare of states, the production, design, enforcement and justification of international public goods cannot be left to intergovernmental power politics and piecemeal engineering. The US proposals after the Second World War for a coherent set of Bretton Woods Agreements and the UN Charter focused on 'hegemonic leadership' and rights and obligations of state actors. This book claims that – as multilevel governance of interdependent international public goods has become the most challenging policy task in the twenty-first century – the current under-supply of international public goods requires embedding IEL into stronger constitutional, cosmopolitan and democratically justifiable foundations.

Economists and political scientists tend to distinguish three major varieties of public goods with different regulatory problems and 'production strategies'[57]:

(i) 'Single best efforts public goods' may be supplied unilaterally or 'minilaterally', for instance by investing in the development of medicines (such as polio vaccine) for preventing pandemics and by engineering technology for avoiding other potential catastrophes (such as 'geoengineering' as an option for preventing climate change).

(ii) 'Weakest link public goods' may be undermined if one or a few state(s) (for example poor or 'failed states') do not cooperate, for instance in polio eradication as a global public good or in nuclear non-proliferation and control of other weapons of mass destruction.

(iii) 'Aggregate efforts public goods' can be supplied only through collective action, which may not come about without incentives for cooperation and sanctions of non-cooperation. As discussed in chapter I, their collective supply tends to be confronted not only with numerous 'collective action problems' like 'free-riding' and other 'prisoner-dilemmas'. Global aggregate public goods also tend to be composed of numerous national and regional public goods and to interact with functionally related, other public goods. For instance, an efficient world trading system – which may be conceptualized as a non-rival and non-excludable public good beneficial for all consumers and trading countries (in contrast to the WTO or free trade agreements as 'club goods') – cannot properly function without a liberal (ie, liberty-based) legal and dispute settlement and international payments system (as 'intermediate public goods').

Distinguishing the different kinds of public goods and related regulatory problems may assist in designing the rules and institutions necessary for overcoming 'collective action problems'. For instance:

[57] *cf* S Barrett (2007) 22 ff.

- 'Best shot public goods' may be provided by private or public, national institutions (eg, research foundations for combating tropical diseases and promoting geoengineering) with little resort to international law and institutions (eg, for protection of patent rights, financial support, regulation of non-discriminatory access).
- 'Weakest link public goods' may require multilateral action (eg, authorization by the UN Security Council of humanitarian interventions into 'failed states') and multilateral regulation (eg, of non-proliferation of nuclear products) even if remedial interventions may be carried out by one single 'hegemonic power' (eg, US military intervention in Iraq in order to destroy alleged weapons of mass destruction). The financial and 'sovereign debt' crisis in the EU likewise illustrates how the regional public good of financial stability may be undermined by persistent violations of the EU fiscal and debt disciplines by a few irresponsible governments.
- 'Aggregate efforts public goods' tend to require multilateral treaties and institutions like the UN Charter for the protection of international peace, the IMF and WTO Agreements for the protection of a mutually coherent world trade and payments system, or multilateral agreements on limitation and supervision of environmental pollution. Why is it that some global public goods – postal services by the Universal Postal Union, telephone communications by the International Telecommunications Union – have in fact been protected long since?

This study focuses on 'aggregate international public goods' such as efficient monetary, trading, financial, investment, environmental and rule of law systems that tend to be composed of national and regional public goods and overlap each other in ever more complex ways. Chapters II to VI emphasize that 'principles of justice', cosmopolitan rights, constitutional law, democratic governance and other institutions protecting 'public reason' can be perceived as 'intermediate public legal goods' that are necessary for regulating and legitimizing global economic public goods, especially regarding:

- the constitution of international institutions with limited, delegated powers and 'checks and balances' protecting citizens;
- the distribution of rights, obligations, advantages and costs among cooperating states, non-governmental institutions, third states (eg, 'free riders') and individuals;
- the necessary cooperation among international institutions and coordination of their legal regimes (*cf*, eg, Articles XII–XV, XVIII GATT on cooperation among the IMF and GATT in controlling balance-of-payments restrictions);
- their inevitable 'prioritization' (eg, in Article 103 UN Charter) and conflict prevention mechanisms in order to use scarce resources most efficiently;
- the design of decision-making procedures that reduce the collective action problems (eg, of voluntary rulemaking based on state consent, consensus or 'single undertakings'), and promote 'constitutional principles' like transparency, accountability and rule of law;
- the peaceful settlement of disputes and sanctioning of non-compliance; and
- the coordination of interacting national and international legal regimes, for instance by legal harmonization and respect for national 'margins of appreciation'.

Human rights and constitutional 'principles of justice' say little about the optimal legal design of national and international institutions. As reasonable people may never agree on any comprehensive theory of justice, this study engages extensively in comparative assessments of the relative merits of 'constitutional' and 'institutional choices', alternative procedures for revealing democratic and cosmopolitan preferences and legal and judicial safeguards and 'balancing methods'. Chapters V and VIII emphasize the 'constitutional functions' of international courts for the peaceful settlement of disputes, judicial clarification of contested rules, protection of cosmopolitan rights and 'institutionalization of public reason'. The analysis of more than a hundred national and international court judgments interpreting, clarifying and developing economic rules in the light of relevant constitutional principles and cosmopolitan rights illustrates that judicial decisions may be conceived also as a 'single best effort public good' which – for instance, through cooperation or non-cooperation among competing jurisdictions and 'multilevel judicial governance' in the context of regional economic and human rights conventions and investor–state arbitration systems – remains closely related to 'aggregate effort public goods'. This books emphasizes that cosmopolitan rights and judicial remedies are necessary for 'contestation' and 'countervailing restraints' challenging the vast shift of additional, regulatory powers – as a result of globalization and of its transnational and global regulation – to the executive branches of states, multiple international institutions as well as to private actors with mobile economic resources.

Yet, the institutional safeguards for holding public and private international regulation legally and democratically accountable remain underdeveloped. This study argues that the various 'enabling', 'limiting', 'distributive' and 'corrective' functions of the law of international economic organizations raise corresponding questions of 'constitutional justice', 'distributive justice', 'corrective justice' and 'transitional justice' requiring coherent justifications and institutionalization of 'cosmopolitan public reason' (as discussed in chapters II to VI), notwithstanding the preferences of authoritarian rulers and their diplomats for utilitarian rather than constitutional justifications of IEL.[58] This study makes numerous propositions to reform the 'constitutional' and 'cosmopolitan deficiencies' in international trade and investment regulation, for instance by renegotiating the World Bank Convention establishing the International Center for the Settlement of Investment Disputes (ICSID) in order to make investor–state arbitration procedures more transparent and more coherent (eg, in case of multiple, simultaneous complaints in response to systemic economic crises like Argentina's financial and sovereign debt crises in 2001). In most worldwide economic organizations, international economic regulation continues to be designed in close cooperation among governments and business without effective control by national parliaments, courts and civil society. In contrast to rulemaking inside constitutional democracies, intergovernmental rulemaking often lacks effective constitutional restraints, for instance by human rights, parliamentary and 'deliberative democracy' and judicial remedies of adversely affected citizens. The eight 'GATT Rounds' of multilateral trade negotiations from 1950 to 1994 were characterized by protectionist pressures on trade negotiators and regulators by 'special interests' from

[58] Even though my long-standing arguments for 'cosmopolitan' and 'constitutional reforms' of the GATT and WTO legal and dispute settlement systems (eg, in Hilf and Petersmann (eds) (1993) ch 1; Petersmann (1997), ch 1) have been criticized by GATT/WTO diplomats and by protectionist interest groups as too much constraining 'state sovereignty' and 'realist state interests', this book continues to be based on the 'constitutional premises' developed in my earlier books (notably in Petersmann (1991)), including my long-standing proposition to conceive of international institutions for the collective supply of interdependent, international public goods as a 'fourth branch of governance' which – like the legislative, administrative and judicial branches – require constitutional restraints and democratic legitimation to protect citizens against abuses of power.

agricultural, cotton, textiles, steel, pharmaceutical and other industries in developed countries. In view of the progressive 'regulatory capture' of national and intergovernmental lawmakers by powerful interest groups and their professional lobbies, a 'package deal' replacing GATT 1947 and the 1979 Tokyo Round Agreements by the 1994 WTO Agreement turned out to be the only political option for fundamental legal reforms of the world trading system. The failure of the 153 WTO members to reach consensus on new 'Doha Development Round agreements' during the Doha Round negotiations from 2001 has led to increasing criticism from environmental groups, human rights groups, public health organizations, labour unions and LDCs challenging 'injustices' and 'imbalances' of the world trading system.[59] In spite of worldwide criticism of the gap between the declared objectives of IEL and the realities on the ground, governments fail to agree on the needed economic, political, legal and institutional reforms. For instance, can the reality of 'interest group politics' in intergovernmental negotiations be overcome without using the 'constitutional techniques' that succeeded in limiting abuses of power and 'regulatory capture' by vested self-interests inside constitutional democracies, such as constitutional, institutional and competition safeguards of 'general citizen interests', 'checks and balances' and judicial protection of constitutional rights? How can national parliaments control more effectively global rulemaking? Should deficits in 'democratic input legitimacy' in the law of worldwide organizations be compensated by stronger judicial remedies for protection of human rights and rule of law by 'courts of justice'? Are the traditional legal theories of 'monism' and 'dualism', or political 'principal-agent' conceptions of international organizations, appropriate for protecting human rights in multilevel economic governance? If the legitimacy of international law no longer depends only on state consent, but also on consistency with the multilevel human rights obligations of governments and respect for democratic self-determination, how should judges clarify the procedural and substantive 'principles of justice' underlying IEL, especially in intergovernmental disputes where governments often prevent adversely affected private parties from submitting *amicus curiae* briefs complaining of violations of human rights?

The 1944 Bretton Woods institutions and the 1948 Havana Charter for an International Trade Organization were negotiated on the basis of drafts provided by the US government. The failure of the US Congress to adopt legislation empowering the US government to conclude the Doha Development Round negotiations in the WTO and the UN negotiations on climate change prevention illustrate today's lack of leadership by the United States for collective protection of 'global public goods'. As discussed in chapter I, the globalization of markets, of the environment, of international law and communications requires not only new kinds of multilevel regulation of transnational 'market failures' and 'governance failures'. The necessary delegation of limited legislative, administrative and judicial powers to intergovernmental organizations risks undermining democratic and judicial protection of rule of law and individual rights unless intergovernmental decision-making is constitutionally restrained by parliamentary control and judicial protection of individual rights. This requires multilevel constitutional theories recognizing the need for compensating the deficiencies of 'constitutional nationalism' by stronger

[59] *cf* D Zang, 'Divided by Common Language: "Capture" Theories in GATT/WTO and the Communicative Impasse' (2010) 32 *Hastings International & Comparative Law Review* 423–76; R Rosa Cedro and B Furtado Vieira, 'John Rawls' Justice as Fairness and the WTO: A Critical Analysis on the Initial Position of the Multilateral Agricultural Negotiations' (2010) 3(2) *The Law and Development Review*.

'constitutionalization' of foreign policies and of multilevel governance of interdependent public goods.[60]

THE NEED FOR RIGHTS-BASED REGULATION LIMITING THE 'COLLECTIVE ACTION PROBLEMS' IN IEL

Globalization continues to weaken the traditional forms of 'constitutional checks and balances' by national parliaments, limited delegation of powers to national governments and 'courts of justice' protecting the rights of citizens against abuses of public and private power. The ever greater impact of international relations on the domestic welfare of citizens requires new forms of multilevel governance of interdependent public goods and multilevel judicial protection of rule of law in the worldwide division of labour among more than 6 billion citizens. The worldwide crises of the international trading, financial and environmental systems confirm that neither the Bretton Woods Agreements nor the WTO Agreement (as a substitute for the stillborn 1948 Havana Charter for an International Trade Organization) effectively protect consumer welfare, 'sustainable development', human rights and democratic self-governance. The progressive liberalization and regulation of international trade and investments continues to evolve on the basis of bilateral, regional and worldwide agreements which – like the Bretton Woods and WTO agreements – usually refrain from referring to human rights. How should WTO bodies respond to the increasing criticism that WTO law and other areas of IEL are inconsistent with 'principles of justice' and the human rights of the more than one billion poor people living in WTO member countries without adequate access to food, water, sanitation and essential medicines? Does the worldwide recognition of 'inalienable' and 'indivisible' human rights constitute a new 'cosmopolitan' rather than 'state-centred' foundation of IEL? What are the legal consequences of the repeated recognition by all UN member states, since the Universal Declaration on Human Rights (UDHR) of 1948, 'of the inherent dignity and of the equal and inalienable rights of all members of the human family (as) the foundation of freedom, justice and peace in the world' (Preamble UDHR) for the worldwide regulation and governance of markets, competition, private property (as a precondition for private freedom), freedom of profession, freedom of association (including the right to strike), freedom of commercial opinion and the necessary legal limitations of economic freedoms to protect social justice and the environment?

This study analyzes 'constitutional problems' of IEL from the perspective of rational and reasonable citizens and their constitutional rights rather than from the perspective of governments. It challenges – from the perspective of human rights, constitutional democracies, economics and political 'public choice' theories – the normative legitimacy of the often non-transparent, inefficient and arbitrary ways of modern international

[60] On the need for protecting the collective human rights obligations of UN member states not only at national, but also at international levels see ch IV and ME Salomon, *Global Responsibility for Human Rights: World Poverty and the Development of International Law* (Oxford: OUP, 2007). On the dependence of multilevel protection of human rights and of democratic self-governance on multilevel protection of transnational rule of law, see chs V and VIII as well as G Palombella and N Walker (eds), *Relocating the Rule of Law* (Oxford: Hart Publishing, 2009). On the 'globalization of constitutional law' and functionally limited 'multilevel constitutionalism', see chs II to V and F Venter, *Global Features of Constitutional Law* (Nijmegen: Wolf Legal Publishers, 2010).

economic regulation. Yet, it also takes into account that rational citizens in the 193 UN member states are unlikely to ever agree on any comprehensive theory of justice or of 'global constitutionalism' in international relations. IEL will continue to be driven primarily by economic rationality. Yet, it requires constitutional reforms protecting human rights, 'democratic constitutionalism' and peaceful resolution of the ubiquity of conflicts of interests 'in conformity with principles of justice', with due respect for legitimately diverse views of citizens and governments on how civil, political, economic, social and cultural rights should be mutually reconciled at national and international levels of governance. Chapters I to IV argue that – from the perspective of reasonable citizens – the 'constitutional legitimacy' of IEL depends primarily on its consistency with human rights and constitutional democracy rather than on utilitarian welfare arguments. The book's normative claim – ie, that the 'collective action problems' in the supply of global 'aggregate public goods' can be overcome only on the basis of multilevel protection of cosmopolitan rights, transnational rule of law and respect for 'constitutional pluralism' at national and international levels – is strongly influenced by the revolutionary reforms of European economic law since the Second World War, not only within the EU and among the 30 member states of the EEA, but increasingly also in the more than 25 free trade agreements of the EU with ever more third countries in Europe and beyond (eg, Chile, Mexico and Korea).[61] The rights-based, multilevel constitutional protection of a 'social market economy' in European law is bound to remain contested by citizens and governments with different preferences and diverse 'constitutional experiences', such as Anglo-Saxon democracies without constitutional protection of economic and social rights, Asian countries with Confucian traditions emphasizing social duties rather than individual legal rights and non-liberal countries.

THE NEED FOR COORDINATING LEGAL REGIMES ON THE BASIS OF 'MULTILEVEL CONSTITUTIONAL PLURALISM'

This study claims that the prevailing conceptions of 'international law among sovereign states' and of international economics neither ensure collective supply of global public goods nor effectively coordinate the ever larger plurality of national, regional and worldwide legal systems in conformity with human rights and democratic constitutionalism. Contrary to the authoritarian beliefs of some human rights advocates, international market competition – as a citizen-driven, decentralized information and adjustment-mechanism for coordinating the autonomous actions of billions of producers, investors, traders and consumers participating in the worldwide division of labour – is an indispensable complement of human rights. Yet, contrary to the beliefs of Anglo-Saxon 'market fundamentalists', neither economic markets nor 'political markets' (democracy) can function efficiently and legitimately without

- '*enabling constitutions*' empowering citizens and governments to collectively supply interdependent public goods;
- '*limiting constitutions*' limiting the ubiquity of 'governance failures' and 'market failures' by rights-based regulation empowering adversely affected citizens and courts of justice to protect equal rights of citizens; as well as

[61] *cf* European Commission, 'Trade, Growth and World Affairs – Trade Policy as a Core Component of the EU's 2020 Strategy' COM (2010) 612 (Brussels, 9 November 2010).

- functionally limited, *multilevel constitutional safeguards* for the collective supply of supplementary, international public goods and for reconciling competing, increasingly overlapping 'partial constitutional regimes' with due respect for 'constitutional pluralism'. Some Anglo-Saxon common law theories argue that human progress is best achieved in private 'common law societies' by imposing as few restrictions as possible on 'natural liberties', rational utility maximization and self-regulating markets. This study proceeds, by contrast, from Kant's assumption of the antagonistic nature and conflicts of interests dominating human competition, which call for multilevel constitutional protection of equal liberties and transnational rule of law in all human interactions at national, transnational and international levels. Protection of consumer welfare in the global division of labour depends on multilevel legal restraints of 'market failures', 'governance failures', 'discourse failures' and other conflicts of interests.

As inside constitutional democracies, a modern theory of IEL must analyze questions of rulemaking, administration, adjudication and compliance not only from the standpoint of governments, but from the perspective of citizens, their constitutional rights and the need for multilevel judicial protection of transnational rule of law. Just as democracies can remain stable over time only as a 'constitutional democracy' whose constitution, legislation, administration, adjudication and 'deliberative democracy' must be 'anchored' in an 'overlapping consensus' (Rawls) on 'principles of justice', so must citizen-oriented conception of IEL in the twenty-first century be 'constitutionally anchored' and justified by 'principles of justice' as defined by human rights, democratic constitutionalism and legitimate 'constitutional pluralism'. Economic analyses of 'market failures' and 'public choice' analyses of 'governance failures' must be supplemented by 'constitutional choice' analyses of 'constitutional failures' and by 'comparative institutional economics' evaluating alternative decision-making processes, like citizen-driven market processes, political processes and judicial procedures.[62]

IEL regulates transnational economic cooperation in incomplete ways in response to 'demand for regulation' by citizens, governments and non-governmental organizations adversely affected by 'market failures' or 'governance failures'. Due to 'rule-following' and 'Westphalian path-dependence', intergovernmental regulation all too often continues focusing on reciprocal rights and obligations of governments without providing for legal, democratic and judicial accountability of governments vis-à-vis citizens. In the modern age of human rights and constitutional rights, authoritarian 'law-as-command' theories are no longer sufficient for justifying the validity of, and compliance with, international economic rules. Westphalian conceptions of 'international law among states' often fail to offer efficient and effective instruments for the collective supply of international public goods, as explained in chapter I. As the relevant 'rules of recognition' should be applied in conformity with human rights and other constitutional restraints of power, the interpretation and development of IEL may legitimately differ – as discussed in chapters II to IV – depending on the constitutional rules and conceptions of 'justice' prevailing in different jurisdictions. Chapters V and VIII discuss numerous case studies

[62] *cf* the interdisciplinary constitutional, economic and 'public choice' analyses of multilevel economic regulation in Hilf and Petersmann (eds) (1993). On participation-oriented 'comparative institutional analysis' of alternative decision-making processes like markets, political processes and judicial procedures, see NK Komesar (1994).

where 'courts of justice' clarifying incomplete, often vaguely drafted and contested rules of IEL justified their decisions also in terms of human rights and other 'constitutional principles' like non-discriminatory treatment of citizens and 'proportionality' of government restrictions aimed at protecting and 'balancing' competing individual rights. Economic analysis of law, cost-benefit analyses and comparative 'institutional choices' (eg, between markets, political government interventions and alternative rules and institutions) risk offering an incomplete analysis of regulatory problems. Reviewing multilevel 'constitutional choices' for constituting, limiting and supplementing legislative, administrative and judicial powers and participatory rights of citizens has proven to be of crucial importance for the success of economic integration in Europe, for instance compared with the failures of many regional trade agreements in Africa and in the Americas to create non-discriminatory conditions of market competition. Justice – as the oldest paradigm of law – requires not only that IEL must remain justifiable in terms of principles of human rights, constitutional democracies and other 'principles of justice'. Constitutional principles of justice will remain effective only to the extent they are supported by legislatures, administrations, courts and citizens as shared 'public reason'. Respect for the legitimate diversity of moral, legal, economic and political theories of justice suggests that the legitimacy and appropriate design of IEL in the twenty-first century have become more complex than most theories (eg, on 'global administrative law' and 'conflicts law' conceptions of IEL) admit. 'Constitutional pluralism' emphasizes the need for respecting this legal complexity without indulging in any utopia of a 'common philosophy' on 'global constitutionalism'.

THE STRUCTURE OF THIS BOOK

The book begins by discussing *normative questions* which tend to be neglected by legal practitioners, diplomats and civil servants working in national ministries of foreign affairs and worldwide economic organizations like the Bretton Woods institutions, the UN Conference on Trade and Development (UNCTAD) and the WTO.

Chapter I explores how IEL should be designed in order to protect more effectively 'global aggregate public goods' (like a mutually beneficial trading, financial and environmental system preventing climate change) that are beneficial for all citizens but can neither be supplied by individual states nor through private markets because their benefits are 'non-excludable' (eg, they cannot be withheld practicably from one individual without withholding them from others) and 'non-rival' (eg, their consumption by one individual does not diminish their availability for others). Chapter I claims that the current lack of coherent legal and political strategies for transforming national and regional into global public goods requires 'integrating' the different private and public, national and international conceptions of multilevel economic regulation to improve the problem-solving capacity of IEL and its 'constitutional functions' for empowering citizens to increase their individual and social welfare through mutually beneficial, rules-based cooperation. Chapter I makes the empirical and normative claim that – as substantiated by numerous case studies, notably in chapters V and VIII – the multilevel judicial protection of the EU common market rules, the EEA common market rules, of the human rights guarantees in the European Convention on Human Rights (ECHR) as well as of transnational commercial, investment and arbitration law offers four diverse examples of 'cosmopolitan legal orders' that have proven empirically and normatively more successful in protecting transnational rule of law for the benefit of citizens than the state-centred 'Westphalian conceptions' of IEL underlying the Bretton Woods Agreements, GATT and WTO law.

Chapter II discusses the emergence of 'multilevel constitutional restraints' and 'global administrative rules' in regional and worldwide 'economic integration law' in order to limit the disintegrating effects of 'legal fragmentation' and transform 'legal pluralism' into a mutually coherent rule of law system on the basis of 'common constitutional principles' governing national and international law. Rights-based conceptions of international economic regulation call for stronger constitutional restraints of multilevel economic governance aimed at correcting 'market failures' and subjecting 'governance failures' to multilevel 'constitutional checks and balances' in order to protect human rights and democratic constitutionalism more effectively. The terms 'constitutionalism', 'constitutionalization', constitutional pluralism and 'human rights coherence' of IEL are explained.

Chapter III uses Kant's theory of multilevel constitutional protection of equal liberties and Rawls' theory of constitutional protection of 'public reason' for explaining why – contrary to power-oriented, allegedly 'realist' claims that political morality and justice do not reach beyond the boundaries of states – the legitimacy of international law and transnational 'rule of law' no longer depend only on state consent, but on multilevel protection of constitutional rights and democratic self-government. The human rights jurisprudence of the ECJ, the EFTA Court and the European Court of Human Rights (ECtHR) illustrate why human rights are essential not only for empowering individuals, but for promoting horizontal and vertical coherence of interdependent, national and international legal systems and jurisdictions. The current financial and environmental crises illustrate the need for limiting the ubiquitous 'moral hazards' in economic relations by multilevel constitutional protection of 'public reason' and 'countervailing rights' of citizens. As explained by Kant and by other modern theories of cosmopolitanism, rights-based 'multilevel constitutionalism' is not only morally required; it offers also the politically most 'realist' strategy for limiting abuses of public and private power for the benefit of citizens by promoting 'participatory' and 'deliberative democracy' as necessary complements of parliamentary and representative democracy.

Chapter IV examines the diverse strategies for making multilevel economic regulation (for example of market competition and property rights) consistent with the human rights obligations of governments at national, regional and worldwide levels with due respect for legitimately diverse conceptions of human rights, constitutional democracies and 'corporate social responsibilities'. The legitimacy and effectiveness of IEL depend on its 'human rights coherence' and on support by an 'overlapping consensus' on principles of justice and 'public reason' justifying international economic rules. Hence, economic liberties must be interpreted in conformity with all other constitutional rights. Contrary to authoritarian conceptions (eg, by Schmitt) of human nature and politics as endless power struggles between friends and foes, constitutional and cosmopolitan conceptions of modern IEL aim at reducing antagonistic conflicts on the basis of 'universalizable' principles of justice and fair procedures justifying and clarifying contested rules by means of legislation, administrative and judicial clarification, 'deliberative democracy' and 'proportionality balancing' of the civil, political, economic, social and cultural dimensions of fundamental rights.

Chapters I to IV criticize the prevailing 'Westphalian view' – ie, that IEL must be conceived and further developed as 'international law among states' – not only for unduly neglecting the customary law requirement of interpreting international treaties and settling international disputes 'in conformity with principles of justice' and the human rights obligations of all UN member states. IEL also fails to protect 'sustainable development', human rights and other 'global public goods' by means of an international 'social market economy' protecting equal, or at least fair opportunities for citizens in rich and poor countries to live the life they have reason to value. Chapter V explains why human rights, the 'overlapping nature' of most international 'aggregate public goods' and the 'collective action problems' require citizen-driven 'struggles for rights' (Jhering) and for multilevel protection of transnational 'rule of law', with due respect for the reality and normative legitimacy of 'constitutional pluralism' and for legitimately diverse conceptions of justice as an explicit objective of national and international legal systems. The judicial functions of courts of justice and human rights require respect ('judicial comity') for the interdependence and mutually coherent interpretation of legal systems for the benefit of citizens.

Chapter VI claims that human rights and justice also require that IEL rules must remain justifiable in terms of formal as well as substantive principles of justice governing national, transnational and international economic regulation; the 'human rights coherence' and democratic legitimacy of multilevel legal and judicial protection of transnational 'rule of law' must be justified by an 'overlapping consensus' on principles of justice, respecting 'reasonable disagreement' among countries and citizens with diverse preferences and often conflicting self-interests; as the intergovernmental structures of UN law have failed to protect and fulfil the promise of UN human rights (as proclaimed in Article 28 UDHR) to a just international economic and constitutional order, the decision of WTO members to keep the WTO outside the system of UN Specialized Agencies remains justifiable, for instance in view of the fact that WTO membership is open to non-state entities (like Hong Kong and the EU) which have not been admitted to UN institutions.

Chapter VII argues that – notwithstanding the need for respecting legitimate 'constitutional pluralism' at national and international levels of governance – multilevel protection of interdependent public goods requires far-reaching changes also in the law of international organizations outside the UN system, like the WTO. For instance, the WTO practices of 'member-driven governance' and decision-making on the basis of consensus and 'single undertakings' has led to institutional paralysis blocking initiatives for protecting international public goods. The universal duties to protect human rights entail constitutional and cosmopolitan duties to reform IEL by adjusting the 'Bretton Woods system' of the 1940s and the WTO to the citizen-driven structures of modern globalization, human rights law and constitutional democracies. All three Bretton Woods institutions – the IMF, the World Bank and the WTO (as the late step-child of the still-born International Trade Organization as envisaged by the 1948 Havana Charter) – face legitimacy and accountability crises due to their inadequate rules, decision-making procedures and 'governance failures' in protecting efficient trading, financial, development and human rights systems. The necessary constitutional reforms are unlikely to come about 'top-down' by 'G20 recommendations' and intergovernmental agreements unless citizens, civil society, parliaments and courts insist more strongly on challenging intergovernmental power politics from the perspective of human rights, 'deliberative democracy' and other constitutional 'checks and balances'. Chapter VIII concludes that the past focus on 'constitutional nationalism' – as illustrated by the refusal of some Supreme Court justices (eg, in the United States) to refer to international and 'foreign law', as well as by the one-sidedly inward-looking focus of members of national parliaments (eg, US congressmen) on their political dependence on local constituencies and 'election campaign financing' by organized interest groups – must be limited by multilevel 'constitutional conceptions' of international guarantees of freedom, non-discrimination and rule of law for the benefit of citizens and their cosmopolitan rights. National and international courts should cooperate in interpreting IEL in conformity with modern human rights and in strengthening 'multilevel constitutional restraints' protecting international public goods like transnational rule of law in the global division of labour.

MULTILEVEL CONSTITUTIONALISM AND COSMOPOLITAN CONCEPTIONS OF IEL DEPEND ON 'STRUGGLES FOR RIGHTS'

Since the beginnings of written history (eg, in the books of the Hebrew bible and the Greek *Ilias*), rivalry among individuals, groups and people is described as the major driving force of social, economic and political relations.[63] The human rights declarations of 1776 and 1789 resulted from revolutions of citizens claiming inalienable human rights vis-à-vis oppressive governments. In the UN human rights declarations of 1948, 1993 and 2008, governments universally acknowledged that 'human rights are the first responsibility of governments'.[64] European history and the jurisprudence of European courts illustrate how transforming moral and legal human rights into constitutional democracies protecting common markets and civil, political, economic and social human rights across frontiers requires 'struggles for justice'. The main conclusion of this study is that the twenty-first century must be used by citizens, parliaments, governments and 'courts of justice' for transforming IEL into a more legitimate and more effective instrument for protecting cosmopolitan rights and interdependent public goods. IEL must be conceptualized no longer only in the 'Westphalian tradition' of 'international law among states', but as 'law of peoples' (Rawls) and cosmopolitan 'international law among citizens' entitled to stronger legal and judicial protection of their human rights and other constitutional rights in international economic regulation. The 'regulatory failures' of IEL require legal and judicial limitations of the foreign policy discretion of governments and of private self-regulation by multinational corporations. As many politicians, diplomats, rent-seeking industries and authoritarian governments resist such legal reforms and judicial accountability, civil society and 'courts of justice' must insist on greater respect for 'principles of justice' justifying reinterpretation of existing rules of IEL in conformity with human rights and rule of law for the benefit of citizens.

[63] *cf* E Frankel (ed), *The Illustrated Hebrew Bible* (New York: Stewart, Tabori & Chang, 1999) 23, 29, who identifies family rivalries (eg, since the murder of Abel by his brother Cain) and power politics (like the forced exodus and 'diaspora' of Jews following the repeated conquests of Jerusalem by the Babylonian, Egyptian, Persian and Syrian Empires) as two major themes of human history since antiquity.

[64] For the texts see: D van Gunsteren and B Fassbender (eds), *Menschenrechterklärung. Universal Declaration of Human Rights* (Munich: European Law Publishers, 2009); the quoted text is from the 1993 Vienna Declaration on Human Rights.

The book aims at contributing to the necessary search for 'cosmopolitan public reason' justifying and promoting constitutional reforms of modern IEL. Just as the pervasive conflicts of interests in international economic regulation originate inside the limited reasonableness of individuals, so must legal protection of 'cosmopolitan public reason' in IEL focus on legal and judicial protection of the individual's human rights, constitutional rights, rule of law, general consumer welfare and peaceful settlement of disputes with due respect for 'reasonable disagreement'. UN law protects 'sovereign equality of states' claiming a monopoly for the coercive enforcement of law within their national jurisdictions, including for their 'primary responsibility' of protecting the human rights of their citizens. Yet, European human rights and economic law illustrate that multilevel constitutional and judicial protection of human rights and of other principles of justice can operate as the most important driving force for cosmopolitan reforms of IEL limiting domestic 'governance failures' and justifying 'duties to protect' human rights across national boundaries. The diverse modes of regional economic integration law (eg, inside the EU, the EEA, NAFTA and MERCOSUR) confirm that respect for 'constitutional pluralism' offers diverse, albeit imperfect 'checks and balances' limiting abuses of public and private power in transnational cooperation among free citizens and democratic governments. The fact that the existing worldwide monetary, trade and environmental agreements are based on legal principles that emerged first at national and bilateral levels (eg, in the US trade agreements based on the US Reciprocal Trade Agreements Act of 1934) suggests that the needed reforms of IEL may be most effective if they evolve 'bottom-up' based on 'best practices' rather than on the basis of premature claims of global 'top down regulation'.

The human rights revolutions which have occurred since the eighteenth century, the successful trade liberalization across Europe during the second half of the nineteenth century, the 'labour law revolution' following the First World War and the international human rights revolutions, decolonization and worldwide economic integration following the Second World War, illustrate that citizen-driven 'struggles for rights' and judicial 'piecemeal reforms' of Westphalian 'treaties among sovereign states' are often necessary before political agreement on new worldwide rules and institutions may be feasible. This book offers numerous examples why, eg, international dispute settlement systems have become more effective if they were supported and legitimated by involving citizens, non-governmental organizations and civil society rather than only states.[65]

The financial crisis that began in 2008 and its destruction of private savings worth trillions of US dollars are reminders that – wherever economic and social rights of citizens are not effectively protected – abuses of power, selfish egoism and the 'banality of evil' (Arendt) risk to prevail. The failure of the IMF to limit the ever larger balance-of-payments imbalances by using the IMF surveillance powers granted in Article IV of the IMF Agreement, the failure of the G20 to agree on new multilateral adjustment disciplines for monetary and exchange rate policies as part of a new 'Bretton Woods III Agreement',[66] or the failure of

[65] *cf* GC Shaffer and R Meléndez-Ortiz (eds), *Dispute Settlement at the WTO. The Developing Country Experience* (Cambridge: CUP, 2010), whose empirical country-studies demonstrate that not only developed countries (like the US and EU member states), but also LDCs have used WTO dispute settlement proceedings most effectively whenever governmental complaints were politically, financially and legally supported by domestic industries, non-governmental organizations and civil society based on domestic legislation granting procedural rights and incentives for private parties to petition for WTO dispute settlement complaints.

[66] R Zoellick, President of the World Bank Group, proposes that the 'development of a monetary system to succeed "Bretton Woods II", launched in 1971, . . . should include possible changes in International Monetary

EU member states and EU institutions to comply with their constitutional obligations to 'avoid excessive government deficits' (Article 126 TFEU) illustrate that reforms of modern IEL cannot be left to politicians alone. Nor can correction of 'market failures' be left to private self-regulation, as illustrated by the fierce opposition from self-interested bankers against increasing the equity requirements of banks in order to reduce banks' systemic risks and 'moral hazards' that contributed to the near collapse of the financial system at the expense of taxpayers.

This study illustrates in numerous case studies that, the less IEL protects 'democratic input legitimacy', the stronger is the need for 'deliberative democracy' and judicial review of the consistency of international economic regulation with constitutional restraints like human rights, transparent rulemaking, due process of law, 'proportionality' of restrictions of individual rights and legal safeguards of 'output legitimacy.' Chapter VIII explains why – in ever more fields of IEL – transparent, independent, impartial and multilevel judicial review and 'balancing' of legislative and administrative restrictions of individual freedoms – based on 'suitability' (efficiency), necessity (rationality) and 'reasonableness tests' (proportionality *stricto sensu*) as constitutional preconditions for lawful governmental restrictions of constitutional rights – is becoming the hallmark of rights-based constitutionalism and the 'ultimate rule of law' (Beatty). Governments and business usually focus their economic rulemaking on reciprocal rights and obligations without justifying economic regulation in terms of principles of justice. In contrast to political institutions and business, the constitutional mandates of 'courts of justice' may require judges to justify their interpretation and application of 'under-theorized' economic rules in terms of 'administration of justice'.[67]

'PUBLIC JUSTICE' (KANT) IN IEL WILL ALWAYS REMAIN CONTESTED

The legal implications of 'principles of justice' for resolving specific disputes often remain contested and require judicial deference towards national 'margins of appreciation', 'reasonable disagreement' and 'constitutional pluralism'. Hence, it is also understandable that – notwithstanding the two statues representing 'peace' and 'justice' at the

Fund rules to review capital as well as current account policies, and connect IMF monetary assessments with WTO obligations not to use currency policies to remove trade concessions. This package approach to economic cooperation reaches beyond the G20 dialogue' and 'supplies a growth and monetary agenda that parallels the G20 financial sector reforms' *Financial Times* (8 November 2010) 13. Zoellick's proposals for considering the use of gold as part of a new monetary 'Bretton Woods III' Agreement provoked widespread public criticism of a return to some gold standard (which JM Keynes chastised as 'a barbarous relic'), for instance because gold's stabilizing properties are 'largely mythical' and 'unrepresentative of the economy': 'any reserve currency needs a supply that can grow as rapidly as global trade. Gold supply falls significantly short of this basic requirement': *Financial Times* (9 November 2010) 2, 10.

[67] *cf* G Sartor, *Doing Justice to Rights and Values: Teleological Reasoning and Proportionality in Judicial Review* (Florence: EUI Law Department Working Paper, 2010) 2–3: 'doing justice in interpersonal relationships depends on duly taking into account all the *valuable interests* at stake, both individual and collective, namely all interests that deserve (legal) protection. If justice consists in making choices that best respond to all valuable interests, then doing justice seems to involve two aspects, maximization and balancing: a just choice should maximize the benefit resulting from the aggregation of the choice's impacts on the relevant interests (maximization), taking into account the relative importance of these interests (balancing)'. On the ancient distinctions between case-specific 'particular justice' and abstract principles of 'justice' (eg, in the 'Thomist sense' of understanding 'justice' generically as the sum of all virtues), see already Acquinas, *Summa Theologiae* (Allen: Benzinger Bros, 1947) question 58.

entrance of the WTO headquarters – trade diplomats inside the Centre William Rappard focus on a rules-based trading system and leave it to 'deliberative democracy' and 'courts of justice' to clarify the perennial controversies over the 'social justice' of international economic regulation. According to WTO member governments, there is no need for incorporating human rights into WTO law. Legal and judicial interpretation of WTO rules in conformity with human rights and the 1994 WTO Decision on the mutual coherence of trade and environmental policies, like the 1996 WTO Ministerial Declaration rejecting 'the use of labour standards for protectionist purposes' and calling for cooperation with the International Labour Organization as 'the competent body to set and deal with [labor] standards', are widely perceived as more appropriate examples for promoting legal coherence among IEL and human rights than incorporating UN human rights obligations into WTO law, eg, following the controversial precedent of incorporating intellectual property treaty obligations into the WTO Agreement on Trade-Related Intellectual Property Rights (TRIPS).[68] Respect for the plurality of justifications of reasonable economic rules in terms of diverse 'principles of justice' is more important than the elusive search for worldwide agreement on how to define the formal, procedural and substantive dimensions of 'social justice' and legitimacy in IEL. Yet, public discussion and legal clarification of the 'public reason' of the dangerously inadequate international economic order at the beginning of the twenty-first century are necessary for transforming IEL into a more effective tool for protecting human rights of citizens all over the world. As illustrated by the progressive transformation of European economic integration law, 'paradigm shifts' in favour of cosmopolitan conceptions of IEL must take place first inside the minds of individual citizens, politicians, lawyers and judges before they may eventually become accepted by governments as integral parts of positive IEL.

This book does *not* offer a systematic description of IEL, for instance of its historical evolution, legal subjects and steering mechanisms, the main international economic organizations and dispute settlement systems in IEL, the multilevel regulation of international monetary and trade relations, international competition, transports, communications and other services, investment relations, international government procurement, commodity markets, intellectual property rights and other fields of international economic regulation. The purpose of this book is rather to reconsider basic systemic questions and regulatory problems of international economic regulation in the twenty-first century. For instance:

1. How should IEL, its 'systemic' nature, legitimate objectives, 'primary rules of conduct' and 'secondary rules' of recognition, adjudication and enforcement be conceived in the twenty-first century? Does IEL constitute a 'legal system' for multilevel economic governance?
2. Does IEL need to be justified by theories of justice? Is the prevailing conception of 'public international law among sovereign states' consistent with the human rights obligations of all UN member states? Do human rights require a cosmopolitan conception of IEL (as, eg, in the common market regulations of the EU and the EEA) in order to protect human rights and consumer welfare more effectively?

[68] *cf* C Thomas, 'The WTO and Labour Rights: Strategies of Linkage' in Joseph, Kinley and Waincymer (eds) (2009) 257 ff. See also the joint study by the ILO and WTO Secretariats on 'Trade and Employment: Challenges for Policy Research' (Geneva, 2007), which emphasized mutual synergies among labour, social and trade policies and acknowledged labour rights as fundamental rights that may be relevant context for interpreting WTO rules.

3. Is the 'constitutionalization' of IEL by means of multilevel regulation and limitation of abuses of economic power the logical continuation of postwar decolonization of international economic relations? Why did governments fail after the First World War, but succeed after the Second World War to reconstruct a liberal international economic order? Why has the transformation of GATT 1947 into the WTO legal system been so much more successful than the attempts at reforming international monetary, financial, investment and environmental law?
4. What are the main causes and origins of the current crises in the international trading, financial, development and environmental systems? Are the related failures of IEL the inevitable fate of humanity in view of the 'rational egoism' of individuals and the ubiquitous 'market failures' and 'governance failures'?
5. Does multilevel governance of interdependent national, regional and worldwide public goods require a multilevel constitutional theory? Are cosmopolitan rights and transnational rule of law necessary for regulating the 'collective action problems' in the decentralized supply of interdependent 'aggregate efforts public goods'?
6. How are the major theoretical approaches in international relations theories and international law related to each other? Do the legitimacy and effectiveness of IEL require an 'overlapping consensus' on principles of justice justifying international economic regulation? Can the 'fragmented' private and public, national and international legal sub-systems of IEL be coordinated without recourse to some coherent theory of 'multilevel constitutional pluralism'?
7. Are the experiences of 'constitutionalism' and 'constitutionalization' relevant for limiting 'market failures' and 'governance failures' in international economic regulation? How should the ambiguous terms 'constitution', 'constitutionalism', 'constitutionalization' and 'constitutional pluralism' be defined in the context of IEL? Have state constitutions become 'partial constitutions' in a globally integrating world where individuals and national communities are increasingly influenced by events originating abroad such as global markets, financial crises, health pandemics, terrorism and environmental pollution?
8. Are the 'principles' underlying international monetary, trade, financial, investment and environmental law mutually coherent? Should economic courts interpret treaty rules by 'balancing' economic principles with human rights principles? Does the universal recognition of human rights influence the interpretation of the 'rules of recognition' of public international law as defined in Article 38 ICJ Statute? Why is it that citizens, NGOs, parliaments, governments, courts of justice and international organizations (like the EU) often have such different views about the appropriate interpretation of IEL rules?
9. What is the legitimate role of 'courts of justice' in interpreting and clarifying IEL rules, principles, individual rights, market access commitments and 'public interest' regulation? Are courts of justice the only branch of government that has to justify its decisions – as independent 'exemplars of public reason' (Rawls) – on the basis of constitutional principles of justice? Is impartial and independent judicial review closer to the ideal dimension of law than political and parliamentary rulemaking based on majority politics? Is judicial discourse based on laws, precedent and legal dogmatics only a special case of general practical discourse open to moral arguments concerning rights and justice, ethical arguments concerning individual and collective identities and pragmatic means-end arguments?

10. Does the potential 'tyranny of majority politics' require judicial protection of constitutional citizen rights also in relation to intergovernmental economic regulation? Why are governments so often requesting courts to exercise judicial deference in respect of requests by citizens for judicial review of intergovernmental restrictions of individual economic liberties and property rights (eg, in case of UN 'smart sanctions' against individuals without judicial remedies, EU trade restrictions in manifest violation of WTO and EU guarantees of freedom, non-discrimination and rule of law)? Was the EU Regulation of 11 May 2010 on the introduction of a European Financial Stability Facility aimed at stabilizing the European financial system consistent with EU law (eg, Article 122:2 TFEU, the 'no bailout' clause in Article 125 TFEU, the 'principle of conferral' of limited powers)?[69]
11. Why do many economic courts refer only rarely to the customary law requirement (as codified in the Preamble of the VCLT) of interpreting international law, and settling disputes over the interpretation of treaties, 'in conformity with the principles of justice' and human rights? Why is this customary law requirement of 'constitutional interpretation' so often ignored by GATT/WTO dispute settlement panels and investor–state arbitrators?
12. What are the legal interrelationships between multilevel human rights law, multilevel 'constitutional law' (eg, providing for cooperation among independent 'courts of justice') and multilevel economic guarantees of equal freedoms, non-discrimination and judicial protection of rule of law (as in European free trade agreements)? Do multilevel human rights and multilevel economic guarantees of freedom, non-discrimination and rule of law rest on common 'principles of justice'? How can the 'functional unity' of IEL be defined, if it exists at all?
13. What are the constitutive building blocks of a 'highly competitive social market economy' (Article 3 TEU)? Can the citizen-oriented approach to European economic law serve as a model for citizen-oriented interpretations of international trade, investment and environmental law beyond Europe? Can the 'collective action problems' impeding global public goods be resolved without recourse to the 'constitutional methods' used for national and regional public goods? What kinds of WTO reforms would a constitutional approach to IEL require?
14. Can parliamentary democracy remain effective in a globally integrating world without stronger protection of deliberative, participatory and 'cosmopolitan democracy' and stronger judicial remedies? Should IEL be evaluated in terms of its contribution to protecting human rights? Is the EU Charter of Fundamental Rights and its distinction between dignity rights, liberty rights, equality rights, solidarity rights, citizen rights and rights to justice consistent with the different distinctions between civil, political, economic, social and cultural human rights in UN law?
15. Do the 'principles of justice' underlying UN law enable governments to supply 'international public goods' effectively? Which 'constitutional principles' are important for limiting the collective action problems in supplying interdependent public goods?

[69] For the view that this EU Regulation No 407/2010 (OJ L118/1 of 12 May 2010) was inconsistent with Arts 122:2, 125, 127:5 and 352 TFEU see: M Seidel, 'Aktuelle Probleme der Europäischen Währungsunion' (2010) 4 *Integration* 334–49.

Lawyers, politicians and economists are likely to answer these questions in diverse ways depending on their normative premises. The conclusions at the end of this study, summarizing my own answers as elaborated in the eight chapters, are kept deliberately brief; for this book – which was drafted during my busy years as head of the Law Department of the European University Institute at Florence, when the dramatic changes in the international financial, trading and environmental systems required ever more revisions of the text – evolved, unfortunately, into a much longer manuscript than originally envisaged. This book differs from other textbooks on IEL by its 'constitutional' and interdisciplinary approaches. Their two methodological and normative premises are based on positive law and should not be misunderstood as 'utopian idealism': First, the human rights obligations of all UN member states require interpreting treaties, and settling related disputes, 'in conformity with principles of justice' and human rights challenging the prevailing 'Westphalian power politics' and its under-supply of public goods demanded by citizens. Secondly, human rights and the collective action problems impeding the supply of international public goods also require regulating the limited reasonableness of human beings, 'majoritarian governance' and intergovernmental power politics by constitutional and cosmopolitan rights and multilevel, judicial protection of transnational rule of law for the benefit of citizens. Westphalian conceptions of government in terms of promoting 'state interests' (as defined by rulers and their diplomats) must be limited by constitutional conceptions of multilevel, democratic self-governance.

Throughout the book, my arguments are illustrated with more than a hundred case examples from diverse fields of economic and human rights adjudication – which may render the reading of some of the text more difficult for those not familiar with adjudication in these often very diverse, national and international jurisdictions. The philosophical and constitutional premises of this study will inevitably remain contested, especially from the perspective of non-democratic countries, Anglo-Saxon 'majoritarian democracies' and 'Washington interest group democracy' with its often 'corrupting influence of money' on economic rulemaking. European 'multilevel constitutionalism' and its underlying 'constitutional economics' differ fundamentally also from the utilitarian 'dollar-sterling diplomacy' dominating the Bretton Woods conferences in the 1940s.[70] The study refers extensively to relevant legal, political and economics literature in the hope of promoting more public discussion on the methodological problems of IEL and its changing 'rules of recognition'.[71] Each chapter begins with short summaries and overviews of the main arguments so that each chapter can be read as a complementary essay; the disadvantage of this conception of the eight chapters is some repetition of the 'cosmopolitan premises' of each chapter. As the book focuses on legal, political and economic *principles* underlying the historically grown thicket of thousands of IEL *rules*, it avoids getting lost in systematic *descriptions* of many 'technical details' of the ever more complex international monetary, trade, financial, investment, development and environmental regulations. The normative and methodological premises are summarized in 25 tables and illustrated by discussing judgments of international tribunals and domestic courts

[70] *cf* the classic analysis by RN Gardner, *Sterling-Dollar Diplomacy: Anglo-American Collaboration in the Reconstruction of Multilateral Trade* (Oxford: OUP, 1956) and the revised 1980 edn: *Sterling-Dollar Diplomacy in Current Perspective: The Origins and Prospects of our International Economic Order* (New York: Columbia University Press, 1980). I wish to thank Richard Gardner for many stimulating discussions at Florence and New York on the issues analyzed in the following chapters.

[71] The books listed in the bibliography are cited in the footnotes in abbreviated form.

in developed and less-developed countries. Thanks are due to my EUI research assistants Johanna Croon and Anna Pitaraki, as well as to the participants in my annual doctoral seminars on *European and International Economic Law – Constitutional Problems of Law and Economics* at the European University Institute in Florence, for frank criticism of some of the texts. All mistakes are my own. Hopefully, the imperfections of this book will prompt other researchers and practitioners of IEL to further debate and clarify the moral and constitutional foundations of multilevel economic regulation as well as the practical relevance of the 'human rights revolution' and 'judicial revolution' in European economic law for more cosmopolitan conceptions of worldwide IEL.

I

How Should International Economic Law be Designed in Order to Protect 'Interdependent Public Goods' More Effectively?

INDIVIDUAL AND SOCIAL life are characterized by progressive discovery and realization – through 'trials and errors' – of the complexity of human nature, like our sentiments, emotions, animal instincts, rationality, limited social reasonableness and search for 'equilibrium' in our quest for self-realization, social cooperation and exploration of the limits of the 'human condition'.[1] Most people – even if they define their identity in terms of social, cultural and political narratives (eg, as members of a family, social community or polity) – devote most of their professional and much of their private life to economic activities like producing, trading and consuming private and public goods and services. As barter, money and trade are of existential importance for satisfying basic human needs through social cooperation, monetary and trade regulation are among the oldest fields of law.[2] Since the rights-based American and French revolutions in the eighteenth century, constitutional theory claims that all legal and governance institutions must be justified by legal and institutional protection of human rights and other 'principles of justice' necessary for promoting respect for human dignity, 'public reason' and rule of law limiting rational egoism, moral hazards and the ubiquity of conflicts among individuals. This study argues that – just as the inability to predict the 2008 economic crisis requires economists to review the mathematical models of their 'dismal economic science' in favour of more humane conceptions of the *homo economicus* – the inability of governments to protect international financial stability and other 'global public goods'[3] calls for a

[1] The books by Frans de Waal, *Our Inner Ape: The Best and Worst of Human Nature* (London: Granta Books, 2005) and *Primates and Philosophers: How Morality Evolved* (Princeton: Princeton University Press, 2006), emphasize the mental and moral continuity in the social behaviour of humans and other animals. On the controversial conceptions of the relationship between the human mind (eg, the psychological capacities of sensation, perception, memory, cognitive and cogitative powers, vision, emotions and volition) and the human body (eg, the brain) see: M Freeman and O Goodenough (eds), *Law, Mind and Brain* (Burlington: Ashgate, 2009).

[2] *cf* WJ Bernstein, *A Splendid Exchange. How Trade Shaped the World* (New York: Monthly Press, 2008); N Ferguson, *The Ascent of Money: A Financial History of the World* (New York: The Penguin Press, 2008).

[3] On the defining characteristics of 'public goods', the 'collective action problems' impeding the supply of international 'public goods' (like the 'jurisdictional gap', the 'participation gap', 'incentive gap' and 'prisoner dilemmas') and on the increasing democratic insistence on devolving decision-making powers to the lowest possible level ('subsidiarity') in order to promote 'stakeholder participation' in the decentralized implementation and enforcement of multilevel regulation, see: I Kaul, I Grunberg and MA Stern (1999). While economic analysis of public goods has a long standing (*cf* M Olson, 1971), legal analysis of international regulation of public goods remains rare; *cf* P Drahos, 'The Regulation of Public Goods' in KE Maskus and JH Reichman (eds) (2005) 46–64.

'paradigm change' in multilevel economic governance.[4] In order to become more legitimate and more supported by civil society, the traditionally state-centred conceptions of intergovernmental monetary, trade, development and environmental regulation must be supplemented by 'constitutional' and 'cosmopolitan conceptions' of IEL. Such citizen-oriented conceptions are bound to be opposed by many governments and multinational corporations benefiting from the current 'regulatory gaps', 'regulatory capture', lack of effective parliamentary control of international economic regulation and lack of judicial accountability for many welfare-reducing 'governance failures.' As stated by Machiavelli in *The Prince* (1513):

> [T]here is nothing more difficult to execute, nor more dubious of success, nor more dangerous to administer than to take the lead in the introduction of a new order to things. Because the innovator has for enemies all those who have done well under the old conditions, and lukewarm defenders in those who may do well under the new.[5]

OVERVIEW OF CHAPTER I

Section 1 gives an overview of the evolution of IEL since the trade-liberalization agreement between the United Kingdom and France in 1860 up to the world financial crisis since 2008. Section 2 follows from the regulatory failures in IEL and from its 'two paradoxes of liberty' that there is a need for a 'paradigm change' in international economic regulation in favour of cosmopolitan and 'constitutional' conceptions of multilevel economic regulation for the benefit of citizens; arguably, the multilevel judicial protection of the EU common market rules by national courts and the ECJ, of the EEA common market rules by national courts and the EFTA Court, of the human rights guarantees in the ECHR by national courts and the European Court of Human Rights (ECtHR), as well as of transnational commercial, investment and arbitration law by national courts and transnational arbitral tribunals offers four diverse examples of 'cosmopolitan legal orders' that have proven empirically and normatively more successful in protecting transnational rule of law for the benefit of citizens than the state-centred 'Westphalian conceptions' of IEL underlying the Bretton Woods Agreements, GATT and WTO law. Section 3 discusses and compares five diverse conceptions of IEL. It suggests that – from a human rights perspective – the evolution of worldwide international economic regulation remains characterized by 'constitutional failures' such as the unnecessary poverty of more than one billion people living without effective access to water, sanitation, food, essential medicines or rule of law. The universal recognition of human rights by all UN member states calls for stronger legal and judicial safeguards for interpreting, developing and enforcing the 'primary rules' and 'secondary rules' of IEL for the benefit of citizens

[4] The term 'governance' is derived from the Latin word *gubernare* referring to both steering and regulating the course of actions. The proposed 'paradigm shift' in economic governance and in its legal regulation refers to the need for charting a new course in interpreting IEL and producing public goods: like a captain of a boat has to chart the course agreed with the boat passengers, IEL must no longer be interpreted only in terms of rights and obligations of the rulers; the constitutional rights of citizens as the 'democratic principals' of 'government agents' require stronger legal protection, notably by courts of justice as 'independent and impartial guardians' of rule of law. As stated in the UDHR, the human rights obligations of all UN member states require 'that human rights should be protected by the rule of law' (Preamble UDHR) in all fields of government regulation.

[5] P Bondanella and M Musa (eds), *Machivelli* (New York: Penguin Books, 1979) 94.

and their constitutional rights. Section 4 identifies five major 'collective action problems' in the supply of global public goods such as an efficient world trading and financial system, protection of the environment and international rule of law. As inside constitutional democracies, overcoming the transnational collective action problems requires stronger constitutional restraints on multilevel economic governance based on international rulemaking, rule administration and judicial protection of international rule of law and rights of citizens in their decentralized, market-driven cooperation in support of international public goods. The constitutional and 'public goods' theories and 'methodological pluralism' applied in Chapter I reject the methodological claim of international relations theories (like realism, institutionalism and functionalism) focusing one-sidedly on power, security and states as the most important actors; they proceed from 'normative individualism' rather than power politics and utilitarianism as legitimate value premise of modern IEL and argue that 'public choices' (eg, by legislatures, governments and courts) should be analysed and justifiable in terms of consent, democratic politics and representative rulemaking by rational and reasonable citizens as 'democratic principals' of government agents with limited, delegated powers.

1 TRIALS AND ERRORS IN INTERNATIONAL ECONOMIC REGULATION: HOW SHOULD IEL BE EVALUATED?

Since the nineteenth century, economic mercantilism, colonialism and imperialism were increasingly challenged by economic liberalism based on Smith's and Ricardo's economic theories for a mutually beneficial division of labour exploiting the absolute and comparative advantages of countries (eg, in terms of natural and human resources) in producing goods and services. Economic mercantilism and colonialism had been shaped by power politics of the rulers in order to increase government revenue (eg, as a means for increasing national power) and reduce the scarcity of resources. The liberal, ie, liberty-based international division of labour in the production of traded goods and services, by contrast, tends to be driven by demand and supply of citizens, market competition and the utilitarian propensity of rational human beings to maximize satisfaction of human needs and preferences through efficient use of resources (eg, by buying less expensive goods and services imported from abroad).[6]

A mutually beneficial international division of labour requires mutually coherent monetary and trade regulation. From the Cobden–Chevalier trade agreement of 1860 between the United Kingdom and France until the First World War, the European system of bilateral trade agreements, most-favoured-nation commitments and convertibility of national currencies into gold or silver had promoted several decades of liberal trade, monetary stability and economic growth.[7] Following the First World War, the various worldwide economic conferences convened in the framework of the League of Nations lacked leadership and failed to recreate a multilateral monetary and trade system. The banking crisis on Wall Street in 1929 evolved into a worldwide economic depression when the trade barriers enacted by the 1930 Smoot-Hawley Tariff Act of the US Congress

[6] On the influence of economics on the formation of international law, the economic assumptions of 'methodological individualism' (ie, individuals seek to maximize their preferences) and 'normative individualism' (ie, individuals are the only valid source of values), and on the formation and application of national and international rules and related allocation of jurisdiction, see: JP Trachtman (2008).

[7] On the historical evolution of IEL see: EU Petersmann (1991) 31 ff.

triggered worldwide payments and trade restrictions, insolvencies of banks, economic recession and unemployment across North America and Europe. The dramatic restrictions of international payments and trade entailed economic, social and political disintegration during the 1930s ushering in political dictatorships in many European countries and the Second World War. Based on draft agreements proposed by the US government, the 1944 Bretton Woods Agreements, the 1945 UN Charter, the law of UN Specialized Agencies and GATT 1947 responded to these dramatic experiences of 'governance failures' by laying the multilateral, legal and institutional foundations for more than 60 years of international trade expansion, economic integration and historically unprecedented economic welfare in developed and many less-developed countries.

The Bretton Woods Agreements, GATT and the WTO: success stories?

At the 1944 Bretton Woods Conference, the drafters of the International Monetary Fund (IMF) and World Bank Agreements emphasized the mutually complementary functions of international monetary, financial and trade rules and institutions. Article IV of the IMF Agreement required each member state 'to collaborate with the Fund to promote exchange stability, to maintain orderly exchange arrangements with other members, and to avoid competitive exchange alterations' on the basis of 'par values' (defined in gold or US dollars); discriminatory monetary practices and exchange restrictions were prohibited subject to exceptions for countries without convertible currencies. Article V provides for drawing rights and stand-by arrangements enabling member states to draw on the financial resources of the Fund in case of balance of payments problems.

The unilateral termination of the gold convertibility of the US dollar on 15 August 1971 entailed the end of the par value system. The 1978 amendment of the IMF Agreement requires each member state to promote 'orderly exchange arrangements' by

1. pegging the value of its currency to the currency of another member or to the Fund's Special Drawing Rights;
2. through cooperative arrangements with other members (like regional monetary systems); or
3. any other exchange arrangements (including floating exchange rates) subject to the prohibition of manipulation of exchange rates (like competitive devaluations).

The more all major currencies floated against each other (except within the European Monetary System), the more the IMF surveillance functions pursuant to Article IV became focused on LDCs; requests from developed countries for balance-of-payments assistance from the IMF became increasingly rare.[8] The quota, voting and governance systems of the IMF – providing EU member states with seven directors on the IMF executive board, compared with only one for the United States and 12 for the 161 less-developed IMF members – discriminates against the emerging economies like Brazil, China and India. The IMF has also failed to regulate the imbalances of currency reserves and volatile capital flows resulting from the large US trade deficit and the associated surpluses of China, Japan, Germany and oil exporting countries (the bilateral trade deficit between China and the United States was $252 billion in November 2010). The

[8] *cf* AF Lowenfeld, 'The International Monetary System: A Look Back over Seven Decades' (2010) 13 *JIEL* 575–95.

'conditionality' of the IMF's financial assistance based on the 'Washington consensus' (eg, that 'crony capitalism', corruption and weak regulation had been major causes of the financial crises in Asia and Russia during the 1990s) has become more and more contested among LDCs. The recent involvement of the IMF in the financing of the public debt of Greece and Ireland – without a clear legal basis in the absence of exchange rate and balance of payments problems of these eurozone member countries – raises broader problems of the 'constitutional legality' of such financial assistance beyond the limited legal mandate in the IMF Agreement.

The current 187 member states of the IMF progressively realized their statutory objectives 'to facilitate the expansion and balanced growth of international trade' through international monetary cooperation, promotion of 'orderly exchange arrangements' and 'the establishment of a multilateral system of payments in respect of current transactions between members' (Article I IMF Agreement). The replacement, since August 1971, of the fixed exchange rate system based on the US dollar by the unilateral introduction and subsequent legalization of floating currencies limited the supervisory, lending and regulatory functions of the IMF essentially to LDCs with debt crises and balance-of-payments problems.[9] The participation of the IMF in the conditional financial assistance for the eurozone member countries Greece and Ireland in 2010 illustrated the capacity of the IMF to assume new tasks in preventing international financial and monetary crises. Hence, the Bretton Woods Agreements can be viewed as a success story, especially if compared with the monetary disorder before the Second World War. Also, the 186 member states of the World Bank Group – including the International Bank for Reconstruction and Development (IBRD 1944), the International Finance Corporation (IFC 1956), the International Development Association (IDA 1960), the International Centre for the Settlement of Investment Disputes (ICSID 1965) and the Multilateral Investment Guarantee Agency (MIGA 1985) – progressively expanded their financial and technical assistance to LDCs around the world.[10]

The IMF and World Bank rules, their independent funds and three-tiered governance institutions (boards of governors, boards of executive directors in continuous residence at Washington, and permanent staff directed by the IMF Managing Director and World Bank President, respectively) are based on international treaties ratified by their more than 180 member states. The rejection by the US Congress of the 1948 Havana Charter for an International Trade Organization entailed that GATT 1947 never entered into force as international treaty law. It continued to be applied only on a 'provisional basis' subject to 'grandfather exceptions' for existing trade restrictions and 'waivers' for additional trade restrictions in the United States and other countries, without adequate financial and institutional resources. The statutory objectives of GATT 1947 – ie, to contribute to 'the substantial reduction of tariffs and other barriers to trade and to the elimination of discriminatory treatment in international commerce' – were, to some extent, realized through eight successive 'GATT Rounds' of multilateral trade negotiations. The latter prioritized powerful interests in developed countries, for instance in liberalization of industrial tariffs, restrictions of cotton, textiles and agricultural imports from LDCs, legalization of agricultural subsidies, regulation of worldwide product standards and technical regulations as applied in industrialized countries and unilateral enforcement of

[9] *cf* ibid.

[10] For collections of these international economic agreements and other basic legal instruments of international economic law see, eg: P Kunig, N Lau and W Meng (eds) (1993); S Zamora and RA Brand (1990).

intellectual property rights through trade sanctions (eg, based on section 301 of the US Trade Act). Due to the 'consensus practices' in the GATT dispute settlement system, the adoption of many GATT dispute settlement reports was 'vetoed' by powerful trading countries. GATT 1947 remained dominated by intergovernmental power politics aimed at 'rule by law' without effective constitutional guarantees of 'rule of law' for the benefit of citizens. GATT contracting parties failed to regulate systemic 'market failures' (like restrictive business practices) as well as 'governance failures' (such as discriminatory anti-dumping and government procurement practices); general consumer welfare was neither mentioned nor effectively protected as an objective of GATT rules.[11]

In 1995, GATT 1947 was replaced by the WTO, which now administers more than 30 worldwide agreements on trade in goods, services and trade-related intellectual property rights among 156 WTO members (2012) covering more than 90 per cent of world trade. By acceding to GATT and the WTO and integrating into the legal framework of the worldwide division of labour, ever more less-developed GATT and WTO member countries, such as Brazil, Chile, China, India, Singapore and South Africa, succeeded in promoting their rapid economic, social and legal development, thereby lifting hundreds of millions of poor citizens out of poverty.[12]

The limits of 'Westphalian IEL': international poverty, financial, economic and environmental crises

From a legal perspective focusing on the statutory rules and objectives of the Bretton Woods Agreements, GATT, the WTO, the more than 250 regional trade agreements (RTAs) and more than 2800 Bilateral Investment Treaties (BITs), IEL could be described as one of the most successful fields of international law since the Second World War. Such a positive assessment might be justified notably from the perspective of the 30 developed OECD countries (which tend to consume up to 80 per cent of the world's resources) as well as from a historical perspective recalling the failures of the international legal system following the First World War. Yet, the 'Westphalian focus' on rights and obligations of governments asserting 'sovereignty' over their domestic territories and people neglects that human rights, democracy, non-discriminatory conditions of competition and consumer welfare are not effectively protected in many LDCs. From a human rights perspective, the unnecessary poverty of some two billion people living on two dollars per day or less, and the more than three billion people living outside rule of law and democratic governance[13] – notably in 'failed states' and resource-rich LDCs governed by non-democratic rulers – illustrate the many 'dark sides' of IEL. Systemic governance failures have also been revealed by the financial crises since 2008, the climate change crisis, the intergovernmental distortions of the world trade system by the long-standing discrimination against cotton, textiles and agricultural imports from LDCs, and by the inadequate WTO decision-making procedures impeding further liberalization and regulation of world trade during the WTO Doha Round negotiations since 2001. The enormous complexity of the worldwide, regional and

[11] *cf* RM Gadbaw, 'Systemic Regulation of Global Trade and Finance: A Tale of Two Systems' (2010) 13 *JIEL* 551–74.

[12] For a detailed analysis and criticism of the international trading system, see ch VII.

[13] *cf* Commission on Legal Empowerment of the Poor, *Making the Law Work for Everyone: Report of the Commission on Legal Empowerment of the Poor*, vol I, especially chs 2 and 3 (Geneva: UN, 2008).

bilateral economic agreements and national regulations governing the international division of labour among more than six billion producers, investors, traders and consumers in 193 UN member states also render effective *domestic*, democratic and parliamentary control increasingly illusionary. Apart from these and other shortcomings of worldwide economic agreements focusing on 'sovereign rights' and obligations of states, there are increasing doubts of whether the existing *system of IEL* and of its multilevel governance will be able to cope with what the presidents of the leading economies described – at their 'G20 summit meeting' at Pittsburgh in September 2009 – as the 'critical transition from crisis to recovery to turn the page on an era of irresponsibility and to adopt a set of policies, regulations and reforms to meet the needs of the 21st century global economy'.[14]

In their 2009 Pittsburgh Summit Declaration, the G20 leaders recalled that

> when we last gathered in April, we confronted the greatest challenge to the world economy in our generation. Global output was contracting at a pace not seen since the 1930s. Trade was plummeting. Jobs were disappearing rapidly. Our people worried that the world was on the edge of a depression . . . Our forceful response helped stop the dangerous, sharp decline in global activity and stabilize financial needs. Industrial output is now rising in nearly all our economies. International trade is starting to recover. Our financial institutions are raising needed capital, financial markets are showing a willingness to invest and lend, and confidence improved . . . as the work of recovery continues, we pledge to adopt the policies needed to lay the foundation for sustained and balanced growth in the 21st century.

The G20 Summit Declaration includes numerous proposals for institutional and regulatory reforms of the international monetary, banking and financial systems; for 'new steps to increase access to food, fuel and finance among the world's poorest'; for promoting 'energy market transparency and market stability'; for fighting trade protectionism, dealing with the threat of climate change (eg, by phasing out inefficient fossil fuel subsidies) and for successfully concluding the Doha Development Round negotiations in the WTO as well as negotiations on a new Kyoto II Protocol complementing the UN Framework Convention on Climate Change (UNFCCC). Yet, by the end of 2011, little progress had been achieved in worldwide negotiations on new international financial regulation and supervisory mechanisms, modernization of international financial and development institutions, more secure access to international food and energy, further WTO agreements on liberalization and regulation of world trade, implementation of the Millennium Development commitments for poverty reduction and new environmental agreements on carbon reductions and climate change prevention. The US Dodd–Frank Consumer Protection and Financial Reform Act of July 2010 and the large number of EU regulations reforming EU fiscal, budgetary, financial, monetary and economic disciplines, institutional supervision and financial support mechanisms focused on *domestic regulatory problems* inside the EU and the US. Many transnational regulatory problems highlighted by the international financial crisis since 2008 – and by the 'great depression' in 2009 (the biggest since the 1930s) – remained unresolved. For instance, market failures in private international banking and financial services are inadequately regulated (eg, 'toxic financial instruments', excessive risk-taking and executive bonuses of 'banks that are too big to fail', oligopolistic structures of credit-rating agencies). Related government interventions trigger international disputes (eg, concerning 'bail-outs' of domestic banks, discriminatory aircraft subsidies). Also

[14] Leaders Statement: The Pittsburgh Summit, 24–25 September 2009, Preamble, para 1, available at: www.pittsburghsummit.govmediacenter.

international prevention, supervision and 'restructuring' of private and public debt defaults lack adequate regulation.

Table 1: Regulatory problems of the international financial crisis

- Government housing credit subsidies and lax monetary and banking policies promoted a 'real estate bubble' (notably in the US) whose collapse led to over 20% of defaults of sub-prime mortgages and systemic contagion within the banking and financial system.
- 'Securitization' of sub-prime mortgages entailed massive defaults on 'toxic financial products' and government bailouts of mortgage agencies and related financial institutions.
- In 2009, the financial crisis turned into a 'great recession' prompting additional government rescue packages for banks and other industries.
- Banking supervision systems failed to prevent excessive risk taking, inadequate risk assessments and excessive remuneration practices focusing on annual performance.
- In spite of coordinated responses by the IMF, the Financial Stability Board and the G20 enabling increased lending facilities and institutional reforms of the IMF, the macro-economic imbalances continued and gave rise to monetary disputes (eg, over undervaluation of the Chinese renminbi) and trade disputes (eg, over the 'buy America' clause in the US stimulus package).
- The previously fragmented systems of financial regulation and supervision in the EU were replaced in November 2010 by a new European financial supervisory framework based on a European Systemic Risk Board and three new European supervisory authorities: the European Banking Authority, the European Insurance and Occupational Pensions Authority and the European Securities and Markets Authority.
- The G20 approved in November 2010 the Basel III Agreement on increasing the minimum capital requirements for banks. Several states introduced legislation for additional deposit guarantee schemes and for taxing banks in order to finance funds for the orderly resolution of bank failures. Yet, major regulatory problems remained unresolved such as: how to prevent excessive risk-taking by banks and 'banks that are too big to fail'? how to wind them down in case of bankruptcy? how to restructure sovereign debts in case of government insolvency?
- The EU adopted a first regulation on credit rating agencies aimed at improving transparency and reducing conflicts of interest. The EU Commission also adopted proposals for regulating 'financial derivatives', their 'over the counter' (OTC) trading and 'short selling'.
- The Eurozone countries and the IMF provided several hundred billions of Euros financial support for financing the sovereign debts of Greece, Ireland and Portugal. The European Central Bank purchased more than €100 billion of government debts of Greece, Ireland and Portugal in 'secondary markets', and made available about a trillion of euros for private banks inside the Eurozone, thus blurring the limits of monetary, financial and fiscal policies.
- In March 2011, the EU Council approved an amendment of Article 136 TFEU providing for a 'European Stability Mechanism' as well as the 'Euro Plus Pact' in order to respond more effectively to the growing public debt, budget deficits and refinancing problems of EU states violating the 'convergence disciplines' set out in Article 126 TFEU.

The need for limiting 'Westphalian embedded liberalism' by cosmopolitan rights

The worldwide financial crisis has revealed fundamental flaws and conflicts of interests in multilateral institutions as well as in domestic fiscal and financial regulation and supervision of banking practices, credit rating agencies, housing subsidies, government bailouts of private industries and 'sovereign debts'. The ten years of Doha Round negotiations in the WTO, the protracted negotiations on preventing irreversible climate change and the inability of governments to meet their self-imposed 'Millennium Development goals'[15] (eg, to better protect the more than two billion poor people living on two dollars or less per day) illustrate systemic problems of rulemaking in worldwide organizations: many governments have the power to obstruct consensus-based universal agreements; responsible leadership by the United States, Europe, Brazil, India or China (= the 'BRICs') becomes more and more rare; and 'Westphalian agreements' treat citizens as mere objects without effective protection of their fundamental rights. In contrast to the crises of the international financial, trading and economic systems during the 1930s, the WTO legal and institutional system succeeded in preventing a rampant protectionism and a breakdown of the international trading system. However, there is a need for strengthening the capacity of IEL to transform intergovernmental power politics into welfare-enhancing cooperation among citizens for the collective supply of private and 'public goods'. As discussed in detail in chapters II, III and VII, the Bretton Woods Agreements, GATT/WTO law and their underlying 'embedded liberalism' reserve sovereign rights of states to limit 'market failures'[16] and provide 'public goods'[17] through non-discriminatory regulation and government interventions aimed at avoiding welfare-reducing trade discrimination and competitive distortions. Yet, due to the ideological East–West and North–South divides following the Second World War and decolonization, the focus of these agreements on sovereign rights fails to protect the human rights of citizens.

Global economic integration means that ever more economic activities of citizens – like working, investing, saving, producing and consuming goods and services, coordinating autonomous economic activities in different countries, settling related disputes, preventing environmental pollution and related costs – are influenced by international law. Citizens participate in the global division of labour in order to enhance their welfare without fully understanding the complex interactions among rules and principles governing the world economy. They usually have limited knowledge of complex financial products, 'securities trading', 'proprietary investing' and of the systemic risks caused by bankruptcies of banks that financed the 'housing bubble' in the United States and triggered the international financial crisis of 2008. Hence, the need for consumer protection and for preventing that 'rational ignorance' of citizens vis-à-vis international economic regulation is being abused by 'political capture' and collusion between periodically elected politicians and powerful interest groups, such as

[15] *cf* MDG Gap Task Force Report, *Delivering on the Global Partnership for Achieving the Millennium Development Goals* (UN, 2008) which – as stated by UN Secretary-General Ban Ki-Moon in his preface – 'makes clear that while there has been progress on many fronts, the delivery on commitments has been deficient and has fallen behind schedule' (at iii).

[16] On 'market failures' and 'governance failures' to protect general consumer welfare against speculative 'credit bubbles', 'housing bubbles' and the resultant economic depression since 2008 see: RA Posner, *A Failure of Capitalism. The Crisis of 2008 and the Descent into Depression* (Cambridge: Harvard University Press, 2009). On the need for reconsidering the economic 'Washington Consensus' see: N Serra and JE Stiglitz (eds), *The Washington Consensus Reconsidered: Towards a New Global Governance* (Oxford: OUP, 2008).

[17] On the defining characteristics and 'collective action problems' of 'public goods' see Kaul, Grunberg and Stern (1999); I Kaul et al (eds) (2003); S Barrett (2007); T Sandler, *Global Collective Action* (Cambridge: CUP, 2004).

- trading companies enjoying '(neo)colonial privileges' (eg, for trading and selling bananas from former colonies inside the EU above market prices);
- producer interests dominating the eight 'GATT Rounds' of multilateral trade negotiations from 1948 until 1994 by lobbying for subsidies and welfare-reducing restrictions of trade in cotton, textiles, agricultural and other products;
- investor interests protected and often privileged by more than 2800 BITs; and
- patent holders and pharmaceutical companies benefiting from the WTO Agreement on Trade-Related Intellectual Property Rights (TRIPS).

For centuries, governments have cherished discretionary trade and economic policy powers enabling politicians and diplomats to tax domestic citizens and distribute 'protection rents' at the expense of consumer welfare, without effective legal and judicial remedies of adversely affected citizens and often without effective democratic control. The lack of references to general consumer welfare and to human rights in the Bretton Woods Agreements, GATT, BITs and WTO law reflects this power-oriented 'Westphalian bias' on rights and obligations of states and on protection of foreign policy discretion of the rulers rather than on human rights and democratic governance. The insufficient rules protecting 'global public interests' vis-à-vis special interest group politics entail that international rule of law and other international public goods continue to be undermined by 'rent-seeking' interest group pressures to the detriment of general citizen interests. For instance, prior to the entry into force of the WTO Agreement on 1 January 1995, trade policies were often characterized by secretive diplomatic negotiations on restrictions of trade (eg, in cotton, textiles, bananas, beef, steel, automobiles and other traded products and services) to the detriment of general consumer welfare; the continuing lack of their effective parliamentary control reflects authoritarian governance paradigms of past centuries when rulers could freely ignore the general interests of their citizens.

According to Nobel Prize economist Joseph Stiglitz, the 'near-death experience' of the 2008 financial crisis discredited not only the 'market fundamentalism' advocated by many economists –ie, the notion that unfettered markets, all by themselves, can ensure economic prosperity and growth – in the same way as the fall of the Berlin wall discredited communism.[18] The shifting of the lending risks to investors in 'toxic assets' also reminded ordinary citizens of the ubiquitous conflicts of interests in economic markets, for instance among sellers (interested in high prices) and buyers (interested in low prices), or bankers and managers of private equity funds maximizing their individual profits at the expense of 'shareholder value' and taxpayers covering the bailouts of 'banks that were too big to fail'. The destruction of private savings and investments worth trillions of dollars during the financial crisis of 2008 illustrated that 'rational ignorance' towards international economic regulation and complex financial transactions risks entailing high economic and social costs. It was only during the second half of 2010 that European and American lawmakers finally adopted a series of legislative measures aimed at resolving some of the regulatory problems of the global banking and financial crisis. The failure of the US Congress to adopt 'fast-track legislation' enabling the US government to conclude the WTO 'Development Round' negotiations as well as the 'Kyoto II negotiations' on preventing climate change, like the uncertain future of the international

[18] *cf* JE Stiglitz (2010).

financial and monetary systems, illustrate the need for reviewing how IEL can be transformed into a more effective instrument for protecting consumer welfare, human rights and other general citizen interests.

Citizens all over the world are increasingly affected by economic crises like the breakdown of parts of the international banking and financial system since 2008. Like UN human rights conventions, worldwide economic agreements tend to treat citizens as mere objects of interstate regulation without empowering and protecting individuals as 'democratic owners' of legitimate governance institutions by means of enforceable rights to rule of law (eg, compliance with WTO law) and effective judicial remedies. Notwithstanding increasing rights of 'access to justice' at national levels, UN human rights law and many fields of IEL remain dominated by paternalistic conceptions of 'diplomatic protection' that leave individuals often without effective judicial remedies against governmental violations of international economic and human rights agreements.[19] As long as diplomats continue interpreting 'state sovereignty' as involving rights of governments to freely violate international rules (eg, of WTO law) without judicial remedies of adversely affected citizens, rule of law cannot be effectively protected in the international division of labour among citizens. The now more than 2800 BITs protecting rights of foreign investors that can be enforced through investor–state arbitration and national courts – albeit without adequate guarantees of 'balancing' investor rights with all other constitutional rights and human rights[20] – illustrate that citizen-oriented reforms of IEL are politically feasible also outside regional economic integration law.

This study argues that, from a human rights perspective, IEL should promote general consumer welfare and transnational rule of law for the benefit of citizens through more effective legal and judicial remedies protecting cosmopolitan rights of individuals engaged in mutually beneficial, transnational economic cooperation. Citizens, civil society, parliaments and domestic 'courts of justice' are rightly reluctant to support and apply intergovernmental rules (like WTO law) that do not refer to protection of human rights, consumer welfare and rule of law for the benefit of citizens and fail to prevent economic, environmental, food, health, poverty and political crises and related 'governance failures'. Without stronger legal protection of cosmopolitan rights of citizens participating in, or being adversely affected by, international economic cooperation, the economic and social benefits of the global division of labour risk being undermined. Just as European economic law and the EU Charter of Fundamental Rights emphasize that the individual rights of EU citizens 'entail responsibilities and duties with regard to other persons, to the human community and to future generations' (Preamble of the EU Charter of Fundamental Rights), so must IEL strengthen cosmopolitan citizen rights, 'corporate social responsibilities' and incentives for more accountable government conduct and rule of law.

Also beyond the economy, climate change and the extinction of animal and plant species demonstrate that the universally accepted goal of 'sustainable development' requires

[19] The 2009 Optional Protocol to the International Covenant on Economic, Social and Cultural Rights (ICESCR) was ratified by only three states in 2010 and will not come into force until 10 states have ratified it. The non-ratification of the ICESCR by the United States reflects the opposition by many governments against effective legal and judicial protection of economic and social human rights. The 2009 Optional Protocol offers individuals only a political complaint procedure rather than judicial remedies; if their economic, social and cultural rights are violated at national levels, individuals may seek justice at international level by communications to the UN Committee on Economic, Social and Cultural Rights.

[20] *cf* PM Dupuy, F Francioni and EU Petersmann (eds) (2009).

overcoming the false dichotomies of the economy, the environment and human welfare. Because decisions and actions affecting the environment are largely taken in the context of economic activities, 'sustainable development' requires integrating environmental protection into economic regulation – as prescribed in EU law since 1987 (Article 6 EC) and recognized in ever more international court judgments[21] – in order to 'internalize' environmental costs of polluting activities by producers and consumers. The inadequacy of parliamentary and judicial control of intergovernmental economic and environmental regulation is further reinforced by non-transparent 'network governance' and 'private–public partnerships' in international economic regulation.

The need for limiting intergovernmental 'network governance' by cosmopolitan rights

Until the First World War, international law regulated essentially the external, 'international' relations among states. International trade transactions were governed by national private law systems based on the assumption that – while application of foreign *public law* was perceived as a potential threat to the national sovereignty of the *forum* state – foreign *private law* systems reflected general principles (eg, of contract law and tort law) in common law and civil law countries that could be applied also in foreign courts (eg, based on judicial *comitas*). The ever more comprehensive government regulation of international economic transactions since the First World War entailed that the paradigm of an 'international private law society' governed by neutral private law principles (including autonomously agreed 'law merchant' and private arbitration) was increasingly challenged by claims that 'conflicts law' – in the sense of national and international rules coordinating the transnational effects of competing private law and judicial systems across borders – had to respect national government interests and 'public interests' in the *forum* state.[22]

Since the Second World War, international movements of goods, services, persons, capital and related payments are increasingly regulated by public IEL coordinating, regulating and harmonizing national trade, monetary, investment, labour and environmental laws and other regulations at national, regional and worldwide levels. The universal recognition of human rights by all UN member states entailed that individual and collective exercises of economic liberties and property rights (such as patents for essential medicines), and their legal regulation (such as privatization of essential services like access to water), were recognized – at least inside constitutional democracies – as legal problems not only of private law, economic legislation and administrative regulation, but also of human rights law and constitutional law. As the regulatory problems, constitutional restraints and 'collective action problems' differ among policy areas, multiple forms and institutions of sector-specific, multilevel governance emerged – such as financial governance by the G5, G7, G8 or G20. In contrast to *national governments* governing by means of national law, *international governance* by governmental, intergovernmental and non-governmental actors remains characterized by multiple legal bases, non-transparent procedures and participants differing among policy areas. The regulation and management

[21] *cf* most recently the case concerning pulp mills on the river Uruguay; *Argentina v Uruguay*, ICJ judgment, 20 April 2010.

[22] *cf* B Currie, 'The Constitution and the Choice of Law' in *Selected Essays on the Conflict of Laws* (Durham: Duke University Press, 1963) 188 ff, who argued that laws, statutes and common law rules also pursued 'governmental interests', and courts were neither legitimated nor well equipped to engage in 'judicial balancing' of competing state interests.

of international movements of goods, services, persons, capital and payments overlap and interact in complex ways that remain incomprehensible to most citizens.

One major hypothesis of this study is that 'rights-based' European conceptions of multilevel economic regulation – notably among the 27 EU member states and the 30 EEA member states, but also among the 47 member states of the ECHR and in worldwide commercial, investment and arbitration law – illustrate the political practicality of 'cosmopolitan legal orders' that can 'internalize' harmful economic, environmental and legal 'externalities' more effectively by providing adversely affected citizens and countries with 'countervailing rights' and judicial remedies. The diverse forms of rights-based 'cosmopolitan governance' in Europe have also proven to be more effective in overcoming collective action problems in creating and regulating international markets and peaceful settlement of transnational disputes among citizens than other international organizations. European economic integration, its multilevel legal regulation and multilevel judicial interpretations continue to transform the plurality of national legal systems and European treaty regimes (eg, of the EC, EU and EEA Treaties and the ECHR) into new kinds of 'integration law' based on a plurality of claims to legal validity derived from state sovereignty, human rights, international law and 'community law'. The dialectically evolving acceptance – by European governments, European courts, national courts, parliaments and civil society in Europe – of functionally limited claims to legal primacy of diverse forms of European human rights and economic regulation remains embedded in worldwide treaties (like UN law, WTO law) and reinforces multilevel legal and judicial protection of cosmopolitan rights and transnational rule of law throughout Europe far beyond 'Westphalian guarantees' of rights and obligations of states.

Table 2: From 'Westphalian IEL' to regionally or functionally limited 'cosmopolitan IEL'

- **Westphalian IEL** focuses on reciprocal rights/obligations among 'sovereign states' and separation of international from national legal systems without compulsory jurisdiction (eg, of UN tribunals) for peaceful settlement of disputes; the treatment of citizens as mere objects, the lack of effective protection of 'transnational rule of law' and of human rights and ineffective parliamentary and democratic control of UN law in many states undermine the moral and democratic legitimacy of 'Westphalian international law'.
- **Cosmopolitan IEL** focuses on rights and obligations of individuals and their multilevel legal and judicial protection across national frontiers in conformity with UN and WTO law; it thereby protects transnational rule of law and strengthens the 'constitutional limits' of state sovereignty, popular sovereignty and 'constitutional justice', for instance in regional EU law, EEA law and the ECHR.
- **EU law** integrates international and national, legal and judicial guarantees of common market freedoms, transnational rule of law, human rights and other cosmopolitan rights on the basis of multilevel constitutional principles (eg, of legal primacy, direct effect and direct applicability of EU legal rules) and EU institutions.
- **EEA law** integrates international and national, legal and judicial guarantees of common market freedoms, transnational rule of law, human rights and other cosmopolitan rights on the basis of more deferential constitutional principles (eg, of quasi-primacy and quasi 'direct applicability' of EEA rules after their incorporation into domestic law) and EEA institutions.
- **ECHR law** has evolved into a multilevel system protecting human rights and access to justice in the legal and judicial systems of the 47 member states for the benefit of more than 800 million citizens.

- **Law merchant** (*lex mercatoria*) continues to evolve into cosmopolitan commercial, investment and arbitration law with multilevel judicial protection of individual freedoms (eg, of contract), property rights and transnational rule of law empowering citizens.

Worldwide and regional economic integration regimes outside Europe, by contrast, continue to be dominated by state-centred and often hegemonic structures, as illustrated by the predominance of the United States in the North American Free Trade Agreement (NAFTA), of Brazil in the South American Common Market (MERCOSUR), of South Africa in the Southern African Development and Economic Community (SADEC) and of China and India in Asian trade agreements. The ECJ, the European Free Trade Area (EFTA) Court and the ECtHR imposed far-reaching obligations on national courts to provide stronger judicial protection for individuals seeking to enforce European law in national courts. The regional and national courts in most regional economic and human rights regimes outside Europe, by contrast, have tended to refrain from similar 'multilevel judicial governance' (eg, in the sense of adjudicating not only specific disputes but jointly developing the interpretation, interactions and synergies of national and international legal systems in order to strengthen cosmopolitan rights and judicial remedies of citizens). Hence, the multilevel European constitutional and economic law has so far influenced only few regional agreements outside Europe, such as the common market law and judicial system of the Andean Community. Most countries outside Europe remain unwilling to submit to supranational institutions like those of the EU. Yet, the more than 2800 BITs providing for decentralized enforcement of international treaty obligations reflect increasing recognition of the need for transforming IEL into a more effective tool for protecting economic welfare and transnational rule of law.

The need for more effective regulation of the 'collective action problems' impeding the supply of 'global public goods'

Cosmopolitan IEL in Europe focuses on equal freedoms of citizens and other cosmopolitan rights and can be interpreted, as explained in chapter III, in terms of Kantian moral and constitutional theories. Public goods theory offers a different, economic approach to analysing collective action problems in providing mutually beneficial public goods. The climate change crisis and the destruction of biodiversity illustrate the 'tragedy of unregulated commons' and the emphasis by economists that the economic concept of public goods includes also 'public bads': without appropriate regulation, self-interested individuals, acting independently and rationally, risk depleting shared limited resources even if this is not in anyone's long-term interest.[23] As overuse of shared 'common goods' (like the earth's atmosphere) and other 'market failures' are caused by 'rational egoism', the 'collective action problems' in protecting 'common goods' and 'collective public goods'[24] confirm the need for constitutional regulation mandating

[23] The 'tragedy of the unregulated commons' was first described by G Hardin, 'The Tragedy of the Commons' (1968) 162 *Science* 1243–48. Using the example of a common pasture shared by local herders, Hardin explained the long-term degradation of the pasture by the unequal division of costs and benefits: the individual herder gains all the short-term advantages from adding additional animals, but the long-term disadvantage from overuse of the pasture is shared among all herders unless they can agree on 'enclosure' and privatization of commons.

[24] The different types of 'single best effort public goods', 'weakest link public goods' and 'aggregate effort public goods' and their diverse regulatory problems were discussed in the Introduction (*cf* fn 57 and related

individuals and institutions to correct 'market failures' and 'governance failures' on the basis of constitutionally agreed 'principles of justice' that must become an integral part of the legal order by means of democratic legislation, administrative regulation, judicial remedies and other accountability mechanisms. 'Governance failures' in the collective supply of international public goods – like transnational rule of law, human rights, mutually beneficial common markets, democratic peace and 'sustainable development' – are, likewise, caused by 'rational egoism' and harmful 'externalities' that can often be 'internalized' most effectively by providing adversely affected citizens and states with 'countervailing rights' and institutional and judicial remedies.

Inside states, the constitutional and legislative rules and institutions for the collective supply of 'public goods' tend to acknowledge this need for actionable rights of individuals, like *procedural rights* (eg, of access to information, participatory decision-making, access to justice) and *substantive cosmopolitan rights* (eg, based on human rights, common market and competition rules, environmental permit/sanctions systems). Modern social welfare states also acknowledge the social and redistributive problems and need for 'trade-offs' if costly public goods do not benefit everyone equally. The collective supply of *transnational* public goods raises similar economic, political and legal problems of 'social justice'. Yet, at the international level, the Westphalian paradigm of 'international law among sovereign states' continues to be abused by many governments for restricting and redistributing domestic consumer welfare for the benefit of domestic interest groups and political constituencies, and for 'externalizing domestic problems' (eg, of 'sovereign debts' and pollution of the environment) to the detriment of third countries. The frequent 'democratic deficits', inadequate parliamentary control and weak 'output legitimacy' of international organizations are often due to the pursuit of self-interests by governments and diplomats in denying citizens cosmopolitan rights (eg, to transnational rule of law) in order to limit the legal and judicial accountability of governments for failures of intergovernmental diplomacy. As discussed in the Introduction, the different types of 'single best effort public goods', 'weakest link public goods' and 'aggregate effort public goods' entail different 'collective action', multilevel governance and regulatory problems. Empirical evidence suggests that – just as almost all UN member states have adopted national constitutions in order to protect public national goods more effectively – also multilevel governance in international institutions for the collective supply of international public goods requires delegation of limited governance powers subject to constitutional safeguards and restraints. Arguably, multilevel constitutional approaches in European institutions have been more effective in protecting transnational public goods (like common markets) than intergovernmental, regulatory

text). Economists distinguish 'pure global public goods' that are non-excludable and non-rival (like moonlight) from impure public goods that are non-excludable but rival (like the atmosphere and other 'common pool resources') or non-rival but excludable ('club goods' like international organizations, patented and published inventions). Private goods, by contrast, tend to be made excludable and rival by means of private property rights. While some global public goods are well provided (like communication and transport networks), others are overused (like straddling fish stocks, the ozone layer) or under-provided (like public health care, environmental stability). Access to some global public goods remains restricted (eg, industrial use of patented knowledge requires payment of royalties). Certain non-rival, human-made 'collective goods' are made non-exclusive on a global scale (eg, respect for international law). Certain natural public goods are deliberately left in the global public domain (eg, global gene pools to promote biodiversity preservation).

approaches outside Europe.[25] Without more coherent regulatory approaches enlisting and empowering also individuals, business and civil society in the joint production of public goods, intergovernmental 'top-down approaches' of UN law – as illustrated by the intergovernmental coordination approach of the United Nations Environmental Programme (as discussed below) – fail protecting human rights, rule of law and other, interrelated international public goods in many UN member states. Also environmental law principles like 'polluter pays', 'precautionary protection', 'sustainable development', prohibition of transboundary harm, and 'common but differentiated responsibilities' can hardly become effective without rights-based, participatory regulation and 'private–public partnerships' within a 'constitutional bottom-up framework' limiting 'governance failures' and protecting international public goods for the benefit of citizens.

Collective supply of global public goods has become the most challenging foreign policy problem of the twenty-first century. Globalization entails ever stronger, horizontal as well as vertical interdependencies among national and transnational economic, political and legal systems. Increasing numbers of *national public goods* can no longer be protected effectively without simultaneous regulation of interdependent *international public goods* (like an efficient trading and financial system, protection of the environment). The history of European integration confirms that collective supply of international public goods requires rules, institutions and governance mechanisms that go beyond those of the Westphalian system of 'international law among sovereign states'. Likewise, the postwar economic 'Washington consensus' and 'Washington security doctrine' continued focusing one-sidedly on state interests and on power-oriented conceptions of international law and foreign policies. Collective supply of 'aggregate global public goods' depends on additional rules and institutions limiting the five main 'collective action problems' impeding supply of many international 'aggregate public goods'.

The jurisdictional gap

States are incapable of providing 'aggregate efforts global public goods' without international cooperation. New forms of multilevel governance are required in international organizations with limited, international jurisdiction in order to overcome 'prisoner dilemmas' in decentralized coordination among states and cooperation among citizens.

The governance gap

Most intergovernmental organizations are unable to regulate and govern the collective supply of international public goods effectively. New forms of multilateral, multilevel rules with limited constitutional, legislative, administrative and judicial functions are often required. The existing forms of intergovernmental rulemaking at worldwide levels tend to lack adequate rules and institutions for multilevel governance of interdependent public goods in ways that are supported by domestic citizens as 'just' (eg, legally and democratically justified).

[25] *cf* M Carbone, 'Supporting or Resisting Global Public Goods? The Policy Dimension of a Contested Concept' (2007) 13 *Global Governance* 179 ff (referring to European states as more active supporters of multilevel governance for collective supply of international public goods than hegemonic states like the United States, China or Brazil).

The incentive gap

The inherent temptation of free-riding in the collective supply of international public goods – whose consumption is by definition 'non-excludable' and 'non-rival' – requires common, but differentiated responsibilities not only among states, but also for civil society and business. Examples include financial incentives for poor countries that provide transnational environmental services by protecting tropical forests that are of global importance for bio-diversity and carbon-reduction. Consensus-based WTO negotiations lack adequate financial and other incentives for less-developed WTO members (eg, in terms of capacity-building, trade facilitation) to participate in and support new WTO rules limiting market failures (eg, by means of WTO competition and environmental rules) and protecting global public goods (eg, in terms of promoting international food and energy security). Rules must be justifiable – at all levels of multilevel governance – in terms of satisfying the reasonable interests of all affected citizens and governments. Multilevel regulation of citizen-driven market competition should provide for stronger participation rights and legal remedies, for instance by empowering citizens to enforce international trade, competition and investment rules in domestic courts against arbitrary violations of the rule of law.

The participation gap

The need for inclusive consensus-building and worldwide participation requires leadership, incentives and financial assistance for 'capacity building' by 'coalitions of the willing' so that all relevant public and private actors cooperate in the collective supply of global public goods. Citizen-driven economic and environmental systems cannot function legitimately and effectively without the right of all affected citizens to participate in multilevel decision-making and have recourse to legal and judicial remedies against unjustified restrictions of individual rights and market distortions.

The rule of law gap

The inevitable *legal fragmentation* among hundreds of national, international and transnational legal regimes interacting in the supply of many global public goods risks undermining legal predictability and transnational rule of law. It requires legal protection of legitimately diverse conceptions of justice, human rights and 'constitutional pluralism' as common legal foundations for the collective supply of global public goods. Transnational rule of law must be promoted by recognizing, 'balancing' and reconciling competing rights and constitutional claims on the basis of common constitutional principles, like the human rights obligations of all UN member states; the legitimate diversity of national constitutional traditions and democratic preferences must be respected. As interstate rules may lack democratic legitimacy and may unduly restrict individual rights, transnational 'rule of law' – as a constitutional, jurisdictional and judicial restraint protecting equal individual rights against abuses of 'rule by law' – may require and justify departures from state-centred interpretations of 'rule of international law'.

Unresolved 'public choice' problems in the supply of global public goods

Modern 'public choice theory' and 'behavioural economics' emphasize that the human rationality of the *homo economicus*' private choices in economic markets within the existing rules may not differ from the rationality of the *homo politicus*' choices in 'political markets' for new rules. Hence, the increasing regulation – at private and public, national and international levels – of transnational economic activities often pursues not only national and international 'public interests' like governmental correction of 'market failures' and collective supply of public goods; economic regulation (eg, of financial markets) is often 'simply an instrument (. . .) which market actors lobby for, deploy, avoid, or simply ignore in the pursuit of their own interests'.[26] The inadequate financial market regulation and banking supervision resulting in the financial crisis of 2008, like the powerful lobbying and political opposition against new international regulation of 'hedge funds', 'banking bonuses' and 'credit-rating agencies', illustrate that banking and company laws often protect business interests more effectively than consumer welfare and 'shareholder value'. Similarly, public international trade law continues to be all too often manipulated by producer lobbies and regulators for the benefit of powerful 'producer interests' at the expense of consumer welfare, which is nowhere mentioned in WTO law. Since 2008, the lack of congressional legislation for enabling US leadership in concluding the Doha Development Round negotiations and an environmental agreement on prevention of climate change illustrated the limited 'problem-solving capacity' even of the world's 'single superpower' to remedy obvious 'market failures' and 'regulatory failures'. According to former Vice-President Al Gore, 'the failure by the Senate to pass legislation intended to cap American emissions before the Copenhagen meeting guaranteed that the outcome would fall far short of even the minimum needed to build momentum toward a meaningful solution'. 'Global political paralysis has thus far stymied work not only on climate, but on trade and other pressing issues that require coordinated international action'.[27] The periodical US elections and the dependence of US congressmen on financial election campaign contributions from rent-seeking lobbies entail additional political paralysis (eg, impeding US leadership in the WTO Doha Round negotiations) and inward-looking isolationism in the US Congress: 'Now nobody can'.[28]

Adam Smith had already discovered during the eighteenth century that – within an appropriate structure of 'laws and institutions' – the pursuit of individual interests can further the interests of others without requiring individual agents to understand the overall structure of the regulatory system. Why do citizens and governments fail to agree on such 'laws and institutions' transforming the current economic, environmental, food

[26] *cf* J Black, 'Empirical Legal Studies in Financial Markets: What have we Learned?' LSE Law, Society and Economy Working Papers 4/2010, 1.

[27] *cf* A Gore, 'We Can't Wish Away Climate Change' *International Herald Tribune* (1 March 2010) 8, according to whom the reasons for the heightened opposition to constraints on the use of carbon-based fuels as our principal source of energy are primarily economic: 'some industries and companies whose business plans are dependent on unrestrained pollution of the atmospheric commons . . . are ferociously fighting against the mildest regulation – just as tobacco companies blocked constraints on the marketing of cigarettes for four decades after science confirmed the link of cigarettes to diseases of the lung and the heart'. For 'public choice' analyses of foreign trade laws and policies in Europe and North America see the contributions, eg, by CK Rowley, W Thorbecke, B Hindley and V Curzon Price to M Hilf and EU Petersmann (eds) (1993) pt V.

[28] *Financial Times* (5 November 2010) 12.

and poverty crises into mutually beneficial cooperation? Why – in spite of many years of preparatory work and of international negotiations – did governments fail to conclude the Doha Development Round negotiations in the WTO and the worldwide negotiations on a Kyoto II Protocol on climate change prevention? Can IEL resolve the ubiquitous conflicts between private self-interests and 'public interests' in international markets without 'constitutional safeguards' like judicial protection of rule of law and of individual rights which have proven to be indispensable for peaceful and mutually beneficial cooperation among citizens inside constitutional democracies? Is the reality of national and international governance failures in the collective supply of global public goods the inevitable consequence of the 'Westphalian public international law ideology' of benevolent governments maximizing 'state interests' without recognizing citizens as legal subjects and 'democratic owners' of international law?

2 THE 'TWO PARADOXES OF FREEDOM' REQUIRE A 'PARADIGM CHANGE' IN IEL: FROM 'WESTPHALIAN' TOWARDS 'COSMOPOLITAN IEL'?

Historical experience shows that both 'economic markets' as well as 'political markets' are characterized by the 'paradox of liberty': non-discriminatory conditions of competition promoting consumer welfare and other common self-interests of reasonable citizens can be protected over time only within a framework of constitutional and competition rules limiting abuses of private and public power. Rawls' *Theory of Justice* explains why, as illustrated by constitutional democracy in the United States, citizens have to seek agreement on 'principles of justice' and progressively institutionalize them through a 'four-stage sequence'[29] of constitutional and legislative rulemaking, administrative rule application and judicial rule clarification and rule enforcement supported by citizens and their 'public reason'. This study argues that – in view of the lack of effective international competition rules and constitutional restraints of foreign policy powers the rules and basic principles governing international monetary, trade, financial and investment relations often operate in favour of more powerful competitors to the disadvantage of weaker parties and consumers; they require being reviewed and reformed for the benefit of citizens with due regard to 'ideal' economic, political and legal theories as well as to 'realistic public choice explanations'. For instance, why has the rules-based IMF legal system failed to effectively regulate international monetary and financial relations? Why are so many international financial regulations 'soft law instruments' without effective monitoring and compliance by self-interested private actors?[30] Why have LDCs insisted on terminating the WTO negotiations on trade-related competition rules in full knowledge that lack of competition rules reduces consumer welfare and legal accountability for restrictive business practices inside LDCs?

[29] J Rawls (1971) 195 ff.

[30] The 'soft law' character of much of international financial regulation is illustrated by the 'Financial Stability Board Charter' of September 2009, whose Charter 'is not intended to create any legal rights or obligations' (Art 16). The FSB is serviced by a secretariat located in Basel at the Bank for International Settlements (*cf* Art 15), which – in spite of being an intergovernmental organization among 57 member central banks – carries out most of its work through informal consultations and recommendations (eg, on capital adequacy and reserve requirements of banks). The inadequate transparency, supervision and monitoring by national and international institutions (like the BIS and FSB) of regulatory competition and non-compliance with non-binding financial standards reinforce the 'moral hazards' in financial practices.

The 'economic paradox of freedom': market freedoms risk destroying themselves without competition rules and constitutional safeguards

Since the Second World War, almost a hundred countries have adopted new competition laws and constitutions aimed at protecting open markets and constitutional freedoms of citizens. Just as democratic constitutions pursue an 'enabling function' as well as a 'limiting function' (as discussed in chapter II), competition laws aim at 'constructing markets' in order to enhance their 'productive capacity'– and social welfare-functions as well as at 'embedding markets' by prohibiting and regulating restraints of competition (as illustrated in Table 3 below) and reconciling economic and non-economic interests.[31] As discussed in chapter VII, there is today worldwide recognition that economic and social welfare of citizens depends on rules and institutions limiting 'market failures' as well as 'governance failures'. Yet, most UN Specialized Agencies for the liberalization and regulation of international trade and services – like postal services regulated by the Universal Postal Union, telecommunications services regulated by the International Telecommunications Union, air transport services regulated by the International Civil Aviation Organization, maritime services regulated by the International Maritime Organization – prescribe no effective competition disciplines or focus one-sidedly on 'effective protection against unfair competition' (Article 10*bis* of the 1883 Paris Convention on Protection of Industrial Property administered by the World Intellectual Property Organization) without providing for international antitrust rules protecting freedom of competition and consumer welfare (eg, against market segmentation by means of patent rights and licensing agreements). The 1948 Havana Charter provided for detailed rules limiting restrictive business practices as well as governmental distortions of international trade and competition (eg, through subsidies and state-trading enterprises). The non-ratification of the Havana Charter by the United States entailed that transnational restrictive business practices and many government distortions of international trade and competition eluded effective legal constraints unless – in case of international practices with anti-competitive distortions also inside the American and European markets – the EU and US antitrust laws were unilaterally extended – on the basis of the 'effects doctrine' and other justifications of 'unilateral jurisdiction' – to transnational restrictive business practices.[32]

Following the abandonment of the Havana Charter in 1950, governments pursued transnational competition policies in the context of three complementary strategies aimed at promoting 'convergence' among national, regional and international competition rules and policies as well as synergies with other economic and trade rules:[33]

1. *Competition law approaches* rely essentially on unilateral application of domestic competition laws and policies of powerful trading countries (notably American and European antitrust laws and policies) to foreign firms and restrictive business practices abroad on the basis of diverse jurisdictional and 'effects doctrines'. Yet, in

[31] On the 'constructive' and 'embedding' functions of competition laws and policies see: D Gerber (2010) ch 1. On the 'enabling', 'limiting', 'regulatory' and 'justificatory functions' of constitutions see chapters II and III below.

[32] *cf* ibid, ch 3.

[33] *cf* EU Petersmann, 'Competition-oriented Reforms of the WTO World Trade System: Proposals and Policy Options' in R Zäch (ed), *Towards WTO Competition Rules* (The Hague: Kluwer, 1999) 43–71; Gerber (2010) chs 2–4.

spite of increasing international cooperation among domestic competition authorities based on bilateral and multilateral cooperation agreements (eg, among the EU and the US competition authorities, the regional 'European Competition Network', the worldwide 'International Competition Network' (ICN) among more than 80 competition authorities) and non-binding multilateral guidelines for 'best practices' and 'model competition rules' (as elaborated by the OECD, UNCTAD and the ICN), many domestic competition laws exempt export or import cartels. As government-supported restraints of competition (eg, for telecommunication services, shipping cartels), conflicting merger control decisions[34] or unilateral enforcement of national antitrust rules against foreign firms may generate international conflicts and 'blocking statutes' abroad, unilateral, extra-territorial enforcement of national competition rules is increasingly recognized as an inadequate and ineffective approach to regulating and preventing international competition problems.[35] Even though governments responded to the financial crises since 2008 by giving priority to *domestic* regulatory reforms, the threats by banks, investment funds and rating agencies to relocate and 'out-source' to other jurisdictions ('race to the bottom') confirmed the need for international legal coordination and competition disciplines.

2. *Regional economic integration law approaches* increasingly provide for mutual adjustment of trade and competition rules in the context of regional free trade agreements (like the EFTA, EEA, EU, NAFTA, the Andean Common Market, the Australia/New Zealand Free Trade Agreement) in order to protect regional market integration and cross-border competition against both governmental and private market access barriers and distortions. The European network of national and European competition authorities, like the rights-based enforcement of multilevel competition laws in national and European courts in all 30 EEA member countries, has developed unique learning processes for innovative 'constitutional', legal and 'economic approaches' as to how multilevel trade, common market, competition, environmental and social rules need to be mutually adjusted in order to protect a 'highly competitive social market economy' (Article 3 TEU) based on 'a system ensuring that competition is not distorted' (Protocol No 27 to the TFEU). In accordance with the 'four-stage sequence' suggested by Rawls, the dynamic, multilevel interactions between constitutional, legislative, administrative and judicial clarifications of rights-based competition rules have enabled European governments to limit regulatory abuses (eg, of anti-dumping laws) that nationalist competition regimes have failed to overcome (eg, in NAFTA countries like the United States without effective constitutional restraints on subsidies and discriminatory market access barriers like anti-dumping duties).
3. The proposals for negotiating *worldwide competition rules in the* WTO – for instance, for an 'International Antitrust Code' as a Plurilateral Trade Agreement in terms of Annex 4 of the WTO Agreement,[36] or for integrating multilateral competition rules

[34] An illustration was the prohibition of the proposed merger between the General Electric Co and Honeywell Inc by the EU Commission on 3 July 2001, in spite of the clearance of this merger by US antitrust authorities.

[35] *cf* Gerber (2010) ch 8 and the case studies in CA Jones and M Mitsushita (eds), *Competition Policy in the Global Trading System* (The Hague: Kluwer, 2002) pt II.

[36] The text and detailed comments on this code are published in H Hauser and EU Petersmann (eds), *International Competition Rules in the GATTWTO System* (special issue of the *Swiss Review of International Economic Relations* (St Gallen: Rueger, 1994); W Fikentscher and U Immenga (eds), *Draft International Antitrust Code* (Baden-Baden: Nomos, 1995).

into the worldwide WTO rules on trade in goods, services and trade-related intellectual property rights[37] – were discussed in the WTO Working Group on Trade and Competition from 1997 until 2003 when the WTO ministerial Conference decided to discontinue these discussions at the request of less-developed WTO member countries.[38] As the lack of competition disciplines undermines consumer welfare notably in LDCs without competition laws and impedes effective international trade liberalization in the WTO (notably in areas such as anti-dumping laws, regulated services like telecommunications, air transport and financial services, government procurement, trade-related intellectual property rights), the resumption of international negotiations on integrating multilateral competition rules into the WTO legal and dispute settlement system – following the conclusion and domestic implementation of future Doha Round Agreements – may be only a matter of time. While the Havana Charter approach of a worldwide 'big bang competition code' was over-ambitious, many LDCs criticized during the Doha Round negotiations the opposition by the United States to considering not only *private*, but *government-supported* restraints of competition (like US shipping cartels and anti-competitive anti-dumping practices). The diverse national, regional and worldwide initiatives for more effective competition disciplines remain complementary, long-term policy tasks. The now more than 100 WTO member countries with national competition law, the increasing cooperation among national competition authorities in the context of bilateral and multilateral agreements (like the ICN), the WTO disputes over government support for anti-competitive restraints of competition[39] and the WTO negotiations over regulated services (like telecommunications and financial services) make it likely that future WTO negotiations on the interactions of trade and competition rules will be more successful than in the past.

Why does IEL fail to effectively restrain 'unreasonable', welfare-reducing restraints of competition – such as those illustrated in Table 3 – by private as well as by public economic actors in international economic relations? Why did governments fail to progressively develop the IMF Agreement into a more effective legal and institutional framework for regulating and preventing worldwide monetary and financial crises like those which have occurred since 2008? Why did governments succeed in transforming the 'soft' GATT 1947 rules into the world's most successful, worldwide legal and compulsory dispute settlement system, albeit often based on 'second-best' rules and principles as agreed in the 1994 WTO Agreement and in the Doha Round Declaration of 2001? Does the failure of WTO negotiations on international competition disciplines justify the conclusion that worldwide regulation of abuses of private and public regulatory powers must evolve 'bottom-up' based on support from national and regional governments, regulators, civil

[37] *cf* EU Commission, 'Competition Policy in the New Trade Order: Strengthening International Cooperation and Rules' (report of a Group of Experts from the EU Commission with J Immenga and EU Petersmann, 1995); EU Petersmann, *The Need for Integrating Trade and Competition Rules in the WTO World Trade and Legal System* (Geneva: Graduate Institute for International Studies, 1996).

[38] For an overview of the various proposals from WTO members see: Petersmann (n 33); Jones and Mitsushita (n 35) chs 16 and 20; Gerber (2010).

[39] *cf* E Fox, 'The WTO's First Antitrust Case – Mexican Telecom: A Sleeping Victory for Trade and Competition' (2006) 9 *JIEL* 271 ff. The 2004 panel report (WTDS204R) – which found, inter alia, that Mexico's support for anti-competitive price-fixing practices violated Mexico's GATS commitments – was adopted without appeal. The panel findings were reviewed and also endorsed in a joint meeting of the OECD trade policy and competition policy committees.

society and 'epistemic communities' of experts? How can the overall coherence and synergies of monetary, trade, financial, competition, investment and environmental regulation be promoted and 'embedded' into domestic democratic and constitutional systems in order to avoid hostility and opposition to markets from those who have no voice or are adversely affected by international competition?

Table 3: The economic 'paradox of liberty': economic freedoms risk being destroyed without rules limiting unreasonable restraints of competition

Horizontal restraints: 'Hard core cartels' among firms in an oligopolistic market (eg, on price fixing, output restrictions, market division, customer allocation, collusive tendering) and other anticompetitive cooperation between firms selling competing products. While 'naked' cartels tend to be prohibited, the anti- and pro-competitive effects of other horizontal cooperation need to be balanced (eg, based on a 'rule of reason', individual exemptions or group exemptions).

Vertical restraints: Distribution strategies between manufacturers, suppliers or distributors such as tying (the sale of one good is conditioned on the purchase of another), exclusive dealing (the seller requires the buyer to purchase products only from the seller), territorial restraints (the seller requires the buyer/distributor to re-sell the product within a limited geographical area) and resale price maintenance (the seller requires the buyer to re-sell the product only at a specified price). While resale price fixing tends to be generally prohibited, the pro- and anticompetitive effects of other vertical restraints need to be evaluated (eg, misuse control).

Abuses of intellectual property rights: Technology licensing arrangements abusing the monopoly-like position of IPR holders, eg, through non-competition clauses (eg, 'grantback': the licensee is required to assign inventions made in the course of working the transferred technology back to the licensor) or non-contestation clauses (the licensee is prevented from contesting the validity of the IPR or other rights of the licensor). IPR abuses might be subject to the general competition rules on horizontal and vertical restraints.

Abuses of market dominance: Dominant firms accounting for a significant market share (eg, of 40 per cent or more) may attempt to monopolize a market eg, through excess prices, price discrimination, predatory low prices, refusal to deal or vertical restraints. Rules against the abuse of a dominant position may be conduct-oriented (eg, a general prohibition against monopolizing and foreclosure of competition) or result-oriented (eg, prohibition of predatory pricing only if the losses can be recouped).

Mergers and acquisition policies: Horizontal, vertical or conglomerate mergers may reduce competition or increase efficiency. Merger policies may be designed to ensure the contestability of markets by preventing a monopoly (price-setting by a single seller), monopsony (price-setting by a single buyer) or oligopolistic market power. But acquisition policies may also be used for industrial policy purposes.

Public undertakings and enterprises with special privileges: In view of their market power (eg, financial independence), they may be required to behave according to market principles (Article XVII GATT). Exclusive trading rights and monopolies may be prohibited.

National competition laws and institutions reflect the needs, interests and values of the states in which they operate rather than the regulatory needs of global markets.

Multilevel regulation based on international law and international institutions can compensate the 'protection biases' of national legal systems by limiting nationalist discriminations and protecting economic freedoms and other cosmopolitan rights in international cooperation among citizens. It remains contested to what extent such international legal disciplines for multilevel governance should be designed as 'global administrative law' (GAL) based on national, notably US federal administrative practices (like criminal law rules against conflicts of interests, 'notice and comment' rulemaking, deferential judicial review of administrative action by agencies operating under a federal statute subject to congressional oversight), which were designed for a constitutional system with effective parliamentary control of delegated, administrative powers and may not fit international governance systems without effective oversight by national parliaments and with countries having diverse constitutional traditions of multilevel regulation, judicial review and protection of individual rights. As IEL fails to regulate the 'paradox of freedom' also in respect of 'unreasonable', welfare-reducing *governmental* restrictions of international trade and competition, GAL may need to be embedded by *constitutional principles* common to the member states and adjusted to the particular structures and limited mandates of the international organizations concerned similar to national and European administrative law systems inside constitutional democracies.

The 'political paradox of freedom': economic policy discretion risks destroying itself without multilevel constitutional restraints

The state-centred 'Westphalian system' of international law emerged from the power struggles against the Church, the Holy Roman Empire, feudalism and – following the peace treaties of Westphalia (1648) – from struggles against imperialism and colonialism in support of a new system of states with 'sovereign equality' (Article 2 UN Charter). Even though the 'international law of coexistence' continues to be increasingly supplanted by 'international law of cooperation',[40] the 'international law among states' and its basic premises – like 'sovereign equality of states', foreign policy discretion and intergovernmental cooperation in international organizations composed by states and represented by diplomats emphasizing 'member-driven governance' – continue to dominate international state practices. The purchase by the European Central Bank of hundreds of billions of government bonds from over-indebted EU member countries and banks without a clear, democratically approved mandate – neither in the EU Treaty[41] nor from national parliaments in conformity with the national constitutional law principles of parliamentary responsibility over public revenues, expenses and budgetary decisions[42] –

[40] *cf* W Friedmann (1964).

[41] Arguably, the 'bailout prohibition' of Art 125 TFEU ('The Union shall not be liable for or assume the commitments of central governments' . . .) and of Art 123 ('Overdraft facilities or any other type of credit facility with the European Central Bank . . . in favour of Union institutions, bodies, offices or agencies, central governments . . . shall be prohibited, as shall the purchase directly from them by the European Central Bank . . . of debt instruments') prohibits the ECB buying government debts from over-indebted EU member governments and banks. The textual argument used by the ECB – that the text of Art 123 TFEU does not prohibit indirect purchases of government bonds in secondary markets – remains contested as it blurs the distinction between monetary and fiscal policies (the latter remaining a national competence under EU law in conformity with the 'subsidiarity principle') and risks undermining the objective of the bailout prohibition of Art 125 TFEU.

[42] In the German Constitutional Court judgment of 7 September 2011 on the constitutionality of Germany's participation in the international treaty establishing the European Financial Stability Mechanism, the Court

illustrates the 'political paradox of freedom', ie, the risk of abuses of economic policy powers that are inadequately constitutionally constrained (eg, by the 'bailout' prohibition in Article 125 TFEU and by inadequate EU safeguards of democratic governance based on 'rule of law') and risk undermining the democratic legitimacy of economic governance. The international negotiations on overcoming the crises in the international trade, financial, environmental and development systems remain dominated by the self-appointed 'Group of 20', UN bodies (such as the IMF and the World Bank), the WTO and ever more complex intergovernmental networks of national ministries, international agencies (eg, the Bank for International Settlements at Basel) and other experts (eg, from central banks). Even though the failures to conclude the Doha Round negotiations in the WTO since 2001, to prevent the financial crises which have occurred since 2008 as well as climate change, are widely attributed to 'regulatory failures' (such as inadequate supervision and regulation of financial markets and currency manipulations), the 'crisis management' continues to be dominated by the very same governments and agencies with often inadequate democratic control by national parliaments and citizens. For instance, since 2008, the US Congress has adopted neither trade legislation nor environmental legislation enabling US leadership for concluding the WTO and climate change negotiations. The 2600 pages of the US Congress' Dodd–Frank Consumer Protection and Financial Reform Act of July 2010 focus on domestic regulation and domestic interest group demands (eg, regarding bailouts, capital requirements and bonus practices of US banks and the government-sponsored mortgage finance companies Fannie Mae and Freddie Mac) without changing the anticompetitive concentration of a few 'systemically important' US banks 'that are too big to fail',[43] and without precise guidance for reforming the international monetary and financial system. As discussed in chapter VII, protection of human rights is rarely mentioned in the intergovernmental negotiations of trade and finance experts in the WTO, G20 and the Bretton Woods institutions.

This study argues that the ever more comprehensive human rights obligations acknowledged by all UN member states since the entry into force of the UN Charter in 1945 call for cosmopolitan conceptions of IEL and stronger 'constitutional restraints' of intergovernmental regulation of the worldwide division of labour where production, investments, trade, environmental pollution and consumption of scarce resources tend to be driven by *private* actors: neither the international coexistence of liberal states, authoritarian states, totalitarian and 'rogue states' nor the continuing importance of 'state capitalism' (as illustrated by 'sovereign wealth funds' and state-enterprises in China, Russia, Saudi Arabia and other countries) justify excluding cosmopolitan reforms of IEL, as they have been successfully realized in European economic law inside the EU and EEA. In order to overcome the international economic, financial and environmental crises and supply 'global public goods' more effectively, IEL must no longer be conceived only as 'international law among states' but also as a 'law of peoples' and cosmopolitan law limiting the discretionary foreign policy powers of the rulers by empowering producers, investors, traders and consumers to engage in mutually beneficial economic cooperation across frontiers – with rights of citizens and corresponding duties of governments to protect rule of law and

emphasized that Art 38 of the German Basic Law protects the parliamentary representation of German citizens and the inalienable, democratic responsibility of the German Parliament to control important budgetary decisions (2 BvR 98710, 148510 and 109910).

[43] *cf* A Ross Sorkin, *Too Big to Fail* (New York: Viking, 2009).

human rights. More than in most other areas of international law, treating citizens as mere objects of IEL undermines the effectiveness of international economic and environmental regulation,[44] its support by citizens and the legitimacy of IEL, which derives from its contribution to protection of human rights and to democratic self-governance no less than from promotion of general consumer welfare as explained by welfare economics. Similar to theories of justice focusing on the basic structure of society and on its systemic impact on the life chances of each individual,[45] UN human rights instruments rightly emphasize the 'indivisibility' of civil, political, economic, social and cultural human rights which makes their mutual reconciliation, 'balancing' and 'optimization' through constitutional, legislative, administrative and judicial protection the central problem of democratic governance systems, also in IEL. The prevailing, utilitarian focus in IEL on 'efficient welfare maximization' cannot legitimately ignore that discriminatory, governmental trade restrictions redistributing domestic welfare and competitive opportunities in favour of rent-seeking producer interests raise constitutional problems.

This study argues that cosmopolitan (re)interpretations of the normative foundations of modern IEL are necessary for regulating the 'collective action problems' in the supply of public goods more effectively and enhancing respect for the legitimate diversity of constitutional democracies (eg, their often diverse human rights conceptions). The main conclusion is that – similar to multilevel constitutionalism inside federal states limiting multilevel governance at local, state and federal levels in order to enable collective supply of public goods – multilevel constitutional restraints of the pervasive abuses of international economic regulation are required also at transnational levels by means of international law and institutions promoting collective supply of global public goods and protecting the constitutional rights and 'legal empowerment' of citizens across frontiers. The local, state and federal levels of multilevel governance must be integrated – together with additional 'cosmopolitan levels of governance' – in coherent 'multilevel constitutional structures' (as illustrated by Cottier's paradigm of a 'common constitutional house')[46] protecting citizens and democratic supply of public goods inside as well as beyond 'constitutional democracies' by means of transnational 'deliberative democracy', 'participatory democracy' and stronger 'constitutional checks and balances'. The less effective *parliamentary democracy* regulates the challenges of global governance, the more it is necessary to protect *participatory* and '*deliberative democracy*' based on cosmopolitan rights and rule of law beyond state borders in mutually beneficial economic cooperation among citizens. As 'market failures' and 'governance failures' originate in the rational egoism and limited reasonableness of individuals, they must be limited not only by intergovernmental regulation and judicial protection of rule of law among states; there is also a need for stronger constitutional protection and democratic support of 'cosmopolitan public reason' based on multilevel legal, institutional and judicial protection of cosmopolitan rights and corresponding responsibilities in IEL – with due respect for 'reasonable disagreement' among citizens and democracies with legitimately diverse

[44] In contrast to global economic and environmental governance which eludes unilateral national regulation, states and national governments remain the most important guarantors of human rights, democratic self-government and national security. Yet, the 2004 UN report by a Panel of Eminent Persons on 'We the Peoples: Civil Society, the United Nations and Global Governance' UN Doc A58817 (11 June 2004) rightly emphasized that the effectiveness and legitimacy of the UN system also depends more than ever on cooperation of states with civil society and other international and non-governmental organizations.

[45] *cf* Rawls (1971) 7, 9–10, 54.

[46] *cf* T Cottier, 'Towards a Five-Storey House' in C Joerges and EU Petersmann (eds) (2011) ch 17.

constitutional traditions. The different governance levels of legal and institutional protection of human rights and other citizen rights must be controlled 'bottom-up' by citizens using their participatory rights and representative institutions, with due respect for legitimate 'constitutional pluralism'.[47]

Diversity of constitutional approaches to economic regulation

Trade and its legal regulation have dynamically evolved since ancient times, notably since the transition from economic mercantilism, imperialism and colonialism to multilateral liberalization and regulation of international trade in the framework of the General Agreement on Tariffs and Trade (GATT 1947).[48] It was first in the framework of the US Constitution of 1787 that 'principles of justice' and human rights were progressively institutionalized through democratic legislation, administration and judicial protection of fundamental rights enabling a citizen-driven, common market among today's 50 states. The US common market law continues to be supplemented by more and more regional free trade agreements (like NAFTA) with third countries and US participation in worldwide monetary, trade and investment rules. The WTO Agreement remains the only worldwide agreement ratified by the US Congress with worldwide guarantees of non-discriminatory market access, prohibitions of non-tariff trade barriers, harmonization of international trade regulation and a compulsory dispute settlement system committed to 'providing security and predictability to the multilateral trading system' (Article 3 WTO Dispute Settlement Understanding). The 'constitutional dimensions' of the WTO legal and dispute settlement system are illustrated by the regular review, criticism and adoption of the so far more than 200 dispute settlement panel and appellate reports by the WTO membership in the WTO Dispute Settlement Body; this rapidly expanding WTO jurisprudence clarifies contested interpretations of WTO rules and progressively develops WTO law as illustrated by the domestic implementation of most WTO dispute settlement rulings. Yet, the perceptions of intergovernmental and 'judicial rule clarification' in the WTO 'in the shadow' of previously agreed principles, rules and jurisprudence differ considerably among diplomats, civil society and courts of justice.[49] Just as, in spite of President FD Roosevelt's revolutionary initiatives for 'a world founded upon four essential human freedoms' including also 'freedom from want' and 'freedom from fear', the United States has ratified only a small number of UN human rights

[47] N Walker, 'The Idea of Constitutional Pluralism' (2002) 65 *Modern Law Review* 317 ff, contrasts the reality of multilevel 'heterarchical constitutional pluralism' with the past, national 'constitutional monism'. On the diverse conceptions and practices of 'constitutional pluralism' see ch II and, eg, M Avbelj and J Komarek (eds), 'Four Visions of Constitutional Pluralism' EUI Law Working Paper No 21 (2008). My use of the terms 'constitution', 'constitutionalism' and 'constitutionalization' is explained in ch II. On the diversity of theories of justice for the constitutional design of democratic self-governance and representative legislative, administrative and judicial institutions see: EU Petersmann, 'Constitutional Justice and the Perennial Task of "Constitutionalizing" Law and Society through "Participatory Justice"' EUI Working Paper Law 2010/03. On the particular problems of 'transitional justice' in post-conflict societies reconciling the need for 'criminal justice' with other human needs (eg, in terms of 'democracy building' and protecting human rights) see: MC Bassiouni (ed), *Post-Conflict Justice* (Ardsley: Transnational Publishers, 2002); N Roht-Arriaza (ed), *Transitional Justice in the 21st Century* (New York: CUP, 2006).

[48] On the historical evolution of private and public, national and international trade law and its multilevel interrelationships see: EU Petersmann, 'Principles of World Trade' in R Wolfrum (ed) (2010).

[49] *cf* RH Steinberg, 'Judicial Lawmaking at the WTO: Discursive, Constitutional and Political Constraints' (2004) 98 *AJIL* 240 ff.

conventions and ILO labour and social law conventions, US diplomats perceive the WTO primarily as a framework for advancing US trade interests rather than for protecting transnational rule of law, consumer welfare or 'multilevel constitutionalism' for the benefit of citizens.[50]

As human rights say little about the optimal constitutional, legislative, administrative, international and judicial design of economic regulation, comparative analyses are of crucial importance – albeit often neglected. My 1991 book, *Constitutional Functions and Constitutional Problems of International Economic Law*, compared the diverse 'multilevel constitutional regulation' of common markets in federal states in the United States and Europe as well as in EC law; it argued that international liberalization of trade with third states derived its democratic legitimacy not only from utilitarian values, but from extending basic constitutional principles like equal liberties, non-discrimination and rule of law for the benefit of citizens.[51] Since the 1960s, today's 500 million EU citizens are experiencing ever more profound transformations of nation states through European economic integration law as historical, social learning processes revealing the 'transformative potential' of international law for transforming centuries of periodic wars in Europe into peaceful, mutually beneficial cooperation among citizens across state borders. Beginning in the 1950s with the ECHR and the European Coal, Steel, Economic and Atomic Energy Communities, European law continues to fundamentally change national legal systems and individual, social and political conduct – not only inside the 30 member states of the EEA, but also in their relations with third countries which have universally accepted the EU as a new international actor and 'rule of law community' different from states. Both in the EU as well as in the EEA, citizens and national parliaments have accepted the 'judicial transformations' of EU law, EEA law and also of the ECHR into 'constitutional instruments' protecting fundamental rights of citizens. While similar regional transformations of IEL may be possible in regional trade agreements in Africa (eg, SADEC), in the Amercias (eg, the Andean Common Market) and Asia (eg, among the four Chinese customs territories), the constitutional legitimacy of judicial rule clarification and progressive development of IEL for the benefit of citizens and their constitutional rights remains deeply controversial in worldwide organizations like the WTO.

Are there lessons from the rights-based, citizen-oriented 'constitutional approaches' to international economic and environmental regulation in Europe for global economic governance and for its legal regulation? Why is it that trade has given rise to increasingly complex systems of private and public, national, regional and worldwide regulation,

[50] On the US' distrust and hegemonic use of international law, as illustrated also by its non-ratification of the 1948 Havana Charter for an International Trade Organization and by the US insistence on US veto rights in the Bretton Woods institutions and 'grandfather rights' under GATT 1947, see eg: P Sands, *Lawless World: America and the Making and Breaking of Global Rules* (London: Penguin Books, 2005). The continuing influence of President Roosevelt's State of the Union speech of 6 January 1941 is reflected in the recognition in the Outcome Document of the 2005 World Summit 'that all individuals, in particular vulnerable people, are entitled to freedom from fear and freedom from want, with an equal opportunity to enjoy all their rights and fully develop their human potential' (UN Doc ARES601 of 24 October 2005, para 143). US financial and trade policies remain, however, dominated by the strong lobbying influence of US industries (eg, Wall Street banks, steel industries benefiting from anti-dumping protection) and their election campaign contributions in exchange for governmental protection of private 'rent-seeking'. The 'functional use' of the term 'constitutionalism' as a political method for limiting abuses of power by using constitutional principles, rules of a higher legal rank and institutional 'checks and balances', and the distinction between 'enabling, constraining and supplemental constitutionalization', are explained in ch II, section 3.

[51] *cf* Petersmann (1991).

whereas the financial crisis of 2008 revealed a 'black hole' in the international regulation of the financial transactions and accountability of banks, credit rating agencies, hedge funds and investment funds? Are the human rights obligations of all UN member states relevant legal context for interpreting international economic rules, for instance in the WTO disputes over China's political censorship and related restrictions of intellectual property rights and individual freedoms of expression and information? Similar to the American philosopher Rawls' description of the historical evolution of American constitutionalism as a leading example of founding a constitutional democracy on 'principles of justice' through a 'four-stage process', this study uses the diverse European experiences of extending constitutional democracy to multilevel governance for the collective supply of international public goods – like the European common market and the diverse treaty-based systems for multilevel judicial protection of human rights and rule of law in the EU, the EEA as well as in the 47 member states of the ECHR – as important examples for the worldwide task of protecting international public goods more effectively. The constitutional and judicial protection of economic and social rights in constitutional democracies in LDCs (like Brazil, India and South Africa),[52] and the comparatively weaker constitutional and judicial protection of economic and social rights in many industrialized 'common law countries' (like Australia, Canada, New Zealand and the United States),[53] illustrate that 'constitutional pluralism' remains a political reality reflecting legitimately diverse conceptions of human rights and constitutional self-government. As explained in chapter II, respect for 'constitutional pluralism' offers also the most convincing method for coordinating national and international constitutional regimes in a globally integrating world composed of hundreds of diverse, but increasingly interdependent national and international legal systems with different 'rules of recognition', law-creating procedures and often conflicting claims to legal validity, political autonomy and legitimacy. The jurisprudence of European courts illustrates that transnational rule of law cannot be effectively protected in international relations on the basis of hierarchical claims and simplistic 'monism versus dualism debates'. Conflicting constitutional claims often need to be reconciled by weighting, 'optimizing' and 'balancing' multiple rights and constitutional values in transparent procedures respecting the 'heterarchy' of other constitutional systems, due process of law, 'reasonable disagreement' and institutional deference towards national or transnational 'margins of appreciation', as discussed in chapters V and VIII.

The need for a 'paradigm change' in international economic and environmental regulation

This book argues in favour of a 'paradigm change'[54] in IEL – similar to the citizen-oriented paradigm shift in European economic law based on bottom-up 'multilevel constitutionalism' – in order to protect human rights and constitutional rights of citizens more effectively

[52] *cf* V Gauri and DM Brinks (eds), *Courting Social Justice. Judicial Enforcement of Social and Economic Rights in the Developing World* (Cambridge: CUP, 2010).

[53] *cf* RE Howard-Hassmann and CE Welch (eds) (2006); Hilf and Petersmann (eds) (1993).

[54] On periodic 'paradigm shifts' in scientific research challenging the assumptions of a scientific community in order to resolve social problems more effectively see: TS Kuhn, *The Structure of Scientific Revolutions* (Chicago: University of Chicago Press, 1962).

in international economic regulation. A citizen-oriented, rights-based conception of IEL is a constitutional precondition for reducing the collective action problems in global economic and environmental governance in order to supply international public goods more effectively. The continuing 'global warming pollution' illustrates not only the urgency of overcoming the false dichotomy of the international economy, the environment and constitutional democracy; as international 'market failures' (like pollution of the environment) and 'governance failures' are caused by individual conduct of citizens and politicians, the necessary protection of 'sustainable development' calls for additional 'constitutional restraints' on such conduct. 'Public justice' – as defined by human rights, constitutional and legislative rights of citizens and 'rule of law' – must be protected more effectively beyond state borders in order to enhance stakeholder participation, legitimacy and effectiveness in international rulemaking and rule enforcement. As it is citizens who produce and consume goods and services, invest their savings, pollute the environment, compete in economic markets and shape democratic governance, citizens must be recognized as legal subjects and 'democratic owners' of IEL with individual rights and responsibilities to challenge harmful 'market failures' as well as 'governance failures'. Discretionary foreign policy powers to restrict mutually beneficial trade, distort competition among citizens and permit adverse environmental pollution run counter not only to welfare economics, but also to the constitutional mandates of governments to promote consumer welfare and human rights. In order to protect citizens more effectively against abuses of foreign policy powers, the rules and institutions of IEL must be interpreted no longer only as 'international law among states', but as protecting cosmopolitan rights of individuals and democratic self-governance of peoples, as in European economic and human rights law. Human rights require conceiving markets no longer as neutral arenas for private competition but rather as 'constitutional constructs' which – like the common market governed by EU law – can protect general consumer welfare, non-discriminatory conditions of competition, 'sustainable development' and human rights only in a multilevel legal framework protecting constitutional, legislative, administrative and judicial guarantees of equal citizen rights and common 'public interests' of citizens.

Just as collective supply of private and public goods inside constitutional democracies depends on consumer-driven competition and citizen-driven governance within a constitutional framework limiting legislation, administration and adjudication, so does collective supply of international public goods depend on stronger constitutional restraints on intergovernmental regulation, administration and judicial settlement of disputes for the benefit of citizens and their constitutional rights. The importance of international rule of law and of the WTO legal and world trading system for the collective supply of many other global public goods – like international food security, energy security and climate change prevention – illustrates the systemic interdependence of many 'overlapping public goods'. As discussed in the following chapters, promoting stronger 'constitutional legitimacy' of IEL raises numerous controversial questions on which citizens and governments often legitimately disagree. For instance, do individual 'market freedoms' have constitutional foundations (eg, in constitutional freedoms of expression, profession, property and other human and labour rights)? Are there corresponding constitutional obligations limiting governmental restrictions and collective exercises of market freedoms (eg, by corporate obligations to respect and protect human rights in the exercise of private economic power)? How should the limits of 'reasonable disagreement' among citizens and of 'constitutional pluralism' reflecting diverse conceptions of human rights and of democratic self-governance be defined? Is it appropriate for WTO law and other worldwide agreements to leave the answers to such controversial questions to individual governments, 'deliberative democracy' and 'courts of justice' whenever they have to reconcile and 'balance' conflicting constitutional claims?

Cosmopolitan conceptions of IEL require 'human rights coherence' of international economic regulation

Most textbooks on IEL, including a recent research handbook in international economic law,[55] follow the Anglo-Saxon tradition of analyzing IEL from the national perspective of legislative, administrative and intergovernmental regulators on the basis of welfare economics and political 'public choice constraints'. They neither explore the controversial 'constitutional foundations' of international private and public economic regulation, such as freedom of expression, freedom of profession, contractual freedom and private property as legal preconditions for the proper functioning of 'markets'. Neither do they acknowledge the role of such rights for market competition and its role as citizen-driven dialogues about values and decentralized information, coordination and sanctioning mechanisms. Instead, IEL tends to be perceived as an instrument of government regulation without much regard to its constitutional foundations and the 'constitutional coherence' of IEL. Textbooks on IEL focus ever more on *descriptions* of 'positive IEL' without exploring the human rights problems underlying international economic regulation.

This study proceeds from the normative premise that – in view of the human rights obligations of all UN member states – the legitimacy of IEL in the twenty-first century depends on its 'human rights coherence'. UN human rights instruments derive 'inalienable' human rights as constitutional limitations of all governance powers not only from 'respect for human dignity' as a universally recognized 'moral imperative' of human reasonableness and inherent rights of every human being;[56] they also acknowledge that the right to popular self-determination may justify diverse 'constitutional contracts' on how to define, and mutually balance, constitutional rights and the delegation of limited governance powers in a particular democracy. Particular national and regional human rights conceptions, including the premises of this study as summarized in Table 4 and explained in chapter III, will remain inevitably contested among countries and citizens with different human rights traditions and diverse human rights conceptions. Law as a 'social fact' and integral part of culture must respect that states and democratic legislatures may legitimately implement UN human rights obligations in diverse ways at national and regional levels, especially in the field of economic and environmental regulation.[57] As discussed in subsequent chapters, it remains rare that national or international courts conclude that democratic economic legislation (eg, restricting tobacco advertising and biotechnological uses in Europe, regulating night work of bakers in the US, nationalizing industries or restricting cultural and land rights of indigenous people in LDCs) is violating human or constitutional rights such as freedom of commercial expression, other economic freedoms, property rights, cultural rights, access to justice and other due process rights.

[55] *cf* AT Guzman and AO Sykes (eds), *Research Handbook in International Economic Law* (Cheltenham: Edward Elgar, 2007).

[56] *cf* J Morsink (2009).

[57] *cf* L Rosen, *Law as Culture* (Princeton: Princeton University Press, 2006); Howard-Hassmann and Welch (eds) (2006).

Table 4: The political 'paradox of liberty': economic freedoms also risk being destroyed without constitutional restraints and 'human rights coherence' of IEL

- The human rights obligations of all UN member states entail that human rights – as 'the foundation of freedom, justice and peace in the world' (UDHR) – are the constitutional foundations of the legitimacy also of IEL. 'Equal freedoms' as 'first principle of justice' and welfare economics justify liberalization of mutually beneficial international division of labour among free citizens. Protection of human rights by rule of law across frontiers requires limiting 'market failures' as well as 'governance failures' by means of constitutional and institutional restraints of abuses of public and private power.
- Human rights require treating citizens as subjects and 'democratic principals' of international regulation of mutually beneficial economic cooperation among citizens. Just as economic competition derives its constitutional legitimacy from protecting equal freedoms and general consumer welfare, so does international economic regulation derive its constitutional legitimacy from protecting equal rights of citizens and constitutionally agreed 'public goods.' Unnecessary poverty, violation of human rights, treatment of citizens as mere objects and environmental pollution undermine the legitimacy of the 'Westphalian paradigm of IEL'.
- Multilevel economic regulation requires multilevel constitutional protection of equal rights and judicial protection of rule of law. IEL should be conceived not only as 'international law among states', but also as 'law of peoples' and 'cosmopolitan law' protecting cosmopolitan freedoms, including individual rights to rule of law and judicial protection of precise and unconditional international guarantees of freedom, non-discrimination, rule of law and social justice.
- The UN principles of 'sovereign equality of states' and of 'self-determination of peoples' and the 'subsidiary function' of UN human rights law, justify national and regional diversity of human rights conceptions. IEL must respect reasonable disagreement about interpreting human rights.
- **Policy conclusion**: Just as constitutional principles are not explicitly repeated in all domestic laws, so does the 'human rights coherence' of IEL not necessitate explicit references to human rights in worldwide economic agreements. The intergovernmental practice of separating economic regulation from human rights protection on the basis of 'exception clauses' recognizing sovereign rights to protect human rights is politically justifiable and does not curtail the human rights obligations of WTO members (eg, Article XX GATT must be construed in conformity with the human rights obligations of WTO members).

All UN member states are likely to claim that their economic laws and multilevel economic regulation are consistent with their human rights obligations under national and international law. In order to make 'human rights coherence' a meaningful standard of review, chapters II and III emphasize the constitutional dimensions of human rights to democratic self-governance and of access to justice. History confirms not only that governments can protect human rights effectively only in the context of 'constitutional democracies' with delegation of limited legislative, administrative and judicial powers for the protection of the constitutional rights and general interests of citizens; in IEL, effective protection of constitutional rights, human rights and consumer welfare has proven possible only in the context of legal systems which constitutionally limit abuses of legislative, administrative and judicial powers.

Cosmopolitan conceptions of IEL must promote transnational rule of law on the basis of respect for legitimate 'constitutional pluralism'

Since the UDHR of 1948, worldwide, regional and national human rights instruments call for 'equal protection of the law' (Article 7) and of human rights 'by the rule of law' (Preamble UDHR). According to Article 28 UDHR, '(e)veryone is entitled to a social and international order in which the rights and freedoms set forth in this Declaration can be fully realized'. 'In the exercise of his rights and freedoms, everyone shall be subject only to such limitations as are determined by law solely for the purpose of securing due recognition and respect for the rights and freedoms of others and of meeting the just requirements of morality, public order and the general welfare in a democratic society' (Article 29). The inadequate constitutional and judicial protection of 'rule of law' in transnational economic relations, and the apparent lack of 'input legitimacy' (eg, in terms of parliamentary participation and protection of human rights) of many intergovernmental economic regulations, entail that the democratic legitimacy of IEL and its consistency with basic principles of constitutional democracies and constitutional rights are increasingly challenged by civil society. Transnational 'rule of law' in the worldwide division of labour among billions of citizens governed by hundreds of 'fragmented' national and international legal regimes depends less on the legal formalism of state-centred conflict rules (such as *lex specialis*, *lex posterior*, *lex superior*) and related hierarchical claims (eg, to legal primacy of international law over domestic law) than on the consistency of IEL with human rights and 'democratic constitutionalism'.

Overcoming the existing regulatory failures of IEL requires clarifying its 'constitutional foundations' with due respect for the legitimate diversity of individual preferences, human rights conceptions, constitutional and democratic traditions. The more general consumer welfare, non-discriminatory competition and rule of law are disregarded by self interested politicians (eg, in order to grant 'protection rents' to protectionist lobbies in exchange for political support), the more it becomes necessary to limit regulatory abuses by independent judicial review of international economic regulation. European economic integration confirms that many regulatory problems of IEL cannot be effectively resolved without citizen-oriented 'constitutional reforms' committing multilevel economic regulation to stronger protection of consumer welfare and human rights. One of the most important historical experiences in virtually all states has been that – notwithstanding the reality and legitimacy of 'constitutional pluralism' – collective supply of national public goods has proven possible only within 'constitutional structures' protecting individual and democratic self-governance (*cf* Table 5). In addition to this necessary 'input legitimacy' of IEL in terms of 'human rights coherence' and democratic participation, 'good governance' may have other sources of legitimacy – like results-based legitimacy (such as economic efficiency enhancing general consumer welfare), legitimacy deriving from 'rule of law' and from systemic 'checks and balances', 'deliberative legitimacy' and procedural legitimacy.[58] Multilevel constitutionalism, as explained in chapter II, aims at legal protection and promotion of the diverse legal sources of substantive, procedural, democratic, deliberative, results-based and order-based legitimacy.

[58] The various moral and legal foundations of 'legitimate governance' are emphasized in the vast literature on 'good governance' and 'global administrative law'; see, eg: DC Esty, 'Good Governance at the Supranational Scale: Globalizing Administrative Law' (2006) 115 *Yale Law Journal* 1490–1562, 1515 ff.

By contrast, proposals for promoting 'good governance' on the basis of 'global administrative law' principles are often based on moral propositions rather than on positive international law. The citizen-oriented approach advocated in this book argues for reinterpreting and progressively developing IEL in light of the human rights obligations and constitutional restraints of UN member states.

Table 5: 'Democratic constitutionalism' as an additional condition of the legitimacy of multilevel economic regulation

- Democracy can be sustained over time only as constitutionally limited democracy. Individual and democratic self-governance depend on protection of human rights and democratic supply of other public goods in the context of long-term constitutional principles, rules and procedures of a higher legal rank approved by 'the people'. Such norms must constitute and limit post-constitutional democratic law-making, administration, 'judicial governance' and individual self-governance at local, national and transnational levels.
- The exercise of human rights inevitably entails 'deliberative democracy' based on citizen-driven economic markets as well as 'political markets' as decentralized 'dialogues about values', information and coordination mechanisms. Depending on the preferences of citizens, democratic constitutionalism may provide for legitimately diverse forms of representative parliamentary democracy, direct participatory democracy and 'deliberative democracy' in order to limit 'market failures' (such as restrictive business practices, other abuses of market power, harmful external effects, information asymmetries) and provide 'public goods'.
- Protection of human rights and rule of law in multilevel economic governance entails 'multilevel constitutional problems' that go beyond those of the state-centred 'Westphalian system' of 'international law of coexistence' and 'international law of coordination' among sovereign states. Respect for human rights requires resolving these problems with due respect for legitimate 'constitutional pluralism' and legitimately diverse conceptions of human rights (eg, in case of national or institutional 'margins of appreciation').
- **Policy conclusion:** Democratic constitutions recognize international law as a necessary complement of national legal systems for the supply of public goods in a globally integrating world. Rule of international law must remain consistent with human rights and democratic constitutionalism. If transnational disputes cannot be prevented by mutual agreements or third-party mediation, dispute settlement should be delegated to independent 'courts of justice' for impartial 'administration of justice' based on due process of law and cooperation among courts.

IEL can protect many public goods only in mutually coherent 'multilevel constitutional frameworks' protecting human rights, 'public reason' and transnational rule of law

The main claim of this study is that collective supply of international public goods (like transnational rule of law, protection of biodiversity and 'carbon sinks' in tropical forests) requires subjecting regulatory powers to stronger 'constitutional checks and balances'. For instance, parliamentary review and judicial protection of individual rights and rule of law in international economic regulation should empower citizens, protect their human rights across frontiers and hold governments accountable for their often arbitrary violations of international rule of law. The customary law requirement of settling international disputes 'in conformity with the principles of justice and international law', including human rights – as explicitly recalled in the Preamble of the VCLT – reflects this need for stronger legal and judicial protection of international rule of law for the benefit of all citizens benefiting from the worldwide division of labour. Just as democratic self-governance requires constitutional restraints on legislative, administrative and judicial powers to protect the constitutional rights of citizens, so does multilevel protection of international public goods beyond 'constitutional democracies' require multilevel constitutional safeguards of the common interests and human rights of citizens. The main arguments explaining this need for a multilevel constitutional framework protecting human rights and cosmopolitan 'public reason' for the supply of international public goods more effectively are summarized in Table 6 and discussed in chapter II.

Table 6: 'Multilevel constitutional pluralism' as a necessary legal framework for collective supply of 'interdependent aggregate public goods'

- Just as citizens in all states have found it necessary to establish (un)written constitutions for democratic supply of national public goods, so do transnational 'collective action problems' in the supply of international public goods require 'constitutional principles of justice' and their protection by transnational rulemaking, multilevel administration and judicial protection of rule of law. European law illustrates the legitimate diversity of functionally limited 'treaty constitutions' (like the ECHR, the EU and EEA treaties) and the need for respecting legitimate 'constitutional pluralism' in protecting interdependent public goods.
- The need for 'multilevel constitutionalism' is confirmed by the 'composite nature' of aggregate public goods like human rights, rule of law and sustainable development, whose international protection must build on their local and national protection in conformity with 'principles of subsidiarity'. National and cosmopolitan constitutionalism constitutes multilevel 'constitutional houses' with interdependent floors protecting citizens in their transnational cooperation and multilevel governance for transnational public goods.
- Transnational law and 'governance' must limit 'nationalist government failures' such as 'harmful external effects' and welfare-reducing discrimination in national legislation, administration and adjudication. For instance, the 'discourse failures' inside states underlying harmful 'transnational externalities' must be counteracted by 'institutionalized leadership' for promoting 'global public reason' in support of international public goods (eg, independent institutions for monitoring, precautionary assessment, early warning, coordination and legislative proposals concerning international public goods following the example of the EU Commission as guardian of 'community interests'). National democracy must be supplemented by transnational 'deliberative democracy' and 'participatory democracy' in order to promote democratic support for international public goods and limit national 'government failures'. Multilevel legislative, executive and judicial governance powers and institutions must remain constitutionally limited and subject to rule of law and mutual 'checks and balances'.
- **Policy conclusion**: The 'overlapping nature' of separate international legal regimes (such as trade and environmental treaties) for the protection of interrelated 'public goods' (like an efficient world trading system and protection of the environment) requires promotion of legal coherence and transnational rule of law. If disputes cannot be prevented through multilevel regulation, their settlement should be entrusted to multilevel judicial protection of transnational rule of law for the benefit of citizens based on coherent 'principles of justice' (such as 'judicial cooperation' and 'comity' among courts, individual access to justice,

due process of law). Overcoming the 'collective action problems' in the supply of global public goods also requires other 'cosmopolitan principles of justice' such as 'common but differentiated responsibilities' for co-financing of international public goods and for promoting 'coalitions of the willing', 'capacity building', 'duties to protect' and 'solidarity on the ground' in protecting 'common concerns'.

3 THE NEED FOR INTEGRATING THE FIVE COMPETING CONCEPTIONS OF IEL

Similar to the story of the blind men touching different parts of an elephant and describing the same animal in contradictory ways, private and public, national and international lawyers tend to describe and analyze IEL from very diverse perspectives, for instance as: (1) public international law; (2) 'global administrative law'; (3) 'conflicts law'; (4) multilevel constitutional regulation; or (5) multilevel economic regulation of the economy. The state-centred 'Westphalian conception' of international law, which emerged from the power struggles against the Church, the Holy Roman Empire and colonialism in support of a new system of states with 'sovereign equality' (Article 2 UN Charter) continues to dominate UN law in spite of the ever more comprehensive human rights obligations acknowledged by all UN member states. Textbooks on IEL tend to describe and analyze IEL from competing perspectives.

IEL as 'public international law regulating the international economy'

International state practice and most textbooks on IEL focus on the 'Westphalian conception' of IEL and on international rights and duties among states and international organizations regulating governmental restrictions of international movements of goods, services, persons, capital and related payments among states.[59] The 1944 Bretton Woods Agreements establishing the IMF and the World Bank, the 1945 United Nations Charter, GATT 1947 and the UN Specialized Agencies engaged in regulating international services – like the Universal Postal Union, the International Telecommunications Union, the International Civil Aviation Organization and the International Maritime Organization – were all negotiated by states, under the leadership of the most powerful industrialized countries, and provide for reciprocal rights and obligations among states. As governments tend to view international economic treaties as instruments for advancing state interests, they remain reluctant to delegate policy powers (eg, for supervision of monetary, trade, development and labour policies) to worldwide organizations. Hence, 'member-driven governance' focuses on state interests as defined by domestic rulers and organized interest groups, often with systemic biases inside less-developed and non-democratic countries to the detriment of general citizen interests. Powers for intergovernmental rulemaking, administration and adjudication tend to be allocated to separate international organizations, but usually without effective legal and judicial restraints of state sovereignty and without guarantees of effective domestic implementation of treaty obligations. For instance, many less-developed countries in Africa do not appear to have

[59] See, eg, AH Qureshi and AR Ziegler (2007) ix: 'This book focuses on that branch of Public International Law which is concerned with international economic relations between States'.

incorporated the 1994 WTO Agreement into their domestic legal systems or to have adjusted their national trade and economic legislation accordingly. Coordination among the hundreds of separate, intergovernmental organizations remains 'member-driven' and decentralized. The 'general exceptions' included into their international treaties enable each state to depart from economic treaty obligations to protect non-economic 'public interests' (eg, pursuant to Articles XX and XXI GATT).

'Public international law conceptions' of international economic regulation, based on the sources of international law and 'rules of recognition' as defined in Article 38 of the Statute of the International Court of Justice (ie, treaties, customary law, general principles of law), are sometimes criticized for their 'dangerously naïve tendency towards legalism – an idealistic belief that law can be effective even in the absence of legitimate institutions of governance'. They are especially attacked if they neglect that 'whatever their professed commitments, all nations stand ready to dispense with international agreements when it suits their short- or long-term interests'.[60] 'Public international law approaches' tend to leave domestic rule implementation to the sovereign discretion of states without providing citizens with effective legal and judicial remedies in case of non-compliance. The democratic legitimacy and contribution to 'rule of law' of such foreign policy discretion remains contested, for instance if non-democratic governments deny individual economic rights and restrict human rights like freedom of expression.[61] Arguably, the focus on rights and obligations of states rather than of citizens explains why most worldwide agreements have failed to protect human rights and other 'global public goods' effectively.

IEL as functionally interrelated 'private and public, national and international economic regulation' based on 'constitutional nationalism'

This alternative conception of IEL as multilevel economic regulation, which underlies many international trade and investment agreements, focuses on the functional unity of private and public, national and international regulation of the economy[62] and on the advantages of decentralized forms of market regulation and dispute settlement as provided for in Chapters 11 and 19 of the North American Free Trade Agreement (NAFTA) as well as in EEA law. This 'multilevel economic law perspective' emphasizes 'constitutional nationalism' (as discussed in chapter VIII) and potential synergies of public–private partnerships. It stresses that private regulation can supplement and complement incomplete, intergovernmental regulations and offer decentralized enforcement mechanisms (like commercial arbitration, investor–state arbitration, Article 1904 NAFTA dispute settlement panels established at the request of private complainants and replacing domestic tribunals reviewing anti-dumping and countervailing duty orders in NAFTA

[60] EA Posner (2009), who claims that 'most European scholars are global legalists' with an 'excessive faith in the efficacy of international law' who lose 'sight of the social function of law' (at xii); Posner justifies the 'pattern of American international lawbreaking' (at xi) on grounds of national cost-benefit analyses by the foreign policy elites.

[61] See, eg, the WTO Appellate Body report, 'China – Publications and Audiovisual Products' (WTDS363ABR) adopted 19 January 2010.

[62] See, eg, EU Petersmann, 'International Economic Theory and International Economic Law' in RSJ Macdonald and DM Johnston (eds), *The Structure and Process of International Law* (The Hague: Kluwer, 1983) 239 ff.

countries). Such private–public co-regulation may increase the legitimacy, effectiveness and scope of economic regulation. It may justify legal presumptions – as it is the case in the WTO Agreements on Technical Barriers to Trade (TBT) and Sanitary and Phytosanitary Measures (SPS) – that privately agreed production standards, product standards and (phyto)sanitary standards are consistent with public international law rules unless they are successfully challenged in intergovernmental dispute settlement proceedings.[63] Yet, private–public partnerships also risk facilitating 'protectionist collusion' and restrictive business practices to the detriment of consumer welfare.

Multilevel economic regulation at public and private levels lacks a single unifying rule of recognition in view of its broad coverage of private and public, national and international sub-systems of IEL. It understands IEL as interdependent regulatory practices, including the 'private ordering' of the international division of labour among billions of producers, investors, traders and consumers in 193 UN member states. The synergies, functional interrelationships and 'optimal levels' of public regulation (eg, by means of competition law, banking law, investment law, labour law, environmental law) and private regulation (such as 'corporate governance' of the ever larger share of world trade carried out inside multinational corporations) are perceived as major regulatory problems. 'Multilevel economic regulation' approaches tend to be critical of authoritarian 'top-down conceptions' of intergovernmental economic regulation. For instance, they draw attention to the ineffectiveness of most intergovernmental commodity agreements (eg, for coffee, cocoa and tin) aimed at guaranteeing 'stable, fair and remunerative' commodity prices. Yet, they recognize (eg, in NAFTA Chapter 19 on multilevel judicial review of national antidumping and countervailing duty determinations, and NAFTA Chapter 11 on investor–state arbitration) that international legal and procedural guarantees may be necessary for limiting 'protection biases' in national laws and institutions. Identifying the 'optimal level of legal regulation', and promoting mutual synergies between private and public, national and international economic regulation, are perceived as central regulatory challenges:

- Private international law – such as the national and international rules coordinating the effects of domestic private laws across borders by harmonizing private law systems, allocating jurisdiction and providing for mutual recognition and enforcement of judgments and arbitral awards – offers decentralized systems for self-governance across borders (eg, based on contract law, company law, competition law, tort law) subject to control by national governments and decentralized enforcement by domestic courts or arbitration. As illustrated by investor–state arbitration and private litigation against transnational corporations (eg, under the US Aliens Tort Act), such decentralized self-governance may be more efficient and offer more effective legal and judicial remedies than centralized governance systems.[64]
- Private law enables not only the pursuit of private interests (such as settlement of individual conflicts among private parties), but also of public and social interests. For instance, national courts may exercise judicial comity vis-à-vis foreign jurisdictions or judicial deference vis-à-vis domestic government interests.

[63] On the many problems of such legal presumptions see the contributions by T Hüller, ML Maier, R Howse, H Schepel and others to C Joerges and EU Petersmann (eds) (2006) chs 9 to 14.

[64] See the examples discussed by R Wai, 'Conflicts and Comity in Transnational Governance: Private International Law as Mechanism and Metaphor for Transnational Social Regulation' in Joerges and Petersmann (eds) (2006) 229–62. See also the contributions by C Joerges, R Nickel and F Rödl in R Nickel (ed), *Conflict of Laws and Laws of Conflict in Europe and Beyond* (Antwerp: Intersentia, 2010).

- The increasing number of international treaties harmonizing certain areas of international private law, coordinating national jurisdictions (eg, by means of providing for mutual recognition and enforcement of foreign civil, commercial and arbitral judgments in national courts), or limiting the legitimate scope for private self-regulation (eg, by means of international competition rules, public risk regulation limiting private standard setting, ICAO rules limiting private self-regulation of international air transport in the context of the International Air Transport Association), illustrate potential synergies of dovetailing public and private economic rules and institutions.

Table 7: IEL as a multilevel legal system composed of private and public, national and international economic regulation

- Regulatory task: Promotion of mutually beneficial international movements of goods, services, persons, capital and related payments empowering individuals to enhance economic welfare and enjoy their human rights.
- 'Empowering', 'limiting' and 'regulatory functions' of IEL:
- *National private law* (eg, economic freedoms, contract law, property rights, commercial arbitration, conflict rules) empowers citizens to engage in mutually beneficial cooperation and limits governmental restrictions.
- *National public law* (eg, constitutional, monetary, trade, investment, environmental laws and regulations) restrains 'market failures' as well as 'governance failures' and protects 'public goods'.
- *International public law* (eg, IMF, GATT, WTO, ITU, ICAO, and ILO law, ICSID, MEAs, RTAs, BITs, codes of conduct) limits harmful 'external effects' and promotes transnational protection of 'public goods'.
- **Regulatory problems**: How to reconcile human rights, national sovereignty and domestic welfare with international liberalization and regulation? How to maintain economic and 'legal order' among 'fragmented' national, bilateral, regional and worldwide legal regimes and institutions?

Multilevel constitutional conceptions of IEL

The diverse 'multilevel constitutional approaches to IEL' emphasize that the legitimacy and effectiveness of IEL – as an instrument for promoting consumer welfare and human rights of domestic citizens – depend on its consistency with national and international human rights obligations and other constitutional obligations of governments. Such approaches are practised by the ECJ, the EFTA Court and the ECtHR in cooperation with national courts and protect rule of law for the benefit of citizens, with due respect for the legitimate diversity of constitutional democracies. The legal primacy of constitutional rules over post-constitutional rulemaking may justify granting international treaties only an infra-constitutional legal rank in domestic legal systems and excluding 'direct applicability' of international law rules in domestic courts. As international law's claim (eg, in Article 27 VCLT) to legal primacy over domestic law must remain subject to constitutional restraints, constitutional democracy may require higher levels of *national* protection of human rights than the minimum standards prescribed in *international* human rights treaties. However, whenever international guarantees of freedom, non-discrimination and rule of law go beyond those of national legal systems – as in many areas of IEL – constitutional democracy may justify using IEL for limiting 'constitutional failures' and 'government failures' of nation states. For instance, European economic law empowers European citizens to invoke and enforce the fundamental rights guarantees of European law in national courts vis-à-vis welfare-reducing, national restrictions of mutually beneficial economic cooperation among citizens across frontiers. Human rights law justifies the practice of virtually all national constitutions to subject the incorporation of international rules into the domestic legal system to constitutional safeguards like respect for human rights and parliamentary ratification of treaties, often subject to 'later-in-time rules' protecting the sovereign right of parliaments to override the domestic law effects of international treaties by later legislation. In Europe, 'multilevel economic regulation' is designed and reviewed in 'multilevel constitutional systems' which legitimately vary. Its legal and judicial assessment depends on whether the economic regulations are governed by EU constitutional law as interpreted by the ECJ, EEA law as interpreted by the EFTA Court, or by the ECHR as interpreted by the ECtHR in close cooperation with national courts operating in diverse multilevel systems of 'constitutional democracy'.[65]

This study claims that only citizen-oriented 'constitutional bottom-up approaches' to IEL can effectively protect human rights and limit the 'collective action problems' in the supply of international public goods. The common market and rule of law system of the 30 EEA member countries illustrate the potential variety of combining diverse national and international constitutional rules and institutions. Without linking international rules to their domestic 'constitutional foundations', top-down 'public international law conceptions' of IEL risk failing to protect consumer welfare and human rights effectively. As human rights protect *individual* as well as *collective exercises* of fundamental freedoms (eg, property rights owned by corporations, collective labour rights exercised by trade unions), human rights and constitutional law must also protect the institutions necessary for such collective exercises of fundamental rights. For instance, they must safeguard private property, private companies, private newspapers and private markets as 'dialogues about values' among producers and consumers and citizen-driven information mechanisms coordinating supply and demand. Without constitutional, legislative and administrative protection and regulation of market competition and judicial protection of individual rights, the ubiquitous conflicts among private and public interests cannot be effectively protected over time in economic markets.

IEL as 'conflicts law' inspired by international private law approaches?

Economic globalization continues to link hundreds of diverse national and international legal systems and thousands of governmental and non-governmental regulations. It impacts on international trade and comparative advantages of producers, investors and countries competing to attract investments and other scarce resources. This competition and rivalry make some private lawyers emphasize:

[65] On these complex, functional interrelationships between national, regional and worldwide economic rules see the contributions of K Mortelmans, 'The Interdependence of International, European and National Economic Law: The European Community Example' and EU Petersmann, 'Constitutional Functions of International Economic Law' in PV Dijk et al (eds), *Restructuring the International Economic Order: The Role of Law and Lawyers* (The Hague: Kluwer, 1987) 14 ff, 49 ff.

- the reality of conflict and contestation in transnational society;
- the inevitable limits of 'top-down global governance';
- the lessons from private international law for coordinating and resolving conflicts among jurisdictions, among government regulations, and among transnational governance mechanisms; and
- the advantages of using private international law concepts for resolving 'conflicts among multiple systems of rules of both state and private ordering'.[66]

They also draw attention to the social functions and *public policy* goals of private law and private litigation by private 'attorneys general' who, through the pursuit of their own interests, may also serve social purposes of regulation. For example, individuals may claim compensation in litigation related to product liability, environmental harms, restrictive business practices and corporate accountability for human rights violations. The ever greater influence in IEL of transnational, *private* 'advocacy networks' and transnational, *private* litigation against multinational companies, human rights violators and host states of foreign direct investors, illustrates the systemic importance of 'adversarial legalism' as a tool of transnational governance. Private 'conflict of laws' doctrines (like the effects doctrine, judicial restraint doctrines, principles for mutual recognition of foreign standards and court judgments) may assist in resolving the coordination problems resulting from competing private and *public regulation* systems. They may also facilitate coordination among regulatory authorities, representation in national regulatory bodies of all adversely affected foreign interests and reduce other regulatory gaps favouring business interests in transnational private ordering (for instance through contracts and international commercial arbitration privileging the asymmetric mobility of business actors as compared with consumers and workers). Private law experiences may argue for mediating 'conflicts of normative orders' among national and international public law regimes by use of 'judicial comity'. National courts may not only pay deference towards their own legislatures in case of cross-jurisdictional conflicts of policy, but also to legitimate interests of foreign jurisdictions and transnational governance procedures. Such conflict rules may promote judicial protection of transnational 'principles of cosmopolitan justice'.[67]

Yet, does this increasing confrontation of private and public international law with common regulatory problems – such as the need for overcoming their 'methodological nationalism' and parochial legacies of discriminating against foreigners – justify conceptualizing IEL as 'conflicts law'?[68] This chapter argues that the recognition by all UN member states of human rights obligations and other constitutional restraints of governance powers requires justifying IEL in terms of human and constitutional rights of citizens rather than only in terms of economic utilitarianism or private law principles. 'Conflicts law principles' of private law for determining whether foreign jurisdictions, conflicting government regulations and transnational governance mechanisms 'deserve recognition' are no substitute for the necessary review of the 'human rights coherence' of IEL. They cannot replace legal and judicial 'balancing' of constitutional principles and human rights in applying and interpreting IEL 'in conformity with principles of justice'

[66] Wai (n 64) 230.

[67] *cf* Wai (n 64) emphasizing 'the value of both conflict and comity in the relationship among regulatory orders, whether they be public or private, domestic or foreign, or international or transnational' (at 262).

[68] As suggested by C Joerges, 'Three-Dimensional Conflicts Law as Constitutional Form' in Joerges and Petersmann (eds) (2011) ch 15.

and the human rights obligations of governments, as required by national and international law.[69]

IEL as 'global administrative law' (GAL)?

An increasing number of administrative lawyers argue that

> (m)uch global regulatory governance – especially in fields as trade and investment, financial and economic regulation – can now be understood as administration, by which we include all forms of law-making other than treaties or other international agreements on the one hand and episodic dispute settlement on the other.[70]

As multilevel economic governance aims at regulating the conduct not only of states, but also of private actors, they acknowledge that the traditional inter-state paradigm of international law needs to be adjusted to the pluralistic and cosmopolitan regulatory realities. GAL approaches wish to ensure that 'global regulatory decision-makers are accountable and responsive to all of those who are affected by their decisions.' For instance, 'the challenges faced by the WTO can be addressed by greater application of GAL decision-making mechanisms of transparency, participation, reason-giving, review and accountability to the WTO's administrative bodies including its councils and committees and the Trade Policy Review Body'. GAL principles and procedures should be strengthened in three dimensions:

1. The efficacy and legitimacy of the internal WTO governance structures and decision-making procedures could be improved by strengthening transparency, participation, reason-giving and the law-making role of the WTO's regulatory, administrative and adjudicatory bodies.
2. In the vertical interrelationships between the WTO and its regulation of members' domestic administrations, the incorporation of GAL principles and procedures into domestic administrative rules and procedures could strengthen rule of law, transparency of trade regulation, uniform and impartial administration, due process of law and judicial review.
3. In the increasingly close 'horizontal linkages' among different global regulatory institutions, the WTO should recognize (eg, pursuant to the WTO Agreements on Sanitary and Phytosanitary Standards and Technical Barriers to Trade) regulatory standards issued by other global regulatory bodies only if generated through transparent procedures and 'regulatory due process' affording rights of participation and based on 'public reason' supported by the decisional record and reflecting fair consideration of all affected interests.

The focus of 'GAL norms' on the procedural elements of administrative law has 'served not only to secure implementation of the substantive norms of liberalized trade

[69] For my criticism of Joerges' proposals for reinterpreting IEL as 'conflicts law' see: EU Petersmann, 'The Future of International Economic Law: A Research Agenda' in Joerges and Petersmann (eds) (2011) ch 18. On the need for defining law not only by authoritative issuance and social efficacy of rules, but by principles of justice see: R Alexy, *The Argument from Injustice* (Oxford: OUP, 2010). According to Alexy, only 'extreme injustice' and violations of human rights affect the validity of legal rules.

[70] R Stewart and R M Ratton Sanchez Badin, 'The WTO and Global Administrative Law' in Joerges and Petersmann (eds) (2011) ch 16. The following quotations in the text are from these authors.

but also to promote broader goals including open administration, even-handed treatment of foreign citizens, and the rule of law'. Thereby, the standards are seeking 'to provide safeguards against abuse of power, counter-factional capture, and temper the tunnel vision of specialized regulatory bodies'. Yet, GAL proponents acknowledge that – due to the absence of democratic legislation and democratic accountability at the global level – 'procedural mechanisms alone may be relatively ineffective in overcoming disparities in power and the biases of specialized mission-oriented organizations'. 'To the extent GAL procedures enable a broader range of social and economic actors and interests, especially those that tend to be disregarded, to more effectively scrutinize and have input to decisions and also foster broader discussion and debate, they may also promote a democratic element in global regulatory governance'.

GAL without constitutional restraints?

GAL policy proposals have emerged as pragmatic responses to the 'accountability gaps' in the administrative practices of international institutions and the recognition that the 'ultimate aim of many of these regimes is to regulate the conduct of private actors rather than states; private actors including NGOs and business firms and associations as well as domestic government agencies and officials'.[71] Yet, the legal context of administrative activities of international organizations with limited competences differs fundamentally from national constitutional and administrative laws. For instance:

- The constitutional constraints and parliamentary control characteristic of administrative law inside constitutional democracies are absent in the law of worldwide organizations. GAL proposals by US administrative lawyers seem to imply the underlying US constitutional law constraints without explaining why the particular features of US constitutional and administrative law (such as limited judicial review pursuant to the 'Chevron doctrine' in view of congressional regulation and oversight of delegated administrative powers) should be appropriate for worldwide organizations that elude effective parliamentary control in most states.
- Most worldwide organizations offer no effective judicial remedies for adversely affected citizens, with a few exceptions such as the UN and ILO Administrative Tribunals protecting international civil servants, Part XI of the UN Law of the Sea Convention regarding deep seabed mining, WIPO arbitration concerning disputes over internet domain names and World Bank inspection panels.
- Many worldwide organizations offer frameworks for intergovernmental coordination rather than for independent administration (eg, of the lending activities of the World Bank Group). Their review and dispute settlement procedures – like the 'compliance procedures' of multilateral environmental agreements identifying, reviewing and restricting harmful activities – are often politicized and lack the independence necessary for 'administration of justice'.

The administrative law practices of international organizations and courts remain embedded in their specific legal contexts of 'primary' and 'secondary law'. GAL advocates acknowledge the lack of international agreement on a uniform 'constitutional foundation'

[71] Stewart and Sanchez Badin (n 70).

or 'rule of recognition' for determining GAL principles, rules and practices by the diverse private and public, national and international actors. Nor is there agreement on new customary GAL resulting from the often informal, administrative and legal practices in different institutional contexts with limited jurisdictions and diverse memberships of states.

European integration has given rise to ever more comprehensive 'European administrative law' based on common 'administrative constitutionalism' constituting and limiting national and European administrative practices in the implementation of EU and EEA law.[72] The administrative law dimensions of the law of *worldwide organizations*, by contrast, tend to remain contextual (ie, limited and defined by their respective constitutional rules), fragmented and diverse. These characteristics impede the emergence of general, universally agreed 'global administrative law'. Without more thorough empirical, comparative and contextual legal research into the transformation of administrative practices into positive 'global law', GAL claims risk being criticized as wishful thinking rather than as methodologically convincing determinations of positively existing international law. For instance, Kingsbury's concept of 'law' in GAL research[73] has been rightly criticized as a 'natural law interpretation'[74] of the 'general principles of public law' without methodologically convincing determinations of positively existing law. Kingsbury admits that the 'legal constitution of the global administrative body' by 'a kind of constitution-making' amounts to an international exercise of 'constitutive power' and 'constitutionalist commitment to publicness'.[75] Yet, rather than exploring the constitutional principles governing the 'primary law' and 'secondary law' of international organizations and of their judicial interpretation at regional and worldwide levels,[76], Kingsbury claims: 'Constitutionalism implies a coherence of structure which global legal and institutional arrangements do not currently have . . . While constitutive power is certainly exercised internationally, international constitutionalism in its richer forms is still, at most, in *statu nascendi*'. Arguably, Kingsbury's methodological assumptions are inconsistent with the reality of 'constitutional pluralism'. They risk contributing to 'GAL claims' that are incompatible with both the diversity of administrative law practices in international organizations and the contextual contingency of administrative law systems.[77]

The 'market for regulation': international relations theories and IEL approaches

Law – as one among many other political instruments for social ordering – tends to be influenced by the self-interests of private and public actors, their political, economic and

[72] *cf* E Fisher, 'Beyond the Science/Democracy Dichotomy: The WTO Sanitary and Phytosanitary Agreement and Administrative Constitutionalism' in Joerges and Petersmann (eds) (2006) ch 11.

[73] According to B Kingsbury, 'The Concept of "Law" in Global Administrative Law' (2009) 20 *EJIL* 23 ff, 32–33, 'requirements of publicness in GAL' include the principle of legality, the principle of rationality, proportionality, rule of law and basic human rights, ie, basic constitutional principles (called 'constitutive administrative law' in Kingsbury's terminology). Yet, Kingsbury fails to identify to what extent his 'general principles of public law' are already part of the positive law of international organizations or merely proposals *de lege ferenda*.

[74] *cf* A Somek, 'The Concept of "Law" in Global Administrative Law: A Reply to B Kingsbury' (2010) 20 *EJIL* 985 ff, 990 f.

[75] *cf* Kingsbury (n 73) 34–36.

[76] *cf* N Blokker and H Schermers, *International Institutional Law*, 4th edn (Leiden: Martinus Nijhoff, 2003).

[77] *cf* Petersmann (n 69) 14 ff. The constitutional principles and rules identified by Blokker and Schermers (n 76) as part of the law of international organizations contradict the claims by Kingsbury.

social conceptions of law and the 'public reason' prevailing in particular communities. The fact that private commercial law, monetary and trade regulation and trade agreements have historically evolved over more than 2500 years reflects the ever greater importance of trade for individual and social welfare. Many standards underlying WTO rules – like the most-favoured-nation and national treatment standards – were used and progressively refined in bilateral trade agreements during centuries. In most areas, economic law evolved first at private, local and national levels before being coordinated, liberalized and regulated through ever more bilateral and multilateral international agreements. In democratic countries, economic regulation responds to demands by citizens and other economic actors for regulation of market failures as well as of governance failures by means of private and public, national and international rules and institutions. Just as the multilateral Bretton Woods, WTO and Law of the Sea Agreements were preceded by hundreds of bilateral and regional monetary, trade, shipping and development agreements, so are international investment, financial and environmental relations governed by hundreds of bilateral and multilateral investment, double-taxation, financial and environmental agreements. The 'rules in the books' and the 'law in action' dynamically interact in response to disputes over their interpretation, national application or judicial clarification.

Table 8: 'Protection biases' in 'political markets' for multilevel economic regulation

For centuries, multilevel economic regulation of transnational economic transactions tends to be driven by citizen demand for private and public national regulation and autonomous, bilateral and multilateral transnational regulation of goods, services, persons, capital and related payments, with increasingly complex interrelationships between unilateral, bilateral, regional and multilateral regulation of international monetary, trade and investment relations.

- Demand for economic liberalization > supply of multilevel commercial, monetary, trade, financial and investment regulation
- Demand for regulation of 'market failures' > supply of multilevel competition, banking, social and environmental regulation
- Demand for regulation of 'governance failures' > supply of 'enabling' and 'limiting constitutionalization', GAL, independent regulatory agencies, courts of justice
- Demand for regulation of 'constitutional failures' > international agreements and institutions limiting harmful 'legal nationalism' and promoting transnational 'public goods'
- Demand for regulating 'systemic problems' of IEL > 'integration agreements' like the 2007 Lisbon Treaty limit all regulatory powers by 'constitutional restraints' (such as the 'no bail-out clause' in Article 125 TEU, the EU Charter of Fundamental Rights)

Regulatory problem: 'Regulatory capture' of political regulators for the benefit of powerful producer lobbies in exchange for financial and political support of the regulators can be observed in all countries. 'Public choice' theory explains such 'protection biases' by the fact that concentrated producer interests (including self-interests of regulators) are easier to organize and more successful in lobbying for concentrated 'protection rents' than large social groups with more dispersed common interests, which often remain 'rationally ignorant' towards specific economic regulation accommodating protectionist interests.

State-centred 'top-down conceptions' of IEL, citizen-oriented 'bottom-up conceptions' and 'constitutional conceptions' of IEL are often influenced by international relations theories, such as realism, institutionalism, liberalism and constructivism as the four major political science approaches to, and explanations of, international relations and international law.[78] When, based on my personal experiences as legal advisor in the Uruguay Round Negotiating Groups which elaborated the WTO Dispute Settlement Understanding (DSU) and the institutional framework of the WTO Agreement, I published one of the first books on the GATT/WTO dispute settlement system following the entry into force of the WTO Agreement, I emphasized the need for using these simplifying theories in complementary rather than mutually exclusive ways in order to understand the power-oriented context of WTO rules and their frequent neglect for 'normative individualism' focusing on citizen interests.[79]

Realism

The 'realist' focus on states as the principal actors in international politics, and on their power-oriented pursuit of national security and other state interests, is consistent with the intergovernmental structures of WTO law, with the 'member-driven' nature of reciprocal bargaining in GATT and WTO negotiations, and with the reliance of the WTO dispute settlement system on self-help in case of violations of WTO obligations (eg, recourse to WTO dispute settlement procedures and to countermeasures vis-à-vis WTO members refusing to implement WTO dispute settlement rulings). Yet, the prevailing realist approaches to international relations leave the definition of 'national interests' to the discretion of national rulers. They only inadequately take regard of transnational 'external effects' caused by national protectionism and violations of international law, and lack a coherent theory for the collective supply of international public goods.

Institutionalism

The institutional changes from GATT to the WTO confirm the premise of institutional theories that rational governments can reduce the collective action problems (such as uncertainty and free-riding in intergovernmental negotiations) impeding collective supply of international public goods by deliberately changing the legal and institutional incentives for non-cooperation. The compulsory jurisdiction of WTO dispute settlement bodies for independent, factual as well as legal dispute settlement findings, and the ever stronger influence of judicial clarification of 'incomplete agreements' on intergovernmental rulemaking and domestic legal practices, illustrate how institutional changes have helped WTO members to legally limit their welfare-reducing recourse to unilateral self-help and trade sanctions. European integration suggests that additional institutional changes are necessary for collective supply of international public goods. Examples include notably institutions with independent powers for defending 'community interests' in global public goods (eg, by proposals for collective rulemaking) vis-à-vis conflicting national interests and private interests.

[78] *cf* KW Abbott, 'Toward a Richer Institutionalism for International Law and Policy' (2006) 1 *Journal of International Law and International Relations* 9–34; SR Ratner and AM Slaughter (eds), *The Methods of International Law* (Washington, DC: American Society of International Law, 2004).

[79] *cf* EU Petersmann (1997) 4–24.

Liberalism and rational choice theory

Economists, political scientists and lawyers tend to agree today that – inside citizen-driven markets and constitutional democracies – analyses of the economy, polity and law should proceed from normative individualism (ie, values must be derived from individual consent) and from the assumption of rational choices of individuals confronted with scarcity of resources and with competition among rational egoists for scarce goods and services (eg, educational and medical services, job opportunities). The trade policies of constitutional democracies are primarily shaped by arguments of economic, political and legal liberalism, welfare economics and 'public choices'. They respond to rational pursuit of rent-seeking self-interests, as illustrated by political resistance to trade liberalization by import-competing producers who are often politically more influential and easier to organize than consumer interests in trade liberalization. In all trading countries, the political influence of export industries and import-competing producers on reciprocal market access negotiations forces governments to react to the political pressures, demands and 'rent-seeking' of their domestic constituencies. Legalistic perceptions of states as 'black boxes' maximizing 'public interests' risk neglecting these domestic origins of intergovernmental bargaining, the 'domestic policy functions' of international trade rules (eg, for limiting domestic 'protection biases'), and the policy impact of non-governmental organizations on intergovernmental relations.

Constructivism

The successful transformation of the European 'international law among states' into a European 'community law' protecting peaceful cooperation among 500 million 'EU citizens' across national frontiers confirms that international power politics can be legally limited and transformed by institutional 'checks and balances', constitutional restraints of foreign policy powers, parliamentary control of their exercise, and judicial protection of constitutional rights. It thereby shows that – by limiting the 'realist' focus on state power in intergovernmental relations by constitutional rules of a higher legal rank protecting transnational constitutional freedoms and citizen-oriented 'public reason' – economic integration law can put an end to centuries of power politics among European states. This European experience suggests that rights-based 'cosmopolitan conceptions' of IEL, based on the human rights obligations of states, may similarly contribute to limiting the 'governance failures' in the collective supply of international public goods resulting from 'Westphalian conceptions' of international law and power politics.

Positive law requires methodological pluralism in the interpretation of IEL

The economic theory of comparative advantage explaining the mutually beneficial welfare effects of an international division of labour is often described as the only area of economics where economists from all over the world tend to agree.[80] The economic principles underlying WTO rules, free trade areas, customs unions and trade policies, like the incorporation of natural law assumptions (eg, of human rights) into positive national

[80] For an overview of modern trade theories see, eg: BM Hoekman and MM Kostecki, *The Political Economy of the World Trading System* (Oxford: OUP, 2009).

and international law, have grafted normative and descriptive, economic and political theories of law together. Hence, the arguments of *legal positivism* – that legal rules and principles derive from human enactment pursuant to formal law-creating processes and 'rules of recognition' (Hart) that distinguish 'ought' (which is desirable) from 'is' (which legally exists) and law from other social rules – can no longer obviate the normative question of how incomplete systems of legal rules and principles *ought* to be interpreted in order to realize their declared legal objectives most effectively (such as protecting human rights and economic welfare). The more citizens and governments engage in economic activities using IEL for realizing economic and non-economic objectives, the more important it becomes to clarify the interrelationships between legal, political and economic principles, rules and objectives in the interpretation, application and progressive development of IEL rules.

Most legal principles (like justice and equality) and many rules (like human rights to protection of life, liberty and property) use words with 'open texture' and meanings to be clarified through interpretation by legislatures, governments, courts and 'deliberative democracy'. As discussed in chapter VII, judicial clarification of contested interpretations of 'incomplete agreements' has proven to be of constitutional importance for the application and dynamic evolution of IEL. Human rights challenge positivist claims that legality and the validity of rules do not depend on the moral merit of rules, or that judges exercise discretion when faced with a dispute to which no statute or previous decision applies. The more national and international 'primary rules of conduct' evolve dynamically in response to 'globalization', the more urgent becomes the need for reviewing the 'secondary rules' for changing the law, adjudicating disputes over conflicting legal claims and for identifying valid rules.[81] Cosmopolitan conceptions of IEL call for interpreting the traditional 'rules of recognition' of international law (as codified in Article 38 of the Statute of the International Court of Justice) no longer only from the point of view of governments. Respect for human rights requires examining the *opinio juris sive necessitatis* and the emergence of 'general principles of law' also with due regard to the legal claims of civil society, democratic parliaments and 'courts of justice' as the most principled 'constitutional guardians' of the constitutional rights of citizens (eg, compared with majority decisions in political governance institutions).

A 'constitutional approach' to IEL and to multilevel economic governance beyond Europe?

If IEL is understood as an economic and legal 'system' based on 'primary rules of conduct' and 'secondary rules' for identifying valid rules, changing the law and settling disputes peacefully, then the definition of IEL – either as a sub-system of public international law or as a dynamic integration of private and public, national and international rules and institutions – is likely to influence 'systemic' and 'functional interpretations' of IEL

[81] Law as a union of 'primary rules' of conduct and 'secondary rules' of recognition, change and adjudication is explained by HLA Hart (1994) ch V. Like the 'constitutional distinction' between constitutional, legislative, executive and judicial rules and institutions, the distinction between primary and secondary rules is of crucial importance for understanding the systemic character and dynamic evolution of IEL as an integrated, legal system of private and public, national and international legal sub-systems that can protect 'justice' and human rights across borders only in a multilevel constitutional framework protecting overall coherence, legitimacy and 'public reason'.

rules calling for a coherent understanding of rules and for normative justification of their interpretations. For instance, just as political science recommendations on international relations are shaped by their respective methodologies (eg, of state-centred 'realism', 'institutionalism' and 'constructivism' versus individual-centred 'liberalism'), so are legal interpretations influenced by the diverse conceptions of IEL (eg, of common market rules and related dispute settlement procedures) and of their often diverse normative premises (eg, of investor–state arbitration versus intergovernmental dispute settlement in the WTO). This study infers from the universal recognition of human rights the normative need for applying 'constitutional approaches' to multilevel regulation of economic cooperation among citizens and multilevel governance of interdependent public goods. It is argued that – similar to national economic law which, in constitutional democracies, can be understood only as an integral part of a national constitutional system providing for constitutional rights of citizens and legislative, administrative and judicial institutions designed to protect constitutional rights – the legitimate functions, regulatory problems, systemic nature and dynamic evolution of IEL can be normatively evaluated and coherently developed only in the broader context of the multilevel human rights obligations and common constitutional principles accepted by UN member states. The proposed 'bottom-up multilevel constitutional approach' to international economic regulation shares the 'realist premise' that 'legalism' has no intrinsic value. As Posner put it: 'law cannot control behaviour unless legal institutions support it; without legal institutions – legislatures, enforcers and courts – international law is unavoidably weak'.[82] Yet, in contrast to the often arbitrary 'cost-benefit' justifications of 'utilitarian arguments' for 'efficient violations' of international law, constitutionalism argues for limiting 'rule by law' through constitutional safeguards of 'rule of law' across frontiers based on respect for human rights and the legitimate diversity of constitutional democracies.

4 COLLECTIVE ACTION PROBLEMS IMPEDING 'INTERDEPENDENT AGGREGATE PUBLIC GOODS': CLIMATE CHANGE, ENERGY SECURITY AND THE FUTURE OF THE WTO

The Bretton Woods Agreements and the WTO Agreement tend to describe their treaty objectives in terms of enabling member states to increase their domestic economic welfare through international division of labour based on international movements of goods, services, persons, capital and related payments. Even though the development objectives and monetary, financial and trade policy instruments of the diverse 'Bretton Woods institutions' overlap, the IMF, World Bank and GATT were designed as separate institutions with separate policy instruments and limited powers.[83] The IMF, GATT and WTO Agreements prioritize reciprocal liberalization and regulation of global product markets and of a stable monetary and exchange rate system promoting monetary and price stability and current international payments over liberalization of international factor markets (eg, the flow of capital, diffusion of technology, international migration of labour and human capital).

[82] Posner (2009) xiv.

[83] On the economic theories (such as 'separation of policy instruments', ranking of policy instruments according to their economic efficiencies) and constitutional theories underlying the Bretton Woods Agreements see: Petersmann (1991) chs III and VII.

Table 9: The promotion of sustainable development as an objective of GATT/WTO law

According to the WTO Preamble, the WTO aims at expanding production of, and trade in, goods and services through reciprocal liberalization and regulation of discriminatory market access barriers and market distortions as a means for increasing non-discriminatory conditions of competition, standards of living, attaining full employment and promoting real income, effective demand and 'sustainable development'.
GATT (eg, **Articles III, XVI, XVIII–XXI, XXVIII**) **and GATS** (eg, **Articles VI, XIV–XVIII**) **protect national sovereignty to regulate the domestic economy by non-discriminatory rules and efficient policy instruments** (eg, tariffs and production subsidies rather than non-tariff trade barriers), including sovereign rights to restrict international trade in order to protect non-economic public interests. WTO law reflects the liberal premise that domestic welfare depends on appropriate rules and institutions.
The **1993 and 1994 GATT/WTO Ministerial Declarations on 'Greater Coherence in Global Economic Policymaking'** recognize the need for 'effective cooperation with other intergovernmental organizations that have responsibilities related to those of the WTO' (Article V WTO Agreement), such as cooperation with the Bretton Woods institutions, WIPO and protection and preservation of the environment.
The **2001 Doha Ministerial Declaration** recognized: 'International trade can play a major role in the promotion of economic development and the alleviation of poverty. We recognize the need for all our peoples to benefit from the increased opportunities and welfare gains that the multilateral trading system generates. The majority of WTO Members are developing countries. We seek to place their need at the heart of the Working Programme adopted in this Declaration'.

Why is it that that some *global* public goods (like postal services, telecommunications, maritime and air transports) are so much more effectively provided than many others (like a liberal world trading system), whose under-supply at international levels often adversely affects the supply of related *national* public goods? Section 1 identified the 'jurisdictional gap', the 'governance gap', the 'incentive gap', the 'participation gap' and the 'rule of law gap' as major collective action problems in supplying 'aggregate public goods' like a mutually beneficial world trading system, international energy security, prevention of climate change and international rule of law. This section illustrates why intergovernmental 'top-down regulation' risks failing to overcome these collective action problems without 'bottom-up support' from business, civil society and domestic parliaments, governments and courts. Citizen-oriented conceptions of IEL may also be necessary in view of the 'overlapping nature' of many international public goods like a rules-based world trading system, energy security and mutually coherent carbon emission trading systems necessary for prevention of climate change; for, the economic, legal and democratic arguments for rendering market competition more effective by means of incentives for stakeholder participation, consumer-driven competition, citizen-driven democratic governance, rule compliance and legal and judicial accountability are valid for economic markets no less than for energy markets or decentralized carbon-emission trading systems. All UN member states have acknowledged the need for 'sustainable development' focusing no longer one-sidedly on economic growth, but also on protection of the environment and of human rights as normative bases for evaluating 'human development' (eg, in favour of general consumer welfare rather than particular producer interests). Yet, many governments in UN member states cling to power-oriented interpretations of UN law focusing on 'sovereign equality of states' and foreign policy discretion rather than on protection of human rights, poverty reduction and 'duties to protect' the environment and other 'common concerns' for the benefit of citizens.

Failures of 'Westphalian regulatory top-down paradigms': the example of the UN Environment Programme (UNEP)

Pursuant to the principle that 'form should follow function', UNEP has been established in 1972 as an intergovernmental UN body with multiple functions for monitoring, assessing, coordinating and promoting the environment-related activities of all UN institutions and UN member states. As decisions and actions affecting the environment are confronted with 'free riding problems' and other 'prisoner dilemmas' that are often closely linked to economic and social problems, UNEP was deliberately designed *not* as another specialized UN Agency operating in a separate governance sector, but as a 'programme' integrating and protecting the environment throughout all UN activities, in close cooperation with the UN's 'Environment Coordination Board' that is comprised of the executive heads of all UN agencies under the chairmanship of UNEP's executive director. Following the 1992 UN Environment and Development Conference at Rio de Janeiro, a new UN Inter-Agency Committee on Sustainable Development was established which reports to the UN Commission on Sustainable Development. Yet, due to its scant institutional and financial resources, lack of regulatory powers and many other impediments, UNEP never succeeded in fulfilling its ambitious, catalytic tasks as a leader, monitor and coordinator of environmental protection throughout the UN system. Notwithstanding UNEP's contribution to improving the scientific understanding of environmental problems (eg, by the Intergovernmental Panel on Climate Change jointly established by UNEP and the World Meteorological Organization) and to the promotion of multilateral environmental agreements (like the successful 1987 Montreal Protocol on the protection of the ozone layer), UNEP has fallen short of accomplishing its goals.[84]

The failures of UNEP in protecting the global environment and developing and enforcing more effective UN environmental regulation are largely due to its state-centred development and regulatory models. Treating citizens as mere objects of intergovernmental UN regulation undermines the incentives for reducing environmental pollution and for citizen-driven capacity-building, policy-coherence, domestic rule compliance and accountability. UNEP's inadequate resources and 'capacity gaps' are unlikely to be overcome without stronger involvement of civil society and business as the most important sources of 'market failures' like pollution of environmental resources. Likewise, in the field of 'global warming pollution', the 'cooperation problems' among individuals as well as among countries cannot be resolved without changing the conduct of individual polluters by means of a new 'cooperation culture' based on stronger protection of rule

[84] For a critical analysis see: 'Global Environmental Governance in the 21st Century'. Report from the Global Environmental Governance Forum July 2009, available at: environmmentalgovernance.org. The report emphasizes five core functions for rendering UNEP more effective: (1) monitoring, assessment and early warning; (2) policy and norm development; (3) capacity development; (4) coordination; and (5) enforcement of international environmental disciplines.

of law. Former US Vice-President Al Gore emphasized: 'From the standpoint of governance, what is at stake is our ability to use the rule of law as an instrument of human redemption'.[85] Just as rule of law inside states depends on constitutional rules legitimating governance and protecting rights of citizens, compliance with international environmental duties to prevent transboundary harm cannot be secured without democratic implementing legislation transforming the often vague principles of international environmental law – like the polluter pays principle, the precautionary principle, the principle of common but differentiated responsibilities, the principle of sustainable development and other related international law principles (eg, of equity and good faith) – into fair and precise rules of individual conduct and individual, legal and judicial remedies.[86] Prevention of climate change and many other global public goods cannot be realized without 'private-public partnerships' supported not only by governments, but also by citizens as 'just' (eg, in the sense of justified rulemaking and burden-sharing).[87]

An 'Interagency Statement of the United Nations System', adopted on 30 June 2009 by a group of international organizations including the WTO, emphasized the urgent need for transforming the world economy, based on fossil fuels, into a 'green economy':

> The current financial and economic crisis is throwing millions of people into poverty, especially the most vulnerable in the developing world. This is happening amidst the ongoing food, water, energy, ecosystem and climate crises. Together, these crises are undermining the efforts to achieve the Millennium Development Goals and setting back development progress of the past few decades. . . . The shift towards a green economy requires education for sustainable development including training in new job skills and newly required health systems.[88]

The 'jurisdiction gap' requires multilevel policymaking and rulemaking with stronger safeguards of 'collective self-interests'

Depending on the scale of their impact, economists distinguish between local public goods (like a street sign), national public goods (like national electoral and public health systems), regional public goods (like common management of regional river basins) and global public goods that impact people at a global level and are non-excludable and non-rival in terms of consumption (like UN human rights law). As a result of globalization and increasing openness of national borders, many national public goods are transformed into global public goods calling for cross-border cooperation (eg, in order to protect public health and climate stability). Many environmental problems – like climate change mitigation – relate to 'aggregate public goods': reduction of pollution (emissions) by individual states tends to be efficient only as part of an international agreement providing for complementary reductions by other polluting countries. Such agreements are likely to be negotiated and accepted by the major countries only if the incentive structures for joining the agreement are stronger than the costs of non-participation (eg,

[85] Gore (n 27).

[86] On the lack of coherent UN rules, governance institutions and remedies for coordinating and enforcing the more than one hundred multilateral environmental agreements on the level of polluters and citizens see: D Bodansky, 'Is there an International Environmental Constitution?' (2009) 16 *Indiana Journal of Global Legal Studies* 565–84.

[87] *cf* O Godard, 'Climate Justice. Between Global and International Justice – Insights from Justification Theory', *EUI Working Papers RSCAS* 2011/56.

[88] Cited from the WTO website of 30 June 2009.

in the Montreal Protocol on Substances that Deplete the Ozone Layer).[89] As the costs and benefits of international cooperation and the incentives for collective crisis-management are often unevenly distributed, effective regulation of the collective action problems requires 'community institutions' protecting 'collective self-interests' by proposing, monitoring and enforcing mutually beneficial common rules and state 'duties to protect common concerns'.

Since the earth's atmosphere has the same carbon concentration across all nations due to the uniform and stable diffusion of carbon dioxide throughout the planet's atmosphere, improvements in the quality of the atmosphere resulting from the abatement of carbon can be considered as a 'global public good' benefiting all citizens. On the basis of the 1992 UN Framework Convention on Climate Change (UNFCCC) and its 1997 Kyoto Protocol, many developed countries have undertaken reduction commitments for their greenhouse gas emissions, carbon mitigation as well as 'clean development' commitments in order to prevent climate change and its adverse effects on the global economy (such as agriculture, forestry, fisheries) and on the living conditions of people (notably in countries affected by rising levels of sea waters and of drought). Yet, while the EU claims that its carbon emission 'cap and trading system' is realizing the EU commitment to reduce greenhouse gas emissions by 8 per cent until the year 2012 (based on 1990 emission levels), many signatories of the Kyoto I Protocol continue to increase their greenhouse gas emissions. The two national economies with the largest shares in greenhouse gas emissions, China and the United States, have rejected any legally binding carbon reduction commitments under the Kyoto I Protocol. Even if all major countries accept carbon reduction commitments, global climate change governance beyond the expiry of the Kyoto I Protocol commitments in 2012 will succeed in transforming social conduct into 'green economies', and in adapting to the problems of climate change (such as climate change refugees), only by also involving non-state actors more actively through new rules, public–private partnerships (eg, for reducing carbon emissions and realizing 'clean development mechanisms') and market-based incentives.[90] As in economic integration law, the multilevel EU environmental law and carbon emission trading system have also emerged as a major source of innovation in environmental governance for promoting sustainable development across states within a multilevel constitutional framework.[91]

The 'jurisdiction gap' impeding the collective supply of public goods needs to be reduced on the basis of the 'matching principle': the regulatory authority should match the scope of the regulatory problem so that cost-benefit calculations in multilevel cooperation and regulation can be made correctly without harmful 'externalities' and 'free-riding'.[92] Hence, there is a need for stronger worldwide environmental institutions and 'cost-internalization'.[93] Global environmental harms, like climate change, need to be addressed by multilevel local, national and worldwide environmental regulation which – in view of the economic and competitive distortions and diminishing social welfare caused by pollution – must be dovetailed with economic and social regulation.

[89] *cf* the case study of the 'Montreal Protocol' in Barrett (2007) 77 ff.

[90] *cf* F Biermann, P Pattberg and F Zelli (eds) (2010).

[91] For case studies see: J Scott (ed), *Environmental Protection. European Law and Governance* (Oxford: OUP, 2009).

[92] *cf* M Olson (1971) 46–48; DC Esty, 'Breaking the Environmental Law Logjam: The International Dimension' (2008) 17 *NYU Environmental Law Journal* 836 ff.

[93] On proposals for a Global Environment Organization, promoting 'network governance' without a big central bureaucracy, see Esty (n 92) and Biermann, Pattberg and Zelli (eds) (2010).

Environmental policymaking – including 'issue spotting, problem specification, harm evaluation, policy option assessment, cost-benefit analysis, rulemaking, program implementation, enforcement, evaluation and program refinement'[94] – and involvement of business and other non-governmental organizations continue to be much less developed at global levels than at national and regional levels (eg, in the EU and NAFTA). 'Optimal intervention' directly at the source of pollution requires 'subsidiarity' prioritizing local and national environmental regulation and promotion of innovative 'green technologies' by 'Tieboutian regulatory competition' within internationally agreed framework rules that can be justified as fair, equitable and efficient.

The 'incentive' and 'participation-gaps' require 'common but differentiated responsibilities' of governments and incentives for private participation

The UNESCO World Heritage Convention illustrates how 'weakest link public goods' can be effectively protected if a poor host country is unable, but willing to provide the international public good (like a world heritage site) with external assistance. Geo-engineering approaches to counteract the effects of greenhouse gas emissions illustrate how the 'aggregate efforts public good' of greenhouse gas mitigation may be transformed into a 'single best effort public good', ie, 'from an exceedingly complicated regulatory regime to a simple . . . problem in international cost sharing' with much less regulatory challenges.[95] Taking into account the different varieties and related collective action problems of international public goods can reduce their collective governance problems, such as lack of state consent and non-participation in collective supply of 'aggregate efforts public goods'. The legal design of the 'input legitimacy' (eg, in terms of inclusive decision-making procedures) of public goods regimes, of the distribution of their costs and of their supervision, compliance and dispute settlement mechanisms tends to be of crucial importance for overcoming problems of 'free riding' and non-participation.

Developed countries bear responsibility for most of the past build up of greenhouse gases since industrialization and for climate change as 'the biggest market failure the world has ever seen'.[96] As the capacities and 'opportunity costs' of adapting to climate change are distributed unequally among individual citizens as well as among individual countries (such as LDCs with large populations without access to electricity), the UNFCCC provides for 'common but differentiated responsibilities' (Article 3.1 UNFCCC). The future implementation of the various UNFCCC principles[97] entails numerous 'collective action problems' in elaborating mutually consistent trade, environmental, competition and investment rules. For example, one of the few outcomes of the Copenhagen conference in December 2009 was a commitment by developed countries to transfer, by 2020, $100 billion a year in support of carbon mitigation and climate adaptation policies in LDCs, including for 'reduction of emissions from deforestation and forest

[94] Esty (n 92) 841.

[95] *cf* T Schelling, 'The Economic Diplomacy of Geoengineering' (1996) 33 *Climatic Change* 303–07.

[96] N Stern, *The Economics of Climate Change: The Stern Review* (Cambridge: CUP, 2007).

[97] Such as taking into account 'the specific needs and special circumstances of developing country Parties' (Art 3.3), 'cost-effective' climate change policies in order to ensure 'global benefits at the lowest possible cost' (Art 3.3) and promotion of an 'open international economic system' promoting 'sustainable development' without measures constituting 'a means of arbitrary or unjustifiable discrimination or a disguised restriction on international trade' (Art 3.5).

degradation' (REDD). Changing deforestation and forest degradation requires changing local and national laws, institutions and financial incentives. The climate change legislation in Europe and North America envisages that carbon taxes and quantitative restrictions of carbon emissions (eg, by means of tradable permits) in developed countries risk also being undermined by relocation of polluting industries ('carbon leakages'). The systems will be weakened unless imports from third countries without equivalent carbon reduction commitments are subjected to 'border adjustment measures', with due respect for the principle of 'common but differentiated responsibilities' as provided for in the UNFCCC.[98]

The Kyoto Protocol's 'flexibility mechanisms' (such as 'emission trading', 'joint implementation', the 'clean development mechanism') offer parties numerous options for cost-effective implementing measures in conformity with WTO rules.[99] The need for market-based approaches relying on 'economic instruments' (such as carbon emission trading systems) is increasingly recognized.[100] LDCs have no reduction commitments under the Kyoto I Protocol and account for only about 40 per cent of current carbon dioxide emissions; yet, as they are expected to become the largest emitters during the next twenty to thirty years, the historical emissions of industrialized countries 'will eventually count for very little in future climate change if the major emerging countries continue to emit without stringent restrictions'.[101] A future agreement on the allocation of reduction commitments, 'mitigation commitments' (eg, for reducing fossil fuel subsidies, enhancing 'carbon sinks' in forests) and 'adaptation commitments' (eg, by enhancing the capacity of states and ecosystems to cope with the consequences of climate change) will hardly be possible without 'fair procedures' and principles of 'procedural justice' as well as 'substantive justice' that governments, national parliaments and citizens can accept as democratically legitimate. While developed countries committed – at the 'Group of 8' summit meeting in Italy in July 2009 – to reduce their greenhouse gas emissions by 80 per cent up to the year 2050, it was only in the 'Copenhagen Accord' of December 2009 and the 'Durban agreement' of December 2011 that a group of LDCs (such as Brazil, China, India and South Africa) accepted political commitments to reduce their carbon emissions as of 2020. An EU communication of 10 September 2009 offered annual EU payments of up to €15 billion for carbon reduction and climate adaptation measures in LDCs as part of an ambitious Kyoto II Protocol. According to the EU Commission, up

[98] As the carbon emission limits agreed under the Kyoto I Protocol end in 2012, the EC Directive 2009/29/EC of 23 April 2009 envisages a 'carbon equalization system' and the extension of the European Emission Trading System to imports (by requiring importers to acquire emission allowances corresponding to the carbon embedded in the imported goods). On the applicable WTO rules and European and North American climate change regulations see: GC Hufbauer, S Charnovitz and J Kim (2009); N Mizulin, 'The EC Experience in Creating an Internal Energy Market: Lessons for the WTO' in J Pauwelyn (ed), *Global Challenges at the Intersection of Trade, Energy and the Environment* (Geneva: The Graduate Institute, 2010) 67–73. On the legal controversies over 'border measures' (especially border taxes on production inputs that are not physically incorporated into the products concerned) see also: 'Trade and Climate Change. A report by UNEP and the WTO (Geneva, 2009) 98 ff; EU Petersmann, 'International Trade Law and International Environmental Law: Environmental Taxes and Border Tax Adjustment in WTO Law and EC Law' in RL Revesz (ed), *Environmental Regulation, the Economy and Sustainable Development* (Cambridge: CUP, 2000) 136 ff.

[99] On WTO-consistent incentive schemes for promoting renewable energies and reducing greenhouse gas emissions see: T Cottier, O Nartova and SZ Bigdeli (eds), *International Trade Regulation and the Mitigation of Climate Change* (London: Cameron & May, 2009); E Vranes, *Trade and the Environment* (Oxford: OUP, 2009) pt IV.

[100] *cf* J Freeman and CD Kolstad (eds), *Moving to Markets in Environmental Regulation: Lessons from Twenty Years of Experience* (New York: Oxford University Press, 2006).

[101] Godard (n 87), 12.

to half of the annual cost of LDCs of about €100 billion for mitigating greenhouse gas emissions should be financed by developed and emerging economies (such as Brazil, China and India); up to €38 billion per year could be financed by private participants in a global 'carbon market' for the trading of pollution permits and private investments in green technologies in LDCs; the remainder should be financed by the budgets of other LDCs.

Apart from the problems of 'free-riding' and an equitable burden sharing of the cost of climate change prevention, the characteristics of 'public goods' – such as their non-excludable and non-rival use benefiting all citizens – entail additional 'collective action problems'. These impede their collective supply in a decentralized world composed of 193 UN member states with often conflicting 'national interests' and related conflicts of interests among individuals (eg, due to their rational egoism and competition for scarce resources).[102] The manifold interrelationships between the negotiations on a Kyoto II Protocol, on international energy security and on the successful conclusion of the Doha Round negotiations in the WTO are illustrated by the need for regulating subsidies for 'clean energies', oil and gas transit regimes, liberalization of environmental goods and services, transfer of environmental technologies, related intellectual property rights, carbon taxes and border tax adjustments. Collective supply of 'international public goods' like climate change prevention, energy security and an efficient world trading system, in turn, depends on additional 'global public goods'. Legal security is needed for the investments into effective climate change prevention (eg, investments for efficient production, transportation and distribution of fossil-based and alternative, renewable energies). In order to become effective, carbon reduction commitments and complementary financial transfer commitments must be embedded into legally binding agreements as well as into domestic implementing legislation with supervisory institutions supported and controlled by national parliaments and citizens.

How can such horrendously complex negotiations in different *fora* with different memberships among countries with conflicting interests (eg, energy exporting countries interested in high prices versus energy importing countries interested in low prices) be successfully concluded without the negotiators getting lost in coordination and collective action problems, as it happened at the Copenhagen conference on a Kyoto II Protocol in December 2009? How should governments prioritize the hundreds of specific regulatory problems in their negotiations on the climate change regime, on concluding the Doha Round and WTO accession negotiations (eg, with important energy suppliers like Russia that became a WTO member in 2012) and on international energy security? Should governments seek bilateral solutions (eg, in the context of the new EU–Russia Cooperation and Partnership Agreement) or multilateral guarantees of energy security (eg, based on the Energy Charter Treaty and the OECD's International Energy Agency at Paris)? How and where should disputes over the inevitable conflicts of interests and over sub-optimal, unilateral regulations be settled peacefully? What are the 'optimal levels' of regulating energy security and energy markets?

[102] *cf* Kaul, Grunberg and Stern (1999) whose book focuses on the 'jurisdictional gap', the 'participation gap', 'incentive gap' and 'prisoner dilemmas' in the collective supply of international public goods; Kaul et al (eds) (2003).

The need for promoting 'private–public partnerships' subject to legal restraints

Maximization of consumer welfare through worldwide division of labour, development of 'clean industries' for prevention of climate change, and international energy security are global public goods that must be realized primarily by business and consumer-driven competition in decentralized frameworks of appropriate laws and institutions. Just as democratic self-governance depends on citizen-driven 'deliberative', 'participatory' and 'representative democracy', so does the collective supply of economic, environmental and many other public goods depend on private–public partnerships in correcting 'market failures' (eg, by means of decentralized enforcement of appropriate competition rules, common market, environmental and labour market rules). These partnerships may also serve the collective supply of 'public goods' (like prevention of climate change by business initiatives for carbon reductions, decentralized 'carbon trading' and development of clean industries).

Almost all international economic organizations closely cooperate with non-governmental organizations to pursue their regulatory objectives more effectively and more legitimately. Examples include the cooperation of representatives of employers, employees and governments in the tripartite governance structures of the ILO; the UN's 'Global Compact' with more than 5000 transnational corporations in order to promote 'corporate social responsibility'; the IMF's cooperation with private banks and financial institutions; the WTO's cooperation with non-governmental organizations for the elaboration of technical standards, sanitary and phytosanitary standards and preshipment inspection standards; the ICAO's cooperation with private airlines associated in the International Air Transport Association; and the ITU's cooperation with private telecom companies. The multilevel internet governance involving the EU, states and non-governmental organizations – like the Internet Corporation for Assigned Names and Numbers (ICANN) and 'Top-Level Domain' Registries organized as private non-profit organizations[103] – illustrates why governments may successfully delegate parts of the governance of global goods (like the internet) to flexible private–public partnerships. The latter may, if subjected to appropriate legal restraints, enhance the effectiveness of multilevel regulation (eg, by using decentralized knowledge and enforcement mechanisms) and its input and output legitimacy (eg, by cooperating with civil society organizations). They may also foster the use of flexible 'soft law instruments' (such as private forest certification under the supervision of the Forest Stewardship Council, private company codes on corporate social responsibility, ILO recommendations) where governments are not yet willing to accept 'hard law agreements'. As discussed in subsequent chapters, international dispute settlement and enforcement procedures in international trade, investment, environmental and regional economic integration law have proven to be much more effective if governments enlist private market actors by offering incentives for decentralized prevention of international disputes (eg, by judicial remedies in domestic courts) and decentralized enforcement of competition and environmental rules. Yet, in order to avoid welfare-reducing 'protectionist collusion' among public and private actors, private–public partnerships must be subjected to legal safeguards and democratic supervision.

[103] *cf* R Uerpmann-Wittzack, 'Multilevel Internet Governance Involving the EU, Nation-States and NGOs' in A Follesdal, RA Wessel and J Wouters (eds) (2008) 145–68; D McLean (ed), *Internet Governance: A Grand Collaboration* (New York: United Nations ICT Task Force, 2004).

The plurality of international negotiation *fora* and competing jurisdictions require legal and judicial coordination of separate international regimes

The legal and governance system of the WTO is more comprehensive than that of the UNFCCC and of its Kyoto I Protocol (which expires in 2012 and was not ratified by, eg, the US) or that of the geographically limited Energy Charter Treaty (ECT). Yet, many governments object to coordinating all the interrelated trade, competition, environmental and energy regulation problems in the WTO. There is broad agreement today that the multitude of different negotiation *fora* and organizations involved in negotiations on international trade, environmental and energy regulation remains an inevitable fact of diplomacy in an interdependent, legally and politically fragmented world composed of competing, national and international legal and political regimes and often conflicting national interests. The Copenhagen conference of December 2009 confirmed that consensus-based UN negotiations, like consensus-based WTO negotiations, risk failing without leadership by smaller 'coalitions of the willing'. In addressing the problems of energy security and of climate change regulation, governments have to comply with their many other existing legal obligations, for instance under WTO law and BITs. Hence, the success of separate negotiations depends on their coordination in order to preserve the mutual coherence of separate legal regimes. For instance, international energy security will depend on trade and transit rules protecting the supply of energy services and access to infrastructures such as oil and gas pipelines. That such factors are already taken into account in international trade regulation shows the example of Ukraine's specific WTO commitments on pipeline transportation in its WTO Protocol of Accession. The effectiveness of such trade and transit rules may depend on complementary investment rules setting incentives for creating a Europe-wide pipeline network. Coordination of the complementary environmental, energy, trade and investment regimes may succeed only to the extent that 'rule by law' can be limited through guarantees of 'rule of law' (eg, in case of disputes among energy export countries and transit countries interrupting energy transportation to third countries). Institutions protecting rule compliance and legal as well as judicial remedies against non-compliance and 'free-riding' are of crucial importance. As explained in chapter II, the greater the complexity of multilevel governance problems, the greater is the need for 'checks and balances' protecting transnational rule of law.

In accordance with the economic theory of 'optimal policy intervention',[104] the separate legal regimes (eg, of the UNFCCC, the ECT, WTO law, BITs) give priority to diverse policy instruments in their pursuit of different policy objectives. The Kyoto Protocol focuses on carbon reduction commitments, 'clean development mechanisms' and financial transfer commitments. WTO law regulates and prioritizes trade policy instruments (such as tariffs, subsidies and non-tariff trade barriers) according to their respective economic efficiency.[105] Investment promotion and protection rules in BITs, and production management in the context of the Organization of Petroleum Exporting Countries, are based on respect for national 'public interests' and reconcile private and public interests on the basis of principles of non-discrimination, transparent policymaking and 'fair and equitable treatment'. In view of this legitimate diversity of legal regimes with different memberships aimed at realizing complementary policy objectives, international

[104] *cf* Petersmann (1991) 57 ff.
[105] This is further explained in ch VII.

consensus on global regimes and on 'global governance' integrating the diverse trade, environmental and investment rules – as it has been possible in regional agreements like the ECT and EU law – will remain rare. Incomplete governance regimes, decentralized 'regulatory competition' (eg, among bilateral energy transportation pipelines), and sub-optimal 'countervailing measures' are bound to remain permanent 'collective action problems' whose costs need to be limited by transnational rule of law.

Under international law, every state has to respect all its international legal obligations simultaneously. As there are no 'self-contained' international legal regimes isolated from the general rules of international law, the legal coordination of the various treaty regimes depends not only on the specific treaty provisions, but also on other relevant international law rules (eg, on interpretation of successive treaties with overlapping subjects). Disputes over these often vague, substantive and formal principles of international law (like '*lex specialis*', '*lex posterior*', '*lex superior*') for the coordination of treaty regimes are inevitable in a world composed of 193 UN member states. Respect for the legitimate diversity of international legal regimes entails that, for example, the negotiators of the Kyoto II Protocol should *not* attempt to regulate all the 'interface problems' of climate change rules with WTO law. Once international agreement has been reached on a Kyoto II Protocol regulating the 'first best policy instruments' for preventing climate change, WTO members could subsequently clarify the relevant WTO legal disciplines for using 'second best trade policy instruments' (like border carbon taxes, 'green subsidies', export taxes) in support of their climate change commitments under the Kyoto II Protocol and their energy policy commitments under other international treaty regimes (like the ECT). In spite of the limited jurisdiction of international dispute settlement bodies that were set up for enforcing only specific treaty rights and obligations (eg, under the WTO and BITs), judicial procedures and the customary rules of international treaty interpretation offer sufficiently flexible principles and rules. In contrast to hierarchical domestic legal systems, international treaties are usually perceived as horizontal systems of legal norms that must and can be construed in mutually coherent ways as required by the customary law requirement of 'systemic integration' (Article 31 VCLT); the practice of international courts confirms that most 'inter-regime conflicts' can be avoided by interpreting separate treaty regimes and obligations of their member states in mutually coherent ways without need for resorting to claims of legal hierarchy (eg, based on the *jus cogens* core of human rights). The legitimacy of such 'interpretative reconciliation' and 'judicial coordination' of separate treaty regimes may also depend on taking into account 'principles of justice' and human rights obligations of governments as explicitly recalled in the Preamble of the VCLT.[106] Just as 'regulatory competition' among international organizations may limit abuse of power by 'checks and balances', so do competition, 'judicial dialogues' and 'judicial comity' among competing jurisdictions in the interpretation of treaties and settlement of related disputes limit potential abuses of legal and institutional 'centralization'.

Sequencing and forum choice problems in multilateral negotiations

As discussed in chapters II to VI, modern theories of justice and of constitutional democracies (like Rawls' *Theory of Justice*) explain why the legitimacy and effectiveness of

[106] *cf* EU Petersmann, 'Administration of Justice in the WTO: Did the WTO Appellate Body Commit "Grave Injustice"?' (2009) 8 *The Law & Practice of International Courts and Tribunals* 329–74.

rulemaking, rule application and judicial clarification and enforcement of rules depend on compliance with agreed 'constitutional principles of justice'. European integration law and WTO law confirm that intergovernmental rulemaking for the collective supply of international public goods (like common market rules for a mutually beneficial international division of labour among the 30 member countries of the EEA) is confronted with 'constitutional problems' (eg, of democratic legitimacy and consensus-building) similar to those inside democracies. The 'principles of justice' necessary for overcoming 'collective action problems' at worldwide levels are only incompletely defined in UN law, the UNFCCC and WTO law. For instance, the exact content of human rights obligations of UN member states and of 'sustainable development' often remains contested. Transforming such principles into specific rights and obligations through rulemaking in diverse international organizations with overlapping jurisdictions (such as the UNFCCC, the WTO, regional economic and energy organizations), and creating coherent institutions for rule application and judicial rule clarification and enforcement, pose controversial 'strategic questions.' For example:

- Should the environmental, trade and investment rules necessary for preventing international climate change be kept separate and negotiated successively in specialized jurisdictions like the UNFCC, the WTO, the ECT, the OECD and its International Energy Agency and BITs? Can such separate negotiations remain mutually coherent without prior agreement on their underlying 'principles of justice' (such as the financial and legal implications of 'common but differentiated responsibility')?
- Could the prospects for a 'global package deal' be enhanced by following the example of the ECT, which integrates environmental, trade and investment rules into one single treaty regime? Would a similarly integrated Kyoto II Protocol, or a complementary WTO Agreement on Trade and Climate Change, receive the global support necessary for effective climate change prevention?
- Which worldwide, regional and national institutions should be mandated with administering, coordinating, monitoring and enforcing the necessary 'carbon emission trading' systems, 'carbon leakage' safeguards and financial transfers for carbon mitigation and adaptation measures in LDCs?
- To what extent should domestic implementation of Kyoto II disciplines be left to individual governments and states in spite of past experiences that intergovernmental rules risk remaining ineffective unless citizens, local and non-governmental organizations (like energy companies) are enlisted in the decentralized enforcement of the rules by recognizing them as legal subjects with effective rights and remedies?

UN law and its 'Westphalian paradigm' have notoriously failed to protect rule of international law for the benefit of citizens through collective rulemaking, rule application and rule enforcement. Intergovernmental rules are often not effectively applied and enforced in all member states due to inadequate legal and judicial remedies in domestic courts and inadequate 'capacity building'.[107] A future Kyoto II Protocol risks suffering the fate of many other multilateral environmental agreements that failed to realize their environmental objectives (like protection of biodiversity) effectively. The failure of UN

[107] The 1998 Aarhus Convention on Access to Information, Public Participation in Decision-Making and Access to Justice in Environmental Matters offers more legal and judicial remedies and 'compliance mechanisms' than any *worldwide* multilateral environmental agreement, *cf* A Andrusevych, T Alge and C Clemens (eds), *Case-Law of the Aarhus Convention Compliance Committee 2004–2008* (Lviv: RACSE, 2008).

law to provide for a compulsory 'international judiciary' also deprives UN member states from the 'strategic option' to delegate clarification of 'incomplete agreements' to independent and impartial 'courts of justice' clarifying disputed interpretations case-by-case through principle-oriented, reasoned judgments after listening to all parties concerned. As worldwide negotiations on environmental and financial 'first-best policy instruments' for climate change prevention and the subsequent clarification of 'second-best trade policy instruments' in the WTO and regional trade organizations are bound to remain incomplete, legal and judicial remedies in WTO dispute settlement bodies, regional and national courts are of crucial importance for peaceful dispute settlement and for legal security (eg, regarding national carbon taxes and 'clean energy subsidies') in the collective supply of international public goods.

Best alternative to a negotiated agreement (BATNA)?

Political negotiations, legal dispute settlement strategies and alternative dispute prevention procedures are interrelated in complex ways.[108] The 'BATNA strategy' suggested by the Harvard School of dispute settlement explains why the EU, the United States and other leading participants in the Kyoto II Protocol negotiations emphasize their determination to resort to unilateral policy alternatives (like national and regional carbon emission trading systems and unilateral border adjustment taxes) if UN member states fail to agree on global disciplines for carbon emission reductions and 'carbon leakages' in a new Kyoto II Protocol. Public choice theory explains why countries often succumb to domestic pressures and 'free-riding strategies' undermining international legal disciplines. The negotiations by important energy exporting countries (like Russia and other former member countries of the USSR) on their accession to the WTO offered similar 'BATNA options' for insisting on 'WTO-Plus commitments' (following the example of China's Protocol on accession to the WTO) if negotiations on 'first-best policy instruments' for energy security and energy transit regimes in the ECT and in EU–Russia partnership and cooperation agreements fail. Similarly, decentralized investor–state arbitration proceedings based on the ECT, on regional free trade agreements (like Chapter 11 of NAFTA) and on BITs may offer foreign investors more effective legal and judicial remedies against discriminatory restrictions of energy investments and energy trade than diplomatic dispute settlement procedures under WTO law or under a Kyoto II Protocol to the UNFCCC.

The environmental objectives of a future Kyoto II Protocol cannot be achieved without respect for the WTO legal and dispute settlement system. The negotiators of the Kyoto II Protocol should explicitly acknowledge the existing obligations under WTO rules, notwithstanding the frequent disagreement on how the incomplete and often unclear WTO disciplines should be applied to environmental policy instruments like border tax adjustments and emission trading systems. The negotiations on environmental 'first-best policy instruments' could be facilitated by an explicit mandate of WTO members to the WTO Committee on Trade and Environment to review the applicability, and any necessary adjustments, of WTO disciplines impacting on climate change

[108] *cf* Petersmann (1991) 66 ff; EU Petersmann, 'Prevention and Settlement of Transatlantic Economic Disputes' in EU Petersmann and M Pollack (eds) (2003) 3–64.

policies. Such demarcation of jurisdictions could de-politicize Kyoto II Protocol negotiations and give additional *impetus* to the WTO Development Round negotiations on liberalization and regulation of environmental goods, environmental services and 'green subsidies'. If WTO members cannot agree on worldwide commitments, they should promote 'plurilateral agreements' with limited membership (pursuant to Annex 4 of the WTO Agreement) and regional commitments (pursuant to Articles XXIV GATT, V GATS) as second-best policy alternatives.

'Environmental justice', burden-sharing and 'governance-design problems'

From a historical perspective and in terms of per capita pollution, the contribution of individual citizens in less-developed countries (like China and India) to green house gas emissions resulting from consumption of energy derived from fossil fuels is much smaller than the average contribution of citizens in industrialized countries. What are the implications of 'environmental justice principles' like the 'polluter pays principle' and the UNFCCC principle of 'common but differentiated responsibility' in order to promote equitable burden sharing of the inevitable costs of climate change prevention without obstructing satisfaction of basic human needs?[109] The Copenhagen conference of December 2009 confirmed that – without agreement on the legal and financial implications of 'climate justice principles' – LDCs may not consent to future Kyoto II disciplines. Nor are their citizens likely to comply with climate change disciplines whose allocation of 'adjustment costs' and redistribution of 'competitive benefits' among states and citizens are not perceived as legitimate.

In view of the importance of future climate change agreements for the welfare of billions of people and the traditional lack of effective enforcement mechanisms and judicial remedies in worldwide environmental agreements, voluntary rule compliance by governments and private citizens (eg, climate-polluting business and consumers) must be promoted by *multilevel* rights and obligations. It must be supported by multilevel monitoring mechanisms and multilevel legal as well as judicial remedies. Intergovernmental top-down approaches have all too often failed to change individual conduct at domestic and local levels. Many UN environmental agreements are not effectively implemented due to their failure to involve citizens by means of financial incentives and enforceable rights. Without transforming principles of 'global environmental justice' into enforceable rights and obligations of citizens and their governments, a UN climate change convention is unlikely to effectively limit climate change pollution by billions of citizens and companies in all UN member states.

Even if UN member states should reach international agreement on legitimate principles for 'global climate change governance', the history of past UN environmental agreements suggests that the appropriate design of climate change rules and institutions will remain confronted with numerous 'governance problems'. For instance:

[109] For an overview of diverse, individualist and collectivist conceptions of the 'polluter pays principle' (eg, focusing on individuals or states as 'polluters' and as bearers of rights to emit greenhouse gases) and other principles of 'environmental justice' and on the importance of protecting important individual and social interests by means of rights and judicial remedies, see Godard (n 87) and eg: S Caney, 'Cosmopolitan Justice, Responsibility and Global Climate Change' (2005) 18 *Leiden Journal of International Law* 747–75.

- Do UNEP and the UNFCCC Secretariat offer a sufficient institutional framework for negotiating and progressively developing UNFCCC Protocols? Is protection of the global environment feasible without a World Environmental Organization with the five core functions of (1) monitoring, assessment and early warning (eg, of fraudulent 'carbon trading'); (2) policy and norm development; (3) capacity development (eg, for the controversial technological dimensions of 'carbon sequestration'); (4) coordination; and (5) enforcement of international environmental disciplines?
- Can global public goods be collectively supplied as long as states focus on their 'national interests' (eg, in bilaterally agreed pipelines and alternative energy transportation networks) without effective constraints by international institutions mandated to protect common interests in international public goods?
- Will private investors supply the financial resources for the private investments and technology transfers necessary for the transition from fossil fuels to renewable energies without stronger legal protection of investment security and of intellectual property?
- As the 'European model' of negotiating 'integrated' trade, investment, environmental and energy rules with effective legal and judicial remedies can hardly be repeated at worldwide levels, would incorporation of 'plurilateral energy security agreements' (like the ECT) into the WTO legal and dispute settlement system as an optional 'plurilateral trade agreement' (pursuant to Annex 4 of the WTO Agreement) offer sub-optimal second-best solutions? How should civil society and governmental support for more 'participatory forms' of citizen-driven, transnational 'multilevel governance' and (sub)national forms of implementing international trade and environmental rules be designed?

How to avoid 'secondary conflicts' undermining international law and institutions

Under the Kyoto I Protocol, the agreed carbon emission reduction commitments of developed countries appear to have reduced carbon emissions only marginally, for instance much less than the carbon emission reductions caused by the worldwide financial crisis and economic recession since 2008. Past experiences with global negotiations on UN environmental agreements (including the Copenhagen conference in December 2009) suggest that transforming the 1992 UNFCCC and 1997 Kyoto I Protocol principles into more precise and more effective carbon reduction commitments by all major UN member states requires many years of progressive consensus-building, rulemaking, rule administration and rule enforcement. During this transition period of continuing climate pollution in many countries, recourse to sub-optimal safeguard measures – like national and EU border adjustment taxes aimed at preventing 'carbon leakage' and circumvention of carbon taxes – as well as to related dispute settlement proceedings (eg, in the EU and WTO jurisdictions) may be inevitable. Such 'secondary conflicts' arising from lack of agreement on, and non-compliance with, 'primary rules of conduct' risk overburdening international organizations like the WTO whose compulsory jurisdiction for trade-related disputes attracts ever more complaints concerning 'competitive distortions' caused by 'second-best policies' (like trade-distorting national aircraft subsidies) adopted in the absence of international first-best disciplines (like more precise competition and subsidy rules). They may also undermine the 'functionally limited legitimacy' of organizations like the WTO, for instance if dispute settlement rulings limiting recourse to trade policy sanctions are perceived by civil society as obstacles to 'saving the world' from global warming.

Lessons for worldwide climate change negotiations?

All UN member states have made the historical experience that democratic supply of 'national public goods' for the benefit of citizens and their human rights has required 'legal systems' protecting the legitimacy and effectiveness of rulemaking and 'rule of law' by means of five different kinds of rules and institutions: (1) constitutional; (2) legislative; (3) administrative; (4) judicial; and (5) international rules and institutions for democratic governance and protection of constitutional rights by means of 'rule of law'. This study argues that, similar to the adoption of national constitutions by almost all UN member states (including a few unwritten 'common law constitutions'), the collective supply of 'international public goods' requires functionally limited, multilevel 'constitutional systems' limiting the complex 'collective action problems' among states and among citizens by international rules and institutions with constitutional, legislative, administrative and judicial functions, in close cooperation with domestic legal systems implementing international rules at national and sub-national levels. The diverse forms of European integration law (eg, in the EU, EEA and ECHR) illustrate the 'enabling', 'limiting' and 'supplementing functions' of functionally limited, international 'treaty constitutions'. They demonstrate that extending constitutionalism beyond the nation state and integrating the different local, national and international layers of legal, economic and environmental governance can succeed only by strengthening constitutional rights of citizens, rule of law, respect for democratic governance and allocation of powers in conformity with principles of 'subsidiarity'. Like the multilevel 'European constitutional houses', the multilevel constitutional framework necessary for global governance must be built bottom-up and derives its democratic legitimacy from respect for human rights and for national constitutional democracies.[110]

Table 10: The need for a 'paradigm shift' in designing IEL in order to protect global public goods more effectively

- The prevailing conception of IEL as 'public international law regulating the economy' lacks legitimacy and effectiveness due to its treatment of citizens as mere objects of international law, its neglect of human rights coherence and its incapacity of protecting global public goods. Proposals for transforming national administrative law principles (like the US Chevron doctrine of judicial deference) into 'global administrative law' risk lacking constitutional justification at the international level where parliamentary participation and judicial protection of rule of law remain inadequate.
- The competing conception of IEL as 'multilevel economic regulation' (eg, in trade, investment and environmental agreements) remains too often dominated by industry lobbies to the detriment of general consumer welfare and global public goods (as illustrated by the 2008 financial crisis and its 'regulatory gaps'; one-sided focus on investor interests in investor–state arbitration; prevention of international competition and environmental rules by producer lobbies).

[110] On the images of a 'European house' (as used by former USSR President Gorbachev) and of a five-storey 'constitutional house' for multilevel governance, see Cottier (n 46).

- European 'multilevel constitutionalism' has protected human rights, consumer welfare, international rule of law and 'sustainable development' in the 30 EEA countries more effectively than in other regional regimes. The increasing recourse to regional 'economic coalitions of the willing' must be supplemented by 'functional coalitions' for collective supply of international public goods (eg, countries accepting carbon reduction commitments, emission trading, joint implementation and clean development mechanisms for climate change prevention). EU law confirms that such 'regulatory competition' can promote higher regulatory standards and public goods without a 'race to the bottom'.
- **Policy conclusion**: The history of constitutionalism and of governance failures in the collective supply of international public goods suggests that international economic regulation, like other fields of international law, should be conceived from a constitutional perspective as a 'fourth branch of governance' that can protect international public goods effectively only in 'multilevel constitutional houses' promoting legitimacy and coherence among the local, national, regional and worldwide levels of governance, rule of law and rights of citizens with due respect for legitimate 'constitutional pluralism'.

Multilevel governance for international public goods tends to focus on functionally limited fields like legal protection of an open and mutually beneficial world trading system, international monetary stability and freedom of payments, development assistance for LDCs and protection of the environment and of human rights. Yet, the diverse legal regimes for protecting 'international public goods' are horizontally and vertically interrelated, for example regarding their dependence on international rule of law and functional interrelationships between prevention of climate change, protection of security of energy supplies and maintenance of an open, rules-based trading system. Many policy recommendations for regulating the 'collective action problems' of such 'overlapping international public goods' – as illustrated by Table 11 summarizing policy recommendations for regulating climate change and energy security – go beyond 'Westphalian conceptions' of 'international law among sovereign states'.[111]

Table 11: Policy recommendations for regulating climate change and energy security

- Negotiations on a new agreement replacing the Kyoto I Protocol should prioritize environmental 'first-best policy instruments' (such as carbon-reduction commitments, a global emission trading system, financial and technological promotion of 'clean development mechanisms', etc) without complicating these environmental negotiations by discussion of 'second-best trade policy instruments', and without delaying the conclusion of the overdue Doha Development Round negotiations in the WTO. The 'Copenhagen Accord' of December 2009 and the 'Durban Accord' of December 2011 have significantly clarified some of the environmental objectives. They call for keeping the rise in global temperature to two degrees centigrade, making greenhouse gas reduction commitments more inclusive (eg, by including some LDCs like Brazil, China, India and South-Africa) and clarify the financial assistance obligations by developed countries (eg, to provide up to $100 billion a year by 2020). The political limits of consensus-based UN negotiations require leadership by 'coalitions' of countries willing and capable of making significant environmental, financial and legal commitments.

[111] The policy recommendations are explained in EU Petersmann, 'Climate Change Prevention, Energy Security and the WTO: Collective Action Problems in Promoting Global Public Goods' in Pauwelyn (n 98), 219 ff.

- Clarification and eventual adjustments of applicable WTO disciplines should be left to later WTO negotiations. The WTO Committee on Trade and Environment could prepare negotiations on WTO commitments for international energy and environmental goods and services, border tax adjustments, export taxes, transit trade and tariff regimes, phasing out of fossil fuel subsidies, 'green subsidies' for the transition to carbon-free energy production based on renewable resources, carbon capture and storage technologies.
- Inter-agency cooperation needs to be promoted (eg, for financial assistance by the World Bank Group, promotion of technology transfer by the World Intellectual Property Organization, negotiation of regional energy security systems in the context of the ECT and EU partnership agreements with Russia and other energy exporting countries).
- There may be need for acknowledging that specifically agreed 'compliance/supervision mechanisms' (eg, in a Kyoto II Protocol, investor–state arbitration procedures under the ECT and BITs) may offer more appropriate procedures for the settlement of the inevitable disputes over compliance with carbon reduction commitments, 'competitive distortions' and discriminatory restrictions than would the WTO dispute settlement system.
- Synergies between national and international environmental, energy and trade regimes need to be fostered. This is necessary in view of the fact that the energy sector accounts for over 50 per cent of all greenhouse gas emissions and development of carbon-neutral energies may need to be subsidized. 'Competitive distortions' will make recourse to unilateral 'safeguard measures' politically inevitable (eg, the costs of carbon constraints on production may necessitate border taxes on carbon-intensive imports like steel, aluminium and cement from countries without carbon reduction commitments).
- The domestic 'constituencies' supporting additional international disciplines need to be broadened and supplemented by transnational, multilevel governance structures and involvement of business. There is need for incentives for individual actors, sub-national and non-governmental organizations (eg, research institutes, private standard-setting organizations) to assist in decentralized standard-setting, monitoring, enforcement of new rules on climate protection, energy security and development of 'clean energies'. Contrary to the authoritarian 'Westphalian paradigm' of 'international law among states', citizens must be recognized not only as the ultimate beneficiaries, but as the democratically legitimate 'principals' of international economic regulation. As producers, investors, traders, consumers, polluters and 'democratic principals' of all governance institutions, citizens are the most important legal subjects and self-interested guardians of 'rule of law' in international economic and environmental relations.

Constitutional responses to the five major 'collective action problems' impeding supply of 'aggregate public goods'

The intergovernmental UN approaches have failed to protect human rights and many other international public goods effectively. Rendering multilevel governance more effective requires additional rules and institutions addressing and limiting 'collective action problems' and legitimacy deficits more specifically. For instance:

- The *jurisdiction gap*, ie, the incapacity of every state to provide global 'aggregate public goods' without international cooperation, requires – as in European integration law – promoting international duties of cooperation (eg, among national governments and international organizations, national and international courts) and competition among 'alliances of the willing'. WTO law rightly promotes 'competing liberalization' at worldwide and regional levels, as illustrated by the increasing recourse to free trade areas, customs unions and preferential agreements among LDCs as 'second-best' policies in the absence of worldwide consensus on concluding the WTO Development Round negotiations. Yet, UN law and WTO law remain deficient regarding the task of 'multilateralizing' regional agreements (eg, on human rights, regional security systems, free trade areas, environmental regulation). The jurisdiction gap at national levels must be compensated by conferring international jurisdiction (eg, following the model of the EU Commission) for initiating regulation and protection of global public goods, and for coordinating interdependent 'overlapping public goods regimes'. Multilevel governance may often operate most effectively at *national* rather than international levels, as illustrated by

- the 'global corporate economy' governed by private law structures;
- the decentralized enforcement of European economic law in national courts and by national regulatory agencies (such as competition authorities);
- the governance of the internet based on US corporate law, administrative law and intergovernmental coordination[112]; or
- the use of the US Alien Torts Claims Act for holding multinational corporations legally accountable for abuses of workers' rights in foreign jurisdictions[113],

provided that the overall coherence of multilevel governance remains constitutionally protected.

- The *governance* gap, ie, the inability of most intergovernmental organizations to regulate and govern the collective supply of international public goods democratically and effectively, requires new forms of multilevel constitutional, legislative, administrative and judicial commitments and institutions for collective protection of public goods. European integration law suggests that overcoming discriminatory 'legal nationalism' requires 'international guardians of community interests' like independent commissions with rights to initiate rulemaking and promote 'deliberative democracy' and judicial accountability for violations of common rules. The current coordination of multilevel economic governance in the G20 could be institutionalized (eg, with a secretariat with independent powers of initiative) and extended to multilevel environmental governance. The transformation of the power-oriented GATT 1947 into the rules-based WTO trading system with compulsory, national and international jurisdiction for the peaceful settlement of disputes and judicial protection of rule of law was achieved by 'intergovernmental leadership' of constitutional democracies. Yet, the 'governance failures' in concluding the 'Development Round' negotiations in the WTO illustrate the need for additional governance reforms of the WTO legal system (eg, by establishing a WTO Executive Committee and WTO Legal Committee, broadening the mandate of the WTO Director-General and institutionalizing the interparliamentary cooperation inside the WTO). Most importantly, extending national public goods to international relations requires support by 'private–public partnerships' and non-governmental stakeholders based on legal and judicial protection of individual rights and remedies against violations of international rules.
- The *incentive gap*, ie, the inherent temptation of free-riding in the collective supply of international public goods whose costs and benefits are distributed unevenly, requires

[112] *cf* Uerpmann-Wittzack (n 103).

[113] For examples see: Wai (n 64) and S Sassen, 'Neither Global nor National: Novel Assemblages of Territory, Authority and Rights' (2008) 1 *Ethics & Global Politics* 1–19, 4.

making 'common but differentiated responsibilities' for private and public, national and international actors more effective. UN financial and technical assistance for poor countries (eg, if they provide transnational environmental services by protecting tropical forests that are of global importance for biodiversity and carbon-reduction), like the WTO provisions for capacity-building and trade facilitation assisting less-developed countries in participating in and supporting WTO rulemaking, illustrate how legal and financial incentives for private and public participation in the supply of international public goods may assist in limiting 'governance failures' and promoting equitable sharing of adjustment costs. The European experiences with financial redistribution (eg, by EU regional, structural and development funds), capacity-building and 'human rights conditionality' suggest that only citizen-oriented 'community law' and rights-based 'integration law' may effectively transform power politics (eg, in LDCs) by more effective protection of cosmopolitan rights, development assistance and rule of law.

- The *participation gap*, ie, the need for inclusive consensus-building promoting worldwide participation, requires legal and institutional protection of 'deliberative governance by discussion', institutionalized leadership (eg, by international organizations with mandates for initiating rulemaking for global public goods) and financial assistance for 'capacity-building' by 'coalitions of the willing' so that all relevant public and private actors cooperate in the collective supply of global public goods. International economic and environmental public goods are crucially dependent on private stakeholder participation (eg, industries developing 'green technologies'). As first explained by Kantian legal theories of 'multilevel constitutionalism' promoting citizen-driven 'struggles for equal rights' and 'public justice' and illustrated by the citizen-driven structures of the diverse European economic, legal and human rights regimes, international economic, environmental and legal public goods cannot become effective and legitimate without rights of all affected citizens to participate in multilevel decision-making and have recourse to legal and judicial remedies against unjustified restrictions of individual rights and market distortions.
- The *rule of law gap* inevitably results from the *legal fragmentation* among hundreds of national, international and transnational legal regimes transforming national constitutions into 'partial constitutions' that can no longer secure protection of human rights through centralized, nationalist legal systems. As illustrated by the diverse European legal and judicial regimes, transnational rule of law requires multilevel constitutional restraints on multilevel governance and on their intergovernmental 'rule by law'. Legal predictability, rule of law and legal protection of legitimately diverse conceptions of justice, human rights and 'constitutional pluralism' are essential for the collective supply of global public goods. Transnational rule of law must be promoted by recognizing, 'balancing' and reconciling competing rights and constitutional claims on the basis of common constitutional principles. The balancing must respect legitimately diverse interpretations and diverse national legal implementation of international rules in conformity with different national constitutional traditions and democratic preferences. As intergovernmental rules may lack democratic legitimacy and may unduly restrict individual rights, transnational 'rule of law' – as a constitutional, jurisdictional and judicial restraint protecting equal individual rights against abuses of 'rule by law' – may require and justify departures from the prevailing Westphalian conceptions of 'rule of international law', as illustrated by the *Kadi*-judgments of the ECJ (cf Table 18 in chapter II).

Examining the 'optimal level' of legal regulation of public goods

Once the basic rules and institutions for the collective supply of international public goods have been established (eg, the UN Charter, the Bretton Woods Agreements, the WTO Agreement, the 'constitutions' establishing the ILO, WHO, FAO and UNESCO), the operational activities for the production and protection of public goods often make use of a large variety of public law and private law instruments and public–private partnerships. Some of these international organizations recognize fundamental rights of access to public goods based on human rights (eg, recognized in UN instruments), labour and social rights (eg, recognized by the ILO), the right to education recognized in the UNESCO Constitution, the right to health protection recognized in the WHO Constitution, and the right to food recognized in FAO instruments. But the public and/or private forms of production and protection of public goods (like food security, health services, information and education services) often remain political choices by individual state actors. The European carbon emission trading system for climate change mitigation, the worldwide administration of website addresses by the private, non-profit Internet Corporation for Assigned Names and Numbers (ICANN) discussed in chapter II, the 'UN Global Compact' with thousands of transnational corporations on promotion of 'Corporate Social Responsibility' discussed in chapter IV or the WTO Agreements regulating the cooperation with non-governmental organizations (eg, for the elaboration of technical product and production standards, sanitary, phytosanitary and preshipment inspection standards) discussed in chapter VII are examples for the ever more intense cooperation among public and private institutions in the collective supply of certain international public goods. The human rights approach to IEL, as advocated in chapters III, IV and VII, aims at protecting private and public autonomy and responsibility of individuals and 'peoples' as constitutional foundation for individual and democratic self-development and 'public reason'. From this citizen-oriented, cosmopolitan perspective, 'constitutionalization' of authoritarian, inefficient 'Westphalian governance regimes' and their decentralization to more optimal levels of regulation in conformity with principles of 'subsidiarity' and transnational public–private co-regulation (eg, of internet governance, 'corporate social responsibility'), are important tasks of IEL reforms in the twenty-first century. For example, as discussed in chapter V:

- In transnational commercial law, the 1958 New York Convention on Recognition and Enforcement of Foreign Arbitral Awards provides for a worldwide system of private commercial arbitration as an alternative to judicial remedies in national courts, which sometimes risk being more expensive, slower and potentially biased against foreigners.
- The WTO Preshipment Inspection Agreement provides for private arbitration under the jurisdiction of the WTO and the International Chamber of Commerce as an alternative to WTO dispute settlement procedures among WTO members.
- In international investment law, the 1965 ICSID Convention and the global network of more than 2800 BITs provide for investor–state arbitration as an alternative option to 'espousal' of investor claims by the home state, and to their diplomatic protection and judicial pursuit through politicized, costly and lengthy interstate adjudication in the ICJ.
- In intellectual property law, the Arbitration Centre of the World Intellectual Property Organization (WIPO) and national courts offer decentralized legal and judicial

remedies in view of the fact that the dispute settlement provisions in many WIPO conventions providing for the jurisdiction of the ICJ have never been used so far, and WTO dispute settlement procedures for the enforcement of the WTO Agreement on Trade-Related Intellectual Property Rights are limited to WTO members.

More generally, as many 'impure public goods' can be transformed into 'club goods' by means of public or private regulation (eg, based on property rights, agreements and contracts excluding 'free-riders'), the role of private actors and of transnational private regulation in the production of international public goods becomes increasingly important, notably as a complement of public production and regulation (eg, of food security, health protection, 'corporate social responsibility', freedom of the internet). The traditional assumption that 'non-rivalry' and 'non-excludability' of public goods prevent their supply in private markets for private goods and services, is increasingly challenged, notably for 'impure public goods' and 'single best effort public goods'.[114]

[114] *cf* Barrett (2007) 2 ff.

II

The Emergence of Cosmopolitan IEL Based on Respect for 'Constitutional Pluralism'

PUBLIC INTERNATIONAL LAW has historically evolved as a power-oriented legal system with state-centred 'primary rules' of conduct and incomplete 'secondary rules' about the recognition, amendment and enforcement of 'international law among states'.[1] Whereas the Westphalian 'international law of coexistence' among states focused on protection of state sovereignty, the postwar 'international law of cooperation' promotes ever more international cooperation among governments and citizens based on respect for inalienable human rights to individual and popular self-determination.[2] Yet, as emphasized by Kofi Annan in his final address as UN Secretary-General to world leaders assembled in the UN General Assembly on 19 September 2006, the power-oriented international legal system is widely perceived as 'unjust, discriminatory and irresponsible' and has failed to effectively respond to the three global challenges to the United Nations:

> [T]o ensure that globalization would benefit the entire human race; to heal the disorder of the post-Cold War world, replacing it with a genuinely new world order of peace and freedom; and to protect the rights and dignity of individuals, particularly women, which were so widely trampled underfoot.

According to Kofi Annan, these three challenges – 'an unjust world economy, world disorder and widespread contempt for human rights and the rule of law' – entail divisions that 'threaten the very notion of an international community, upon which the UN stands'.[3]

Chapter I inferred from the crises in the international monetary, financial, trading, environmental and development systems the need for more legitimate and more effective regulation of the 'collective action problems' in supplying international public goods. As inside constitutional democracies and in European economic integration law, also transnational IEL beyond Europe must respond to the economic and political 'paradoxes of liberty' by stronger legal and institutional protection of human rights and

[1] On Hart's concept of law as a unified system of 'primary rules of conduct' and 'secondary rules' of recognition, rulemaking and change of primary rules, and on the influence of 'public reason' on determining what the law is, see HLA Hart (1994) and GK Hadfield and S Macedo, 'Rational Reasonableness: Toward a Positive Theory of Public Reason' University of Southern California Law School Law and Economics Working Paper 127 (2011).

[2] On the distinction between 'international law of coexistence' and 'international law of cooperation' see: W Friedmann (1964).

[3] The speech of Kofi Annan is reproduced in UN document GA/105000 of 19 September 2006. On the need for community-based conceptions of international law see: B Fassbender (2009) 52 ff.

other cosmopolitan rights empowering citizens as legal subjects of IEL to invoke and enforce IEL rules and transnational rule of law for the benefit of citizens. Chapter II argues that – notably in citizen-driven areas of international relations like the worldwide division of labour aimed at efficient satisfaction of consumer demand for scarce goods and services – the human rights obligations of all UN member states require stronger legal and institutional protection of open markets, non-discriminatory conditions of competition and constitutional restraints of multilevel economic governance. In increasingly more areas of IEL, market freedoms, trading rights, investor rights, intellectual property rights, labour, environmental and human rights are being protected by national and international courts for the benefit of citizens. European economic integration law demonstrates most clearly how the welfare and cosmopolitan rights of citizens can be enhanced by interpreting IEL as a citizen-oriented integration and community law protecting individual rights, legal security and reducing transaction costs for the benefit of citizens. Yet, the current approaches to regulating trading rights, investor rights, intellectual property rights, labour rights, environmental rights, common market freedoms, procedural rights of access to justice, property rights and human rights in IEL beyond Europe – as international rights of states, cosmopolitan rights of citizens and/or national constitutional rights – lack legal coherence and are often dominated by bureaucratic self-interests in avoiding legal and judicial accountability for arbitrary violations of IEL.

OVERVIEW OF CHAPTER II

Chapter II begins by describing the changing structures of international law (section 1) and of IEL in particular (section 2), which call for 'constitutional approaches' to international regulation of 'market failures' as well as of 'governance failures'. Section 3 defines the use of the ambiguous terms 'constitution', 'constitutionalism' and 'constitutionalization' of IEL; it also explains why national and international regimes constituting rulemaking, administrative and judicial powers must be coordinated on the basis of respect for 'constitutional pluralism'. Claims of legal primacy of international law and of allegedly 'self-contained regimes' must be reviewed in light of the human rights obligations and legitimately diverse constitutional regimes of UN member states. In order to limit abuses of public and private power, multilevel economic regulation must be subjected to 'democratic checks and balances' (section 4). Section 5 suggests that the legal coherence and legitimacy of IEL depend – especially in areas where governments act as *regulators of private trade*, financial services, investments, savings, competition, consumption and pollution, rather than as *suppliers of intergovernmental public goods* (like monetary and exchange rate stability) – on stronger, multilevel protection of human rights. Rather than treating citizens as mere objects of intergovernmental economic regulation, citizens must be legally empowered to participate in the international division of labour on the basis of 'cosmopolitan rights', enabling them to challenge the ubiquity of 'market failures' and 'governance failures' caused by rational pursuit of self-interests and 'moral hazards' in transnational economic regulation. More inclusive rulemaking and citizen-driven rule enforcement will render transnational rule of law more effective than if IEL rules are imposed by governments without recognizing corresponding cosmopolitan rights to transnational rule of law.

1 FROM 'INTERNATIONAL LAW AMONG STATES' TO 'GLOBAL LEGAL PLURALISM': THE NEED FOR COMPARATIVE CONSTITUTIONAL AND INSTITUTIONAL ANALYSES

Chapter I described how the postwar transformation of the 'international law of coexistence' among sovereign states into an ever vaster 'international law of cooperation' (Friedmann) among 193 UN member states entailed ever more national and transnational legal regimes with autonomous rulemaking and rule enforcement systems. In particular in transnational economic regulation by transnational corporations (TNCs) and by intergovernmental networks of national regulators, traditional conceptions of law based on coercive enforcement of rules by the state are often neither descriptively correct nor normatively desirable in view of the advantages of voluntary, decentralized rule compliance, coordination and rule enforcement in the international economic cooperation among millions of producers, investors, traders and consumers. The incomplete legal regulation of the fragmentation and potential synergies among the multiplicity of transnational legal regimes corresponds ever less to traditional conceptions of law as a system of governance by a recognized authority establishing and faithfully enforcing rules that are *general*, *stable*, *public*, *prospective*, *clear*, *not contradictory* and acknowledged by citizens as *just*.[4] The 'centrifugal' forces driving this 'global legal pluralism' often aim at avoiding existing constitutional and legal disciplines in industrialized countries by 'rule shopping', 'forum shopping' and allocating specific economic activities to foreign or transnational jurisdictions where stakeholders benefit from existing inequalities of power and resources. The traditional conceptions of 'sovereign equality' among states coexisting in non-hierarchical, multiple sovereign legal orders can no longer explain the hundreds of sub-national, transnational and supranational legal regimes allocating powers to non-state actors and acknowledging more and more human rights and transnational economic and labour rights of citizens. Yet, it remains deeply contested to what extent 'global legal pluralism' protects the diversity of human values and communities (especially of 'mobile actors' that have the resources necessary for benefiting from transnational legal regimes) or requires stronger constitutional and institutional safeguards in order to protect human rights and public goods more effectively. Even if state sovereignty is increasingly limited by the universal recognition of human rights, of popular self-determination and by UN humanitarian interventions aimed at protecting citizens against gross human rights violations by their own governments (as in the case of Kosovo and Libya), there is agreement that a 'global constitutional and institutional top-down redesign' ('big C Constitutionalism') and 'systemic integration' of the existing legal pluralism is neither politically feasible nor normatively desirable.

The worldwide agreements establishing the postwar Bretton Woods institutions (IMF, World Bank, International Finance Corporation, International Development Association), GATT 1947 and the WTO have promoted progressive liberalization of governmental barriers to international trade and related payments by means of reciprocal market access commitments among states, financial adjustment assistance and legal requirements that internal regulation of economic transactions, of 'market failures' and 'public interests' should remain non-discriminatory. The worldwide framework agreements are

[4] *cf* LL Fuller (1969).

supplemented by hundreds of regional agreements (eg, establishing free trade areas, customs unions, common markets) and thousands of bilateral agreements about, inter alia, protection of foreign investments, international air, maritime and rail transport, postal and telecom services, avoidance of double taxation, and cooperation regarding tax evasion. The intensity of multilevel economic regulation differs among the various sectors of international movements of goods, services, persons, capital and related payments. International trade in goods and many services (like international transports, postal and telecommunication services) have become subject to ever more private and public, national, regional and worldwide regulation and 'legal harmonization', for instance of production and product standards aimed at protecting consumers and the environment by means of technical, sanitary and phytosanitary standards and risk-assessment procedures. In international monetary and financial regulation, by contrast, the breakdown of the IMF system of fixed exchange rates in 1971 reduced the regulatory functions of the IMF and entailed a return to greater, national 'monetary sovereignty'; compared with international trade law, national monetary and financial regulation remains less 'harmonized' by international monetary and financial regulation.[5] Apart from regional agreements providing for liberalization of financial services and investments (eg, in the EU, EEA and NAFTA) most of the more than 2800 bilateral investment treaties (BITs) focus on protection standards like national treatment, most-favoured nation treatment, full protection and security, fair and equitable treatment, access to justice, necessity of emergency measures, and 'umbrella clauses' transforming contract obligations into treaty obligations of the host state. Most BITs leave the regulation of 'market failures' – like restraints of competition, other abuses of power and harmful 'external effects' (like pollution of the environment) – to the national jurisdiction of states.[6]

The need for comparative constitutional and institutional analyses

As explained by Rawls, in view of the 'fact of reasonable pluralism' and 'the fact that in a democratic regime political power is regarded as the power of free and equal citizens as a collective body', the democratic exercise of coercive power over one another is democratically legitimate only when 'political power . . . is exercised in accordance with a constitution (written or unwritten) the essentials of which all citizens, as reasonable and rational, can endorse in the light of their common human reason'.[7] Arguably, the human rights obligations of all UN member states entail that the moral justifiability and effectiveness also of multilevel governance of citizen-driven IEL in the twenty-first century depends on a 'four-stage sequence' (Rawls) of constitutional, legislative, executive and judicial clarification of principles, rules and 'public reason' supported by citizens.[8] Comparative analyses of national constitutions and of their regulation of multilevel economic governance (eg, based on limited delegation of regulatory powers to international organizations, incorporation of primary and secondary international law into domestic

[5] *cf* AF Lowenfeld, 'The International Monetary System: A Look Back over Seven Decades' (2010) 13 *JIEL* 575 ff.

[6] *cf* R Dolzer and C Schreuer (2008).

[7] J Rawls, (2001) 41.

[8] On the 'four-stage sequence' of legitimate rulemaking inside constitutional democracies like the United States see: J Rawls (1971) 195 ff.

legal systems) reveals an enormous diversity of constitutional, institutional and legislative approaches also among constitutional democracies.[9] Even though all UN member states have adopted national (written or unwritten) constitutions and international human rights commitments, they don't share a common 'public reason' justifying multi-level regulation of IEL and of transnational rule of law. Human rights say little about the necessary 'institutional choices' among alternative economic, political, legislative, administrative and judicial institutions at private and public, local, state, federal and international levels of economic governance. Yet, institutional choices tend to be strongly influenced by constitutional conceptions of justice, for instance in Anglo-Saxon countries prioritizing 'parliamentary sovereignty' (eg, in the United Kingdom) or civil and political rights over economic and social rights (eg, in the United States). As discussed in chapters III and IV, diverse conceptions of human rights, constitutional and cosmopolitan rights often explain diverse conceptions of IEL and of related 'institutional choices'. The choices of alternative social decision-making processes may have far-reaching effects on the economic transaction costs of market participants, their democratic participation, 'public interests' in promoting consumer welfare, private self-interests in promoting producer welfare, political self-interests and 'public choices' of regulators, the correction of 'market failures' and 'governance failures' and on judicial interpretations of legal rules and principles.[10]

Both democratic constitutionalism and welfare economics tend to evaluate 'welfare' in terms of methodological and normative individualism focusing on the preferences of individuals. Also international trade law, investment, labour, social, environmental and regional economic integration law increasingly focus – like human rights law – on protection of *individual* rights like EU citizen rights, human rights, 'market freedoms', labour and social rights, investor rights and intellectual property rights. In certain areas, they entail the emergence of citizen-oriented 'cosmopolitan economic integration law' aimed at promoting mutually beneficial cooperation not only among governments, but also among individuals, people and their parliamentary representatives.[11] Yet, due to the diverse national constitutional traditions of protecting economic and social rights (like economic freedoms, property and labour rights), the worldwide, regional and functional economic and legal regimes tend to regulate the allocation of regulatory powers, institutional decision-making processes and individual rights in often diverse ways without mutually coherent conceptions of 'embedded liberalism', constitutional protection and institutionalization of 'public reason', democratic participation and 'distributive justice'. The more than 70 regional trade agreements concluded since the failure of the 2003 WTO Ministerial Conference to advance conclusion of the 'Doha Round negotiations' illustrate that regional and inter-regional agreements (like the EU free trade agreements with Chile, Mexico and Korea) are increasingly perceived as alternative *fora* not only for trade liberalization, but for trade regulation and non-economic cooperation.[12] The recent initiatives for transforming regional free trade areas into, for instance, an ASEAN

[9] *cf* the comparative legal and interdisciplinary analyses in M Hilf and EU Petersmann (eds) (1993).

[10] *cf* G Shaffer and JP Trachtman, 'Interpretation and Institutional Choice at the WTO' (2011) 52 *Virginia Journal of International Law* 1–52.

[11] *cf* EU Petersmann, 'From the Hobbesian International Law of Coexistence to Modern Integration Law: The WTO Dispute Settlement System' (1998) 2 *JIEL* 175–98. On the difficulties of liberalizing international movements of persons see: JP Trachtman (2009).

[12] *cf* EU Petersmann, 'The WTO and Regional Trade Agreements as Competing *Fora* for Trade Liberalization and Trade Regulation' in L Bartels and F Ortino (eds) (2006) 281–312.

Community, a Southern African Development and Economic Community (SADEC), a South American Common Market (MERCOSUR,) Andean and Central American Economic Communities reflect the European experience that the success of regional trade liberalization and market integration depend on embedding them into broader legal, institutional, social and political frameworks supported by citizens and non-governmental constituencies. Similar to regional economic integration law complementing worldwide economic agreements, the increasing number of regional human rights instruments (eg, in the Americas, Africa and Europe) complements UN human rights instruments by offering stronger, multilevel guarantees of human rights and judicial remedies, for instance by protecting private property, freedom of commercial expression, freedom of association and freedom of profession also in transnational economic cooperation; by protecting individuals against abuses of public power, both regional economic and human rights courts increasingly recognize individuals as primary subjects of international law.[13]

IEL as a 'layered', multilevel legal system with dynamically changing interactions: courts of justice as guardians of the systemic unity of IEL?

In IEL, many specialized legal regimes emerged and developed in response to pressures from diverse actors interested in protecting transnational trading rights, investor rights, intellectual property rights and other 'market freedoms', economic, labour, social and procedural rights and corresponding responsibilities. For instance, the 'investor-driven' evolution of international investment law and adjudication, the 'producer-driven' evolution of international trade law and adjudication and the 'tripartite' evolution of international ILO convention and 'core labour standards' have resulted in legal regimes and 'interpretive communities of economic law practices' prioritizing certain economic and social rights subject to general 'public interest clauses' acknowledging the need for reconciling such economic and social rights with other public interests and non-economic rights. This necessary 'balancing' and reconciliation of economic and non-economic legal regimes tends to be allocated to national and international rulemaking, administrative and judicial institutions and procedures which – for instance, in the case of specialized investor–state arbitral tribunals and WTO dispute settlement bodies – risk favouring powerful economic actors without adequate regard to overlapping, non-economic legal regimes such as human rights, ILO and environmental agreements. Even though legal and jurisdictional pluralism may enhance 'voice' and 'discursive spaces' for non-state actors, the asymmetric access to specialized economic regimes and institutions with limited mandates does not guarantee a fair balancing of all legal interests affected by economic decision-making processes.

The discussion – in chapter I, section 3 – of five competing conceptions of IEL illustrated the ever more complex evolution of the international economic order into a 'layered legal system' based on private and public, national, regional and worldwide rules, institutions and 'governance networks'. The frequent disagreements among lawyers and

[13] On the conception of national sovereigns as 'agencies of the international law system' see: J Waldron, 'Are Sovereigns Entitled to the Benefit of the International Rule of Law?' (2011) 22 *EJIL* 315–43. On the dynamic evolution of regional human rights instruments and institutions see, eg: C Krause and M Scheinin (eds) (2009) pt III.

judges on the best conceptualization of the relationships between the different levels of the international legal system, their dynamic interactions and the legal interpretation of state-centred and citizen-oriented economic rules reflect the diverse 'constitutional infrastructures' at national and regional levels of economic regulation, as discussed in the following chapters. The state-centred, power-oriented 'international law of coexistence' and the 'intergovernmental law of cooperation' continue to shape the regional and worldwide 'economic integration law', for instance by:

- privileging industrialized countries in the composition and voting rules of IMF bodies;
- prioritizing trade interests of developed countries in GATT and WTO negotiations;
- regulating international financial transactions on the basis of standards used in developed countries;
- providing for investor–state arbitration and producer-driven trade adjudication favouring powerful, mobile economic actors; and
- focusing, often one-sidedly, on protection of economic rights without explicit acknowledgment of the human rights obligations of all UN member states and the 'social corporate responsibilities' of TNCs.

In contrast to hierarchical domestic legal systems, international courts tend to resolve most norm conflicts and legal constraints resulting from 'regime-interactions' through 'harmonious interpretation' and 'balancing' of different rights and obligations pursuant to the 'systemic integration paradigm' underlying the customary methods of treaty interpretation (as codified in the Preamble and Article 31 VCLT) rather than by claims of legal hierarchy of human rights (as advocated by many Anglo-Saxon human rights lawyers) or power-oriented claims of prioritizing 'national interests' (as defined by politicians and industry lobbies). Human rights based hierarchies (eg, based on the concept of peremptory norms or *jus cogens* and Article 103 UN Charter) vis-à-vis other international legal obligations have been emphasized in human rights courts and European courts committed to protection of fundamental rights, but only rarely in other transnational and international judicial bodies with different functional emphasis.[14] Bilateral, regional and worldwide economic agreements dynamically interact in diverse ways. For instance, due to the reciprocity principle, regional free trade areas and the worldwide WTO commitments tend to go far beyond the autonomous guarantees of freedom of trade in national trade laws. The WTO Agreement on Textiles and Clothing provided a successful multilateral framework for the progressive phasing out (by 2005) of thousands of bilaterally agreed restrictions of international trade in cotton and textiles. The 1965 World Bank Convention on the Settlement of Investment Disputes between States and Nationals of other States (ICSID Convention) succeeded in setting up a multilateral framework for the settlement of hundreds of investor–state disputes through investor–state arbitral awards that can be enforced through national judicial remedies. Efforts at 'multilateralizing' BITs through OECD negotiations on a Multilateral Agreement on Investments had to be abandoned, however, in 1998 in view of strong opposition from civil society groups.[15] In contrast to the 'constitutional jurisprudence' of the ECJ, the EFTA Court and the ECtHR engaging in comprehensive 'balancing' of economic law and constitutional rights, investor–state arbitration and WTO dispute settlement rulings

[14] *cf* the case studies in: E De Wet and J Vidmar (eds), *Norm Conflicts and Hierarchy in Public International Law: The Place of Human Rights* (Oxford: OUP, forthcoming 2012).

[15] *cf* Dolzer and Schreuer (2008) 26.

tend to resolve disputes without clarifying the 'constitutional principles of justice' and human rights obligations limiting economic regulation and adjudication.

Bilateral economic agreements (such as investment, air transport and double taxation agreements) thrive mainly in areas where governments are not (yet) willing to submit to multilateral legal disciplines. For example, the *multilateral* IMF guarantees of freedom of current payments and avoidance of discriminatory currency practices (*cf* Articles VI, VIII IMF Agreement) have successfully replaced hundreds of previously *bilateral* payments and exchange agreements. Some bilateral and multilateral agreements provide for individual rights (eg, pursuant to Article VIII:2 IMF Agreement) and judicial remedies that are enforceable in national or international courts (eg, foreign investor rights enforceable through investor–state arbitration and domestic courts). The hundreds of dispute settlement rulings based on bilateral, regional and worldwide economic agreements progressively limit power-oriented, intergovernmental structures of IEL and strengthen transnational rule of law. As discussed in subsequent chapters of this book, the case law of regional economic courts and regional human rights courts increasingly interacts, for example in the judicial protection by the ECtHR of freedom of commercial speech, private property and intellectual property rights as parts of human rights,[16] and in the protection of human and constitutional rights by the ECJ against interferences by EC measures, state measures and private economic organizations.[17]

Whether fragmentation and overlaps among international legal regimes are mutually harmful or beneficial can often be determined only case by case depending on the particular cooperation problems. Similarly, the 'optimal' horizontal allocation and delimitation of jurisdiction among states and among international organizations, like the vertical allocation of rights and responsibilities among individuals, local, national and international institutions, will often remain controversial due to diverse value preferences and their distributive consequences for citizens, governments and non-governmental organizations. The resultant incompleteness of many international legal regimes often prompts governments to delegate the settlement of related disputes to international and transnational dispute settlement institutions. The law of some international organizations and the legally binding rulings of international courts and other dispute settlement institutions assert legal supremacy not only in 'vertical relations' vis-à-vis national laws (*cf* Articles 103 UN Charter, XVI:4 WTO Agreement, 27 VCLT); they introduce legal hierarchies and constitutional 'checks and balances' also in the 'horizontal relations' among the legislative, administrative and judicial institutions of international organizations and among the different levels of their primary and secondary law (*cf* Articles IX, XVI:3 WTO Agreement). The worldwide legal disciplines on regional agreements (*cf* Articles XXIV GATT, V GATS), on bilateral agreements (*cf* Article 11 of the WTO Safeguards Agreement, the WTO Agreement on Textiles and Clothing) as well as on unilateral restrictions of states are progressively strengthened by means of compulsory jurisdiction of international dispute settlement bodies (eg, pursuant to Articles 16, 17 and 23 DSU). This chapter explains why such legal rules and compulsory jurisdictions of a higher legal rank can serve 'constitutional functions' for legal protection of freedom, non-discrimination, rule of law and welfare-increasing cooperation among citizens

[16] *cf* L Helfer, 'The New Innovation Frontier? Intellectual Property and the European Court of Human Rights' (2008) 49 *Harvard International Law Journal* 1–52.

[17] *cf* B De Witte, 'Balancing of Economic Law and Human Rights by the European Court of Justice in PM Dupuy, F Francioni and EU Petersmann (2009) 197–207.

across national frontiers. In increasingly more fields of IEL, national and international courts interact in their judicial clarification and justification of functional interrelationships between national and international economic law.[18] The multiplication of regulatory claims, jurisdictions and competing interpretations proposed by changing political majorities in parliaments and in intergovernmental negotiations entails that the task of clarifying and justifying the normative unity of IEL is often delegated to courts of justice, whose judicial reasoning tends to be more independent, impartial, principle-oriented, systemic and transparent than political majority decisions depending on particular circumstances.

2 THE EMERGENCE OF MULTILEVEL 'CONSTITUTIONAL LAW', 'GLOBAL ADMINISTRATIVE LAW' AND 'LEGAL CONSTRUCTIVISM' IN IEL

In international economic relations, the 'horizontal international law among states' is increasingly transformed by the hierarchical structures of the law of international organizations and the universal recognition and multilevel regulation of human rights with corresponding *erga omnes* obligations of governments based on a *jus cogens* core. The ever more comprehensive, multilevel regulation and globalization of economic, environmental, legal and political relations transforms IEL into a cosmopolitan 'international law of states, peoples and citizens' with complex legal layers, governance networks and interactions of private and public, national and international economic regulation.

Diverse forms of multilevel economic governance

In addition to the traditional forms of national and international governance by legislative, executive and judicial institutions and of decentralized coordination in markets and civil society, the increasing liberalization and globalization of international economic relations continues to generate ever more new forms of transnational governance, notably by means of 'co-production of norms and public goods' by public–private decision-making networks involving different levels of public authority.[19] The types of actors involved and the extent of their involvement, the decision-making procedures, institutions and co-production of norms and public goods vary enormously. Five basic types of international economic regulation (eg, of exchange rates, investments, production, trade, competition, consumption, goods, services, social and environmental standards, transnational movements of capital, persons and communications) can be distinguished[20] and interact in manifold ways that often lack transparency:

1. International treaties and intergovernmental organizations at worldwide and regional levels (such as the WTO and the more than 250 regional trade agreements), which

[18] *cf* the case studies of interactions among Brazilian, MERCOSUR and WTO dispute settlement rulings on Brazilian import restrictions of retreaded tyres: N Lavranos (ed), 'Multilevel Judicial Governance between Global and Regional Economic Integration Systems: Institutional and Substantive Aspects' EUI Working Paper MWP 2009/41.

[19] *cf* A Héritier and M Rhodes (eds) (2011).

[20] *cf* B Kingsbury, N Krisch and R Stewart, 'The Emergence of Global Administrative Law' (2005) 68 *Law and Contemporary Problems* 15 ff.

increasingly also protect private rights (eg, in the EC) and private judicial remedies (eg, in the World Bank's International Centre for the Settlement of Investment Disputes).

2. Informal intergovernmental networks among domestic regulatory agencies (such as the Basel Committee of national bank regulators, the International Competition Network among more than 65 national competition authorities).
3. National authorities implementing international economic rules and policies subject to international regulation and multilevel constitutional restraints (eg, resulting from multilevel judicial review by national and international courts).
4. Hybrid public–private 'regulatory partnerships', such as the worldwide administration of website addresses by the private, non-profit Internet Corporation for Assigned Names and Numbers (ICANN), which is subject to the regulatory supervision by the United States and closely cooperates with the World Intellectual Property Organization (WIPO) (eg, concerning the peaceful settlement of domain name disputes through WIPO arbitration procedures and the already more than 15,000 WIPO arbitration awards).[21]
5. Private regulatory bodies such as the International Organization for Standardization (ISO) for the international harmonization of standards that are also used as a legal basis for intergovernmental trade regulation (eg, in the WTO Agreement on Technical Barriers to Trade); or the International Chamber of Commerce (ICC) whose private rules and commercial arbitration are closely connected with national and intergovernmental regulatory systems (see, for instance, the private 'Independent Review Procedures' administered jointly by the ICC and the WTO in order to determine the compliance by public and private parties with the WTO Agreement on Preshipment Inspection).

Synergies of multilevel constitutional constraints of multilevel economic governance

Almost all UN member states have adopted constitutions that constitute national polities, citizen rights and limited government powers, subject governments to constitutional restraints and international legal obligations and commit government policies to constitutionally defined objectives (like protection of human rights) and 'constitutional checks and balances'. All democratic constitutions, including functionally limited 'treaty constitutions' (eg, establishing rulemaking, executive and judicial powers in the EU, EEA and ECHR), acknowledge the need for six basic types of rulemaking – constitutional, legislative, administrative, judicial, international and private – necessary for democratic self-governance. One defining element of constitutional democracies is that all six types of rulemaking and related institutions interact and compete in their search for protecting human rights and other 'principles of justice'. The institutionalization and evolution of the 'public reason' necessary for maintaining democratic self-governance legitimately differ among countries depending on their historical experiences and democratic preferences, for instance regarding the controversial relationships between majoritarian political institutions, non-majoritarian regulatory agencies and courts of justice. From a

[21] *cf* R Uerpmann-Wittzack, 'Multilevel Internet Governance involving the EU, Nation-States and NGOs' in A Follesdal, RA Wessel and J Wouters (eds) (2008) 145–68.

constitutional perspective, both political and judicial institutions are 'agents' with limited constitutional mandates. The constitutional and democratic legitimacy of independent 'courts of justice' protecting constitutionally agreed rights of citizens is not inherently weaker than the legitimacy of majoritarian, political processes that tend to be less independent and less constrained by 'principles of justice'. As emphasized by comparative constitutional and institutional analyses, the comparative advantages of constitutional, legislative, administrative, judicial and intergovernmental processes depend on which institution is in a better position to protect the constitutional values inherent in the relevant rules and arbitrate competing legal claims.[22]

This book began by describing why national diplomats, members of parliaments and organized interest groups so often disagree on the rules, principles and institutions necessary for limiting the 'collective action problems' in supplying global public goods that are beneficial for all citizens, for instance due to 'capture' by vested interests of intergovernmental rulemaking on trade liberalization, financial regulation and protection of the environment. Globalization demonstrates that national constitutions alone can neither protect human rights across frontiers nor secure the collective supply of global public goods. The more the self-development of citizens depends on consuming foreign goods and services (eg, imported food and medicines for millions of poor people in LDCs, imported energy resources sustaining production and consumption in industrialized countries), the more national constitutions turn out to be 'incomplete constitutional safeguards' that can no longer realize many of their objectives without complementary 'transnational constitutional safeguards' protecting open markets, human rights and limiting abuses of power also in transnational and international relations.[23] The ever more intense intergovernmental cooperation for the collective supply of 'international public goods' leads to increasingly complex forms of multilevel governance in international organizations limiting national policy powers by multilevel legal restraints. Since the 1919 Constitution (*sic*) Establishing the ILO, many other constituent agreements of international organizations – such as the FAO, the WHO and UNESCO – are officially named 'constitutions' in view of the fact that they

- constitute an international legal order with legal primacy over national laws of member states (eg, pursuant to Article 27 VCLT);
- create new legal subjects and hierarchically structured institutions with limited governance powers;
- provide for institutional checks and balances (eg, among rulemaking, administrative and dispute settlement bodies in the WTO and judicial review of state measures);
- legally limit the rights of member states (eg, regarding withdrawal, amendment procedures, dispute settlement procedures);

[22] *cf* nn 9 and 10 and N Komesar, *Imperfect Alternatives: Choosing Institutions in Law, Economics and Public Choice* (Chicago: Chicago University Press, 1994); N Komesar, *Law's Limit: The Role of Courts, the Rule of Law and the Supply and Demand of Rights* (Chicago: Chicago University Press, 2001); M Poiares Maduro, *We the Court – The European Court of Justice and the European Economic Constitution* (Oxford: Hart Publishing, 1998).

[23] See, eg: EU Petersmann, 'Multilevel Trade Governance Requires Multilevel Constitutionalism' in C Joerges and EU Petersmann (eds) (2006) ch 1; DM Johnston, 'World Constitutionalism in the Theory of International Law' in RSJ Macdonald and DM Johnston (eds), *Towards World Constitutionalism. Issues in the Legal Ordering of the World Community* (The Hague: Kluwer, 2005) 3–30; R Uerpmann-Wittzack, 'The Constitutional Role of Multilateral Treaty Systems' in A von Bogdandy and J Bast (eds) (2006) 147–81.

- provide for the collective supply of 'public goods' that – as in the case of the above-mentioned treaty constitutions (of the ILO, WHO and UNESCO) – are partly defined in terms of human rights (such as core labour rights, the human rights to health, food and education); and often
- operate as 'living constitutions' whose functions – albeit limited in scope and membership – increasingly evolve in response to changing needs of citizens for international cooperation in the supply of public goods.

Worldwide 'treaty constitutions' differ fundamentally from national constitutions, for example by their limited policy functions and less effective constitutional restraints (eg, on intergovernmental and national policy powers). State-centred international lawyers therefore prefer to speak of 'international institutional law',[24] 'global administrative law'[25] or of an intergovernmental 'constitutionalism lite'.[26] However, in view of the interdependencies between international and national public goods (like efficient markets), international organizations for the collective supply of international public goods are more and more indispensable for the proper functioning of national organizations for the collective supply of national public goods. Human rights and their moral value premises (normative individualism) require designing national and international governance as an integrated, multilevel constitutional framework for the protection of citizen rights, democratic self-government and cooperation among free citizens across frontiers.[27] Multilevel *international constitutionalism* is a functionally limited, but necessary complement to *national constitutionalism* which, only together, can protect human rights and democratic self-government more effectively across frontiers in a globally integrating world.

The European 'social market economy' (Article 3 TEU), and its 'system ensuring that competition is not distorted' (Articles 101 ff, Protocol 27 TFEU), confirm that markets can operate as efficient, decentralized information, allocation, coordination and sanctioning mechanisms for a spontaneous division of labour among citizens only if market competition remains legally embedded in a framework of non-discriminatory trade, competition and social rules and governance institutions. Similarly, global markets can operate efficiently – as discussed in more detail in chapters VII and VIII – only if the dynamic interrelationships between private and public, national and international actors, regulators and the diverse layers of legal regulation are coordinated by multilevel 'constitutional rules'. Even though national *Constitutions* have much more comprehensive functions (eg, for constituting democratic self-governance of 'We the People' within a national territory), functionally limited *treaty constitutions* supplement national constitutions by empowering, limiting, regulating and justifying international institutions for the collective supply of transnational public goods that are becoming increasingly important for the welfare of

[24] *cf* N Blokker and H Schermers, *International Institutional Law*, 4th edn (Leiden: Martinus Nijhoff, 2003).

[25] *cf* Kingsbury, Krisch and Stewart (n 20); R Stewart and M Ratton Sanchez Badin, 'The WTO and Global Administrative Law' in C Joerges and EU Petersmann (2011) ch 16; E Fisher, 'Beyond the Science/Democracy Dichotomy: The WTO Sanitary and Phytosanitary Agreement and Administrative Constitutionalism' in Joerges and Petersmann (eds) (2006) 327–49.

[26] *cf* J Klabbers, 'Constitutionalism Lite' (2004) 1 *IOLR* 31, 45.

[27] On the 'constitutional functions' of international organizations as a 'fourth branch of government' see: EU Petersmann, 'Constitutionalism and International Organizations' (1996) 17 *Northwestern Journal of International Law & Business* 398, 415 et seq. On this view – ie, that both states and international organizations should be conceived as agents for the benefit of citizens, with constitutionally limited, delegated powers similar to government agencies inside constitutional democracies – see also: Waldron (n 13).

citizens[28] The worldwide financial crisis of 2008, like the climate change crisis and poverty crises in so many UN member states, illustrate the lack of adequate rules and multilevel governance institutions protecting the common citizen interests in international financial risk regulation, banking supervision, carbon-reduction commitments, promotion of 'clean energies', reduction of unnecessary poverty and protection of human rights. In the international financial crises since 2008, the 'market disciplines' (like the spread of interest rates on government bonds of euro member states depending on their indebtedness and domestic competitiveness) often succeeded in imposing more effective restraints on domestic 'market failures' as well as 'governance failures' than intergovernmental rulemaking among governments, central banks and financial regulators.

'Constitutional functions' of WTO law

None of the supporters of 'multilevel constitutionalism' claims that international 'treaty constitutions' constituting, limiting, regulating and justifying international rulemaking, executive and judicial powers for the collective supply of international public goods are, or should become, constitutions in the same sense as national constitutions. In line with the diverse national constitutional traditions, constitutional approaches to multilevel governance differ inevitably. Unsurprisingly, advocates (eg, in the United States) of using 'hegemonic international law' for advancing 'national interests' (eg, as defined by political majorities and interest groups) oppose limiting foreign policy discretion and multilevel governance by additional constitutional restraints, especially if they perceive 'international governance without government' and international law as 'antidemocratic' due to their remoteness from the national *demos* and popular politics.[29] Rights-based conceptions of constitutional democracy acknowledge the crucial role of international law for protecting constitutional rights and public goods across national boundaries. For instance, the notion of a functionally limited 'WTO constitution' is being used in view of

- the comprehensive rulemaking, executive and (quasi) judicial powers of WTO institutions;[30]
- the 'constitutionalization' of WTO law resulting from the jurisprudence of the WTO dispute settlement bodies;[31]
- the *domestic* 'constitutional functions' of GATT/WTO rules, for example for protecting constitutional principles (like freedom, non-discrimination, rule of law, proportionality of government restrictions) and domestic democracy (for instance, by limiting the power of protectionist interest groups) for the benefit of transnational cooperation among free citizens;[32]

[28] On the diverse 'constitutional functions' of IEL in terms of an 'enabling constitution' (eg, protecting international economic transactions among producers, investors, traders and consumers through mutually coherent 'constituent principles' of contract law, corporate law, trade and investment law, monetary law, legal liability, etc) and a 'limiting constitution' (eg, limiting 'market failures' and 'governance failures' resulting from abuses of private and public power) supplementing national constitutions for the collective supply of national 'public goods' see already: EU Petersmann (1991) chs III and VII.

[29] *cf* J Rubenfeld, 'Unilateralism and Constitutionalism' (2004) 79 *NYU Law Review* 1971, 2017 f.

[30] See JH Jackson (1998).

[31] See DZ Cass, 'The Constitutionalization of International Trade Law: Judicial Norm-Generation as the Engine of Constitutionalization' (2001) 11 *EJIL* 39–75.

[32] On the need to distinguish the 'foreign policy functions' of international rules from their 'domestic policy functions' see: Petersmann (1991); JO McGinnis and ML Movsesian, 'The World Trade Constitution'

- the *international* 'constitutional functions' of WTO rules, for example, for the promotion of 'international participatory democracy' (eg, by holding governments internationally accountable for the 'external effects' of their national trade policies, by enabling countries to participate in the policy making of other countries)[33] and of the enhancement of 'jurisdictional competition among nation states'[34] and 'the allocation of authority between constitutions';[35]
- in view of the necessity of 'constitutional approaches' for a proper understanding of the law of comprehensive international organizations that have used constitutional terms, methods and principles for more than 50 years (see, eg, the 'Constitutions' of the ILO, WHO, FAO, UNESCO and EU);[36] or
- in view of the need to interface and coordinate different levels of governance on the national and international level.[37]

All these constitutional approaches agree that the WTO should not simply be viewed in narrow *economic* terms, for example, as an institution promoting economic welfare through trade liberalization. WTO rules and policies also pursue *political* as well as *legal* objectives that are no less important than the economic benefits from liberal trade. The guarantees of private 'rights to import and export', intellectual property rights, private access to independent courts and rule of law in the 2001 WTO Protocol on the accession of China and the contribution of WTO dispute settlement rulings enforcing these rights to protection of constitutional principles inside China (like protection of independent trade courts, rule of law, commercial freedom of information and expression),[38] illustrate these 'constitutional dimensions' of WTO law. The introduction of open markets and rule of law on the basis of China's WTO obligations, including a system of independent trade courts (supervised by a chamber of the Chinese Supreme Court specializing in WTO law), like the foundation of the EU's customs union on the respective customs union obligations of all EU member states under GATT/WTO law, offer evidence that GATT/WTO law can operate as a revolutionary 'transformation agreement' for the benefit of citizens. Similarly, the exclusion of Chinese citizens from the benefits of the multilateral trading system for over 40 years following China's withdrawal from the GATT in 1949 illustrated the unnecessary poverty which nationalist and protectionist government policies can inflict on citizens.

(2000) 114 *Harvard Law Review* 511–605; PM Gerhart, 'The Two Constitutional Visions of the World Trade Organisation' (2003) 24 *University of Pennsylvania Journal of International Economic Law* 1–75, contrasts the 'inward-looking, economic vision of the WTO' in helping member countries addressing internal political failures with the 'external, participatory vision of the WTO' helping WTO members to address concerns raised by policy decisions in other countries.

[33] See, eg, PM Gerhart, 'The WTO and Participatory Democracy: The Historical Evidence' (2004) 37 *Vanderbilt Journal of Transnational Law* 897–934.

[34] See JO McGinnis, 'The WTO as a Structure of Liberty' (2004) 28 *Harvard Journal of Law and Public Policy* 81–88.

[35] J Trachtman, 'The Constitutions of the WTO' (2006) 17 *EJIL* 623–46.

[36] See, eg: Petersmann (1991); N Walker, 'The EU and the WTO: Constitutionalism in a New Key' in G de Búrca and J Scott (eds) (2001).

[37] T Cottier and M Hertig, 'The Prospects of 21st Century Constitutionalism' (2003) 7 *Max Planck Yearbook of United Nations Law* 261.

[38] See WTO document WT/L/432 of 23 November 2001, part I, section 2, and the recent WTO dispute settlement rulings enforcing China's WTO obligations vis-à-vis Chinese censorship restrictions on the importation and distribution of certain 'cultural' or 'content' goods and services (WT/DS363/AB/R adopted on 19 January 2010).

WTO law as 'global administrative law' (GAL)?

As discussed in chapter I, section 3, the diverse constitutional conceptions of IEL are challenged – notably in Anglo-Saxon and other polities without constitutional protection of economic freedoms and social rights of citizens – by 'Westphalian' conceptions, GAL conceptions, multilevel economic regulation conceptions and 'conflicts of law' conceptions of IEL. In a recent article, Stewart and Sanchez Badin argue that 'the challenges faced by the WTO can be addressed by greater application of GAL decision-making mechanisms of transparency, participation, reason-giving, review and accountability to the WTO's administrative bodies including its councils and committees and the Trade Policy Review Body'.[39] Yet, from the perspective of constitutional democracies that protect economic and social rights as fundamental freedoms and constitutional rights, GAL conceptions[40] risk neglecting the constitutional dimensions of economic regulation. In ever more countries, economic and social rights of citizens, and the 'rule of law' conditions for their administrative restriction, are based on human rights, constitutional rights, democratic legislation and judicial review. The frequent focus of GAL proponents on 'accountability' in terms of *ex post* review and administrative remedies reflects Anglo-Saxon traditions of leaving economic regulation to democratic majorities without constitutional guarantees of economic freedoms. Alternative definitions of GAL – for instance, as including requirements of publicness, generality of law and 'constitutive administrative law' constituting and limiting the legal authority of administrative bodies and administrative practices[41] – also risk obscuring the constitutional and human rights foundations of 'common constitutional principles' limiting administrative powers. Proposals that GAL approaches – like the emergence of European administrative law systems in monarchical and authoritarian states during the nineteenth century – should focus on 'rule by law' rather than on protection of human rights and 'rule of law', run counter to the human rights obligations of all UN member states and the 'constitutional functions' of administrative law as 'applied constitutional law'.

Inside constitutional democracies, administrative law refers to one among several other function(s) of governance – like constitution making, democratic legislation, administration, adjudication and foreign policymaking for international peace, rule of law and the collective supply of other international pubic goods. National democratic constitutions and 'treaty constitutions' (like the EU Treaty) define, and constitutionally limit, the objectives, legitimacy, legal principles, lawful instruments, institutions and limited powers of economic administration based on the premise (as explained in theories

[39] Stewart and Ratton Sanchez Badin (n 25).

[40] *cf* Kingsbury, Krisch and Stewart (n 20) 15 (conceiving 'global administrative law as the legal mechanisms, principles and practices, along with supporting social understandings, that promote or otherwise affect the accountability of global administrative bodies, in particular by ensuring that these bodies meet adequate standards of transparency, consultation, participation, rationality and legality, and by providing effective review of the rules and decisions these bodies make')

[41] *cf* B Kingsbury, 'The Concept of "Law" in Global Administrative Law (2009) 20 *EJIL* 23 ff, 31: 'Publicness is a necessary element in the concept of law under modern democratic conditions. The claim is that the quality of publicness, and the related quality of generality, are necessary to the concept of law in an era of democratic jurisprudence'. According to Kingsbury, the principles of legality, rationality, proportionality, rule of law and human rights are 'requirements of publicness' and 'the object of much GAL research and practice' (at 32–33). Rather than invoking a vague 'administrative law principle' of 'publicness', it is argued in this study that multilevel human rights law offers more precise 'constitutional principles' limiting administrative practices.

of justice from Kant to Rawls) that all legislative, administrative and judicial governance activities derive their legitimacy from constitutional 'principles of justice' as defined in national constitutions. Since the Second World War, such principles of justice are also increasingly recognized in the law of international organizations – like the human rights obligations under the UN Charter, the right to health protection protected by the WHO Constitution (*sic*), the right to education protected by the UNESCO Constitution (*sic*), the right to food protected by the FAO Constitution (*sic*), labour rights protected by the ILO Constitution (*sic*) and the human rights guarantees of the EU Charter of Fundamental Rights and the ECHR. The 2007 Treaties on European Union (TEU) and on the Functioning of the European Union (TFEU), for instance, begin by defining the 'principles' and 'common provisions having general application' before defining the institutions and limited, delegated powers of the EU. In the modern 'age of rights',[42] national and international administrative regulations and decisions increasingly impact on individual rights. The universal recognition of human rights entails that the constitutional limits of administrative powers can no longer be separated from administrative law and from its judicial review (*cf* Table 12). It remains to be clarified to what extent constitutional and GAL principles recognized in regional economic law and jurisprudence have also become appropriate standards of legal and judicial review of worldwide economic law and jurisdictions.

Table 12: Human rights and IEL: judicial protection of fundamental rights in the administration of the EC's common agricultural market organizations

The EC's common agricultural policy has given rise to hundreds of judicial complaints challenging the legality of EC regulations, directives, decisions, and of national implementing measures. For instance, in Case 29/69, *Stauder v City of Ulm*, ECR 1969, 419, Stauder successfully challenged – by invoking his constitutional right to respect for human dignity (Article 1 German Basic Law) – a requirement in an EC scheme for the reduction of the surplus of butter that the eligibility of social security recipients to receive subsidized butter was dependent on revealing their names and addresses. In Case 44/79, *Hauer v Rheinland-Pfalz*, ECR 1979, 3272, Hauer invoked her constitutional rights of freedom of profession and private property (Articles 12, 14 German Basic Law) in order to challenge the refusal – based on an EC regulation – of an authorization to plant new vines on her property; the ECJ – while acknowledging that these fundamental rights are part of the principles of Community law as reflected in the 'constitutional traditions common to the Member States' and the ECHR – concluded that the EC restrictions of these rights were not disproportionate to the objectives of the Community's structural agricultural policy. By recognizing fundamental rights as general principles of EU law and by reviewing whether legislative and administrative restrictions of fundamental rights are compatible with the EU principles of non-discrimination and proportionality (including requirements of 'suitability', 'necessity' and 'proportionality *stricto sensu*), the ECJ offers effective constitutional protection to fundamental rights.

[42] *cf* N Bobbio, *The Age of Rights* (Cambridge: Polity Press, 1996); L Henkin, *The Age of Rights* (New York: Columbia University Press, 1990).

Constitutional and administrative law principles may have different legal ranks

Kingsbury's proposal to view the primary and secondary law of international organizations as integral parts of 'global administrative law' obscures the function of constitutional rules to operate as 'checks and balances' protecting citizens against abuse of administrative powers. International law recognizes that such constitutional safeguards (eg, in treaties constituting international organizations) are beyond the limited powers of administrative bodies and constitutionally limit the legitimate scope of 'secondary administrative law' adopted by international organizations. Constitutional law and administrative law pursue separate constitutional functions, as acknowledged by principles of 'separation of powers' inside constitutional democracies and in European law. As emphasized by the ECJ in its review of national and EU measures inconsistent with human rights,[43] the multilevel human rights obligations of states constitutionally limit the 'rules of recognition' by recognizing only such rules and institutions as legitimate and valid which respect these multilevel human rights obligations and their underlying 'constitutional principles of justice'; administrative practices violating human rights obligations cannot be recognized as valid law on constitutional grounds, as rightly emphasized by the ECJ and by national courts in Europe.

Similarly, national administrative assessments of 'risks to human health' pursuant to the WTO Agreements on Sanitary and Phytosanitary Measures and TRIPS, and judicial review of national health protection measures by WTO dispute settlement bodies,[44] are limited by principles of transparency, non-discrimination, necessity, proportionality and rule of law whose legal foundations go beyond administrative law and administrative discretion. These 'constitutional principles' may require deference by international courts whenever such principles are interpreted by national jurisdictions depending on their respective constitutional and human rights obligations in order to avoid conflicts between IEL (eg, WTO obligations under the TRIPS Agreement to grant patent protection for pharmaceuticals) and human rights (eg, of access to essential medicines).[45] As discussed in chapter III, multilevel human rights law may justify invocation of higher national and regional human rights standards as relevant context for interpreting WTO exceptions (eg, to protect human health) inside states even if the corresponding UN human rights guarantees prescribe only lower minimum standards.

Hence, Anglo-Saxon proposals to distinguish 'constitutive administrative law', 'substantive administrative law' and 'procedural administrative law' as 'three categories of public global administrative activity' – without any reference to multilevel human rights

[43] See ch III, section 4 and joined cases C-402/05P and C-415/05 P, *Kadi and Al Barakaat International Foundation v Council of the EU and Commission of the European Communities*, Judgment (3 September 2008), para 284: 'It is also clear from the case-law that respect for human rights is a condition of the lawfulness of Community acts (Opinion 2/94, paragraph 34) and that measures incompatible with respect for human rights are not acceptable in the Community (Case C-112/00, *Schmidberger* [2003] ECR I-5659, paragraph 73 and case-law cited)'.

[44] *cf* M Matsushita, 'Human Health Issues in Major WTO Dispute Cases' (2009) 4 *Asian Journal of WTO & International Health Law and Policy* 1–26.

[45] *cf* ch III, section 4 and H Hestermeyer, *Human Rights and the WTO. The Case of Patents and Access to Medicines* (Oxford: OUP, 2007), who argues that – as the TRIPS Agreement may give rise to conflicts with the customary law obligation of access to life-saving medicines in the face of national health emergencies – customary law requires WTO dispute settlement bodies to interpret TRIPS provisions (eg, on parallel imports, compulsory licences) in conformity with the human rights obligations of WTO members.

and other constitutional limitations of GAL – risk undermining human rights and constitutional democracy. Kingsbury's acknowledgment – that '(c)onstitutive power is exercised internationally, most obviously in the constitution of international organizations'[46] – justifies the more convincing, alternative conclusion that the increasing recognition of 'common constitutional principles' by international courts, investor–state arbitration and other quasi-judicial dispute settlement systems (eg, in the WTO) constitutionally limit GAL and multilevel economic governance. Such functionally limited 'multilevel constitutionalism' reflects the emergence of overlapping 'transnational polities' in regional and functional integration organizations (such as the EU and ILO) for the collective supply of international public goods. Rather than denying the normative reality of 'multilevel constitutional protection' of human and citizen rights against abuse of administrative powers on the obvious ground that centralized 'global Constitutionalism' is neither feasible nor desirable,[47] it is important to acknowledge that functionally limited 'multilevel constitutionalism' (eg, in multilevel human rights law and trade law) – like constitutional democracies – is based on respect for 'constitutional pluralism' and on legitimate diversity of constitutional and human rights conceptions at national, regional and worldwide levels.

From the constitutional perspective of 'rule of law' as a constitutional restraint on 'rule by law', some 'GAL conceptions' of delegated 'private ordering' – for instance, in case of 'privatizing' governmental tasks to commercial security services, health services and other 'services of public interest' – raise doubts about the constitutional validity of some of the 'administrative law' involved.[48] Examining such contested legality of administrative practices vis-à-vis citizens depends on their constitutional justifiability as 'rule of law' rather than on administrative law claims of 'rule by law', 'political welfare' and administrative procedures justifying administrative decisions by 'review, reason-giving and publicity/transparency'.[49] Acknowledgment of the fact that 'there are specific rules of recognition in particular governance regimes' of global administrative law[50] must not obscure the fact that the universal human rights obligations of all UN member states, and the law of international organizations, are also leading to increasing recognition of 'common constitutional principles' limiting the legal validity of international administrative practices. The administration of justice and protection of European human rights standards in the *Kadi* judgment by the ECJ (Table 18) illustrate that UN law might justify multilevel judicial protection of human rights even vis-à-vis UN Security Council sanctions.[51] While European integration has given rise to 'European administrative law'

[46] Kingsbury (n 41) 35.

[47] ibid 36; N Krisch, 'Global Administrative Law and the Constitutional Ambition' LSE Working Paper 2009/10. For a criticism of the unrealistic conception of the UN Charter as the 'constitution of the international community' see: EU Petersmann, 'How to Reform the UN System? Constitutionalism, International Law and International Organizations' (1997) 10 *Leiden Journal of International Law* 421 ff. My description of UN human rights law as part of an emerging 'multilevel human rights constitution' emphasized the functions of human rights to protect individual and democratic diversity and criticized the lack of judicial remedies in UN human rights law.

[48] *cf* D Dyzenhaus, 'The Concept of (Global) Administrative Law' New York University IILJ Working Paper 2008/7, available at: www.iilj.org.

[49] Kingsbury (n 41) 41 ff.

[50] ibid 57.

[51] Joined cases C-402/05P and C-415/05 P, *Kadi and Al Barakaat International Foundation v Council of the EU and Commission of the European Communities*, Judgment (3 September 2008), para 299: 'It follows from all those considerations that it is not a consequence of the principles governing the international legal order under the United Nations that any judicial review of the internal lawfulness of the contested regulation in the

based on common 'administrative constitutionalism'[52] constituting and limiting national and European administrative practices in the implementation of EU and EEA law, the administrative law dimensions of the law of worldwide organizations tend to remain contextual (ie, limited and defined by their respective constitutional rules), fragmented and pluralist rather than being part of a universally agreed 'global administrative law'. Without more thorough empirical, comparative and contextual legal research into the transformation of administrative practices into positive 'global law', GAL claims – including Kingsbury's 'natural law interpretation'[53] of the 'general principles of public law' – risk being criticized as wishful thinking rather than as methodologically convincing determinations of positively existing law.

From authoritarian legal positivism towards constitutional theories of IEL

Since the Second World War, human rights law, economic law and environmental law have evolved into multilevel, global governance systems that continue to fail to protect human rights, rule of law, consumer welfare and the environment effectively in the majority of UN member states. More than 200 years ago, Immanuel Kant had already criticized leading international lawyers ('Grotius, Pufendorf, Vattel and the rest') as 'sorry comforters . . . still dutifully quoted in *justification* of military aggression', whose 'philosophically or diplomatically formulated codes do not and cannot have the slightest *legal* force since states as such are not subject to a common external constraint'.[54] To this day, many international legal practitioners continue to justify 'efficient violations' of international law and intergovernmental power politics without regard to today's universal obligations of all UN member states to respect, protect and promote human rights and democratic self-governance by rule of law. Human rights activists and civil society increasingly call for more responsible ways of national and international regulation of transnational economic, political, legal, social and environmental relations. The 2007 Lisbon Treaty's commitment to promoting 'a highly competitive social market economy' (Article 3 TEU), like the commitment of all UN member states to prevention of climate change as well as to the 'Millennium development goals' of halving the unnecessary poverty of more than one billion people by the year 2015, illustrate the determination of some governments to transform international economic regulation for the benefit of citizens. Can such commitments be realized without creating the constitutional foundations necessary for international rule of law?

State constitutions and federal constitutions regulate social and political cooperation among citizens more comprehensively than functionally limited international 'treaty constitutions' like the ECHR and the 2007 Lisbon Treaty. Yet, the increasing globalization of the economy, of the environment and of international communications reveals that state constitutions have become incomplete 'partial constitutions' that can no longer

light of fundamental freedoms is excluded by virtue of the fact that that measure is intended to give effect to a resolution of the Security Council adopted under Chapter VII of the Charter of the United Nations'.

[52] *cf* Fisher (n 25) ch 11.

[53] *cf* A Somek, 'The Concept of "Law" in Global Administrative Law: A Reply to B Kingsbury (2010) 20 *EJIL* 985 ff, 990 f, who criticizes the lack of clarity in some GAL research on legal and non-legal practices and 'law as it is' and 'law as it is not'.

[54] I Kant, 'Perpetual Peace' in Kant (1970) 101.

effectively protect many citizen interests in a globally integrating world without state participation in international agreements and organizations enabling citizens to benefit from international regulation and cooperation. The less state constitutions remain 'holistic orders' of social life, the more must the 'constitutional functions' of the increasing delegation of limited rulemaking, administrative and judicial powers to international organizations be taken into account. Like national legal systems, IEL as an integrated system of private and public, national and international rules and institutions can protect and promote human rights and rule of law only in a multilevel constitutional framework respecting the legitimate diversity of national constitutional systems and justifying the legitimacy of IEL by coherent 'constitutional interpretations'. European economic integration law and its increasing influence on regional integration agreements beyond Europe (like the EU's free trade agreements with Mediterranean countries, the EU's Cotonou Agreement with LDCs in Africa, the Caribbean and the Pacific) confirm that – with the support of independent 'community institutions' (like the EU Commission and the ECJ) and citizens – 'Westphalian international law among states' can be transformed into functionally limited, multilevel constitutional systems protecting economic rights of citizens across national frontiers. Without such 'community institutions' defending community interests vis-à-vis special interest groups, international economic regulation risks being 'captured' by rent-seeking interest groups and focusing one-sidedly on legal and judicial protection of powerful producer interests – as illustrated by the focus on investor rights in BITs, on producer interests in GATT/WTO law, or by the welfare-reducing discrimination among regional economic agreements in response to protectionist pressures from import-competing producers (eg, agricultural lobbies in Europe and the United States).[55]

This study argues that – just as constitutional democracies and their decentralized enforcement of rule of law depend (as explained by Rawls) on institutionalizing 'public reason' in conformity with constitutional principles of justice which all citizens can support as fair and reasonable – modern IEL must be based on the human rights obligations of all UN member states and on an efficient, transnational rule of law system supported by an 'overlapping consensus' of citizens and governments with due respect for their 'reasonable disagreement' regarding comprehensive, political conceptions of justice and individual conceptions of a good life. Citizens will support international rules and institutions only to the extent that rule compliance is recognized as being beneficial for all and consistent with human rights independent of the diverse, individual conceptions of the good. Hart's positivist conception of international law – as stated in the first edition of his *Concept of Law* (1961) and repeated in the second 1994 edition – as a mere set of 'primary rules of obligation', lacking a unified 'legal system' of primary and secondary rules,[56] is no longer justifiable for rights-based trade, investment and economic integra-

[55] On past proposals for creating a Transatlantic Free Trade Area and the 'protectionist capture' of the EU/US 'Transatlantic Economic Partnership' institutions by producer lobbies see: EU Petersmann and M Pollack (eds) (2003), especially chs 1 and 2.

[56] *cf* Hart (1994) 214: 'It is indeed arguable, as we shall show, that international law not only lacks the secondary rules of change and adjudication which provide for legislature and courts, but also a unifying rule of recognition specifying "sources" of law and providing general criteria for the identification of its rules'. Hart's legal positivism is descriptive in the sense of his claim that law and morals must remain separated (*cf* at 240). As the UN Charter, customary international law and human rights require interpreting treaties, and settling disputes, 'in conformity with principles of justice' and human rights, my own publications challenge 'realist' and positivist 'value neutrality theses' as being inconsistent with the normative tasks of interpreting the 'rules of recognition' of national and international law in conformity with the *jus cogens* and *erga omnes* core of

tion law as interpreted and applied by European jurisdictions and some worldwide dispute settlement systems. The recent failures of the worldwide financial, trade and environmental systems are due, at least in part, to 'Westphalian conceptions' of 'international law among sovereign states' and their neglect for human rights as relevant context for interpreting and applying modern IEL. Human rights justify going beyond Hartian conceptions of international law by emphasizing the constitutional restraints of IEL in order to make multilevel regulation of the worldwide division of labour, and of the collective supply of other international 'public goods', more legitimate and more effective for the benefit of citizens and their human rights.

Similar to the emphasis by European courts on 'common constitutional principles' as constitutional foundation of European economic law, the general principles of law – as defined in Article 38 ICJ Statute as the third legal source of international law complementing international treaties and customary rules – include today human rights principles restraining the recognition and interpretation of IEL rules. The human rights obligations of all UN member states justify deriving the functional unity and normative justification of IEL from respect for human rights and for the legitimate diversity of constitutional democracies. The multilevel human rights obligations of states constitutionally limit the 'rules of recognition' by permitting recognition of only such rules and institutions as legitimate and/or valid which respect 'constitutional principles of justice' as defined in democratic and judicial proceedings.[57] 'Rules of recognition' and their judicial interpretations may legitimately differ among constitutional democracies, international organizations and national and international courts of justice. The coexistence of multiple, national and international constitutional jurisdictions thereby promotes 'constitutional checks and balances', 'deliberative democracy' and multiple review of power-oriented 'Westphalian recognition practices' in light of 'constitutional pluralism'. In contrast to economic and empirical–sociological approaches to interpreting IEL (eg, focusing on the interests of consumers, competitors and other social interests in the interpretation of economic rules), constitutional conceptions of IEL also emphasize the additional need for interpreting IEL in conformity with the human rights obligations of the countries concerned and the constitutional limits of the law of international economic organizations. For instance, conflicts between pharmaceutical patents and human rights of access to essential medicines, or between 'commercial freedom of speech' (eg, in the context of commercial advertising) and 'democratic freedom of speech', may require 'judicial balancing' of competing economic and political principles and judicial justification of the prevailing 'public reason'.

Rights-based constitutional approaches to multilevel regulation of economic cooperation among citizens do not deny the importance of 'economic analysis of law' for

human rights and constitutional rights. In contrast to positivist claims that judges have 'discretion' to decide disputes in the absence of a clear rule of law (*cf* Hart at 136), Dworkin's 'rights thesis' emphasises that – even if positive law may not specify the applicable rights in such 'hard cases' – the judge has to clarify the existing rights by means of 'just interpretation' of the existing rules and principles of law (*cf* R Dworkin (1977) introduction, at vii, 84–86). While Dworkin does not mention 'proportionality balancing' in his work, European courts and Art 52 of the EU Charter of Fundamental Rights recognize 'proportionality' analysis as a principle of constitutional law that is of crucial importance for clarifying rights in view of the indeterminate nature of constitutional systems.

[57] In order to avoid legal uncertainty, only violations of human rights, constitutional rights and other forms of 'extreme injustice' are likely to affect the validity of legal rules; *cf* R Alexy, *The Argument from Injustice* (Oxford: OUP, 2010).

clarifying, for instance, the 'basic principles . . . underlying this multilateral trading system' (Preamble WTO Agreement). These principles are also influenced by 'political economy' objectives as illustrated by the numerous safeguard clauses for protecting import-competing producers. Principles of justice and human rights leave open many questions of 'institutional design', for instance whether international organizations require more independent 'powers of initiative' and of monitoring in order to promote collective supply of international public goods more effectively. Nor do reasonable and stable 'principles of justice' (eg, as defined by human rights) prevent citizens, non-governmental organizations (NGOs), parliaments, governments, courts of justice and international organizations from advancing very diverse views about appropriate interpretations of IEL rules. Legal answers to many interpretive questions do not exist as objective truths to be empirically discovered in the real world; they rather depend on the prevailing 'public reason' and methodologies chosen for interpreting existing norms and developing new rules in order to realize legal, political and economic objectives more effectively. The universal recognition of 'the purposes of the United Nations' in terms of promotion of international cooperation and peaceful settlement of disputes 'in conformity with the principles of justice and international law', including 'promoting and encouraging respect for human rights and for fundamental freedoms for all without distinction as to race, sex, language, or religion' (Article 1 UN Charter), confirms the customary law requirement of interpreting and developing national and international legal systems in conformity with 'principles of justice' and the human rights obligations of states. The Preamble of the 1969 VCLT likewise recalls that 'disputes concerning treaties, like other international disputes, should be settled by peaceful means and in conformity with the principles of justice and international law', including, inter alia, 'respect for, and observance of, human rights and fundamental freedoms for all'.[58] Yet, individual and national conceptions of 'principles of justice', human rights and democratic constitutionalism may legitimately differ among citizens, peoples and countries. UN human rights law often provides only for minimum standards respecting national and regional 'margins of appreciation' for higher constitutional guarantees of fundamental rights and stronger judicial remedies by national and regional 'courts of justice'. European human rights law goes far beyond most UN human rights guarantees, for instance in terms of multilevel judicial guarantees by European courts of equal freedoms, non-discrimination and judicial protection of rule of law as constitutional rights and principles governing European economic integration law. Yet, it remains controversial, both inside and outside Europe, whether multilevel human rights and multilevel economic guarantees of freedom, non-discrimination and rule of law rest on common 'principles of justice'. For instance, are the distinctions between 'negative liberty' and 'positive liberty' in human rights law relevant context for similar distinctions in interpreting *ordo*-liberal conceptions of non-discriminatory competition (as specified in the Lisbon TFEU Protocol 27) and constitutional conceptions for a 'social market economy' (as postulated in Article 3 TEU)? Should international economic courts avoid

[58] Arguably, the Preamble language – 'Having in mind the principles of international law embodied in the Charter of the United Nations, such as . . . universal respect for, and observance of, human rights and fundamental freedoms for all' – refers not only to 'conditions under which justice and respect for the obligations arising from treaties can be maintained', but also to 'principles of justice and international law' in the preceding sub-paragraph, in conformity with the recognition in numerous legal systems that human rights constitute not only individual rights, but corresponding obligations of governments and 'principles of law' to be taken into account in legislation, administration and adjudication.

references to human rights in view of the widespread disagreement on the human rights dimensions of IEL?

The need for clarifying the 'normative premises' of IEL through democratic discourse and 'courts of justice'

The progressive development and expansion of European economic integration law since the 1950s illustrates how much international economic regulation depends on democratic and parliamentary discourses and 'judicial dialogues' among courts progressively clarifying and developing rules and 'public reason' in ways which citizens can understand, approve and politically support. Arguably, the universal recognition of human rights and the effectiveness of international economic regulation also require citizen-oriented conceptions of worldwide IEL based on individual and democratic self-governance and multilevel judicial protection of rule of law in international economic transactions among citizens. The EU Charter of Fundamental Rights, as incorporated into EU law by the 2007 Lisbon Treaty, and its distinction between dignity rights, liberty rights, equality rights, solidarity rights, citizen rights and rights to justice, illustrates that UN human rights law can be implemented at national and regional levels in legitimately diverse ways.

In view of the limited mandates of national and international courts deciding disputes on the basis of the applicable rules of law, and the legal methods of textual, contextual and functional treaty interpretation as codified in the VCLT (notably Articles 31–33), legal positivism has become the generally accepted starting point in research about IEL. Yet, legal positivism and textual interpretations of rules leave open many normative questions. The worldwide recognition – in more than a hundred UN human rights instruments since the entry into force of the 1945 UN Charter – of 'inalienable' human rights 'deriving from respect for human dignity' has incorporated natural law principles as an integral part of positive international law. Such principles may be relevant for interpreting the systemic nature of human rights,[59] the relationships between 'rules' and 'principles' in human rights law and IEL,[60] the legal clarification of 'common, but differentiated responsibilities' in international environmental law and the need for respecting the individual diversity of human beings, of their constitutional democracies and other forms of legitimate, social cooperation.[61] Many past doctrinal disputes among 'legal positivists' and 'natural rights theorists' – for instance, whether positive law includes only 'rules' or also 'principles' of law, and whether judges enjoy discretion in the absence of applicable rules – appear 'outdated' today in view of the explicit recognition and ever greater importance of 'general principles of law' in IEL and the acknowledgment by many courts that, in disputes over the contested meaning of imprecise rules,

[59] On the diverse conceptions of 'economic justice' and 'ecological justice' see, eg: G Chartier, *Economic Justice and Natural Law* (Oxford: OUP, 2009) (examining legal questions of ownership, production, distribution and consumption on the basis of a natural law theory of ethics).

[60] On the distinction between rules (whose limited scope of application and categorical 'if-then structure' apply in an 'all-or-nothing fashion' determining the outcome of a dispute irrespective of any other legal arguments made) and principles (as 'optimization requirements' requiring 'weighing and balancing' among competing principles to be realized in the whole legal order) as mutually exclusive sub-categories of legal norms see: R Alexy (2002).

[61] On the need for respecting 'reasonable disagreement' and the 'morality of conflicts' see J Rawls (1993) and S Besson (2005).

judges must find the 'right answer' through 'administration of justice', judicial clarification and 'balancing' of rules in light of applicable procedures and principles of law.[62] Yet, WTO dispute settlement bodies, investor–state arbitration and other economic courts often pragmatically avoid controversial questions about justice.

In disputes over the interpretation of economic rules, the parties to the dispute often base their conflicting interpretations on competing principles. For example, should freedom of commercial expression in the context of competition, unfair trade and consumer protection laws be construed in order to protect consumers, competitors or deliberative democracy? Do human rights justify interpreting international treaties not only as 'international law among states', but as 'international law among peoples' (as suggested by Rawls) and as 'cosmopolitan law' of citizens (as suggested by Kant) in order to protect individuals against abuses of power? To what extent should empirical, sociological, economic and 'system theories' influence the legal and judicial interpretation of WTO provisions referring to the 'multilateral trading system' and 'dispute settlement system' of the WTO? Why should WTO prohibitions of regulatory discrimination among 'like products' (eg, in Article III GATT) and 'like service providers' (eg, in the context of Article XVII GATS) only focus on economic competition criteria rather than also taking into account human rights as potential justification of regulatory and consumer preferences for goods that are produced without violation of human rights (eg, prohibiting child labour) and do not endanger human rights (eg, to human health protection)? Should governments and judicial review of anti-dumping measures take into account that economic theories (eg, about 'predatory dumping') may not justify imposition of anti-dumping duties on low-cost imports that enhance consumer welfare without undermining competition in the importing country? How should judges respond to 'normative advocacy' (eg, by individuals, private firms, other non-governmental organizations) for citizen-oriented interpretations of international economic rules (eg, regulating privatization of public water services) rather than state-centred interpretations advocated by governments in order to limit their legal and judicial accountability towards citizens?

From retrospective, legal positivism towards participatory 'legal constructivism'

The customary methods of international treaty interpretation give priority to textual, systemic and teleological interpretation methods (as codified in Article 31 VCLT) rather than focusing on the often contested 'historical intentions' of rulemakers (*cf* Article 32 VCLT). As most international economic treaties are concluded among states, textbooks on IEL tend to describe and explain the evolution of IEL as agreed among governments without challenging the often one-sided focus on reciprocal rights and duties of governments rather than of citizens. Similarly, 'economic analysis of law' often analyzes the economic rationale of economic rules (eg, for anti-dumping measures), and their impact on economic competition, consumer welfare and adjudication (eg, the empirical importance of 'private–public partnerships' for the success of complaints in GATT/WTO dispute settlement proceedings), without challenging governmental determinations of

[62] On the increasing resort – in international human rights law, labour law, trade and investment law and adjudication – to 'principle-oriented' interpretations and adjudication see: EU Petersmann, 'Judging Judges: From "Principal-Agent Theory" to "Constitutional Justice" in Multilevel Judicial Governance of Economic Cooperation among Citizens' (2008) 11 *JIEL* 827–84.

'national welfare' (eg, in terms of producer rather than general consumer welfare). This study shares the positivist legal premises that

- positive law must be distinguished from normative proposals for changing the existing rules;
- positive law must therefore also remain separable from moral principles that have not been incorporated into positive law; and
- the efficacy of legal systems requires that 'primary rules' of conduct and 'secondary rules' of recognition, change and adjudication must be established as 'social facts' reflected in social practices and sources of law.

Yet, substituting 'constitutional order' for anarchy in international economic relations requires going beyond descriptive, economic and empirical analyses of IEL by challenging authoritarian *normative legal doctrines* and reinterpreting international economic rules in conformity with the human rights obligations of states and their underlying 'constitutional principles'. Albert Einstein famously remarked: 'We can't solve problems by using the same kind of thinking we used when we created them'. As explained by the New Haven School's conception of international law as a 'constitutive process of authoritative decision-making' by individuals and democratic constituencies,[63] jurisprudence is also about making and developing international law through reasonable policy choices protecting human rights, democratic self-governance and a just social order. The less the 'IEL in the books' succeeds in realizing its development objectives, the stronger becomes the need for reviewing the 'IEL in action' from the diverse legal and policy perspectives of the various actors like individuals, firms, parliaments, intergovernmental lawmakers, national and international administrators, diplomats and judges. Normative legal and constitutional theory concentrates on the reasonable relationships between legal principles, rules and institutions and on their diverse perceptions depending on their 'observational standpoint' (eg, of diplomats, parliaments, international judges, impartial and reasonable citizens, non-governmental civil society organizations). The needed *policy-oriented legal analysis* must also take into account the social, economic and political conditions necessary for realizing legal and constitutional policy objectives.

Democratic and cosmopolitan reforms of IEL depend on 'struggles for rights'

Constitutionalism cannot be understood without the historical insights gained in the 'trials and errors' of 'democratic constitutionalism' – from the ancient Greek city republics to the

[63] On the interdisciplinary 'New Haven methodology' of analyzing national and international law as decision-making processes that are both 'authoritative and controlling' in the pursuit of a 'public order of human dignity' enabling individuals to realize their human aspirations in their 'civic order', proceeding from the equal worth of all individuals and the right to individual self-development as constitutional core values, see: MS McDougal, 'The World Constitutive Process of Authoritative Decision' in MS McDougal and WM Reisman, *International Law in Contemporary Perspective: The Public Order of the World Community. Cases and Materials* (Mineola: Foundation Press, 1981) 191 ff; WM Reisman, S Wiessner and AR Willard, 'The New Haven School: A Brief Introduction' (2007) 32 *The Yale Journal of International Law* 587–94. The policy-oriented 'democratic participant perspective' of the New Haven School is justified in international law by the worldwide recognition of human rights by all UN member states. 'Realist' claims of 'impartial description' of the continuing reality of power-oriented state practices refute neither the normative limitations of state sovereignty by modern human rights law nor the increasing recognition of individual rights and judicial remedies of individuals in ever more fields of positive international law.

2007 Lisbon Treaty on the EU – that law as an instrument of social self-governance cannot remain legitimate and effective without 'principles of justice' and their legislative, administrative and judicial protection and institutionalization through constitutional 'checks and balances' at national and international levels of legal regulation. Without 'participatory' and 'deliberative democracy', the 'public reason' necessary for supporting democratic self-governance and rule of law cannot be maintained over time.[64] Enabling citizens to defend their human rights and constitutional rights promotes 'participatory democracy' and 'deliberative democracy' complementing 'parliamentary democracy' by constitutional limitations on majority politics. The ubiquity of conflicts inside the human mind (eg, among our rational search for professional success and our limited reasonableness towards others), among self-interested individuals as well as among societies competing for scarce resources requires *constitutional* and *constructivist approaches* to law which, as explained in theories of justice from Kant to Rawls, must institutionalize 'public reason'. The legitimately diverse 'constitutional traditions' at national and international levels of regulation must be rendered compatible within a 'multilevel constitutional framework' for interpreting and progressively developing IEL with due respect for the constitutional and human rights obligations of governments vis-à-vis their citizens as the 'democratic owners' of IEL and the main actors in the worldwide division of labour. The normative policy goal of an international legal order protecting human rights requires respect for the legitimate diversity of individual life plans, of democratic communities and of the indeterminacy of many international rules. The needed reforms of IEL require critical review of authoritarian claims to legal domination (eg, based on 'legal privileges' in the allocation of decision-making powers in the Bretton Woods institutions). 'Cosmopolitan interpretations' of international rules may be preconditions for international rule of law and also for democratic support in poor countries that may rightly insist on 'common but differentiated responsibilities' for collective supply of global public goods.

The historical evolution of private law, economic law, constitutional law and of human rights has often been driven by 'struggles for rights' by self-interested citizens challenging abuses of power and resorting to political and judicial remedies:

> The law is not mere theory, but living force. And hence it is that Justice which, in one hand holds the scales in which she weights the rights, carries in the other the sword with which she executes it. The sword without the scales is brute force; the scales without the sword is the impotence of law.[65]

The successful transformation of Europe by citizen-driven European law has confirmed the frequent experiences of European citizens that democratic peace and mutually bene-

[64] On the various 'political inventions' (Riklin) of constitutionalism – like the principles of legality, separation of powers (eg, by means of a 'mixed constitution', separation of legislative, executive and judicial powers), limitation of powers by constitutional rights (including 'inalienable human rights'), democratic participation in the exercise of government powers and social dispersion of power through legal and social protection of weaker parties (like children and women, unemployed and sick people, consumers and employees) – see: A Riklin, *Machtteilung. Geschichte der Mischverfassung* (Darmstadt: Wissenschaftliche Buchgesellschaft, 2006). As explained in my previous publications (*cf* n 28), the Kantian idea of multilevel protection of human rights by multilevel constitutional restraints of foreign policy powers – and its practical application in constitutional democracies and European law – are of constitutional importance for limiting the 'constitutional failures' of UN law in order to strengthen the potential, yet insufficiently realized function of the UN Charter as an international 'constitution of the international community' for the protection of collective security, complementing the diverse national constitutions (*cf* Fassbender (2009)).

[65] R Jhering, *The Struggle for Law* (Chicago: Callaghan, 1915) 1–2.

ficial trade across Europe depend on the 'enlightened courage'[66] of citizens to defend individual and democratic self-governance against power politics and discriminatory boundaries. Rule of law in the EU's common market depends more on its decentralized enforcement by EU citizens than on infringement proceedings by the EU Commission (Article 258 TFEU) or by a member state (Article 259 TFEU) challenging failures by other member states to fulfil EU legal obligations. By enabling EU citizens and non-governmental organizations (like companies, trade unions, other NGOs) to directly invoke and enforce primary and secondary EU law in national courts and EU courts, EU law has become more effective, more citizen-driven and more legally coherent (eg, in terms of limiting the discretion of the EU institutions in selecting and prioritizing infringement proceedings). The decentralized enforcement of EU rules has changed 'public reason' inside the EU by including private interests and private rights more comprehensively than in intergovernmental proceedings focusing on rights of states and of EU institutions which often pursue bureaucratic self-interests (eg, in avoiding legal and judicial accountability for their own violations of EU law and of international treaty obligations).[67]

Kantian and Rawlsian theories of justice suggest that maximum equal liberties must be constitutionally protected – in the economy no less than in the polity – as 'first principles of justice', for instance as in German and European constitutional law (as discussed in chapters III and VI). Such constitutional 'principles of justice' also justify liberal (ie, liberty-based) consumer-driven competition and international trade in economic markets supplementing democratic self-governance in 'political markets' – provided autonomous self-development, mutually beneficial cooperation among free citizens, market failures as well as 'governance failures' are adequately regulated. Democratic support for 'market freedoms' is, however, often impeded by the fact that the thousands of private and public, national and intergovernmental regulations of transnational economic and environmental relations, and their complex interactions, have become incomprehensible for most citizens. It is only by identifying and explaining 'principles of justice' justifying IEL that the 'forest' behind the innumerable 'trees' of IEL can become comprehensible again and democratically supported by citizens. The citizen-oriented principles of modern human rights law and of European economic integration law challenge the *legitimacy* of many state-centred, power-oriented principles underlying trade, financial and environmental regulation beyond Europe, such as authoritarian ideologies of 'member-driven trade governance' in the WTO without any mention of human rights and of general consumer welfare in WTO rules and WTO dispute settlement proceedings. Citizens depend increasingly on traded goods (like food and medicines), related services (like transport, telecommunication and information networks) and on international 'public goods'. The collective production of such public goods – like food security, health security, energy security, freedom of information and climate change prevention – will depend on democratic support and participation by civil society and business no less than on intergovernmental rulemaking. Paternalistic treatment of citizens as mere objects of global economic governance contributes to alienation and 'rational ignorance'

[66] *cf* I Kant, 'What is Enlightenment?' in Kant (1970) 54: 'Enlightenment is man's emergence from his self-incurred immaturity . . . The motto of enlightenment is therefore: *Sapere aude*! Have courage to use your own understanding'.

[67] For examples where lawyers of the EU Commission patently misled the ECJ about EC obligations under GATT law (eg, an unpublished GATT dispute settlement ruling) in order to avoid their own legal and judicial accountability for violations of GATT rules, see: EU Petersmann, 'Darf die EG das Völkerrecht Ignorieren?' (1997) Europäische Zeitschrift für Wirtschaftsrecht 325–31, 651–53.

of citizens in respect of IEL. It is only through a 'democratic paradigm change' in IEL and 'struggles for cosmopolitan rights' that many abuses of secretive intergovernmental rulemaking for the benefit of powerful interest groups and other authoritarian practices can be effectively challenged, like the 'lending privilege' and 'resource privilege' of democratically unaccountable regimes exploiting foreign loans and domestic resources for their self-interests.

Lack of democratic 'input legitimacy' and paternalistic exclusion of citizens as mere objects of IEL also undermine the effectiveness of international regulation. For instance, due to a lack of effective remedies against welfare-reducing violations of WTO guarantees of non-discriminatory market access, many trade disputes are 'politicized' and settled in intergovernmental WTO dispute settlement proceedings rather than in domestic courts. Civil society often cannot hold governments accountable for their international 'governance failures' to protect human rights, as illustrated by the unnecessary poverty of more than one billion people living on one dollar or less per day and the premature death of more than 18 million people per annum due to malnutrition, preventable diseases and other poverty-related causes.[68] The structural changes in European economic and human rights law, international investment law and international criminal law, and the ever greater influence of 'courts of justice' on the interpretation and progressive development of IEL and human rights, were often introduced in response to struggles for more citizen-oriented conceptions of international law. Just as the ever larger number of national democratic constitutions responded to citizen claims for constitutional protection of 'life, liberty and the pursuit of happiness' (as proclaimed in the US Declaration of Independence of 1776) in order 'to establish justice' and 'promote the general welfare' (as stated in the Preamble of the US Constitution of 1789), so depends more effective protection of life, liberty, justice and consumer welfare of citizens on individual and democratic 'struggles for justice' and their legal and judicial protection by parliaments, governments and 'courts of justice'.

3 DEFINING 'CONSTITUTIONS', 'CONSTITUTIONALISM' AND 'CONSTITUTIONALIZATION' OF IEL

The ever more comprehensive literature analyzing and criticizing international law from 'constitutional perspectives' often leads to misunderstandings caused by diverse uses of 'constitutional terms' as well as by the diversity of national and regional constitutional traditions in civil law countries, common law countries and many LDCs. This study uses the terms 'constitution', constitutionalism', 'constitutionalization' and 'constitutional approach' to IEL as explained in my previous publications.[69] *Constitution* refers to a

[68] *cf* T Pogge (2003) 2 ff. On cosmopolitan duties to assist poor people to enjoy their human rights see also: H Shue, 'Global Accountability: Transnational Duties toward Economic Rights' in JM Coicaud, MW Doyle and AM Gardner (eds), *The Globalization of Human Rights* (Cambridge: CUP, 2003) 160 ff.

[69] *cf* Petersmann (1991). For the variety of constitutional conceptions see J Raz, 'On the Authority and Interpretation of Constitutions: Some Preliminaries' in L Alexander (ed), *Constitutionalism* (Cambridge: CUP, 1998) 152 ff. Functional conceptions of 'constitutional rules' are also applied by economists like G Brennan and J Buchanan, *The Reason of Rules: Constitutional Political Economy* (Cambridge: Harvard University Press, 1985), who perceive the basic norms enabling citizens to overcome collective action problems and build stable forms of social, democratic cooperation as constitutive of communities. Political scientists like A Stone Sweet use the following three criteria for defining international regimes as 'constitutional': (1) the regime must establish rights among states or other legal persons that are subject to judicial enforcement; (2) the jurisdic-

coherent set of long-term principles and rules of a higher legal rank constituting the basic order of a political community (eg, in a state), or of a functionally limited community (eg, based on an international 'treaty constitution' for the collective supply of international public goods), with legislative, administrative and dispute settlement functions for the maintenance of rule of law for the benefit of citizens. This general concept of a constitution covers both comprehensive 'big C constitutionalism' for national constitutions and functionally limited 'small c constitutionalism' for 'international treaty constitutions' such as the EU Treaty and the ECHR as interpreted by European courts. Constitutions serve multiple functions, both constituting, constraining, regulating and justifying constitutional rights and governance powers and coordinating national and international legal systems by 'supplementary constitutional restraints' and multilevel rules with interrelated 'constitutional functions'. The main constitutional challenge in the twenty-first century is to protect human rights, rule of law, democratic supply of public goods and judicial protection of individual rights beyond state borders to empower citizens to increase their welfare through mutually beneficial cooperation in the global division of labour. Many international 'treaty constitutions' can serve 'constitutional functions' for protecting equal rights, rule of law, transparent self-governance of citizens across frontiers and for 'constitutionalizing' foreign policy powers even if the respective rules are not formally designated as 'constitutional', for instance in international treaties and in the few countries without a written, national constitution.

Constitutionalism refers to the political method of using constitutional principles, rules and institutions (such as constitutional conventions elaborating constitutional rules) for the collective supply of national and international public goods. Multilevel constitutionalism uses constitutional principles, rules and institutions at national and international levels of governance for the collective supply of international public goods, for instance by constituting and limiting international trade organizations with legislative, executive and judicial powers for protecting transnational rule of law among citizens. The legitimacy of multilevel constitutionalism depends on democratic participation of citizens and on parliamentary, administrative and judicial protection of general citizen interests as defined by human rights and equal constitutional rights.[70]

Constitutionalization refers to legal methods aimed at strengthening constitutional principles, rules and institutions (like protection of constitutional rights by democratic governance and 'courts of justice') in the diverse forms of national and international rulemaking, rule-administration and rule enforcement. Democratic constitutionalism

tion of the regime's 'court' must be compulsory (eg, as in the case of the EC Court, the ECtHR and the WTO dispute settlement bodies); and (3) the dispute settlement methods must be akin to those used by constitutional courts in their adjudication of conflicts between rights and state interests recognized by the regime's constitution: *cf* A Stone Sweet, 'Constitutionalism, Legal Pluralism and International Regimes' (2009) 16 *Indiana Journal of Global Legal Studies* 621 ff.

[70] The term 'constitutionalism' tends to be used today mainly for liberal and cosmopolitan conceptions of constitutions: *cf* M Kumm, 'The Cosmopolitan Turn in Constitutionalism' in JL Dunoff and JP Trachtman (eds) (2009) 258–324. Kumm's 'cosmopolitan constitutionalism' seems to be consistent with my own constitutional arguments: *cf* EU Petersmann, 'How to Constitutionalize International Law and Foreign Policy for the Benefit of Civil Society?' (1999) 20 *Michigan Journal of International Law* 1–30. Constitutions may also exist in non-democratic countries without 'constitutionalism', referring both to substantive as well as procedural rules (eg, establishing governance institutions and the 'secondary rules' defining how other norms are created, interpreted, changed and enforced). On reconciling 'big C' national constitutionalism with 'small c' multilevel constitutionalism in order to better protect common constitutional principles justifying and limiting multilevel economic governance for the benefit of citizens see: Petersmann (1991) 363 ff.

emphasizes the need for systemic 'constitutional constraints' on all governance powers. Politicians and private holders of economic power, by contrast, have self-interests in limiting their legal and judicial accountability. The normative linkages between the diverse individual, democratic, legislative, executive and judicial dimensions of constitutionalism are illustrated by the manifold tasks of 'courts of justice'. Independent and impartial, judicial settlement of disputes over the interpretation and application of rules promotes judicial clarification and continuous adaptation of legal systems to the needs of citizens; it offers citizen-driven modes of 'judicial governance' and – as a principle-oriented 'constitutional restraint' on majoritarian rulemaking by political institutions – can protect individual and democratic diversity against the potential 'tyranny of majority politics', thereby supplementing and constitutionally limiting majoritarian democracy. Also most international trade and investment disputes are initiated – directly or indirectly (eg, in case of diplomatic protection of citizen rights by the home state) – at the request of citizens in order to defend their rights against alleged abuses of private and public power. 'Multilevel judicial governance' is more developed in IEL governing international economic cooperation among citizens than in other fields of international law.[71] Empirical evidence confirms that – notably in regional economic integration law, human rights law and in international investment law – constitutional rights of citizens and their judicial protection have proven to offer the most effective means of empowering citizens to challenge welfare reducing restrictions by governments and business.

Human rights and 'democratic constitutionalism' require 'constitutional approaches' to multilevel economic and environmental regulation

Since the UDHR of 1948, all UN member states have acknowledged in numerous UN human rights instruments – as discussed in more detail in chapter III – their legal obligation to respect, protect and promote 'inalienable' and 'indivisible' human rights, including rights to direct democratic participation in periodical elections of representative governments (*cf* Article 21 UDHR) and rights of 'access to justice'. The universal recognition of obligations to protect 'human rights . . . by the rule of law' (Preamble UDHR) reflects the constitutional insight that all government powers must be constitutionally restrained and legitimated by individual rights and other constitutional rules of a higher legal rank. Almost all UN member states have adopted national constitutions (written or unwritten) and ratified functionally limited, international 'treaty constitutions' for the protection of collective security (eg, based on the UN Charter) and of mutually beneficial economic cooperation. The recognition – that 'everyone is entitled to a social and international order in which the rights and freedoms set forth in this Declaration can be fully realized' (Article 28 UDHR) – explains the increasing linkages between international 'treaty constitutions' and human rights, as illustrated by the explicit mandates in the 'Constitutions' (*sic*) of the ILO, WHO, UNESCO and FAO to protect fundamental labour rights and other fundamental rights to health protection, education and 'freedom from hunger'.

[71] *cf* Joerges and Petersmann (eds) (2006). See also M Shapiro and A Stone Sweet, *On Law, Politics and Judicialization* (Oxford: OUP, 2004) ch 4 (describing adjudication as a particular mode of governance, through which the legal structures of a legal community are continuously adapted to the needs and purposes of citizens and governments).

This need to respect human rights and fundamental freedoms in all transnational relations has been confirmed in numerous UN instruments not only for international economic relations,[72] but also for international environmental and political cooperation. For instance, the 1972 'Stockholm Declaration' of the UN Conference on the Human Environment proclaimed that 'man has the fundamental right to . . . adequate conditions of life, in an environment of a quality that permits a life of dignity and well-being, and he bears a solemn responsibility to protect and improve the environment for present and future generations'.[73] Even though there a few explicit references to economic and environmental regulation in UN human rights instruments, an increasing number of international treaties, court decisions and acts of international organizations recognize that economic and 'environmental issues are best handled with the participation of all concerned citizens, at the relevant level'.[74] Regional and worldwide courts likewise acknowledge that – as Judge Weeramantry observed in his Separate Opinion in the *Gabcikovo-Nagymaros* dispute between Hungary and Slovakia – 'protection of the environment is . . . a vital part of contemporary human rights doctrine, for it is a *sine qua non* for numerous human rights such as the right to health and the right to life itself'.[75] Even though human rights are inherently anthropocentic – while some environmental rules protect the environment per se – there is an increasing jurisprudence by human rights bodies (like the ECtHR and the Inter-American Commission on Human Rights) interpreting human rights guarantees in the light of environmental law.[76] Respect for human rights has been especially important for protecting rights to participate in environmental decision-making and for respecting the legitimate diversity of national and international rules connecting and 'balancing' civil, political, economic, social and environmental rights and regulations.

The explicit commitments to promotion and protection of human rights in the UN Charter as well as in the law of UN Specialized Agencies support this study's claim that the human rights obligations of states, and the constitutional limitation of their government powers, require – as a matter of positive law – constitutional protection of individual rights in transnational economic cooperation. The codification – in the Preamble and Article 31 of the VCLT – of the customary law requirement of interpreting international law in conformity with the human rights obligations of states and other 'principles of justice' supports this 'constitutional requirement' of limiting abuses of public and private power in order to legally protect rights of citizens.[77] As illustrated by the increasing number of UN and UNESCO resolutions on 'duties to protect' citizens against violations of human and cultural rights by their own governments, the government obligations to respect, protect and promote human rights at home and abroad justify

[72] *cf* the 1976 UN General Assembly Resolution A/3281 on the 'Charter of Economic Rights and Duties of States'.

[73] *cf* UN Doc A/Conf 48/14/Rev 1 (1973) 3.

[74] Rio Declaration on Environment and Development, UN Conference on Environment and Development UN Doc A/Conf 151/5/Rev 1 (1992).

[75] *Hungary v Slovakia* [1997] ICJ Rep 7, 88.

[76] *cf* T Stephens, *International Courts and Environmental Protection* (Cambridge: CUP, 2009); D Shelton, 'Developing Substantive Environmental Rights' (2010) 1 *Journal of Human Rights and the Environment* 89 ff.

[77] *cf* EU Petersmann, 'International Trade Law, Human Rights and the Customary International Law Rules on Treaty Interpretation' in S Joseph, D Kinley and J Waincymer (eds) (2009) 69–90.

reconceptualizing sovereignty as responsibility *erga omnes* requiring rights-based, democratic and cosmopolitan reforms of the existing global governance system.[78]

The terms 'constitution', 'constitutionalism' and 'constitutionalization' are used both descriptively as well as prescriptively. From a *descriptive positive law perspective*, it is argued that the constitutional limitation of all government powers entails that legislative, administrative and also intergovernmental regulation must be interpreted with due regard to the constitutional context, the reality of 'constitutional pluralism' and the respective 'principles of justice' incorporated into the legal system concerned. The mere text of many legal rules remains inevitably indeterminate and contested depending on the rational self-interests of different interpreters. For instance, government officials may focus on their 'government discretion'; legislators on their parliamentary or 'democratic discretion'; judges on 'administration of justice'; and citizens are likely to defend their constitutional rights and rational self-interests. In the inevitable 'balancing' and reconciliation of competing rights of domestic and foreign citizens, legislators, administrators, judges and (non) governmental organizations must justify their respective 'weighting' of economic and non-economic values in terms of constitutional principles like respect for human rights, rule of law, and proportionality of government restriction of individual rights.[79] If IEL is explicitly 'founded on the principles of liberty, democracy, respect for human rights and fundamental freedoms, and the rule of law, principles which are common to the Member States', as in Article 6 of the EU's Nice Treaty, such constitutional context may be legally relevant for interpreting economic rules and governance powers.[80] Independent and impartial 'courts of justice' and 'deliberative democracy' are more likely to interpret IEL in conformity with human rights and 'principles of justice' than self-interested political institutions.

From a *prescriptive legal policy perspective*, human rights and other 'principles of justice' may justify 'struggles for rights' by citizens and parliaments for additional legal, parliamentary and judicial 'checks and balances' of intergovernmental regulation. For instance, the progressive transformation of the EC, EU, EEA Treaties and of the ECHR into 'constitutional instruments' for the protection of fundamental rights of European citizens was mainly due to the judicial protection of fundamental rights by the ECJ, the EFTA Court, the ECtHR and national courts at the request of adversely affected citizens, albeit with due judicial respect for the legitimate diversity of national constitutions and the necessary 'subsidiarity' of multilevel regulation of transnational economic cooperation among citizens.[81] Comparative studies of constitutional and judicial protection of

[78] *cf* G Brock, *Global Justice. A Cosmopolitan Account* (Oxford: OUP, 2009). On 'rights constitutionalism' and rights-based conceptions of law and adjudication see: GW Anderson, *Constitutional Rights after Globalization* (Oxford: Hart Publishing, 2005). On the 'ongoing process of a humanization of sovereignty (as) a cornerstone of the current transformation of international law into an individual-centered system' see also: A Peters, 'Humanity as the Alpha and Omega of Sovereignty' (2009) 20 *EJIL* 513–44.

[79] On 'balancing' and 'weighting' of competing rights and legal principles, which are discussed in more detail below (eg, chs III and VIII), see: Alexy (2002) and notably R Alexy, 'The Weight Formula' in J Stelmach, B Brozek and W Zaluski (eds), *Studies in the Philosophy of Law. Frontiers of the Economic Analysis of Law* (2007) 9–28.

[80] *cf* EU Petersmann, 'De-Fragmentation of International Economic Law through Constitutional Interpretation and Adjudication with Due Respect for Reasonable Disagreement' (2008–09) 6 *Loyola University Chicago International Law Review* 209–48.

[81] The Treaty of Lisbon amending the Treaty on European Union and the Treaty establishing the European Community (published in the EU Official Journal C 306 of 17 December 2007 as well as in: The Lisbon Treaty, Foundation for EU Democracy 2008) entered into force on 1 December 2009; it incorporates the 'principle of subsidiarity' into the revised Art 5 TEU and specifies its legal consequences in the 'Protocol on the application of the principles of subsidiarity and proportionality'.

free movements of goods, services, persons, capital and related payments in unitary states, federal states and regional free trade areas and customs unions suggest that the constitutional value of economic freedoms, and the constitutional requirement of 'balancing' and reconciling economic with non-economic freedoms and other constitutional rights, are increasingly recognized by national and international jurisdictions, as illustrated by the judicial protection of investor rights under Chapter 11 of NAFTA or by the case law of the High Court of Australia in relation to the constitutional guarantees of free movement of goods and persons in Section 92 of the Australian Constitution.[82]

4 WHY COSMOPOLITAN LEGAL ORDERS ARE MORE EFFECTIVE AND MORE LEGITIMATE

There is a long tradition in international law doctrine challenging 'states-only conceptions' by 'individualistic conceptions' of international law on the ground that

> (t)here is no rule of international law which precludes individuals and bodies other than States from acquiring directly rights under customary or conventional international law and, to that extent, becoming subjects of the Law of Nations. . . . The conferment of such rights may cover either particular rights or the so-called fundamental rights of the individual in general. With regard to the latter, there is room for the view that having regard to the inherent purposes of international law, of which the individual is the ultimate unit, he is in that capacity a subject of international law . . . there has been an increasing realization that the direct subjection of the individual to the rule of international law is an essential condition of the strengthening of the ethical basis of international law.[83]

In the twenty-first century, there are many reasons not only for an 'open conception' of international law that any legal entity addressed by an international rule can be a legal subject of international law, without any a priori exclusion of international persons. As human rights and constitutional democracy are necessary for protecting private and public autonomy, peaceful discourse and cooperation among free and equal citizens,[84] human rights law also justifies a presumption that – at least in certain fields like human rights and economic integration law where citizens are the main actors, beneficiaries and ultimate sources of value – precise and unconditional guarantees of individual freedom, non-discrimination and rule of law should be interpreted for the benefit of citizens as protecting also individual rights (eg, to hold governments accountable for internationally wrongful acts). Empowerment of citizens sets incentives for decentralized review and enforcement of international rules by self-interested citizens as guardians of the rule of

[82] On the judicial interpretation of the constitutional freedom of interstate trade among the states of the commonwealth of Australia see: G Villalta Puig, *The High Court of Australia and Section 92 of the Australian Constitution* (Sydney: T Reuters Lawbook Co, 2008). For comparisons of constitutional and judicial protection of freedom of trade in Europe, Japan and the United States see: Hilf and Petersmann (eds) (1993). For an analysis of investor–state arbitration see ch VIII.

[83] H Lauterpacht, 'The Subjects of the Law of Nations' in E Lauterpacht (ed), *International Law: Being the Collected Papers of Hersch Lauterpacht* (Cambridge: CUP, 1975) 526 f. On the five different conceptions of personality in international law, their origins and legal manifestations see: R Portmann, *Legal Personality in International Law* (Cambridge: CUP, 2010) 29–242.

[84] On the justification of human rights and democratic decision-making as being logically necessary for discourse, majority decisions and rule of law among free and equal human beings see, eg: R Alexy, 'Discourse Theory and Human Rights' (1996) 9 *Ratio Juris* 209–35 and R Alexy, 'The Dual Nature of Law' (2010) 23 *Ratio Juris* 167–82.

law. National and international human rights law and the human rights obligations of UN member states call for reviewing IEL from the perspective of 'normative individualism': all values protected by governmental measures must be justifiable in terms of human rights of citizens.[85] From the perspective of human rights and constitutional democracies, natural persons – rather than sovereign states – are 'the primary international legal persons and the primary members of the global constitutional community'.[86] The principle of state sovereignty 'has already been relegated to the status of a second-order norm which is derived from and geared towards the protection of basic human rights, needs, interests, and security'.[87]

As 'everyone has the right to recognition everywhere as a person before the law' (Article 6 UDHR, Article 16 ICCPR), human rights call for a 'humanization of international law'.[88] Especially in citizen-driven areas of the global division of labour –like consumer-driven international competition, private investments and savings, international production, trade and migration and international consular protection of citizens abroad[89] – respect for 'human dignity' as a 'human right to have international rights' calls for interpreting IEL rules for the benefit of citizens as protecting individual rights to democratic participation, rule of law and legal and judicial remedies vis-à-vis intergovernmental regulation.[90] As in competition and common market rules inside constitutional democracies and European economic law, citizens must also be legally recognized and constitutionally protected as primary legal subjects in their *transnational* division of labour and economic cooperation across national frontiers, even if governments do not explicitly provide for individual rights. As famously stated by the ECJ:

> [T]he fact that certain provisions of the Treaty are formally addressed to the Member States does not prevent rights from being conferred at the same time on any individual who has an interest in compliance with the obligations thus laid down (see Case 43/75 *Defrenne v Sabena* [1976] ECR 455, para 31). Such consideration must, *a fortiori*, be applicable to Article 48 of the Treaty, which . . . is designed to ensure that there is no discrimination in the labour market.[91]

Regional and worldwide IEL are characterized increasingly by legal and judicial protection of individual trading rights (eg, based on the WTO Protocol for the Accession of China); investor rights (eg, based on BITs); intellectual property rights (eg, based on WIPO conventions and the TRIPS Agreement); labour rights (eg, based on ILO conventions); and other cosmopolitan rights (eg, of individual access to justice).

[85] On 'normative individualism' and human rights as constitutional foundations of modern international law see, eg: F Teson, *A Philosophy of International Law* (Boulder: Westview Press, 1998) 27.

[86] *cf* A Peters, 'Membership in the Global Constitutional Community' in J Klabbers, A Peters and G Ulfstein (2009) 157.

[87] Peters (n 78) 544. On the responsibilities of governments and international organization to protect human rights see: C Verlage, *Responsibility to Protect* (Tübingen: Mohr Siebeck Verlag, 2009).

[88] *cf* T Meron, *The Humanization of International Law* (Oxford: OUP, 2006).

[89] *cf LaGrand Case (Germany v United States)* [2001] ICJ Rep 466, para 77.

[90] On the long-standing international law traditions of recognizing individuals as legal subjects of international law see: Peters (n 86) 158 ff; JE Nijman, *The Concept of International Legal Personality: An Inquiry into the History and Theory of International Law* (The Hague: TMC Asser, 2004).

[91] *cf* Case C-281/98, *Angonese* [2000] ECR I-4139.

Transformation of European economic law into a multilevel constitutional order based on parliamentary, 'participatory' and 'deliberative democracy'

National and European courts of justice interpret national and European economic regulations of international movements of goods, services, persons, capital and related payments with due regard to the human rights obligations and constitutional principles at the respective levels of governance, as explicitly required by Article 2 of the Lisbon TEU:

> The Union is founded on the values of respect for human dignity, freedom, democracy, equality, the rule of law and respect for human rights, including the rights of persons belonging to minorities. These values are common to the Member States in a society in which pluralism, non-discrimination, tolerance, justice, solidarity and equality between women and men prevail.

In European economic law, the agreements establishing the EU, the EEA and the ECHR have been interpreted by national and European courts as 'constitutional instruments' protecting fundamental rights, rule of law and democratic self-governance of European citizens across frontiers, with due respect for the diversity of constitutional democracies in Europe and for their diverse approaches to intergovernmental economic regulation (eg, inside the European Economic Area). The national constitutions in the 27 EU member states, like the EU and EEA treaties, are interpreted and progressively developed as complementary, multilevel constitutional frameworks protecting dignity rights, individual freedoms, equality rights, solidarity rights, citizen rights and rights of access to justice for the benefit of EU citizens, as codified in the EU Charter of Fundamental Rights.[92] The Lisbon Treaty and its 'provisions on democratic principles' (Title II TEU) have further strengthened the role of national parliaments and of the European Parliament in European legislation and decision-making as well as additional forms of 'participatory' and 'deliberative democracy', including rights of EU citizens to petition the EU Commission to 'submit any appropriate proposal on matters where citizens consider that a legal act of the Union is required for the purpose of implementing the Treaties' (Article 11 TEU). In contrast to political rights that tend to be limited to the citizens of the polity concerned (eg, national and EU citizens), legal and judicial protection of civil, economic, social and cultural human rights and of related fundamental freedoms continues to progressively expand across Europe. The EU Treaty guarantees of free movements of persons, freedom of profession and freedom of establishment apply to all EU and EEA citizens and are partly extended to third countries in the context of the EU's free trade agreements with associated third countries. The EU and EEA guarantees of free movements of goods, services, capital and related payments are also legally and judicially protected inside the EEA for the benefit of nationals from third countries lawfully operating inside the EEA. The multilevel judicial protection by national courts, the ECJ and the EFTA Court of 'market freedoms', social rights (eg, to equal pay for equal work of men and women, non-discriminatory access of family members of EU migrant workers to social services) and human rights as fundamental freedoms of EU

[92] On the EU Charter of Fundamental Rights adopted in December 2000 (Official Journal of the EC of 18 December 2000, C 364/1-21), and on its interpretation by national and European courts even prior to its formal incorporation into EU law by the 2007 Lisbon Treaty, see: F Amici, V Papa and E Sacca (eds), *The Courts and the Nice Charter*, available at: www.lex.unict.it/eurolabor/en/research/dossier/dossier12.pdf.

citizens and cosmopolitan rights of nationals from third countries continues to dynamically evolve.[93] The controversies about the judicial 'balancing' of common market freedoms and discriminatory uses of trade union rights by the EC Court of Justice in the 2007 'Laval' and 'Viking disputes', [94] and about the exclusion of certain collective agreements from the scope of EU competition disciplines in the 'Albany' and 'Wouters' judgments of the ECJ,[95] illustrate that the impact of European integration on national and European social rights of EC citizens remains contested in view of the traditionally diverse 'social models' inside EU member states.[96]

Since the 1960s, the 'common market freedoms' of European integration law have brought European citizens unprecedented legal and democratic stability and social welfare across national frontiers. The 'Anglo-Saxon prioritization' of civil and political freedoms over protection of economic 'common law freedoms' and social rights is increasingly overcome in European constitutional and integration law. The non-economic achievements of European economic law – like transnational rule of law, democratic peace and ever more comprehensive constitutional rights of EU citizens at national and European levels of governance – are increasingly recognized as the most important results of the diverse European integration agreements. By contrast, regional and bilateral economic agreements outside Europe – like the North American Free Trade Agreement (NAFTA) and BITs – focus more one-sidedly on legal and judicial protection of investor rights, intellectual property rights and rights of producers in national courts, investor–state arbitration, NAFTA panels (eg, pursuant to Chapter 19 NAFTA) and regional courts (like the Andean Common Market Court) without references to human rights. Beyond Europe, the cosmopolitan ideal – that citizens should be protected by civil, economic and social rights and corresponding obligations and judicial remedies in their worldwide division of labour at home and abroad – tends to be far less protected by international law.

EU decision-making, albeit by necessity slow, is today often more transparent, more constitutionally restrained and more democratically accountable to national parliaments and the European Parliament and democratically elected governments than multilevel economic decision-making in most states outside Europe.[97] The emergence of multilevel

[93] *cf* T Kingreen, 'Fundamental Freedoms'; A Hatje, 'The Economic Constitution'; and J Drexl, 'Competition Law as Part of the European Constitution' in von Bogdandy and Bast (eds) (2006) 549–86, 587–632 and 633–74; HW Micklitz, 'Judicial Activism of the European Court of Justice and the Development of the European Social Model in Anti-Discrimination and Consumer Law' in U Neergaard, R Nielsen and L Roseberry (eds), *The Role of Courts in Developing a European Social Model* (Copenhagen: DJOF, 2010) 25–61.

[94] *cf* L Azoulai, 'The Court of Justice and the Social Market Economy: The Emergence of an Ideal and the Conditions for its Realization' (2008) *CMLR* 1335–56.

[95] *cf* LS Rossi and SJ Curzon, 'An Evolving "Rule of Reason" in the European Market' in G Bongiovanni, G Sartor and C Valentini (eds) (2009) 405–19.

[96] For a criticism of the 'Laval' and 'Viking' jurisprudence of the ECJ from the perspective of 'social justice' see, eg: C Joerges, 'A Renaissance of the European Economic Constitution?' in U Neergaard, R Nielsen and L Roseberry (eds), *Integrating Welfare Functions into EU Law: From Rome to Lisbon* (Copenhagen: DJOF, 2009) 29–52, 29 ff.

[97] This normative judgment is without prejudice to the German Constitutional Court's decision of 30 June 2009 (see Table 13) that the German ratification of the 2007 Lisbon Treaty on the European Union must be complemented by stronger participatory rights of the German Parliament in the voting of German representatives in the EU Council; *cf* the editorial comment on this judgment in (2009) 46 *Common Market Law Review* 1023–33. On the divergent views on whether EU law promotes democracy (eg, in terms of transparent and accountable governance, participation of citizens, parliamentary co-decision, a lively cross-border public space) or whether the EU is structurally inconsistent with democracy (eg, in terms of inadequate protection of political equality and of equal representation of all EU citizens in the European Parliament) see, eg: D Nicol,

'constitutional', 'participatory' and 'deliberative European democracy' continues to transform 'popular' and 'representative democracies' inside EU member states by protecting new, transnational 'market freedoms' and additional civil, political, economic and social rights at national and European levels. The transformation, in 2007, of the former EU Monitoring Centre for Racism and Xenophobia into the Fundamental Rights Agency of the EU reflects the insight that multilevel economic governance must be constitutionally restrained not only by multilevel, democratic as well as judicial 'checks and balances'; there is also a need for providing special expertise for 'protecting rights across borders' and institutionalized monitoring of the human rights dimensions of multilevel governance.[98]

Inadequate parliamentary and democratic control of worldwide IEL

In contrast to European economic integration law, worldwide IEL remains fragmented and based on hundreds of bilateral and multilateral treaties. For instance:

- international movements of goods and related payments are regulated in IMF and WTO law as well as in more than 250 regional trade agreements and product-specific commodity agreements;
- international movements of services are regulated in WTO law, in numerous UN Specialized Agencies (like the International Telecommunication Union, the Universal Postal Union and the International Civil Aviation Organization), as well as in hundreds of bilateral agreements on air transport, maritime transport and telecommunications services; yet, in contrast to the multilevel regulation of product and production standards for trade in goods, the financial regulation and supervision of governments, central banks and financial regulators failed to provide for equivalent prudential standards and 'risk assessment procedures' for trade in financial services and to align incentives in the private financial industry with the public good of financial security and consumer protection (eg, vis-à-vis complex financial derivatives and conflicts of interests due to proprietary trading and asymmetric information of bankers and investment funds);[99]
- international movements of persons are regulated in the law of the ILO, of the International Organization for Migration, in regional economic integration agreements as well as in bilateral agreements on temporary movements of guest workers;[100]
- capital movements and related payments are regulated in the law of the Bretton Woods institutions, WTO law, regional economic integration and other agreements like the Energy Charter Treaty, as well as some 2800 BITs and hundreds of bilateral agreements on taxation and avoidance of double taxation.

'Can Justice Dethrone Democracy in the EU? A Reply to Jürgen Neyer'; and J Neyer, 'Who's Afraid of Justice? A Rejoinder to Danny Nicol' (2012) 50 *Journal of Common Market Studies*.

[98] *cf* O De Schutter, 'The Fundamental EU Rights Agency' in K Boyle (ed), *New Institutions for Human Rights Protection* (New York: OUP, 2009) 92–135; J Greenwood, 'Institutions and Civil Society Organizations in the EU' in B Locher and J Joachim (eds), *Transnational Activism in the UN & the EU* (New York: Routledge, 2009).

[99] *cf* RM Gadbaw, 'Systemic Regulation of Global Trade and Finance: A Tale of Two Systems' (2010) 13 *JIEL* 551–74.

[100] *cf* Trachtman (2009).

Most of these economic agreements do not refer to the human rights obligations of member states. In contrast to democratic legislation inside constitutional democracies, they are not effectively controlled by 'constitutional checks and balances' by parliaments, courts, civil society and 'deliberative democracy'. Intergovernmental rulemaking and policy making in worldwide organizations tends to be dominated by diplomats, bureaucracies and organized interest groups such as cotton, textiles, agricultural and pharmaceutical industries influencing rulemaking in GATT negotiations; agricultural lobbies influencing negotiations in the FAO; telecommunications industries participating in the rulemaking of the International Telecommunications Union; aircraft industries dominating rulemaking in the International Civil Aircraft Organization and International Air Transport Association; or worker and employer organizations represented in ILO bodies.

The frequent lack of 'inclusive decision-making' in intergovernmental rulemaking favours a narrow focus on 'sectoral interests' that may adversely affect general consumer welfare. National parliaments and EU institutions tend to justify democratic legislation in respect of domestic citizens in terms of constitutional principles. Worldwide economic regulation, by contrast, tends to be adopted in the UN, the Bretton Woods institutions and the WTO without references to human rights, to general consumer welfare, democratic citizen participation and to rule of law among citizens. Even if intergovernmental agreements are subsequently ratified by national parliaments, the practical influence of parliaments on changing worldwide treaty rules after years of multilateral negotiations remains all too often marginal. For example, the 1994 Uruguay Round Agreements establishing the WTO were ratified by the German Parliament after a relatively short debate prior to the availability of a complete German translation of the 25,000 pages of treaty text.[101] Since 1999, all WTO ministerial conferences have been accompanied by interparliamentary meetings of parliamentarians from the majority of WTO member states; similar interparliamentary information and consultation networks have been set up for the Bretton Woods institutions. But formal establishment of consultative parliamentary bodies in worldwide organizations remains opposed by many member states, including constitutional democracies like the United States.[102] Empirical studies of parliamentary involvement in, and review of, intergovernmental rulemaking in worldwide organizations confirm that parliamentary control of intergovernmental rulemaking often remains superficial and ineffective; once intergovernmental negotiations have resulted in comprehensive 'package deals' elaborated in secretive negotiations in distant international organizations (like the 1994 Uruguay Round Agreements), any national parliament can hardly unilaterally insist on re-opening and changing the agreed results.[103]

[101] *cf* the country studies on the domestic implementation and parliamentary deliberations of the WTO Agreement in J Jackson and A Sykes (eds), *Implementing the Uruguay Round* (Oxford: Clarendon Press, 1997).

[102] *cf* E Mann, 'A Parliamentary Dimension to the WTO: More than Just a Vision?' in EU Petersmann (ed) (2005) 421–28. On involvement of parliamentarians and civil society in WTO discussions see also the contributions by S Charnovitz, M Hilf, P Eeckhout, EU Petersmann and US Congressman Sawyer to E Baron Crespo (ed), *The Parliamentary Dimension of the WTO* (European Parliament Doc WTO/242, 2006); *WTO Policy Issues for Parliamentarians* (WTO, 2001); *Regional Workshop for Parliamentarians on the Multilateral Trading System* (Commonwealth Parliamentary Association/WTO, 2003); *For A Free, Just and Equitable Multilateral Trading System: Providing a Parliamentary Dimension* (Inter-Parliamentary Union, 2001).

[103] The Uruguay Round Agreements have illustrated that national parliaments in most WTO member countries 'rubber-stamped' the results or, as in many less-developed African countries, did not adopt any implementing legislation. A recent study suggests that, apart from the Swiss Parliament, the US Congress and the European Parliament, most parliaments continue exercising little control over WTO decision-making; *cf* 'The Role of Parliaments in Scrutinising and Influencing Trade Policy – A Comparative Analysis', European Parliament Study (PE 370-166v01-00) December 2005.

As emphasized in the 'Lisbon Treaty judgment' by the German Constitutional Court in June 2009 (Table 13), parliamentary and democratic control of intergovernmental rule-making is essential for protecting democratic self-government against the power-oriented realities of intergovernmental politics. In its judgment of 30 June 2009 on whether the 2007 Lisbon Treaty is consistent with the German constitutional guarantees of democratic governance, the German Federal Constitutional Court identified a 'structural democratic deficit' in the EU governance system. In order 'to guarantee the effectiveness of [German citizens'] right to vote', the Court suspended the German ratification process for the 2007 Lisbon Treaty on the European Union on the ground that the German legislation approving the Lisbon Treaty must provide for more effective rights of parliamentary participation in European lawmaking procedures and treaty amendment procedures.[104]

Table 13: The Lisbon Treaty judgment of the German Constitutional Court of 30 June 2009: constitutional rights to democratic participation in international rulemaking

BVerfG, 2 BvE 2/08 of 30 June 2009, in the context of 'constitutional complaints' by German citizens and 'Organstreit proceedings' by members of the German Parliament against the German Acts ratifying and implementing the 2007 Lisbon Treaty on the European Union: '4.a) The Act Extending and Strengthening the Rights of the Bundestag and the Bundesrat in European Union Matters (Bundestag document 16/8489) infringes Article 38.1 in conjunction with Article 23.1 of the Basic Law insofar as rights of participation of the German Bundestag and the Bundesrat have not been elaborated to the extent required taking into account the provisos that are specified under C.II.3'. '4.b) Before the entry into force of the constitutionally required legal elaboration of the rights of participation, the Federal Republic of Germany's instrument of ratification of the Treaty of Lisbon amending the Treaty on European Union and the Treaty establishing the European Community, signed at Lisbon, 13 December 2007 . . ., may not be deposited. In other respects, the constitutional complaints are rejected as unfounded'. . . . The Court emphasized that the constitutional principles of democratic state, limited delegation of powers and the 'non-transferable identity' (Article 79 GG) of German constitutional law limit German participation in the EU (eg, by requiring approval by the German Parliament of certain decisions adopted under EU law). However, the Court also acknowledged that the Basic Law's openness for EU law (Article 23 GG) calls for restrictive use of judicial review powers.

Is democractic governance possible in intergovernmental economic organizations?

An increasing number of reports by the UN Secretary-General, UN expert reports and UN resolutions acknowledge that – even if the national forms of constitutional and parliamentary democracy cannot be transferred to global levels – the UN should actively promote the diverse forms of 'representative democracy', 'deliberative democracy', 'participatory democracy' and 'contestatory democracy' at international levels.[105] The 2005

[104] An English translation of the judgment of the Constitutional Court is available from: www.bundesverfassungsgericht.de/entscheidungen/es20090630_2bve000208en. html). For critical comments on this judgment see: R Bieber, 'An Association of Sovereign States' (2009) 5 *European Constitutional Review* 391–406.

[105] *Cf* UN Secretary-General, *Agenda for Development* (UN Doc A/478/935 (1994)), paras 118 ff (promoting democracy as good governance); UN General Assembly Resolution of 2001 on *Promoting and Consolidating Democracy* (UN Doc A/55/96); *We the Peoples: Civil Society, the United Nations and Global Governance*,

World Summit Outcome confirmed that 'democracy is a universal value' and that human rights, rule of law and democracy are 'interlinked and mutually reinforcing'.[106] The World Summit 'commitment to support democracy by strengthening countries' capacity to implement the principles and practices of democracy'[107] is increasingly supported by practical UN activities, such as the UN Democracy Fund (established in 2005) and UN monitoring of national elections. In Europe, the ECtHR emphasizes that 'democracy is without doubt a fundamental feature of the European public order' and a legal obligation under the ECHR.[108] Similar to the Council of Europe, the Organization of American States and the African Union are explicitly committed to protection of human rights and democracy. Only a few, non-democratic UN member states continue objecting to claims that UN human rights instruments have given rise to a universal customary law obligation to protect democratic self-governance at national and international levels.[109] Yet, even if democratic self-governance is recognized as a *principle* of UN human rights law (eg, based on the rights set out in Articles 21 UDHR and 25 ICCPR to participate in the conduct of public affairs and to vote in elections, the collective right to self-determination protected by Articles 1 of the ICCPR and ICESCR), human rights and the diversity of national democratic traditions suggest that people and states retain a broad margin of discretion regarding their respective design of democratic procedures, rights and institutions at national and international levels.[110] The 2005 World Summit documents reaffirmed that 'while democracies share common features, there is no single model of democracy'.[111]

National democracy is an indispensable, but insufficient precondition for democratic governance at international levels. The 2004 UN report entitled 'We the Peoples: Civil Society, the United Nations and Global Governance' acknowledged that '(t)he weak influence of traditional democracy in matters of global governance is one reason why citizens of the world are urging greater democratic accountability of international organizations'.[112] Yet, proposals for strengthening parliamentary control over intergovernmental rulemaking by establishing interparliamentary bodies in the United Nations, the World Bank Group and the WTO remain contested and opposed by many countries, including constitutional democracies like the United States.[113] At national levels, constitutional democracies increasingly complement representative, parliamentary democracy

Report of the Panel of Eminent Persons on UN–Civil Society Relations UN Doc. A/58/817 (11 June 2004); A Peters, 'Dual Democracy' in Klabbers, Peters and Ulfstein (2009) 263, 268 ff.

[106] UN Doc A/60/1 (24 October 2005), para 119.

[107] ibid paras 135–36.

[108] *cf* ECtHR, *United Communist Party of Turkey and others v Turkey* App no 133/1996/752/951, Judgment (30 January 1998), para 45.

[109] *cf* J d'Asprémont, *L'Etat non-démocratique en droit international* (Paris: Pedone, 2008) 275 ff.

[110] cf G Sartori, who – in his classical *The Theory of Democracy Revisited. Part One : The Contemporary Debate* (Chatham: Chatham House Publisher, 1987) – criticized the term 'democracy' as a misleading and pompous 'name for something that does not exist' (at 7). T Nagel, *Equality and Partiality* (New York: OUP, 1991) 168 ff argues that – in view of the human diversity and 'reasonable disagreement' on the global scale – 'a legitimate government of the world is not possible'.

[111] UN Doc A/RES/60/1 (24 October 2005), para 135.

[112] UN Doc A/58/817 (11 June 2004) 8.

[113] See (n 102) and M Krajewski, 'Legitimizing Global Economic Governance through Transnational Parliamentarization: The Parliamentary Dimensions of the WTO and the World Bank' University of Bremen Working Paper 136/2010. There are today 155 national parliaments cooperating in the Inter-Parliamentary Union, which has set up a Committee of the Human Rights of Members of Parliaments that reviews complaints concerning freedom of election of parliaments and free exercise of parliamentary mandates (*cf* the website of the IPU: www.ipu.org).

by ever more constitutional guarantees of human rights, constitutional rights, 'participatory democracy' and 'deliberative democracy' (as illustrated by Article 11 TEU on 'citizen initiatives' for EU regulations). The ever greater impact of globalization and fragmented governance on domestic citizens – like the practical limits of parliamentary and other forms of representative democracy beyond national and regional communities – entail that the traditional 'two-track model' of democratic self-government through constitutional and parliamentary democracy inside states, and state consent to interstate rules of international law elaborated through deliberative forms of diplomacy, can no longer realize the democratic ideal that the people decide, through democratic procedures, all policy issues that are politically decidable.[114] The ideal of 'deliberative democracy' that only 'those action norms are valid to which all possible affected persons could agree as participants in rational discourses',[115] calls for a 'four-track model' of democratic self-governance with additional, multilevel guarantees of transnational 'participatory democracy' and 'global deliberative democracy'. In addition to constitutional democracy at national levels and intergovernmental, representative decision-making at international levels, there is a need for stronger, transnational legal and judicial protection of human rights and other cosmopolitan rights enabling citizens to participate more actively in multilevel governance in order to protect cosmopolitan rights against unnecessary or disproportionate intergovernmental restrictions.

Is democratic control of multilevel economic governance possible without transnational rule of law for the benefit of citizens?

Citizen-driven 'participatory' and 'deliberative democracy' depends on empowering citizens by individual rights of participation, information and incentives for monitoring (inter)governmental rulemaking and rule compliance. In most worldwide economic organizations, diplomats continue to insist that intergovernmental rulemaking must remain secret and focus on reciprocal rights and obligations of governments without individual rights to rely on 'rule of law' for the benefit of citizens. When I joined the GATT Secretariat in 1981 as first 'legal officer' ever employed by the GATT Secretariat, trade diplomats emphasized time and again that the success of GATT was due to its 'pragmatism': 'GATT should neither have a Legal Office nor a judicial system for the settlement of trade disputes'. These anti-legal prejudices were cultivated by trade diplomats and non-lawyers inside the GATT Secretariat in order to justify their own power politics and reduce their own legal accountability, for example for the dozens of secretive 'voluntary export restraints' (VERs) imposed by trade politicians from the EC and the US in support of export cartels abroad (eg, for exports of steel and automobiles) to the detriment of consumers in Europe and the United States. The establishment of a GATT Legal Office in 1983 and the replacement of the power-oriented system of 'GATT diplomats jurisprudence' (Hudec) in 1995, by the WTO legal system have significantly strengthened rule of law among WTO members.[116] Now, WTO law ensures compulsory

[114] *cf* S Wheatley (2010).
[115] J Habermas (1996) 107.
[116] For an insider story of my experiences as legal advisor in the GATT Secretariat as well as in the Uruguay Round negotiating groups elaborating the WTO dispute settlement system and WTO institutional framework see: EU Petersmann (1997).

jurisdiction for quasi-judicial settlement of trade disputes by WTO panels, the Appellate Body and arbitration inside the WTO. Compared with GATT 1947, WTO law also stipulates stronger rights empowering LDCs to challenge discriminatory restrictions. For instance, the WTO Agreement on Safeguards explicitly prohibits VERs (Article 11); the WTO Agreement on Textiles and Clothing phases out discrimination against LDCs (*cf* Article 9); and the WTO Dispute Settlement Understanding provides for legal services free of charge for less-developed WTO members involved in WTO dispute settlement proceedings (*cf* Article 27 DSU). Such 'legal correctives' of past discrimination and 'power imbalances' among developed and less-developed states under GATT 1947 were essential preconditions for the political consensus on transforming GATT 1947 into the WTO legal and dispute settlement system. Even though complaints can only be submitted to the WTO dispute settlement system by WTO members,[117] a large part of the more than 400 complaints since the entry into force of the WTO Agreement in 1995 continues to be triggered indirectly by requests from industries.[118] Yet, in most WTO member countries and the EU, citizens have no rights to challenge violations of WTO law by their own governments in domestic courts. Hence, as citizens can neither invoke WTO rules in domestic courts nor rely on compliance with WTO rules by their own governments, they have no incentives for monitoring WTO rulemaking and rule compliance. As long as intergovernmental rulemaking in worldwide economic organizations remains so far away from what 'global justice'[119] would require, most citizens remain 'rationally ignorant' about the complex rules and practices of worldwide economic organizations and their frequent violations by intergovernmental power politics.

5 IEL MUST BE INTERPRETED AND DEVELOPED IN CONFORMITY WITH HUMAN RIGHTS AND 'CONSTITUTIONAL PLURALISM'

Apart from a few common law countries (like Israel, New Zealand and the United Kingdom), almost all UN member states have adopted written, national constitutions which differ depending on their constitutional traditions and the democratic preferences and historical experiences of their citizens. This pervasive reality of 'constitutional pluralism' at national levels is unlikely to change in view of the 'sovereign equality of states' and the human right to popular self-determination as constitutional principles of the UN Charter and of UN human rights law (*cf* Article 1 of the 1966 UN human rights conventions). Just as human rights protect individual and democratic autonomy of interpreting and developing rules of law inside states on the basis of legitimately diverse reasons of morality and 'public reason', so does UN law protect 'pluralist structures' of private and public, national and international legal systems in international relations among states.[120] In contrast to the unifying, steering ambitions of hierarchical 'national foundational Constitutionalism', the 'constitutional principles' underlying UN law and

[117] On the comprehensive WTO guarantees of individual access to domestic courts and commercial arbitration provided for in the WTO Agreement on Preshipment Inspections see: Petersmann (1997) 183, 194 ff.

[118] The procedures provided for in s 301 of the US Trade Law and in corresponding trade laws of other WTO members (eg, the EU Regulation on Trade Barriers) empower industries to petition their respective home governments to initiate dispute settlement proceedings in the WTO challenging foreign trade restrictions.

[119] *cf* Brock (n 78) and D French (ed), *Global Justice and Sustainable Development* (Leiden: Brill, 2010).

[120] On 'pluralism under international law' see: N McCormick, *Questioning Sovereignty* (Oxford: OUP, 1999) ch 7.

international human rights law protect legal diversity, subsidiarity, 'constitutional pluralism' and competing jurisdictions of states and of international and non-governmental organizations with limited legal autonomy.

Democracies tend to proceed from the rebuttable presumption that national law should be construed in conformity with international legal obligations ('consistent interpretation principle') unless national legislators deliberately violate international law.[121] Yet, departures from international rules may be justifiable by domestic constitutional guarantees of human rights and democratic governance if – as in the *Kadi* judgment of the ECJ of September 2008 (*cf* Table 18 and related text) – they protect human rights more effectively than intergovernmental rules and, thereby, strengthen democratic 'checks and balances' on intergovernmental rulemaking.[122] Even though a state 'party may not invoke the provisions of its internal law as justification for its failure to perform a treaty' (Article 27 VCLT), the human rights obligations of states and customary rules of treaty interpretation (*cf* Article 31 VCLT) require interpreting treaty provisions as not preventing states protecting higher standards of human and constitutional rights and democratic governance than those set out in international minimum standards.

National, regional and worldwide 'courts of justice' increasingly insist on their autonomous 'constitutional authority' of 'administering justice' in the settlement of disputes and protecting 'rule of law' in conformity with human rights and other constitutional limitations of governance powers.[123] In rights-based international relations covered by IEL and human rights law, the relationships between the diverse principles, procedures and institutions of national and functionally limited, international 'constitutional systems' are increasingly governed by legal 'checks and balances' and competing claims for protecting human rights and other constitutional rights, democratic self-governance, rule of law and 'public reason' rather than intergovernmental power politics or formal claims to *a priori* legal hierarchies. The 'internal pluralism' inside national and regional 'constitutional democracies' (like the EU) differs from the 'external constitutional pluralism' in the external relations among constitutional democracies and worldwide organizations for the collective supply of international public goods.[124] The universal recognition of human rights, the increasing jurisdiction of international courts and the constitutional legitimacy of the ever stronger, multilevel judicial protection of individual rights offer convincing arguments for coordinating 'legal pluralism' on the basis of cos-

[121] *cf* M Kumm, 'International Law in National Courts; The International Rule of Law and the Limits of the Internationalist Model' (2003) 44 *Virginia Journal of International Law* 19 ff; Wheatley (2010) 370–79.

[122] *cf* M Kumm, 'The Legitimacy of International Law: A Constitutionalist Framework of Analysis' (2004) 15 *EJIL* 907 ff; Wheatley (2010) 376: 'The construction of a multiverse of democratic visions of global governance orders by democratic states will have the practical consequence of democratizing the international law order, providing democratic legitimacy for international law'.

[123] On judicial protection and clarification of 'common constitutional principles' as a means of 'administering justice' in the settlement of international disputes and judicial coordination of the plurality of normative orders see: EU Petersmann, '"Constitutional Justice" Requires Judicial Cooperation and "Comity" in the Protection of "Rule of Law"' in F Fontanelli, G Martinico and P Carozza (eds), *Shaping Rule of Law through Dialogue* (Groningen: Europa Law Publishing, 2009) 1–19. On 'rule of law' as the constitutional, rights-based foundation and jurisdictional protection of a fair and just society limiting unnecessary and disproportionate government restrictions of constitutional rights and governmental claims to 'rule by law' and pursuit of the 'public good' see: T Bingham, *The Rule of Law* (London: Penguin Books, 2010); G Palombella and N Walker (eds) (2009).

[124] On the 'internal' and 'external dimensions' of constitutionalism in the EU and in the jurisprudence of the European Court of Justice see: M Poiares Maduro, 'Courts and Pluralism: Essay on a Theory of Judicial Adjudication in the Context of Legal and Constitutional Pluralism' in Dunoff and Trachtman (eds) (2009) 356–80.

mopolitan principles of human rights, constitutional rights, rule of law and constitutional democracy.[125] Yet, legal perceptions of transnational 'legal pluralism', of its systemic unity and ultimate source of legitimate authority remain inevitably contested,[126] just as 'constitutional interpretations' inside constitutional democracies often remain contested among citizens.[127] National and international courts increasingly acknowledge that claims to 'rule of international law' and to legal certainty and predictability in transnational relations must be limited and balanced by respect for human rights and other constitutional principles of justice.[128] The strong influence of national and European courts on the dynamic evolution of European law suggests that – in international relations – the independent, impartial and 'principled' reasoning of 'courts of justice' based on 'due process of law' may be more likely than political majority decisions to promote order among the different layers of private and public, national, regional and worldwide law and to justify changing interpretations of law by balancing competing rights and clarifying principles of 'constitutional justice'.

'Responsible sovereignty' requires clarifying 'duties to protect' and 'constitutional functions' of IEL

UN and regional human rights bodies increasingly clarify the positive obligations of states under UN and regional human rights conventions to respect, protect and fulfil human rights.[129] Modern economics and theories of justice (eg, those of Rawls) emphasize that the welfare of citizens and their adequate access to essential goods and services depend on 'reasonable rules and institutions' rather than on domestic resources. Hence, the World Development Report 2011 rightly identifies the 'absence of legitimate institutions that provide citizens security, justice and jobs' as the main cause of mass violence and unnecessary poverty in so many countries.[130] Constitutional democracies and European international law recognize that the legal task of 'institutionalizing public reason' depends – also in IEL – on a 'four-stage sequence' of constitutional, legislative, administrative and judicial safeguards of human rights with due respect for 'reasonable disagreement' about particular conceptions for a good life. Civil society increasingly challenges the obvious failures of both UN law and worldwide IEL – which are confronted with ever more crises in international monetary, trade, financial, environmental relations and poverty reduction – to institutionalize 'public reason' in international relations. 'Westphalian intergovernmentalism' reflects 'discourse failures' due to authoritarian treatment of citizens as mere objects of international law and neglect of human rights to reasonable justification of all governance restrictions. If protection and fulfil-

[125] On 'cosmopolitan constitutionalism' see: Kumm (n 70).

[126] *cf* N Krisch, *Beyond Constitutionalism: The Pluralist Structure of Postnational Law* (Oxford: OUP, 2010).

[127] On 'interpretive pluralism' under EU and US constitutional law see: D Halberstam, 'Constitutional Heterarchy: The Centrality of Conflict in the European Union and the United States' in Dunoff and Trachtman (eds) (2009) 326–55.

[128] *cf* J Waldron, 'The Concept of the Rule of Law' (2008) 43 *Georgia Law Review* 1–61; G Palombella, 'The Rule of Law beyond the State: Failures, Promises and Theory' (2009) 7 *International Journal of Constitutional Law* 442–67.

[129] *cf* D Xenos, *The Positive Obligations of the State under the European Convention on Human Rights* (London: Routledge, 2011). On the 'human rights approach' to IEL advocated by UN bodies and the ILO, see ch VII, section 4.

[130] *World Development Report 2011: Conflict, Security and Development* (Washington: World Bank, 2011).

ment of human rights depend on 'responsible sovereignty' and on stronger constitutional 'checks and balances' limiting abuses of regulatory discretion and 'rent-seeking' by powerful interest groups, then there is a need for strengthening the 'constitutional functions' of IEL guarantees of equal freedoms, non-discrimination and transnational rule of law, for instance by cosmopolitan rights empowering citizens to request domestic courts to protect transnational rule of law and ensure the accountability of all delegated governance powers.

Respect for the diversity of national constitutions protecting diverse lists of agreed human rights and constitutional rights calls for clarifying common 'constitutional principles of justice' in international economic regulation, with due respect for the legitimately diverse ways of national regulations of interactions among human rights, economic regulation and judicial protection of constitutional rights.[131] As explained in my 1991 monograph on 'Constitutional Functions and Constitutional Problems of International Economic Law',[132] the necessary 'embedding' of IEL in domestic constitutional systems can be promoted by interpreting multilevel principles of freedom, non-discrimination, rule of law and social justice in mutually consistent ways unless compliance with IEL obligations risks undermining domestic constitutional rights. Treating citizens as legal subjects entitled to 'rule of law' might justify judicial protection in domestic courts also of *international* guarantees of economic freedom, non-discrimination, rule of law and social protection of citizens, as it is increasingly practised in national and European courts.[133] The collective action problems in protecting international public goods confirm that the legal restraints of foreign policy powers deriving from multilevel, legal guarantees of human rights, economic freedoms, democratic participation and judicial protection of rule of law need to be strengthened with due respect for the legitimate diversity of national and regional constitutional traditions.

Chapter III discusses European traditions of legal philosophy which, since ancient Greece, perceive law as an instrument for promoting a just social order. Modern theories of justice (eg, those of Kant to Rawls) explain why 'rule by law' derives its legitimacy from agreed 'principles of justice' and from constitutional protection of 'rule of law' in conformity with human rights and democratic governance. In the dynamically evolving 'European constitutional law' of the EU, the EEA and the ECHR,[134] the 'principles of justice' are increasingly defined in terms of human rights, constitutional democracy and multilevel judicial protection of rule of law. As predicted by the Kantian theory of multilevel constitutionalism and cosmopolitan rights, the most important achievements of the multilevel constitutional guarantees of the EC Treaty, the EU Treaty, the EEA Treaty and the ECHR have been 'democratic peace' and social welfare based on rule of law and on multilevel, judicial protection of fundamental rights of citizens, with due respect for the

[131] *cf* the comparative studies in Hilf and Petersmann (1993).

[132] *cf* Petersmann (1991); the 'constitutional approach' developed in this 'habilitation thesis' (written in the 1980s during my work as legal advisor in the GATT Secretariat at Geneva and in the Uruguay Round Negotiating Groups on the new institutional and dispute settlement rules of the WTO) focused on the 'domestic policy functions' and 'constitutional functions' of IEL inside constitutional democracies rather than on the 'collective action problems' in multilevel governance of interdependent public goods.

[133] *cf* H Keller and A Stone Sweet (eds) (2008).

[134] On the impact of the EU Charter of Fundamental Rights, the future EU membership in the ECHR, the future relationships between the ECJ and the ECtHR and other constitutional changes of the Lisbon Treaty on European constitutional law see: J Wouters et al (eds), *European Constitutionalism beyond Lisbon* (Groningen: Europa Publishing, 2009); B Rittberger and F Schimmelfennig, *The Constitutionalization of the European Union* (London: Routledge, 2009).

diversity of national constitutional traditions and for 'reasonable disagreement', as illustrated by the non-application of many supranational EU law principles in the more decentralized EEA legal system.

Respect for 'cosmopolitan constitutional pluralism' requires exploring to what extent the fragmented national and international legal regimes share common 'constitutional foundations', for instance in UN human rights law and general international law. Chapters III and IV argue that the worldwide recognition – in UN, regional and national human rights law – of 'the inherent dignity and of the equal and inalienable rights of all members of the human family (as) the foundation of freedom, justice and peace in the world' (Preamble of the 1948 UDHR) justifies interpreting the functional interrelationships between national, regional and worldwide guarantees of equal freedoms and rule of law in accordance with the Kantian theory of justice, with due respect for modern human rights law.[135] As explained by Kant, the moral duty and reasonable autonomy (dignity) of human beings to respect equal freedoms of all others justifies not only human rights to equal liberties and to autonomous self-development as man's moral ends; the human right to external freedom, like the moral restraints of our internal freedom of conscience, also carries with it correlative duties to strive for multilevel constitutional protection – in all human interactions at national, transnational and international levels – of equal freedoms and 'public justice'.

Respect for human dignity requires respect for the diversity of individual value preferences, for instance regarding the seven 'basic forms of human flourishing' (ie, life, knowledge, play, aesthetic experience, sociability, practical reasonableness and religion) postulated by natural rights theories.[136] The scarcity of resources, like the unnecessary suffering of more than one billion poor people, also illustrates the need for constitutional protection of individual freedom of choice among competing uses of civil, political, economic, social and cultural liberties. This includes the freedom of enhancing one's consumer welfare and economic resources for self-development through mutually beneficial, voluntary economic cooperation among citizens across frontiers. Natural rights theories (eg, those of Kant) are based on respect for human reason as a social fact and normative goal. The universal recognition of the inalienable rights of human beings deriving from respect for human dignity has transformed the moral task of human rights protection into a legal obligation of positive, national and international law, also permeating IEL as an ever more important instrument for protecting human welfare and human rights. The 'social contracts' justifying democratic governance are today based on positive, constitutional laws rather than on 'natural rights' (as proclaimed by Locke), theories of the 'general will' (as proclaimed by Rousseau in order to justify democratic, yet quasi-totalitarian governance powers of citizens), or on constitutional 'thought-experiments' (as proposed by Rawls). Hence, legal and judicial clarification and protection of the 'inner morality of law'[137] and of a 'world public order of human dignity' (as postulated by the New Haven School) must be examined as problems of *positive law* and

[135] For an earlier explanation of this normative premise of my publications see: Petersmann (n 70).

[136] On contemporary, natural law theories see: J Finnis, *Natural Law and Natural Rights* (London: Clarendon Press, 1980), whose seven 'basic forms of human flourishing' and nine 'basic requirements of practical reasonableness' are not deduced from human nature, but from 'self-evident principles' for a reasonable 'human good' (in conformity with the philosophies of Aristotle and Aquinas) and 'good life'.

[137] *cf* Fuller (1969), who defines the 'morality of law' by eight principles of generality, promulgation, non-retroactivity, clarity, non-contradiction, possibility of compliance, constancy and congruence between declared rule and official action.

legitimate policies. Answers to these constitutional problems and regulatory tasks of IEL must 'fit' constitutional conceptions of law, as explained by Dworkin's theory of 'law as integrity'.[138] Chapter III explains why the Kantian legal theory of multilevel constitutional protection of equal freedoms and rule of law at national, transnational and international levels continues to 'fit' cosmopolitan conceptions of IEL and of multilevel constitutional protection of human rights across frontiers.

[138] On law as an interpretive process under which constitutional rights and 'law as integrity' are paramount, and the judicial function to interpret rules (which apply in an 'all-or-nothing fashion') in the light of legal principles (which have 'the dimension of weight or importance') and policy goals in order to find the 'right answer' fitting best with the constitutional system (rather than 'judicial rulemaking' if the existing rules are unclear and incomplete), see ch VIII and Dworkin (1977).

III

'Civilizing' and 'Constitutionalizing' IEL Requires Cosmopolitan Restraints of Public and Private Power

CHAPTERS I AND II criticized the prevailing conceptions of IEL and argued that more effective regulation of the 'collective action problems' impeding supply of interdependent public goods requires 'constitutionalizing' intergovernmental economic regulation to offer producers, traders, investors, consumers and other 'market citizens' more effective legal and judicial remedies against public and private abuses of power. The following sections 1 and 2 place these constitutional and economic law arguments into the broader context of Kantian and Rawlsian constitutional theories. Most economists perceive globalization as a desirable and irreversible engine of prosperity and progress that has reduced poverty in many countries;[1] even though economists admit 'market failures', they often conceptualize the *homo economicus*, competition and economic policies as if the models of the physical sciences could be applied to society. Civil society, by contrast, often focuses on the dark sides of globalization like pandemics, pollution of the environment and selfish exploitation of profit opportunities through 'corporate imperialism' and transnational organized crime like money laundering, drugs and human trafficking.[2]

Constitutionalism attributes the failures of economists to predict even dramatic economic crises (such as the financial crisis that began in 2008) to the 'constitutional ignorance' (Hayek) of individuals and social sciences: the unpredictable interactions among human sentiments, rational egoism, moral hazards and limited reasonableness of individuals and groups render the global economy unpredictable. In contrast to the focus by economists on individual choices within given rules, constitutional theory focuses on changing the rules and human incentives by 'institutionalizing public reason' based on constitutional 'principles of justice', their legal protection by rules of a higher legal rank and institutional 'checks and balances'. Claims to economic micro and macro-management of 'market failures' by omnipotent governments are seen as a 'pretence of knowledge' (Hayek) that remains dispersed among billions of individuals and cannot be known to any central authority. Hence, constitutional theory focuses on constitutional restraints of abuses of power and countervailing rights of adversely affected citizens to prevent or limit private 'market failures' (like the financial sector irresponsibility which

[1] *cf* M Wolf, *Why Globalization Works. The Case for the Global Market Economy* (New Haven: Yale University Press, 2004); J Bhagwati, *In Defense of Globalization* (New York: OUP, 2004).

[2] *cf* GW Kolodko, *Truth, Errors and Lies: Politics and Economics in a Volatile World* (New York: Columbia University Press, 2011).

caused the Irish banking and financial crisis in 2010) as well as public 'governance failures' (like the fiscal and political irresponsibility that brought about Greece's sovereign debt crisis in 2009).

OVERVIEW OF CHAPTER III

Section 1 explains why the Kantian theory of multilevel constitutional protection of equal freedoms of citizens justifies multilevel constitutional protection of 'market freedoms' and human rights in all human interactions at national, transnational and international levels. Kant's theory of multilevel constitutional protection of cosmopolitan freedoms is not only more rights-based than Anglo-Saxon theories of cosmopolitanism aimed at making international institutions more accountable to civil society by means of 'deliberative' and 'participatory, cosmopolitan democracy';[3] it also better explains the rights-based, multilevel constitutionalism in European economic law and its marked contrast with the libertarian 'common law' and 'majoritarian democracy' traditions in Anglo-Saxon democracies as well as in many LDCs. Section 2 argues that the Kantian theory of constitutional rights protecting 'public justice' offers a coherent justification of multilevel, constitutional limitations of abuses of public and private powers based on 'countervailing rights' and citizen-oriented conceptions of IEL aimed at limiting the ubiquitous conflicts of interests among selfish individuals in their private and 'public choices'. Section 3 compares the constitutional protection of economic liberties in Europe with their inadequate constitutional and judicial protection in US jurisprudence since the 1930s; the constitutional need for reconciling economic liberties with all other constitutional and social rights is emphasized. Section 4 concludes that the 'balancing' of civil, political, economic, social and cultural human rights requires constitutional theories of justice and, as explained by Rawls, a 'four-stage sequence' of 'civilizing' and 'constitutionalizing' multilevel economic regulation by constitutional and legislative rights and judicial remedies.

1 KANTIAN 'MULTILEVEL CONSTITUTIONALISM' AS JUSTIFICATION FOR 'ECONOMIC CONSTITUTIONALISM' IN EUROPEAN ECONOMIC LAW AND IEL

Law as an instrument of governance needs justification. In contrast to the utilitarian traditions of economic regulation in many common law countries, European civil law countries have long traditions of justifying and regulating economic freedoms as integral parts of constitutional law.[4] The need for respecting the positive law reality of 'constitutional

[3] For a discussion of cosmopolitan reforms of the WTO from a perspective of Anglo-Saxon conceptions of participatory and deliberative 'majoritarian democracy' and 'contestability of decision-making' see, eg: R McGrew, 'After Globalisation? WTO Reform and the New Global Political Economy' in T Cottier and M Elsig (eds) (2011) 20, 40 ff.

[4] For a detailed explanation of the rights-based constitutional regulation of economic freedoms in German and Swiss constitutional law since the nineteenth century, and the different common law traditions see: EU Petersmann (1991) ch VIII and M Hilf and EU Petersmann (eds) (1993). On the different British constitutional traditions see: D Nicol (2010). Nicol claims that – due to EU law, the ECHR and WTO law – the British constitutional guarantees of parliamentary freedom and majority politics have become limited by a neo-liberal legal order leaving Britons 'bereft of choice over fundamental aspects of economic governance' (159). Nicol admits that British constitutional law up to the early 20th century protected the vested interests of the ruling

pluralism' is not inconsistent with normative arguments that constitutional, legislative and judicial protection of human dignity and personal freedom – as in German and European constitutional and economic law[5] – justifies a cosmopolitan model for citizen-oriented interpretations of principles of freedom, non-discrimination, rule of law and human rights in the context of international monetary, trade, investment and economic integration agreements. Economic theory offers additional arguments for legal and judicial protection of equal freedoms as the most effective instrument for enabling citizens and countries to increase their economic welfare through trade. Kantian moral and legal theory explains the need for multilevel, constitutional and judicial protection of equal liberties on moral, legal and political rather than economic grounds.

The need for limiting 'moral hazards' in economic regulation

Should citizens, democratic legislatures and courts of justice continue perceiving IEL from the authoritarian 'Westphalian perspective' as 'international law among states' rather than also as a cosmopolitan 'international law of citizens', peoples and their democratic representatives? Globalization has shifted regulatory powers away from parliaments towards government executives and non-governmental organizations (like TNCs) that have rational self-interests in limiting their legal and judicial accountability vis-à-vis citizens, as illustrated by welfare-reducing 'collusion' among periodically elected politicians and rent-seeking industries (eg, granting support for the election of members of parliament in exchange for trade protection) and by other 'regulatory failures' vis-à-vis restrictive business practices, public bailouts of private banks, or pollution of the environment. The transformation of European economic law resulting from interpreting international EC, EU, EFTA and EEA treaty provisions in favour of rights and judicial remedies of citizens illustrates that rights-based interpretations of market regulations for the benefit of citizens can limit trade policy discretion and its 'protection biases' by protecting consumer welfare and general citizen interests more effectively than authoritarian conceptions of economic law focusing only on rights and reciprocal duties of governments or on parliamentary majority politics.

UN human rights law describes 'recognition of the inherent dignity and of the equal and inalienable rights of all members of the human family (as) the foundation of freedom, justice and peace in the world' (Preamble UDHR) and derives from this normative

few. Rather than welcoming human and constitutional rights and judicial remedies of citizens as protecting 'constitutional democracy', Nicol argues for a return to national 'parliamentary sovereignty' based on a purely procedural constitution and 'a global order that . . . does not undermine national autonomy' (160) and reverses neoliberal promotion of the interests of capital holders (38), ie, a legal utopia without constitutional principles of justice.

[5] See Art 6 EU (cited above) and Art 1 German Basic Law on 'Protection of human dignity': '1. The dignity of man is inviolable. To respect and protect it shall be the duty of all public authority. 2. The German people therefore uphold human rights as inviolable and inalienable and as the basis of every community, of peace and justice in the world. 3. The following basic rights shall bind the legislature, the executive and the judiciary as directly enforceable law'. Art 2 Basic Law on 'Rights of liberty' infers from the human right to respect for dignity (Art 1) comprehensive constitutional rights to maximum equal freedoms subject to constitutional and legislative restrictions, as suggested by Kantian legal theory: '1. Everybody has the right to the free development of his personality in so far as he does not violate the rights of others or offend against the constitutional order or morality. 2. Everybody has the right to life and physical integrity. Personal freedom is inviolable. These rights may not be encroached upon save pursuant to a law').

premise that 'everyone has the right to recognition everywhere as a person before the law' (Article 6 UDHR). It recognizes both the moral and reasonable autonomy of individuals as well as 'that human rights should be protected by the rule of law' (Preamble UDHR). Personal autonomy protects not only individual rights to judge for one's self on one's individual conception of a good life; reasonable persons must also recognize the need for limiting individual autonomy by rules of law that determine whether actions are right or wrong. As explained by Kant:

> (H)owever well disposed men might be, . . . individual men, peoples and states can never be secure against violence from one another, since each has its own right to do what seems right and good to it and not to be dependent upon another's opinion about this. So, unless is wants to renounce any concept of Right, the first thing it has to resolve upon is the principle that it must leave the state of nature, in which each follows its own judgment, unite itself with all others (with which it cannot avoid interacting), subject itself to a public lawful external coercion, and so enter into a condition in which what is to be recognized as belonging to it is determined by law.[6]

Even if individual moral judgements are perceived like self-legislation (as suggested by Kant's 'categorical imperative'), 'we do not and cannot simply rely on people's moral self-command or self-restraint' but need lawmaking and institutions based on 'public reason' limiting individual freedom to act on our individual moral judgements.[7] Yet, as rules of law may be iniquitous, responsible enlightened citizenship requires – as emphasized by Kant – making 'public use of one's reason in all matters'[8] in order to review and change rules of law to render them more reasonable and just. The universal recognition of human rights by all UN member states morally requires and legally empowers citizens to review the authoritarian premises of the Westphalian 'international law among states' and its failures to protect human rights, consumer welfare and the environment effectively. For, a 'citizen's allegiance is to the law, not to any particular person's view of what the law is, and he does not behave unfairly so long as he proceeds on his own considered and reasonable view of what the law requires'.[9]

Cosmopolitan 'Kantian interpretations' of multilevel, legal guarantees of equal freedoms in international trade and investment law differ from the authoritarian, state-centred traditions in most countries. Kantian justifications for reinterpreting 'international law among states' for the benefit of citizens are bound to remain contested and resisted – not only by diplomats interested in limiting their legal and judicial accountability, but also by governments privileging civil and political over economic and social rights of citizens. Public discussion remains the best arbiter for evaluating whether the diverse forms of 'cosmopolitan constitutionalism' in the EU and in the EEA could serve as a model for IEL beyond Europe. The worldwide adoption of national constitutions reflects not only the democratic insight that, as explained by Rawls in his controversial

[6] I Kant, *The Metaphysics of Morals* (trans M Gregor) (Oxford: OUP, 1991) 124.

[7] *cf* N McCormick, *Practical Reason in Law and Morality* (Oxford: OUP, 2008) 181: even if citizens are required to comply with legal rules, the law does not cancel the 'validity of the conscientious judgment of any issue by a moral agent. Autonomy in moral judgment means that each person is responsible for her/his view of what is good and bad, right and wrong and can never be overruled on the issue'.

[8] I Kant, 'What is Enlightenment?' in I Kant (1970) 54 ff, 55. Moral duties of citizens to participate in political processes in order to support just laws and institutions are emphasized by many modern legal philosophers like Rawls, according to whom the welfare of citizens depends essentially on their domestic rules and institutions rather than their natural resources.

[9] R Dworkin (1977) 214.

proposals for an international 'Law of Peoples' based on tolerance vis-à-vis non-liberal, albeit decent peoples,[10] constitutional *domestic reforms* are more important preconditions for promoting development than external 'development assistance' (eg, for LDCs) and non-binding pledges to 'good governance';[11] democratic constitutionalism at national levels is also a precondition for multilevel constitutional protection of equal freedoms and human dignity in transnational relations, as suggested by Kantian cosmopolitan constitutionalism.

Kantian 'multilevel constitutionalism' as institutionalized 'public reason' protecting a 'universal law of freedom'

The idea of 'constitutional justice' in the sense of legal and judicial protection of 'rule of law' as an independent restraint of the 'rule by men' and their 'rule by law' belongs to the oldest paradigms of 'justice'.[12] Immanuel Kant was the first legal philosopher who extended his constitutional conception of law (as 'the sum total of those conditions within which the will of one person can be reconciled with the will of another in accordance with a universal law of freedom')[13] and of 'rule of law' to international law. In his proposals for 'Perpetual Peace: A Philosophical Sketch' (1795), Kant explained why – in order to institute lasting peace among rational, antagonistic egoists with limited reasonableness and 'unsocial sociability' – 'all men who can at all influence one another must adhere to some kind of civil constitution' of the three following types:

> (1) a constitution based on the civil rights of individuals within a nation (ius civitatis);
> (2) a constitution based on the international rights of states in their relationships with one another (ius gentium);
> (3) a constitution based on cosmopolitan right, in so far as individuals and states, coexisting in an external relationship of mutual influence, may be regarded as citizens of a universal state of mankind (ius cosmopoliticum).
>
> This classification, with respect to the idea of a perpetual peace, is not arbitrary, but necessary. For if even one of the parties were able to influence the others physically and yet itself remained in a state of nature, there would be a risk of war, which it is precisely the aim of the above articles to avoid.[14]

The Kantian conception of multilevel constitutionalism as a morally necessary 'categorical imperative' for protecting human dignity and equal freedoms of individuals in all their social interactions at national, transnational and international relations reflects

[10] *cf* J Rawls (1999) 108 ff.

[11] For a critical discussion of Rawls' claim that the causes of severe poverty and of other human rights deprivations are domestic to the societies in which they occur, see: T Pogge, 'Do Rawls' Two Theories of Justice Fit Together?' in R Martin and DA Reidy (eds), *Rawls's Law of Peoples* (Oxford: Blackwell, 2007) 206, 217 ff.

[12] On Kant's moral justification of 'public justice' as a 'condition which reason, by a categorical imperative, makes it obligatory for us to strive after' in order to guarantee to all men equal maximum liberties as a human right, see: Kant (n 6) 120–29. On the particular common law ideals of law, and of the judicial duty to decide disputes in accordance with the law of the land, see: P Hamburger, *Law and Judicial Duty* (Cambridge: Harvard University Press, 2008).

[13] I Kant, 'The Metaphysics of Morals' in Kant (1970) 133. Kant follows from his moral 'categorical imperative' that 'every action which by itself or by its maxim enables the freedom of each individual's will to co-exist with the freedom of everyone else in accordance with a universal law is *right*' (at 133). Arguably, this 'categorical imperative' also justifies constitutional protection of equal freedoms of trade subject to appropriate regulation.

[14] *cf* I Kant, 'Perpetual Peace: A Philosophical Sketch' in Kant (1970) 98.

moral self-limitation by rules of a higher rank in order to promote individual and collective self-development of all human faculties. Kantian multilevel constitutionalism also rests on Kant's insight that – since rules cannot specify all the conditions of their own application – the application of every rule requires interposition of an authority determining what the rule should mean in a particular situation, and whether applying the rule might be better than resorting to an exception.[15] Hence,

> (a) constitution allowing the greatest possible human freedom in accordance with laws which ensure that the freedom of each can coexist with the freedom of all the others (not one designed to provide the greatest possible happiness, as this will in any case follow automatically), is at all events a necessary idea which must be made the basis not only of the first outline of a political constitution but of all laws as well.[16]

Kant was also the first legal philosopher emphasizing what most politicians and lawyers outside Europe continue to ignore to date, ie, that the 'problem of establishing a perfect civil constitution is subordinate to the problem of a law-governed external relationship with other states, and cannot be solved unless the latter is also solved'.[17] Kant's proposals for separating and limiting legislative, executive and judicial powers by multilevel constitutional restraints were aimed at institutionalizing and promoting 'public reason' in the sense of political support for the moral judgements of law-appliers in determining what equal freedoms and other 'principles of justice' require in real word conflicts and contestation. According to Kant, it is only through antagonistic, historical learning processes that individuals and states can be expected to progressively transform the lawless state of nature into law-governed national, transnational and international relations protecting 'conditions under which the choice of one can be united with the choice of another in accordance with a universal law of freedom'.[18]

The legitimacy of all governance depends on constitutional restraints

Rawls' *A Theory of Justice* uses Kantian legal theory in order to explain why – in view of the 'fact of reasonable pluralism' and 'the fact that in a democratic regime political power is regarded as the power of free and equal citizens as a collective body' – the democratic exercise of coercive power over one another is democratically legitimate only when 'political power . . . is exercised in accordance with a constitution (written or unwritten) the essentials of which all citizens, as reasonable and rational, can endorse in the light of their common human reason'.[19] EU law regulates the basic principles of the EU's customs union, its 'system ensuring that competition is not distorted' (TFEU Protocol 27), the EU's common market, common policies and the EU's commitment to a 'highly competitive social market economy' at the same constitutional level as the EU guarantees of fundamental freedoms and human rights. Economic theory confirms that human freedom deserves constitutional protection in the economy no less than in the polity. As *foreign policy powers* can be abused for taxing domestic citizens (eg, by means

[15] *cf* I Kant, *Critique of Pure Reason*, V Politis (ed) (Oxford: OUP, 1991) 140 f.
[16] *cf* I Kant, Appendix from 'The Critique of Pure Reason' in Kant (1970) 191.
[17] *cf* I Kant, 'Idea for a Universal History with a Cosmopolitan Purpose' in Kant (1970) 47.
[18] Kant (n 6) 230.
[19] J Rawls (2001) 41.

of tariffs), for restricting their freedoms (eg, by means of non-tariff trade barriers) and for exposing citizens to existential dangers (like wars or global recessions) no less than *domestic policy powers*, the EU's multilevel economic constitutionalism can be justified in terms of Kantian and Rawlsian theories of justice and constitutionalism.[20]

Like multilevel protection of human rights, multilevel constitutional safeguards of equal economic freedoms and fair procedures provide not only for constitutional restraints on 'rule by law'; they empower and protect individuals and law-appliers to interpret and apply the inevitably indeterminate rules in reasonable ways respecting equal freedoms and universal 'principles of justice'. According to Rawls, the legal and political stability of social orders over time depends on legally protecting and maintaining an 'overlapping consensus' on 'principles of justice' among citizens with diverse self-interests by means of 'institutionalizing' principles of justice through constitutional, legislative, administrative and judicial rules and institutions. Also in IEL governing the transnational economic cooperation among citizens, the progressive extension of rule of law depends not only on the 'justice' of national and international rules and on institutionalizing 'reasonable judgments' in applying the rules. Constitutional empowerment of citizens to defend their rights, and constitutional clarification of the 'judicial duties' of courts as independent, impartial guardians of 'rule of law', have likewise proven to be of crucial importance for citizen-driven 'struggles for rights', for instance in the judicial enforcement of the EU citizens' common market freedoms against public and private protectionist restraints. Multilevel constitutional guarantees of citizen rights and judicial remedies promote and enable 'public reason' to prevail in the inevitably antagonistic rivalries among rational individuals and public and private institutions (like TNCs), which often favour instrumental conceptions of 'rule by law' and intergovernmental 'legal regimes' without judicial accountability and democratic supervision.[21]

European multilevel constitutionalism as a model for cosmopolitan IEL?

During the first year after the entry into force of the Lisbon Treaty in December 2009, the 27 EU member states agreed on a vast range of additional fiscal, monetary and financial disciplines, procedural safeguards (eg, for supervision of national budgets) and new institutions (like the Financial Stability Facility, the European Systemic Risk Board and three separate EU agencies to monitor securities, banks and insurance companies) aimed at preventing a continuation of the international financial crisis. Also the 'bail out' agreements for Greece, Ireland and Portugal illustrated that the EU often succeeds more quickly and more comprehensively than other regional or worldwide organizations in using crises as opportunities for improving multilevel governance. Does the *European laboratory* for multilevel governance offer more general policy lessons for the biggest policy challenge of the twenty-first century, ie, to protect international public goods

[20] *cf* EU Petersmann, 'The Foreign Policy Constitution of the European Union: A Kantian Perspective' in U Immenga et al (eds), *Festschrift für Ernst-Joachim Mestmäcker* (Baden-Baden: Nomos, 1996) 433–47.

[21] On 'constitutional approaches' as ways of reducing 'fragmentation' of international legal regimes and limiting instrumental, managerial conceptions of 'rule by law' see also: M Koskenniemi, 'Constitutionalism as Mindset: Reflections on Kantian Themes about International Law and Globalization' (2007) 8 *Theoretical Inquiries in Law* 9–36; A van Aaken, 'Defragmentation of Public International Law through Interpretation: A Methodological Proposal' (2009) 16 *Indiana Journal of Global Legal Studies* 483–512.

more effectively? Does the supranational constitutional law of the EU (as interpreted by national and European courts), or do the more decentralized constitutional structures of EEA law (as interpreted by the EFTA Court) and of the ECHR (as interpreted by the ECtHR), offer models for functionally limited international economic and legal integration beyond Europe and for worldwide, collective supply of international public goods? The 'regional hegemons' in North America (like the United States), Latin America (like Brazil), Africa (like the Republic of South Africa) and Asia (like China, India, Japan and Russia) follow 'realist approaches' to international regulation and oppose submitting their 'state interests' to supranational, regional economic integration law. Yet, as discussed in chapter I, many international public goods – like a liberal world trading system, protection of the environment and of human rights – cannot be secured merely through intergovernmental negotiations without independent guardians of transnational rule of law (like the EU Commission and EU courts in the European common market) and decentralized, rights-based enforcement empowering citizens and courts to protect transnational rule of law. Hence, notwithstanding the unwillingness of most non-European governments to emulate 'European constitutionalism', the European experiences with multilevel constitutional restraints of discretionary foreign policy powers offer important lessons for constitutional reforms of IEL.

Citizen-oriented 'constitutional interpretations' of UN human rights conventions and of other international legal instruments (such as core labour rights protected by the law of the ILO) proceed from normative premises that differ from state-centred interpretations based on 'realist conceptions' of 'international law among states' as well as from functionalist interpretations of international law as 'global administrative law'. As discussed in more detail in chapters IV and VII, 'constitutional interpretations' perceive UN human rights conventions and ILO conventions not only as limiting government powers in relations among states, but as empowering citizens and protecting their individual rights and rule of law. 'Realist' and 'global administrative law' approaches, by contrast, tend to focus on 'state sovereignty' and 'rule by law'. The competing conceptions of IEL reflect the fact that the normative premises underlying many international rules and principles remain contested among governments, parliaments, courts and citizens. For example, realist approaches justify foreign policy discretion by portraying governments as the 'masters' of the law of international organizations and of their 'member-driven governance'. Courts, parliaments and citizens, by contrast, invoke human rights for justifying the counter-claim that national and international governance agents have only limited mandates that must be exercised for the benefit of citizens as the 'democratic principals'. 'Constitutional approaches' argue that the human rights obligations of all UN member states, like the constitutional duties of judges to protect human rights and 'administer justice', justify interpreting national and IEL as a functional unity for promoting consumer welfare and equal rights of citizens by limiting abuses of private and public power. The general principles underlying IEL – such as the 'basic principles underlying this multilateral trading system' (WTO Preamble) and the 'fundamental principles on which the ILO is based' (1944 Philadelphia Declaration of the ILO) – should be clarified in conformity with the human rights obligations of UN member states under UN law (eg, Articles 1, 55, 56 UN Charter). The judicial clarification of the common constitutional principles underlying national and international human rights law, constitutional law and IEL can contribute not only to overcoming the 'fragmentation' of national and international legal systems for the benefit of citizens and of their 'inviolable' and 'indivisible human rights'.[22] It can also help reduce the legitimacy deficits (eg, of intergovernmental majority voting without regard to democratic representation) and 'collective action problems' impeding more effective protection of rule of law and general citizen interests in international relations.

Judicial 'piecemeal constitutionalization' of IEL beyond Europe?

My 1991 monograph on 'Constitutional Functions and Constitutional Problems of International Economic Law' argued that the multilevel guarantees of freedom, non-discrimination and rule of law in GATT law, in the regional customs union law of the EC as well as in German constitutional law justify interpreting national and European trade law and constitutional freedoms of citizens in conformity with the GATT obligations ratified by all national parliaments inside the EC. EU institutions, however, in order to limit their legal and judicial accountability vis-*à*-vis EU citizens for their frequent violations of GATT/WTO law, continue to reject rights of EU citizens and of EU member states to invoke GATT/WTO rules in EU courts – even if EU violations of GATT/WTO legal obligations have been formally established in legally binding WTO dispute settlement rulings, the 'reasonable period' for implementing WTO obligations and terminating illegal measures has expired, and transnational rule of law would better protect the constitutional 'freedom to conduct a business in accordance with Union law' (Article 16 EU Charter of Fundamental Rights), the 'strict observance of international law' (Article 3 TEU) and consumer welfare than welfare-reducing violations of WTO law.[23] The increasingly comprehensive, multilevel judicial protection of rule of law in international trade, investment, intellectual property, criminal and human rights law and adjudication entails increasing calls for judicial protection of cosmopolitan rights beyond Europe, for example by Australian and North American researchers.[24]

The more rulemaking and adjudication in international organizations affect individual rights and 'the legal options available to private entities and persons',[25] the more citizen-oriented reforms of international economic regulation appear necessary to protect general citizen interests in consumer welfare, rule of law and democratic self-governance more effectively. In view of the often one-sided influence of powerful interest groups on

[22] The 'universal, indivisible, interrelated, interdependent and mutually reinforcing' nature of human rights was reaffirmed by all UN member states in numerous human rights instruments such as UN Resolution 63/116 of 10 December 2008 on 'the 60th anniversary of the Universal Declaration of Human Rights' UN Doc A/RES/63/116 (26 February 2009).

[23] For a discussion of the frequent neglect of the 'consistent interpretation' principle, and the denial of 'direct applicability' by EU citizens of precise and unconditional GATT/WTO guarantees, see Tables 16 and 19 and the related text. See also: EU Petersmann, 'Can the EU's Disregard for "Strict Observance of International Law" (Article 3 TEU) be Constitutionally Justified?' in M Bronckers, V Hauspiel and R Quick (eds), *Liber Amicorum* for J Bourgeois (Cheltenham: Edward Elgar Publishing, 2011) 214–25.

[24] *cf* GE Evans, *Lawmaking under the Trade Constitution. A Study in Legislating by the WTO* (Deventer: Kluwer, 2000) who uses the example of the Australian Trade Marks Act of 1995 for illustrating his hypothesis 'that the WTO may be explained as a trade constitution having the capacity to provide a legal framework for the universalization of binding norms of substantive law, which have a significant impact on private individuals at the domestic level' (at 4). For a case study of the contribution of the Andean Tribunal of Justice to protecting rule of law in the Andean Community see: LR Helfer, KJ Alter and MF Guerzovich, 'Islands of Effective International Adjudication: Constructing an Intellectual Property Rule of Law in the Andean Community' (2009) 103 *AJIL* 1–47.

[25] Evans (note 24), using the example of the Australian legislative and administrative implementation of the trade mark provisions in the WTO Agreement on Trade-Related Intellectual Property Rights (TRIPS).

intergovernmental economic regulation and the often weak oversight by national parliaments of intergovernmental rulemaking, multilevel judicial protection of individual rights and citizen participation appear ever more necessary. For example, the one-sided influence of pharmaceutical lobbies in the Uruguay Round negotiations drafting the TRIPS Agreement, or of EU banana lobbies on the EU's illegal import restrictions on bananas from 1993 to 2009, would have been easier to counterbalance if democratic participation of citizens in rulemaking had been regulated in non-discriminatory ways. Cosmopolitan conceptions of IEL can promote the necessary reconciliation of 'state sovereignty', 'popular sovereignty', 'individual sovereignty' and 'global subsidiarity' through decentralized forms of constitutionally restrained, multilevel governance and enable IEL to address more effectively 'global governance problems' like lack of transnational rule of law, mass poverty in many LDCs, climate change, or 'burden-sharing between Wall Street and Main Street' in more transparent and democratically accountable ways.[26]

De-mystification of states through 'constitutionalization' of intergovernmental power politics

Constitutional approaches to IEL aim at limiting not only welfare-reducing abuses of discretionary policy powers and the legitimacy deficits and ineffectiveness of intergovernmental power politics, for instance in case of the frequent 'VERs' concluded among trade politicians during the 1980s which redistributed domestic income and transferred 'protection rents' worth billions of dollars by means of government support for private foreign export cartels (eg, for exports of Japanese automobiles and computers) – without legislative mandate, parliamentary approval and judicial remedies for adversely affected consumers.[27] They also go beyond purely instrumental conceptions of 'rule by law' and intergovernmental 'management' of international economic problems, as well as beyond merely 'moral criticism' of international law.[28] Kantian constitutionalism offers moral and constitutional arguments for cosmopolitan empowerment of citizens through additional constitutional limitations of government powers and corresponding legal rights and judicial remedies based on principles of fairness, justice, equal rights and 'rule of law'. As the legal implications of 'principles of justice' for the design of IEL remain controversial among reasonable people,[29] general principles of 'constitutional

[26] Also the recent proposals for introducing international taxation – such as carbon taxes based on the 'polluter pays principle' or a 'global financial transaction tax' in all G20 countries which, at 0.05 per cent, could yield up to $690 billion a year (*cf* P Steinbrück, 'A tax on trading to share the costs of the crisis' *Financial Times* (25 September 2009) 13) – may be justifiable on cosmopolitan grounds.

[27] For criticism of these illegal 'grey area trade restrictions' see: Petersmann (1991) ch V.2. Both 'realists' and 'constitutionalists' agree 'that we cannot condemn a state merely for violating international law. The question is whether by violating international law a state is likely to change international law for the better from a moral perspective'; *cf* JL Goldsmith and EA Posner (2005) 199. Yet, constitutional approaches argue for 'reinterpreting' international law in conformity with constitutional principles common to national and international legal systems rather than for foreign policy discretion to disregard international legal obligations. The 'basic principles' underlying international agreements (such as the WTO Agreement and ILO Constitution), the human rights obligations of their member states, the customary methods of treaty interpretation, and the constitutional mandates of 'courts of justice' justify 'constitutional interpretations' of international law for the benefit of citizens without endangering legitimate 'state interests'.

[28] eg, by philosophers like T Pogge (2003).

[29] *cf* my responses to the polemic misrepresentations of 'European economic constitutionalism' by its Australian and Canadian critics: EU Petersmann, 'Human Rights, International Economic Law and

justice' need to be progressively clarified through democratic rulemaking, administrative rule application, judicial rule enforcement and 'deliberative democracy', with due respect for the legitimate variety of conceptions of 'international justice' and for the need to clarify them through patient 'conjectures and refutation' (Popper).

The diverse forms of multilevel constitutionalism in the EU, in the EEA as well as in the implementation of the ECHR have contributed to 'demystifying the state and the state constitution'[30] by demonstrating the need for multilevel 'constitutional checks and balances' on discretionary foreign policy powers. They have contributed not only to more transparent, more inclusive and more constitutionally restrained decision-making in intergovernmental, parliamentary and judicial bodies of international organizations and regulatory agencies for the collective supply of international public goods, like the European Central Bank protecting monetary stability of the Euro and the EU's multilevel network of national and EU competition authorities protecting undistorted competition in the EU's common market. In the long European history of constitutionally constraining foreign policy powers,[31] and establishing supranational courts protecting transnational rule of law[32] the transformation of the ECHR, the EC, EU and EEA treaties into 'constitutional instruments' with supranational courts for the protection of rights of citizens has also brought about fundamental changes in *national* constitutional systems across Europe. 'Constitutional analysis' of international law continues to be more widespread in European legal practice and research than in the state-centred international law traditions prevailing outside Europe, notably in 'hegemonic' countries like the United States and China.[33] National courts inside EU member states, like the German

"Constitutional Justice": Rejoinder to Howse' (2008) 19 *EJIL* 995; EU Petersmann, 'Taking Human Dignity, Poverty and Empowerment of Individuals More Seriously: Rejoinder to Alston' (2002) 13 *EJIL* 845–51; EU Petersmann, book review of D Cass, *The Constitutionalization of the WTO* (2006) 43 *CMLR* 890–91.

[30] A Peters, 'The Merits of Global Constitutionalism' (2009) 16 *Indiana Journal of Global Legal Studies* 397 ff, 402.

[31] See already the constitutional proposals by Donato Gianotti in his *Republica Fiorentina* (1534), for avoiding a repetition of the past 'constitutional failures' of the three Florentine Republics from the thirteenth century to 1434, from 1494 to 1512 and again from 1527 to 1530. Due to the lack of republican guarantees (eg, more than 90 per cent of the Florentine population remained without democratic citizen rights) and of restraints on foreign policy powers (eg, concerning the use of mercenary armies, political alliances with foreign kings), the constant power struggles with feudalist rulers finally led the Medici dynasty, in 1532, to establish a hereditary principality; cf D Gianotti, *Republica Fiorentina. A Critical Edition and Introduction*, G Silvano (ed) (Geneva: Librairie Droz, 1990); D Gianotti, *Die Republik Florenz (1534)*, A Riklin and D Höchli (eds) (München: Fink Verlag, 1997).

[32] Early examples of supranational courts in Europe include the ecclesiastical *Sacra Rota Romana* court created in 1331, the Imperial Chamber Court created in 1495, and the judicial remedies under the International Rhine River Organization since 1864, which all had jurisdiction open to individuals and covering several European states; *cf* L Lesaffer, *European Legal History* (The Hague: Kluwer, 2009).

[33] See, eg, Goldsmith and Posner (2005), whose 'theory is that international law emerges from states acting rationally to maximize their interests, given their perceptions of the interests of other states and the distribution of state power' (at 3). This 'state interest as we use the term is not necessarily, or even usually, the policy that would maximize the public good within the state'; 'our use of the term "state interest" is merely descriptive of leaders' perceived preferences and is morally neutral' (at 7). As Goldsmith and Posner 'are more sceptical about the role of international law in advancing international cooperation than most (but not all) international relations institutionalists and most rational choice-minded lawyers' (at 17), they largely ignore the collective action problems and 'constitutional problems' of international economic regulation: 'Information and power asymmetries, as well as the absence of centralized enforcement mechanisms, make international collective action problems difficult to overcome even where there is a plausible argument that the international regime, if successful, would enhance the welfare of every participating state' (at 217); 'the hurdles to cosmopolitan action in a liberal democracy are structural: that too much cosmopolitan sentiment among a citizenry is inconsistent with democratic statehood; that liberal democratic governments cannot act much beyond what citizens will support; and that liberal democratic processes create multiple hurdles to cosmopolitan action' (at 221); 'some

Constitutional Court in its 'Lisbon Treaty judgment' of 30 June 2009 on the constitutional limits for Germany's participation in EU integration,[34] rightly emphasize the constitutionally limited powers and limited democratic legitimacy of international organizations like the EU.[35] Yet, the Court's introverted conception of national democracy as institutionalized reasonableness neglects – similar to Hegel's one-sided idealization of the state as the legal foundation of equal liberties and other individual values[36] – the obvious 'governance failures' of states in the collective protection of 'public goods' beyond national borders. The current financial crisis in the eurozone remains characterized by long-standing violations by EU member states of the EU's legal disciplines for fiscal and debt policies (*cf* Article 126 TFEU); it illustrates, once again, that 'constitutionalizing IEL' remains a perennial challenge.

In order to justify their disregard for 'international public goods', non-European 'realists' like to dismiss 'constructivist experiences' in European integration law as pre-federal 'cooperation among states' that are unifying into a larger state 'akin to the pre-twentieth-century unification efforts in the United States, Germany and Italy'.[37] Yet, such claims are refuted by the fact that a European federal state is no longer perceived as a desirable policy objective by citizens and governments in the 27 EU member states. The current international trade, financial and environmental crises illustrate how intergovernmental power politics fails to protect not only general citizen interests in the collective supply of international public goods like a rules-based financial system protecting individual savings; it also risks undermining transparent, democratic self-governance inside states as illustrated by the repeated German Constitutional Court judgments, at the request of citizens and members of the German parliament, insisting on stronger protection of democratic rights and parliamentary duties in the multilevel governance of the eurocrisis.

State constitutions have become 'partial constitutions' that can protect 'aggregate public goods' only in cooperation with international law

The reality of legal, economic and political 'globalization' continues to transform state constitutions into 'partial constitutions' that can protect general citizen interests in international 'aggregate public goods' (like an efficient world trading system) only in cooperation with international rules and institutions. International law increasingly limits the policy discretion of UN member states by requiring protection of human rights, 'sustainable development' and of other international public goods. Yet, even though international law claims legal primacy vis-*à*-vis conflicting national rules (*cf* Article 27 VCLT), the 'constitutional functions' of IEL are not effectively protected inside most domestic legal systems. For instance, as discussed in chapter I, the internationally

of the global problems may simply be unsolvable' because 'liberal democracies are unlikely to support a cosmopolitan foreign policy' (at 226).

[34] See Table 13 and related text. An English translation of the judgment of the Constitutional Court is available at: www.bundesverfassungsgericht.de/entscheidungen/es20090630_2bve000208en. html).

[35] For critical comments on this judgment see: R Bieber, 'An Association of Sovereign States' (2009) 5 *European Constitutional Review* 391–406.

[36] *cf* GWF Hegel, *Vorlesungen über die Philosophie der Geschichte Band I: Die Vernunft in der Geschichte*, G Lasson (ed) (Heidelberg, 1920) 89 f: 'Alles was der Mensch ist, verdankt er dem Staat; er hat nur darin sein Wesen. Allen Wert, den der Mensch hat, alle geistige Wirklichkeit, hat er allein durch den Staat'.

[37] Goldsmith and Posner (2005) 126, 224.

recognized need for transforming the 'fossil economy' into a 'renewable green energy economy' in order to prevent climate change has not yet created adequate incentives in domestic legal systems for clean energy production, consumption and adaptation measures by all individual, (sub)national and non-governmental producers of greenhouse gas emissions. The collective supply of some 'global public goods' may be based on international competition provided 'market failures' are legally limited by competition, environmental and social rules. Many other international public goods (like protection of international 'energy security', health and food security) can hardly be realized without 'international solidarity' based on redistributive 'principles of justice', like the 'polluter pays principle', collective financing of climate change adjustment measures in poor countries and democratic 'duties to protect common concerns'. The following section 2 argues that mutually complementary, national and international guarantees of political and economic freedom need to be rendered more effective by interpreting them not only as legal restraints of government powers, but as corresponding rights of citizens to transnational rule of law and to legal and judicial protection of equal liberty rights across state borders.

2 KANT'S THEORY OF RIGHTS PROTECTING 'PUBLIC JUSTICE': A COSMOPOLITAN 'FOURTH CONCEPT OF LIBERTY' JUSTIFYING COSMOPOLITAN RIGHTS?

Adverse 'external effects' (like environmental pollution) and other 'market failures' can often be prevented most effectively by prohibitions conferring 'countervailing rights' to adversely affected persons (eg, rights to challenge in courts environmental pollution and restrictive business practices) and setting incentives for complementary governmental and private enforcement of the rules. Rights-based constitutionalism rests on the same insight: constitutional rights and judicial remedies protect citizens more effectively against abuses of government powers than objective constitutional restraints without effective remedies. The 'market failures', 'regulatory failures' and 'constitutional failures' in international economic regulation have their common origin in the rationality of human beings, whose moral hazards, conflicting self-interests and limited reasonableness call for stronger 'constitutional limitations' of selfish 'utility-maximization' and economic regulation. Human rights law and democratic constitutionalism offer coherent frameworks for mutually consistent, national and international regulation of globally interdependent economic activities by focusing not only on states and intergovernmental organizations, but primarily on individuals and their private associations as legal subjects of human rights and of corresponding duties to respect and protect human rights and 'corporate responsibilities' in transnational business activities.[38] The focus of human rights law and constitutional democracies on individual *rights* rather than only on communitarian *duties* runs counter to authoritarian traditions in many countries. Yet, as supply, demand and competition in international economic cooperation are driven by individual producers, investors, traders, consumers and regulators, international economic regulation must proceed from 'normative individualism' as protected by human rights. Economic regulation by means of contract law, tort law, company law, invest-

[38] On the 'UN Guiding Principles on Business and Human Rights' adopted by the UN Human Rights Council on 6 July 2011 see ch IV, section 2.

ment, competition and labour law tends to be rights-based all over the world. The need for specifying and protecting reciprocal rights and corresponding duties of producers, investors, traders, consumers and regulators also in transnational cooperation and competition leads to increasing numbers of international treaties providing for individual market access guarantees and national and international judicial remedies aimed at protecting reciprocal rights and duties of private economic actors.

Legitimately diverse traditions of economic and social constitutional rights

All UN member states have reaffirmed repeatedly their 'commitment towards the full realization of all human rights for all, which are universal, indivisible, interrelated, interdependent and mutually reinforcing'.[39] Yet, UN law leaves states not only discretion as to which human rights conventions they wish to ratify; states also have a large 'margin of appreciation' as to how civil, political, economic, social and cultural human rights should be legally protected, prioritized and reconciled in their domestic legal systems in case of conflicts.[40] The 1966 UN Covenant on Economic, Social and Cultural Rights (ICESCR) focuses on 'the right to work' (Article 6); the 'right of everyone to the enjoyment of just and favourable conditions of work' (Article 7); labour rights and trade union rights (Article 8); the 'right of everybody to social security' (Article 9); protection of the family, mothers and children (Article 10); the 'right of everyone to an adequate standard of living' (Article 11); and the human rights to health (Article 12) and to education (Article 13). Yet, apart from a brief reference to 'safeguarding fundamental political and economic freedoms to the individual' (Article 6.2), the ICESCR does not refer to the economic freedoms of profession, trade and private property which are emphasized in the EU Charter of Fundamental Rights in conformity with the constitutional traditions in EU member states. In national legal systems, human rights tend to be protected by constitutional or legislative rights, administrative practices and judicial remedies. The lack of universal agreement on economic liberties reflects the tradition in many common law countries of protecting freedom of contract, freedom of profession and other economic freedoms as common law guarantees rather than as constitutional and human rights. During the seventeenth and eighteenth centuries, English common law judges protected individual freedoms to earn a living as part of their challenges of royal monopolies. Yet, since the 'New Deal' policies during the 1930s, the US Supreme Court no longer protects the 'liberties' guaranteed by the US Bill of Rights as including economic liberties like the right to earn a living – a right which US Supreme Court Justice W Douglas had once called 'the most precious liberty that man possesses'.[41]

The EU Charter of Fundamental Rights expresses the 'indivisibility' of human rights by protecting 'dignity rights', 'liberty rights' and 'equality rights' in the economy no less

[39] See UN Resolution 63/116 on the 60th anniversary of the UDHR adopted on 10 December 2008. Inspired by the 1776 US Declaration of Independence and the 1789 French Declaration of the Rights of Man and of the Citizen, the 1948 Universal Declaration of Human Rights and numerous other UN human rights instruments have recognized the 'inherent nature' of human rights deriving simply from being born into the human family, regardless of any government or court action or inaction; *cf* J Morsink (2009).

[40] In UN Resolution 63/116 (n 39), UN member states 'deplore that human rights and fundamental freedoms are not yet fully and universally respected in all parts of the world. In no country or territory can it be claimed that all human rights have been fully realized at all times for all'.

[41] *cf* T Sandefur (2010).

than in the polity. It thereby also protects the individual liberty to decide which dimensions of civil, political, economic, social and cultural human rights an individual values most. In Europe, 'Hayekian paradigms' and common law paradigms of 'negative liberty' were successfully challenged by 'constitutional paradigms' of 'positive liberty' aimed at *enabling* individuals to live autonomous lives. Rather than focusing one-sidedly on the 'limiting constitution' (eg, *prohibiting* certain state restrictions and impermissible reasons of coercive interferences), human rights and constitutional democracy are construed as also requiring an 'enabling constitution' and social rights protecting not only 'negative freedoms from interference', but also positive, individual '*freedoms to*' develop one's individual and social lives autonomously and participate meaningfully in democratic self-governance. 'Horizontal effects' of human rights and constitutional rights in the 'private sphere' are today recognized also beyond Europe in ever more national jurisdictions.[42] Yet, *ordo*-liberal proposals for worldwide WTO guarantees of protecting consumer welfare through non-discriminatory competition rules, like human rights approaches to IEL for establishing a 'social market economy' and protecting socio-economic rights as preconditions for an autonomous life,[43] continue to be opposed by many governments outside Europe.[44] Some human rights lawyers, notably from countries that remain committed to 'parliamentary sovereignty' (like Australia, England, New Zealand) or to constitutional prioritization of civil and political rights over economic and social human rights (like the United States), claim that constitutional protection of economic rights risks 'prioritizing' economic over social rights.[45] Yet, claims for prioritizing civil and political rights and leaving economic and social rights to democratic majority legislation disregard the 'indivisibility' of human freedoms and the need for their 'constitutional balancing' in order to limit public and private abuses of economic power.

The financial crisis on Wall Street in 2008 demonstrated, once again, the economic and social risks of international economic liberalization based on Anglo-Saxon 'efficient market hypotheses' and economic majority legislation dominated by rent-seeking interest groups.[46] The 'great Depression' leading to the Second World War prompted many

[42] For a comparative study of the different constitutional methods of protecting 'horizontal effects' of constitutional rights in relations among private persons see: D Oliver and J Fedtke (eds), *Human Rights and the Private Sphere: A Comparative Study* (London: Routledge-Cavendish, 2007); A Sajo and R Uitz (eds), *The Constitution in Private Relations* (Utrecht: Eleven International Publishing, 2005).

[43] *cf* S Fredman, *Human Rights Transformed: Positive Rights and Positive Duties* (Oxford: OUP, 2008).

[44] *cf* EU Petersmann, *The Need for Integrating Trade and Competition Rules in the WTO World Trade and Legal System* (Geneva: Graduate Institute of International Studies, 1996); EU Petersmann, 'Time for Integrating Human Rights into the Law of the World Trade Organization: Lessons from European Integration Law for Global Integration Law' Harvard Law School Jean Monnet Working Paper 7/2001; EU Petersmann, 'WTO Core Principles and Trade and Competition' in B Hawk (ed), *International Antitrust Law & Policy, Annual Proceedings of the Fordham Corporate Law Institute* (2004) 669–84.

[45] See, eg, P Alston, 'Resisting the Merger and Acquisition of Human Rights by Trade Law: A Reply to Petersmann' (2002) 13 *EJIL* 815–44. Alston, Howse and other Anglo-Saxon critics of constitutional protection of economic liberties disregard the comprehensive 'balancing' of economic and non-economic rights by legislatures and courts throughout Europe.

[46] The efficient market hypothesis as advanced mainly by Anglo-American business lobbies and policymakers – ie, that market prices reflect all relevant information, that financial markets tend towards equilibrium and accurately reflect all available information about the future, that deviations from equilibrium occur randomly by exogenous shocks and that regulators can count on the market to correct its excesses – is today widely considered to have been empirically falsified by market imperfections (such as asymmetries in information) and selfish market distortions (eg, by bankers granting themselves excessive bonus rewards for their risky speculation at the expense of shareholder value and consumer welfare); *cf* A Brender and F Pisani, *Global Imbalances and the Collapse of Globalised Finance* (Brussels: Centre for European Policy Studies, 2010); L Ahamed, *Lords of Finance: The Bankers Who Broke the World* (New York: Penguin Press, 2009); G Akerlof

more European countries to adopt 'constitutional approaches' to the postwar regulation of economic and 'political markets' at national and European levels. The US Supreme Court, however, has – since the 1930s – stopped reviewing economic legislation in terms of 'substantive due process' in favour of a much more deferential 'rational basis test', resulting essentially in 'legislative freedom from judicial restraint' in most areas of economic legislation.[47] The global financial crisis which started in 2008 has prompted many countries to adopt new legislation limiting abuses of public and private governance powers and 'market distortions' through additional monetary, financial and fiscal regulation, new financial supervisory institutions and safeguard mechanisms for consumer protection in financial markets. Yet, without stronger constitutional and judicial protection of individual rights and remedies against the ubiquitous abuses of power in economic and financial markets, majoritarian economic legislation pretending to institutionalize 'public reason' and consumer protection in IEL risks failure.[48]

Kant's theory of limiting the 'unsocial sociability' of individuals by constitutional and cosmopolitan rights: a cosmopolitan 'fourth concept of liberty'

In his *Critique of Pure Reason*, Kant explained how our human understanding of the empirical world is influenced by a priori categories of human reasoning (like space, time, causality, necessity). Kant's *Critique of Practical Reason* perceived the human capacity of moral and reasonable 'judgment', 'enlightenment' and the individual's rule over oneself as social facts and as defining characteristics of human freedom.[49] Kant's theory of rights aimed at institutionalizing 'public reason' and 'public justice' on the basis of cosmopolitan rights in order to reinforce the incentives for mutually beneficial, peaceful cooperation even if the human nature (such as individual freedom of judgement) is unlikely to change. Kant's theory can also be interpreted as justifying legal and judicial empowerment of individuals to protect themselves against adverse 'external effects' caused by the ubiquity of 'market failures' and 'governance failures' in transnational cooperation among citizens: constitutional protection of an individual 'general freedom of action' (eg, as provided for in Article 2 of the German Basic Law) complements other, more narrow conceptions of liberty – like specific 'negative liberties from constraint', 'positive liberty to political inclusion' and individual 'freedom to judge for oneself'[50] – by empowering citizens and courts to challenge and review all government restrictions of

and R Shiller, *Animal Spirits: How Human Psychology Drives the Economy and Why It Matters for Global Capitalism* (Princeton: Princeton University Press, 2009); A Smithers, *Wall Street Revalued: Imperfect Markets and Inept Central Bankers* (Chichester: John Wiley & Sons, 2009).

[47] *cf* Sandefur (2010) 11 ff, 123 ff.

[48] On constitutional and judicial protection of 'public reason' as the appropriate response to the problems of 'pretence of knowledge' (Hayek) in international economic regulation see: EU Petersmann, 'Can International Public Goods be Supplied without Multilevel Constitutional Democracy and "Constitutional Justice"?' in R Nickel (ed) (2010) 61–116.

[49] For English translations and a brief comparison of Kant's three critiques of 'pure reason', 'practical reason' and of the 'power of judgment' see : CJ Friedrich (ed), *The Philosophy of Kant. Immanuel Kant's Moral and Political Writings* (New York : Modern Library, 1993).

[50] *cf* S Fleischacker, *A Third Concept of Liberty. Judgment and Freedom in Kant and Adam Smith* (Princeton: Princeton University Press, 1999), who focuses his 'third concept of liberty' – different from Isaiah Berlin's distinction between 'negative liberty *from* constraint' and 'positive liberty *to* political inclusion' – on 'the important human skill known as "judgment", and construes freedom above all as that which enables one to judge for oneself' (4, 251 ff).

individual freedom that are not sufficiently justified as being necessary and proportionate for protecting equal rights of citizens or other public interests.[51] Such a 'cosmopolitan fourth freedom' is particularly justified in mutually beneficial economic cooperation among citizens across frontiers subject to democratically approved restrictions reconciling economic freedoms with other constitutional rights.

Kant's theory of human autonomy and natural rights to equal freedoms proceeds from a substantive account of human nature (such as the inborn moral consciousness of adults, their 'idea of reason', natural needs and desires as social facts) that emphasizes both the proper moral and legal ends that humans should strive for, as well as the anthropological and political limits of human perfectibility in the historical struggles for progressive enlightenment and human reasonableness. Rather than inferring human rights from libertarian claims to self-ownership or conceptualizing them as a gift from God (as argued by Locke), Kant's moral theory deduces a universal human right to external liberty from the morality, autonomy, rationality and reasonableness (dignity) of man.[52] In order to transform the political reality of authoritarian 'rule by law' and protect equal human rights by 'rule of law' to be based on a 'universal law of freedom', Kant's legal theory emphasizes the need for protecting equal human rights through multilevel constitutional limitations of governance powers in all human interactions at national, international and transnational levels of social relations.[53] Yet, Kant's theory of the antagonistic nature of individual and social self-development acknowledged the 'unsocial sociability of men', who can develop their human reasonableness only through competition and social cooperation regulated by law (eg, in families, communities, states, transnational and international social cooperation).[54] As individuals joining society remain self-interested, rational egoists with only limited social reasonableness, the political history of progressive enlightenment through constitutional protection of equal human rights progresses through dialectic struggles for 'public justice' rather than through reasonable constructivist design, as illustrated by the popular support for the democratic revolutions in America and France during the eighteenth century which Kant welcomed as historical evidence of the progressing humanity.[55] The constitutional protection of cosmopolitan rights respecting equal legal autonomy of individuals and other 'principles of justice' provides the moral justification of, and unifying link between, national and international 'rule of law'.[56]

[51] The diverse conceptions of liberty and justice are further discussed in section 3 and ch VI.

[52] On Kant's unique connection of morality (in terms of acting from duty rather than inclination), freedom (in terms of autonomous rather than heteronomous action) and reason (in terms of categorical rather than hypothetical imperatives), and Kant's rejection of utilitarian, libertarian and virtue-based conceptions of distributive justice, see eg: T Sandel, *Justice. What's the Right Thing to Do?* (New York: Farrar et al, 2009) 104 ff. For a criticism of the prevailing interpretation of Kant's theory of rights see: G Beck, 'Immanuel Kant's Theory of Rights' (2006) 19 *Ratio Juris* 371–401.

[53] See Kant (1970) and ch III, section 1.

[54] *cf* Kant (1970) 42–45.

[55] In *The Contest of Faculties* (1798), Kant explained why the constitutional reforms resulting from the 'parliamentary revolution' in seventeenth century England and from the democratic revolutions in eighteenth century America and France offered objective evidence of progress in the history of human civilization and of the development of human 'faculties'. Even though Kant admitted the uncertain future of the constitutional reforms introduced by the revolutions in France and the United States and rejected a 'right to rebellion' that risked leading to anarchy, he perceived the public enthusiasm about the constitutional limitations of abuses of monarchical powers as empirical evidence of the progressive nature of these reforms, *cf* Kant (1970) 176 ff.

[56] In view of his perception of man as a free, moral and rational agent, Kant considered legal and governmental coercive powers to be justifiable only for 'guaranteeing negative liberty' and 'dispensing justice equally' (C Taylor, 'Kant's Theory of Freedom' in Z Pelczynski and J Gray (eds), *Conceptions of Liberty in Political*

Arguably, Kant's theory of rights remains the only constitutional theory for multilevel protection of human rights and fundamental freedoms which offers a coherent historical explanation and moral as well as legal justification of the transformation of European nation states into multilevel constitutional systems protecting equal fundamental freedoms across frontiers – first inside some European confederations and federal states (like Germany and Switzerland) and, since the 1960s, inside the EC, among the 30 member states of the EEA, in the context of EU and EEA free trade agreements with third countries (eg, Turkey) and, increasingly, also among the 47 member states of the ECHR as interpreted and progressively developed in the thousands of judgments and decisions of the ECtHR. The multilevel judicial protection of civil, political, economic and social rights of European citizens by the ECJ, the EFTA Court, the ECtHR and national courts remained the most dynamic 'integration motor' for transforming the international ECHR, EC and EEA treaties into constitutional instruments protecting equal constitutional rights of European citizens across frontiers.[57] Similar to Adam Smith's moral argument that individuals must reconcile their 'moral sentiments' and commercial self-interests through legal principles of justice,[58] Kant's constitutional theory of rights offers additional reasons why IEL in the twenty-first century must be interpreted with due respect for the human rights and fundamental freedoms of the billions of producers, investors, traders, consumers and citizens participating in the worldwide division of labour in order to satisfy their human needs for autonomous self-development. Like Montesquieu, Adam Smith and many other philosophers, Kant emphasized the importance of international trade which – due to the mutually beneficial nature of voluntary trade transactions – offers citizens and governments strong reasons for protecting equal freedoms and rule of law across frontiers in order to enlarge their human capacities and freedom of choice.

The limits of parliamentary democracy in the supply of global public goods must be compensated by legal and judicial protection of 'cosmopolitan rights'

The adverse effects of the global economic, climate and security crises on the welfare of consumers and citizens all over the globe illustrate how the economic challenges of development are closely interlinked with legal, political, social and institutional challenges to protect human rights and limit abuses of power more effectively. The 'crisis management' by most national parliaments focuses on *domestic* regulation without effective initiatives for, and parliamentary control of, intergovernmental rulemaking, administration and adjudication in worldwide organizations for the collective protection of global public goods. The political incapacity since 2008 of the democratic majority in both houses of the US Congress to approve national legislation enabling the US government to exercise

Philosophy (London: Athlone Press, 1984) 114, 118). Respect for human autonomy (as the reasonable capacity of human beings to exercise their 'negative freedoms' in conformity with self-imposed moral laws respecting equal freedoms for all others) requires voluntary understanding and reasonable self-restraint: 'actions are morally good not because they conform to a substantive ideal of moral perfection, but because they are willed in a certain (rational) manner': Beck (n 52) 384.

[57] *cf* EU Petersmann, 'Human Rights, International Economic Law and "Constitutional Justice"' (2008) 19 *EJIL* 769–98.

[58] *cf* F Forman-Barzilai, *Adam Smith and the Circles of Sympathy: Cosmopolitanism and Moral Theory* (Cambridge: CUP, 2010).

leadership for concluding the WTO Doha Round negotiations, for negotiating an international agreement on financial regulation and banking supervision to prevent a repetition of the global financial crisis, or for an international agreement on prevention of climate change, illustrates this limited capacity of parliamentary governance to secure global public goods. Even the Dodd–Frank legislation on financial reforms, finally approved by the US Congress in July 2010, focuses only on certain financial sector reforms inside the United States and delegates most of the regulatory tasks to new financial and supervisory US authorities. As its more than 2000 pages are riddled with special interest provisions, its impact on financial reforms remains unpredictable and incomprehensible for most citizens.

'Cosmopolitanism',[59] like human rights, emphasizes the 'common humanity', responsibility and need for legal recognition of the equal worth of human beings in spite of their diversities and conflict of interests. Reasonable citizens share many common objectives in life, as reflected in their demand for 'human rights', democratic self-governance, private and public goods and services like access to education and information. Yet, the human search for discovering and realizing one's unique personality also entails antagonistic instincts to give priority to rational self-interests over conflicting interest of others.[60] Most collective action problems impeding supply of 'public goods' originate in 'bounded rationality' and 'moral hazards' of individuals,[61] for example when individual confidence in 'efficient markets' prompted central bank officials (like Alan Greenspan) to assume that private bankers maximize shareholder value, or whenever 'animal spirits' (like greed) aggravated 'market failures' in the financial and banking crisis which began in 2008.[62]

The conflicting self-interests and limited reasonableness of competing individuals, and the constitutional requirement of respecting human autonomy (eg, in the sense of individual autonomy and responsibility) even in the absence of adequate legal restraints (eg, limiting rational self-interests by communitarian 'principles of justice'), make 'market failures' as well as 'governance failures' inevitable facts of life in all human societies at national and international levels. Many international agreements following the Second World War referred to the historical experiences of 'constitutional failures' – like 'man's inhumanity to man' and the inherent tendencies of freedom and competition to destroy

[59] *cf* KA Appiah, *Cosmopolitanism: Ethics in a World of Strangers* (New York: Norton & Co, 2006).

[60] On man as a violent animal and the devastating development effects of mass violence in so many countries see the 2011 Development Report by the World Bank on *Conflict, Security and Development* (Washington: World Bank, 2011), which identifies the main domestic and international causes of mass violence in terms of the 'absence of legitimate institutions that provide citizens security, justice and jobs'. Poor countries are the most vulnerable to such costly governance failures like the piracy in the Horn of Africa and the Indian Ocean (the annual costs of which are estimated at about $2 billion).

[61] On the controversial conceptions of the relationship between the human mind and the brain, and on the criticism of Descartes' 'dual substance doctrine' separating the mind from the body (eg, in contrast to the Aristotelian conception of the soul as a biological capacity as illustrated by neuro-scientific correlations between mental and brain activities), see: MR Bennet and PMS Hacker, *Philosophical Foundations of Neuroscience* (Oxford: Blackwell, 2003). Human rights rest on normative ideas of personal autonomy and responsibility that are inconsistent with neuro-scientific reduction of the mental to the physical (eg, comparing mental activities to a physically pre-determined computer programme or – as claimed by F Crick, *The Astonishing Hypothesis* (1995) 3 – to 'no more than the behaviour of a vast assembly of nerve cells and their associated molecules'). Human rights law proceeds from the Kantian premise of human autonomy, ie, it is the human person – and not only the human brain – which engages in autonomous human activities entailing human responsibilities.

[62] *cf* Akerlof and Shiller (n 46); J Fox, *The Myth of the Rational Market. A History of Risk, Reward and Delusion on Wall Street* (New York: Harper Business, 2009).

themselves ('paradox of freedom') – by emphasizing the need for international economic, humanitarian, criminal and human rights law to prevent a repetition of economic depressions, genocide, racial discrimination and war crimes.[63] For example, in the Preamble to the 1945 Constitution establishing the United Nations Educational, Scientific and Cultural Organization (UNESCO), the 193 member states justify the UNESCO rules and institutions in the following terms:

> Since wars begin in the minds of men, it is in the minds of men that the defences of peace must be constructed . . . the education of humanity for justice and liberty and peace are indispensable to the dignity of man and constitute a sacred duty which all the nations must fulfil in a spirit of mutual assistance and concern.

One major task of human, constitutional and cosmopolitan rights is to supplement and constrain individual rationality by 'public reason' empowering individuals to engage in 'struggles for their rights' and for 'rule of law' as moral duties.[64] Empirical evidence confirms that citizens restrained by constitutional safeguards of 'communitarian solidarity' often reason and behave differently inside constitutional democracies compared with their actions as utility-maximizing rivals in under-regulated global markets, or as national government representatives in power-oriented worldwide organizations. The 'bounded rationality' of individuals, and the contribution of constitutionalism to enhancing 'public reason', offer anthropological and normative reasons for Kant's moral proposition of an individual-based 'cosmopolitan law' protecting equal freedoms beyond state borders through multilevel constitutional guarantees promoting 'struggles for rights' and for transnational rule of law.

'Countervailing rights' as decentralized incentives for limiting 'market failures'

From a constitutional perspective focusing on equal human liberties as 'first principle of justice', the systemic risks of the inevitable 'market failures' go far beyond economics, for example in view of their simultaneous 'discourse failures' undermining 'public reason' as well as the legitimacy of economic regulation. International trade, investment, economic integration law and environmental law protect mutually beneficial economic transactions through ever more legal and judicial guarantees which often respond to past regulatory failures, as in the case of the successful judicial remedies and US countermeasure holding the British Petroleum company legally and financially accountable for the oil spill caused in the Gulf of Mexico.[65] International regulation of transnational monetary and financial transactions, by contrast, remains characterized by obvious 'governance failures' in the regulation and supervision of credit markets, mortgage-backed securities and other financial and banking practices that provoked the global financial crisis in 2008.[66] Just as the oil pollution crisis in 2010 and the 'climate change' crisis are

[63] *cf* L Chand Vohrar et al (eds), *Man's Inhumanity to Man: Essays on International Law in Honour of Antonio Cassese* (The Hague: Kluwer Law International, 2003).

[64] On 'life of the law as a struggle', and on 'the struggle for his rights as a duty of the person whose rights have been violated' as well as a 'duty to society', see: R Jhering, *The Struggle for Law* (Chicago: Callaghan, 1915) chs II to IV. On 'democracy as public reason' see: A Sen (2009) 321 ff.

[65] On the much less successful judicial remedies in the Bhopal chemical incident in India see ch IV.

[66] *cf* Brender and Pisani (n 47); H James, *The Creation and Destruction of Value* (Cambridge: Harvard University Press, 2009), explains the differences between the stock market crash of 1929 and ensuing

triggered by individually rational, but socially unreasonable pollution, so was the financial crisis in 2008 caused by 'bounded rationality' of financial services transactions – without adequate supervision and consumer protection in what US President Obama denounced as a 'culture of irresponsibility' in financial market practices of bankers, insurers, hedge funds and rating agencies.[67] As in the financial crisis of 1929, governments responded by nationalist safeguard measures without adequate international coordination (eg, of national bailouts of domestic banks and car industries), often at the expense of their 'Millennium Development commitments' for LDCs and without agreement on stricter international disciplines on the selfish rationality of profit-maximizing bankers, investors, insurers, hedge funds and rating agencies.

WTO law and regional trade agreements contributed to preventing a recurrence of the unilateral trade protectionism that had caused the breakdown of the international trade and financial system during the 1930s. Yet, if 'public reason' requires constitutionally and democratically justified, procedural as well as substantive restraints on the instrumental rationality of individuals[68] to limit abuses of power, then the lack of reasonable regulation of international financial markets continues to threaten the welfare of billions of citizens all over the world, for instance by enabling a continuation of the same banking practices that provoked the 2008 financial crisis. The new EU regulations setting up a European Systemic Risk Board (intended to detect risks to the European financial system and to issue early risk warnings when needed) – assisted by three new EU supervisory authorities in the areas of banking, insurance and securities as well as new EU procedures for supervision of national fiscal policies and annual budgets – regulate financial markets without strengthening individual rights and judicial remedies.[69] Similar to the inherent powers asserted by national and international 'courts of justice' for discharging their judicial functions of peaceful settlement of disputes and 'administration of justice',[70] human rights require governments to regulate international monetary, financial and environmental risks in ways that also protect the rights and judicial remedies of citizens against abuses of private and public power.

'deglobalization' of the international trading and financial system during the 1930s and the financial crisis of 2008 (when governments could avoid, eg, by means of fiscal activism and coordinated monetary liquidity expansion, a repetition of some of the problems of the 'Great Depression' during the 1930s). Many regulatory challenges of the financial crisis of 2008 differ from those of the 1930s.

[67] On US President Obama's critique of 'greed' of Wall Street bankers and other CEOs 'executive compensation – unmoored from long-term performance or even reality – rewarding recklessness rather than responsibility' see Paul Krugman, 'Out of the Shadows' *International Herald Tribune* (20–21 June 2009) 9; Paul Krugman, 'A belief in rational markets helped lead to a surprise bubble and a crisis' *International Herald Tribune* (5–6 September 2009) 17.

[68] For an overview of procedural and substantive, moral and legal criteria of 'reasonableness' in diverse fields of private and public, national and international law see: G Bongiovanni, G Sartor and C Valentini (eds) (2009).

[69] The 'Treaty on Stability, Coordination and Governance in the Economic and Monetary Union' signed by 25 EU member states in March 2012 provides (in Article 8) for judicial recourse by EU member states to the ECJ and for judicial imposition of financial sanctions against member states violating the 'fiscal compact' (Article 3).

[70] *cf* EU Petersmann, 'Need for a Constitutional Theory of International Economic Adjudication' in PM Dupuy, F Francioni and EU Petersmann (eds) (2009) ch 8. On the distinction between the limited subject-matter jurisdiction of courts (eg, their 'jurisdiction over claims'), their applicable law (to be interpreted and applied by the court) and their inherent jurisdiction (ie, the inherent or implied powers of courts deriving from their nature as a judicial body) see also: AD Mitchell (2008) ch 3.

'Constitutional functions' of cosmopolitan rights for protecting 'struggles for rights' limiting multilevel economic governance

My 1991 monograph explained the 'Constitutional Functions of International Economic Law' in terms of 'constitutional self-commitment theory': like Ulysses when approaching the island of the dangerous *sirens*, rational citizens have reasonable self-interests in limiting abuses of all policy powers, and especially of discretionary *foreign policy powers*, by empowering citizens to act as self-interested guardians of rule of law challenging abuses of regulatory powers by invoking constitutional rights and judicial remedies and, thereby, contributing to 'public reason'.[71] Globalization has increased the dangers resulting from the scant regulation in national constitutions of the importance of international law and international organizations for the supply of public goods.[72] Some countries (like Anglo-Saxon majoritarian democracies) favour, however, utilitarian conceptions of economic law and procedural conceptions of 'parliamentary democracy' leaving national and international economic regulation to majority politics and governmental discretion without substantive constitutional 'principles of justice'.[73] The different continental European tradition of constitutional and judicial protection of economic freedoms, property rights and social rights of citizens – with due regard to non-economic constitutional rights – was justified in my 1991 monograph in terms of respect for human dignity, autonomy, responsibility and diversity of individuals. By interpreting both the 'domestic policy functions' as well as the 'foreign policy functions' of IEL guarantees (eg, in WTO law) of freedom, non-discrimination, rule of law and national sovereignty in conformity with the human rights obligations of states, IEL can contribute to limiting abuses of foreign policy powers for the benefit of citizens, for instance by legally limiting trade policy powers to tax and restrict mutually beneficial trade transactions among citizens for the benefit of domestic producer interests. Just as protection of human rights and of agreed 'principles of justice' (as legal preconditions for democratic supply of national public goods) can remain effective inside constitutional democracies only to the extent 'public reason' is constitutionally protected by democratic, legislative, administrative and judicial institutions, so does collective supply of *international* public goods depend on multilevel constitutional safeguards of 'constitutional justice', rights of citizens, rule of law and democratic accountability of governance institutions limiting abuses of foreign policy powers. As emphasized in the above-mentioned UNESCO Preamble, international law and international organizations must set legal incentives for individuals and governments – for instance, by legal limitations of rational egoism and judicial accountability for predatory financial practices and restrictive business practices – to participate constructively in reasonable multilevel governance for the collective supply of international public goods. Yet, the diversity of individuals, their diverse forms of democratic self-governance at local and national levels and their 'reasonable disagreements' must be duly respected in international economic regulation.

As 'democratic owners' of international law and of all governance institutions in the twenty-first century, citizens must be able to identify themselves as democratic co-authors

[71] *cf* Petersmann (1991).

[72] On the need for 'compensatory international constitutionalization' rendering the 'constitutional functions' of international rules more effective see: A Peters and A Armingeon, 'Introduction – Global Constitutionalism from an Interdisciplinary Perspective' (2009) 16 *Indiana Journal of Global Legal Studies* 385 ff (special issue).

[73] *cf* D.Nicol (2010).

and legal subjects of IEL. Citizens have strong reasons to challenge authoritarian government traditions of disempowering citizens in their international division of labour for the benefit of bureaucratic and other powerful interests. The intergovernmental focus on rights and obligations of governments in the law of most worldwide organizations reflects an unreasonable disregard for the constitutional rights of citizens and the necessary legitimization of multilevel governance institutions by democratic participation of parliaments, civil society and citizens.[74] Discourse in intergovernmental organizations remains dominated by the self-interests of politicians, diplomats and powerful producer lobbies (eg, in granting trade protection in exchange for political support) rather than by general citizen interests, as illustrated by the lack of any reference to consumer welfare in WTO law. Also the statement in the 1919 Preamble of the International Labour Organization (ILO) that 'the failure of any nation to adopt humane conditions of labour is an obstacle in the way of other nations which desire to improve the conditions in their own countries', reflects a misunderstanding of labour law as an 'economic cost' and 'race to the bottom prisoner dilemma'. The characterization of trade liberalization as a 'concession' in Article XXVIII GATT runs likewise counter to economic theory and protection of consumer welfare.[75] From a reasonable citizen perspective, both GATT/WTO law as well as ILO law are better understood as legal frameworks for helping citizens and their democratically elected governments in maximizing reasonable citizen interests, for instance in promoting mutually complementary 'human freedoms', economic welfare, high labour standards and 'social justice' as preconditions for 'democratic peace', rule of law and lower transaction costs.[76]

'Participatory justice' requires cosmopolitan rather than Westphalian conceptions of IEL

Kant's theory of rights and of their multilevel constitutional protection confirms the practical experience in European economic integration law that legal and judicial protection of human rights and of constitutional 'principles of justice' through national and international law depends on legal and democratic empowerment of citizens who have no reason to leave the defence of their common self-interests to the discretion of the rulers. Judicial protection of individual rights and of 'participatory justice' is of particular importance in citizen-driven areas of international relations like economic and environmental cooperation. The emerging 'international markets for tradable carbon emission permits' in the framework of the UNFCCC and its Kyoto I Protocol illustrate how multilevel legal regulation of economic freedoms and property rights may be necessary instruments for supplying also environmental global public goods. For example, regula-

[74] *cf* Petersmann (1991) 423 ff.

[75] On the mutual benefits of international labour and trade law, and the lack of empirical evidence for a 'race to the bottom' (eg, induced by alleged trade and investment gains caused by lower labour rights), see: BA Langille, 'What is International Labor Law For?' (2009) 3(1) *Law and Ethics of Human Rights*.

[76] On the need for justifying international economic regulation in terms of 'constitutional input legitimacy' rather than only in terms of utilitarian 'output legitimacy' see, eg: EJ Mestmäcker, *A Legal Theory without Law. Posner versus Hayek on Economic Analysis of Law* (Tübingen: Mohr Verlag, 2007); Petersmann (1991) chs III, IV and VII. On individual freedom as both the primary objective and the most important means not only of human rights, but also of economic and social law promoting individual self-development 'in conditions of freedom and dignity' (as stated in the 1944 Philadelphia 'Declaration Concerning the Aims and Purposes of the ILO') see: A Sen (2000).

tion of the freedom to emit carbon dioxide in the production and use of fossil-based energies by property rights in tradable permits to emit carbon dioxide can provide market-based incentives for reducing greenhouse gas emissions and for developing alternative 'clean energies'. It is widely expected that the negotiations on prevention of global warming are likely to produce far-reaching changes in the international institutional architecture,[77] with repercussions on the international trading, investment and economic governance systems.

The necessary reforms of IEL must go far beyond legal-institutional issues. Democratic support from parliaments, local governments, NGOs, producers, investors, traders and consumers may not come about unless new IEL rules are recognized as reasonably justifiable and 'socially just'. The democratic and 'constitutional limits' of intergovernmental regulation, and the need for seeking more decentralized, alternative forms of 'bottom-up governance', are illustrated by the repeated failures (discussed in chapter IV) of regulating the impact of transnational business activities on human rights and labour rights through legally binding UN conventions on transnational corporations (TNCs). 'Company codes' for 'corporate social responsibility', multilevel 'certification schemes' (such as the 'Kimberley Process Certification Scheme' for exported diamonds) and decentralized enforcement of investor–state arbitral awards (eg, under the supervision of the International Chamber of Commerce and the International Centre for the Settlement of Investment Disputes) through national courts illustrate the emergence of alternative 'multilevel governance approaches' based on private–public partnerships using both 'hard law' as well as 'soft law rules' such as UN, OECD and ILO guidelines for TNCs. The need for complementing the 'international law among states' by citizen-oriented, participatory forms of economic governance raises complex questions about the interrelationships between human rights, constitutional law and economic regulation.

3 THE NEED FOR RECONCILING ECONOMIC LIBERTIES WITH ALL OTHER CONSTITUTIONAL RIGHTS: FROM 'NEGATIVE' TO 'POSITIVE LIBERTIES' PROTECTING 'HUMAN CAPABILITIES'

The German 'historical school' perceived law as 'the science of liberty' (von Savigny).[78] Responding to the 'constitutional failure' of dictatorship and genocide in Nazi Germany, the constitutional guarantee of a general right to liberty of action and 'free development of the personality' in Article 2 German Basic Law is interpreted by the German Constitutional Court as protecting, prima facie, all individual liberty interests to do or not to do whatever is valued by the individual, including riding horses through public woods,[79] feeding pigeons in public squares,[80] smoking marihuana[81] and importing a particular breed of dog into the country,[82] subject to constitutional and legislative limitations provided they are necessary and proportionate for protecting more important

[77] CF Bergsten in his Preface to GC Hufbauer, S Charnovitz and J Kim (2009) ix.

[78] *cf* LJ Wintgens, 'From Law without a Science to Legal Science without the Legislator: The German Historical School and the Foundation of Law' (2010) 31 *Statute Law Review* 85–106.

[79] BVerfGE 80, 137.

[80] BVerfGE 59, 158.

[81] BVerfGE 90, 145.

[82] BVerfGE 110, 149.

public interests.[83] Similarly, the ECtHR has adopted an expansive understanding of privacy guaranteed under Article 8 ECHR. The elaboration of legal institutions protecting equal freedoms from abuses of private and public power continues to be a core issue of jurisprudence in European human rights and economic law.[84] German and European constitutional law protect economic liberties and related, decentralized decision-making and market competition. Inside the EU and the EEA, these 'market freedoms' are protected not only by common market rules limiting governmental trade barriers, but also by EU competition rules limiting *private* restrictive business practices as well as – in contrast to US antitrust law – *public* restraints and distortions of competition by EU member states and EU institutions. Proposals for negotiating worldwide competition rules complementing the liberal trade rules of the WTO have, however, been opposed by governments in LDCs in spite of the fact that restrictive business practices tend to harm consumer welfare especially in LDCs without effective competition laws.

The enlargement of markets by means of EU law required private and public actors to liberalize private and public restraints on individual freedoms that had been accepted inside EU member states for centuries. The transformation – in European economic integration law – of intergovernmental 'market freedoms' (eg, in the EC and EAA treaties) into constitutional rights of 500 million European citizens, protected by national and European courts also beyond the EU (eg, in EFTA countries like Switzerland), has transformed the European 'private law society' (Böhm) coordinating production, investments, trade and consumption by means of private law (such as contract, corporate and labour law). It also transformed constitutional democracy inside EU member states by multilevel guarantees of economic liberties and free movements of goods, services, persons, capital and related payments across state borders. While the ideas of constitutional liberty protecting civil society in a common market became constitutional law for the first time through the Constitutions of the United States (1789) and France (1791), the cosmopolitan ideal of an international common market with transnational citizen rights protected by multilevel constitutional law has become a social reality for the first time in EU law. In Anglo-Saxon countries, the US Bill of Rights and national constitutions protect personal freedoms without specific references to economic liberties in view of the unwritten 'common law freedoms' of contract, property and freedom of profession and the reliance, in common law countries, on 'enlightenment of society by the rule of law'.[85] Likewise, the ICESCR of 1966 refers neither to freedom of profession and trade nor to protection of private property, notwithstanding its recognition that states should safeguard 'economic freedoms to the individual' (Article 6, paragraph 2). The EU treaties, the ECJ and the EU Charter of Fundamental Rights, by contrast, protect the common market freedoms as integral parts of the constitutional rights and corresponding obligations of EU citizens. Such diverse constitutional traditions often entail diverse approaches to international economic regulation and adjudication.

[83] For an explanation of this constitutional and judicial guarantee of a general right to liberty and the 'balancing' of constitutional rights (that operate also as 'principles' to be optimized in the whole legal order and public interests – without understanding rights as 'trumps' as proposed by Dworkin (1977) 266 – see: R Alexy (2002) ch 7.

[84] For comparative studies see: D Merten and HJ Papier (eds), *Handbuch der Grundrechte*, vol VI (Karlsruhe: Müller Verlag, 2010).

[85] T Bingham, 'The Rule of Law' (March 2007) 66 *Cambridge Law Journal* 67–85.

Should protection of economic liberties be left to majority legislation?

The multilevel constitutional and judicial protection of economic liberties in the EU – based on judicial interpretation and protection of the EU common market rules as individual rights – remains contested outside the EU, notably in Anglo-Saxon countries without constitutional protection of comprehensive liberty rights and human rights in the economy no less than in the polity.[86] My 1991 monograph criticized 'Hayekian conceptions' of multilevel legal protection of a 'constitution of liberty' – as reflected in the laws of Anglo-Saxon democracies, the 1944 IMF Agreement and GATT 1947 – for their neglect of the necessary 'social embedding' of the international division of labour. The 'great transformation' (Polanyi) caused by the financial crisis of 1929, the subsequent breakdown of the international payments and trading system and ensuing 'social disembedding' during the 1930s facilitated the emergence of political dictatorships in many European countries, ushering in the Second World War. My 1991 book argued for constitutional protection of a 'social market economy' based not only on civil and political, but also economic and social rights of citizens. Human rights require supplementing the 'negative liberties from government interferences' – as protected to a limited extent by the common law guarantees of contract law, property law and tort law, the 1944 Bretton Woods Agreements and GATT 1947 – by 'positive liberties' necessary for human self-realization and for democratic communities committed to constitutional principles of justice.

The social injustice caused by judicial interpretations of liberty rights as merely 'negative liberties from government interferences' were illustrated by the civil rights cases in the United States: the judicial protection of private liberty to choose contractual partners prompted the US Supreme Court to annul congressional legislation prohibiting racial discrimination that did not result from state action.[87] Similarly, in the US Supreme Court decision in *Lochner v New York* (Table 14), the US Supreme Court annulled social legislation in the state of New York prescribing a maximum limit for hours of work. The Court protected the freedom of bakers to enter into contracts with their employers on whatever terms the parties were able to agree. In both cases, the Supreme Court conceived the 'private law society' as a neutral realm of private liberty and self-regulation, which the judiciary must protect against legislative encroachment even if the democratic legislation aimed at preventing racial discrimination in housing markets or abuses of power in labour markets. The 'Lochner era' until the 1930s remained characterized by one-sided judicial interpretations of the common law freedom of contract as a constitutional liberty without adequate judicial regard to other constitutional principles like the need for balancing economic and social constitutional rights.[88]

[86] For a critical review of 'the failures of both Canada and the United States to protect the economic rights of all their citizens' (at 5) see: RE Howard-Hassmann and CE Welch (eds) (2006). On the judicial abandonment of protecting 'substantive due process of law' and constitutional guarantees of economic liberty vis-à-vis economic interest group legislation based on a 'rational basis' see: BH Siegan (1980); Sandefur (2010).

[87] 109 US 3 (1883).

[88] *cf* W McCormack, 'Lochner, Liberty, Property and Human Rights' (2005) 1 *New York University Journal of Law & Liberty* 433 ff, who acknowledges that the 'Lochner' decision is justly criticized for protecting the property and contract claims of the strong against the weak; but this judgment also continued protecting a general concept of liberty that flowed from English common law traditions regarding personal autonomy. If the Supreme Court – in the *Slaughter House* cases – had recognized the right of occupation claimed by the New Orleans butchers as part of their liberty protected by due process, then the reformers of the later

Table 14: *Lochner v New York*, 198 US 45 (1905): Constitutional protection of 'negative liberty' in labour markets without regard to 'social justice'?

Lochner v New York, 198 US 45 (1905): The Supreme Court invalidated a state law limiting the hours of labour in bakeries to ten a day or sixty a week on the grounds that (a) state police power was overreached as the occupation of baker was not dangerous to health; and (b) the statute interfered with the rights of individuals and deprived them of freedom of contract protected by the due process clause of the Fourteenth Amendment.
Regulatory problem: To what extent does the due process clause protect economic liberties ('substantive due process')? Are state laws protecting discriminatory interferences into the common law freedoms of contract and private property? Is constitutional protection of 'negative liberties' (eg, in the sense of 'contractual self-government') sufficient for securing social justice in labour markets? How should 'courts of justice' reconcile and 'balance' diverse constitutional and human rights? Is the assumption by the US Supreme Court in the post-1937 era convincing that virtually every economic regulation pursues public rather than private purposes and affects all private interests in the same way? Why does the 'rational basis test' of the US Supreme Court (= 'procedural due process') offer no adequate standard for reviewing the reasonableness of economic regulation and for reconciling private and democratic self-government?

When the Supreme Court, first in 1937 and definitively since 1941, gave up striking down economic and social legislation on the ground of violation of 'substantive due process' (as protected by the due process clauses in the Fifth and Fourteenth Amendments), the judiciary – rather than engaging in 'judicial balancing' of competing constitutional principles in judicial review of majoritarian economic legislation – 'essentially abandoned the field to legislatures because social and economic issues ultimately rested on policy judgments not amenable to resolution pursuant to anything resembling legal reasoning'.[89] Today, many Americans find it bizarre that 'economic freedom would be protected by the Constitution in the same way that it protects rights of religious freedoms or privacy',[90] or that judges should strictly scrutinize democratic economic regulation redistributing domestic income and distorting competition for the benefit of rent-seeking industries. Yet, if the main purpose of constitutional democracy is to protect the equal human rights of citizens against abuses of private and public power, is it reasonable to expect that constitutional protection of equal liberties and other human rights can always be secured through majoritarian legislation and administration by periodically elected governments without constitutional and judicial clarification and reasoned 'balancing' of economic and social rights? American antitrust laws are, accord-

nineteenth and early twentieth centuries would have been on notice that economic rights existed and could justify social reforms. Only the dissenting minority judges in the *Slaughter House* cases accepted an unwritten 'right to pursue a lawful employment in a lawful manner, without other restraint than such as equally affects all persons' (83 US (166 Wall.) 36 (1873) 418). McCormack's conclusion – 'Liberty may well be a convenient term for summarizing much of the content of human rights. If so, then the *Lochner* experience may prove helpful to decision-makers across the globe' (at 475) – argues for a 'generalized notion of human dignity and liberty' that would be more similar to judicial review in European constitutional law.

[89] M Tushnet (2008) 185; for a criticism of the judicial abandonment of 'economic due process review' on the ground that the judiciary must protect *all* liberty rights, including equal economic liberties of citizens against majoritarian interest-group regulation and pervasive 'market failures', see: Siegan (1980).

[90] Sandefur (2010) 292.

ing to the US Supreme Court, 'the Magna Charta of free enterprise . . . They are as important to the preservation of economic freedom and our free enterprise system as the Bill of Rights is to the protection of our fundamental freedoms'.[91] Antitrust law illustrates not only that economic legislation may, indeed, serve 'constitutional functions' for protecting consumer welfare against abuses of market power by offering citizens effective judicial remedies against 'market failures'.[92] The absence – in most European countries prior to the entry into force of the 1957 EEC Treaty[93] – of effective competition laws limiting restrictive business practices demonstrated the frequent reality that legislative majorities may be dominated by rent-seeking interest groups preventing effective protection of equal freedoms and social justice. Similarly, the lack of adequate health insurance of millions of US citizens prior to the adoption of new federal health legislation in 2009 demonstrated that social justice may be secured neither by market competition nor by majoritarian, parliamentary legislation without constitutional and judicial protection of social rights.

From 'negative liberties' to legal and judicial protection of 'positive constitutional liberty' committed to social justice

Chapters V and VI discuss how – similar to the US Constitution's commitment to securing 'the blessings of liberty to ourselves and our posterity' (Preamble) – modern theories of justice (from Kant to Rawls) and ever more constitutional democracies acknowledge equal liberties as the 'first principle of justice'.[94] Yet, the central term of democratic and economic liberalism – liberty – often remains unclear and deeply contested. In his essay on 'Two Concepts of Liberty',[95] Isaiah Berlin distinguished 'negative liberty' (in the sense of *freedom from constraints* and from interferences by other people) from 'positive liberty' (in the sense of *freedom to act* as a legal subject of democratic self-governance). Positive liberties to participate in democratic self-government require civil and political rights, for instance of individual access to institutions protecting justice, education and participation in democratic elections. Likewise, economic self-governance through division of labour requires constitutional protection of open markets based not only on 'negative freedom' such as prohibitions of internal market access barriers as provided for in most national constitutions; 'positive liberties' (eg, to petition competition authorities and courts for legal protection against abuses of market power) may be no less necessary for protecting non-discriminatory conditions of competition. The *Lüth* case, in which the German Constitutional Court – in the context of a private 'constitutional complaint' – held a politically motivated, private boycott to be justifiable on grounds of freedom of expression illustrates this potentially 'direct effect' of constitutional rights on the interpretation of private law and 'market freedoms.' Today's prevailing view in European

[91] *United States v TOPCO Assoc Inc*, 405 US 596, 610 (1972).

[92] On the decentralized enforcement of US antitrust law see: CA Jones, *Private Enforcement of Antitrust Law in the EU, UK and USA* (New York: OUP, 1999); on the inherent tensions between freedom of contract, freedom of competition and liberal democracy see: G Amato, *Antitrust and the Bounds of Power* (Oxford: Hart Publishing, 1997).

[93] *cf* DJ Gerber, *Law and Competition in Twentieth Century Europe: Protecting Prometheus* (Oxford: OUP, 1998).

[94] *cf* J Rawls (revised edn, 1999) sections 11 (two principles of justice) and 32 (the concept of liberty).

[95] I Berlin, *Liberty*, revised edn H Hardy (ed) (Oxford: OUP, 2002) 166 ff.

constitutional law is based on this constitutional and judicial protection of constitutional rights as constituting an 'objective order of values' that affects public as well as private law: 'every provision of private law must be compatible with this system of values, and every such provision must be interpreted in its spirit'.[96]

Table 15: *Lüth*, BVerfGE 7 (1956) 198: Constitutional protection of 'positive liberty' in economic markets (freedom of expression)

- The *Lüth case*, German Constitutional Court, BVerfGE 7 (1958), 198: The Constitutional Court admitted a private 'constitutional complaint' and confirmed that fundamental constitutional rights (such as the general personality right and freedom of expression protected by Articles 2 and 5 of the Basic Law) could legally justify a private boycott against a film produced by a former Nazi film director (who had produced the anti-semitic film *Jud Süss*): apart from granting individual rights, constitutional rights also prescribe objective constitutional values that apply to the whole legal order and must be taken into account in judicial interpretation of general private law clauses (such as the civil court injunctions against the boycott based on the private law prohibition of intentionally harming another 'in a manner offensive to good morals').

From *ordo*-liberal theories of economic rights to social and cosmopolitan justice?

Inside constitutional democracies, citizens tend to be recognized as legal subjects with individual rights and judicial remedies against legislative and administrative restrictions of individual rights. The postwar Bretton Woods Agreements and GATT/WTO law, however, provide only for international rights and obligations of governments without directly empowering citizens and protecting individual rights by judicial remedies. The universal recognition of human rights entails that theories of 'natural liberty' (eg, in favour of market economies indifferent to wealth distribution), like theories of 'fair equality of opportunity' (eg, privileging individual talent), are increasingly challenged by rights-based theories of justice constitutionally constraining duty-based and goal-based conceptions of 'good governance'. While '*first generation civil and political rights*' are often (mis)conceived as 'negative liberties' (eg, focusing on prohibitions of interference with the right-holder's freedom), '*second generation economic, social and cultural rights*' tend to be interpreted as 'positive claim-rights' (eg, of access to essential medical care, food, housing and education). '*Third generation human rights*' – which focus on collective 'solidarity rights' to social and economic development, protection of the environment, democratic governance and, as already proclaimed in Article 28 of the UDHR, to the entitlement of 'everyone . . . to a social and international order in which the rights set forth in this Declaration can be fully realized' – continue to remain even more controversial. The following chapters infer from the universal recognition of human rights that the regulation of mutually beneficial, international economic cooperation among citizens should be based on rights-based conceptions of modern IEL recognizing citizens as

[96] BVerfGE 7, 198 (15 January 1958); *cf* H Rösler, 'Harmonizing the German Civil Code of the 19th Century with a Modern Constitution – The Lüth Revolution 50 Years Ago in Comparative Perspective' (2008) 23 *Tulane European and Civil Law Forum* 1 ff.

'primary legal subjects' and sources of all constitutional values. As international division of labour has proven to be the most important tool for enhancing economic welfare, IEL should be interpreted as entitling and empowering citizens to challenge welfare-reducing, protectionist border restrictions of their equal freedoms and other discriminatory market access barriers. Legal protection of human rights and of general consumer welfare calls for cosmopolitan restraints on multilevel economic governance, for instance by stronger 'institutional checks and balances' and judicial protection of rule of law. Human rights and constitutional rights limit utilitarian conceptions of 'law and economics', for instance if a purely economic focus on 'total wealth maximization' in the allocation of goods and other resources to those people who value them most (as determined by their willingness and ability to pay more for the resources) entails social injustice inconsistent with human rights of access to essential goods and services at affordable prices.

The '*ordo*-liberal approach' – as advocated first by the 'Freiburg School of law and economics' in the 1930s[97] – prepared the intellectual foundations for the EU's functionally limited 'economic constitution' based on common market and competition rules aimed at systematic limitation of economic 'market failures' (like cartelization and other restrictive business practices) as well as of government failures (like welfare-reducing border restrictions). The national as well as European monetary, competition, trade and common market regulation and EU institutions continue to dynamically evolve into a multilevel constitutional framework protecting monetary stability, common market freedoms of 500 million European citizens, their consumer welfare and other public goods like human rights, rule of law and the environment.[98] My 1991 monograph justified such 'constitutional conceptions of economic liberties' – building on similar constitutional approaches in the process of creating common markets inside federal states (like Germany and Switzerland) – subject to the proviso that 'fundamental economic freedoms' (like the common market freedoms protected by the ECJ and national courts inside the EU) must be construed and protected with due regard to other civil, political, social and cultural rights of citizens, as reflected by the 'proportionality balancing' of civil, political, economic and social rights in the case law of German and European courts. Raz has argued that 'negative freedom, freedom from coercive interferences, is valuable in as much as it serves positive freedom and autonomy'.[99] Similarly, constitutional and judicial protection of economic liberties is necessary not only for protecting citizens against abuses of public and private power, but for enabling individuals to gain the resources necessary for assuming control of their own lives and for constitutional protection of autonomous, individual as well as communal self-development.[100]

[97] *cf* F Böhm, *Wettbewerb und Monopolkampf* (Tübingen: Mohr, 1933); F Böhm, *Die Ordnung der Wirtschaft als geschichtliche Aufgabe und rechtsschöpferische Leistung* (Tübingen: Mohr, 1937); Petersmann (1991) 63 ff.

[98] On the EU's 'economic constitution' see, eg: Immenga et al (eds) (n 20).

[99] J Raz, *The Morality of Freedom* (Oxford: OUP, 1986) 410.

[100] *cf* Petersmann (1991) 334 ff; EU Petersmann, 'Human Rights and International Trade Law: Defining and Connecting the Two Fields' in T Cottier, J Pauwelyn and E Bürgi (eds), *Human Rights and International Trade* (Oxford: OUP, 2005) 29–94. For a detailed explanation of an autonomy-based, Kantian understanding of constitutional liberty see: Fleischacker (n 50).

The need for strengthening the social welfare functions of IEL

My 1991 monograph concluded that European economic integration law should extend the regulatory objectives of *ordo*-liberalism – as reflected in European competition and common market rules – in conformity with the 'social market economy approach' advocated by German postwar governments on the basis of Germany's constitutional commitment to a social welfare state. In view of the ever more comprehensive human rights guarantees in EU law, Article 3 TEU now explicitly commits the EU to 'a highly competitive social market economy, aiming at full employment and social progress, and a high level of protection and improvement of the quality of the environment'.[101] As discussed in chapters VII and VIII, the judicial activism of the ECJ in protecting non-discrimination and social integration of EU citizens exercising their EU market freedoms and claiming access to universal services illustrates the need for legal and judicial reconciliation of economic freedoms with social rights and human rights. The ECJ judgments in the 2007 *Viking* and *Laval* cases reconciling economic and social rights contributed to the clarification of the EU's 'social market economy' by 'judicial balancing' of the 'common market freedoms' of EU citizens with the rights of trade unions.[102] Similarly, the 'dignity rights' protected in Title I of the EU Charter of Fundamental Rights may justify interpreting 'common market freedoms' and the 'liberty rights' protected in Title II of the Charter in terms of autonomy-based 'positive liberties'.[103]

Human rights, social rights and social welfare functions continue to be progressively strengthened as integral parts of European economic and integration law. Worldwide IEL should likewise promote the necessary 'social embedding' of open market economies by means of multilevel, constitutional protection of human, social and labour rights to limit 'market failures' more effectively and provide for 'global public goods'. As explained in chapter VIII and increasingly recognized also by economists (like Nobel Prize laureate Amartya Sen) and political philosophers (like Nussbaum), 'sustainable development' – as explicitly recognized as an objective of the WTO in the Preamble to the WTO Agreement – must be construed in conformity with the human rights obligations of states in order to promote mutual synergies between civil, political, economic, social and environmental rights and empower individuals to develop their 'human capacities'.[104] The UN Resolutions on the 'Right to Development' since 1986 have likewise considered development and human rights as two sides of the same process allowing the realization of civil, political, economic, social and cultural rights and other fundamental freedoms by expanding the capabilities and choices of individuals.[105]

[101] The Lisbon Treaty on the EU (OJ C/306 of 17 December 2007) entered into force on 1 December 2009.

[102] See Table 25 and related text.

[103] On competing constitutional conceptions of liberty rights see Fleischacker (n 50) and K Möller, 'Two Conceptions of Positive Liberty: Towards an Autonomy-based Theory of Constitutional Rights' (2009) 29 *Oxford Journal of Legal Studies* 757–86.

[104] On 'development as freedom' and substantive 'opportunity to achieve' see: A Sen, *Rationality and Freedom* (Cambridge: Harvard University Press, 2002) ch 17 on 'Markets and Freedoms'; Sen (2000), explaining the mutually reinforcing synergies among different types of 'instrumental freedoms' for self-development. On the 'capabilities approach' interpreting human rights as legal entitlements to develop one's 'human capabilities' and a 'life worthy of human dignity' see MC Nussbaum, *Frontiers of Justice* (Cambridge: Harvard University Press, 2006) 69 ff; MC Nussbaum, 'Beyond the Social Contract: Capabilities and Global Justice' in G Brock and H Brighouse (eds), *The Political Philosophy of Cosmopolitanism* (Cambridge: CUP, 2005) 196 ff.

[105] *cf* S Marks, *Report of the High Level Task Force on the Implementation of the Right to Development on its 6th Session* (Geneva: UN Doc A/HRC/15/WG.2/TF/2, January 2010).

4 LIMITATION OF 'PROTECTION BIASES' BY INTERPRETING IEL IN CONFORMITY WITH HUMAN RIGHTS AND 'COSMOPOLITAN CONSTITUTIONALISM'

Chapter III has argued that 'civilizing' and 'constitutionalizing' political markets (democracy) as well as economic markets require an 'overlapping consensus' on constitutional principles of justice and their constitutional, legislative, executive and judicial protection on the basis of constitutional rights and human rights in order to limit abuses of regulatory powers. Economic policy powers include powers to tax domestic citizens (eg, by means of tariffs); restrict their freedoms (eg, by quantitative restrictions); redistribute income among domestic groups (eg, by means of subsidies); and distort competition for the benefit of powerful interest groups (eg, by granting monopoly powers and other restraints of competition). As concentrated producer interests are easier to organize than large groups with dispersed interests (like taxpayers and consumers), regulatory discretion tends to be influenced and 'lobbied' in all countries by rent-seeking producer interests benefiting from concentrated 'protection rents' which rational consumers are likely to neglect.[106] Hence, protection of general consumer welfare depends on constitutional rules protecting open markets, non-discriminatory conditions of competition and judicial remedies against protectionist abuses of regulatory powers and of democratic majority decisions. This is particularly so in the field of foreign economic policy powers in view of the longstanding 'realist traditions' of avoiding substantive constitutional restraints on foreign policy powers.[107]

Table 16: Access to justice as a constitutional safeguard against the 'protection biases' in IEL?

Access to justice as an individual right is protected in diverse ways in national and international human rights instruments (eg, Article 8 UDHR, Article 13 ECHR, Article 47 EU Charter of FR, Articles 3 and 7 African Charter of Human and People's Rights, Articles 8 and 25 Inter-American Charter of Human Rights) as well as in numerous IEL treaties (eg Article X GATT, BITs, RTAs).

Regulatory problem: To what extent should individual access to justice be protected in IEL in view of the fact that monetary, trade and other economic policy powers include powers to tax domestic citizens, restrict their freedoms, redistribute income among domestic groups and distort competition for the benefit of powerful interest groups? Should judicial remedies also offer safeguards against 'procedural biases' and 'regulatory capture' by concentrated producer interests that are easier to organize and more successful in lobbying for concentrated 'protection rents' than large social groups with more dispersed common interests and 'rational ignorance' towards specific economic regulation accommodating protectionist

[106] On information asymmetries, 'discourse failures' and 'protection biases' in discretionary economic regulation as explained by 'public choice theory' (eg, in the publications by M Olson and G Stigler and briefly summarized in Table 8, see: Petersmann (1991) 6 ff, 112 ff; M Olson, *The Logic of Collective Action. Public Goods and the Theory of Groups* (Cambridge: Harvard University Press, 1962); M Olson, *The Rise and Decline of Nations. Economic Growth, Stagflation and Social Rigidities* (New Haven: Yale University Press, 1982). On public choice explanations of trade protectionism see the case studies in Hilf and Petersmann (eds) (1993) pt V.

[107] *cf* the comparative studies of the diverse constitutional law traditions of regulating 'foreign affairs' in Hilf and Petersmann (eds) (1993).

interests? Does the history of rights-based competition law and common market regulation confirm that constitutional rights and other 'countervailing rights' of citizens offer the most effective remedies against protectionist 'governance failures' as well as 'market failures'? Is it true that – the more regulatory discretion is constitutionally restrained by equal freedoms and principles of non-discriminatory competition and access to justice (eg, inside the EU's common market) – the more effectively general citizen interests can be protected? Why does the US Supreme Court's deferential 'rational basis standard' of judicial review of economic legislation protect only 'procedural due process of law' whereas all European and international courts review also 'substantive due process' of economic legislation?

Emergence of cosmopolitan IEL in spite of reasonable disagreement on its constitutional foundations

Sections 1 and 3 justified the emergence of 'cosmopolitan economic rights' – first in transnational commercial, arbitration and human rights law and, since the 1960s, in regional economic integration law, international trade, investment and intellectual property (*cf* Table 2) – not only on grounds of rights-based moral, constitutional and economic arguments. Today's universal commitment by all UN member states to 'the full realization of all human rights for all, which are universal, indivisible, interrelated, interdependent and mutually reinforcing'[108] was also seen as justifying the claim that – today – the human rights obligations of all UN member states can no longer be limited to their function as 'negative' and 'positive' civil and political rights; UN member states are also required, albeit to different degrees (eg, depending on their ratification of human rights conventions), to protect economic, social and cultural 'autonomy rights' (eg, to protection of private property at national and international levels), whose precise content often remains contested. Sections 1 and 2 also recalled the 'constitutional function' of cosmopolitan rights to empower citizens by means of 'countervailing rights' to challenge the ubiquity of abuses of regulatory powers – notably in transnational economic relations, where organized interest groups influence discretionary economic regulation in order to obtain 'protection rents' at the expense of poorly organized, general interests of consumers and taxpayers.

The often 'reasonable disagreement' among countries on the constitutional foundations, scope and contents of human rights, economic rights and cosmopolitan rights may be justifiable in terms of both human rights law, constitutional law and economic law. Since the American and French revolutions of the eighteenth century, human rights law evolved at national and international levels in three successive phases:

- first, as inalienable *civil and political rights*, which are increasingly protected as 'positive rights' to inclusive decision-making (eg, prohibiting racial and gender discrimination) rather than only as 'negative rights' against arbitrary government restrictions;
- secondly, protection of *economic, social and cultural rights* remains more contested depending on the diverse national constitutional traditions; to date, the number of ratifications of the 1966 UN Covenant on Economic, Social and Cultural Human Rights remains smaller (160 parties by August 2009) compared with the ICCPR (164

[108] UN Resolution 63/116 of 10 December 2008 on the 60th anniversary of the Universal Declaration of Human Rights.

parties by August 2009), and Article 2 of the ICESCR provides for more flexible legal obligations to implement economic, social and cultural rights compared with the implementation obligations of Article 2 of the ICCPR; the legal 'integration' of human rights and economic law in European integration law, as illustrated by rights to free movement and non-discriminatory treatment of workers and of EU citizens inside the EU, goes far beyond what is prescribed in the regional economic integration law outside Europe;[109]

- thirdly, legal protection of collective '*third generation rights*' – like rights to development and to protection of the environment – remains even more contested. Yet, all UN member states have recognized collective rights (eg, to popular self-determination and development) and corresponding 'duties to protect' citizens against gross human rights violations by their own governments, notwithstanding the diverse conceptions of constitutional, parliamentary and participatory democracy among UN member states.

Human rights and cosmopolitanism share at least the following three principles: first, values must be derived from respect for human beings (normative individualism); secondly, individuals must be treated equally as sharing a universal legal status; and thirdly, this equal legal status must be recognized generally and globally calling for 'cosmopolitan constitutional safeguards' of human rights and cosmopolitan rights beyond state borders limiting both 'state sovereignty', 'popular sovereignty' and power-oriented dichotomies of national and international law. Sections 1 to 3 argued that Kant's theory of 'multilevel cosmopolitan constitutionalism' offers not only convincing normative justifications for empowering citizens through cosmopolitan rights limiting abuses of public and private powers in multilevel economic governance and economic cooperation among citizens across frontiers. It was also argued that the human rights obligations of UN member states, the 'consistent interpretation principles' recognized in national and international legal systems, and 'cosmopolitan interpretations' of 'state sovereignty' and 'popular sovereignty' may justify interpreting *existing IEL rules* (eg, in international trade, investment and intellectual property law) as also protecting cosmopolitan 'trading rights', 'investor rights', 'intellectual property rights', consumer and citizen rights and judicial remedies: an interpretation and protection of modern IEL for the benefit of citizens and of their human rights may 'fit best' (in the sense of Dworkin's interpretation maxim) the constitutional duties of governments to protect the human rights of citizens more effectively at home and in the international cooperation among citizens.

Section 3 emphasized that the constitutional legitimacy of economic rights depends on their legal and judicial 'balancing' with all other constitutional and human rights. It was noted that – in contrast to the constitutional guarantees of economic liberties like freedom of profession in national constitutions of European countries (eg, Article 12 German Basic Law) as well as in EU law (eg, Articles 15 and 16 EU Charter of Fundamental Rights) – the US Supreme Court ceased protecting freedom of profession as an implicit guarantee of the US Bill of Rights. US Supreme Court judges once had protected individual economic freedoms – like the freedom to earn a living as 'the most

[109] *cf* F Fuders, 'Economic Freedoms in MERCOSUR' and L Lixinski, 'Human Rights in MERCOSUR' in MT Franca Filho, L Lixinski and MBO Giupponi (eds), *The Law of MERCOSUR* (Oxford: Hart Publishing, 2010) 87–130, 351–64.

precious liberty that man possesses'[110] – under the US Constitution's contract clause and 'due process' guarantees. Yet, since the 'New Deal Supreme Court's 1934 landmark judgment in *Nebbia v New York*, this constitutional and judicial protection has been replaced with more narrow, positivist interpretations of the Bill of Rights; the now prevailing, extremely deferential 'rational basis test' recognizes parliamentary and government discretion to regulate economic freedoms as long as the regulation remains 'rationally related to a legitimate government interest'.[111] The link between personal liberty and economic rights was recognized by the US Supreme Court in respect of property rights: 'In fact, a fundamental interdependence exists between the personal right to liberty and the personal right to property: Neither could have meaning without the other'.[112] Also US antitrust law was recognized by the US Supreme Court 'as important to the preservation of economic freedom and our free enterprise system as the Bill of Rights is to the protection of our fundamental freedoms'.[113] Yet, US courts tend to exercise judicial deference towards democratic majority regulation even if – as in the case of the 2600 pages of the Dodd–Frank Wall Street Reform and Consumer Protection Act, which had been drafted by the US Congress in close cooperation with financial lobbies and became law in the US in July 2010[114] – economic regulation seems to redistribute income among domestic groups in discriminatory and selective ways.

Legal and judicial remedies of citizens vis-à-vis abuses of multilevel economic governance powers often remain inadequate

Transnational rule of law and rights of citizens (as 'democratic principals' of multilevel economic governance) are even less protected against abuses of regulatory powers at intergovernmental levels. The Constitution of the International Labour Organization (ILO) remains one of the few worldwide agreements acknowledging the systemic interrelationships between labour rights, human rights and economic freedoms. The ILO's 1944 Philadelphia Declaration (amending the 1919 ILO Constitution) proclaimed, inter alia: 'All human beings, irrespective of race, creed or sex, have the right to pursue both their material well-being and their spiritual development in conditions of freedom and dignity, of economic security and equal opportunity'. Yet, most international economic agreements establishing international economic organizations offer citizens no effective legal and judicial remedies against abuses of their regulatory powers. For instance, the intergovernmental crisis management in the Bretton Woods institutions and the

[110] *Barsky v Board of Regents*, 347 US 442, 472 (1954) (Justice WO Douglas dissenting).

[111] *Nebbia v New York*, 291 US 502, 537 (1934). For a criticism of this standard of review, of inadequate judicial protection of economic liberties and the lack of judicial 'proportionality review' of economic regulation in the United States, see: Siegan (1980) and Sandefur (2010).

[112] *Lynch v Household Finance Corp*, 405 US 538, 552 (1972).

[113] See (n 91) and related text.

[114] *cf* Dodd–Frank Wall Street Reform and Consumer Protection Act, Pub Law No 111-203, 124 Stat 1376 (2010). For instance, the Dodd–Frank legislation remedied neither the financial dominance of 'banks that are too big to fail' nor many of their inherent 'moral hazards' (eg, to privatize profits and socialize losses at the expense of taxpayers). The US Federal Housing Finance Agency, which regulates the two government-owned mortgage finance companies Fannie Mae and Freddie Mac, revealed in October 2010 that the combined losses of these two companies could cost the US taxpayer as much as $363 billion: *Financial Times* (22 October 2010) 2. The US government housing policies and their incentives for lenders to approve mortgages to un-creditworthy borrowers are often cited as a major cause of the financial crisis and credit bubble in the United States.

International Bank of Settlement failed to protect consumers and investors against the destruction of billions of dollars of private bank investments and pension funds, the emergence of huge financial imbalances[115]and inadequate supervision of rating agencies, hedge funds, sub-prime securities and bonus practices of international banks that are 'too big to go bankrupt' in spite of their over-indebtedness. The massive financial assistance granted by the IMF for resolving public sector insolvency in Greece, or private insolvency of banks in Ireland, lacked any clear legal basis in the IMF Statutes: 'It is strange for the IMF to be lending to a region which has a reserve currency and no balance of payments problem'.[116] The purchases by the European Central Bank of Greek, Irish, Italian, Portugese and Spanish government bonds worth hundreds of billions of euros – even though the market value of governments bonds from these over-indebted countries was being down-graded in financial markets – were likewise criticized as testing the legal limits of EU law (eg, the 'bailout' prohibitions in Articles 123-125 TFEU and the limited mandate of the European Central Bank for temporary liquidity assistance rather than for financing of structural, long-term fiscal deficits). EU Law and the ECJ offer EU citizens no effective legal and judicial remedies against many violations of EU law (eg, the persistent violations of the budgetary disciplines and debt limits prescribed in Article 126 TFEU) and of the EU's disregard for its constitutional requirement of 'strict observance of international law', for instance in case of violations of the EU's WTO obligations to the detriment of EU citizens.[117]

The tripartite institutional structure of the ILO and the rights-based dimensions of some international economic and environmental agreements (such as the 1998 Aarhus Convention on Access to Information, Public Participation in Decision-Making and Access to Justice in Environmental Matters) have limited 'Westphalian intergovernmentalism' in certain areas of economic and environmental regulation. For instance, the 1998 ILO Declaration on Core Labour Standards and the 2008 ILO Declaration on Social Justice for a Fair Globalization (as discussed in chapter VI) focus on individual rights, basic needs and progressive development of rights-based economic and social regulation rather than only on rights and obligations of states. International monetary and financial regulation, by contrast, fails to protect private consumers against the risks of complex financial instruments and other 'market failures' in financial services. The normative ideal of 'government of the people, by the people, and for the people' – based on transparent 'governance by discussion' and accountable 'representative' and 'participatory democracy' – is increasingly elusive in international economic regulation dominated by special interest groups and non-transparent, intergovernmental 'deal-making'. A 'real new world order' must be based not only on 'horizontal' international networks among national legislative, executive, judicial and other government institutions (like regulatory

[115] The IMF lacks a mandate to regulate private financial flows. Bilateral IMF consultations pursuant to Arti IV of the IMF Agreement with countries facing balance of payments problems have turned out to be less appropriate for responding to the huge imbalances in the monetary and financial system since 2008 than the multilateral 'assessment process' undertaken in the G20 group of leading economies, including both deficit and surplus countries.

[116] *Financial Times* (23 November 2010) 4. Due to IMF voting rights based on shareholder contributions, IMF decisions and governance structures continue to be dominated by Europe and the United States; they are rightly criticized by many LDCs for their lack of 'representativeness', notwithstanding the inclusion of nine 'emerging economies' into the G-20 meetings since 2008.

[117] *cf* Petersmann (n 23).

agencies);[118] intergovernmental 'bureaucratic bargaining systems'[119] must also be constitutionally restrained by new forms of transnational 'participatory democracy' based on legal and judicial protection of cosmopolitan rights of citizens and parliamentary and civil society participation in the 'agenda setting' and 'public scrutiny' of intergovernmental rulemaking. The more economic, environmental and legal 'globalization' continues to transform nation states, the stronger becomes the need for adjusting representative and constitutional democracy at national levels to new forms of rights-based 'cosmopolitan democracy'.[120] Transnational democratic governance regimes, like national constitutional democracies, can reconcile competing private and public interests only on the basis of 'checks and balances' institutionalizing 'public reason' and protecting cosmopolitan rights by judicial remedies against abuses of public and private power.

Why 'civilizing' and 'constitutionalizing' IEL depends on 'access to justice' and on multilevel judicial protection of constitutional rights

Both human rights law, constitutional law and modern economic law are based on essentially similar constitutional structures such as:

- limited delegation of powers from 'we the people' to legislative, executive and judicial institutions mandated to protect equal rights of citizens by transparent rulemaking and non-discriminatory administration of 'rule of law';
- ubiquity of conflicts between (a) human rights, constitutional rights and economic rights pleaded by citizens and (b) legislative and administrative measures adopted as being necessary for protecting public interests and justifying restrictions of individual rights;
- claims by individuals of 'access to justice' requesting independent review by 'courts of justice' of whether governmental restrictions of individual rights respect due process of law and do not go beyond what is 'necessary' and 'proportionate' for protecting legitimate public interests; and
- dynamic processes of legislative, administrative and judicial clarification of indeterminate rules and 'public reason' based on 'deliberative democracy', 'balancing' and progressive development of principles and rules in response to pressures from civil society.

Human rights tend to be effectively protected inside states only in the context of 'constitutional democracies' empowering individuals and limiting abuses of public and private power. Sections 1 and 2 inferred from the antagonistic nature of competitive, human interrelationships as well as from the history of constitutionalism that the progressive realization of 'democratic constitutionalism' and of 'social market economies' depends on 'struggles for rights', as illustrated by the citizen-driven English, American, French

[118] *cf* AM Slaughter (2004).

[119] RA Dahl, 'Can International Organization be Democratic?' in I Shapiro and C Hacker-Cordon (eds), *Democracy's Edges* (Cambridge: CUP, 1999) 19 ff, 33.

[120] *cf* D Held, *Democracy and the Global Order: From the Modern State to Cosmopolitan Governance* (London: Polity Press, 1995) 23: 'national democracies require an international cosmopolitan democracy if they are to be sustained and developed in the contemporary era. Paradoxically, perhaps, democracy has to be extended and deepened within and between countries for it to retain its relevance in the future'. On the numerous problems of promoting 'cosmopolitan democracy' see: *Symposium: Envisioning a More Democratic Global System* in (2007) *Widener Law Review* XIII 243–446.

and EU 'rights revolutions' and the judicial protection of ever more cosmopolitan rights by European courts. UN law and most worldwide organizations fail to protect human rights, rule of law and 'sustainable development' effectively due to their intergovernmental legal structures and lack of adequate 'constitutional safeguards'. For example, the failures to regulate international banking and financial markets in ways preventing the sudden destruction of stock market value and savings of citizens worth trillions of US dollars during the financial crisis which began in 2008, to limit environmental pollution leading to life-threatening climate change and to reduce unnecessary poverty and human rights violations in so many UN member states, reveal profound failures of UN law to realize its self-proclaimed objectives. As discussed in chapter I, without using international law and international organization more constructively for overcoming collective action problems impeding collective supply of international public goods, national democracies risk being ever less capable of protecting the human rights of their citizens in the globally integrating world economy.

In order to make global governance for the collective supply of 'global public goods' more legitimate and more effective, multilevel economic regulation must be designed and justified more coherently vis-à-vis citizens in terms of human rights and constitutional 'principles of justice.' This is especially true for intergovernmental regulation of *private* conduct of producers, investors, traders and consumers. My 1991 study of 'Constitutional Functions and Constitutional Problems of International Economic Law' focused on multilevel judicial protection of international guarantees of freedom, non-discrimination and rule of law in the collective supply of *national public goods* and *European public goods* inside constitutional democracies (such as judicial protection of the common market freedoms inside the EU). This book focuses on (re)interpreting and (re)constructing IEL in order to better respond to general citizen interests and 'constitutional problems' in the collective supply of *global public goods*. Both studies emphasize that, using the 'principal–agent model' of political and constitutional theorists, multilevel cooperation among national and international courts of justice is of constitutional importance for protecting transnational rule of law for the benefit of citizens in multilevel economic regulation. As illustrated by the emergence of 'global constitutionalism' and judicial 'proportionality review' by ever more national and international courts,[121] 'courts of justice' have constitutional mandates not only for protecting the constitutional rights of citizens vis-à-vis discriminatory majority politics and unjustified administrative restrictions; they are also 'trustee courts' mandated to ensure that the constitutional rules adopted by 'the people' are respected in majoritarian, multilevel economic rulemaking.[122]

The more international trade and economic cooperation become indispensable sources of consumer welfare in more and more countries (eg, in terms of national food, health and energy security), the more protection of human rights requires exploring the synergies and 'linkages' between legal and judicial interpretations of human rights,

[121] *cf* A Stone Sweet and J Matthews, 'Proportionality and Global Constitutionalism' (2008) 47 *Columbia Transnational Law Review* 73 ff.

[122] On the relationship between 'constitutional review *qua* ideal representation of the people' and parliamentary legislation see: B Ackerman, *We the People: Foundations* (Cambridge: HUP, 1991); R Alexy, 'The Dual Nature of Law' (2010) 23 *Ratio Juris* 167–82. On judicial review as a defining feature of global constitutionalism and the different uses of 'delegation theory' for justifying judicial review on the basis of often indeterminate constitutional rules and principles see: K Alter, 'Agents or Trustees? International Courts in their Political Context' (2008) 14 *European Journal of International Relations* 33–63.

constitutional rights and IEL guarantees of freedom, non-discrimination, protection of property and the general 'exception clauses' in international economic treaties acknowledging the political priority of non-economic 'public interests'. The task of 'globalizing embedded liberalism' through multilevel protection of human rights in order to make the global economy work better for all is also increasingly emphasized by human rights lawyers and UN human rights bodies. Yet, the various reports by the UN High Commissioner for Human Rights on the human rights dimensions of WTO law and investment law illustrate that many governments remain reluctant to endorse human rights approaches to economic regulation in worldwide economic organizations in view of the many controversies over the potential relevance of human rights for interpreting IEL.[123] In contrast to long-standing Anglo-Saxon traditions of prioritizing 'parliamentary sovereignty' and 'majoritarian democratic regulation' vis-à-vis protection of equal constitutional rights in the area of economic and social regulation of cooperation among citizens,[124] the European constitutional and judicial traditions acknowledge that human rights and 'courts of justice' – as guardians of the human rights of access to justice[125] and essential parts of the 'constitutional checks and balances' limiting the abuses of government powers – may justify interpreting, clarifying and justifying IEL rules by connecting specific human rights obligations with the legal interpretation and judicial protection of rules and principles of IEL. By ensuring, at the request of citizens, that national and European economic and human rights protections evolve in mutually consistent ways, national courts as well as the ECJ, the EFTA Court and the ECtHR promote 'cosmopolitan public reason' in European law.

Judicial interpretation of IEL in conformity with human rights: diverse traditions of protecting freedom of commercial speech

Customary international law requires interpreting treaties and settling international disputes in conformity with the human rights obligations of UN member states – as explicitly recalled in the VCLT (Preamble and Article 31) as well as in the jurisprudence of the ICJ and of many regional courts.[126] Yet, if the parties to an international dispute – as in the United States' WTO complaint against *China-Publications and Audiovisual Products*[127] – neither invoke human rights nor challenge the sovereign right of 'content control' of internet services, intergovernmental dispute settlement bodies may have good reasons to avoid references to human rights and 'principles of justice'. The UN covenants on civil and political rights (ICCPR) and economic, social and cultural rights (ICESCR) – notwithstanding their ratification by some 160 UN member states – continue to lack ratification by important member countries of worldwide economic organizations.[128]

[123] These reports are discussed in ch VII, section 4; see also: D Kinley (2009).

[124] *cf* RA Epstein, *Supreme Neglect. How to Revive Constitutional Protection for Private Property* (New York: OUP, 2008); Tushnet (2008); Sandefur (2010). D Nicol (2010), by contrast, emphasizes in ch 1 that freedom of Parliament to decide remains at the core of British constitutionalism and democracy.

[125] *cf* F Francioni (ed), *Access to Justice* (Oxford: OUP, 2008).

[126] *cf* EU Petersmann, 'Administration of Justice in the WTO: Did the WTO Appellate Body Commit "Grave Injustice"?' (2009) 8 *The Law and Practice of International Courts and Tribunals* 329–74.

[127] See the WTO Appellate Body Report in WT/DS363/AB/R, adopted in January 2010.

[128] For instance, the ICCPR has not been ratified by China; the ICESCR has not been ratified by the United States.

Governments often disagree on whether UN human rights law is legally relevant for interpreting and applying the law of worldwide organizations. Civil society, by contrast, increasingly claims that intergovernmental regulations, or sub-contracting supply of essential services (such as access to water, food and essential medicines) to non-governmental organizations, risk circumventing the human rights obligations of states. European courts (like the ECJ and the ECtHR) and European lawyers increasingly admit that non-ratification of human rights treaties by specialized international organizations is no convincing legal argument against holding states accountable for human rights violations resulting from their implementation of the law of international organizations.[129] State obligations to respect, protect and promote human rights also require governments to prevent violations of human rights by intergovernmental and non-governmental organizations – even if international organization with separate legal personality may be formally bound only by customary human rights obligations and *not* by the state-centred UN human rights conventions.

The founding fathers of modern economics (like Adam Smith and David Ricardo) emphasized the importance of appropriately regulated free trade for the protection of individual and political freedom, rule of law and justice.[130] Today, the complex inter-relationships between liberal economic, political and legal orders are acknowledged by ever more leading economists (from Friedman to Sen).[131] As discussed in chapters IV and VII, the UN High Commissioner for Human Rights emphasizes the need for interpreting IEL rules in conformity with the human rights obligations of states. Yet, human rights also protect individual and democratic diversity and may require respect for 'reasonable disagreement', notably in areas of economic regulation (such as freedom of commercial speech) where national constitutional traditions legitimately differ between countries. As illustrated by the *Hertel* case in the ECtHR (summarized in Table 17), constitutional, legislative and judicial protection of 'freedom of commercial speech' may legitimately differ depending on whether

- freedom of trade and profession is constitutionally protected (as in EU law and Swiss law);
- courts protect 'commercial speech' as part of general constitutional guarantees of freedom of expression (as in US constitutional law and in the ECHR); and
- freedom of commercial speech has to be 'balanced' with other constitutional values or has to be interpreted in the context of specific laws protecting undistorted and fair competition.[132]

[129] *cf* A Clapham, *Human Rights Obligations of Non-State Actors* (Oxford: OUP, 2006); HG Schermers and N Blokker, *International Institutional Law. Unity within Diversity*, 3rd edn (Deventer: Kluwer, 1995) para 1574.

[130] See, eg, A Smith, *An Inquiry into the Nature and Causes of the Wealth of Nations*, 1776/1976 edn RH Campbell, AS Skinner, WB Todd (eds) (New York: Random House), noting that the benefits which commerce can bestow on individual freedom are 'by far the most important of all effects' of liberal trade (at 412).

[131] *cf* M Friedman, *Capitalism and Freedom* (Chicago: University of Chicago Press, 1982) arguing that 'economic freedom is . . . an indispensable means toward the achievement of political freedom' (at 8); Sen (2000) arguing (eg, in ch 2) that economic and political freedom can mutually support each other.

[132] *cf* J Krzeminska-Vamvaka, *Freedom of Commercial Speech in Europe* (Hamburg: Verlag Dr Kovac, 2008); R Shiner, *Freedom of Commercial Expression* (Oxford: OUP, 2003).

Table 17: *Hertel v Switzerland*, judgments of the European Court of Human Rights: judicial deference vis-à-vis freedom of commercial speech in Europe?

ECtHR, judgment of 25 August 1998 (Rep. 1998-VI, fasc.87) and decision of 17 January 2002 (ECHR 2002-I, no 53440/99): In response to legal challenges by the Swiss Association of Manufacturers and Suppliers of Household Electrical Appliances of the applicant's publications on 'Microwave ovens: a health hazard; irrefutable scientific evidence', a Swiss commercial court issued an injunction under the Unfair Competition Act prohibiting the applicant from making public statements that food cooked in microwave ovens was a danger to health in that it was carcinogenic. The injunction was confirmed by the Swiss Federal Court. In the 1998 judgment of the ECtHR, the majority found that the injunction violated freedom of expression as protected by Article 10 ECHR because the injunction was not 'necessary in a democratic society' for protecting the rights of producers and traders of microwave ovens; some minority opinions argued for judicial deference towards the judicial interpretations of freedom of commercial speech by the Swiss courts which had criticized the public statements concerning dangerous effects of microwaved food for their lack of mentioning the scientific differences of opinion regarding any health dangers. A 1999 judgment by the Swiss Federal Court confirmed that Hertel was free to express his views provided that he did not give the false impression that his views were scientifically proved findings. In view of the careful 'balancing' of the freedom of expression and of the rights under the Unfair Competition Act, the 2002 decision of the ECtHR considered the 1999 Federal Court judgment – and its judicial interference with the applicant's freedom of expression – to be proportionate to the public interests pursued; the second complaint by Hertel was thus rejected as inadmissible and manifestly ill-founded.

Due to the diverse national constitutional contexts and democratic preferences, citizen-oriented interpretations of IEL rules in the case law of the ECJ, the EFTA Court, the ECtHR and national courts throughout Europe often remain contested among citizens and may be rejected in other jurisdictions and organizations with different conceptions of economic regulation. For instance, a Latvian constitutional court decision of December 2009 examined the challenge by pensioners of parliamentary pension legislation reducing pension payments in order to comply with IMF budget deficit reduction targets. The Constitutional Court found the legislative restrictions in violation of the individuals' right to a pension as protected by Article 109 of the Latvian Constitution and Article 9 ICESCR; as the international creditors had not explicitly stipulated reductions in pension payments which threatened the minimum essential payments guaranteed by the fundamental right to social security, the Court asserted the legal primacy of constitutional and human rights law over unnecessarily drastic interpretations of international loan agreements.[133]

Diverse traditions of reconciling human rights with intellectual property rights

The increasing recognition of citizens as subjects of legal rights and judicial remedies in human rights law, IEL, international environmental and criminal law was often due to

[133] For a discussion of the case see: 'Latvian Constitutional Court Upholds Right to Social Security despite IMF Pressure to Implement Fiscal Austerity Measures' (June 2010) 12 *ESCR Justice Monthly Case Law Update*.

national and international courts rather than to explicit provisions in intergovernmental treaties. For instance, even though the 1883 Berne Convention for the Protection of Literary and Artistic Works and the 1886 Paris Convention for the Protection of Industrial Property did not explicitly provide for 'direct applicability' and judicial protection of their respective treaty guarantees in national courts, many courts in European countries protected individual copyrights and patent rights as individual rights in conformity with these international treaty guarantees. At the international level, regional and worldwide economic courts (like the ECJ, the EFTA Court, the Andean Common Market Court, the WTO dispute settlement bodies) as well as human rights courts (like the ECtHR) continue to protect intellectual property rights as integral parts of economic law as well as of the protection of property rights in human rights conventions.[134] Yet, proposals by the UN High Commissioner for Human Rights that the World Intellectual Property Organization (WIPO) and the WTO should interpret, apply and develop intellectual property rights in the context of a 'human rights-based approach' with due regard for the human right to health protection, have so far remained without official responses in view of the controversies among the WIPO and WTO member states on how human rights can help identify solutions for social problems related to intellectual property rules like

- the protection of traditional knowledge and traditional cultural expressions that are in the public domain;
- the transfer of medical technology in order to promote the human right to health;
- the transfer of agricultural technology for promoting the human right to food; or
- the limitations of copyrights in education materials necessary for promoting the human right to education.[135]

The GATT, GATS and WTO Agreement on Trade-Related Intellectual Property Rights (TRIPS) include explicit provisions acknowledging sovereign rights of WTO members to protect human, animal and plant life and health. WTO dispute settlement practice illustrates that health concerns may influence the interpretation of WTO rules in many diverse ways, such as, for instance

- different kinds of asbestos may not be considered as 'like products' (eg, in terms of Article III GATT) if their inherent health risks considerably differ;
- legal distinctions between product and production standards for protecting health from unsafe products may have to be justified in terms of 'risk assessment' procedures and public international standard-setting procedures recognized in relevant WTO Agreements (eg, on sanitary and phytosanitary standards and technical barriers to trade) in order to distinguish legitimate safeguards from protectionist measures to ward off competition from foreign imports;
- private food safety standards (eg, concerning pesticide residues) may need to be justified under the SPS and TBT Agreements;

[134] *cf* FM Abbott, 'WTO Dispute Settlement Practice relating to the TRIPS Agreement' in F Ortino and EU Petersmann (eds) (2004) 421–54; Helfer, Alter and Guerzovich (n 24) 1–47; L Helfer, 'The New Innovation Frontier? Intellectual Property and the European Court of Human Rights' (2008) 49 *Harvard International Law Journal* 1–52.

[135] *cf* UN Commission on Human Rights, *Report of the High Commissioner on the Impact of the Agreement on Trade-Related Aspects of Intellectual Property Rights on Human Rights*, UN Doc E/CN.4/SUB.2/2001/13 (2001); *How Human Rights Can Inform the WIPO Development Agenda* (Geneva: 3D, 2010).

- WTO members confronted with urgent disease outbreaks (eg, avian 'swine flu') or food contamination (eg, melamine) might be able to justify precautionary measures even in the absence of complete information and scientific evidence (eg, as provisional measures permitted under the SPS Agreement);
- liberalizing international health services (like tele-diagnostic, tele-radiology, laboratory testing, international movements of nurses and medical personnel) and regulating them in GATS commitments may contribute to protection of human rights;
- innovation of pharmaceuticals, procurement of patented medicines, combating of counterfeit medicines and management of health-related intellectual property rights are likely to be influenced by the TRIPS Agreement.

Many developed WTO members negotiate 'TRIPS plus' standards in bilateral and regional agreements going beyond the minimum standards of the TRIPS Agreement. A group of mainly developed countries has also negotiated an Anti-Counterfeiting Trade Agreement which was signed by more than 20 industrialized countries and the EU in December 2011.[136] As this agreement encompasses far broader subject matter than trademark counterfeiting and copyright piracy as defined in the TRIPS Agreement, it could modify or eliminate a number of the due process protections incorporated in the TRIPS Agreement for persons accused of infringements of intellectual property rights. Less-developed WTO members criticize some of the TRIPS provisions, inter alia, on the ground that intellectual property rights standards conceptualized in industrialized countries (like Article 27.3(b) of the TRIPS Agreement concerning plant variety protection) neither protect traditional knowledge and community-owned, traditional medicines in LDCs nor set market incentives for research in tropical diseases affecting poor countries. The TRIPS Agreement requires all WTO members – subject to transition phases for LDCs – to protect pharmaceutical patents enabling temporary monopoly prices; yet, in case of health pandemics (like HIV/AIDS in many LDCs, terror threats of using anthrax in the United States and Canada in 2001, 'bird flu' and 'swine flu' pandemics) such patents and related pricing practices risk preventing individuals from enjoying their human right of access to essential medicines.[137] The TRIPS Agreement recognizes the rights of WTO members 'to protect public health and nutrition, and to promote the public interest in sectors of vital importance to their socio-economic and technological development' subject to the proviso 'that such measures are consistent with the provisions of this Agreement' (Article 8). Hence, the patent protection requirements of the TRIPS Agreement and the limited scope of the 'WTO flexibilities' (eg, in Article 31 TRIPS Agreement and the WTO 'waivers' from Article 31(f) granted in 2003 and 2005 for compulsory licenses for the supply of 'generic drugs') risk violating the human rights obligations of WTO members.[138]

[136] In view of the widespread criticism of this Agreement as being inconsistent with Internet freedom and with access to life-saving medicines, the EU Commission requested in February 2012 an advisory opinion from the ECJ on the legal consistency of this Agreement with EU law.

[137] *cf* H Hestermeyer (2007).

[138] In this sense Hestermeyer (2007) 294–95: 'the general obligation to grant pharmaceutical patents is sufficient to create a "conflict" between the TRIPS Agreement and the human rights provision on access to medicine', notwithstanding the fact that – under the TRIPS Agreement – 'Members enjoy considerable latitude in the implementation of those provisions' (eg, least-developed countries benefit from a transition period until 1 January 2016 with respect to pharmaceutical products and until 1 July 2013 with respect to most other TRIPS Agreement obligations). The transition period that allowed many other LDCs with production capacities to manufacture drugs – like Brazil and India – to refuse product patent protection for pharmaceuticals expired on

As of 31 May 2010, 28 WTO Members plus the EU (acting also on behalf of its 27 member states) had notified their acceptance of the 2005 WTO Protocol of Amendment to the TRIPS Agreement, whose new Article 31*bis* would make permanent the 2003 waiver enabling compulsory licensing of medicines predominantly for export to countries with insufficient or no capacity in the pharmaceutical sector.[139] As the Article 31*bis* Amendment will become effective on acceptance by two-thirds of WTO Members, the deadline for acceptance was extended repeatedly. Yet, the 2003 waiver decision remains in effect for each WTO Member until it has accepted the Amendment. So far, Canada remains the only WTO member which has issued a compulsory license under the waiver for exports of pharmaceuticals to Rwanda. Even though the waiver was promoted as a means of facilitating the supply of needed medicines to sub-Saharan Africa, Zambia has remained the only country in sub-Saharan African – by the spring of 2010 – that notified acceptance of the Protocol of Amendment. It remains unclear whether this reluctance by LDCs to ratify the TRIPS Amendment can be interpreted as confirming the view that the existing 'legal flexibilities' under the TRIPS Agreement are sufficient for protecting human rights of access to essential medicines.

'Balancing' of diverse human rights must be justifiable by 'principles of justice'

As a generic concept, 'justice' refers to the need for justifying law and governance on the basis of principles of procedural, distributive, corrective or 'commutative justice' or principles of equity. Reconciling and 'optimizing' civil, political, economic, social and cultural human rights in a world of scarce resources requires clarifying the national and international human rights dimensions of IEL through – as explained by Rawls – a 'four-stage sequence' of constitutional, legislative, administrative and judicial principles, rules and 'public reason' necessary for protecting and reconciling human, constitutional and other rights of citizens.[140] UN law (eg, Article 1 of the UN Charter) and customary law (as codified in the VCLT) acknowledge this need for interpreting international law and settling international disputes 'in conformity with principles of justice' and the human rights obligations of states. But courts also have to respect the legitimate reality of 'constitutional pluralism' as illustrated by the diversity of human rights traditions in countries which have deliberately refrained from ratifying certain human rights conventions and pertinent ILO conventions. Can judicial clarification of 'principles of justice' in IEL help in reducing disagreement on how economic rules should be reconciled with social and other non-economic obligations of the countries concerned? Or should 'courts of justice' proceed more pragmatically and clarify the often contested meaning of 'incomplete' IEL rules and principles without referring to concepts of justice?

The inquiry, in chapters V and VI, into 'principles of justice' underlying modern IEL proceeds from Rawls' *A Theory of Justice* as the most widely respected justification of 'constitutional democracy' in the twentieth century. According to Rawls, the democratic legitimacy of legal systems derives from respect for mutually agreed 'principles of

1 January 2005. The formal amendment of Art 31(f) of the TRIPS Agreement in December 2005 has not yet entered into force due to the insufficient number of ratifications.

[139] See: www.wto.org/english/tratop_e/trips_e/amendment_e.htm.

[140] *cf* J Waldron, 'Socioeconomic Rights and Theories of Justice' New York University School of Law Public Law & Legal Theory Working Paper 10-79 (November 2010).

justice' which, in order to enable an 'overlapping consensus' among citizens with diverse self-interests and often conflicting conceptions for a good life, must be institutionalized and protected over time by means of constitutional, legislative, administrative and judicial rules and institutions promoting 'public reason' and compliance with the constitutional rules. In view of the 'fact of reasonable pluralism' and 'the fact that in a democratic regime political power is regarded as the power of free and equal citizens as a collective body', Rawls emphasizes that exercise of coercive power over one another is democratically legitimate only on the basis of constitutional rules which all citizens can endorse in the light of their common human reason.[141] European constitutional law proceeds from the same basic insight that the overall stability and democratic legitimacy of European economic law depend on respect for 'principles of justice' that have become part of the EU's constitutional, legislative, administrative and judicial rules and institutions in order to maintain an 'overlapping consensus' among European citizens, with due respect for their diverse conceptions for a good life and social justice. UN human rights laws reflect this constitutional insight by acknowledging the need for 'recognition of the inherent dignity and of the equal and inalienable rights of all members of the human family (as) the foundation of freedom, justice and peace in the world', as recalled in the Preambles of the UDHR of 1948 and of numerous UN human rights conventions.

Chapters III to VI perceive, in accordance with Kantian and Rawlsian legal theory, indivisible equal liberty rights as the 'first principle of justice' and 'foundation of freedom' in the sense of UN human rights law. Respect for human dignity also requires respecting individual freedom to decide which civil, political, economic, social or cultural dimensions of liberty an individual values most. In order to also protect equal liberties as 'first principle of justice' in transnational economic cooperation among citizens, they must be interpreted –in the multilevel regulation of economic freedoms (eg, of contract law, freedom of profession, freedom of association, corporate accountability, private property, commercial speech, free movements of goods, services, persons, capital and related payments) – in conformity with human rights and 'multilevel cosmopolitan constitutionalism', as first explained by Kant. German and European constitutional and economic laws are founded on Kantian principles of respect for human dignity and multilevel constitutional protection of fundamental freedoms in the economy as well as in the polity. Yet, the ever more comprehensive guarantees of civil, political, economic, social and cultural human rights in national constitutions, regional human rights conventions and UN human rights law rightly go beyond the liberal Kantian principles of justice as well as beyond Rawls' proposals for an international 'law of peoples' based on minimal conceptions of UN human rights law. The multilevel constitutional and judicial protection of 'dignity rights', comprehensive liberty rights and other human rights in European economic integration law, as well as in the EU Charter of Fundamental Rights, confirm that Kantian cosmopolitanism offers a flexible framework for multilevel legal protection of human rights and of economic freedoms in mutually supportive ways.[142] European conceptions of common market freedoms as 'fundamental rights' and of their judicial interpretation in conformity with multilevel human rights guarantees remain contested outside Europe, notably in Anglo-Saxon legal systems prioritizing civil and political rights over economic and social human rights. Just as Rawls later limited his

[141] *cf* Rawls (2001) 41.

[142] *cf* also Fleischacker (n 50) x: 'Kant's moral philosophy, as John Rawls has shown, can be used to support a welfare state on other than utilitarian grounds'.

initial, Kantian definition of the 'first principle of justice' in terms of maximum equal freedoms as going beyond what reasonable people may be willing to politically accept,[143] so may worldwide institutions and international courts outside Europe find it more realistic to define the 'first principle of justice' underlying IEL in terms of more narrow conceptions of 'equal freedoms' as in UN human rights law and Anglo-Saxon democracies refusing ratification of the ICESCR. Also the Rawlsian 'difference principle' and other 'principles of justice' in IEL may be defined in conformity with UN and regional human rights law. Additional 'procedural justice principles' have been clarified in the jurisprudence of international courts and in international agreements (like WTO law) on special and differential treatment of poor countries.

One major policy conclusion of this chapter III is that the 'constitutional problems' of economic regulation necessitating democratic constitutionalism *inside* states – like the inevitable social conflicts resulting from the rational egoism and limited reasonableness of citizens as well as from abuses of public and private power to the detriment of consumer welfare and other public goods – require even stronger safeguards of individual 'access to justice' and democratic participation in *transnational* economic regulation. In order to be legitimate and effective, intergovernmental regulation of the worldwide division of labour, and of the collective supply of other 'global public goods', require 'constitutional justification' of international rules as reasonable self-restraints protecting human rights, constitutional rights and cosmopolitan rights of citizens engaged in, and benefiting from the worldwide division of labour. The decentralized enforcement – at national and international levels – of the EU/EEA competition rules against restrictive business practices, as well as of the EU/EEA common market freedoms against welfare-reducing national border discrimination, based on judicial interpretation of state-centred EU/EEA economic rules in terms of EU citizen rights and cosmopolitan rights illustrate that rights-based, cosmopolitan reforms of IEL are no utopian fantasy; they depend on respecting and empowering citizens by democratic institutions and 'courts of justice' to challenge abuses of public and private governance powers.

Human rights and democracy may justify 'reinterpreting' international law: the example of the ECJ's *Kadi* judgment

Legal and constitutional pluralism emphasize that conflicts among national and international jurisdictions can often be resolved most convincingly on the basis of common constitutional principles, 'balancing' and 'judicial dialogues' rather than by reference to formal rules and hierarchical legal claims of 'monist' or 'dualist' rather than 'pluralist' relationships between national and international legal systems. International treaties require not only good faith implementation (Article 26 VCLT) and legal priority vis-à-vis domestic law (Article 27 VCLT); related disputes must also be settled in 'conformity with the principles of justice' and 'human rights and fundamental freedoms for all' (Preamble VCLT). Constitutional, democratic and 'judicial deficits' of intergovernmental economic regulation may 'delegitimize' international rules and justify their non-application by domestic courts, as illustrated by the *Kadi* judgments of the ECJ making

[143] On the late Rawls' 'normative realism' so as to keep normative reflection in touch with what is politically feasible see: 'The Idea of Public Reason Revisited' in Rawls (1999) 129 ff.

the domestic implementation of 'smart sanctions' imposed by the UN Security Council conditional on respect for human rights and judicial remedies (*cf* Table 18). National courts in constitutional democracies, and European courts, often refuse to apply international rules that are perceived as inconsistent with human rights and constitutional principles of 'public order', or with judicial deference vis-à-vis foreign policy discretion, reciprocity principles of international treaties and intergovernmental dispute settlement procedures.[144] In its *Kadi* judgment of 3 September 2008, the ECJ held that EC Council regulations implementing 'targeted economic sanctions' imposed by the UN Security Council were invalid due to their inconsistency with the constitutional principles and fundamental rights of EC law.

Table 18: *Kadi v Council* (C-402/05 P and C-415/05 P, [2008] ECR I-6351): multilevel judicial protection of human rights vis-à-vis multilevel economic regulation

Joined Cases C-402/05P and C-415/05P, *Kadi* and *Al Barakaat Foundation v Council of the EU*, judgment of the ECJ, 3 September 2008: The ECJ (Grand Chamber) set aside the appealed judgments of the Court of First Instance of 21 September 2005, annulled Council Regulation (EC) No 881/2002 of 27 May 2002 imposing certain specific restrictive measures directed against certain persons and entities associated with the Al-Qaeda network and the Taliban, and maintained – so far as concerned the appellants – the effects of Regulation No 881/2002 for a period of up to 3 months so as to allow the Council to remedy the infringements found. As 'the Community is based on the rule of law, inasmuch as neither its Member States nor its institutions can avoid review of the conformity of their acts with the basic constitutional charter, the EC Treaty, which established a complete system of legal remedies and procedures designed to enable the Court of Justice to review the legality of acts of the institutions', the Court asserted jurisdiction for reviewing the EC legislation implementing a UN Security Resolution. The Court emphasized 'that the obligations imposed by an international agreement cannot have the effect of prejudicing the constitutional principles of the EC Treaty, which include the principle that the Community acts must respect fundamental rights, that respect constituting a condition of their lawfulness which it is for the Court to review'. Even though 'the European Community must respect international law in the exercise of its powers', including 'observance of the undertakings given in the context of the United Nations', it is 'not a consequence of the principles governing the international legal order under the United Nations that any judicial review of the internal lawfulness of the contested regulation in the light of fundamental freedoms is excluded'. The Court found that 'the rights of the defence, in particular the right to be heard, and the right to effective judicial review of those rights, were patently not respected'. 'In the circumstances of the case, the imposition of the restrictive measures laid down in the contested regulation in respect of Mr Kadi . . . constitutes an unjustified restriction of his right to property'.

Arguably, judicial insistence on interpreting and applying international treaties in conformity with human rights is justified also by the recognition in the UN Charter and in numerous UN human rights instruments that – in order 'to establish conditions under

[144] *cf* JO McGinnis and I Somin, 'Should International Law be Part of our Law?' (2007) 59 *Stanford Law Review* 1175–248; A Buchanan and R Powell, 'Constitutional Democracy and the Rule of International Law: Are they Compatible?' (2008) 16 *Journal of Political Philosophy* 326–49; J Goldsmith and D Levinson, 'Law for States: International Law, Constitutional Law, Public Law' (2009) 122 *Harvard Law Review* 1791–868; M Kumm, 'The Cosmopolitan Turn in Constitutionalism' in JL Dunoff and JP Trachtman (eds) (2009) 274 ff.

which justice and respect for the obligations arising from treaties and other sources of international law can be maintained' (Preamble of the UN Charter) – civil, political, economic and social 'human rights should be protected by the rule of law' (Preamble UDHR). As discussed in chapter II, section 4, increasing numbers of UN member states recognize and protect human rights of access to justice, democratic governance and everyone's 'right to take part in the government of his country, directly or through freely chosen representatives' (Article 21 UDHR), as well as everyone's entitlement 'to a social and international order in which the rights and freedoms set forth in this Declaration can be fully realized' (Article 28 UDHR). In order to comply with the human rights requirement that 'in the exercise of his rights and freedoms, everyone shall be subject only to such limitations as are determined by law solely for the purpose of securing due recognition and respect for the rights and freedoms of others and of meeting the just requirements of morality, public order and the general welfare in a democratic society' (Article 29 UDHR), courts of justice must review whether national and international governance institutions have exercised their limited powers with reasonable regard to human rights and democratic participation. Chapter VIII discusses in more detail how, even in disputes focusing on private commercial interests and investor rights, IEL restrictions may require justification in terms of human rights and other 'principles of justice', for instance in view of the fact that private investor interests have to be reconciled with adversely affected social interests.

The main proposition of this chapter is that – without cosmopolitan conceptions of constitutional democracy and IEL aimed at stronger protection of transnational rule of law based on respect for cosmopolitan rights and 'principles of justice' – the multilevel regulation of economic cooperation and of protection of human rights through private and public, national, transnational and international rules and institutions risks remaining incoherent, ineffective and lacking democratic legitimacy. Reasonable citizens with diverse preferences and different constitutional traditions will often disagree on the interpretation of 'principles of justice' and of human rights at international levels, just as they tend to disagree on 'principles of justice' and economic and social rights inside constitutional democracies.[145] Hence, constitutional, legislative and judicial clarification of 'principles of justice' and human rights depends on respect for 'reasonable disagreement', impartial procedures and legal, political and social equality of opportunity in democratic and judicial decision-making processes.[146] The legitimacy of international economic regulation requires promoting 'public reason', 'deliberative democracy' and an 'overlapping consensus' (Rawls) through public discourse and legal as well as judicial

[145] Even inside the United States, there is – as explained by R Dworkin, *Is Democracy Possible Here?* (Princeton: Princeton University Press, 2006) – pervasive disagreement between conservatives and democrats on human rights and democracy. Dworkin argues for basing constitutionalism on two basic principles of human dignity, ie, first, that each human life is intrinsically and equally valuable and, secondly, that each person has an inalienable personal responsibility for realizing her unique potential and human values in her own life. According to Dworkin, 'a legitimate government must treat all those over whom it claims dominion not just with a measure of concern but with *equal* concern' (at 103).

[146] On these constituent elements of legal and democratic legitimacy in majoritarian political processes see: W Sadurski, *Equality and Legitimacy* (Oxford: OUP, 2008). As unequal distribution of resources may entail 'power inequalities' and democratic 'discourse failures', deliberative democracy may require redistributive, communitarian policies: 'citizens must possess a certain level of income and resources if they are to develop the basic capacities necessary to be effective participants in democratic deliberation' (K Knight and J Johnson, 'What Sort of Equality Does Deliberative Democracy Require?' in J Bohman and W Rehg (eds), *Deliberative Democracy: Essays on Reason and Politics* (Cambridge: MIT Press, 1997) 279 ff).

clarification of how IEL can protect human rights, legal equality, general consumer welfare and respect for other 'principles of justice' more effectively. The welfare of a society cannot be judged alone by indicators of economic utility or in terms of institutionalization of ideal 'principles of justice'. IEL must also be evaluated in terms of its contribution to empowering citizens to enjoy and defend their human rights, develop their human capacities and remove specific injustices piecemeal as long as constructing a 'just international economic order' based on agreed principles of justice remains beyond the reach of humanity.

Justice requires stronger, multilevel judicial protection of economic and social rights

The adoption of 'Human Rights Acts' in ever more common law countries (like Canada, New Zealand, the United Kingdom), and of regional human rights conventions and regional courts in the Americas, Africa and Europe, has considerably enhanced rights-based conceptions of 'constitutional democracy'[147] and of judicial review of economic regulation at national and regional levels. Judicial protection of economic and social rights (eg, to healthcare, housing, freedom of association) is also increasingly accepted in countries outside Europe, albeit subject to often 'weaker remedies' compared with judicial protection of civil and political rights.[148] International trade and investment law continues to limit the regulatory discretion of governments by ever more precise trade, investment and double-taxation agreements providing for individual rights and judicial remedies. The ICJ – in its *Barcelona Traction* judgment of 5 February 1970 – found the limited impact of the dynamic evolution of international investments on the customary international law rules on diplomatic protection 'surprising'. More recently, the ICJ's *Diallo* judgment of 24 May 2007 acknowledged the increasingly 'residual' nature of the exercise of diplomatic protection and recourse to the ICJ in investment disputes: 'The role of diplomatic protection has somewhat faded, as in practice recourse is only made to it in rare cases where treaty regimes do not exist or have proved inoperative'. [149] International monetary and financial regulation, by contrast, often fails to provide for effective legal disciplines and judicial remedies for international financial and banking practices with disastrous effects for consumer welfare and citizens adversely affected by national monetary crises and bankruptcies of banks.[150]

Reforms of IEL empowering citizens and protecting consumer welfare are unlikely to come about without cosmopolitan, multilevel governance approaches and judicial protection of enforceable, individual rights similar to those which enabled European citizens and courts to transform Europe's *ordo*-liberal 'economic constitution' into a 'social market economy' with effective legal and judicial protection of human and social rights in all

[147] *cf* Nicol (2010) who argues, however, for returning to the procedural, British conception of democracy as defined – in ch 1 – by the ideas of: (1) contestability of all legal norms (= no self-evident truths shall be enshrined as supreme law); (2) ideological neutrality of constitutional rules; and (3) accountability of rulers to citizens.

[148] *cf* Tushnet (2008); V Gauri and DM Brunks (eds) (2008); BG Ramcharan (ed) (2005).

[149] *cf Belgium v Spain* [1970] ICJ Rep 3; *Guinea v Congo* (Case concerning Diallo) [2007] ICJ Rep 64 (Preliminary Objections).

[150] For a case study of Argentina's financial crisis in 2001/2002 see: W Burke-White, 'The Argentine Financial Crisis: State Liability under BITs and the Legitimacy of the ICSID System' (2008) 3 *Asian Journal of WTO & Health Law and Policy* 199–234.

30 member states of the EEA. The more state-centred, international approaches (including UN human rights conventions) fail to effectively empower citizens and to limit abuses of public and private governance powers in international economic regulation, the more obvious becomes the need for extending legal and judicial protection of cosmopolitan rights beyond state borders to investors, producers, workers, traders, consumers, legitimate civil society organizations and democratic citizens as legal subjects of IEL and 'democratic owners' of intergovernmental organizations. As emphasized in the EU Charter of Fundamental Rights in conformity with a long-standing European tradition of constitutional conceptions of equal freedoms and related responsibilities, 'rights entail responsibilities and duties with regard to other persons, to the human community and to future generations' (Preamble EU Charter as incorporated into EU law by the 2007 Lisbon Treaty). As discussed in chapter I, multilevel governance for effective supply of international public goods must more actively involve individuals and non-governmental organizations (like transnational corporations, trade unions and NGOs) as legal subjects and duty-bearers of IEL. As in European economic and human right law, citizens have reasonable, common self-interests in limiting the widespread 'intergovernmental collusion' to the detriment of citizen rights and of consumer welfare (eg, in intergovernmental trade negotiations focusing on 'diplomatic protection paradigms' and producer welfare rather than on general consumer welfare) by stronger 'constitutional checks and balances' protecting cosmopolitan rights of citizens. Both empirical evidence and normative reasoning[151] confirm that the emergence of a transnational 'human rights and rule of law culture' in IEL cannot be achieved without stronger empowerment of citizens for 'struggles for justice' insisting on legislative, administrative and judicial protection of civil, political, economic and social human rights in economic regulation, notably by interpreting IEL in conformity with human rights and constitutional rights. The Kantian theory of individual rights, as discussed in sections 1 and 2, explains why securing 'the greatest freedom' for the benefit of citizens depends on 'the most precise specification and preservation of the limits of this freedom in order that it can co-exist with the freedom of others'.[152] This holds true no less in multilevel economic governance than inside constitutional democracies where the need for interpreting economic rules in conformity with human rights and constitutional rights has become accepted by increasing numbers of countries.

[151] On the necessity of procedural and substantive rules protecting the 'reasonableness of law', and on the distinction between economic rationality (eg, efficiency) and moral reasonableness of rules, see: R Alexy, 'The Reasonableness of Law' in Bongiovanni, Sartor and Valentini (eds) (2009) 5–15.

[152] Kant (n 17) 45. On autonomy-based, modern conceptions of 'equal freedoms' in terms of civil, political, economic, social and cultural human rights and constitutional rights in European constitutions, regional and UN human rights instruments see: Möller (n 103).

IV

Legal and Political Strategies for Making Multilevel Economic Regulation Consistent with Human Rights

SCIENTIFIC AND POLICY conceptions can operate as intellectual barriers to alternative, more effective conceptions. Just as a fly inside a bottle may see neither the glass barrier nor the way out,[1] so do the prevailing, power-oriented conceptions of IEL and of self-regulating markets fail to protect important, general citizen interests. Chapter I has argued that – from the perspective of citizens and their constitutional rights – nationalist conceptions of intergovernmental power politics based on 'hegemonic international law among states' are among the major reasons for the 'constitutional failures' of IEL to protect human rights, rule of law, general consumer welfare and other international public goods more effectively.[2] Chapters II and III emphasized the need for 'cosmopolitan constitutionalism' protecting cosmopolitan rights and rule of law in the global division of labour for overcoming the 'globalization paradox',[3] ie, that governments depend increasingly on international law and worldwide organizations but fear and neglect them: just as democracy can remain effective over time only as 'constitutional democracy' protecting constitutional rights against abuses of power, so can human rights and rule of law be effectively protected in transnational economic relations only by extending 'constitutional guarantees' for cosmopolitan rights, democratic 'input legitimacy' of IEL and judicial protection of cosmopolitan rights vis-à-vis public and private abuses of power, with due respect for the legitimate reality of 'constitutional pluralism'. This chapter explores how legal, institutional and judicial protection of individual rights by multilevel guarantees of equal freedoms, non-discrimination and rule of law needs to be further developed so that human rights, constitutional law and economic law operate in mutually coherent ways and overcome the 'global disorder' of fragmented legal regimes with due respect for the legitimate diversity of national and regional human rights conceptions. Just as the ECtHR construed the ECHR as a 'collective enforcement of rights in the Universal Declaration of Human Rights',[4] so should IEL be presumed –

[1] *cf* LJ Wittgenstein, *Philosophical Investigations* (Oxford: Basil Blackwell, 1968), who defined the aim of his philosophy as 'showing the fly the way out of the bottle' (para 309).

[2] On the prevailing 'realist conceptions' of international law as a power-oriented instrument for advancing state interests in an anarchic world where 'global public goods' cannot be collectively supplied, see: JL Goldsmith and EA Posner (2005).

[3] For a criticism of this paradox see: AM Slaughter (2004).

[4] In *Behrami and Saramati v France, Norway and Germany*, Judgment of the ECtHR (2 May 2007) (App nos 71412/01, 71412/01 and 78166/01), the Court began by recognizing that all contracting parties of the ECHR are also UN member states, and that one of the ECHR's aims is the 'collective enforcement of rights in the Universal Declaration of Human Rights'. Similarly, the ECJ construes national and EU human rights

notably in relations among constitutional democracies – to be a consistent implementation of the human rights obligations of UN member states justifying rights-based interpretations and judicial review of IEL.

OVERVIEW OF CHAPTER IV

Section 1 recalls that – even in the EU which is constitutionally committed to 'strict observance of international law' (Article 3 TEU), including 'respect for the principles of the United Nations Charter and international law' (Article 21 TEU) – the legal requirements of 'consistent interpretation' and 'transnational rule of law' have not prevented EU member states and EU institutions from violating their European monetary and international WTO obligations to the detriment of EU citizens, as illustrated by more than 40 GATT/WTO dispute settlement findings of illegal EU restrictions and the frequent unwillingness of EU institutions to comply with WTO dispute settlement rulings (eg, on illegal restrictions of imports of bananas, hormone-fed beef, genetically modified products) even after the end of the 'reasonable period' for terminating illegal WTO measures. Section 2 discusses the UN Global Compact for 'corporate social responsibility' and its obvious limits in protecting human rights, labour rights, the environment and anti-corruption principles in the 'corporate governance' of the more than 6000 transnational corporations (TNCs) and 2000 other non-governmental organizations (NGOs) from civil society participating in the Global Compact. Section 3 explains why, so far, both WTO law and European economic integration law can be interpreted in conformity with the human rights obligations of their member states. Yet, as discussed in section 4, WTO law fails to adequately protect human rights in the domestic implementation of WTO rules, for instance regarding patent rights that entail price increases of life-saving pharmaceuticals depriving poor people from access to generic medicines. Similarly, as discussed in section 5, while international trade liberalization tends to promote individual freedom of trade and competition, WTO law fails to adequately protect freedom of commercial speech and non-discriminatory conditions of competition for the benefit of consumers.

1 'DISORDER AMONG FRAGMENTED LEGAL ORDERS': WESTPHALIAN VERSUS COSMOPOLITAN CONCEPTIONS OF THE EXTERNAL RELATIONS LAW OF THE EU

National human rights instruments, constitutional democracies and also *regional regulation* of human rights and economic integration legitimately differ among countries depending on their legal traditions, democratic preferences, available resources and specific regulatory problems. Chapters I to III concluded that respect for 'reasonable disagreement' and for the legitimate diversity of constitutional democracies require

guarantees in conformity with the ECHR and – in the *Kadi* case (table 18 and related text) – construed UN law as not preventing protection of higher human rights standards inside the EU. On the international 'disorder of normative orders' see: N Walker, 'Beyond Boundary Disputes and Basic Grids: Mapping the Global Disorder of Normative Orders' (2008) 6 *International Journal of Constitutional Law* 376 ff. On the function of 'courts of justice' to review the overall coherence of legal systems and of majority legislation on the basis of 'principles of justice' see: EU Petersmann, 'Human Rights, International Economic Law and "Constitutional Justice"' (2008) 19 *EJIL* 769–98.

basing multilevel governance of interdependent public goods on individual and democratic self-governance, 'cosmopolitan constitutionalism' and 'subsidiarity' of regulation as closely as possible to the citizens concerned. How can the constitutional necessity of more effective protection of human rights and of rule of law in multilevel governance of global public goods be reconciled with the 'reasonable disagreement' among citizens over the national and international legal design of human rights and democratic governance institutions? Can this 'constitutional paradox' – ie, that national constitutional freedoms also protect disagreement over how to 'constitutionalize' the political reality of intergovernmental power politics – be resolved? Are 'struggles for human rights' – as in the 'English parliamentary revolution' during the seventeenth century, the American and French 'human rights revolutions' during the eighteenth century, the 'anti-colonial' and 'anti-communist revolutions' during the twentieth century, or in the recent popular revolutions in Arab countries – legitimate responses to disregard for human rights and abuses of discretionary governance powers, as recalled in many human rights declarations?[5] What lessons does European economic law – where protection of human rights and constitutional rights as integral parts of EU and EEA law was initiated by national and European courts in response to citizen requests rather than by intergovernmental agreements[6] – offer for international economic regulation beyond Europe? Can constitutional citizen rights to participate in democratic self-governance be extended beyond local and national 'communitarian democracies' to global governance for 'cosmopolitan democracy'? How should 'majority politics' by means of parliamentary rulemaking be reconciled with 'non-majoritarian politics' by independent regulatory agencies and 'courts of justice' with limited, delegated powers? Chapter III explained why multilevel economic regulation of mutually beneficial economic cooperation among citizens requires justification in terms of 'cosmopolitan constitutional principles' of human rights, subsidiarity, due process of law, democratic self-governance and judicial protection of constitutional rights. This chapter shows why many diplomats and TNCs oppose limiting their regulatory powers by human rights and cosmopolitan constitutionalism .

Do multilevel human rights, constitutional and economic guarantees of equal freedoms, non-discrimination and rule of law rest on common principles of justice?

Chapter III explained why, from the perspective of Kantian 'cosmopolitan constitutionalism', liberal (ie, liberty-based) economic agreements and human rights conventions can be understood as protecting complementary dimensions of equal freedoms, non-discrimination, rule of law and human welfare. Respect for human autonomy requires, according to Kant, leaving the individual prioritization of civil, political, economic, social and cultural dimensions of human freedom to each individual rather than to paternalistic decisions of the rulers. National and regional constitutional laws proceeding from respect for human dignity, like the German Basic Law of 1949 and the EU

[5] *cf* the Preamble to the UDHR of 1948: 'Whereas it is essential, if man is not to be compelled to have recourse, as a last resort, to rebellion against tyranny and oppression, that human rights should be protected by the rule of law'.

[6] As neither the 1951 European Coal and Steel Community Treaty nor the 1957 European Economic Community Treaty referred to human rights, the ECJ declined to apply human rights as unwritten part of European law prior to the *Stauder case* in 1969 (see Table 21 and related text).

Charter of Fundamental Rights, rightly protect economic freedoms (like freedom of profession, freedom of association and private property) no less than civil, political and social freedoms necessary for individual and social self-development, subject to constitutional, democratic and judicial 'balancing' of human rights and constitutional rights in their mutual interactions.[7]

International trade agreements have been concluded since ancient times (eg, among the Greek, Roman and north African city republics in the Mediterranean) in order to protect reciprocal access of traders and consumers to foreign markets and promote domestic welfare through trade. Reciprocal trade commitments often protect legal guarantees of economic freedoms far beyond what governments are willing to legally protect unilaterally. The reasons for this reciprocity principle are primarily political rather than economic; economic theory is almost unanimous in emphasizing that the 'comparative advantages' resulting from *unilateral* trade liberalization (eg, in terms of consumer welfare, enhanced import competition, specialization and productivity of domestic producers) may offer more 'gains from trade' than maintaining trade protection in the absence of *reciprocal* liberalization by trading partners.[8] It is only in the context of citizen-oriented common markets and free trade agreements that intergovernmental reciprocity principles are constitutionally limited by legal and judicial protection of individual freedoms of trade, such as the 'common market freedoms' of some 500 million European citizens protected in EU and EEA law and 'directly applicable free trade rules' in external trade agreements of the EU with third countries in Europe and Africa.

Most human rights conventions have emerged after the Second World War with international treaty structures (eg, in terms of rights and obligations of states) aimed at protecting equal freedoms at home and abroad supplementing the economic freedoms promoted by free trade and common market agreements. For instance, legal and judicial protection of equal economic freedoms limiting abuses of power in 'economic markets' aims at protecting human autonomy similar to legal and judicial protection of equal freedoms limiting abuses of power in citizen-driven 'political markets'.[9] Yet, UN human rights conventions also reveal fundamental differences compared with international economic agreements such as WTO law. For instance:

- Some constitutional democracies support human rights conventions primarily for 'foreign policy reasons', as illustrated by the non-ratification of many UN human rights conventions by the United States, or by the non-adoption of effective implementing legislation in common law countries (eg, prior to the adoption of 'Human Rights Acts' in Australia, Canada, England and New Zealand) based on claims that Anglo-Saxon democracies offer more effective safeguards of human rights than diplomatically negotiated UN treaty rules.
- Some countries (eg, in Eastern Europe) have ratified human rights conventions (like the ECHR) in order to meet the 'human rights conditionality' of their membership in regional organizations (like the EU and the Council of Europe).

[7] The Preamble of the EU Charter of Fundamental Rights explicitly 'reaffirms . . . the rights as they result, in particular, from the constitutional traditions and international obligations common to the Member States' including 'the case-law of the Court of Justice of the European Union and of the European Court of Human Rights'. On the judicial practices of 'constitutional balancing' in IEL see ch VIII.

[8] *cf* EU Petersmann, 'Principles of World Trade' in R Wolfrum (2010).

[9] *cf* EU Petersmann, 'Human Rights and International Trade Law: Defining and Connecting the Two Fields' in T Cottier, J Pauwelyn and E Bürgi (eds) (2005) 29–94.

- Some customary rules of treaty interpretation and of reciprocity (eg, in case of treaty violations) may not be applicable to human rights conventions protecting 'inalienable' human rights.[10]
- Human rights conventions often provide only for 'minimum standards' that leave contracting states with a large 'margin of appreciation' regarding their domestic implementation of the treaty standards in the particular context fitting their national democratic traditions. WTO law, by contrast, often requires *higher* standards of legal protection (eg, for non-discriminatory market access, sanitary risk assessment procedures, protection of intellectual property rights, judicial remedies) that go far beyond the autonomous trade legislation in most countries.
- UN human rights conventions guarantee neither individuals nor their home states effective judicial remedies at national and international levels against violations of human rights. WTO law provides for judicial remedies at national and international levels that are effectively used not only by WTO members (eg, in more than 440 WTO dispute settlement proceedings 1995–2012) but also by individuals and companies at national and international levels (eg, by means of WTO dispute settlement proceedings initiated by governments at the request of domestic companies). Paradoxically, the ratification of UN human rights conventions by many UN member states seems to be often due to the 'impunity' of human rights violations in UN and many domestic jurisdictions. Non-democratic rulers violating human rights are often not afraid of review by UN bodies due to the lack of effective legal and judicial remedies.

Reasonable citizen interests in transnational 'rule of law' versus interests of diplomats in limiting their legal and judicial accountability vis-à-vis citizens

'Critical legal studies' emphasize, inter alia, that

- law may not resolve all social problems ('principle of indeterminacy');
- legal reasoning is sometimes biased ('principle of anti-formalism');
- legal doctrines may encapsulate incoherent points of view ('principle of contradiction'); and
- even 'consensus rules' may fail to be a decisive factor in social behaviour ('principle of marginality').[11]

Such claims may be particularly justified in respect of UN law and modern IEL, for instance whenever 'realist theories' are invoked by political scientists and economists for justifying particular interpretations of UN, WTO or EU rules as 'efficient breaches' of the law.[12] Similarly, national governments, parliaments, international officials, national or international judges, interest groups, NGOs and reasonable citizens often justify their competing interpretations of UN, WTO or EU rules by 'eclectic' references to the customary methods of treaty interpretation.[13] Inside constitutional democracies, legal interpreta-

[10] *cf* M Kamminga and M Scheinin (eds), *The Impact of Human Rights Law on General International Law* (Oxford: OUP, 2009).

[11] *cf* R Wacks, *Philosophy of Law: A Very Short Introduction* (Oxford: OUP, 2006) 96 f.

[12] See the brief discussion of international relations theories in ch I, section 3 on 'Competing Conceptions of IEL'.

[13] On the arbitrary disregard of the customary methods of international treaty interpretation in dispute settlement practices under GATT 1947 see: EU Petersmann (1997) 66 ff, 84 ff. On the widespread disregard

tions of the law by the rulers may be challenged by citizens in democratic institutions and courts on the basis of human rights and constitutional remedies. In the law of worldwide organizations, by contrast, diplomats often claim an 'interpretative monopoly' in order to limit their legal and judicial accountability in respect of domestic citizens, as illustrated by the deliberate avoidance of references to human rights in WTO dispute settlement proceedings and in investor–state arbitration under the ICSID Convention.

EU law and the ECJ emphasize that 'rule of law' and comprehensive judicial remedies of citizens against national or EU violations of the law are 'constitutional principles' of European law.[14] International agreements of the EC have been recognized long since (eg, pursuant to Article 300 paragraph 7 EC Nice Treaty, now Article 218 TFEU) as constituting 'integral parts of the Community legal system' with a legal rank superior to unilateral EC regulations. Yet, in order to protect the political 'freedom of manoeuvre'[15] of the EU institutions, the ECJ has consistently refused to protect EU citizens and individual EU member states against harmful economic and legal effects of EU majority decisions restricting international trade in manifest violation of the EU's WTO obligations and constitutional commitment to 'strict observance of international law' (Article 3 TEU). From a legal perspective, the arguments by the ECJ against 'direct applicability' of GATT/WTO provisions and against legal and judicial accountability of the EU vis-à-vis both EU member states as well as EU citizens adversely affected by EU violations of WTO obligations are inconsistent with both WTO law and the 'rule of law' commitments of EU law:[16]

- In contrast to the initial claims by the ECJ, most GATT and WTO prohibitions of tariffs, non-tariff trade barriers and trade discrimination are more precise and unconditionally drafted than, eg, the vague customs union rules of the EU Treaty.
- As in EU law and free trade agreements concluded by the EC, the mere existence of safeguard clauses and of exceptions does not prevent 'direct applicability' of precise and unconditional free trade rules as long as such exceptions have not been invoked by the EU.
- The ECJ's questioning of the legally binding nature of both WTO obligations and WTO dispute settlement rulings ignores a consistent GATT/WTO jurisprudence that WTO members are legally obliged to comply with both WTO obligations and WTO dispute settlement rulings by terminating illegal measures promptly or within a 'reasonable period of time'.[17]

– even in the leading textbooks on WTO treaty interpretation by J Pauwelyn (2003) and I van Damme (2009) – for 'principles of justice' and human rights as relevant context for the interpretation of WTO rules see: EU Petersmann, 'Administration of Justice in the WTO: Did the WTO Appellate Body Commit "Grave Injustice"?' (2009) 8 *The Law and Practice of International Courts and Tribunals* 329–74.

[14] *cf* L Lenaerts, 'The Rule of Law and the Coherence of the Judicial System of the European Union' (2007) 44 *CMLR* 1625–59.

[15] This term continues to be used by the EU institutions and the ECJ (eg, in joined cases C-120 and C-121/06 P, *FIAMM* [2008] ECR I-6513, para 119) as the main justification for their disregard of legally binding WTO obligations and dispute settlement rulings.

[16] On this WTO case law, and the similar ECJ deference (in the *Intertanko* case of 2008) vis-à-vis EU obligations under the UN Convention on the Law of the Sea, see: EU Petersmann, 'Can the EU's Disregard for "Strict Observance of International Law" (Article 3 TEU) be Constitutionally Justified?' in I Govaere, R Quick and M Bronckers (eds) (2011) 214–25; M Dani, 'Remedying European Legal Pluralism: The *FIAMM* and *Fedon* Litigation and the Judicial Protection of International Trade Bystanders' (2010) 21 *EJIL* 303–40.

[17] *cf WTO Appellate Body Repertory of Reports and Awards 1995-2010*, 4th edn (Cambridge: CUP, 2011) 658 ff, 962 ff.

- Many WTO rules and WTO dispute settlement rulings also explicitly recognize their objective of protecting rights of individual traders (eg, 'trading rights' in the sense of the WTO Protocol on the Accession of China), property rights (eg, intellectual property rights protected by the TRIPS Agreement) and judicial remedies of traders and other economic actors (eg, under GATT Article X, the WTO Agreement on Preshipment Inspection): 'The purpose of many of these disciplines, indeed one of the primary objects of the GATT/WTO as a whole, is to produce certain market conditions which would allow . . . individual activity. . . . It is through improved conditions for . . . private operators that Members benefit from WTO disciplines'.[18]
- Contrary to the misinterpretation of Article 22 DSU proposed by the EU Commission and accepted by the ECJ, the possibility offered by Article 22 DSU – in case of non-compliance with WTO dispute settlement rulings – of avoiding lawful trade sanctions by offering additional trade liberalization in no way affects the legal obligation of terminating illegal WTO restrictions.
- EU law prescribes 'rule of law', including 'strict observance of international law' (Articles 3, 21 TEU) and does not confer on the EU powers to violate international treaties ratified by national parliaments (like the WTO Agreement). This argues for interpreting the fundamental rights of EU citizens to effective legal and judicial protection (*cf* Article 19 TEU, Articles 6 and 13 ECHR) in conformity with the EU's 'consistent interpretation requirement'[19] and the fundamental rights to freedom of trade and profession in conformity with EU law (*cf* Article 16 EU Charter of Fundamental Rights) as justifying a legal presumption that – once the 'reasonable period of time' for the implementation of WTO dispute settlement rulings has expired – EU citizens can rely on judicial protection of the rule of law unless the EU institutions justify a political necessity of violating WTO law to the detriment of citizens.
- Even if the EU were allowed to exceptionally justify the political necessity of violating WTO rules, the EU Court should protect adversely affected EU citizens by recognizing an extra-contractual liability of the EU to compensate the private damage caused by such unlawful EU violations of WTO obligations.

The frequent violations of the rule of law in the external trade relations of the EU, similar to the widespread disregard for the EU Treaty's fiscal disciplines for members of the European Monetary Union, confirm that 'rule of law' among citizens and democratic self-governance in accordance with international agreements ratified by parliaments cannot be maintained without effective judicial remedies against opportunistic violations of the law by political majority decisions in order to accommodate protectionist pressures and short-term self-interests of politicians.

[18] *US-Section 301–310 of US Trade Act of 1974*, WTO Panel Report adopted on 27 January 2000, WT/DS152/R, para 7.72.

[19] On the ECJ's 'consistent interpretation jurisprudence' (eg, in Case C-377/98 *Netherlands v European Parliament and Council* [2001[ECR I-7079) see: GI Fiorelli, 'WTO as a Parameter for the EC Legislation through the 'Consistent Interpretation Doctrine' in C Dordi (ed), *The Absence of Direct Effect of WTO in the EC and Other Countries* (Turin: G Giappichelli Editore, 2010) 121–33.

Table 19: Lack of judicial remedies of EU citizens against EC import restrictions for bananas in violation of WTO and EC law (1992–2009)

Since the 1993 GATT Panel report (DS32/R) up to the WTO compliance panel and WTO Appellate Body reports adopted in December 2008 (WT/DS27/AB/RW2/Ecuador and WT/DS27/AB/RW/USA), there have been more than a dozen GATT/WTO dispute settlement findings confirming the illegality of the EC import restrictions on bananas. The report by the WTO Director-General of December 2009 (WT/DS361/2, WT/DS364/2) on his good offices regarding the complaints by Colombia and Panama against the EC import restrictions on bananas mentioned that – in December 2009 – the WTO General Council had taken note of a 'Geneva Agreement on Trade in Bananas' signed by the EU with Latin American suppliers and the US. Since the 1990s, there have been more than 40 complaints in the ECJ at the request of adversely affected EU citizens, European companies and Germany challenging the legality of the same EC import restrictions on bananas. All the ECJ judgments disregarded – essentially on political grounds (such as lack of 'direct effect' of WTO obligations in foreign jurisdictions, respect for the EC's 'freedom of manoeuvre' to violate treaty obligations ratified by parliaments) – the GATT and WTO dispute settlement findings and manifest violations by the EC of its precise and unconditional WTO obligations to maintain non-discriminatory market access for trade in bananas. The ECJ also declined legal liability of the EU for compensating the damage caused by lawful trade sanctions of third WTO member countries to the detriment of EU companies which remained without judicial remedies against EC violations of WTO law. Economists estimated the annual 'protection costs' of the illegal banana restrictions to be equivalent to an annual tax on EU consumers – for the benefit of a few European banana companies controlling the privileged banana imports from former colonies – to be in the order of billions of euros.
Question: Is such lack of judicial remedies of EU citizens against manifest violations of EC obligations to respect WTO law, and against harmful trade retaliation by third WTO members, democratically justifiable in an international 'rule of law community' that nowhere provides for EC competences to violate international treaty obligations ratified by parliaments inside the EU? Why did the ECJ enforce WTO obligations vis-*à*-vis EU member states but not vis-*à*-vis the EU institutions even if EU member states had requested EU compliance with WTO law and have no access to judicial remedies in the WTO?

Lack of judicial protection of rule of law in the EU's external relations undermines the EU's internal market and rule of law to the detriment of EU citizens

The successful realization of the EU's internal market was to a large extent due to the legal and judicial protection of the EC Treaty's 'market freedoms' for movements of goods, services, persons, capital and related payments as individual rights enforceable in national and European courts. Arguably, the ECJ's enforcement of the EC's customs union obligations under GATT law (as explicitly incorporated into Articles 28–33 TFEU) as an 'integral part of the Community legal system'[20] for the benefit of EU citizens could

[20] According to the ECJ, international agreements concluded by the EC become an 'integral part of the Community legal system' (Case 181/73, *Haegeman* [1974] ECR 449). Even though GATT 1947 had never been ratified by the EC, the ECJ recognized – in the *International Fruit Company* (Joined Cases 21-24/72, [1972] ECR 1219) – that, due to the legal succession of the EC to the GATT rights and obligations of EC member states, also GATT law had become an integral part of the Community legal system.

have avoided many of the more than 40 GATT/WTO dispute settlement findings of discriminatory EC trade restrictions or distortions violating GATT/WTO obligations, notably in the case of EC restrictions (eg, on imports of bananas, hormone-fed beef and biotech products) that were illegally maintained even after the 'reasonable period' (in terms of Article 21 DSU) for their termination had long expired. The EU institutions' self-interests in avoiding legal and judicial accountability for their illegal redistribution of domestic income for the benefit of protectionist interest groups (like European banana trading companies) offer no constitutionally convincing justification for disregarding 'strict observance of international law' (Article 3 TEU) to the detriment of EU citizens.

In *International Fruit Company*, the ECJ confirmed the claim by the EC Commission that the flexibility of GATT provisions and GATT's safeguard clause, reciprocity principle and dispute settlement system entailed that GATT rules could not be invoked and enforced by individuals in European courts. This legal reasoning was widely criticized in view of the fact that most GATT prohibitions are drafted in more precise and unconditional terms than the often vague customs union rules of the EC Treaty which were likewise subject to safeguard clauses and exceptions. As the ECJ recognized the 'direct applicability' of trade provisions in reciprocal free trade agreements (eg, with Greece) and in other preferential trade agreements without effective dispute settlement and enforcement systems (eg, in the Yaundé Convention), the ECJ itself admitted in its *Kupferberg* judgment that 'the fact that the courts of one of the parties consider that certain of the stipulations in the agreement are of direct application whereas the courts of the other party do not recognize such direct application is not in itself such as to constitute a lack of reciprocity in the implementation of the agreement'; 'the mere fact that the contracting parties have established a special institutional framework for consultations and negotiations *inter se* in relation to the implementation of the agreement is not in itself sufficient to exclude all judicial application of that agreement'.[21] The political nature of the ECJ's GATT jurisprudence became obvious when – in *Commission v Germany* – the Court had no hesitation in enforcing GATT/WTO rules at the request of the EU Commission against an EC member state failing to implement its GATT/WTO obligations.[22] In *Chiquita v Commission* and *Van Parys*,[23] the EU Commission and the Court revealed their disregard for WTO law by claiming that – even after the end of the 'reasonable period' granted for complying with WTO dispute settlement rulings – the EU's commitments under the WTO legal and dispute settlement system could not be invoked by EU citizens in EU courts. Yet, the Court's reference to the 'institutional balance' between the political and judicial EU institutions offered no constitutional justification of why the alleged 'Community interest' in political 'freedom of manoeuvre' under Article 21.6 DSU (concerning prevention of lawful sanctions by third countries by additional trade concessions of the EU) requires violating precise and unconditional WTO obligations which the EU ratified for the benefit of EU citizens.

In *Intertanko*, the ECJ extended its judicial refusal to review the legality of EC acts in light of WTO law to the EC's obligations under the UN Convention on the Law of the Sea: 'UNCLOS does not establish rules intended to apply directly and immediately to individuals and to confer upon them rights or freedoms capable of being relied upon

[21] Case 104/81, *Kupferberg* [1982] ECR 3641, paras 13–21.

[22] Case C-61/94 [1996] ECR I-3989.

[23] Cases T-19/01 [2005] ECR II-315; C-377/02 [2005] ECR I-1465.

against States, irrespective of the attitude of the ship's flag State'.[24] The 2010 'Proposal for a Council Decision authorizing the signature and provisional application of the Free Trade Agreement between the EU and its Member States and the Republic of Korea' provides for explicit treaty provisions excluding direct effect of the 'new generation' of EU free trade agreements.[25] In *FIAMM*,[26] the ECJ further confirmed its jurisprudence rejecting private actions for damages caused by EU non-compliance with WTO obligations (eg, the illegal restrictions on imports of bananas notwithstanding 15 GATT/WTO dispute settlement rulings between 1993 and 2009). Even though a few ECJ judgments interpret national and secondary EC rules in conformity with pertinent WTO obligations, the Court often disregards the 'consistent interpretation principle' if complainants invoke WTO dispute settlement rulings against the EC or interpret general principles of EU primary law (like non-discrimination) in conformity with the pertinent WTO obligations of the EU. Without explaining why the 'Community interest' justifies violating GATT/WTO law to the detriment of EU citizens, the EU institutions appear to increasingly disregard – for political reasons – the EU's constitutional commitments to 'strict observance of international law' (Article 3 TEU), thereby undermining also the EU's constitutional principle of effective judicial protection of individual rights (as reflected in Articles 19 TEU, 6 and 13 ECHR, 47 EU Charter of Fundamental Rights). A 'political question exception' might be justifiable in individual cases to the extent that EU institutions can convincingly demonstrate that EU compliance with rule of law, and its judicial protection for the benefit of EU citizens, could undermine legitimate 'Community interests' in WTO and UNCLOS dispute settlement procedures. Yet, as EU law prevents EU member states from invoking international judicial remedies (eg, in the WTO and UNCLOS) against EU majority decisions violating international obligations to the detriment of legitimate legal and trading interests of outvoted EU member states, the ECJ's refusal to review complaints by EU member states challenging such violations of international law[27] amounts to denial of justice without justification in terms of 'Community interests'. Claims by the EU Commission for 'freedom of manoeuvre' to violate international legal obligations, and judicial impunity for power politics at the expense of adversely affected EU citizens,[28] undermine the constitutional legitimacy of the EU.

Lessons from European economic law for 'constitutionalizing' IEL?

The multilevel regulation and judicial protection of public goods inside the EU, the EEA and the ECHR confirms the experience of all constitutional democracies that 'collective action problems' in protecting international public goods require constitutional and judicial protection of rights and responsibilities not only of governments, but also of citizens. Hence, as explained in chapter I, the prevailing conceptions of 'international law among sovereign states', 'global administrative law' and multilevel economic regulation must be

[24] Case C-308/06 [2008] ECR I-4057, para 64.

[25] *cf* Art 8, EU Commission document COM (2010) 135 final. On the almost 30 free trade agreements concluded by the EU with third states, and on the proposed 'new generation' of EU free trade agreements focusing on more comprehensive trade liberalization with the EU's major trading partners, see: EU Commission, *Global Europe: Competing in the World* COM (2006), 567 final.

[26] Joined cases C-120 and 121/06P [2008] ECR I-6513.

[27] *cf* Case C-280/93, *Germany v Commission* [1994] ECR I-3989.

[28] *cf* Dani (n 16) 303–40.

integrated into more coherent, multilevel governance limited by multilevel constitutional restraints and 'principles of justice' as defined by the human rights obligations of UN member states. Even though the 'internal constitutional pluralism' inside national and regional legal regimes (like the EU, EEA and ECHR) legitimately differs from their external 'international legal pluralism' with other UN member states, chapters II and III concluded that IEL in the twenty-first century – like European economic law – derives its 'input legitimacy' from legal and judicial protection of constitutional rights in transnational cooperation among citizens based on 'cosmopolitan constitutionalism'.

Chapters II and III challenged Anglo-Saxon conceptions of democracy in terms of 'parliamentary freedom to decide' and related 'realist' perceptions of IEL as an instrument of utilitarian power politics for advancing the most powerful *domestic interests* (eg, of import-competing producers of cotton, textiles, shoes, bananas and steel) at the expense of general citizen interests (like equal freedoms and non-discriminatory conditions of competition promoting general consumer welfare). In contrast to the selfish arguments of rent-seeking interest groups and periodically elected politicians that domestic courts should refrain from applying GATT/WTO obligations of the governments concerned unless governments invoke their rights in domestic courts (eg, in order to enforce WTO obligations vis-à-vis state governments inside the US and the EU), judicial deference to governmental 'rule by law' was criticized as possibly undermining legitimate expectations of citizens to be protected by 'rule of law' in their mutually beneficial economic cooperation across national boundaries.[29] The legal advocates of the EU Commission insist that EU citizens should have no legal remedies against the frequent disregard by the EU institutions for their WTO obligations to protect freedom, non-discrimination and rule of law in international trade.[30] In view of the more than a dozen GATT/WTO dispute settlement findings on the illegality of EC import restrictions on bananas and hormone-fed beef from 1993 up to 2008, the refusal by EU institutions and European courts to protect 'reasonable expectations' of EU citizens to rely on the EU's constitutional commitments to respect 'the rule of law' (Article 2 TEU) and 'strict observance of international law' (Article 3 TEU) lacked constitutional and democratic legitimacy. As illustrated also by the persistent non-compliance by most EU member states with the EU prohibitions of 'excessive government deficits' (Article 126 TFEU), 'rule of law' for the benefit of citizens cannot remain an effective constitutional restraint without judicial remedies against non-compliance by governments with their self-imposed, international legal obligations ratified by parliaments.

The inadequate legal protection of 'rule of law' for the benefit of citizens is symptomatic of a broader 'constitutional problem' of IEL to be explored in more detail in chapter V: does collective supply of international public goods in mutually beneficial economic cooperation among citizens require following the 'constitutional paradigm' of national legal systems limiting 'rule by law' (eg, by parliamentary majorities, governments, administrations, regulatory agencies) by constitutional and judicial safeguards of 'rule

[29] *cf* EU Petersmann, 'Multilevel Judicial Governance of International Trade Requires a Common Conception of Rule of Law and Justice' in WJ Davey and JH Jackson(eds) (2008) 91 ff.

[30] See the power-oriented justifications by members of the EC legal services of EC violations of WTO law: eg, PJ Kuijper, 'WTO Law in the European Court of Justice' (2005) 42 *CMLR* 1313–41 (according to whom the European courts should neither review the EC's violations of WTO law, as determined by legally binding WTO dispute settlement rulings, nor offer EU citizens legal remedies against violations of WTO law nor hold the legal advocates in the EU accountable for such EU violations of international law).

of law'? European economic law confirms the historical experiences that compulsory jurisdiction of national and European courts for protecting the 'rule of law' for the benefit of citizens is a necessary precondition for 'rule of law communities' sharing a common conception of legality based on a common conception of normative legitimacy of international legal regimes. Yet, IEL traditions differ depending on whether national legal systems prioritize reasonable interests of citizens in the rule of law or the rational self-interests of politicians in policy discretion and in reducing their legal and judicial accountability for welfare-reducing discrimination in favour of rent-seeking interest groups (eg, Greek governments persistently violating fiscal, monetary and rule of law obligations under EU law in exchange for support from local constituencies).

The negative Dutch and French *referenda* rejecting the 2004 Draft Treaty establishing a Constitution for Europe, like the negative Irish referendum of 2008 rejecting the 2007 Lisbon Treaty, illustrated that reasonable citizens are unlikely to support 'international treaty constitutions' whose complex rules remain incomprehensible to most citizens and are so easily discarded by politicians.[31] The case law by European courts progressively transforming, since the 1960s, the international structures of the treaties establishing the EC, the EU, the EEA and the ECHR into 'European constitutional law' for the benefit of European citizens evolved in response to requests by citizens for citizen-oriented 'constitutional interpretations' and judicial protection of individual rights. Yet, it was also in response to complaints by citizens that national constitutional courts (like the German Constitutional Court) have repeatedly insisted on the constitutional limits of intergovernmental interpretations expanding the scope of EU competencies (eg, for issuing joined eurobonds entailing an unpredictable German financial responsibility for 'sovereign debts' of other eurozone member states).[32] European economic integration law limits not only the jurisdiction, discretion and decision-making powers of multilevel economic regulation in the EU; the legal and judicial protection of fundamental rights of EU citizens by international rules and institutions of a higher legal rank also aims at protecting 'constitutional input legitimacy' of European economic regulation. Yet, the evolution of a new 'European public reason' – as illustrated by democratic delegation of only limited regulatory powers to EU institutions, judicial protection of the EU's 'market freedoms' as fundamental rights, and 'judicial balancing' of such 'market freedoms' with all other human rights and fundamental rights of affected EU citizens – remains deeply contested by vested interests. Also beyond Europe, democratic acceptance and judicial interpretation of international economic rules are increasingly influenced by whether citizens and people recognize and support international rules and global governance as democratically legitimate and 'just'. The more international law is understood as seeking to establish and institutionalize systems of legitimate, multilevel governance and 'authoritative judgment' in order to protect the human rights of citizens beyond national borders, the more it becomes necessary to review the 'rules of recognition', institutions,

[31] A letter by a member of the European Parliament published in the *Financial Times* on 2 July 2008 (at 10) illustrates the problem: 'The infuriatingly stupid claim by French foreign minister Bernard Kouchner that "no one understands the EU institutions . . . not even me" (FT, 1July) is on par with the assertion – nay, boast – during the referendum campaign by Ireland's EU Commissioner Charlie McCreevey and premier Brian Cowen that they had not read the Lisbon treaty. These are either attempts to pose as populist "one of the boys" or an admission that they are not fit to occupy positions in, respectively, the EU Council of Ministers and current Presidency, European Commission and European Council'.

[32] *cf* the judgment of the German Constitutional Court (7 September 2011) (2 BvR 987/10, 1485/10 and 1099/10) clarifying the constitutional limits for Germany's participation in eurozone bailouts.

legitimacy and design of international law in light of the human rights obligations of all UN member states.[33]

This chapter argues that the European 'human rights approaches' and 'constitutional approaches' – which enabled transforming power-oriented European 'international law among states' into citizen-oriented economic integration law and 'multilevel constitutional law' – offer important lessons for reforming IEL beyond Europe. The 'constitutional paradox' of the need for strengthening the 'constitutional' and 'human rights dimensions' of IEL, in spite of the lack of universal agreement on the normative assumptions underlying human rights and economic regulation, can be reduced by inducing citizens, parliaments and 'courts of justice' to interpret and progressively develop IEL in conformity with their own, often legitimately diverse conceptions of 'principles of justice' and human rights, as required by the customary methods of interpreting international law. The increasing cooperation among national and international dispute settlement bodies in regional trade agreements outside Europe, such as MERCOSUR,[34] NAFTA[35] and the Andean Common Market,[36] suggests that the example of judicial cooperation among national and European courts in the interpretation of European economic law might also promote 'judicial comity' and 'cosmopolitan constitutionalism' in other fields of IEL like international investment, intellectual property and regional economic integration law. The case studies in the remainder of this chapter illustrate that cosmopolitan legal theories of multilevel constitutional protection of equal freedoms and transnational rule of law justify multilevel, judicial protection of transnational rule of law for the benefit of citizens and their constitutional rights also beyond European economic law.

Promoting synergies in multilevel economic and human rights governance: political, judicial and civil-society approaches

The prevailing 'realist', state-centred and power-oriented conceptions of international economic regulation in worldwide organizations leave the definition of 'input-legitimacy' (eg, in terms of domestic negotiation mandates) and 'output-legitimacy' (eg, in terms of welfare-increasing effects of trade liberalization) to 'member-driven governance'. Worldwide economic organizations avoid references to human rights as standards for international rulemaking because of fear of undue 'politicization' of international negotiations in view of the international disagreement on the human rights dimensions of IEL and of relevant 'principles of justice'.[37] Human rights bodies and members of parlia-

[33] *cf* Kamminga and Scheinin (eds) (n 10); P Capps (2009).

[34] *cf* N Lavranos (ed), 'Multilevel Judicial Governance between Global and Regional Economic Integration Systems: Institutional and Substantive Aspects' EUI Working Paper MWP 2009/41; MT Franca Filho, L Lixinski and MBO Giupponi (eds), *The Law of MERCOSUR* (Oxford: Hart Publishing, 2010).

[35] *cf* the case law of Art 1904 NAFTA panels applying the 'consistent interpretation principle' (as recognized in the US 'Charming Betsy doctrine') and remanding US anti-dumping determinations as being inconsistent with legally binding WTO dispute settlement rulings; *cf* JA Huerta-Goldman, 'Trade Remedies Disputes – Reciprocal Relationship between WTO and NAFTA Tribunals' in F Fontanelli, G Martinico and P Carozza (eds) (2010) 319–44.

[36] LR Helfer, KJ Alter and MF Guerzovich, 'Islands of Effective International Adjudication: Constructing an Intellectual Property Rule of Law in the Andean Community' (2009) 103 *AJIL* 1–47.

[37] *cf* G Sampson (ed), *The WTO and Global Governance* (Tokyo: UN University Press, 2008) who emphasizes in his Foreword 'that the WTO should not be responsible for the non-traditional trade issues that have

ments counter that – since the legitimacy of international 'governance', like that of national 'governments', depends on protecting 'human rights . . . by the rule of law' (Preamble UDHR) – there are good reasons for evaluating international agreements and WTO negotiations in terms of their contribution to poverty reduction and protection of human rights (eg, of adequate access to food and medicines). For instance, 'justice as fairness' may explain the neglect of power-oriented WTO negotiations by many LDCs in view of the injustice resulting from the long-standing violations of WTO obligations by developed countries (eg, vis-à-vis cotton exporting developing countries of Africa, banana exporting countries from Latin America) and the marginal development dimensions of the Doha Round.[38] The perception of intergovernmental negotiations as mere instruments for promoting *national* 'producer welfare' of powerful lobbies risks aggravating the 'collective action problems' in supplying international public goods.[39] Hence, WTO Director-General Pascal Lamy has argued for a 'Geneva consensus' that 'opening of markets is necessary to our collective well-being' provided 'strong safety nets help correct the imbalances between winners and losers at the national level' and trade can 'act as a vector for the reinforcement of human rights'.[40] The annual 'public *fora*' of WTO diplomats with NGOs on reforms of the world trading system contribute to more differentiated perceptions of the WTO in civil society.[41]

This chapter discusses political approaches (section 2), judicial approaches (section 3) and pressures from civil society (section 4) for promoting 'human rights coherence' of IEL. The state-centred focus in UN law on international rights and obligations of states has entailed that UN human rights conventions do not offer individuals effective legal and judicial remedies, apart from a few Optional Protocols providing for political complaints procedures. Some regional human rights conventions and constitutional democracies provide for stronger guarantees of economic liberties (eg, of freedom of profession, freedom of commercial speech and private property) and judicial remedies at national and regional levels of regulation. Section 2 gives an overview of past failures to conclude legally binding UN agreements on a 'UN Code of Conduct for TNCs' and other UN norms on business and human rights complementing the legally non-binding OECD Guidelines for Multinational Enterprises and the ILO Tripartite Declaration of Principles concerning Multinational Enterprises and Social Policy. Section 2 also mentions the increasing number of initiatives for 'private–public partnerships' – on worldwide, regional, national and private levels (such as 'company codes' and other private undertakings monitored by governmental and non-governmental organizations) – for specifying, certifying and monitoring obligations of TNCs aimed at protecting human rights in the production and sale of specific products like diamonds, tobacco and breast milk powder, as well as in decentralized supply chains of inputs for TNCs that may not be effectively monitored in less-developed host countries. Multilevel governance and surveillance of private sector 'human rights impacts' illustrate that multilevel implementation

gravitated towards it' (at xiv), and 'that the WTO already has the institutional and legal flexibilities to accommodate both the non-trade issues now confronting it, and those that may come its way in the future' (at xv).

[38] *cf* L Arbour and S Majlessi, 'Placing Human Rights in the Geneva Consensus' in Sampson (n 37) 149 ff.

[39] *cf* the contributions by P Lamy, S Ostry and B Koenders on the 'global governance challenges' of the WTO in Sampson (n 37) 37–111.

[40] 'Towards Shared Responsibility and Greater Coherence: Human Rights, Trade and Macroeconomic Policy', speech by Pascal Lamy (13 January 2010), cited from the WTO website.

[41] *cf* S Joseph, *Blame it on the WTO? A Human Rights Critique* (Oxford: OUP, 2011).

of human rights, economic rules (such as WTO rules on technical, sanitary and phytosanitary product and production standards), ILO Conventions and legally binding 'core labour standards' (eg, monitored by tripartite ILO bodies and non-governmental organizations) becomes increasingly complex and may contribute to reducing the 'governance gaps' in the law of worldwide organizations.[42]

Chapter IV concludes that the global economic, environmental and political crises cannot be overcome unless multilevel economic and environmental regulation is more effectively constrained by human rights and other constitutional restraints of the ubiquitous abuses of private and public power in transnational relations. EU law, EEA law, the ECHR and NAFTA illustrate legitimately diverse approaches to subjecting private and public governance mechanisms at local, national, transnational and supranational levels to more coherent 'constitutional checks and balances'. In order to promote 'global public goods' more effectively, worldwide regulation of transnational, private and public economic and environmental activities must legally empower, coordinate and restrain more effectively the diverse private, (inter)governmental and non-governmental actors at local, national, transnational and international levels. The Westphalian paradigm of centralized 'government' in 'sovereign states' through hierarchical laws and regulations becomes increasingly outdated in view of the reality of multilevel governance mechanisms based on private and public, national and international institutions, networks, rules and market mechanisms as decentralized information, coordination and sanctioning mechanism responding to demand by consumers and supply by producers. In order to remain legitimate, multilevel economic governance must offer citizens new participatory, deliberative and accountability mechanisms that can be justified and supported by citizens as protecting individual rights, judicial remedies and democratic self-governance of civil society.

2 GLOBALIZING 'EMBEDDED LIBERALISM' THROUGH UN HUMAN RIGHTS LAW? THE LIMITS OF THE 'UN GLOBAL COMPACT' FOR 'CORPORATE SOCIAL RESPONSIBILITY'

John Ruggie, in his role as 'UN Special Representative on the issue of human rights and transnational corporations and other business enterprises', began his 2008 report on 'Protect, Respect and Remedy: A Framework for Business and Human Rights'[43] by recalling the obvious fact that markets are no gift of nature. Their functioning depends on appropriate legal regulation:

> Markets function efficiently and sustainably only when certain institutional parameters are in place. The preconditions for success generally are assumed to include the protection of property

[42] Governance mechanisms for steering and coordinating decentralized actions in civil society (eg, through families, market competition, non-governmental organizations and corporate governance), in political society (eg, through political parties and their competition for votes), in states and international organizations tend to be based on numerous, interrelated sub-systems. Their typologies, interactions, social differentiation and fragmentation tend to be analyzed and classified by economists, social and political scientists, cyberneticists and lawyers in diverse ways. *cf* J Pierre, *Debating Governance* (Oxford: OUP, 2000); I Bache and M Flinders (eds), *Multi-level Governance* (Oxford: OUP, 2004); H Schepel, *The Constitution of Private Governance* (Oxford: Hart Publishing, 2005).

[43] UN Doc A/HRC/8/5 (7 April 2008); a revised version of the report was re-submitted in document A/HRC/14/27 (9 April 2010).

> rights, the enforceability of contracts, competition and the smooth flow of information. But a key prerequisite is often overlooked: curtailing individual and social harms imposed by markets. History demonstrates that without adequate institutional underpinnings, markets . . . may even become socially unsustainable.[44]

As discussed in chapter VII, the dependence of economic development on laws and institutions has been emphasized since the publications of Adam Smith more than two centuries ago. Property rights, contract, company, bankruptcy, banking and investment law, competition and trade laws, and legal security based on 'rule of law' are necessary, yet insufficient legal conditions for the proper functioning of economic markets. The need for a systemic 'order policy' creating the constituent and regulative principles of a 'social market economy', correcting 'market failures', supplying 'public goods' and promoting the overall coherence of the interdependent economic, legal, political and social orders was emphasized and explained by the economists and lawyers cooperating in the German 'Freiburg school of *ordo*-liberalism' during and after the Second World War.[45] The diverse degrees of 'legal integration' in the EU, the EEA, the EU's free trade or mere cooperation agreements with third countries, NAFTA and the common market in South America (MERCOSUR) illustrate how citizens and their government representatives often disagree on the necessary scope of legal harmonization inside economic integration and trade agreements depending on their respective social and political systems.

The need for multilevel legal, institutional and social 'embedding' of economic liberalism

In his 1944 book *The Great Transformation*, Karl Polanyi explained the corrosion of the social institutions of the prewar liberal trading system – due to the political transformations caused by the First World War – as a major reason for the postwar failures to re-establish the prewar liberal trading system and for the rise of fascism and dictatorships in Europe during the 1930s. The 'social dis-embedding' of workers, soldiers, families and other parts of populations in Europe lent support to populist calls for authoritarian and protectionist countermeasures promising new kinds of 'social integration' and radical reforms of market competition.[46] In a 1983 article, Ruggie refuted political science claims that the stability of liberal international economic regimes had depended on hegemonic leadership by Great Britain during the liberal trading system from 1860 up to the end of the nineteenth century and, since the Second World War, by the United States during the Bretton Woods system. Ruggie complemented Polanyi's analysis by arguing that the relative stability and economic openness of the Bretton Woods agreements were due also to their 'embedded liberalism compromise' based on multilateral treaty rules protecting sovereign rights to correct 'market failures', provide social 'public goods' and to resort

[44] UN Doc A/HRC/8/5 (7 April 2008), para 1.

[45] For a discussion of the 'school of *ordo*-liberalism' at Freiburg University, the 'Chicago school' of 'law and economics', the 'Virginia school of public choice' and the relevance of economics (notably of the economic theories of 'optimal intervention' and 'separation of policy instruments') for the legal design of national and international economic law see: EU Petersmann (1991) chs III and IV.

[46] K Polanyi, *The Great Transformation: The Political and Economic Origins of our Time* (Boston, MA: Beacon Press, 1944/reprint 2001). On the problem of keeping transnational markets 'socially embedded' see: C Joerges and J Falke (eds), *Karl Polanyi, Globalisation and the Potential of Law in Transnational Markets* (Oxford: Hart Publishing, 2011).

unilaterally to 'safeguard measures' (eg, pursuant to GATT Articles VI, XVII to XXI) protecting import-competing producers, their workers or consumers against 'injurious imports' or socially disruptive adjustment costs of import competition.[47] Ruggie referred to Polanyi's analyses as illustrating the political dangers of 'dis-embedded economic orders' based on ideologies of 'self-regulating markets' (during the nineteenth century trading system) or of their authoritarian, protectionist management through nationalist interventions (during the interwar period in the 1920s and 1930s). The economic liberal multilateralism following the Second World War owed its stability not only to the hegemonic leadership of the United States, but to the 'shared legitimacy of a set of social objectives to which the industrial world had moved, unevenly but . . . as a single entity'.[48]

The political hypothesis developed in Ruggie's article of 1983 – ie, that a liberal international economic regime may remain stable and relatively autonomous in spite of the hegemon's relative decline – is consistent with the increasingly important roles of the EU, Japan, China, India, Brazil and other emerging 'trading powers' and the relatively declining influence of the United States in the GATT/WTO legal and trading system. In another article published in 2003, Ruggie argued that economic globalization undermines the premises of the postwar 'embedded liberalism compromise' (eg, national economies engaged in external trade and investment transactions) and 'threatens to leave behind merely national social bargains'. In order to survive in the twenty-first century, embedded liberalism needs to be re-established on the global plane by promoting the emerging 'global public domain: an arena of discourse, contestation and action organized around global rule-making – a transnational space that is not exclusively inhabited by states, and which permits the direct expression and pursuit of human interests'.[49] According to Ruggie, 'we are a long way from turning rich country consumers, the employees of transnational corporations or even dedicated activists into global citizens'. The necessary institutionalization of a new 'global public domain' with 'more inclusive forms of global governance', and more effective regulatory actions by states, are more likely to be triggered by the 'transnational corporate sector' and by its 'key bridging role' between national communities and the global economy than via 'international corporatism' and idealist calls for 'cosmopolitan democracy'.[50]

The 'UN Global Compact' and 'Corporate Social Responsibility': examples for civilizing the 'global public domain'?

In another article in 2004, Ruggie asserted that the 'UN Global Compact' (UNGC) – launched in 1999 as a joint initiative of five UN agencies (the UN Development Programme, ILO, the UN Industrial Development Organization, the UN Environmental Programme and the UN Office on Drugs and Crimes) and the UN High Commissioner of Human Rights – in cooperation with now more than 6000 companies, 2000 non-business NGOs

[47] J Ruggie, 'International Regimes, Transactions and Change: Embedded Liberalism in the Postwar Economic Order' (1983) 36 *International Organizations* 379 ff.

[48] ibid 398.

[49] J Ruggie, 'Taking Embedded Liberalism Global: The Corporate Connection' in D Held and M Koenig-Archibugi (eds), *Taming Globalization: Frontiers of Governance* (Cambridge: Polity Press, 2003) 3 ff.

[50] ibid 28. Note that 'European cosmopolitanism' protects not only individual rights, but also rights of companies and of other non-governmental organizations under EU and EEA law and the ECHR.

and local UNGC networks based in more than 135 countries[51] – constitutes a 'new global public domain'. Its ten principles concerning the protection of human rights, core labour standards, the fight against corruption, the protection of the environment and of sustainable development are intended to be mainstreamed into global business activities and to 'catalyse' business support of UN goals through partnerships between business and UN agencies, civil society and governments, and other transnational CSR activities.

Table 20: The ten principles of the 'UN Global Compact' for 'corporate social responsibility' of international business

The Compact requests companies to embrace, support and enact, within their spheres of influence, 10 principles based on UN covenants in the areas of human rights, labour standards, the environment and anti-corruption:

Human rights	
Principle 1	Businesses should support and respect the protection of internationally proclaimed human rights; and
Principle 2	should ensure that they are not complicit in human rights abuses.
Labour rights	
Principle 3	Businesses should uphold the freedom of association and the effective recognition of the right to collective bargaining;
Principle 4	the elimination of all forms of forced and compulsory labour;
Principle 5	the effective abolition of child labour; and
Principle 6	the elimination of discrimination in respect of employment and occupation.
Environment	
Principle 7	Businesses should support a precautionary approach to environmental challenges;
Principle 8	undertake initiatives to promote greater environmental responsibility; and
Principle 9	encourage the development and diffusion of environmentally friendly technologies.
Anti-corruption	
Principle 10	Businesses should work against corruption in all its forms, including extortion and bribery.

These principles shall be transformed into practice by articulating 'legitimate social purposes' and contributing to the emergence of new 'accountability systems', such as voluntary 'company codes' for good 'corporate governance' and voluntary 'corporate social reporting'.[52] The increasing involvement of non-state actors in promoting the human rights dimensions of transnational business activities is seen as empirical evidence for non-governmental organizations 'playing public roles to compensate for governance gaps and governance failures at global and national levels'.[53] Ruggie illustrates this 'iconic case of civil society action to redress imbalances in global rule-making' by 'its

[51] UN Global Compact Annual Review – Anniversary Edition (New York: UN, June 2010) 9–10.

[52] J Ruggie, 'Reconstituting the Global Public Domain: Issues, Actors and Practices' (2004) 10 *European Journal of International Relations* 499 ff.

[53] ibid 520 ff.

role in defeating the Multilateral Agreement on Investment, strongly supported by TNCs and international business associations'. In the absence of any prospect of 'legally binding regulation at the global level' due to lack of 'political will or even capacity' on the part of states and the political opposition of TNCs to such global UN regulation, Ruggie presents emerging, multilevel economic and social governance for promoting the human rights dimensions of transnational business activities as 'a historically progressive platform by creating a more inclusive institutional arena in which . . . other social actors, including CSO, international organizations and even states, can graft their pursuit of broader social agendas onto the global reach and capacity of TNCs'.[54] Ruggie admits that legal and institutional adaptations through transnational governance networks 'raise serious accountability issues'. But such transnational governance via networks and private–public partnerships may also promote more inclusive reasoning and collective learning processes compared with intergovernmental reasoning excluding civil society affected by intergovernmental market regulation.[55]

A UN legal framework for transnational business and human rights?

Transnational 'law merchant' (*lex mercatoria*) governing transnational business transactions has existed and evolved for centuries on the basis of freedom of contract, customary business practices (like 'bills of exchange'), standard clauses for specialized commercial, banking, transport and insurance contracts and their interpretation and enforcement by national courts and commercial arbitration.[56] Decolonization, the globalization of TNCs and the ever more comprehensive legal dimensions of their business practices, as illustrated by thousands of investor–state contracts and hundreds of related arbitration proceedings, have prompted the emergence of increasingly specialized 'transnational law'.[57] Yet, in spite of references in UN human rights instruments (eg, Article 29 UDHR) to duties and responsibilities of everyone towards the community, proposals for legally binding UN agreements on a 'Code of Conduct for Transnational Corporations'[58] and on 'UN Norms on Business and Human Rights'[59] only led to draft texts that remained controversial among many UN member states. TNCs, and also some trade unions, opposed attempts to impose on companies – directly under international law – the same range of human rights duties that states have accepted for themselves under human rights treaties, ie, 'to promote, secure the fulfilment of, respect, ensure respect of and protect human rights'. The UN draft code on TNCs, which never became international treaty law, included only a brief clause requiring corporations to respect human rights:

[54] ibid 507 ff.

[55] J Ruggie, 'The UN and Globalisation: Patterns and Limits of Institutional Adaptation' (2003) 9 *Global Governance* 301–21.

[56] *cf* EU Petersmann, 'Principles of World Trade' in R Bernhardt (ed), *Encyclopedia of Public International Law*, no 8 (The Hague: Kluwer, 1985) 530–39.

[57] *cf* D Vagts and H Steiner, *Transnational Legal Problems* (Mineola, NY: Foundation Press, 1968).

[58] The 1983 draft code and revisions are reproduced in UN Doc E/1990/94, *Development and International Economic Cooperation: Transnational Corporations* (1990); for comprehensive analysis see: P Muchlinski, *Multinational Enterprises and the Law* (Oxford: OUP, 2007).

[59] The 2003 draft text is reproduced in UN Doc E/CN.4/Sub.2/2003/12/L.11, *Responsibilities of Transnational Corporations and Other Business Enterprises with Regard to Human Rights* (2003); a *Commentary on the Norms on the Responsibilities of Transnational Corporations and other Business Enterprises with regard to Human Rights* is published in UN Doc E/CN.4/Sub.2/2003/Rev.2 (26 August 2003).

> Transnational corporations shall respect human rights and fundamental freedoms in the countries in which they operate. In their social and industrial relations, transnational corporations shall not discriminate on the basis of race, color, sex, religion, language, social, national and ethnic origin or political or other opinion. Transnational corporations shall conform to government policies designed to extend equality of opportunity and treatment.[60]

The 2003 UN draft norms on business and human rights focused on labour rights, such as the prohibition of forced and child labour, a safe and healthy working environment, remuneration ensuring an adequate standard of living, freedom of association, right to collective bargaining, equal opportunity and non-discrimination for example, of women and indigenous people. They also addressed broader aspects of the right to development, like the prohibition of companies to 'engage in trade that is known to lead to human rights or humanitarian law violations'. In their allocation of human rights responsibilities to corporations, states, the UN as well as to various non-governmental entities, the draft norms defined their 'primary approach' in the following terms:

> States have the primary responsibility to promote, secure the fulfilment of, respect, ensure respect of and protect human rights in international law as well as national law, including ensuring that transnational corporations and other business enterprises respect human rights. Within their respective spheres of activity and influence, transnational corporations and other business enterprises have the obligation to promote, secure the fulfilment of, respect, ensure the respect of and protect human rights recognized in international as well as national law.[61]

The Preamble of the UN draft norms inferred from about 30 UN human rights instruments since the 1948 UDHR that not only states, but also businesses were 'obligated to respect' under international law the 'generally recognized responsibilities and norms' arising under UN human rights instruments.[62] As the scope of direct duties of corporations under UN human rights law remained controversial, the UN High Commissioner for Human Rights was requested to further clarify the concurrent state and corporate responsibilities for observance of human rights. The 2005 report by the UN High Commissioner conceded the existence of 'gaps in understanding the nature and scope of the human rights responsibilities of business' because the 'international instruments give little guidance . . . which human rights are relevant to the activities of business'. The report explained why the scope of human rights responsibilities of business, and their observance within corporate operations, could vary depending on factors such as the 'sphere of influence' and particular business transactions of TNCs.[63]

The 2008 report by the UN Special Representative on business and human rights, J Ruggie, on 'Protect, Respect and Remedy: a Framework for Business and Human Rights'[64] proposed a 'strategic policy framework' based on the following three principles:

1. The *states' duty to protect against human rights abuses by third parties*, including corporate actors, has become a well-established principle of international human rights law requiring states not just to refrain from actively interfering with human

[60] UN draft code (n 60) para 14.

[61] UN draft norms (n 61), para 1.

[62] For a detailed analysis of this claim see: A Clapham, *Human Rights Obligations of Non-State Actors* (Oxford: OUP, 2006).

[63] The *Report of the UN High Commissioner on Human Rights on the responsibilities of transnational corporations and related business enterprises with regard to human rights* of 15 February 2005 is published in UN Doc E/CN/4/2005/91 (the quoted text is from para 88).

[64] See (n 45): UN Doc A/HRC/8/5 (7 April 2008).

rights, but also to intervene through appropriate regulation and judicial remedies. The aim is to prevent private actors – including both natural and legal persons like corporations – within their jurisdiction from harming human rights, for instance by polluting air and land,[65] harming indigenous people's land,[66] or by violating trade union rights.[67] This state duty to protect may also apply to the activities in other countries of 'corporate nationals' and of subsidiaries controlled by the parent company.
2. The *corporate responsibility to respect all human rights* exists independently of states' duties and may potentially relate to numerous human rights that may be impacted by business activities. Yet, since companies are 'specialized economic organs (of society), not democratic public interest institutions', the scope of their corporate responsibility for human rights 'cannot and should not simply mirror the duties of states'. It requires 'due diligence' in the sense of 'a process whereby companies not only ensure compliance with national laws but also manage the risk of human rights harm', with due regard to the particular risks created by company activities.[68]
3. Human rights law also requires '*effective access to remedies*' based on state regulation and company rules, including judicial remedies, state-based non-judicial remedies (such as interventions by national regulatory agencies and human rights institutions) as well as non-state, non-judicial voluntary remedies (such as company level grievance mechanisms). While states retain some discretion as to how to provide a remedy against a violation of human rights, the remedy must be 'accessible and effective' with 'appropriate judicial and administrative mechanisms for addressing claims of rights violations under domestic law'.[69]

On 16 June 2011, the UN Human Rights Council finally endorsed the 'Guiding Principles on Business and Human Rights: Implementing the UN "Protect, Respect and Remedy" Framework' proposed by the UN Special Rapporteur Ruggie.[70] The final report of the Special Representative on the issue of human rights and transnational corporations of 21 March 2011 emphasizes:

> The Guiding Principles' normative contribution lies not in the creation of new international law obligations but in elaborating the implications of existing standards and practices of States and businesses; . . . While the Principles are universally applicable, the means by which they are realized will reflect the fact that we live in a world of 192 UN Member States, 80,000 transnational enterprises, 10 times as many subsidiaries and countless millions of national firms, most of which are small and medium-sized enterprises. When it comes to means for implementation, one size does not fit all.[71]

[65] *cf*, eg, the Judgment by the ECtHR (19 February 1998), *Guerra v Italy*, App no 00014967/89, 26 European Human Rights Reports (1998) 357.

[66] *cf*, eg, the Judgment by the Inter-American Court of Human Rights (31 August 2001), *The Mayagna Awas Tingni Community v Nicaragua*, IACtHR Series C no 79.

[67] *cf*, eg, Judgment by the ECtHR (13 August 1981), *Young, James and Webster v United Kingdom*, App no 7601/76, 4 EHRR (1981) 38.

[68] *cf* (n 45 paras 24–25, 53–55. Ruggie does not suggest changing the traditional interpretation that UN human rights conventions impose legal obligations to protect human rights on states alone without also imposing direct obligations and responsibilities on TNCs for violations of UN human rights obligations.

[69] UN Human Rights Committee, General Comment No 31 of 26 May 2004 (UN Doc CCPR/C/21/ Rev.1/ Add. 13, para 15).

[70] *cf* UN Doc A/HRC/RES/17/4 (6 July 2011).

[71] UN Doc A/HRC/17/31 (21 March 2011), paras 14–15.

Shortcomings of the UN Global Compact

In describing diverse 'governance gaps' resulting from the 'rapid market expansion' during the 1990s, the 2008 report on 'Protect, Respect and Remedy: A Framework for Business and Human Rights'[72] also referred to 'lessons to be drawn from earlier periods. The Victorian era of globalization collapsed because governments and business failed to manage its adverse impact on core values of social community'; fascism and communism in the twentieth century were 'championed in the name of social protection against economic forces controlled by "others"', and responded to failed attempts to 'restore a laissez-faire international economy after World War I'.[73] What kind of 'social embedding' does economic globalization require in the twenty-first century in order to become socially supported and politically stable? What has been the 'transformative impact' of the Global Compact in the absence of independent and transparent monitoring, complaint and enforcement procedures?

The 2008 and 2011 reports recommend, inter alia, that the UN – notwithstanding its lack of powers for protecting human rights through 'command and control' measures – should lead 'intellectually and by setting expectations and aspirations' for the implementation of the 'respect, protect and remedy framework'.[74] The UN Human Rights Council supported the 'Protect, Respect and Remedy' Framework developed by the Special Representative and – based on Ruggie's final report of March 2011[75] – approved by consensus, on 16 June 2011, 31 'Guiding Principles for Business and Human Rights' as well as the establishment of a Working Group of independent experts with the task of promoting the implementation of the Guiding Principles and reporting annually to the Human Rights Council and the UN General Assembly. At the OECD Ministerial Council meeting of 25 May 2011, 42 governments adhering to the OECD Guidelines for Multinational Enterprises also agreed on an updated text of these OECD Guidelines taking into account the final report by Ruggie. Does this 'UN leadership' adequately reflect earlier historical lessons? The growing number of companies and non-governmental organizations participating in the UN Global Compact and in the regular consultations on the 'Guiding Principles for business and human rights' is motivated by manifold economic and non-economic motives.[76] The Global Compact Secretariat claims that

[72] *cf* UN Doc A/HRC/8/5 (n 45), para 104.

[73] *cf* ibid para 83.

[74] *cf* ibid paras 105 ff. Ruggies's contention that the key responsibility of corporations is to *respect* human rights and their responsibility to *protect* remains largely 'negative' in nature, remains contested; *cf* D Bilchitz, 'The Ruggie Framework: An Adequate Rubric for Corporate Human Rights Obligations?' (2010) 7 *International Journal of Human Rights* 198 ff.

[75] Report of the Special Representative of the Secretary-General on the issue of human rights and transnational corporations and other business enterprises, John Ruggie, UN Doc A/HRC/17/31 (21 March 2011). According to this report (para 6), the 'Framework rests on three pillars. The first is the State duty to protect against human rights abuses by third parties, including business enterprises, through appropriate policies, regulation, and adjudication. The second is the corporate responsibility to respect human rights, which means that business enterprises should act with due diligence to avoid infringing on the rights of others and to address adverse impacts with which they are involved. The third is the need for greater access by victims to effective remedy, both judicial and non-judicial'.

[76] See: ME Porter and MR Kramer, 'Strategy and Society: The Link between Competitive Advantage and Corporate Social Responsibility' (2006) *Harvard Business Review* 1–16. For a critical evaluation of the 2011 update of the *OECD Guidelines for Multinational Enterprises* see J Evans, 'Responsible Business Conduct: Re-Shaping Global Business' *Columbia FDI Perspectives* No 50 (7 November 2011).

> in a short period of ten years, the Global Compact stands as the world's largest, global responsibility initiative. As of 1 June 2010, over 8,000 signatories – 6,000 from business and 2,000 from civil society and other non-business groups – based in more than 135 countries were committed to implementing the Global Compact principles into business practices and taking actions to advance UN goals, such as the Millennium Development Goals.[77]

According to Guiding Principle 1, 'States must protect against human rights abuses within their territory and/or jurisdiction by third parties, including business enterprises. This requires taking appropriate steps to prevent, investigate, punish and redress such abuse through effective policies, legislation, regulations and adjudication'. The corporate responsibility to respect human rights is defined in Guiding Principles 11 to 15 in the following terms:

> 11. Business enterprises should respect human rights. This means that they should avoid infringing on the human rights of others and should address adverse human rights impacts with which they are involved.
>
> 12. The responsibility of business enterprises to respect human rights refers to internationally recognized human rights – understood, at a minimum, as those expressed in the International Bill of Human Rights and the principles concerning fundamental rights set out in the International Labour Organization's Declaration on Fundamental Principles and Rights at Work.
>
> 13. The responsibility to respect human rights requires that business enterprises:
>
> (a) Avoid causing or contributing to adverse human rights impacts through their own activities, and address such impacts when they occur;
> (b) Seek to prevent or mitigate adverse human rights impacts that are directly linked to their operations, products or services by their business relationships, even if they have not contributed to those impacts.
>
> 14. The responsibility of business enterprises to respect human rights applies to all enterprises regardless of their size, sector, operational context, ownership and structure. Nevertheless, the scale and complexity may vary according to these factors and with the severity of the enterprise's adverse human rights impacts.
>
> 15. In order to meet their responsibility to respect human rights, business enterprises should have in place policies and processes appropriate to their size and circumstances, including
>
> (a) A policy commitment to meet their responsibility to respect human rights;
> (b) A human rights due-diligence process to identify, prevent, mitigate and account for how they address their impacts on human rights;
> (c) Processes to enable the remediation of any adverse human rights impacts they cause or to which they contribute.

Many NGOs criticize that the lack of effective monitoring, complaint and sanctioning procedures leaves the actual performance and consistency of company practices with the Guiding Principles unclear. There seems to be no evidence that investor–state arbitration tribunals and other dispute settlement *fora* have used these principles and commitments for clarifying the scope of legal 'corporate social responsibility' obligations (eg, in the 'judicial balancing' of legitimate investor expectations and the rights of host states to protect public interests). A recent doctoral thesis criticizes Ruggie's publications, including his 2008 UN report, for neglecting Polanyi's insight that the proper functioning and

[77] UN Global Compact Annual Review – Anniversary Edition (New York: UN, June 2010) 6.

social stability of market economies depend not only on their 'legal and institutional embedding', but also on a 'social embedding' of market-driven production, investments, trade and labour markets.[78] For, Ruggie specified neither the impact of economic globalization on labour law and on 'social dis-embedding' (such as weakening trade union representation, 'informal employment' of workers in less-developed countries, 'feminisation' of 'precarious work', increasing mobility of workers in decentralized supply chains) nor the means for reinforcing labour rights regimes, such as reforms of employment contracts, site-level worker representation, corporate law and 'social citizenship' remedies based on expanded procedural and substantive worker rights. According to O'Brien, 'multilevel transnational social governance' – including the ideal of 'workplace democracy' in corporations as 'social institutions', judicial enforcement of labour and social rights – may not be adequately protected by the recommendations of Ruggie.

Ruggie's pragmatic reliance on existing human rights, labour and social rights may have been influenced by his limited mandate as UN Special Representative for business and human rights as well as by the fact that UN/ILO proposals for wide-ranging reforms of corporate laws, labour rights and social rights at national and international levels continue to be controversial in many UN member states. Only some 'soft law forms' of transnational 'social governance' – such as those based on the OECD Guidelines for Multinational Enterprises, the ILO Tripartite Declarations of Principles concerning Multinational Enterprises and Social Policy, and a few other intergovernmental undertakings regarding promotion of 'company codes' referring to human rights obligations and related certification and accreditation systems (eg, governed by the Kimberley Protocol on 'conflict diamonds') – benefit from support by US government institutions and US-based TNCs.[79] The US government claims that – notwithstanding the longstanding US refusal to ratify most ILO conventions and many UN human rights conventions (such as the 1966 ICESCR) – economic, social and labour rights are adequately protected in US federal or state laws and policies.[80] Yet, empirical US investigations suggest a high degree of actual violations of labour laws in low-wage workplaces in the United States.[81]

Government and parliaments in many Anglo-Saxon countries and LDCs claim 'parliamentary sovereignty' over economic and social regulation without recognizing constitutional rights of citizens to economic freedoms. The neglect in UN human rights conventions of the welfare functions of private property and economic freedoms (like freedom of profession, open markets, non-discriminatory conditions of competition, prohibition of restrictive business practices harming consumer welfare) may be compensated by international economic regulation and domestic implementing legislation protecting economic liberties and property rights in transnational economic cooperation, as illustrated by the legal and judicial guarantees of market freedoms and property rights in

[78] CHM O'Brien, 'Human Rights and Transnational Corporations: For a Multi-level Governance Approach' (doctoral thesis defended at the European University Institute, Florence, October 2009).

[79] For a useful overview and analyses of these various instruments and related practices see O'Brien, ibid. The 1998 and 2008 ILO Declarations on core labour standards for decent work conditions are discussed in chs VI and VII.

[80] On inadequate legal protection of economic and social rights in Canada and the United States see: RE Howard-Hassmann and CE Welch (2006). Even though only few economic, social and labour rights are protected in US constitutional law and US federal laws, they are protected in some US state laws.

[81] According to the *International Herald Tribune* of 5–6 September 2009, a comprehensive 2009 investigation of labour law violations in the United States has 'cast an appalling light' on labour law violations in low wage workplaces in the urban economy of the United States (at 6).

EU and EEA law.[82] Yet, the neglect for effective protection of social and labour rights in the constitutions and laws of many countries outside Europe render the political success of UN proposals for multilevel, legal and institutional protection of social and labour rights uncertain.

Lack of adequate legal and judicial corporate accountability: the example of the Bhopal gas tragedy

Corporate laws often differ from country to country. According to the jurisprudence of the ICJ, the state of incorporation retains exclusive jurisdiction over a corporation even if the company is controlled by another corporation in a different state.[83] The EU model of transnational, legal and judicial protection of socio-economic rights, of individual and group representation in transnational companies,[84] and the role of courts in developing a 'European social model'[85] remain highly controversial outside Europe. There is increasing recognition that legal and judicial accountability of TNCs for socially harmful company activities remains inadequate in many countries. In the EU, most member states introduced effective economic, social and labour rights, environmental protection and related judicial remedies for transnational relations only in the context of their implementation of EU law, including the EU's international legal obligations as an 'integral part of the Community legal system' (pursuant to Articles 300 EC Nice Treaty, 216 TFEU). In the United States, by contrast, the US Congress and most courts are opposed to judicial enforcement in US courts of most international treaty obligations of the government (eg, under UN human rights law, WTO law and ILO conventions). Only in the context of free trade area agreements (like Chapters 11 and 19 of NAFTA), investment, environmental and human rights agreements is multilevel judicial protection of individual rights becoming more effective also outside Europe.[86]

Due to the difficulties of litigating a transnational environmental tort against the perpetrator company abroad, the famous *Trail Smelter* dispute over transboundary environmental pollution caused by Canadian smelter companies was settled through interstate arbitration between the United States and Canada. The arbitral tribunal emphasized that it was 'not sitting to pass upon claims presented by individuals or on behalf of one or more individuals by their Government.'[87] Since the Second World War, the number of national court proceedings involving private complaints against violations of human rights, labour rights and environmental laws by TNCs continues to increase. But the recent judgment of an Indian court at Bhopal in June 2010 in the 23-year-old lawsuit over the toxic gas leak from a Union Carbide pesticide factory in 1984 illustrated the often

[82] On such 'constitutional functions' see: Petersmann (1991); D Nicol (2010).

[83] Case concerning *Barcelona Traction Company (Second Phase, Belgium v Spain)* [1970] ICJ Rep 3, 42.

[84] *cf* A Lo Faro, *Regulating Social Europe: Reality and Myth of Collective Bargaining in the EC Legal Order* (Oxford: Hart Publishing, 2000); S Giubboni, *Social Rights and Market Freedom in the European Constitution* (Cambridge: CUP, 2006).

[85] *cf* U Neergaard, R Nielsen and L Roseberry (eds), *The Role of Courts in Developing a European Social Model* (Copenhagen: DJOF, 2010).

[86] *cf* G Winter (ed), *Multilevel Governance of Global Environmental Change* (Cambridge: CUP, 2006); Bache and Flinders (eds) (n 42). See also the 'judicial balancing' of economic and human rights in the MERCOSUR arbitral award of 6 September 2006 in the 'Bridges case' between Argentina and Uruguay: *cf* L Lixinski, 'Human Rights in MERCOSUR' in Filho, Lixinski and Giupponi (eds) (n 36) 351 ff.

[87] *USA v Canada* (Trail Smelter Case), UN Repertoire of International Arbitration Awards (1941), 1905, 1912.

insufficient legal and judicial accountability of TNCs for grave violations of human rights, labour rights and environmental law.[88]

The Bhopal accident killed thousands and injured more than half a million citizens. In 1987, the US Court of Appeals had affirmed the decision of a US District Court judge to transfer the civil litigation for damages – at the request of Union Carbide – from US courts to Indian courts since Union Carbide India Ltd was a 'separate entity, owned, managed and operated exclusively by Indian citizens in India', and there were additional procedural grounds for considering US courts as *forum non conveniens*.[89] The US Supreme Court in October 1993 refused to hear an appeal of this federal court judgment, thus definitely preventing victims of the Bhopal disaster from seeking damages in a US court. The Indian court judgment of June 2010 found Union Carbide India Ltd and seven executives of the company guilty of causing death by criminal negligence, required the company to pay a fine of 500,000 rupees ($10,870) and sentenced each individual to two years in prison and payment of 100,000 rupees ($2175), the maximum punishment allowed by Indian law. All seven defendants were released on bail shortly after the judgment, and all are expected to appeal against the decision. In 1999, the government of India and Union Carbide had already reached a settlement on the company's civil and criminal liability, under which the company paid $470 million (ie, the insurance sum plus interest, 85 per cent less than the initially $3 billion claimed in the lawsuit). In May 2011, the Indian Supreme Court rejected a petition filed by the Indian Central Bureau of Investigation seeking a harsher punishment for the accused in this case and declined to reopen the 1984 Bhopal gas disaster case.

The contrast with the 2010 BP oil spill disaster in the Gulf of Mexico and with BP's speedy establishment of a $20 billion compensation fund illustrated the disparity between the administration of justice for the Bhopal tragedy in India and for BP's 'Deepwater Horizon' oil spill in the United States. Proposals for 'globalizing embedded liberalism through multilevel protection of human rights' are unlikely to succeed without stronger judicial remedies for the domestic enforcement of human rights, social, labour and environmental rights. Yet, the use of the US Alien Tort Claims Act of the eighteenth century[90] for suing corporations under this Act has recently become contested when a Second Circuit Court of Appeals denied corporate liability under the Act.[91] Also UN law fails to effectively protect citizens against violations of human rights by governments and private actors like TNCs.

3 'HUMAN RIGHTS COHERENCE' OF EUROPEAN ECONOMIC LAW AND REASONABLE DISAGREEMENT ON THE 'HUMAN RIGHTS COHERENCE' OF IEL BEYOND EUROPE

Chapter I explained why the legitimacy and effectiveness of multilevel regulation of a mutually beneficial world trading, monetary, financial, environmental, development and

[88] For a regular documentation of case law on corporate legal accountability, including the lawsuits in Indian and US courts against Union Carbide/Dow (re Bhopal), see: *Corporate Legal Accountability Quarterly Bulletin*, published by the Business & Human Rights Resource Centre at London (www.business-humanrights.org).

[89] *cf* S Baughen, 'Corporate Accountability and the Law of Tort: The Inconclusive Verdict of Bhopal' University of Manchester Working Paper 16 (1993).

[90] 28 USC 1350.

[91] *Kiobel v Royal Dutch Petroleum*, 2010 US App. LEXIS 19382 (2d Circuit 2010).

legal system in the twenty-first century depend on 'human rights coherence' (Table 4) and 'democratic constitutionalism' (Table 5). But it was also emphasized that – in view of the need to respect legitimate 'multilevel constitutional pluralism' (Table 6) – the human rights coherence of IEL beyond Europe remained contested due to the lack of effective, multilevel legislative and judicial protection of human rights as in the law of the EU and of the EEA. This section gives an overview of protection of human rights in European economic law and explains why there continues to be reasonable disagreement on the constitutional foundations and human right coherence of regional and worldwide IEL beyond Europe. It then argues, as explained in chapters II and III, for reconsidering the 'constitutional foundations' and 'rules of recognition' of IEL in order to 'constitutionalize' economic rules and institutions through citizen-oriented interpretations of IEL, as already suggested in Table 7 on the need for a rights-based 'paradigm shift in multilevel economic regulation' to strengthen constitutional protection not only of rights and obligations of sovereign states, but also of their citizens. Transforming and 'civilizing' IEL requires clarifying numerous questions such as:

- Why has parliamentary ratification of UN conventions on human rights failed in so many states and areas of IEL to protect human rights and rule of law more effectively in the worldwide division of labour among citizens?
- Do the human rights obligations of UN member states require complementing the 'horizontal conceptions' of UN human rights conventions by 'vertical safeguards' protecting cosmopolitan rights and remedies of citizens in domestic laws and institutions more effectively?
- Does democratic governance require legal recognition of citizens as the main actors in the international division of labour and as the main legal subjects of IEL? Does such a citizen-oriented, democratic conception of IEL require interpreting the sources of international law (eg, as codified in Article 38 of the ICJ Statute) no longer exclusively from the perspective of states and diplomats, but with due regard also to the *opinio juris sive necessitatis* of citizens, civil society, parliaments and 'courts of justice'?
- What is the 'optimal level' of legal regulation of economic human rights and other 'public goods' protecting individual access to scarce resources of 'existential importance' such as water, food and essential medicines? Should such rights be protected by human rights, constitutional rights, legislative, administrative and/or 'judicial rights' (eg, guaranteeing individual access to essential services like water, food and medical services)? Should economic rights of producers, investors, traders and consumers be protected by national and international human rights law, national and European constitutional law (like the multilevel European guarantees of freedom of profession, property rights and 'market freedoms'), or by economic legislation, administration, judicial remedies and specific international agreements (eg, on intellectual property rights and freedom of the internet)?[92] Should public policies provide public goods directly (eg, through rules, taxes, subsidies, public production) or more indirectly, such as through such regulation as competition policy, price controls of essential medicines, intellectual property rights and health policies? What is the best jurisdictional level for multilevel regulation of local, national and transnational public goods that are often

[92] *cf* KE Maskus and JH Reichman (2005), who argue that important public goods (as basic research, education, public health, protection of the environment) increasingly depend on the exercise and regulation of private rights over technical inputs and information goods.

interrelated in complex ways (eg, in the case of promotion of public knowledge by intellectual property rights whose temporary, legal monopolies may simultaneously create entry barriers and restrict competition)? Under what conditions can privatization of public services and of industrial know-how and technologies serve public interests?

Interpretation of European economic law in conformity with human rights

In the leading 1963 case *Van Gend en Loos*, which established the 'direct effect' of EU (*ex* EEC) Treaty rules, the Court inferred from 'the spirit and general scheme' of the European Economic Community (EEC) Treaty – notably from its provisions for preliminary rulings (Article 267 TFEU) and for direct effect of EC regulations (Article 288 TFEU) – that

> the Community constitutes a new legal order of international law for the benefit of which the states have limited their sovereign rights, albeit within limited fields, and the subjects of which comprise not only Member States but also their nationals. Independently of the legislation of Member States, Community law therefore not only imposes obligations on individuals but is also intended to confer upon them rights which become part of their legal heritage. These rights arise not only where they are expressly granted by the Treaty, but also by reason of obligations which the Treaty imposes in a clearly defined way upon individuals as well as upon the Member States and upon the institutions of the Community.[93]

These citizen-oriented interpretations of EU Treaty rules were based on functional rather than human rights arguments. As neither the 1951 European Coal and Steel Community (ECSC) Treaty nor the 1957 EEC Treaty referred to human rights, the Court declined – prior to its *Stauder* judgment of 1969 – to review Community acts and state measures in light of human rights.[94] In its preliminary ruling regarding Stauder's complaint that an EC requirement of revealing the names and addresses of beneficiaries of 'surplus butter' would infringe his basic right to dignity as protected by Article 1 of the German Basic Law, the Court asserted for the first time that protection of human rights is part of the general principles of EC law.[95]

Table 21: ECJ case law on human dignity as legal context for interpreting European economic law

In Case 29/69 *Stauder* [1969] ECR 419, the Court confirmed for the first time that protection of human rights is part of the general principles of EC law. Stauder claimed that an EC requirement conditioning the distribution of subsidized butter to poor people on disclosure of the name of the recipient violated his constitutional right to respect for dignity protected by the German Basic Law. The ECJ interpreted the EC rule in conformity with human rights as not requiring identification of the name. In Case C-377/98 *Netherlands v European Parliament and EU Council* [2001] ECR I-7079, the Court emphasized that 'it is for the Court

[93] Case 26/62, *Van Gend en Loos* [1963] ECR, 1, 12.
[94] For instance, in the supranational but functionally limited ECSC, the Court held that it lacked competence to examine whether an ECSC decision amounted to an infringement of fundamental rights as recognized in the constitution of a member state: Case C-1/58 *Storck* [1959] ECR 43.
[95] Case 29/69, *Stauder* [1969] ECR 419.

of Justice, in its review of the compatibility of acts of the institutions with the general principles of Community law, to ensure that the fundamental right to human dignity and integrity is observed' (paragraph70). In the *Omega* Case C-36/02 [2004] ECR I-9609, the ECJ acknowledged that the restriction of common market freedoms (to import and offer laser games involving shooting at human targets with laser pistols and simulating the killing of people) in the town of Bonn could be justified as necessary for the protection of human dignity despite the fact that the German conception of protecting human dignity as a human right was not shared by all other EC member states, and other towns inside Germany had not decided to restrict similar market freedoms.

The ECJ has clarified in numerous subsequent judgments that fundamental rights – as part of the general principles of Community law – limit interferences by member states, by the EU institutions and also by non-governmental institutions (such as trade unions). For instance:

- In the *Hauer* case of 1979, the applicant challenged an EC prohibition of the new planting of vines as infringing her fundamental rights to freedom of profession, trade and property. The Court acknowledged these fundamental freedoms as part of Community law but found that the EC restrictions were not disproportionate to the structural objectives pursued by the EC's common agricultural policy.[96]
- In its second *tobacco advertising* judgment of 2006 concerning Germany's challenge of an EC Directive banning advertising for tobacco products as a disproportionate restriction of freedom of commercial expression, the Court concluded again 'that the Community legislature did not, by adopting such measures, exceed the limits of the discretion which it is expressly accorded'.[97]
- The need for balancing competing human rights (such as freedom of expression versus protection of human health) was explicitly emphasized in the *Bodil Lindqvist* case. The Court found that the EU Directive on the free movement of personal data within the common market also aimed at safeguarding fundamental rights of individuals; the Directive contained the 'mechanisms allowing these different rights and interests to be balanced' (eg, rights to privacy versus freedom of expression).[98]
- The 'margin of appreciation' enjoyed by member states in their legislative protection of human rights was emphasized in the *Dynamic Medien* case concerning German legislation restricting the sale by mail order of video cassettes in order to protect children against injurious media material. The judges held that 'it is not indispensable that restrictive measures laid down by the authorities of a Member State to protect the rights of the child (. . .) correspond to a conception shared by all Member States as regards the level of protection and the detailed rules relating to it (. . .) As that conception may vary from one Member State to another on the basis of, *inter alia*, moral or cultural views, Member States must be recognized as having a definite margin of discretion'.[99]

[96] Case 44/79, *Hauer* [1979] ECR 3727.

[97] Case C-380/03, *Germany v Parliament and Council* [2006] ECR I-11573 (*cf* paras 155 ff: 'When a certain amount of discretion is available, review is limited to an examination of the reasonableness and proportionality of the interference. This holds true for the commercial use of freedom of expression in a field as complex and fluctuating as advertising').

[98] Case C-101/01, *Bodil Lindqvist* [2003] ECR I-12971, paras 84 ff.

[99] Case C-244/06, *Dynamic Medien*, Judgment (14 February 2008), paras 39 ff.

- The duties of EC member states to protect the common market freedoms also against private restrictions (not covered by EC competition law) were emphasized by the ECJ in the '*Spanish strawberries* dispute': France had violated the freedom of movement of goods by not preventing violent acts committed by French farmers preventing the sale of Spanish strawberries.[100] In the *Schmidberger* case, the Court accepted, however, that the governmental authorization of private demonstrations for the protection of the environment could restrict – for almost 30 hours – the common market freedom of the German transporter Schmidberger to move his goods to Italy *via* the Brenner motorway in Austria. This restriction was justifiable by the need to protect the human rights to freedom of expression and assembly of demonstrators: 'Since both the Community and its Member States are required to respect fundamental rights, the protection of those rights is a legitimate interest which, in principle, justifies a restriction of the obligations imposed by Community law, even under a fundamental freedom guaranteed by the Treaty such as the free movement of goods'.[101]
- The two judgments in the *Laval* and *Viking* cases of December 2007 (see Table 25) focused directly on the 'horizontal effects' and the need for judicial 'balancing' of common market freedoms and other fundamental rights (like freedom of association and freedom to strike) in relations between private parties (eg, private firms and trade unions): An English court requested a preliminary ruling on whether trade union actions aimed at preventing the Finnish ferry operator Viking from re-flagging one of its ferries to Estonia (in order to compete with cheaper Estonian shipping lines) unduly restricted freedom of establishment and services inside the EU. The ECJ confirmed that rights of workers to associate and take collective actions were protected by the EU legal order and could legitimately limit common market freedoms. Yet, the Court indicated that strike actions rendering intra-Community relocation impossible could be inconsistent with the proportionality requirement of EU law.[102] In its preliminary ruling on the request by a Swedish Labour Court whether blockades by Swedish trade unions amounted to an unlawful interference with the freedom of establishment and freedom to provide services of the Latvian building company Laval, the ECJ held that – in the particular context of Sweden's implementation of the EC's labour law directives – the collective actions had disproportionately restricted the common market freedoms of Laval.

As of 1975, the increasingly extensive case law of the EC courts explicitly refers to the ECHR and protects more and more human rights and fundamental freedoms in a wide array of Community law areas. The ECJ protects civil, political, economic, social and labour rights, drawing inspiration 'from the constitutional traditions common to the Member States and from the guidelines supplied by international treaties for the protection of human rights on which the Member States have collaborated or of which they are signatories'.[103] Since 1989, the ECHR has been characterized by the ECJ as having 'special significance' for the interpretation and development of EU law[104] in view of the fact

[100] Case C-265/95, *Commission v France* [1997] ECR I-6959.

[101] Case C-112/00, *Schmidberger* [2003] ECR I-5659, paras 74 ff.

[102] *cf* Cases C-438/05, *Viking*, judgment of 11 December 2007, and,C-341/05, *Laval*, Judgment of 18 December 2007; for critical comments: J Malmberg and T Siegeman, 'Industrial Action and EU Economic Freedoms: The Autonomous Collective Bargaining Model Curtailed by the ECJ' (2008) *CMLR* 1115–46.

[103] See, eg, Opinion 2/94 ECHR, [1996] ECR I-1759, para 33.

[104] Joined Cases 46/87 and 222/88, *Hoechst* [1989] ECR 2859, para 13.

that the ECHR was the only international human rights convention mentioned in Article 6 EU Nice Treaty. In the 1990s, the EC courts began referring to individual judgments of the ECtHR.[105] In reconciling economic freedoms guaranteed by EC law with human rights guarantees of the ECHR that admit restrictions, the courts have clarified that all interests involved have to be weighed 'having regard to all circumstances of the case in order to determine whether a fair balance was struck between those interests', without giving priority to the economic freedoms of the EC Treaty at the expense of other fundamental rights.[106] The EU courts have also adjusted their case law to new developments in the case law of the ECtHR[107] and differentiate, as in the case law of the ECtHR, between judicial review of EU measures, state measures and judicial review of private restrictions of economic freedoms in the light of other fundamental rights.[108]

Reasonable disagreement about the constitutional foundations of common markets

The economic theory of markets, human rights and democratic constitutionalism were 'Western inventions' that have spread over the entire world. Even though all UN member states are committed to protection of common markets at national levels, the normative foundations underlying consumer-driven market competition, human rights and multilevel trade regulation remain controversial also among 'constitutional democracies', especially in federal states and non-unitary, regional common markets like the EU.[109] My 1991 book comparing the constitutional regulation of foreign trade law and policies in the eighteenth century constitution of the United States, the nineteenth century constitution of Switzerland, the twentieth century postwar constitution of Germany and in the 'treaty constitution' of the EU illustrated that – even among constitutional democracies which reject procedural Anglo-Saxon conceptions of democracy in terms of 'parliamentary sovereignty' and 'freedom to decide' – multilevel trade regulation follows diverse constitutional paradigms. For instance, while the 'commerce clause' in Article I of the US Constitution provides for objective constitutional restraints on discriminatory trade barriers by states restricting or distorting the common market inside the United States, the Swiss and German Constitutions protect the common markets in their respective federal

[105] *cf* Case 13/94, *P v S* [1996] ECR I-2143, para16.

[106] *cf* Case C-112/00, *Schmidberger* [2003] ECR I-5659.

[107] In Case C-94/00, *Roquette Frères* [2002] ECR I-9011, para 29, for example, the ECJ referred explicitly to new case law of the ECtHR on the protection of the right to privacy of commercial enterprises in order to explain why – despite having suggested the opposite in the ECJ's earlier judgment in *Hoechst* – such enterprises may benefit from Art 8 ECHR: 'For the purposes of determining the scope of that principle in relation to the protection of business premises, regard must be had to the case-law of the European Court of Human Rights subsequent to the judgment in *Hoechst*. According to that case-law, the protection of the home provided in Article 8 of the ECHR may in certain circumstances be extended to cover such premises (see, in particular, the judgment of 16 April 2002 in *Colas Est and Others v France, not yet published in the Reports of Judgments and Decisions)* and second, the right of interference established by Article 8(2) of the ECHR might well be more far-reaching where professional or business activities or premises were involved than would otherwise be the case'.

[108] *cf* M Emberland, *The Human Rights of Companies. Exploring the Structure of ECHR Protection* (Oxford: OUP, 2006); B de Witte, 'Balancing of Economic Law and Human Rights by the European Court of Justice' in PM Dupuy, F Francioni and EU Petersmann (eds) (2009) 197–207.

[109] On the very diverse practices and conceptions of governing national and international common markets see the literature in n 42 and S Bell and A Hindmoor, *Rethinking Governance. The Centrality of the State in Modern Society* (Cambridge: CUP, 2009); W Heere (ed), *From Government to Governance* (The Hague: TMC Asser Press, 2004).

states also by individual economic freedoms; the 'common market freedoms' and competition rules in the EU 'treaty constitution' are based on international treaty guarantees with legal primacy, direct effect and direct applicability inside the national legal systems of EU member states; but the diverse forms of agreed, international extensions of EU common market rules to EEA member countries, other EFTA states and to ever more third countries in Europe and the Mediterranean often have weaker 'domestic law effects' inside the domestic legal systems of third states. In the twenty-first century, the ever more comprehensive human rights obligations of UN member states entail that multilevel economic regulation can be justified no longer only in terms of 'factual input legitimacy' (eg, in terms of consent of citizens based on traditional acceptance of rules, charismatic leadership of rulers, and rationality of law and governance as explained by Max Weber) and 'output legitimacy' (eg, in terms of socially beneficial effects of the rules and rulers concerned); only 'informed, democratic consent' and outcomes consistent with constitutional and human rights (eg, to protection of general consumer welfare rather than only producer welfare) can legitimize rules and rulers.[110] My 1991 monograph inferred two constitutional policy arguments from the rights-based, constitutional law traditions in American and European democracies:

- First, democratic self-government and rule of law for the benefit of citizens require that parliaments, governments and courts in constitutional democracies interpret their domestic constitutional and trade laws in conformity with their self-imposed international guarantees of freedom, non-discrimination and rule of law in international trade as duly ratified by domestic parliaments. This 'consistent interpretation principle' will strengthen 'popular sovereignty' over domestic regulation, which the 1944 Bretton Woods Agreements and GATT 1947 also protect by far-reaching exceptions authorizing unilateral restrictions of international economic transactions so as to protect non-economic public interests (eg, pursuant to GATT Articles XVIII to XXI).
- Secondly, parliaments, governments and courts should consider applying – under mutually agreed conditions (such as international reciprocity) – precise and unconditional, international guarantees of economic freedom, non-discrimination and rule of law not only as 'intergovernmental rights and obligations'; such legal guarantees should be applied also for the benefit of citizens as mutually agreed individual freedoms limiting national trade policy discretion, just as BITs and European free trade agreements are applied for the benefit of citizens and their rights. Cosmopolitan rights to economic freedom and transnational rule of law can extend constitutional guarantees of freedom, non-discrimination and rule of law to transnational economic cooperation among citizens based on mutually consistent interpretations of multilevel trade and economic regulation without prejudice to the diverse human rights traditions of countries. Diplomats and trade politicians have protectionist self-interests in resisting such 'constitutionalization' of their trade policy discretion and legal accountability vis-à-vis citizens. Hence, it is important to challenge claims that interpretation of IEL remains a 'Westphalian privilege' of rulers and diplomats.

[110] On this distinction between 'input-legitimacy' (eg, government by the people) and 'output-legitimacy' (eg, government for the people) see: FW Scharpf, *Governing in Europe: Effective and Democratic?* (Oxford: OUP, 1999).

Human rights require citizen-oriented interpretations of 'rules of recognition' in IEL

International law historically evolved as a system of reciprocal rights and obligations of states – without international institutions with centralized lawmaking, administrative and judicial functions for protecting rights of citizens across national borders.[111] Chapters I to III argued that the universal recognition of 'the inherent dignity and of the equal and inalienable rights of all members of the human family (as) the foundation of freedom, justice and peace in the world' (Preambles of the UDHR, ICCPR and ICESCR) require interpreting international human rights law and IEL no longer only as 'international law among states', but also as a 'cosmopolitan law of individuals'. Since the UN Charter commitments to 'universal respect for, and observance of, human rights and fundamental freedoms for all', including 'self-determination of peoples' (*cf* Articles 1, 55 UN Charter), hundreds of UN human rights instruments approved by UN member states acknowledge and legally define the legal entitlements of individuals and peoples to protection of human rights at all levels of multilevel 'governance'. Arguably, cosmopolitan interpretations of IEL and citizen-oriented interpretations of international 'rules of recognition'[112] are more consistent with UN human rights law than the Westphalian conceptions of international law defended by authoritarian rulers and many diplomats in order to justify their powers:

- Respect for human dignity and human rights requires that 'everyone has the right to recognition everywhere as a person before the law' (Article 6 UDHR, Article 16 ICCPR). The human rights to democratic self-governance and to an 'effective remedy' (eg, pursuant to Article 2 ICCPR) should be interpreted in conformity with the customary law principles of state responsibility[113] and reparation of injury suffered by individuals unless limited by treaty law and democratic legislation.
- In citizen-driven areas like the international division of labour and its legal regulation by IEL, explicit legal recognition of judicial remedies – as in Article 3 DSU providing that the 'dispute settlement system of the WTO is a central element in providing security and predictability to the multilateral trading system' – should be interpreted also for the benefit of individuals: precise and unconditional guarantees of equal freedoms of trade, non-discriminatory conditions of competition, rule of law and individual judicial remedies (eg, pursuant to Articles X GATT, VI GATS, 42 ff TRIPS Agreement) must be presumed to protect rule of law not only in relations among governments (as agents of citizens), but also in favour of private citizens engaged in, and benefiting from, mutually beneficial economic cooperation across frontiers.

[111] *cf* J Goldsmith and D Levinson, 'Law for States: International Law, Constitutional Law, Public Law' (2009) 122 *Harvard Law Review* 1791–868.

[112] On the distinction between 'primary rules of obligation' (requiring human beings to do or abstain from certain actions) and 'secondary rules' for changing law, adjudicating disputes and identifying valid rules ('rules of recognition') and the distinction between 'justice or injustice of the *law*' and 'justice or injustice of the administration of the law' see: HLA Hart (1994) 81–94, 160–61. Hart acknowledged (eg, at 107) that – in determining what the law is – a widespread public consensus on reasonableness and justice may have to be taken into account.

[113] *cf* Arts 30 and 31 of the draft codification prepared by the International Law Commission in 2001 (UN Doc A/CN.4/L.602, Rev.1), providing for cessation of illegal acts, non-repetition, reparation including restitution, compensation, rehabilitation or satisfaction.

- Governments and domestic 'courts of justice' should interpret domestic laws and regulations in conformity with international obligations ratified by parliaments in order to protect equal freedoms, non-discriminatory conditions of competition, rule of law and individual rights across frontiers for the benefit of citizens, subject to democratic legislation. As convincingly argued by the New Haven School's 'policy approach',[114] international law should be interpreted and applied not only as a system of intergovernmental rules; the democratic legitimacy, 'rules of recognition' and effectiveness of international law depend on more comprehensive legal decision-making processes determining 'public reason' with due respect for human rights, 'representative democracy', 'deliberative democracy' and 'participatory democracy'. Public review of intergovernmental agreements by parliaments, 'courts of justice' and civil society deliberations scrutinizing representative government participation in international rulemaking need to be strengthened, as illustrated by the now regular interparliamentary conferences at WTO ministerial meetings since 1999, the annual 'public *fora*' of the WTO with civil society organizations and the admission of public meetings and 'amicus curiae' submissions in WTO dispute settlement proceedings. The *opinio juris* determining the scope of international rules must be interpreted in conformity with human rights, other principles of justice and democratic 'public reason' as protected by relevant constitutional systems.

Interpreting WTO rules with due regard to human rights: the example of the right to health protection

Human rights advocates often criticize the WTO for its alleged democratic deficit and for adverse impacts of WTO rules on the human rights to health, labour rights, the right to food, poverty reduction and 'sustainable development'.[115] Chapters I to III argued that – in worldwide organizations representing more than 150 member states with often non-democratic governments – 'human rights coherence' (*cf* Table 4), democratic constitutionalism (*cf* Table 5), respect for 'multilevel constitutional pluralism' (*cf* Table 6) and for the legitimate diversity of constitutionally agreed 'principles of justice' may offer more appropriate benchmarks for evaluating the legitimacy of IEL than the legitimately diverse conceptions of democracy (or *demoi*-cracy in multilevel governance). It was further mentioned that international trade law, investment law, intellectual property and economic integration law increasingly differ from other areas of international law by the ever larger number of national and international court decisions clarifying and progressively developing IEL for the benefit of individual rights and 'rule of law' among producers, investors, traders and consumers (*cf* Table 2). The judicial recognition of cosmopolitan rights – for instance, by protecting investor rights based on BITs as genuine, individual property rights rather than only as procedural rights to enforce rights of

[114] In addition to the literature cited in ch II, fn 63, see also: R Higgins, 'Conceptual Thinking about the Individual in International Law' (1978) 24 *New York Law School Review* 11–29; WM Reisman, 'A Judge's Judge: Justice Florentino P Feliciano's Philosophy of the Judicial Function' in S Charnovitz, D Steger and P van den Bossche (eds), *Law in the Service of Human Dignity* (Cambridge: CUP, 2005) 3–10. The German Constitutional Court decision of 30 June 2009 (table 13) on the inconsistency of the German legislation on implementation of the 2007 Lisbon Treaty on EU is illustrative of the increasing judicial protection of individual constitutional rights against encroachment by international treaties.

[115] *cf* Joseph (n 41).

capital-exporting states vis-à-vis host states – reflects the increasing impact of individuals, non-governmental organizations and courts on the recognition and interpretation of economic law in the light of 'principles of justice' and human rights.[116] Arguably, human rights and judicial administration of justice increasingly change the 'rules of recognition' in IEL by justifying judicial review of state-centred conceptions of international law in order to protect rights of citizens, as illustrated by the interpretation of European economic law in terms of individual 'common market freedoms', related fundamental rights and judicial remedies as well as by the increasing admission of *amicus curiae* briefs by citizens and other third parties adversely affected by investor–state disputes.[117]

Rights and duties under WTO law tend to be limited to WTO members, notwithstanding a few WTO provisions (eg, in the WTO Agreements on Preshipment Inspection, TRIPS, Government Procurement and the WTO Protocol on the Accession of China) providing for individual procedural rights, trading rights, intellectual property rights and judicial remedies (eg, of individual access to arbitration in the WTO for disputes among exporters and preshipment inspection companies). The sovereign rights of WTO members to protect public interests like 'human, animal or plant life or health' are confirmed in numerous WTO provisions (eg, in Articles XX GATT, XIV GATS, 8 TRIPS Agreement) without any reference to human rights. The drafting of these treaty clauses acknowledging the priority of certain non-economic over economic public interests is justifiable in view of the sovereign freedom of states to protect public interests by means of constitutional, legislative, human rights, administrative and/or judicial rights and obligations. Yet, as subjects of international law, states and international organizations (like the EU and the WTO) are presumed to be legally bound by general international law (including human rights obligations) unless the specific nature of the rules prevents their application (eg, due to the limited jurisdiction of international organizations). There are no WTO provisions indicating any intention of WTO members to 'contract out' of their customary and conventional human rights obligations to the extent that 'inalienable' human rights have not acquired the status of *jus cogens*. Access to essential medicines, for instance, is protected not only in many national constitutions, regional and UN human rights conventions as part of the human right to health (eg, as protected in Article 12 and 15.1(b) of the ICESCR) and of the human right to life (eg, as protected by Article 6 of the ICCPR);[118] all WTO member states (except Liechtenstein) are also members of the World Health Organization (WHO), whose Preamble, regulations and 193 member states are recognizing that 'the enjoyment of the highest attainable standard of health is one of the fundamental rights of every human being without distinction of race, reli-

[116] On the broader phenomenon of 'Judges: Constructing a Global Legal System' in fields like human rights law, IEL and international criminal law see chs V and VIII as well as Slaughter (2004) ch 2.

[117] On criticism of international investment law as one-sidedly privileging foreign investor rights over democratic market regulation see: D Schneiderman, *Constitutionalizing Economic Globalization. Investment Rules and Democracy's Promise* (Cambridge: CUP, 2008). On *amici curiae* submissions in international trade and investment adjudication see: J Harrison, 'Human Rights Arguments in *Amicus Curiae* Submissions: Promoting Social Justice?' in Dupuy, Francioni and Petersmann (eds) (2009) 396–421. If the customary law requirement of 'settling disputes in conformity with the principles of justice' is recognized as an integral part of national and international 'rules of recognition', then national and international courts may have sufficient jurisdiction and 'margin of appreciation' for interpreting and reconciling international economic rules in conformity with the respective domestic constitutional requirements of 'public order' and respect for principles of democracy, human rights and dispute settlement in conformity with 'principles of justice'.

[118] *cf* H Hestermeyer (2007) 102 ff (with numerous references to literature, state practice and to the General Comment No 14 on the right to health, adopted by the UN Committee on Economic, Social and Cultural Rights).

gion, political belief, economic or social condition'.[119] As individual rights to protection of health have become recognized in more than one hundred national constitutions[120] as well as in UN human rights instruments[121] and regional human rights conventions, international dispute settlement bodies may challenge the view (eg, as argued by some US diplomats) that the WHO and UN legal instruments reaffirming the right to health protection have not yet evolved into legally binding obligations to protect a human right to health.[122] They may also argue that the consistent UN, WHO and WTO legal practices offer relevant context for interpreting the WTO declarations on the 'TRIPS Agreement and Human Health' and related 'WTO waivers' for compulsory licences for generic medicines in conformity with human rights obligations of WTO members to protect human health. Even though UN, WHO and WTO member states do not agree on the scope of legal obligations to protect human health and access to essential medicines, the successive WTO measures for protecting access to essential medicines must be presumed to be in conformity with the human right to health protection as relevant context for interpreting WTO law. This legal presumption was recently also confirmed by WTO Director-General Pascal Lamy in a speech on human rights, trade policy and the WTO.[123]

'Participatory justice' as justification of cosmopolitan IEL?

Chapters II and III argued that interpreting IEL and settling related disputes in conformity with human rights is not only an explicit requirement of customary international law recognized in the VCLT; it also promotes basic principles of justice protecting equal liberties, rule of law and cosmopolitan rights in the globally interdependent economy for the benefit of citizens. Since ancient Greek law, justice has been recognized as the ultimate objective and 'justifying principle' of legal systems. Arguably, the legitimacy of international legal regimes without a *demos* (including IEL) may be better evaluated by 'principles of transnational justice' (eg, in terms of legal and judicial protection of human rights, rule of law, individual rights to reasonable justification of restrictions of freedom, individual access to courts) than in terms of state-centred, democratic principles which – like equal voting powers of citizens, representative parliamentary legisla-

[119] *cf* Hestermeyer (2007), who points out (at 112) that the Preamble also adopted a new definition of health going far beyond the previous understanding of health as the absence of disease: 'Health is a state of complete physical, mental and social well-being and not merely the absence of disease or infirmity' (WHO Preamble).

[120] *cf* E Kinney and B Clark, 'Provisions for Health and Health Care in the Constitutions of the Countries of the World' (2004) 37 *Cornell International Law Journal* 285–355.

[121] Examples include Art 25 UDHR, Art 12 ICESCR, Art 5(e) of the 1969 Convention for the Elimination of all Forms of Discrimination, Arts 11 and 12 of the 1981 Convention on the Elimination of all Forms of Discrimination against Women and Art 24 of the 1989 Convention on the Rights of the Child.

[122] *cf* BCA Toebes, *The Right to Health as a Human Right in International Law* (Antwerpen: Intersentia/Hart, 1999) who rightly concludes that WHO member states 'have to comply with the right to health as set forth in the Preamble to the WHO Constitution' (at 33).

[123] See the speech by Lamy of 13 January 2010 (n 40). Hestermeyer (2007) claims: 'There is nothing in the operative part of the [WHO] Constitution that would allow us to infer a right to health under the document' (at 114), notwithstanding his admission that the constant reaffirmation of the right to health has contributed to the establishment of the right under customary international law: 'Access to life-saving medicines in the face of national health emergencies, particularly pandemics is protected as customary international law and a general principle and thus binding on all states. State practice shows that the United States, while persistently objecting to a right to health with a larger scope, does not object to this limited rule' (at 296).

tion, government powers to tax and redistribute income for the benefit of the poor – do not exist in most international legal regimes.[124] If justice is defined narrowly in terms of peaceful settlement of disputes in conformity with human rights and due process of law,[125] then the multilevel judicial protection of transnational rule of law and cosmopolitan rights in ever more areas of IEL is justifiable not only by the customary law rules of international treaty interpretation, but as a requirement of justice.

Human rights have been claimed and become constitutionally recognized first in domestic legal systems, notably in England, France and the United States as fundamental principles necessary 'to establish justice' (Preamble of the US Constitution). The main function of their 'inalienable' and 'indivisible' legal nature is to empower and protect individual autonomy and the 'plurality' of human actions as defining elements of 'the human condition';[126] legally enforceable rights contribute to the 'constitutionalization' and 'civilization' of politics by limiting arbitrary 'domination' and requiring democratic and judicial justification of all government interferences into the fundamental freedoms and other rights of citizens. Thanks to international human rights law and European constitutional law as the most important *international* legal systems for protecting fundamental rights of individuals through basic rules of a higher legal rank and 'constitutionalized structures of justification' (eg, in multilevel court proceedings),[127] the 'horizontal structures' of the classical 'international law among sovereign states' are progressively transformed into more vertical 'constitutional structures'. As international human rights often permit higher standards of protection at national levels, the legal hierarchies in national and international human rights law, constitutional law and international law must be determined in substantive rather than in formalistic terms by democratic lawmakers and national and international 'courts of justice' clarifying and protecting individual rights.[128] Notwithstanding proposals for maintaining UN human rights law as 'horizontal legal systems' providing for rights and obligations among states,[129] the European and Inter-American human rights conventions justify the claim

[124] *cf* J Neyer, 'Not Democracy: Legitimacy in the European Union' (2010) 48 *Journal of Common Market Studies* 903–21. On the right to justification see: R Forst, *Das Recht auf Rechtfertigung* (Frankfurt: Suhrkamp, 2007).

[125] *cf* EU Petersmann, 'Justice as Conflict Resolution: Proliferation, Fragmentation and Decentralization of Dispute Settlement in International Trade Law' (2006) 27 *University of Pennsylvania Journal of International Economic Law* 273–366. The diverse theories and 'principles of justice', and the 'right to justification' as an integral part of 'maximum equal freedoms' as 'first principle of justice' (in terms of Kantian and Rawlsian theories of justice), are discussed in chapter VI.

[126] *cf* H Arendt, *The Human Condition* (Chicago: Chicago University Press, 1958).

[127] *cf* Neyer (n 124) 910; Forst (n 124) 270–87. On the interrelationships between constitutional and human rights see: G Neuman, 'Human Rights and Constitutional Rights: Harmony and Dissonance' (2003) 55 *Stanford Law Review* 1863 ff.

[128] *cf* S Gardbaum, 'Human Rights as International Constitutional Rights' (2008) 19 *EJIL* 749–68, discussing arguments that human rights law is evolving into constitutional law also at the international level, characterized by a higher legal rank (eg, of *jus cogens* obligations) and by entrenchment against ordinary methods of legal amendment or repeal by national legal acts (eg, in view of the fact that UN human rights conventions include no provisions on termination or withdrawal, and the UN Human Rights Committee declared – in its General Comment 26 of 1997 – that a state may not withdraw from the ICCPR). As the ECHR has become incorporated into the domestic legal systems of all 47 member states, the ECHR – similar to the human rights guarantees of EU law – operates increasingly as a constitutionalized regional system of fundamental rights of citizens (*cf* H Keller and A Stone Sweet (eds), *A Europe of Rights. The Impact of the ECHR on National Legal Systems* (Oxford: OUP, 2008). Even though international human rights law often provides only for minimum standards that may be lower than those in national human rights laws, it tends to protect human rights more specifically in transnational and international relations beyond the jurisdiction of national human rights laws.

[129] *cf* JH Knox, 'Horizontal Human Rights Law' (2008) 102 *AJIL* 1–47.

that effective protection of human rights requires interpreting international human rights and constitutional rights (eg, the fundamental rights of EU citizens guaranteed in EU law, the social and labour rights protected by the ILO Constitution) as empowering *individuals*. Such actionable rights can limit abuses of governance powers, serve as 'balancing principles' for 'optimizing' individual rights and corresponding obligations of governments and citizens depending on the particular circumstances and require governments to justify restrictions of freedom with convincing arguments in parliaments and 'courts of justice'.[130]

Rights-based conceptions of justice and of constitutionalism differ from republicanism (eg, in ancient Athens, classical Rome, the Italian Renaissance republics) by their '*contractual* justification' (rather than 'Aristotelian justification') of democratic polities and of constitutional constraints on government powers in order to secure man's freedom. Arguably, the recognition – in modern theories of justice (from Kant to Rawls) – of maximum equal legal freedom of all human beings as the 'first principle of justice' also justifies cosmopolitan conceptions of IEL.[131] UN human rights law and regional human rights conventions confirm not only that human rights are becoming the common, normative foundation of modern national and international law in the twenty-first century; they also require justifying UN law and IEL in terms of *normative individualism* and rights-based 'constitutionalism' rather than by feudalist or communitarian traditions of power struggles (eg, for 'mixed constitutions' maintaining constitutional privileges of monarchs, Houses of Lords, churches or communist rulers limiting equal individual rights).[132] International human rights law 'does not simply replicate domestic bills of rights – or substitute for them where lacking – in that, by externalizing the limits in significant ways, it takes constitutionalism to a new stage in its historical development'.[133] By clarifying the human rights foundations of international law, international human rights law also contributes to a citizen-oriented 'paradigm change' of the power-oriented 'international law among states'. As illustrated by the *Kadi* judgments of the European Court of First Instance of September 2005 and by the EC Court in September 2008, the practice of governments to define the *jus cogens* core of human rights narrowly (eg, focusing on the rights to life, freedom from slavery, torture and other 'inhuman treatment') in order to limit their legal and judicial accountability is increasingly challenged by national and international courts.[134] Yet, as discussed below, national legal systems

[130] On these dual functions of human rights and other constitutional rights as *rules*, as well as *principles* for optimizing rules depending on what is factually and legally possible in the particular circumstances, see R Alexy (2002) ch 3. Art I-9, para 3 of the 2004 Treaty Establishing a Constitution for Europe acknowledged these dual functions in the following terms: 'Fundamental rights, as guaranteed by the European Convention for the Protection of Human Rights and Fundamental Freedoms and as they result from the constitutional traditions common to the Member States, shall constitute general principles of the Union's law'. On the different American conception of fundamental rights as 'trumps' (rather than as principles and presumptive shields that may be justifiably limited and overridden by conflicting rights and public policy objectives) see: R Dworkin (1977).

[131] On differences between Kantian and Rawlsian principles of justice (such as Rawls' later limitation of his 'first principle of justice' on grounds of 'normative realism') see ch VI.

[132] For a discussion of 'rights constitutionalism' in the context of globalization see: GW Anderson, *Constitutional Rights after Globalization* (Oxford: Hart Publishing, 2005).

[133] Gardbaum (n 128) 768.

[134] *cf* the broad interpretation of UN human rights as international *ius cogens* and constitutional limitation of intergovernmental powers by the EC Court of First Instance in Cases T-315/01 (*Kadi v Council and Commission)* and T-306/01 (*Yusuf v Council and Commission*), Judgments (21 September 2005): (2005) *Common Market Law Reports* 1334. On appeal, the EC Court – in joined cases C-402/05P and C-415/05 P, *Kadi and Al Barakaat International Foundation v Council of the EU and Commission of the European*

often legitimately differ on how human dignity rights, liberty rights and other human rights should be protected in transnational economic regulation.

IEL must respect reasonably different conceptions of human rights and 'human dignity'

Many national constitutions (such as Article 1 of the German Basic Law of 1949), regional human rights instruments (such as Article 1 of the EU Charter of Fundamental Rights) and UN human rights instruments derive human rights from respect for the human dignity of all human beings, who 'are endowed with reason and conscience and should act towards one another in a spirit of brotherhood' (Article 1 UDHR). This universal recognition of human dignity as requiring legal protection of national and universal human rights can be construed as a universally agreed 'constitutional contract' on the 'constitutional status' and entitlement of every individual to 'inalienable' and 'indivisible human rights' vis-*à*-vis all governance institutions (eg, also in labour law aimed at protecting 'dignity of labour' vis-à-vis abuses of economic power).[135] A comparative analysis of the case law of national and international courts suggests agreement on only a few 'core elements' of human dignity, like the requirements that (1) every human being possesses an intrinsic worth, merely by being human; (2) this intrinsic worth must be recognized and respected by others in terms of legal entitlements to human rights; (3) also the state must be seen to exist for the sake of the individual human being, and not vice versa. Beyond these core elements, the legal meaning and judicial interpretation of 'dignity' may legitimately vary among jurisdictions according to their respective democratic preferences (eg, on how to deal with moral and religious questions relating to abortion, physician-assisted suicide, biogenetics and neuroscience).[136] Arguably, just as the interpretation of the US Constitution remains influenced by its commitment to protection of inalienable human rights 'retained by the people' (as stated in the Ninth Amendment), so must IEL be interpreted in the twenty-first century in conformity with the partly 'invisible constitution' of multilevel human rights law limiting the governance powers of all UN member states, including their intergovernmental powers exercised in international organizations.[137]

Communities, Judgment (3 September 2008) (*cf* table 18 and related text) – emphasized that 'the principle of effective judicial protection is a general principle of Community law' (para 335) and requires that 'the obligations imposed by an international agreement cannot have the effect of prejudicing the constitutional principles of the EC Treaty, which include the principle that all community acts must respect fundamental rights, that respect constituting a condition of their lawfulness which it is for the Court to review in the framework of the complete legal system of legal remedies established by the Treaty' (para 285). In its most recent *Kadi* judgment of 30 September 2010 (Case T-85/09, n.y.r.), the EU General Court exercised 'in principle the full review' (paras 126, 171) 'so long as the re-examination procedure operated by the Sanctions Committee clearly fails to offer guarantees of effective judicial protection' (para 128); as the Court found that the applicant's rights of defence and his right to effective judicial review had been infringed and the restriction of his right to property was unjustified and disproportionate, the Court annulled Commission Regulation (EC) No 1190/2008 of 28 November 2008 amending for the 101st time Council Regulation (EC) No 881/2002 imposing certain restrictive measures against certain persons and entities associated with Usama bin Laden, the Al-Qaeda network and the Taliban, in so far as it concerned Mr Kadi.

[135] *cf* EU Petersmann, 'Human Rights, Markets and Economic Welfare: Constitutional Functions of the Emerging UN Human Rights Constitution' in F Abbott, C Breining and T Cottier (eds) (2006) 29–67.

[136] *cf* C McCrudden, 'Human Dignity and Judicial Interpretation of Human Rights' (2008) 19 *EJIL* 655–724; EU Petersmann, 'Biotechnology, Human Rights and International Economic Law' in F Francioni (ed), *Biotechnology and International Human Rights* (Oxford: Hart Publishing, 2007) 229–73.

[137] *cf* Petersmann (n 135) and LH Tribe, *The Invisible Constitution* (Oxford: OUP, 2008).

Chapters III and VI argue that, in the field of IEL, the citizen-driven structures of the worldwide division of labour and of its multilevel, legal regulation justify interpreting 'human dignity' in accordance with the Kantian conception of human dignity as the moral autonomy and reasonable capacity of human beings of exercising their freedom of choice in a 'just' manner respecting the equal autonomy and maximum equal freedom of all others.[138] This moral 'categorical imperative' aims at legal protection of equal freedoms under the rule of law and justifies a 'private law society' subject to appropriate rules and institutions aimed at promoting non-discriminatory conditions of competition by limiting private and public abuses of market power and other restraints of competition.[139] According to Kant, respect for human dignity and justice requires treating human beings as ends in themselves, respecting their moral choices and protecting maximum equal freedom of individuals and the promotion of 'public reason' through ever more precise, national, international and cosmopolitan constitutional rules.[140] As everybody 'may seek his happiness in whatever way he sees fit, so long as he does not infringe upon the freedom of others to pursue a similar end which can be reconciled with the freedom of everyone else within a workable general law',[141] treating a person as an 'end in herself' and respecting her freely chosen objectives require legal protection of a human right to maximum equal freedom in the economic area no less than in other areas of human cooperation. For only the individual herself can know, and legitimately decide on, his own ends and personal self-development. As discussed in chapter III, democratic legislation reconciling equal freedoms should aim at *enabling* individuals to live autonomous lives in constitutional democracies with open, citizen-driven markets embedded into constitutional and cosmopolitan guarantees of social justice.

[138] According to Kant, 'freedom constitutes man's worth', and 'freedom (independence from the constraints of another's will) insofar as it is compatible with the freedom of everyone else in accordance with a universal law, is the sole and original right that belongs to each human being by virtue of his humanity' (*cf* I Kant, 'The Metaphysics of Morals' in I Kant (1970) 136)); equality and all other human rights derive from this universal birthright of freedom. Justice requires, according to Kant, exercising one's freedom in accordance with the moral 'categorical imperative' that individuals and a just constitution must allow the 'greatest freedom' for each individual along with 'the most precise specification and preservation of the limits of this freedom so that it can coexist with the freedom of others'. As civil, political, economic and social human rights need to be mutually reconciled and restricted by democratic legislation, the broad Kantian definition of the 'first principle of justice' also entails a comprehensive 'right to justification' of all governmental restrictions of human freedom.

[139] On Kant's moral 'categorical imperatives' for acting in accordance with universal laws ('Act only in accordance with that maxim through which you can at the same time will that it become a universal law'), for respecting human dignity by treating individuals and humanity as ends in themselves ('So act that you use humanity, whether in your own person or that of another, always at the same time as an end, never merely as a means') and for respecting individual autonomy ('the idea of the will of every rational being as a will giving universal law') and individual right ('Any action is right if it can coexist with everyone's freedom according to a universal law'), see also: AW Wood, *Kant's Ethical Thought* (Princeton: Princeton University Press, 1999). On Kant's social and historical theories of the antagonistic human nature promoting market competition and constitutional 'rules of justice', and on Kant's moral imperative of transforming the 'lawless freedom' in the state of nature into lawful freedom through ever more precise national, international and cosmopolitan constitutional rules see also: EU Petersmann, 'How to Constitutionalize International Law and Foreign Policy for the Benefit of Civil Society?' (1999) 20 *Michigan Journal of International Law* 1–30.

[140] Like Hobbes, Kant regarded the natural condition of the relations among men and states as a state of war that could be terminated only through a 'constitutional contract' which – in contrast to Hobbes – required limiting abuses of governance powers in all human interactions at national, international and transnational levels, *cf* I. Kant, 'Perpetual Peace' in Kant (1970) 98.

[141] Kant, 'On the Common Saying: This May be True in Theory, but it does not Apply in Practice' in Kant (1970) 74.

Inadequate protection of the 'indivisibility' of human rights in IEL

Judged from the perspective of the Kantian 'first principle of justice', UN human rights law and IEL remain highly imperfect legal systems that do not effectively limit abuses of public and private power. For instance, the indivisibility of human dignity and human liberty is recognized in numerous human rights instruments like the 1993 Vienna Declaration adopted by the UN World Conference on Human Rights: 'All human rights are universal, indivisible and interdependent and interrelated'.[142] Even though some UN human rights conventions separate civil and political human rights (as protected in the ICCPR) from economic and social human rights (as protected in the separate ICESCR), the holistic conception of the 'indivisibility' of human rights – based on our common humanity and dignity – continues to be acknowledged in numerous human rights instruments since its first affirmation in the UDHR of 1948. The ECJ has acknowledged that respect for human rights – including a 'human right to respect of human dignity' – is a condition of the lawfulness of acts of the EU institutions, even if EU acts implement UN Security Council decisions that assert legal primacy (Article 103 UN Charter).[143] The ECtHR has likewise recognized in a series of judgments that the human rights guarantees of the ECHR also apply whenever states implement intergovernmental rules adopted in international organizations.[144] Such court judgments confirm that national and international human rights also limit *foreign policy* powers even if they are being exercised collectively in intergovernmental organizations. Contrary to the reasoning of the EU Court of First Instance in the *Kadi* and *Yusuf* judgments which declined jurisdiction to review UN Security Council resolutions beyond the limited scope of universal *jus cogens*, it is consistent with the subsidiary functions of UN human rights law to protect higher standards of constitutional and human rights in national and regional legal systems also vis-à-vis UN Security Council measures unduly restricting human rights.[145]

[142] Para 5 of the Declaration, reproduced in: *The UN and Human Rights 1945–1995* (UN: New York, 1995) 450.

[143] In joined cases C-402/05P and C-415/05P (n 134), the ECJ emphasized that EC measures implementing UN Security Council sanctions must remain in conformity with EC constitutional law and the human rights guarantees of the ECHR.

[144] See Case *Bosphorus v Ireland*, App no 45036/98, ECtHR Grand Chamber judgment (30 June 2005): 'a Contracting Party is responsible under Article 1 of the Convention for all acts and omissions of its organs regardless of whether the act or omission in question was a consequence of domestic law or of the necessity to comply with international legal obligations' (para 153). 'In . . . establishing the extent to which State action can be justified by its compliance with obligations flowing from its membership of an international organisation to which it has transferred part of its sovereignty, the Court has recognised that absolving Contracting States completely from their Convention responsibility in the areas covered by such transfer would be incompatible with the purpose and object of the Convention' (para 154). 'State action taken in compliance with such legal obligations is justified as long as the relevant organisation is considered to protect fundamental rights, as regards both the substantive guarantees offered and the mechanisms controlling their observance, in a manner which can be considered at least equivalent to that for which the Convention provides' (para 155).

[145] Art 53 of the VCLT defines a 'peremptory norm of general international law' as 'a norm accepted and recognized by the international community of States as a whole as a norm from which no derogation is permitted and which can be modified only by a subsequent norm of general international law having the same character'. The *jus cogens* core of UN human rights is smaller than that of European human rights and constitutional law. In the *Kadi* and *Yusuf* cases (n 136), the Court of First Instance examined the consistency of sanctions imposed by the UN Security Council and EC implementing regulations only with regard to the *jus cogens* core of UN human rights to make use of one's property, the right to a fair hearing and the right to an effective judicial remedy; the Court wrongly claimed that it had no jurisdiction to examine whether the EC implementation of the UN sanctions was also consistent with the broader guarantees of fundamental rights in European Community law. The legal consistency of the listing of alleged terrorist groups with European human rights

Yet, as discussed above, constitutional protection of 'market freedoms' as fundamental rights and their appropriate 'balancing' with communitarian values remain controversial also among constitutional democracies, especially in Anglo-Saxon countries which focus on 'parliamentary sovereignty' and do not provide for comprehensive constitutional protection of economic and social rights vis-à-vis majoritarian economic regulation. As most individuals spend most of their time working in order to earn scarce resources necessary for survival and personal self-development, they have hardly any reason to value economic, social and cultural rights (such as rights to education, freedom of profession, private property) less than their respective civil and political rights. Already in 1968, the Proclamation of the UN Conference on Human Rights at Teheran had acknowledged that: 'since human rights and fundamental freedoms are indivisible, the full realization of civil and political rights without the enjoyment of economic, social and cultural rights is impossible'.[146] In UN General Assembly Resolution 63/116 of 10 December 2008 on the sixtieth Anniversary of the UDHR, all UN member states reaffirmed 'our commitment towards the full realization of all human rights for all, which are universal, indivisible, interrelated, interdependent and mutually reinforcing'. The 'indivisibility' of liberty rights protects the individual autonomy to decide how much an individual values and develops the civil, political, economic, social and cultural dimensions of his or her life and resists external domination. It remains contested to which extent respect for human dignity and for the indivisibility of human rights remains compatible with democratic prioritization of certain human rights dimensions, such as the prioritization of civil and political human rights in some Anglo-Saxon democracies, of economic and social human rights in some communist countries (like China and Cuba), and of democracy-building and satisfaction of basic needs in post-conflict societies (eg, limiting 'criminal justice' by truth commissions and other 'transitional justice' procedures). The multilevel constitutional protection of civil, political, economic, social and cultural rights in European constitutional and economic law goes far beyond the legal protection of citizens in other regional legal regimes.

The impact on IEL of diverse conceptions of human and constitutional rights to liberty

The disagreement over the 'indivisibility' of human rights reflects diverse conceptions over human and constitutional rights to liberty, as discussed in chapters III and VI. Anglo-Saxon jurisdictions often interpret the human right to liberty (Article 3 UDHR) narrowly in terms of freedom of bodily movement. Some other constitutional democracies protect equal freedoms as 'first principle of justice' (in terms of Kantian and Ralwsian legal philosophy) not only through specific liberty rights, but through a general

law was also challenged in the ECtHR which elaborated a concept of presumed compliance of the EC with the ECHR: 'the Court finds that the protection of fundamental rights by EC law can be considered to be . . . "equivalent" . . . to that of the Convention system' (ECtHR decision of 23 May 2002 on App no 6422/2002, para 165); judge Ress rightly emphasized in his concurring opinion that the 'concept of a presumption of convention compliance should not be interpreted as excluding a case-by-case review by this Court of whether there was really a breach of the Convention' (para 2 of the Opinion).

[146] *The UN and Human Rights 1945–1995* (note 143) 247. All human rights derive from the same ethical basis of respect for human dignity and 'may be viewed as prerequisites for one another', *cf* K Raes, 'The Philosophical Basis of Economic, Social and Cultural Rights' in P Van der Auweraert et al (eds), *Social, Economic and Cultural Rights: An Appraisal of Current European and International Developments* (Antwerpen: Maklu, 2002) 43 ff, 44.

constitutional right to liberty (as recognized in Article 2 of the German Basic Law) in order to offer additional constitutional protection to the legal autonomy of citizens against arbitrary, public and private interferences into their liberties. This also includes protection against restriction of individual freedom of action resulting from *multilevel* governance, for instance if *intergovernmental* restrictions adopted in distant international organizations lack a constitutional foundation in the national legal system.[147] There is increasing recognition that constitutional commitment to respect for human dignity also requires legal protection of 'positive liberties' by means of social rights (eg, to education and health protection) in order to effectively empower individuals to develop their 'human capacities' autonomously.[148] The diversity of provisions and institutional safeguards for social rights in national and regional laws, UN and ILO conventions reflects not only diverse legal conceptions for designing social rights as 'indivisible parts' of human rights;[149] constitutional agreement on how to reconcile and 'institutionalize' civil, political, economic and social rights is also inevitably influenced by democratic preferences and the scarcity of resources for effective protection of social rights. Legal and judicial remedies for enforcing civil, political, economic and social rights differ enormously among countries and jurisdictions.[150] Comprehensive constitutional guarantees of individual access to courts (eg, in German law) may better protect individual liberty against arbitrary political restrictions, for instance by offering judicial review of the 'necessity' (rationality) and 'proportionality' (reasonableness) of governmental restrictions on the basis of equal constitutional rights and judicial 'administration of justice'.[151]

Constitutional guarantees of a general right to liberty (including 'market freedoms' as protected in EU law) are not recognized in many constitutional democracies. Their recognition was often motivated by prior experiences of dictatorship (as in Germany) and related abuses of foreign policy powers. The multilevel constitutional guarantees of 'free movement of persons, services, goods and capital, and freedom of establishment' as 'fundamental freedoms' protected by EU and EEA law across the 30 member countries of the EEA are explicitly based on 'the values of respect for human dignity, freedom, democracy, equality, the rule of law and respect for human rights' (*cf* Article 2 TEU). In common law countries, by contrast, the common law tends to protect specific liberties

[147] On the constitutional protection in Germany of a general right to liberty, complemented by specific constitutional liberty rights and other civil, political, economic, social and cultural rights, see Alexy (2002) notably ch 7.

[148] On the 'capabilities approach' in human rights law and philosophy see, eg, MC Nussbaum, *Frontiers of Justice. Disability, Nationality, Species Membership* (Cambridge: Belknap Press of Harvard University Press, 2006) 69 ff. The German Constitutional Court, for example, recognizes a human right to respect and protection of human dignity based 'on an understanding of the human being as an intellectual and moral creature capable of freely determining and developing itself. The Basic Law conceives of this freedom not as that of an isolated and autonomous individual, but as that of an individual related and bound to society' (BVerfGE vol 45, 187, at 227). This reconciliation of the principle of negative liberty with the social interdependence of the individual is explained by the Court in the following terms: 'the individual must submit himself to those limits on his freedom of action which the legislature sets in order to maintain and support social co-existence within the limits of what is generally acceptable according to the relevant subject-matter, and so long as the independence of the person remains guaranteed' (BVerfGE vol 4, 7, at 16). The Constitutional Court derives from the human right to dignity individual social rights of access to the resources necessary for a life in dignity, *cf* D Merten and HJ Papier (eds), *Handbuch der Grundrechte* vol II (Heidelberg: Müller Verlag, 2006) § 40 ('Leistungsrechte') §44 ('Schutzplichten').

[149] *cf* EU Petersmann, 'On "Indivisibility" of Human Rights' (2003) 14 *EJIL* 381–85.

[150] See, eg, M Tushnet (2008).

[151] See ch VIII and Alexy (2002) ch 7.

without constitutional protection of a general right to liberty.[152] Since the judicial abandonment of 'substantive due process' review of economic legislation in the 1930s, US constitutional law protects individual economic freedom and a common market mainly by democratic legislation based on constitutional requirements of a rational, legal basis for governmental restrictions of economic liberty;[153] the US constitutional, antitrust and other legislative guarantees of a common internal market inside the United States appear to be comparatively more effective than the corresponding legislation in some other Anglo-Saxon federal states like Canada, where national markets remain restricted by numerous provincial market access barriers. Since US courts acknowledge deference vis-à-vis economic legislation by the US Congress, most lawyers see no need for US courts to engage in the kind of 'strict judicial scrutiny' of governmental restrictions of economic freedom as it is practised by European courts, WTO dispute settlement bodies and investor–state arbitral tribunals. Legitimately diverse constitutional and democratic traditions and differentiations of civil, political, economic, social and cultural rights must be respected; yet, there are also good reasons for the different classification of fundamental rights in the EU Charter of Fundamental Rights and for the 'strict judicial scrutiny' of national and EU restrictions of common market freedoms and human rights in the *transnational* division of labour and social cooperation among citizens across frontiers. According to German constitutional traditions, human and constitutional rights also express objective, constitutional principles that must be taken into account in the whole legal order. Constitutional and judicial protection of a general right to liberty and of 'common market freedoms' can strengthen the reasonableness of IEL by offering individuals legal and judicial remedies against unnecessary or disproportionate restrictions of equal freedoms.[154] Even if national constitutional traditions legitimately differ from country to country, there are important arguments for basing legal and judicial remedies against abuses of multilevel governance powers on the cosmopolitan principle that multilevel governance restrictions of individual freedom require constitutional and democratic justification and judicial remedies.

[152] *cf* TTS Allan, Law, *Liberty and Justice* (Oxford: OUP, 1993) 135–43. DZ Cass (2005) claims that in 'mature constitutional systems, for example in the United States, Canada and Australia', neither individual economic freedom nor other individual rights are 'a matter considered essential to constitutionalization in the received tradition of constitutionalization' (at 168, 176, 191); yet, Cass ignores comparative constitutional law beyond common law countries.

[153] *cf* FL Morrison and RE Hudec, 'Judicial Protection of Individual Rights under the Foreign Trade Laws of the United States' in M Hilf and EU Petersmann (eds) (1993) 91–133, 92 f; BH Siegan (1980); T Sandefur (2010).

[154] For a discussion of the German Constitutional Court case law on the general right to liberty as protecting 'human freedom of action in the widest sense', subject to broad constitutional limitation clauses, see: Alexy (2002) ch 7. In view of Art 93:1 German Basic Law on 'constitutional complaints, which can be raised by anyone on the grounds that their constitutional rights . . . have been infringed by a public authority', the German Constitutional Court has held: 'Everyone can allege by way of constitutional complaint that a law limiting his freedom of action does not belong to the constitutional order because it infringes (either procedurally or substantively) individual provisions of the Constitution or general constitutional principles and thus that it infringes his constitutional right under Article 2:1 Basic Law' (BVerfGE vol 6, 32, at 41). While such judicial accountability may be perceived as unnecessary in longstanding democracies, it appears justified vis-à-vis multilevel governance by international organizations far away from effective parliamentary oversight.

4 THE DERIVATIVE NATURE OF MULTILEVEL REGULATION OF HUMAN RIGHTS: LEGAL PROTECTION OF ACCESS TO ESSENTIAL MEDICINES, WATER AND PRIVATE PROPERTY

Numerous national and UN human rights instruments recognize (eg, in the Preambles of the ICCPR and ICESCR 1966) that civil, political, economic, social and cultural human rights 'derive from the inherent dignity of the human person'. This 'derivative nature' of human rights is consistent with the Kantian claim that respect for human dignity justifies a right to equal liberties under the rule of law as the most basic human right. As discussed in chapter III, Kant argued that 'all men who can at all influence one another must adhere to some kind of civil constitution' aimed at protecting 'public justice' on the basis of multilevel, constitutional guarantees of equal freedoms that must be institutionalized in all human interactions at national, transnational and international levels in order to institute lasting peace among rational, antagonistic egoists with 'unsocial sociability'.[155] In conformity with this Kantian derivation of a multilevel constitutionalism from respect for human dignity, the 'Charter of Fundamental Rights of the European Union' – adopted first by the EU institutions as a political declaration in December 2000 and incorporated into EU law by the 2007 Lisbon Treaty (Article 6 TEU) – explicitly confirms that the national, international and transnational protection of human rights and constitutional rights in European law is 'founded on the indivisible, universal values of human dignity, freedom, equality and solidarity'.[156]

Reasonably different philosophies of human and constitutional rights

The apparent agreement in UN human rights instruments on deriving human rights from respect for human dignity has not prevented a variety of diverse religious, cultural, consensual, reason-based biological or instrumentalist conceptions of human rights, which are unlikely to convince those who do not share the religious and cultural value premises, refuse to consent, or disagree with biological and instrumental conceptions of human rights.[157] Such diverse approaches to justifying human rights as moral and constitutional principles may entail diverse interpretations of human rights (like freedom of religion, freedom of opinion and expression) depending on the normative premises of the interpreter. Discourse justifications derive human rights from principles of freedom and equality that are necessarily implied in human discourse practices among reasonable human beings that treat each other as free and equal discourse partners. Existential justifications of human rights complement the discursive justification of human rights as

[155] *cf* Kant (1970) 98 f. The Kantian proposals for multilevel constitutionalism based on an international (con)federation among peoples in republican states protecting equal, cosmopolitan rights of citizens remain vague in view of the pluralism of potential constitutional and institutional architectures. Kant emphasizes the dangers of 'paternalist' world government and the advantages of decentralized forms of self-government based on inalienable rights (eg, to equal freedoms, property and independence of citizens as autonomous law givers for themselves as well as for 'the right of every people to give itself a civil constitution of the kind that it sees fit, without interference from other powers', Kant, at 182).

[156] *cf The Lisbon Treaty* (Foundation for EU Democracy 2008) 198 ff. On basing a modern conception of international law on respect for human dignity see: Capps (2009).

[157] *cf* R Alexy, 'Menschenrechte ohne Metaphysik?' (2004) 52 *Deutsche Zeitschrift für Philosophie* I 15–24; S Gosepath and G Lohmann (eds), *Philosophie der Menschenrechte*, 2nd edn (Frankfurt: Suhrkamp, 1999); Besson/Tasioulas (2010), sections 15–17.

social facts by the existential claim that not only respect for human dignity and reasonableness of human beings, but our existential choices in real life require perceiving ourselves as 'discursive creatures' that can fully develop their autonomy only if they assert human rights, challenge abuses of power and 'institutionalize public reason'. The transformation of moral human rights into positive law and their progressive 'optimization' in all fields of law are influenced by cultural diversity, claims to legal recognition of explicit or derived human rights and contestation as to how human rights and other rights should be defined and mutually 'balanced'. The UN General Assembly Resolution of 28 July 2010 on 'The human right to water and sanitation', like the corresponding UN Human Rights Council Resolution of 30 September 2010 affirming that this human right 'is derived from the right to an adequate standard of living', illustrate that the lack of *explicit human rights* entitlements in human rights conventions (like a human right of access to potable water) does not prevent international recognition of *derived human rights* inferred from explicitly recognized rights as being necessarily implied in positive human rights law.[158]

Hence, the moral foundations of human rights remain important for interpreting 'incomplete human rights law' and for the self-understanding of citizens and institutions in rights-based legal systems vis-à-vis claims by rulers denying citizens legal and judicial protection of human and other cosmopolitan rights. The 'Jasmine revolution' in north African countries in 2011 illustrates that denial by authoritarian rulers of human rights can often be overcome only by individual and democratic struggles of citizens defending their inalienable rights. It remains controversial whether and to what extent this existential 'democratic, social responsibility' of citizens for their own constitutional order and domestic welfare limits, as claimed by Rawls, *extraterritorial* human rights duties of assisting individuals and 'sovereign people' in foreign jurisdictions. This study argues that the universal recognition of 'inalienable' and 'indivisible human rights', and of corresponding government obligations to respect, protect and fulfil human rights in their respective jurisdictions, entail that 'human rights coherence' (*cf* Table 4) has become a constitutional requirement also for IEL. Multilevel regulation of the international division of labour must be designed so that human rights are not violated by governments and private economic actors, for instance if the latter collude with non-democratic rulers in exploiting citizens by abusing the 'lending privilege' and 'resource privilege' of countries in ways enriching corrupt rulers. Governmental duties (eg, of lending and borrowing countries) to protect human rights at home and abroad, and private duties to respect human rights (eg, of private banks administering bank transfers for non-democratic rulers), must be interpreted in mutually coherent ways for the benefit of citizens and their human rights. Globalization and the increasing civil society claims of human rights obligations also of international and non-governmental organizations challenge traditional conceptions of human rights law, for example, that human rights obligations are exclusively incumbent on states. Since its *Kupferberg* judgment in 1982, the ECJ has consistently held that – if international agreements do not determine their domestic law effects inside the internal legal orders of the contracting parties – the Court of Justice can decide not only whether clear, precise and unconditional treaty obligations can be

[158] For a discussion of these recent UN resolutions, their legal relevance for recognizing 'derived human rights' and their derivation in political and judicial practices from diverse human rights (eg, to life, health and an adequate standard of living) see: P Thielbörger, *The Right(s) to Water*, EUI doctoral thesis defended in December 2010 (Florence: European University Institute, 2011).

invoked by individuals and EU member states in domestic courts;[159] the ECJ's jurisprudence has even acknowledged a presumption in favour of 'direct effects' unless the nature and structure of the agreement exclude it.[160] It is only more recently that the EU Commission has begun to insert into free trade agreements concluded by the EU (eg, into Article 14.15 of the Draft EU–Canada Comprehensive Economic and Trade Agreement), or into the EU Council Decisions on the conclusion of free trade agreements, explicit provisions denying direct effect for the benefit of citizens: 'The Agreement shall not be construed as conferring rights or imposing obligations which can be directly invoked before Union or Member States courts and tribunals'.[161] As discussed in chapter V, similar 'Westphalian conceptions' of EU powers are reflected in the recent EU Commission proposals to terminate the existing rights of EU investors under BITs among EU member countries to have direct access to individual legal and judicial remedies in investor–state arbitration.

Legitimately diverse forms of regulating human rights: the example of the human rights to health and to access to water

Since the recognition of a fundamental right to health protection in the Preamble of the 1946 Constitution establishing the World Health Organization (in force since 1948 and ratified by now 193 WHO member countries), individual rights to protection of health have become recognized in more than one hundred national constitutions[162] as well as in increasing numbers of UN human rights instruments[163] and regional human rights conventions. In its 'General Comment No 14' on the 'Right to the Highest Attainable Standard of Health', the UN Committee on Economic, Social and Cultural Rights has interpreted the right to health as an inclusive right extending not only to the right to timely and appropriate health care, but also to a 'wide range of socio-economic factors that promote conditions in which people can lead a healthy life', including 'the underlying determinants of health, such as food and nutrition, housing, access to a safe and potable water and adequate sanitation, safe and healthy working conditions, and a healthy environment'.[164] The overlapping elements of the right to health protection and of the human right to life illustrate the indivisible nature and often difficult demarcation lines of complementary human rights, which may be implemented and protected in domestic legal systems through constitutional, legislative, administrative or only judicially recognized rights. The diversity of national health protection systems among UN member states shows that access to essential goods and services (like medicines and medical services) may be legitimately regulated in different ways.

The close interrelationships between the human right to health, property rights, economic freedoms, trade and intellectual property law were illustrated by the 2001 WTO

[159] Case 104/81, [1982] ECR, 3641, para 17.

[160] *cf* M Mendez, 'The Legal Effects of Community Agreements: Maximalist Treaty Enforcement and Judicial Avoidance Techniques' (2010) 21 *EJIL* 83–104.

[161] Art 8 of the Council Decision (2011/265/EU) implementing the 2010 EU–Korea Free Trade Agreement, OJ 2011 L127/1.

[162] *cf* n 120 and related text.

[163] *cf* n 121 and related text.

[164] UN Committee on Economic, Social and Cultural Rights, *General Comment No 14*, adopted in May 2000 (E/C.12/2000/4).

Declaration on 'The TRIPS Agreement and Public Health', the 2003 WTO 'waiver' facilitating the granting of compulsory licences by exporting countries for production and supply of essential medicines to LDCs without pharmaceutical manufacturing capacity and the WTO Decision of 6 December 2005 on the 'Protocol amending the TRIPS Agreement'. The latter is, according to its Preamble, designed 'to find an expeditious solution to the problems of the difficulties that WTO Members with insufficient or no manufacturing capacities in the pharmaceutical sector could face in making effective use of compulsory licensing under the TRIPS Agreement'.[165] A symposium jointly held by the WHO, WIPO and the WTO in July 2010 emphasized that pharmaceutical industries, as profit-driven firms rather than humanitarian enterprises, operate in response to economic and market forces that cannot fix prices only according to their affordability among the poor; hence, there is a need for legal and institutional coordination of health, trade and intellectual property policies, for instance in fields such as incentives for innovation of medicines, research in neglected tropical diseases, drug procurement, drug pricing, intellectual property, trade and competition policies and regulation to ensure the quality, safety, access to and efficacy of medicines. As such rules and drug prices tend to vary from country to country, views continue to differ on whether the flexibilities of the WTO's TRIPS Agreement are sufficient and whether 'TRIPS plus' disciplines are warranted, for instance regarding the protection of traditional medicines in LDCs and the controversial seizures or detentions of generic medicines in transit in the EU.[166] While the vast majority of medicines on the WHO essential medicines list are not under patent protection, the more advanced HIV/AIDS drugs (known as 'second line antiretroviral treatments') and treatments for drug-resistant tuberculosis continue to be protected by patents.

Similar to the diverse legal forms of protecting access to essential medicines and public health, the legal protection of access to water as a human right, a constitutional right, legislative, administrative or judicial right legitimately differs among countries due to their 'margin of appreciation' in designing legal and administrative protection of access to essential services. In view of the fact that more than 1.2 billion people remain without access to safe potable water and almost 2 million children die every year for want of clean water and access to clean sanitation, UN human rights bodies have called for worldwide recognition of a human right of access to water deriving from the human right to health.[167] Depending on their respective legal traditions and available water resources, national legal systems protect access to water in diverse ways, for example, as a human

[165] On this amendment of the TRIPS Agreement, which has not yet entered into force, see WTO document WT/L/641 (8 December 2005); on the drafting history see: Hestermeyer (2007) ch 5. On the considerable variations in the approaches of LDCs regarding their domestic implementation of TRIPS obligations see: C Deere, *The Implementation Game: The TRIPS Agreement and the Global Politics of Intellectual Property Reform in Developing Countries* (Oxford: OUP, 2011).

[166] For detailed analyses see: Hestermeyer (2007); Maskus and Reichman (n 92) pts II and III.

[167] *cf* E Riedel and P Rothen (eds), *The Human Right to Water* (Berlin: Berliner Wissenschafts-Verlag, 2006); SC McCaffrey, 'The Human Right to Water' in EB Weiss, L Boisson de Chazournes and N Bernasconi-Osterwalder (eds), *Fresh Water and International Economic Law* (Oxford: OUP, 2005) 93–115. The UN Commission on Human Rights and its Special Rapporteur for Water noted that 'the right to drinking water and sanitation is an integral part of officially recognized human rights and may be considered a basic requirement for the implementation of several other human rights' (UN Doc E/CN.4/Sub.2/2002/10, para 32). According to General Comment No 15 adopted by the UN Committee on Economic, Social and Cultural Rights, the human right to water entitles everyone to sufficient, safe, acceptable, physically accessible and affordable water for personal and domestic uses.

right deriving from the human right to life (eg, as protected by India's Supreme Court) or from the human right to health (eg, as protected by the High Court of South Africa); as a constitutional right (eg, in Belgium and many LDCs); as a legislative right (eg, in France); or as administrative rights protected and derived by domestic courts from general constitutional and legislative principles (eg, in Germany).[168]

Similar to the different levels and legal sources of human, constitutional, legislative or administrative rights protecting access to water, the corresponding obligations of governments and non-governmental organizations (eg, corporate human rights obligations) may be based on different levels and sources of international, constitutional, legislative, administrative or judicial regulation, including private law commitments by private providers and distributors of water. The international and transnational dimensions of rights of access to water remain controversial, notably regarding obligations of 'water-rich countries' to supply 'water-deficit countries' and their citizens with needed water resources. The respective choices of national and international human rights approaches, constitutional, legislative, administrative and judicial approaches to the regulation of access to water resources legitimately vary (eg, among water-rich, developed countries like Canada and Finland and water-poor LDCs in sub-Saharan Africa) and interact in diverse ways. Even in the absence of explicit human rights and constitutional guarantees of access to water in some constitutional democracies, domestic laws may effectively protect legally secure access of citizens to water under affordable and non-discriminatory conditions. Such 'legal pragmatism' may be consistent with international human rights guarantees and may also facilitate resolution of international water conflicts.[169]

Legitimately diverse constitutional safeguards of private property rights

The legal regulation of access to medicines, food, water and to education inevitably involves constitutional questions of reconciling the regulation of property rights with the regulation of scarce natural resources and intellectual inventions (eg, for medicines and education materials). Just as people have diverse views on the constitutional, majoritarian and participatory design of 'democracy', they often disagree on whether respect for human dignity requires protection of freedom of profession and of private property as human rights, constitutional rights, legislative rights or mere 'common law freedoms' at national and international levels. The African, European and Inter-American human rights conventions protect private property or 'peaceful enjoyment of possessions' (Article 1 of Protocol 1 to the ECHR). But most UN human rights conventions include no corresponding guarantees of private property in view of the postwar disagreement among communist, democratic and less-developed countries on how to translate the 'right to own property' protected in Article 17 UDHR[170] into precise treaty rights and obligations. Utilitarian economists and some human rights advocates view property rights and market freedoms as mere *instruments* for promoting savings, investments and

[168] *cf* n 120 and H Smets, *The Right to Water in National Legislations* (Paris: Agence Française de Développement, 2006); P Thielbörger (n 158).

[169] *cf* U Luterbacher and E Wiegandt, 'Cooperation or Confrontation: Sustainable Water Use in an International Context' in Weiss et al (n 167) 11 ff.

[170] Art 17 reads: 'Everyone has the right to own property alone as well as in association with others. No one shall be arbitrarily deprived of his property'.

more efficient production and allocation of goods and services, notwithstanding the fact that efficient satisfaction of consumer demand serves human values of crucial importance for social justice.[171] Libertarian and other rights-based theories of justice perceive property as the chief bastion of private autonomy and 'civilization'. John Locke justified property rights as moral entitlements to self-ownership and to the fruits of one's labour provided the valuable good (or the added value of the good) was produced without violating the rights and basic needs of others.[172] Hegel's *Philosophy of Right* perceived the appropriation, ownership and alienation of property as expressions of the will, personality, independence and self-development of the owner in relation to objects and to other persons who must respect property rights and may perceive the personality of individuals (eg, of an artist) in light of their property (eg, artworks). This often close interrelationship between personality and property illustrates that – just as property may be an existential component of the autonomy, personality, and social recognition of an individual – deprivation of property may imply an attack on the personality of the owner.[173]

Legal philosophers like Raz emphasise the role of property rights as constituent elements of an autonomous life with privacy, material security, and 'positive freedom' which should be limited only to protect the freedom of others, and requires respect for the fruits of lawful individual choices.[174] As property rights include the right to dispose of one's property by means of voluntary transactions, the various moral justifications of legal protection of property rights also justify private rights to sell or purchase property rights in goods and capital in private markets. As 'enabling devices for individual autonomy',[175] markets and their various social functions as decentralized information, coordination and sanctioning mechanisms can be justified not only on grounds of economic efficiency and as incentives for exertion, creativity, and decentralised coordination of autonomous actions; they are also preconditions for, and inevitable consequences of individual autonomy and for a free, informed and accountable society, subject to democratic legislation limiting and regulating 'market failures' in the public interest.

[171] *cf* eg, R Posner, *The Economics of Justice* (Cambridge: Harvard University Press, 1981); EU Petersmann, 'Morality, Human Rights and International Economic Law: Towards Cosmopolitan Market Integration Law?' in HD Assmann and R Sethe (eds), *Recht und Ethos im Zeitalter der Globalisierung* (Baden-Baden: Nomos, 2004) 53–86.

[172] *cf* the 'Essay Concerning the True Origin, Extent and End of Civil Government' in J Locke, *Two Treatises of Government* (1689) paras 27–41, where Locke assumes that, in a state of nature without money, persons must limit their unilateral appropriations to a proportional share so that 'enough, and as good' for others is left. Locke's labour theory as the moral justification of just property acquisition raises numerous problems (*cf* JW Harris, *Property and Justice* (Oxford: OUP, 1996); J Waldron, *A Right to Private Property* (Oxford: OUP, 1988)). Notably Locke's views on self-ownership and property rights over one's body are inconsistent with respect for human dignity: individuals have personality rights over their bodies and can claim property rights over body parts only to the extent that such body parts could be separated with the consent of the person (eg, hair) and without violating one's human dignity.

[173] *cf* GWF Hegel, *The Philosophy of Right*, trans Knox (Oxford: OUP, 1965); JE Penner, *The Idea of Property in Law* (Oxford: Clarendon Press by OUP, 1997).

[174] *cf* J Raz, *The Morality of Freedom* (Oxford: OUP, 1986) 372–75; AR Coban, *Protection of Property Rights within the European Convention on Human Rights* (Oxford: OUP, 2004) 65–77.

[175] *cf* J Gray, *The Moral Foundations of Market Institutions* (London: IEA Health and Welfare Unit, 1992) eg, at 3.

5 'HUMAN RIGHTS FUNCTIONS' OF MULTILEVEL ECONOMIC REGULATION? FREEDOM OF COMPETITION, FREEDOM OF TRADE AND FREEDOM OF COMMERCIAL SPEECH

The preceding examples illustrate that at least some internationally agreed human rights (eg, to protection of equal liberties, freedom of profession, private property, health protection and access to water) may be protected in domestic laws in legitimately diverse ways. It was further emphasized that human rights, constitutional rights and 'principles of justice' are closely interrelated. For instance, if justice is understood as an individual right to equal liberties and to a 'constitutionalized legal structure of justification' of restrictions of equal liberties, constitutional democracies may have a broad 'margin of justification' of whether and how human rights should be protected by constitutional, legislative, administrative, judicial and international rules, procedures and remedies. Hence, as emphasized in my 1991 monograph, administrative and economic law guarantees of access to essential goods and services (like water) may serve 'human rights functions' and 'constitutional functions' even if the national administrative regulations do not explicitly refer to internationally recognized human rights or to constitutional rights of access to water, medicines, food or other essential goods and services supplied by international trade.

Ordo-liberal economists point to the interdependence of economic, legal and social orders. Civil, political, economic and social freedoms are interconnected and can strengthen each other, as illustrated by Sen's claim that famine has rarely emerged in constitutional democracies. Yet, the contribution of the diverse economic instruments to human rights protection often remains contested also among economists. From the perspective of 'law and economics', most economic and legal problems can be regarded as problems of finding an optimum set of rules and institutions constituting and delimiting autonomy, coordinating autonomous specialized activities in ways which harmonize private and social advantages and promoting 'relative stability'.[176] Also human rights arguments for perceiving IEL from a citizen perspective as an instrument for protecting human rights – notably for empowering individuals to acquire the resources necessary for living their lives in dignity, for freely developing their diverse human capacities and for challenging governmental restrictions that are not justifiable in terms of human rights – can be rationalized on grounds of making economic markets, market regulation and individual uses of scarce resources more efficient and effective, for instance by protecting individuals against adverse effects of market regulation. Trade policies are rarely designed for promoting human rights. Trade diplomats often oppose human rights arguments in order to 'de-politicize' intergovernmental trade negotiations and reduce their own legal and judicial accountability vis-à-vis consumers for protectionist abuses of trade policy powers. Similarly, human rights advocates frequently neglect economic arguments that the availability of scarce resources for enjoyment of human rights depends on the design of IEL for a welfare-increasing division of labour among individuals.[177] From a citizen-

[176] *cf* Petersmann (1991) 27–94.

[177] *cf* EU Petersmann, 'Taking Human Dignity, Poverty and Empowerment of Individuals More Seriously: Rejoinder to Alston' (2002) 13 *EJIL* 845–51. In contrast to Alston's authoritarian conception of economic development, D Kinley (2009) argues for 'recognition, indeed appreciation, of the global economy's role in pursuing the ends aspired to by these same human rights standards' (at 204–05). Kinley acknowledges that many governments are not pursuing human rights as their primary objectives, and also trade unions in developed

perspective, economic transactions derive their legitimacy not only from consent to voluntary agreements (eg, among the seller and the buyer) which are often influenced by restrictive business practices or entail harmful 'external effects' for third parties (eg, resulting from waste and pollution in rich countries, or from protectionist discrimination against imports of cotton, textiles, agricultural and other competitive goods from poor countries). The 'input legitimacy' of market regulation and of market transactions (such as sales of diamonds) also depends on respect for human rights, including individual freedoms and related social rights to produce, acquire, possess and sell scarce goods and services necessary for individual self-development. State-centred conceptions of 'international law among sovereign states', like 'realist dualism' separating rule of law inside states from rule of law in transnational relations among citizens, often neglect the 'empowerment functions' and 'human rights functions' of IEL for enabling citizens to increase their welfare through voluntary cooperation across state borders with due respect for human rights.

Inside constitutional democracies, economic and social laws usually aim at protecting general citizen interests like consumer welfare, non-discriminatory conditions of competition, rule of law and 'decent work conditions'; all such 'public interests' may be justified also in terms of respect for human rights.[178] WTO law and most other worldwide economic treaties, however, do not require governments to protect consumer welfare and other general citizen interests as defined by human rights.[179] For instance, consumer welfare and rule of law are nowhere mentioned in WTO law. The DSU aims at protecting legal security for the rights and obligations of WTO members without offering citizens effective legal and judicial remedies against non-compliance with WTO law. Economic analysis may be important for identifying the most efficient regulatory options, for instance by assisting in evaluating which of the alternative legal systems for protecting individual rights – like human rights law, constitutional law, legislation, private law and international agreements – can protect economic and social rights of citizens most effectively, and how the interactions among different 'layers of legal regulation' should be regulated in order to reduce transaction costs of citizens. Yet, many regulatory problems of IEL involve value questions, for instance regarding the legitimate role of courts in their review of governmental restrictions and as guardians of 'rule of law' in transnational economic cooperation among citizens. 'Public reason' and democratic self-determination require respecting the legitimate 'margin of appreciation' of democratic lawmakers regulating the interrelationships between the constitutional, political, economic and social dimensions of equal freedoms of citizens.

countries may not 'give a damn about workers in the Third World' (at 67, quoting a high-ranking American trade union leader).

[178] On maximization of consumer welfare as the ultimate goal of competition law and policy see, eg, RH Bork, *The Antitrust Paradox. A Policy at War with Itself* (New York: Basic Books, 1978); on other competition policy objectives (like protecting equal freedoms of small competitors against abuses of market power) see: CD Ehlermann and LL Laudati (eds), *European Competition Law Annual 1997: Objectives of Competition Policy* (Oxford: Hart Publishing, 1998); H Hovenkamp, *The Antitrust Enterprise. Principle and Execution* (Cambridge: Harvard University Press, 2005).

[179] *cf* EU Petersmann, *The Need for Integrating Trade and Competition Rules in the WTO World Trade and Legal System* (Geneva: Graduate Institute of International Studies, 1996). On the failure of the WTO negotiations on WTO competition rules see: DJ Gerber (2010) 101 ff, 321 ff.

Legitimately diverse regulation of freedom of competition and freedom of trade

In the EU, the common market freedoms and competition rules of the EU Treaty are legally and judicially protected as 'fundamental freedoms' of individuals with legal primacy, direct effect and 'direct applicability' in the domestic laws of the 27 EU member states.[180] The ECJ rightly avoids 'human rights language' in its legal protection of 'common market freedoms', which form part of the EU's 'primary law guarantees' requiring constitutional and judicial protection – with due regard for all other constitutional rights and human rights. The EU Treaty prohibitions of tariffs, non-tariff trade barriers and trade discrimination – notwithstanding their formulation in terms of rights and obligations of governments – have been construed by the ECJ as directly applicable *individual freedoms* of trade inside the common market as well as objective constitutional principles that must be protected by European courts as fundamental rights: 'the principles of free movement of goods and freedom of competition, together with freedom of trade as a fundamental right, are general principles of Community law of which the Court ensures observance'.[181]

Individual 'freedom to conduct a business in accordance with Community law and national laws' (Article 6 EU Charter of Fundamental Rights) and 'freedom of competition' are, likewise, constitutionally and judicially protected in European law.[182] Especially the freedom of movements of workers and other persons, access to employment and the right of establishment have been described by the ECJ as 'fundamental freedoms'[183] or 'a fundamental right which the Treaty confers individually on each worker in the Community'.[184] By contrast, the corresponding GATT and WTO prohibitions of tariffs, non-tariff trade barriers and trade discrimination continue to be construed by most WTO members, including the EU and its member states, as rights and obligations of governments without corresponding rights and obligations of their citizens.[185] Even though goods and services are produced and consumed by individuals and WTO dispute settlement panels have emphasized that 'one of the primary objects of the GATT/WTO . . . is to produce certain market conditions which would allow . . . individual activity to flourish' by protecting the international division of labour against discriminatory trade restrictions and other distortions,[186] the same dispute settlement panel also emphasized: '(n)either the GATT nor the WTO has so far been interpreted by GATT/WTO institu-

[180] *cf* T Kingreen, 'Fundamental Freedoms' and A Hatje, 'The Economic Constitution' in A von Bogdandy and J Bast (eds) (2006) 549 ff, 587 ff.

[181] Case 240/83, *ADBHU* [1985] ECR 531, para 9.

[182] In European competition law and policy, it remains contested whether pursuit of 'consumer welfare' should be based on a 'total welfare standard' (as argued eg, by GJ Werden, *Essays on Consumer Welfare and Competition Policy*, SSRN, March 2009) or whether competition law also requires limiting discretionary governance powers for redistributing 'consumer benefits' to rent-seeking enterprises ('producer welfare'); *cf* G Monti, 'Article 81 EC and Public Policy' (2002) 39 *CMLR* 1057 ff; EU Petersmann, 'Legal, Economic and Political Objectives of National and International Competition Policies: Constitutional Functions of WTO "Linking Principles" for Trade and Competition' (1999) 34 *New England Law Review* 145 ff.

[183] Case C-55/94, *Gebhard* [1995] ECR I-4165, para 37.

[184] Case 22/86, *Heylens* [1987] ECR 4097, para14.

[185] See section 1 above and, for a recent overview and criticism of the ECJ case law: A Arcuri and S Poli, 'What Price for the Community Enforcement of WTO Law?' EUI Working Paper Law (2010).

[186] *United States – Sections 301–310 of the Trade Act of 1974*, WTO Panel report adopted on 27 January 2000, WT/DS152/R, paras 7.73 *et seq*.

tions as a legal order producing direct effect'.[187] Yet, even if WTO agreements create rights and obligations only for WTO members, the latter remain free to confer rights to invoke and enforce WTO rules and 'consistent interpretations' of domestic trade rules also on private traders, producers and consumers.

In the United States, the 'commerce clause' in Article I, section 8 of the US Constitution is interpreted by the courts as a constitutional prohibition of discriminatory or unnecessary state restrictions of the common market inside the United States[188] without protecting individual 'fundamental freedoms' similar to the 'market freedoms' of EU citizens. US law tends to protect individual economic freedoms and competition rules by legislation rather than by constitutional guarantees. Since the 1930s, the strong constitutional and judicial protection in the Fifth Amendment of the US Constitution ('Nor shall private property be taken for public use without just compensation') has been progressively abandoned in favour of parliamentary majority regulation of private property rights.[189] Economic freedom of profession and freedom of trade are subject to parliamentary majority legislation of the US Congress without effective constitutional protection of economic liberty rights of citizens.[190] The economic legislation may serve 'constitutional functions', as illustrated by the statement of the US Supreme Court that 'antitrust laws . . . are the Magna Charta of free enterprise. They are as important to the preservation of economic freedom and our free enterprise system as the Bill of Rights is to the protection of our fundamental freedoms'.[191] With regard to transnational trade, the Supreme Court has emphasized that

> no one has a vested right to trade with foreign nations, which is so broad in character as to limit and restrict the power of Congress to determine what articles (. . .) may be imported into this country and the terms upon which a right to import may be exercised.[192]

'Law as communication': diverse regulation of freedom of commercial speech

If national and international legal systems are perceived as constitutionally structured forms of agreed law creation,[193] the constitutional and judicial protection of individual and democratic freedom of expression and information is of constitutive significance for all legal systems. The need to communicate is a defining characteristic of all dimensions of society. Should freedom of expression be legally and judicially less protected in the

[187] WT/DS152/R (n 188) para.7.72. The Panel notes: 'The fact that WTO institutions have not to date construed any obligations as producing direct effect does not necessarily preclude that in the legal system of any given Member, following internal constitutional principles, some obligations will be found to give rights to individuals. Our statement of fact does not prejudge any decisions by national courts on this issue'.

[188] *cf* Morrison and Hudec (n 153) 91 ff.

[189] *cf* RA Epstein, *Supreme Neglect. How to Revive Constitutional Protection for Private Property* (New York: OUP, 2008).

[190] *cf* Siegan (1980); Morrison and Hudec (n 153); Tushnet (2008); Sandefur (2010).

[191] *United States v Topco Assoc Inc*, 405 US 596, 610 (1972).

[192] *Buttfield v Stranahan*, 192 US 470, at 493 (1904). While this decision could have been interpreted to imply the existence of a 'right to trade with foreign nations' subject to democratic legislation, subsequent court decisions have quoted from the 1904 judgment only 'that no one has a vested right to trade with foreign nations'. The Court of Appeals for the Federal Circuit explained this absence of a 'right to trade' in terms of majoritarian democracy: 'When the people granted Congress the power "to regulate Commerce with foreign Nations" (. . .) they thereupon relinquished at least whatever right they, as individuals, may have had to insist upon the importation of any product' (*Arjay Associates Inc v Bush*, 891 F.2d 891, 898 (Fed. Cir. 1989).

[193] *cf* D Nelken (ed), *Law as Communication* (Oxford: OUP, 1996).

economy and private society than in the democratic dimensions of individual and collective self-governance in the polity? Is 'commercial speech' – such as communicative acts by commercial actors pursuing commercial aims or 'mixed speech' in commercial contexts – entitled to constitutional protection? National constitutional law in Europe (eg, Article 5 of the German Basic Law) and the ECHR proceed from the presumption that all speech, whatever its content, comes within the protection of freedom of speech under Article 10 ECHR. The constitutional key question is the legal justifiability of permissible restrictions on the basis of legislative, administrative and judicial 'balancing' of competing interests, for instance in the context of consumer protection law, competition law and unfair trade legislation. The 'necessity test' may be less strict with regard to restrictions of commercial statements (eg, tobacco advertising) than in the case of political speech.[194] As far as the ECHR is concerned, states may enjoy a wider 'margin of appreciation' regarding restrictions of commercial speech than in the case of restrictions of political speech which enjoys a higher level of constitutional protection.

In many Anglo-Saxon democracies, 'double standards' of *constitutional protection* of civil and political rights and only *legislative protection* of economic and social rights have a long tradition. In the United States, they reflect deliberate parliamentary and judicial choices during the 1930s in favour of prioritizing civil and political rights (protected by strict judicial scrutiny) over economic and social rights (with more deferential judicial review of legislative and administrative restrictions). The dichotomy seems to have contributed to the US Supreme Court's protection of speech under the First Amendment to the US Constitution on the basis of different categories of speech: some deserve full protection (eg, political speech), some less protection (eg, commercial speech like 'purely commercial advertising' or 'mixed speech' including both commercial and non-commercial statements) and some no protection at all (eg, obscene speech, libel, child pornography, threats). In *Virginia State Board of Pharmacy v Virginia Citizens Consumer Council Inc*, commercial speech was defined as 'a speech that does nothing more than propose a commercial transaction'.[195] In a subsequent judgment, the Supreme Court defined commercial speech as an expression which 'not only serves the economic interest of the speaker, but also assists consumers and furthers the societal interest in the fullest possible dissemination of information'.[196] In view of the potential variety of 'commercial speech' and 'mixed speech' in border areas between 'commercialized politics' and 'politicized business', the method of 'judicial balancing' in the multilevel, constitutional adjudication by European courts rightly avoids abstract definitions and 'categories' of speech in favour of more flexible 'balancing criteria': content, speaker's right, speaker's motive, context of the speech, hearer's right, necessity to face critical statements about one's own commercial activity and the right to strike back serve as criteria in the judicial determination of the appropriate level of protection of the speaker and of the public (eg, other competitors and consumers). The more the commercial speech has the ability of contributing to a public debate on matters of public interest (as in the *Hertel case* summarized

[194] *cf* J Krzeminska-Vamvaka, *Freedom of Commercial Speech in Europe* (Hamburg: Verlag Dr Kova , 2008) 20; see the judgment of the ECtHR (20 November 1989) in *Markt Intern Verlag GMBH v Germany*, 12 EHRR 161.

[195] *Virginia State Board of Pharmacy v Virginia Citizens Consumer Council Inc*, 425 US 748, 762 (1976). The Court emphasized that 'people will perceive their own best interests only if they are well enough informed, and (...) the best means to that end is to open the channels of communication rather than to close them' (at 770).

[196] *Central Hudson Gas and Electricity Corporation v Public Service Commission*, 447 US 557, 561 (1980).

in Table 17), the more constitutional law may limit the margin of appreciation of the legislator. Protection of fair competition and consumer protection may justify legal limitations that may not be permissible outside the context of economic market regulation.

Diverse conceptions of the complementary regulatory functions of human rights law, constitutional law and economic law

Individual rights tend to be protected by diverse legal systems, like human rights law, constitutional law, legislation, private law and international agreements (eg, on protection of intellectual property rights). Each of these interrelated legal systems may rest on diverse value premises. For instance:

- National, regional and universal human rights tend to be derived from respect for human dignity as 'inalienable' rights of every human person.
- Constitutional rights tend to focus on citizenship in national or transnational communities (eg, in case of EU citizenship pursuant to Articles 18 *ff* TFEU).
- Legislative rights (like patent rights) may be designed by democratic majority decisions of legislatures, or by intergovernmental agreements, as efficient policy instruments rather than on the basis of respect for human dignity or other constitutional principles. They may protect rights of everyone, or of only certain individuals (like 'nationals' of WTO Members pursuant to Article 1 of the TRIPS Agreement), depending on the procedural and substantive conditions specified in the legislation and agreements concerned.

Human rights (eg, as *erga omnes* rights and obligations with a *jus cogens* core), constitutional rights (eg, with a higher legal rank in national or European law), legislative rights (eg, of intellectual property rights protected in national legislation) and private rights (such as contractual licences to use private patents and copyrights) differ considerably depending on their legal status. Their respective legal and judicial remedies may likewise differ depending on whether the rights are protected as part of national and/or international human rights law, constitutional law, legislation or private law and arbitration. The universal recognition of human rights may require reviewing the interrelationships between the human rights dimensions, constitutional, legislative or contractual dimensions of economic and social rights. As discussed above, the case law of national and European economic courts and human rights courts on 'freedom of commercial speech' differs considerably depending on whether commercial speech is perceived as part of the constitutional and human rights guarantees of 'freedom of speech' (as in the jurisprudence of the German Constitutional Court and the ECtHR) and on how courts 'balance' the related economic interests (eg, of producers and consumers) and non-economic interests involved. Similarly, 'rules of reason' in European competition law may have to be interpreted not only in terms of their economic objectives of promoting productive efficiency and consumer welfare, but also from human rights perspectives.[197] The judicial methods of national and international courts regarding the interpretation and mutual 'balancing' of economic rules and human rights differ according to their respective 'constitutional mandates', 'judicial cooperation among courts', their judicial

[197] *cf* L Serena Rossi and SJ Curzon, 'An Evolving "Rule of Reason" in the European Market' in G Bongiovanni, G Sartor and C Valentini (2009) 405–20.

conceptions of 'constitutional law', 'majoritarian' and 'deliberative democracy' and the judicial willingness to interpret domestic laws in conformity with the international legal obligations of the state concerned.

Reasonable citizens with diverse conceptions for a good life and for a 'just society' are never likely to agree on any comprehensive conception of 'international justice' for designing and interpreting national and international human rights law, related constitutional law and IEL in mutually coherent ways. IEL must respect this legitimate diversity of national and regional 'constitutional systems' for protecting human rights. Even though the globalization of human rights and of economic interdependence require re-examining the 'basic principles of justice' (eg, as defined by human rights) and constitutional foundations of international economic regulation, the legitimacy of IEL will continue to depend on respect for democratic diversity and 'reasonable disagreement' among citizens. Just as human rights bodies tend to interpret human rights treaties from the perspective of citizens rather than their rulers (eg, by denying that the transfer of jurisdiction over Hong Kong in 1997 from the United Kingdom to China could abrogate – in view of China's non-ratification of the International Covenant for Civil and Political Rights – the civil and political human rights which the United Kingdom had accepted under the ICCPR for the benefit of Hong Kong citizens),[198] so should economic courts of justice interpret IEL with due respect for the rights of citizens as the 'democratic principals' of government agents.

'WTO plus disciplines': protection of individual trading rights, property rights and judicial remedies in the 2001 WTO Protocol on the Accession of China

Constitutional democracies promote economic welfare by *national* legal guarantees of freedom of contract and trade, freedom of speech, freedom of profession, a common market, private property, the rule of law, judicial remedies, competition rules and other legal preconditions for a well-functioning, national market economy. Hence, in view of such *national* legal guarantees, *international* trade agreements among constitutional democracies may not need specific trade rules providing for such freedoms, property rights, individual access to courts and other institutional pre-conditions in national legal systems for mutually beneficial trade and market competition. By contrast, trade agreements with non-democracies lacking such national legal guarantees often include 'WTO plus disciplines' going beyond WTO legal disciplines.[199] The negotiations on the accession of China to the WTO illustrate that – if the legal preconditions for a well-functioning market economy are guaranteed neither at national level nor in WTO law – constitutional democracies may find it necessary to insist on specific 'WTO plus commitments' to protect individual freedoms to import and export, property rights and

[198] See UN Doc CCPR/C/79/Add.57: 'The Human Rights Committee – dealing with cases of dismemberment of States parties to the International Covenant on Civil and Political Rights – has taken the view that human rights treaties devolve with territory, and that States continue to be bound by the obligations under the Covenant entered by the predecessor State. Once the people living in a territory find themselves under the protection of the International Covenant on Civil and Political Rights, such protection cannot be denied to them by virtue of the mere dismemberment of that territory or its coming within the jurisdiction of another State'. 'In this regard, the Committee points out that the parties to the Joint Declaration have agreed that all provisions of the Covenant as applied to Hong Kong shall remain in force after 1 July 1997'.

[199] *cf* Chang-fa Lo, *WTO-Plus Issues in Free Trade Agreements* (Taipei, 2010).

individual access to independent courts offering effective judicial remedies.[200] The WTO Protocol on the Accession of China thereby compensates perceived deficiencies in national legal and economic systems by international agreements and institutions (such as the WTO and its dispute settlement bodies) committing countries to adjust their domestic legal and economic systems to the requirements of IEL. The Accession Protocol demonstrates – in the words of WTO Director-General Pascal Lamy – 'how WTO membership can benefit both the acceding country and the wider WTO family of nations':[201] joining the WTO helped China to reform its domestic legal system by introducing major legal commitments to transparency, non-discrimination, due process of law, judicial protection of individual 'trading rights' and intellectual property rights, and institutions (like independent courts) for legal and judicial protection of rule of law in the field of international economic cooperation. China's integration into the economic, legal and political world trading system based on WTO law also contributed to promoting mutually beneficial cooperation and rule of law in China's internal relations with the Chinese customs territories of Hong Kong, Macao and Taiwan, which continue to be autonomous WTO members in spite of the 'one China policy' followed by most UN member states as well as in China's external relations with WTO members.

The WTO membership of the four separate Chinese customs territories of the People's Republic of China, Hong Kong, Macau and Taiwan, and China's far-reaching market access commitments and 'WTO plus obligations' for legal and judicial protection of individual 'trading rights', property rights and individual rights of access to independent and impartial courts can be perceived as examples for 'constitutional functions' of WTO law. They protect economic freedom, private rights, rule of law and judicial remedies not only in *transnational* relations among WTO members, but also *inside* countries for the benefit of producers, investors, traders and consumers. The simultaneous WTO memberships of four different customs territories of China serves 'constitutional functions' also for the world trading system based on WTO law. Just as there have never been WTO dispute settlement proceedings among the EU as a WTO member and the 27 EU member states as additional WTO members, there have not been any WTO dispute settlement proceedings so far among the four Chinese WTO members.[202] The free trade agreements concluded between China, Hong Kong and Macau, like the trade liberalization agreements concluded between China and Taiwan since November 2008, make it likely that trade disputes among these WTO members will be settled bilaterally outside the WTO, or through private recourse to domestic courts or arbitration inside China, rather than through intergovernmental WTO dispute settlement proceedings. Yet, the legal recognition – by all UN and WTO member states – of the People's Republic of China as the single sovereign Chinese UN member state does not exclude the applicability of the

[200] *cf* the 2001 WTO Protocol on the Accession of the People's Republic of China, WT/L/432 (23 November 2001). For a comprehensive analysis of the impact of WTO law on the introduction of independent courts and judicial protection of freedoms of trade and intellectual property rights in China see: Chien-huei Wu, *The WTO Memberships of China, Taiwan, Hong Kong/China and Macau/China: Their Contribution to Judicial Settlement of Trade Disputes* (Florence: EUI doctoral thesis 2009).

[201] P Lamy in his Foreword to E Lam, *China and the WTO. A Long March towards the Rule of Law* (The Hague: Kluwer, 2009).

[202] Up until October 2010, China had been a complainant or defendant in 16 WTO disputes. In some of these dispute settlement procedures, Taiwan intervened as a third party. For a complete list of WTO dispute settlement procedures with references to relevant WTO documents see the WTO Dispute Settlement Body's annual reports, for instance in document WT/DSB/W/460 (2011), as well as the WTO Appellate Body Annual Reports (eg WT/AB/15 of June 2011).

WTO rules for the settlement of disputes among the four Chinese WTO members, for instance if one of them were to request multilateral WTO dispute settlement and WTO arbitration procedures rather than bilateral dispute settlement on the basis of Chinese law and of the ever larger number of bilateral agreements between China, Hong Kong, Macau and Taiwan. Similarly, as the ECJ does not offer EU member states legal remedies for reviewing legal compliance by the EU institutions with their WTO obligations, WTO dispute settlement bodies may find it legally difficult to deny the right of WTO members to establishment of a WTO dispute settlement panel if an EU member state should ever request establishment of a WTO dispute settlement panel in order to review alleged violations of WTO law by majority decisions of EU bodies which deny that EU member state any judicial remedies under EU law.

'TRIPS plus obligations' as obstacles to human rights?

Conceptions of human rights, democracy and 'constitutionalism' vary enormously among WTO member countries.[203] The 2004 Constitution of the People's Republic of China explicitly refers to human rights; yet, proposals for strengthening civil and political human rights and democratic governance continue to be subject to censorship by the Chinese government, and most constitutional guarantees cannot be legally enforced in China's domestic courts. The enormous economic welfare and legal reforms inside China resulting – since China's 1995 application to accede to the WTO – from the adjustments of China's laws and economic policies to the requirements of WTO law made the 'domestic policy functions' of WTO rules obvious to all Chinese citizens.[204] Had China, rather than withdrawing from GATT in 1949, conducted its economic and trade policies in conformity with GATT rules since 1948, the impoverishment of hundreds of millions of Chinese citizens could have been avoided. Open 'political markets' and democratic freedoms continue to be mistrusted by the Chinese communist party as potential threats for its political power and for the legal and political unity of China. This fear resembles the concerns expressed by some German scholars (like Carl Schmitt) who – in the face of the 'constitutional problems' of Germany's Weimar Republic during the 1930s – emphasized 'the limits of legality and sought its solution in charismatic legitimacy'[205] rather than in constitutionalization of the economy as well as of the polity.[206]

[203] On the variety of democratic theories and related constitutional traditions among countries see: R Dahl, *A Preface to Democratic Theory* (Chicago: Chicago University Press, 2006) 2–4.

[204] Also the potential 'constitutional functions of IEL' in domestic legal systems are increasingly discussed among Chinese academics. The translation into Chinese language, by Professor He Zhipeng (Jilin University Law School), of my book on *Constitutional Functions and Constitutional Problems of International Economic Law* (Beijing: Higher Education Press, 2005) prompted several Chinese doctoral researchers to explore the obvious relevance of 'constitutionalism' for national and international trade and economic regulation inside China.

[205] The quotation is from E Kennedy, *Constitutional Failure. Carl Schmitt in Weimar* (Durham: Duke University Press, 2004) 187.

[206] On C Schmitt's arguments during the Weimar Republic that 'the primacy of individual freedom and private interest . . . worked against democratic unity', see Kennedy (n 205). On the competing 'constitutional theories' during Germany's Weimar Republic (1919–33), for example the political weaknesses of H Kelsen's 'pure theory of law' as well as of R Smend's and H Heller's 'integration theories' compared with C Schmitt's theories justifying dictatorial 'decisionism' and emergency powers by Hitler, see: D Dyzenhaus, *Legality and Legitimacy: Carl Schmitt, Hans Kelsen and Hermann Heller in Weimar* (Oxford: Clarendon Press by OUP, 1997). On 'constraint theory' underlying democratic constitutionalism and 'constitutions as pre-commitment devices' see: J Elster, *Ulysses Unbound* (Cambridge: CUP, 2000).

Contrary to the predictions of an avalanche of WTO disputes challenging violations of intellectual property rights in China, the 2009 WTO panel report on 'China – Intellectual Property Rights'[207] was the first WTO case regarding enforcement of intellectual property rights in China. The panel's finding of an inconsistency of Article 4 of China's Copyright Law (which denies enforcement of copyrights or related rights with respect to works, performances and sound recordings that have not been authorized for publication or distribution) with China's obligations under Article 5(1) of the 1971 Berne Convention, as incorporated into Articles 9.1 and 41.1 TRIPS Agreement, was not appealed. Yet, the panel did not support the additional US claim that China had failed to comply with its obligations to establish criminal procedures and penalties for cases of wilful trademark counterfeiting and copyright piracy on a commercial scale sufficient to provide a deterrent; the panel generally faulted the United States for providing insufficient evidence of counterfeiting in China as might support its claim that China was failing to adequately deter counterfeiting and piracy. The panel emphasized in its 'concluding remarks' that 'the Panel's mandate was limited to a review of whether those alleged deficiencies, based upon an objective assessment of the facts presented by the parties, are inconsistent with those specific provisions of the TRIPS Agreement'.[208] Arguably, WTO dispute settlement findings on the illegal denial of copyright to certain works depending on their content also shield the authors' human right to benefit from the moral and material interests in their work, notwithstanding the focus by the parties to the dispute as well as by the WTO Panel on copyrights without any reference to human rights.[209]

The WTO Appellate Body report on 'China – Publications and Audiovisual Products' of 21 December 2009 confirmed China's rights to invoke Article XX GATT in order to justify economic regulations departing from China's commitments under its Protocol of Accession. The Appellate Body upheld the panel's finding that a number of Chinese restrictions on the importation and distribution of publications, audiovisual products, sound recordings and films were WTO-inconsistent and not 'necessary' to protect public morals within the meaning of Article XX(a) GATT because there were 'reasonably available alternative measures' that would be less trade restrictive and would equally enable the Chinese government to exercise sole responsibility for conducting 'content review'.[210] These WTO Appellate Body findings – even though confirming the illegality of China's allowing only state-approved and state-owned companies to import foreign reading materials (like books, periodicals and newspapers), audiovisual products, sound recordings and films – risk having negative repercussions on freedom of expression in China. Yet, the parties to the dispute and the reasoning of the WTO Appellate Body focused on 'trading rights' protected in the WTO Protocol on the Accession of China without any

[207] WT/DS362/R (26 January 2009).

[208] ibid para 8.5.

[209] On authors' rights as an expression of 'the inherent dignity and worth of all persons' distinct from intellectual property rights see Comment No17, adopted by the UN Committee on Economic, Social and Cultural Rights in 2005 (UN Doc E/C.12/GC/17 (12 January 2006)), on 'The Right of Everyone to Benefit from the Protection of the Moral and Material Interests Resulting from any Scientific, Literary or Artistic Production of which he or she is the Author' (Art 15, para 1(c) of the ICESCR). The WTO panel report concluded that – even if Art 17 of the 1971 Berne Convention for the Protection of Literary and Artistic Works could justify applying censorship for reasons of public order – 'there is no reason to suppose that censorship will eliminate those rights entirely with respect to a particular work' (para 7.132).

[210] *cf* WT/DS363/AB/R (21 December 2009).

reference to human rights like authors' rights and freedom of expression.[211] In spite of widespread hopes that legal protection of economic freedoms is bound to promote also political and personal freedoms,[212] China continues to censor the information flows to and from China and refuses ratification of the UN Covenant on Civil and Political Rights. Absent any references by the parties to the human rights dimensions of censorship and of related denial of authors' rights, both the WTO Panel as well as the WTO Appellate Body would have risked criticism of inappropriate 'judicial activism' if they had ventured to interpret WTO law in light of human rights that remain contested by the parties to the dispute as well as by third WTO members.[213]

Article 7 of the TRIPS Agreement explicitly acknowledges that

> the protection and enforcement of intellectual property rights should contribute to the promotion of technological innovation and to the transfer and dissemination of technology, to the mutual advantage of producers and users of technological knowledge and in a manner conducive to social and economic welfare, and to a balance of rights and obligations.

Article 8 of the TRIPS Agreement further recognizes that:

> 1. Members may, in formulating or amending their laws and regulations adopt measures necessary to protect public health and nutrition, and to promote the public interest in sectors of vital importance to their socio-economic and technological development, provided that such measures are consistent with the provisions of this Agreement.
>
> 2. Appropriate measures, provided that they are consistent with the provisions of this Agreement, may be needed to prevent the abuse of intellectual property rights by right holders or the resort to practices which unreasonably restrain trade or adversely affect the international transfer of technology.

In contrast to the 'general exceptions' in GATT Article XX and GATS Article XIV, Articles 7 and 8 of the TRIPS Agreement specify 'objectives' and 'principles' of – rather than 'general exceptions' to – the TRIPS Agreement. Yet, it remains to be seen whether the TRIPS Agreement offers WTO members less legal flexibilities for reconciling WTO rules and human rights compared with the GATT and the GATS. The inclusion of 'TRIPS plus commitments' into free trade agreements concluded by developed countries, like the Anti-Counterfeiting Trade Agreement (ACTA) concluded in December 2011 among more than 30 developed and less-developed WTO members, reflect the political determination of mainly developed countries to protect intellectual property rights beyond the worldwide guarantees of the TRIPS Agreement in order to further curb

[211] For a criticism see: T Broude, 'It's Easily Done: The China-Intellectual Property Rights Enforcement Dispute and the Freedom of Expression' The Hebrew University of Jerusalem Faculty of Law Research Paper No 22-2009 (October 2009).

[212] On a visit to China in 1998, US President Clinton proclaimed: 'In this global information age, when economic success is built on ideas, personal freedom is essential to the greatness of a nation'. One year later, President Bush made a similar point: 'Economic freedom creates habits of liberty. And habits of liberty create expectations of democracy . . . Trade freely with the Chinese and time is on our side' (quoted from the *Financial Times* (19 January 2010) 9).

[213] Note, for instance, that Art 9 of the TRIPS Agreement explicitly excludes (inter alia at the request of the United States) Article *6bis* of the Berne Convention and authors' rights derived therefrom. Broude (n 211) concludes: 'Human rights will be considered in trade disputes – perhaps – only if a party makes explicit claims to that effect. The US could have claimed, but refrained from claiming, that Article 17 Berne should be interpreted in light of Article 15(3)(c) ICESCR and Article 19 ICCPR (. . .) It would have been naïve to expect the US to couch its business-based complaint in human rights terms' (at 16).

counterfeiting and piracy.[214] Yet, as illustrated by India's WTO complaint against the seizure of Indian generic medicines in European ports (while en route to countries in Africa or Latin America), LDCs and human rights organizations challenge such 'TRIPS plus commitments' as possibly unduly discouraging the legal flexibilities of the TRIPS Agreement for countries wishing to limit intellectual property rights to better protect human rights to health, food and education.[215] Similar disagreements among WTO members continue to exist as to the legal necessity of the WTO 'waiver' of 30 August 2003, as well as of the formal 2005 amendment of the TRIPS Agreement providing for a new Article 31 *bis*, for enabling compulsory licensing of medicines predominantly for export to LDCs without sufficient production capacity in the pharmaceutical sector. By 2010, only one WTO member country had actually invoked the WTO waiver for issuing a compulsory licence (by Canada for medical exports to Rwanda) and only one sub-Saharan African country (Zambia) had notified its acceptance of the WTO Protocol of Amendment, which will become effective only on acceptance by two-thirds of the 155 WTO members.

[214] *cf The Anti-Counterfeiting Trade Agreement (ACTA): A New Obstacle to Human Rights?* Information note 10 (June 2010), published by 3D-> Trade, Human Rights, Equitable Economy (www.3dthree.org).

[215] *cf How Human Rights Can Inform the WIPO Development Agenda*, Policy Brief 4 (April 2010), published by 3D-> Trade, Human Rights, Equitable Economy (www.3dthree.org).

V

Regulating the 'Tragedy of the Commons' and 'Interdependent Public Goods' Requires Transnational Rule of Law

CHAPTER I EXPLAINED how 'the tragedy of the unregulated commons' (such as the ozone layer, the world climate and other 'global commons') requires multi-level regulation and allocation of property rights to avoid harmful overuse of common resources. But it also referred to the potential 'tragedy of the anti-commons' whenever too many uncoordinated property rights and 'sovereign rights' in the 193 UN member states may impede collective supply of international public goods. Hence, both democratic self-governance and collective supply of interdependent public goods require coherence among national and international legal regimes based on transnational rule of law for the benefit of citizens. For instance, international environmental law and its basic principles[1] – such as the polluter pays principle, the principle of preventive action, the precautionary principle, the customary law requirement of environmental impact assessments to prevent significant, transboundary environmental harm,[2] and the principle of 'common but differentiated responsibilities' – must remain consistent with 'sustainable development' as an 'integration principle' (as explicitly recognized in Article 11 TFEU) to regulate the interrelationships between economic, environmental and human rights law in mutually coherent ways (eg, the impact of anthropogenic climate change on people and biological diversity). Chapter I also discussed how collective supply of man-made, interdependent 'collective public goods' is confronted with 'collective action problems' such as 'jurisdiction gaps', 'governance gaps', 'participation gaps', 'incentive gaps' and 'rule of law gaps' in multilevel governance of interdependent 'public goods'. Chapters I and II concluded that more effective regulation of these 'collective action problems' requires integrating state-centred 'Westphalian conceptions' of IEL with 'global administrative law', multilevel economic law, constitutional and private law conceptions of IEL.

Chapters III and IV argued that the necessary 'civilization' and 'constitutionalization' of IEL require a multilevel, constitutional framework based on the liberal premise of modern economics and theories of justice (eg, of Rawls) that the welfare of states depends on their domestic rules and institutions: just as trade liberalization enables citizens and each country to increase domestic welfare and productivity, so is multilevel

[1] *cf* P Sands, *Principles of International Environmental Law*, 2nd edn (Cambridge: CUP, 2003).

[2] The customary law character of this environmental impact assessment requirement was emphasized by the ICJ in its judgment of 20 April 2010, *Case Concerning Pulp Mills on the River Uruguay (Argentina v Uruguay)*, paras 203–19.

regulation of other international public goods of no less constitutional significance for citizens than *national* regulation of 'market failures' impeding efficient supply of private goods and services demanded by consumers. The non-excludable and non-rival use of '*pure public goods*' excludes their supply in private markets and requires collective public regulation with due respect for the legitimate diversity ('margin of appreciation') of national conceptions of human rights, democratic self-governance and 'constitutional pluralism'.[3] Supply of '*impure public goods*' that are either rival but non-excludable ('common pool goods' like the ozone layer) or non-rival but excludable ('toll goods' like patented inventions whose industrial use for producing knowledge-related goods may require payment of royalties), tends to depend on 'private–public partnerships' and multilevel regulation. Chapters I to IV discussed why some public goods need to be regulated and supplied directly (eg, by means of national constitutions and legislation), whereas other public goods may be supplied indirectly, for instance by privatizing public services and subsidizing affordable prices for the poor in order to protect their human rights of access to food, water, essential medicines and work opportunities. The increasing 'governance failures' to protect international public goods (like consumer protection in financial markets) illustrate the inadequate integration of the diverse private and public, national and international regulatory conceptions. In view of the ubiquity of abuses of private and public power and the functional interdependencies among many (inter) national public goods, multilevel governance requires stronger multilevel constitutional restraints and multilevel protection of transnational rule of law based on an 'overlapping consensus' and 'common constitutional principles', which – in worldwide organizations – are likely to remain more limited than those defined in Article 2 TEU for the EU and its 27 member states as well as in the ECHR as common constitutional safeguards vis-à-vis multilevel governance throughout Europe (eg, in the EU, EEA, EFTA, Council of Europe, OSCE). Hence, as illustrated by the structural coherence of UN human rights law and regional human rights conventions and between WTO law and regional free trade agreements, 'multilevel human rights coherence' (Table 4), 'democratic constitutionalism' (Table 5) and 'multilevel constitutional pluralism' (Table 6) may legitimately differ depending on the level of regulation and the specific problem areas. For instance, even though democratic identification and participation of citizens will remain most effective at local and national levels, the often inadequate parliamentary control of multilevel economic regulation can be compensated by multilevel judicial protection of human rights and economic rights of producers, investors, traders, consumers and non-governmental organizations participating in the worldwide division of labour. Chapter IV explained why the 'derivative nature' of human rights and 'constitutional pluralism' entail a multiplicity of legitimately diverse ways of constitutional, legislative, administrative, judicial and international regulation and protection of human rights (eg, of access to water, health protection and essential medicines), economic freedoms (eg, of freedom of profession, freedom of competition and trade, freedom of commercial speech) and property rights (eg, in intellectual property and its industrial use). IEL must be designed, limited and interpreted in ways ensuring its consistency with legitimately diverse conceptions of human rights and constitutionalism.

[3] *cf* Y Shany, 'Toward a General Margin of Appreciation Doctrine in International Law' (2006) 17 *EJIL* 907 ff.

OVERVIEW OF CHAPTER V

Chapter V elaborates on why the legal fragmentation and 'pluralism' among the private and public, national and international legal sub-systems of IEL require a pluralist conception of transnational rule of law to promote rules-based self-government, legal predictability and decentralized enforcement of IEL for the benefit of citizens. The multilevel legal and judicial protection of access to justice, trading rights, intellectual property rights and investor rights in the context of bilateral, regional and worldwide trade and investment agreements, and the increasing recourse to legal and judicial 'balancing' of economic rights with other fundamental rights (eg, to human health protection and access to essential medicines), require promoting legal coherence, transnational rule of law and reduction of transaction costs in the global division of labour among autonomous citizens and companies all over the world. The more effective private rights and judicial remedies are protected across frontiers (eg, in terms of judicial enforceability of investor–state arbitral awards in domestic courts), the more effective transnational rule of law tends to operate for the benefit of citizens. Section 1 illustrates why the competing conceptions of 'rule of law' in the private and public, national and international sub-systems of multilevel 'network governance' need to be reconciled on the basis of common constitutional principles – such as judicial comity, the 'consistent interpretation principle', respect for legitimate 'constitutional pluralism' and 'proportionality balancing' of competing rights and obligations –to protect transnational rule of law and rights and obligations not only of governments, but also of citizens as the main actors and principal 'sources of value' in the international division of labour. Section 2 describes the 'judicialization' of international commercial and investment law as an example of how commercial and investment arbitration can promote legal security based on common constitutional principles in initially fragmented, 'incompletely theorized' and contested areas of IEL. Section 3 explains why 'network governance', 'compensatory constitutionalization' of multilevel governance and the emerging 'common law of adjudication' can limit abuses of power in IEL and promote transnational rule of law. Section 4 discusses the limits of multilevel judicial protection of transnational rule of law and the 'constitutional functions' of IEL for protecting human rights and constitutional rights of citizens.

1 THE DIVERSE CONCEPTIONS OF IEL RISK UNDERMINING TRANSNATIONAL 'RULE OF LAW'

Due to their diverse conceptions of international economic rules, diplomats, economists, public international lawyers, private lawyers, administrative and constitutional lawyers often disagree on how the complex interrelationships between private and public, national and international rules and policies should be theoretically coordinated. For instance:

- *Public international lawyers* tend to focus on 'international law among states' and on intergovernmental bargaining such as reciprocal commitments among governments for trade liberalization and intergovernmental dispute settlement proceedings. Westphalian conceptions of international law prioritize rights of states over rights of citizens and focus on coercive enforcement of rules by state authorities; for instance, judges in worldwide dispute settlement bodies (like the ICJ, ITLOS, WTO dispute settlement bodies) perceive themselves as 'agents' of the state parties to the dispute rather than as 'trustee courts' of a broader legal community including all citizens that may be adversely affected by intergovernmental dispute settlement proceedings. Cosmopolitan conceptions of IEL, by contrast, perceive sovereign states and governments as constitutionally limited agents of their citizens and emphasize the need for decentralized enforceability of rules by the citizens as democratic principals and self-determining agents.[4] Even though customary international law (as codified in the VCLT) requires interpreting treaties and settling international disputes 'in conformity with principles of justice' and the human rights obligations of states, the frequent international disagreement on how to interpret 'principles of justice' and human rights prompts WTO dispute settlement bodies and investor–state arbitral tribunals to avoid references to 'justice' and human rights.

- *Private lawyers* tend to focus on international transaction law and private commercial arbitration among private economic actors and on reducing conflicts among national legal systems, for example by allocating the jurisdiction to one single country for the settlement of commercial disputes, often without adequate regard to the constitutional limits of private party autonomy and to the public law dimensions of transnational dispute settlement proceedings (eg, in case of investor–state arbitration requiring judicial 'balancing' of private and public interests). The medieval law merchant (*lex mercatoria*) in Europe illustrates the long-standing traditions of commercial law and institutions relying on non-state enforcement and 'social punishment' of rule violations. As private arbitrators tend to perceive their mandates from the perspective of 'agents' and the 'contractual autonomy' of the disputing parties, they are often reluctant to take into account third party interests (eg, of civil society NGOs submitting amicus curiae briefs).[5] They often prefer mediation and ad hoc solutions of disputes over general arguments of justice and 'right answers' (Dworkin) that may be essential for decentralized compliance with, and self-enforcement of, rules.
- *Administrative lawyers* perceive many areas of IEL – such as the WTO agreements coordinating rules for customs administration, national government procurement procedures, national sanitary measures, technical standards or intellectual property regulation – as 'global administrative law'.[6] Yet, the systemic context of administrative law in constitutionally limited legal systems and the need for constitutional limitations of administrative powers in IEL are often neglected.[7]

[4] For a discussion of these competing conceptions of international law and of international courts see: J Waldron, 'Are Sovereigns Entitled to the Benefit of the International Rule of Law?' (2011) 22 *EJIL* 315–43; A Stone Sweet and F Grisel, 'Transnational Investment Arbitration: From Delegation to Constitutionalization?' in PM Dupuy, F Francioni and EU Petersmann (eds) (2009) ch 7.

[5] *cf* F Schwarz, 'Limits of Party Autonomy in International Commercial Arbitration' in C Knahr, C Koller, W Rechberger and A Reinisch (eds), *Investment and Commercial Arbitration – Similarities and Divergences* (Utrecht: Eleven Publishing, 2010) 73–96.

[6] *cf* RB Stewart and M Ratton Sanchez Badin, 'The WTO and Global Administrative Law' in C Joerges and EU Petersmann (eds) (2011) 457–94.

[7] G Van Harten and M Loughlin, 'Investment Treaty Arbitration as a Species of Global Administrative Law' (2006) 17 *EJIL* 121–50, admit that 'the defining features of global administrative law are rather fluid' (at 121 f). As there is no centralized system of administration in international law, international regimes make use of diverse legal approaches limiting the administrative functions of states to different degrees. On the impact of administrative law arguments in investor–state arbitration see: H Perez Loose, 'Administrative Law and International Law: The Encounter of an Odd Couple' in PHF Bekker, R Dolzer and M Waibel (eds) (2010) 380–405.

- *Constitutional lawyers* and regional economic and human rights courts[8] increasingly acknowledge the constitutional dimensions of IEL, such as the need for preventing and settling the inevitable conflicts of interests and disputes among citizens and governments by means of 'judicial balancing' of economic rights with non-economic rights and public interests on the basis of common constitutional principles (like legality, non-discrimination, necessity and proportionality of government restrictions of individual rights). Yet, constitutional lawyers often focus one-sidedly on 'state interests' without adequate regard to the 'constitutional functions' of IEL for the collective supply of international public goods, for instance by limiting and compensating national 'governance failures' and protecting cosmopolitan rights in the global division of labour. The value premises of democratic constitutionalism – such as 'normative individualism' and respect for legitimately diverse value preferences that need to be reconciled on the basis of common constitutional principles of justice and other constitutional 'checks and balances' – differ fundamentally from power-oriented conceptions of 'international law among states'. Especially in areas like human rights and IEL which depend on decentralized coordination among citizens and decentralized enforcement of rules by individual agents, shared social systems of 'cosmopolitan public reason' recognizing citizens as legal subjects of international law are of constitutional importance for maintaining transnational rule of law.[9] The UN 'Guiding Principles for Business and Human Rights', as approved in June 2011,[10], may contribute not only to the clarification of legal human rights obligations, but also to 'public reason' and respect for human rights in transnational business practices and related government practices.

The diverse conceptions of the interrelationships between overlapping national and international legal systems often entail diverse conceptions of 'rule of law'. For instance:

- A *formal understanding of rule of law* is often promoted by commercial lawyers and utilitarian, free-market economists. For example, according to Nobel-Prize economist FA Hayek, rule of law 'means that government in all its actions is bound by rules fixed and announced beforehand – rules which make it possible to foresee with fair certainty how the authority will use its coercive powers in given circumstances, and to plan one's individual affair on the basis of this knowledge'.[11] Yet, *substantive conceptions of rule of law* have emphasized since antiquity that rule of law differs from 'rule by law' and 'rule by men' in terms of additional legal safeguards such as judicial protection of principles of justice (eg, legal equality, due process of law) and judicial enforcement of law vis-à-vis all private persons as well as public authorities.[12]

[8] *cf* the comparative law contributions by B de Witte, P de Sena, U Kriebaum and P Nikken on 'Judicial Balancing of Economic Law and Human Rights Law in Regional Courts' in Dupuy, Francioni and Petersmann (eds) (2009) chs 9–12.

[9] On Rawls' theory that constitutional laws ought to be supported by public reasons that all citizens can share in spite of their disagreement on any comprehensive doctrine of truth and a good life, and the need for basing law on a system of shared commitments by citizens in order to predict how others will behave and support reasonable governance principles, see recently: GK Hadfield and S Macedo, 'Rational Reasonableness: Toward a Positive Theory of Public Reason' *University of Southern California Law and Economics Working Paper* 127 (2011).

[10] See ch IV, section 2.

[11] FA Hayek, *The Road to Serfdom* (London: IEA, 1944) 54.

[12] In his later works such as *The Constitution of Liberty* (1960), Hayek emphasized the need for general legislation and judicial protection as defining elements of rule of law: it is 'because the lawgiver does not know

- *Human rights approaches to rule of law*, as reflected in the call of the UDHR for 'equal protection of the law' (Article 7) and of human rights 'by the rule of law' (Preamble UDHR), emphasize that the making, administration and implementation of law derive their 'input legitimacy' and 'output legitimacy' from respecting, protecting and fulfilling civil, political, economic, social and cultural human rights as 'the foundation of freedom, justice and peace in the world' (Preamble UDHR); 'everyone is entitled to a social and international order in which the rights and freedoms set forth in this Declaration can be fully realized' (Article 28); 'in the exercise of his rights and freedoms, everyone shall be subject only to such limitations as are determined by law solely for the purpose of securing due recognition and respect for the rights and freedoms of others and of meeting the just requirements of morality, public order and the general welfare in a democratic society' (Article 29).
- *Democratic approaches to rule of law* share the basic premise of human rights approaches that the only legitimate interest a government is entitled to pursue is that of its citizens and other subjects. Yet, democratic approaches often focus less on human rights and constitutional rights than on parliamentary, popular and 'communitarian discourses' (eg, in terms of 'deliberative democracy'), majority voting and 'representative governance' in defining 'national interests' in domestic legislation, administrative, judicial and foreign policy measures. Proponents of 'deliberative democracy' may perceive the individual self-interest and the common 'public interest' as two mutually consistent sides of the same coin. Proponents of majoritarian democracy admit that the majority interests may run counter to the minority interests. Rights-based conceptions of liberal democracy often emphasize the 'constitutional functions' of courts of justice as ultimate guardians of constitutional rights vis-à-vis abuses by democratic majority decisions.
- *'Constitutional justice' approaches to rule of law* emphasize the constitutional function of supreme courts as 'exemplars of public reason'[13] and instruments of reasoned, social ordering[14] by means of independent, impartial interpretation, application, clarification and enforcement of legal principles, rules, rights and obligations in fair procedures protecting 'procedural' as well as 'substantive justice' (eg, in the presentation of proof, reasoned arguments by all affected parties and reasoned, equitable and peaceful settlement of disputes). Just as common law and civil law systems have evolved by means of judicial clarification and enforcement of principles and rules, so does international rule of law depend on judicial clarification of international rules in

the particular cases to which his rules will apply, and it is because the judge who applies them has no choice in drawing the conclusions that follow from the existing body of rules and the particular facts of the case, that it can be said that laws and not men rule' (at 153). On 'rule of men' as domination, and 'rule of law' as non-domination, see: P Pettit, *Republicanism: A Theory of Freedom and Government* (Oxford: OUP, 1997). L Fuller (1969), identifies (in ch 2) eight moral requirements as being constitutive of 'rule of law' (*ie*, generality, clarity, promulgation, stability, consistency of rules and social behaviour, non-retroactivity and non-contradictory nature of rules which must also not require the impossible). J Raz (1979) 214 ff, emphasizes the need for additional requirements (such as judicial independence, judicial review, fair hearings).

[13] According to Rawls (1993) 231 ff, 'in a constitutional regime with judicial review, public reason is the reason of its supreme court'; it is of constitutional importance for the 'overlapping, constitutional consensus' necessary for a stable and just society among free, equal and rational citizens who tend to be deeply divided by conflicting moral, religious and philosophical doctrines. The content of the Rawlsian 'public reason' comprises substantive principles of justice (such as fundamental rights) as well as procedural principles of justice (such as due process of law, independence and impartiality of courts, democratic governance).

[14] For common law conceptions of rule of law and 'adjudication as a form of social ordering' see: LL Fuller, 'The Forms and Limits of Adjudication' (1978) 92 *Harvard Law Review* 353–409.

incomplete agreements as well as on judicial cooperation among courts in different jurisdictions to coordinate fragmented national and international legal regimes.[15] The Kantian constitutional ideal of protecting equal liberties by means of constitutional restraints on abuses of public and private power in all human interactions inside countries, among countries as well as in transnational relations of citizens vis-à-vis foreign states requires judicial protection of international and transnational rule of law no less than rule of law inside constitutional democracies.[16]

Which conception of IEL is most likely to promote transnational rule of law?

Chapter II distinguished five conceptions of IEL, ie: (1) IEL as public international law regulating the international economy; (2) IEL as 'global administrative law'; (3) IEL as multilevel public economic regulation; (4) IEL as private and public, national and international regulation of the transnational economy within multilevel constitutional constraints; and (5) international private law conceptions of IEL like Joerges' 'three-dimensional conflicts law'. The different perspectives of each conception may favour different dispute settlement methods. For example, the United States accepted membership in the IMF, the World Bank and in GATT 1947 only subject to US veto powers and adopted many global governance decisions unilaterally (eg, on the termination of the gold–dollar convertibility in August 1971); subsequent decisions by the Bretton Woods institutions (eg, on 'floating exchange rates', GATT 'waivers' legalizing certain cotton, textiles and agricultural trade restrictions) were often responses to unilateral decisions taken by the US government or US Congress. Conceptions of 'hegemonic international law' and power politics by rent-seeking interest groups also explain the insistence by many governments (eg, in the US legislation implementing the results of GATT Rounds of multilateral trade negotiations) that worldwide economic treaties (like GATT and WTO law) are not enforceable in domestic courts. Even though WTO guarantees – similar to UN human rights conventions – could be interpreted as protecting equal freedoms and non-discriminatory treatment of citizens in transnational relations, governments and rent-seeking interest groups pursue self-interests in avoiding legal and judicial accountability for their redistribution of income among domestic groups by means of discriminatory protectionism.

Also 'global administrative law' approaches tend to be concerned more about administrative 'rule by law' and intergovernmental regulation of 'public interests' than about constitutional limitations of national and international governance powers to protect human rights and 'rule of law'. Constitutional approaches to IEL emphasize that the collective supply of global public goods – like international legal security and a mutually

[15] On the dependence of international rule of law on multilevel judicial protection of 'constitutional justice' see: EU Petersmann, 'Judging Judges: From "Principal-Agent Theory" to "Constitutional Justice" in Multilevel Judicial Governance of Economic Cooperation among Citizens' (2008) 11 *JIEL* 827–84; R Higgins, *Themes and Theories: Essays, Speeches and Writings in International Law* (Oxford: OUP, 2009) 19–43. As explained in ch 2, section 2, the term 'constitutionalism' is used here for denoting a political and legal method for constituting governance authorities and limiting their delegated powers for the protection of constitutional rights of citizens and human rights.

[16] On the Kantian explanation of multilevel constitutionalism as a precondition for rule of law, see ch 3, sections 1 and 2. For a modern explanation of why foreign policy discretion and 'the government's own freedom of action is not an intrinsic value as it is for individual citizens' see: J Waldron, 'Are Sovereigns Entitled to the Benefit of the International Rule of Law?' *New York University School of Law Working Paper* No 1/2009.

beneficial, efficient world economy promoting general consumer welfare – is confronted with constitutional problems similar to those in national and regional market economies. My 1991 book on *Constitutional Functions and Constitutional Problems of International Economic Law* argued that, from the perspective of reasonable citizens interested in constitutional protection of their individual rights across national frontiers:

- International legal guarantees of private freedoms, property rights, non-discrimination, rule of law and of sovereign rights to protect non-economic public interests – as in WTO law, free trade area agreements as well as in human rights law – should be perceived as parts of the 'empowering constitution' necessary for protecting economic and legal self-government and non-discriminatory conditions of competition in mutually beneficial cooperation among citizens.
- Similarly, international agreements constituting international organizations providing for collective rulemaking and compulsory jurisdiction for the peaceful settlement of international disputes could be conceived as functional parts of a multilevel 'limiting constitution' restraining adverse 'externalities' of national 'governance failures' and other 'collective action problems'.
- Hence, inside economic communities committed to rule of law, domestic courts of justice should interpret domestic laws in conformity with the complementary 'constitutional functions' of IEL to protect equal freedoms of domestic citizens and non-discriminatory conditions of competition in economic cooperation across frontiers. The 'consistent interpretation principle' recognized in national and international legal systems could serve 'constitutional functions' for protecting transnational rule of law.

Diverse conceptions of 'governance failures' and 'constitutional failures' may entail diverse conceptions of transnational rule of law

Chapters III and IV explained why 'constitutional democracies', 'majoritarian democracies' and authoritarian political regimes tend to perceive 'governance failures', 'constitutional failures' and the needed remedies from very different value perspectives. For instance, power-oriented, economic and 'global administrative law' approaches to IEL tend to reject cosmopolitan interpretations of international rules and compulsory jurisdiction of international courts on the ground that the reality of international power politics justifies foreign policy discretion (eg, for 'efficient breaches' of international law) and political 'cost-benefit analyses' regarding whether, and how, international obligations should be complied with by governments. Such conceptions are often linked to communitarian conceptions of democracy focusing on parliamentary discretion to regulate the economy without constitutional protection of economic freedoms and social rights.[17] Constitutional, rights-based conceptions of democracy and of IEL argue, by contrast, that prioritizing government discretion over legal and judicial protection of equal liberties and other citizen rights in international trade and financial relations sets incentives for 'regulatory capture' and other 'constitutional failures' in IEL. Such diverse

[17] Examples include: D Rodnik, *The Globalization Paradox: Democracy and the Future of the World Economy* (New York: Norton, 2011); C Barfield, *Free Trade, Democracy and Sovereignty* (Washington: AEI Press, 2001).

conceptions of 'governance failures' are closely linked to divergent conceptions of rule of law. For example:

- *Market failures* (like abuses of market power reducing consumer welfare, environmental pollution, social injustice) are not effectively regulated and controlled in many areas of IEL, as illustrated by the lack of WTO competition rules prohibiting international restrictive business practices (like export cartels) and by the obvious inadequacy of consumer protection in international financial regulation.
- *Governance failures* (like welfare-reducing trade protectionism, under-regulation of international banking services) are not effectively restrained in many areas of IEL. The WTO system, for instance, continues to treat citizens as mere objects of authoritarian governments without offering producers, investors, traders and consumers effective legal and judicial remedies to protect consumer welfare and rule of law against abuses of discretionary trade policy powers. Even though human rights limit 'state sovereignty', 'popular sovereignty' protects a broad margin of appreciation of how citizens, people and democratic governments protect and 'balance' civil, political, economic and social human rights in IEL.
- Discretionary *'member-driven governance'* in international organizations for the collective supply of global public goods focuses one-sidedly on rights of states, power politics and rent-seeking interest groups rather than on rights of citizens and their common self-interests, for instance in international rule of law and a clean environment. As long as trade governance in the WTO is not democratically controlled by most parliaments and continues to be dominated by 'rent-seeking' pressures from domestic interest groups, 'intergovernmental rule of law' risks undermining consumer welfare, equal freedoms and other rights of citizens.
- Due to the perceived lack of legitimacy of WTO governance dominated by political self-interests of governments in limiting their legal and judicial accountability vis-à-vis domestic citizens for discriminatory trade protectionism, also legally binding WTO dispute settlement rulings are widely ignored by domestic courts.

Legal and 'constitutional pluralism' entails competing conceptions of 'rule of law' in IEL

The reality of legal and 'constitutional pluralism' in multilevel regulation of the worldwide division of labour entails that both national courts inside national constitutional systems as well as international courts in functionally limited, international legal and judicial systems often make competing claims to 'legality' and authoritative interpretations of overlapping multilevel regulation and governance systems. In Europe, conflicts among claims to 'national constitutional supremacy' and claims to 'European constitutional supremacy' have been overcome by pluralistic and dialectic conceptions of the relations between national and European governance based on respect for 'constitutional heterarchy'[18] and for common 'constitutional principles' as they are defined in Titles I and II of the TEU. In the words of Miguel Poiares Maduro, 'any legal order (national or European) must respect the identity of the other legal orders; its identity must not be affirmed in a manner that either challenges the identity of the other legal orders or the

[18] *cf* D Halberstam, 'Constitutional Heterarchy: The Centrality of Conflict in the European Union and the United States' in JL Dunoff and JP Trachtman (eds) (2009) 326–55.

pluralistic conception of the European conception itself'.[19] In their common legal and judicial search for the 'best fit' of national and European legal systems, European courts cooperate ever more closely in clarifying their commitments to common constitutional principles (such as protection of fundamental rights, limited delegation of powers, duties of cooperation, rule of law, respect for 'national identities' as postulated in Article 4 TEU) and engage in transparent 'proportionality balancing' of competing rights and obligations in their multilevel judicial protection of fundamental rights of citizens across the EU and the EEA.

Can the European experience with multilevel judicial protection of transnational rule of law serve as a model for reforms of IEL? The following section 2 on the increasing 'judicialization' of international investment law reveals increasing influences of European jurisprudence. However, the limited number of only one third of UN member states accepting the compulsory jurisdiction of the ICJ pursuant to Article 36 paragraph 2 of the ICJ Statute, the American and French withdrawals of their respective US[20] and French acceptances[21] of this compulsory ICJ jurisdiction and the creation of increasingly specialized international dispute settlement bodies in fields like human rights law, trade law, investment law, intellectual property law, environmental regulation, in the law of the sea as well as in international criminal law, illustrate that the UN Charter ideal of the ICJ as the 'principal judicial organ of the United Nations' (Article 92) has not prevented many fields of international law from remaining dominated by power politics. Many treaty provisions for the optional jurisdiction of the ICJ (eg, under WIPO Conventions and the UN Convention on the Law of the Sea) have never been used. The few cases where international trade and investment disputes have been submitted to the ICJ are widely perceived as examples for the disadvantages of politicized, costly and lengthy disputes among states granting 'diplomatic protection' to their nationals after prior exhaustion of local remedies which, as in the *ELSI* case,[22] might require almost 20 years of litigation in domestic courts.

The very small number – only three – of ECJ judgments in disputes among EC member states since 1953 illustrates that most international trade and investment disputes involve private parties and can be adjudicated most appropriately without transforming private complaints into intergovernmental disputes among states.[23] Also most intergovernmental WTO disputes are triggered by private complaints and could be avoided by enabling private complainants to settle their disputes (eg, about alleged trade discrimination, customs duties, trade-related intellectual property rights) in domestic courts – provided WTO Members (notably the EU and the United States) would not prevent domestic courts from applying WTO law.[24] In the *Diallo* case, the ICJ noted in its judgment on admissibility that the direct access of foreign investors to investor–state arbitration under BITs entailed that most investment disputes were submitted to arbitral tribunals rather

[19] M Poiares Maduro, 'Contrapunctual Law: Europe's Constitutional Pluralism in Action' in N Walker (ed) (2003) 501.

[20] [1984] ICJ Rep 169.

[21] [1974] ICJ Rep 253.

[22] *Case concerning Elettronica Sicula spA (ELSI), United States v Italy*, Judgment [1989] ICJ Rep 15.

[23] On infringement proceedings in the ECJ see: A Arnull, *The EU and its Court of Justice*, 2nd edn (Oxford: OUP, 2006) ch 2.

[24] *cf* EU Petersmann, 'Preventing and Settling Transatlantic Economic Disputes: Legal and Policy Recommendations from a Citizen Perspective' in EU Petersmann and M Pollack (eds) (2003) 3–64, 577–94.

than to the ICJ and other international courts.[25] Yet, proposals for decentralizing and depoliticizing intergovernmental disputes over trade practices vis-à-vis private parties by means of strengthening the *domestic dimensions* of the WTO legal and dispute settlement system – and the underlying conception of empowering citizens and domestic courts to protect 'rule of international law' for the benefit of citizens – continue being opposed by diplomats interested in limiting their legal and judicial accountability, for instance if they use 'hegemonic international law' for the benefit of powerful interest groups at home (eg, cotton, textiles, agricultural and industrial producers dominating trade policymaking in GATT 1947) in exchange for political support. Lawyers perceiving international law as a 'law for states'[26] applaud the diplomatic focus on power-oriented approaches to promoting *national interests* (as defined by government elites and domestic interest groups),[27] for example in view of the fact that WTO law does not explicitly commit governments to promotion of consumer welfare and to individual rights and judicial remedies protecting citizens against non-compliance with WTO law.

The need for transcending and adjusting 'internal legal order approaches' (MacCormick) by acknowledging the globalization of law and the need for cosmopolitan rights

All modern constitutions and most worldwide agreements acknowledge the need to coordinate and regulate the relationships between national and international legal systems in view of their increasing interactions, overlaps and competing claims to legal authority. Hence, 'the globalization of the law, which has been described as creating a form of legal and constitutional pluralism, imposes the recognition and adjustment of each legal order to the plurality of equally legitimate claims of authority made by other legal orders'.[28] Respect for human rights and for legitimate constitutional diversity may require not only respecting the 'internal point of view' internal to legitimately diverse legal systems;[29] the 'permanent fact of reasonable pluralism' (Rawls) may also call for respecting diverse conceptions of 'rule of law' due to the absence of a shared political conception of justice formulated in public reasons. Yet, in 'transnational legal disputes', national and international 'courts of justice' should seek to protect transnational rule of law for the benefit of citizens engaging in mutually beneficial, international cooperation in contexts of interacting and competing legal orders. As proposed by Maduro:

> Such claims of jurisdiction over transnational situations must be accompanied by a commitment to take into account the potential effects of the decision of a particular legal order in other legal

[25] *Diallo* case (*Guinea v Democratic Republic of Congo*) Judgment, 24 May 2007 [2007] ICJ Rep.

[26] *cf* J Goldsmith and D Levinson, 'Law for States: International Law, Constitutional Law, Public Law' (2009) 122 *Harvard Law Review* 1791–868.

[27] For a criticism of such power-oriented conceptions of the WTO dispute settlement system see: EU Petersmann, 'Why Rational Choice Theory Requires a Multilevel Constitutional Approach to International Economic Law – The Case for Reforming the WTO's Enforcement Mechanism' (2008) *1 Illinois Law Review* 359–82.

[28] MP Maduro, 'Legal Travels and the Risk of a Legal Jet-lag: The Judicial and Constitutional Challenges of Legal Globalization in M Monti *et al* (eds), *Economic Law and Justice in Times of Globalization. Festschrift für Carl Baudenbacher* (Baden-Baden: Nomos, 2007) 175–90, 177.

[29] *cf* N MacCormick, *Questioning Sovereignty* (Oxford: OUP, 1999) who distinguishes between the 'internal point of view' of legal systems and their frequent acknowledgement of other, overlapping legal systems without necessarily requiring that one be legally subordinate or hierarchically inferior.

orders. In reality, the global law arising from the regulation of transnational situations ends up being a product of the interaction between different national and international legal orders. In this context, any judicial body (national or international) must reason and justify its decisions in the context of the global legal order in which they are impacting. . . . Such decisions must be grounded in a doctrine that could be applied by any other court in a similar situation, including, in this context, the court of a different legal order.[30]

The latter claim – ie, that courts of justice should justify their settlement of transnational legal disputes in terms of 'universalizable principles' of justice – can be justified most convincingly by the judicial functions of administering justice as well as by the common human rights obligations of all UN member states limiting the legitimate scope for 'constitutional pluralism'.[31] Political governance institutions may assert broader discretionary decision-making powers in view of the often weak constitutional restraints of foreign policy powers under national constitutions. Yet, as discussed in chapters I to IV, if individuals are acknowledged as 'primary subjects' of IEL and courts of justice as the most principled 'constitutional guardians' of individual rights against abuses of power, human rights require treating governments as constitutionally limited agents and trustees of the people; 'it is inappropriate to think that sovereign states are entitled to the same Rule-of-law protections at the international level as individuals are entitled at the municipal level'.[32] Judicial settlements of transnational economic disputes case-by-case and transnational 'judicial dialogues' offer more flexible instruments for adjusting fragmented legal systems than 'constitutional claims' of legal hierarchies and of general prioritization of certain values. Yet, judicial clarification and dispute settlement remain politically contestable by other constitutionally legitimate modes of clarifying, developing and changing 'public reason' through public deliberation, rulemaking and rule application.

Chapters I to IV argued that the diverse conceptions of IEL can be reconciled and integrated most convincingly through multilevel 'consistent interpretations' focusing – as in the diverse forms of economic integration in Europe – on the common constitutional principles underlying national and international rulemaking and multilevel judicial protection of transnational rule of law by 'courts of justice'. Constitutional democracies risk being undermined by intergovernmental regulation unless they promote 'constitutionalization' of intergovernmental power politics through international and judicial protection of 'rule of law', human rights and other 'cosmopolitan rights'. Intergovernmental 'public international law conceptions' of IEL must remain consistent with the 'human rights imperative' of treating citizens as legal subjects and 'democratic masters' of international law and economic cooperation. In international economic relations, transnational rule of law can be maintained most effectively by granting legal and judicial remedies to private participants in the global division of labour with self-interests in decentralized enforcement of

[30] Maduro (n 28) 177 who explains the rationale behind this 'principle of universalizability' by the need for judicial dialogue among legitimately different jurisdictions so as to prevent courts from undermining international legal coherence by 'deciding transnational legal cases in a purely domestic manner'. In addition to respect for constitutional pluralism, coherence and consistency of legal interpretations, and universalizability of judicial reasoning, Maduro further asserts that 'each legal order and its respective institutions (including courts) must be fully aware of the institutional choices involved in any request for their intervention with regard to transnational situations' (at 178), which may justify judicial deference to other jurisdictions or to other, comparatively more appropriate institutions.

[31] *cf* EU Petersmann, 'Do Judges meet their Constitutional Obligation to Settle Disputes in Conformity with "Principles of Justice and International Law"?' (2007) 2 *European Journal of Legal Studies*.

[32] *cf* Waldron (n 4) 315–43.

IEL based on a shared 'public reason'. Human rights law and rights-based, liberal economic integration law offer complementary justifications for a stable, cosmopolitan system of IEL and transnational rule of law for the benefit of citizens participating in the global division of labour.

Obstacles to integrating 'rule of law' in multilevel judicial governance

In Resolution 62/70 of 8 January 2008, the UN General Assembly distinguished the rule of law at the international level and the rule of law at national levels in view of the differences between the primarily 'horizontal structures' of the 'international law among states' and the primarily 'vertical structures' of national legal systems constituting and limiting governance powers vis-à-vis citizens.[33] Yet, as the UN Charter and modern international law require all UN member states to respect, protect and promote human rights also in transnational cooperation among citizens, including rights 'to a social and international order in which the rights and freedoms set forth in this Declaration can be fully realized' (Article 28 UDHR 1948), national and international governments and courts should cooperate in protecting 'international rule of law' for the benefit of citizens in their transnational division of labour. In mutually beneficial transnational economic cooperation among citizens no less than inside democracies, the primary purpose of rule of law should be to protect the human, constitutional and other rights of citizens against abuses of power rather than to protect rights of rulers and welfare-reducing abuses of power vis-à-vis citizens.[34]

Mutually consistent rulemaking and multilevel, judicial protection of 'international rule of law' are likely to strengthen both national as well as international law following the 'plywood principle', as illustrated by the *Kadi* judgment of the ECJ of September 2008 (*cf* Table 18) and by its positive impact on improving legal remedies in decision-making procedures of the UN Security Council's Sanctions Committee. Domestic courts may rightly insist that compliance with international law must remain consistent with human rights and common constitutional principles; vice versa, WTO dispute settlement rulings and investor–state arbitral awards may insist that domestic governments and courts must protect transnational rule of law in conformity with their international legal obligations. From the point of view of citizens, the ever greater impact of multilevel regulation of transnational economic transactions requires 'integrated conceptions of rule of law' in international economic cooperation among producers, investors, traders and consumers. Such common conceptions of rule of law must be based on the common constitutional principles underlying national and international human rights and constitutional law. 'Rule of law'– as a constitutional restraint on 'rule by men' and their often selfish 'rule by law' (eg, in limiting the legal accountability of bank managers for the 'social costs' of bank insolvencies) – can help not only national governments in resisting domestic pressures for illegal, discriminatory border restrictions; it will likewise help international organizations in reducing 'collective action problems' in promoting 'international public goods'.

[33] *cf* A Nollkaemper, 'The Internationalized Rule of Law' (2009) 1 *Hague Journal on the Rule of Law* 74–78; EU Petersmann, 'Multilevel Judicial Governance of International Trade Requires a Common Conception of Rule of Law and Justice' (2007) 10 *JIEL* 529–52.

[34] *cf* Waldron (n 4).

Even inside the EU, the lack of judicial remedies of EU citizens and EU member states against arbitrary EU violations of its WTO obligations (*cf.* Table 19 and related text) illustrates the reluctance of EU institutions to submit to international rule of law and judicial accountability for illegal restrictions of trade to the detriment of EU citizens. Due to the worldwide adoption of national constitutions and international treaties, traditional conceptions of 'government by law and not by men' are increasingly limited by constitutional restraints and international legal obligations. In England, for instance, the traditional claim to 'parliamentary sovereignty' and to legal primacy of later legislation (*lex superior* rule) has become limited by judicial compliance with European law, including the ECHR as specified in the British Human Rights Act of 1998.[35] Chapter VIII discusses in detail how judicial review – by increasing numbers of national and international courts – of the 'proportionality' of legislative and administrative restrictions of individual rights in terms of the 'rationality' (suitability), 'necessity' and 'proportionality *stricto sensu*' of governmental restrictions continues to enhance individual remedies, 'public reason' and the constitutional functions of courts of justice.[36] The successive EU treaties have introduced ever more commitments to 'the principles of liberty, democracy and respect for human rights and fundamental freedoms and of the rule of law' (Preamble TEU): 'The Union is founded on the values of respect for human dignity, freedom, democracy, equality, the rule of law and respect for human rights' (Article 2 TEU), including 'strict observance and the development of international law' and 'the principles of the United Nations Charter' (Articles 3, 21 TEU).

Inside the common market, the ECJ has applied long since stricter standards of judicial review regarding *national* restrictions of common market freedoms compared with *EU* restrictions, especially if EU lawmakers exercised legal discretion or a margin of appreciation concerning complex economic facts. In the 'area of freedom, security and justice' as well as in the common foreign and security policy of the EU, the Lisbon Treaty has further strengthened the jurisdiction of the ECJ and its judicial review.[37] In the areas of WTO law and the UN Convention of the Law of the Sea, by contrast, the ECJ has voluntarily limited its jurisdiction and refuses to judicially review the legality and validity of EU measures in terms of the WTO and UNCLOS obligations in view of the intergovernmental dispute settlement procedures provided for in WTO law and in the Law of the Sea Convention.[38] Hence, even though EU law protects cosmopolitan conceptions of formal and substantive rule of law for the benefit of 500 million EU and EEA citizens in relations among the 30 EEA member states through constitutional restraints of a higher legal rank and multilevel judicial remedies, the scope of judicial review by European courts varies among different areas of European integration law. For instance, in view of the non-applicability of the preliminary rulings procedure of the ECJ to private arbitration, the EU Commission has argued for terminating BITs among EU member states and investor–state arbitration inside the EU – yet, unfortunately, without proposing direct

[35] *cf* FG Jacobs (2007); T Bingham, *The Rule of Law* (London: Allen Lane, 2010).

[36] On this use of 'proportionality analysis' in increasing numbers of international jurisdictions see: A Stone Sweet and J Matthews, 'Proportionality, Judicial Review and Global Constitutionalism' in G Bongiovanni, G Sartor and C Valentini (eds) (2009) 173–214.

[37] *cf* EO Wennerström, *The Rule of Law and the European Union* (Uppsala: Iustus Förlag, 2007); A Hinarejos, *Judicial Control in the EU. Reforming Jurisdiction in the Intergovernmental Pillars* (Oxford: OUP, 2009).

[38] *cf* chapter IV, section 1, and M Mendez, 'The Legal Effects of Community Agreements: Maximalist Treaty Enforcement and Judicial Avoidance Techniques' (2010) 21 *EJIL* 83–104.

access and judicial remedies of investors in EU courts.[39] The limited scope of rule of law and 'justiciability' of EU violations of international law even inside the EU illustrate that judicial protection of rule of law remains dependent on particular contexts and legal cultures.[40] Yet, 'political question doctrines' arguing for judicial self-restraint are less convincing in intergovernmental regulation of economic cooperation among citizens across frontiers: as multilevel regulation is not effectively controlled by most parliaments and national courts, they risk harming legitimate expectations of citizens that multilevel regulation will respect constitutional commitments to 'strict observance of international law' (Article 3 TEU).

The globalization and complexity of IEL require multilevel judicial protection of cosmopolitan rights and transnational rule of law

IEL differs from other fields of international relations in three important dimensions:

1. The number of private and public, (sub)national and international actors participating in the worldwide division of labour and in its legal regulation (eg, of more than half of world trade taking place inside and among some 80,000 TNCs with ten times as many subsidiaries) is much larger than in other areas of international relations.
2. IEL provides for more 'international rule-of-law institutions'[41] (such as international organizations, courts, quasi-judicial dispute settlement procedures, monetary, competition, consumer protection and environmental authorities) supervising and controlling the implementation of international rules and settling disputes arising out of their interpretation than other fields of international law.
3. In order to reduce transaction costs not only for TNCs, but for the millions of national firms and billions of investors, workers and consumers, IEL relies more on decentralized, market-driven information, coordination, steering and sanctioning mechanisms than other fields of international cooperation and regulation.

The increasing complexity and global interdependence of the world economy can be 'governed'[42] efficiently only to the extent that the billions of daily decisions on investments, production, trade, transaction costs and policy coordination remain predictable on the basis of internationally agreed rules and institutions. Economic globalization increases the need for transnational rule of law to 'contain and restrain power, to impose due process and fairness on decision-making and dispute resolution, to make wielders of power accountable for their actions, and to provide redress to those whose rights and expectations have been undermined'.[43] As most international economic transactions are agreed among private producers, investors, traders and consumers in different countries

[39] *cf* H Wehland, 'Intra-EU Investment Agreements and Arbitration: Is European Community Law an Obstacle?' (2009) *ICLQ* 297–320.

[40] *cf* L Pech, '*The Rule of Law as a Constitutional Principle of the EU*' NYU School of Law Jean Monnet Working Paper 04/2009.

[41] *cf* CPR Romano, 'A Taxonomy of International Rule of Law Institutions' Loyola Law School Los Angeles *Legal Studies Paper* No 2010-55.

[42] Governance can be defined in this broader context as 'the process through which the rule systems in place in any social setting are adapted to the needs and purposes of those who live under them'; *cf* A Stone Sweet, 'Judicialization and Construction of Governance' (1999) 32 *Comparative Political Studies* 147.

[43] L Boulle, *The Law of Globalization. An Introduction* (Alpen aan den Rijn: Kluwer, 2009) 397.

with diverse national legal systems, their efficient regulation depends on the legal coherence of private and public, national and international legal systems governing transnational economic relations. 'Top-down' analyses of IEL as a branch of public international law[44] are often based on authoritarian Westphalian conceptions of 'international law among sovereign states' and anachronistic beliefs that the reality of intergovernmental power politics requires national democracies to insist on foreign policy discretion, on separation of national from international law, and on scepticism vis-à-vis worldwide jurisdictions (like the ICJ) that include judges from non-democratic countries and risk enforcing democratically illegitimate conceptions of 'rule of international law';[45] they also often neglect private and public self-interests in circumventing international treaty rules (eg, in commodity and environmental agreements) that are perceived as neither legitimate nor efficient or effective. 'Bottom-up' conceptions of IEL as a citizen-driven, functional unity of private and public, national and international economic regulation[46] often neglect the need for constitutional limitations of multilevel governance powers, as illustrated by the fact that coherent multilateral rules often emerge only in response to systemic conflicts caused by incoherent national rules, bilateral agreements and conflicts of jurisdiction. The more the regulatory needs of the global division of labour continue to lead to ever more bilateral and multilateral economic treaties and related institutions coordinating government regulation of international movements of goods, services, persons, capital and related payments, the stronger becomes the need for protecting transnational rule of law for the benefit of citizens.

The 'globalization' of economic cooperation, communications and of their legal regulation entails an ever more integrated 'global society' where individuals all over the world risk being affected by events abroad, such as a nuclear accident at Chernobyl, a flu pandemic in Mexico, genocide in Africa, war in Afghanistan or a 'culture of irresponsibility' (US President Obama) in banking practices on Wall Street, New York. Just as UN member states have succeeded in supplying *national* public goods only in the context of national, federal or regional constitutional systems committed to protection of human rights, so does the collective supply of *international* public goods depend on complementary rules and institutions for the constitution of legitimate rulemaking, administrative and judicial governance committed to protection of human rights. Both constitutional theory and empirical evidence suggest that – without multilevel constitutional and judicial safeguards of transnational rules of law – the global public goods of a mutually beneficial world trading and financial system, monetary stability, global poverty reduction and environmental protection risk not being supported by citizens as legitimate and, without such support by 'public reason', cannot be effectively secured.

The cosmopolitan principles underlying the human rights obligations of all UN member states and their shared commitments to a liberal (ie, liberty-based) international

[44] Textbooks focusing on public international law include, for instance: I Seidl-Hohenveldern, *International Economic Law,* 2nd edn (The Hague: Kluwer Publishers, 1992); D Carreau, T Flory and P Juillard, *Droit International Economique,* 3rd edn (Paris: Dalloz, 1990); A Lowenfeld, *International Economic Law,* 2nd edn (Oxford: OUP, 2010); AH Qureshi and AR Ziegler (2007).

[45] For a discussion of this 'incompatibility hypothesis' see: EU Petersmann (1991) 288 ff; M Pomerance, *The United States and the World Court as a 'Supreme Court of the Nations': Dreams, Illusion and Disillusion* (Dordrecht: Kluwer, 1996).

[46] *cf* Petersmann (1991); J Jackson, B Davey and A Sykes, *Legal Problems of International Economic Relations,* 5th edn (St Paul: West Publishing, 2008); KM Meessen (ed), *Economic Law as an Economic Good. Its Rule Function and its Tool Function in the Competition of Systems* (The Hague: Kluwer, 2009); C Tietje (ed), *Internationales Wirtschaftsrecht* (Berlin: De Gruyter, 2009).

monetary, trading and investment regime offer the best basis for a reciprocal 'overlapping consensus' on transnational rule of law and 'stability for the right reasons' (Rawls) in international economic relations among citizens and governments which – in spite of their often diverse conceptions of justice – must accept each other as free and equal partners in fair cooperation. Promoting a shared conception of transnational rule of law in international economic cooperation requires transcending the often conflicting conceptions of justice and rule of law in national legal systems in favour of a shared conception of transnational rule of law which reasonable citizens can accept as promoting mutually beneficial, reciprocal cooperation among free and equal citizens. Inside constitutional democracies, 'those who grow up under just basic institutions acquire a sense of justice and a reasoned allegiance to those institutions sufficient to render them stable';[47] in IEL, by contrast, the treatment of citizens as mere objects of intergovernmental rules – often without rights-based legal and judicial remedies against violations of IEL and without adequate competition and social rules protecting consumer welfare and limiting market failures as well as government failures – undermines an overlapping consensus on the democratic legitimacy and distributional fairness of large parts of IEL. Also rent-seeking interest groups that can successfully lobby for income redistribution ('protection rents') by means of governmental economic restrictions or distortions in violation of IEL, may have little incentive to support transnational rule of law and other IEL rules protecting general consumer welfare. As long as governments prioritize rights of governments over rights of citizens in international economic regulation, citizens see little self-interest in supporting intergovernmental rulemaking, and a common 'cosmopolitan ethos' supporting transnational rule of law in international economic relations is unlikely to emerge. As in European economic law, judicial protection of equal cosmopolitan rights by politically independent 'courts of justice' offers the most realistic method of overcoming fragmented, national conceptions of rule of law in transnational economic cooperation. Yet, beyond European economic law, authoritarian Westphalian conceptions of 'international law among sovereign states' continue to be shaped by long-standing beliefs that the reality of intergovernmental power politics requires national democracies to insist on foreign policy discretion, on separation of national from international law and on scepticism vis-à-vis worldwide jurisdictions (like the ICJ) that include judges from non-democratic countries and risk enforcing democratically illegitimate conceptions of 'rule of international law'[48]

2 LESSONS FROM MULTILEVEL JUDICIAL PROTECTION OF TRANSNATIONAL RULE OF LAW IN COMMERCIAL AND INVESTMENT LAW?

The history of transnational commercial law (*lex mercatoria*) is older than the emergence of international trade and investment law based on international 'minimum standards' for the treatment and protection of aliens. Multilevel judicial protection and enforcement of transnational commercial law by national courts and privately agreed, commercial arbitration remains the most successful example of cosmopolitan economic

[47] Rawls (1993) 142.
[48] *Cf* n 45.

law.[49] Commercial arbitrators often disagree on whether international arbitration should be conceived as a component of the national legal order at the seat of arbitration (assimilating the arbitrator to a national judge); as being anchored in a plurality of national legal orders (eg, of all states recognizing and enforcing the arbitration award); or as a transnational arbitral legal order being part of transnational commercial and investment law.[50]

Yet, regardless of their legitimately diverse conceptions, arbitrators and courts increasingly interpret their powers to adjudicate, the applicable rules and procedures governing the arbitration process and the legal effects of arbitral awards with due respect not only for the legal autonomy of the parties and of the arbitrators, but also for the interrelationships of the national and international legal systems involved and for legitimately diverse legal conceptions of national and international public order (*ordre public*). Similar to the recognition and enforcement of commercial arbitration by national courts based on international treaties (such as BITs and the 1958 New York Convention on the Recognition and Enforcement of Foreign Arbitral Awards), the private law and public law dimensions of trade, investment and human rights law are likewise often inseparable. For example, human rights protect both private and public autonomy; most economic transactions among citizens take place from a *private law perspective* of traders, producers, investors and consumers and derive their value from respect for 'normative individualism'. In investor–state arbitration, the legal distinction between 'treaty breaches' (eg, of 'fair and equitable treatment' obligations) and 'contract breaches' (eg, of 'corporate social responsibilities' as recognized in the 2006 'Equator Principles' applied by the World Bank Group), or between 'public interests' (eg, as defined by human rights) and private 'legitimate expectations' of investors (eg, in case of privatization of essential water, health and electricity services), must go beyond dogmatic 'public–private law divides'. As in commercial arbitration, the constitutional limits of private party autonomy and of the freedom of investment arbitrators must be determined in conformity with human rights and public order.

Following the non-ratification of the 1948 Havana Charter for an International Trade Organization, international trade and investment law developed separately. Since the conclusion of the first bilateral investment treaty (BIT) between Germany and Pakistan in 1959, international investment law continues to dynamically evolve:

- The 'first generation' of BITs – until about 1969 – among developed capital-exporting and less-developed, capital-importing countries aimed at clarifying and strengthening the legal protection of foreign investments in host countries without providing for investor–state arbitration. Their protection standards included most-favoured-nation treatment, national treatment, 'fair and equitable treatment' (FET), 'full protection and security', access to justice and fair procedures, emergency clauses (eg, providing for 'necessity', armed conflicts and '*force majeur*') and transfer of funds[51] which reduced the legal insecurity resulting from the post-colonial disagreements on the customary international 'minimum standard' for the protection of foreign property and

[49] On the key principles of transnational commercial law and arbitration see, eg: A Redfern and M Hunter, *Law and Practice of International Commercial Arbitration*, 3rd edn (London: Sweet & Maxwell, 1999).

[50] On these competing conceptions see: E Gaillard, *Legal Theory of International Arbitration* (Leiden: Nijhoff Publishers, 2010); J Paulson, 'Arbitration in Three Dimensions' *LES Law, Society and Economy Working Paper* (London 2/2010).

[51] *cf* R Dolzer and C Schreuer (2008) 119–94.

the payment of 'full, prompt and effective compensation' in case of expropriation of foreign property.

- The 'second generation' of BITs (until about 2003) led to ever more 'common form' BITs based on uniform objectives, structures and standard clauses providing also for investor–state arbitration, notwithstanding important differences among 'European model BITs' (eg, based on a 1967 OECD Draft Convention) and 'American model BITs' (eg, the latter extending non-discrimination standards also to the 'pre-establishment' phase of foreign investments). The increasingly comprehensive legal and judicial protection of foreign investments was also due to increasing recognition that 'FDI-led industrialization' tended to promote more competitive industries than the widespread policies of 'infant industry protection' since the 1960s.[52]
- The 'new generation BITs', concluded from about 2003, acknowledge the need for 'rebalancing' the private and public interests involved in foreign investments, for instance by clarifying the state's rights and duties to regulate and protect public interests. A recent OECD study of 1600 BITs and of their references to environmental concerns noted, for example, an increasing harmonization of investment and environmental policies: the share of newly concluded BITs with explicit environmental references (such as general environmental references in Preambles, explicit recognition of the right to regulate in the environmental policy area, prohibitions of lowering environmental standards for the purpose of attracting investment) exceeded 50 per cent for the first time in 2005 and reached 89 per cent in 2008.[53] Arguably, the non-discrimination requirements in the now more than 2800 BITs and the – by December 2010 – already more than 330 registered ICSID arbitration awards and additional commercial, arbitral awards (eg, based on UNCITRAL rules and the arbitration procedures administered by the London, Paris and Stockholm Chambers of Commerce) promote an increasing 'multilateralization', 'judicialization' and 'constitutionalization' of international investment law by means of investment disputes and precedent-based jurisprudence with ever more coherent interpretations of investment protection standards.[54]
- There are also increasing numbers of regional economic integration agreements providing for liberalization and protection of foreign investments, like the EU and EEA treaties, the Energy Charter Treaty, NAFTA as well as regional economic integration agreements in Africa, Asia and Latin America. Hence, investment tribunals are increasingly willing to interpret bilaterally agreed investment rules in the wider

[52] *cf* T Ozawa, 'The Role of Multinationals in Sparking Industrialization : From "Infant Industry Protection" to "FDI-led Industrial Take-off"' *Columbia University FDI Perspectives* No 39 (New York: 2011).

[53] *cf* K Gordon and J Pohl, 'Environmental Concerns in International Investment Agreements: A Survey' *OECD Working Paper on International Investment* No 2011/1.

[54] In 2010, the number of known investor–state dispute settlement cases filed under international investment agreements increased to 390. But, apart from ICSID, most other arbitration forums do not maintain a public registry of claims. Hence, the total number of treaty-based arbitration cases may be higher. UNCTAD publishes regular overviews of 'Latest Developments in Investor–State Dispute Settlement' (eg, *IIA Issues Note No 1* of March 2011, available at: www.unctad.org/en/docs/ webdiaeia20113 en.pdf). On multilateralization and constitutionalization of investment law see: SW Schill (2009). On the limited number of mutually incoherent arbitration decisions (eg, in the Award of 14 March 2003 in *CME v Czech Republic* and the preceding Award of 3 September 2001 in *Lauder/CME v Czech Republic*, as well as in the two SGS cases: *SGS v Philippines*, Decision on Jurisdiction, 24 January 2004 and *SGS v Pakistan*, Decision on Jurisdiction, 6 August 2003) and the increasing number of ICSID annulment decisions see: SW Schill, 'System-Building in Investment Treaty Arbitration and Lawmaking' (2011) 12 *German Law Journal* 1083–110.

context of concordant treaty practices.[55] The ICJ, however, in the recent *Diallo* case, remained cautious of claims of changes in the customary law rules regarding foreign investments and their diplomatic protection.[56]

Judicial cooperation as a means of limiting abusive *forum* shopping and promoting legal coherence and transnational rule of law

The thousands of bilateral tax and investment agreements with often diverse rules and procedures set incentives for TNCs to engage in 'rules shopping' and 'forum shopping'. The diverse dispute settlement jurisdictions (like national or international courts, treaty-based arbitration or contract-based arbitration) entail risks of mutually inconsistent judgments and conflicting interpretations of IEL. For instance:

- In two investor–state arbitrations – *CME v Czech Republic* and *Lauder v Czech Republic*, the same investor (ie, a Dutch company controlled by the US businessman Ronald Lauder) challenged the same acts by the Czech Republic in two separate arbitration procedures conducted concurrently on the basis of diverse BIT provisions resulting in conflicting awards. In its award of 3 September 2001, an arbitral tribunal operating on the basis of a 1991 US–Czechoslovakia BIT at London found no injury, notwithstanding its finding that the Czech government had acted unfairly in some respect.[57] In a partial award of 13 September 2001, a different arbitral tribunal established under a 1991 BIT between the Netherlands and Czechoslovakia found at Stockholm that the Czech violations of several BIT provisions amounted to a de facto expropriation of CME. A challenge of this award by the Czech government before the competent Court of Appeal at Stockholm – inter alia, on the ground that the arbitrators had disregarded the principles of *lis pendens* and *res judicata* – was rejected. Shortly thereafter, the arbitral tribunal awarded about $250 million in damages to CME.[58]
- Other companies from all over the world have likewise restructured their investments through Dutch companies in order to take advantage of the legal protection and ICSID arbitration procedures offered by Dutch BITs. In *Phoenix Action Ltd v Czech*

[55] *cf Mondev v USA*, ICSID Case No ARB/99/2, Award, 11 October 2002, para 117: 'Investment treaties run between North and South, and East and West, and between States in these spheres *inter se*. On a remarkably widespread basis, States have repeatedly obliged themselves to accord foreign investment such treatment. In the Tribunal's view, such a body of concordant practice will necessarily have influenced the content of rules governing the treatment of foreign investment in current international law'.

[56] *Case Concerning AS Diallo (Republic of Guinea v Democratic Republic of the Congo)* Decision of 24 May 2007 on Preliminary Objections, para 90: 'The fact . . . that various international agreements . . . have established specific legal regimes governing investment protection, or that provisions in this regard are commonly included in contracts entered into directly between States and foreign investors, is not sufficient to show that there has been a change in the customary rules of diplomatic protection ; it could equally show the contrary. The arbitrations relied on by Guinea are also special cases, whether based on specific international agreements between two or more States – or based on agreements concluded directly between a company and the State allegedly responsible for the prejudice to it'.

[57] The award is reproduced in (2002) 14 *World Trade and Arbitration Materials* 35.

[58] The award is reproduced in (2003) 15 *World Trade and Arbitration Materials* 83. For a discussion of such conflicting jurisprudence see: G Sacerdoti, 'The Proliferation of BITs: Conflict of Treaties, Proceedings and Awards' in KP Sauvant (ed), *Appeals Mechanisms in International Investment Disputes* (New York: OUP, 2008) 127 ff. On conflicts avoidance techniques (like joining separately instituted arbitral proceedings into one) see also: Knahr, Koller, Rechberger and Reinisch (eds) (n 5).

Republic, the tribunal dealt with an intra-family transaction intended to shift an investment into a treaty jurisdiction in the middle of a dispute with the host state. The Tribunal stated that it had 'to prevent an abuse of the system of international investment protection under the ICSID Convention, in ensuring that only investments that are made in compliance with the international principle of good faith and do not attempt to misuse the system are protected. . . . It is the duty of this Tribunal not to protect such an abusive manipulation of the system of international investment protection under the ICSID Convention and the BITs'.[59] A subsequent ICSID award in *Mobil Corporation and others v Venezuela* likewise held that transfers and restructuring of companies into a BIT jurisdiction did not confer ICSID jurisdiction over pending disputes.[60]

- A series of recent decisions by ICSID annulment committees challenging the reasoning or findings of ICSID arbitral tribunals in the more than 40 investor–state arbitrations against Argentina's 'emergency measures' during the country's economic and financial crisis in 2001/2002 showed that – even if the limited jurisdiction of annulment proceedings did not permit annulling an arbitral award – the annulment committees nevertheless criticized incoherent arbitral findings and, thereby, influenced the reasoning in related arbitral proceedings.[61]

Table 22: Judicialization and multilateralization of investment disputes

- In contrast to the very limited number of international investment disputes among states in the ICJ, its predecessor (the PCIJ) and in the Permanent Court of Arbitration at The Hague, the hundreds of national and international arbitral awards, court decisions, ICSID annulment decisions and other judgments by specialized dispute settlement bodies (eg, the Iran–US Claims Tribunal) deciding investor–state disputes and enforcing arbitration awards continue to clarify and develop international investment law on the basis of a de facto system of judicial precedents and 'judicial dialogues'.
- The increasing convergence of objectives, structures and protection standards in BITs (eg, national treatment, most-favoured-nation treatment, fair and equitable treatment, full protection and security, protection against direct and indirect expropriation, umbrella clauses transforming contract claims into treaty claims, capital transfer and dispute settlement provisions) and their non-discriminatory application by governments and adjudicators promote a 'multilateralization' (Schill) of rather uniform investment law principles.
- Investor–state arbitrators, BITs and ICSID increasingly promote transparency of arbitration proceedings and of arbitral awards and regard to third-party interests affected by the arbitration (eg, by accepting amicus curiae briefs and engaging in 'proportionality balancing').

The increasing 'judicial dialogues' among investment tribunals and their 'cross-treaty interpretation referring either to BIT practice of wholly unrelated countries or to model treaties or, finally, using teleological interpretation methods'[62] are reflected in the following finding of the tribunal in *Saipem v Bangladesh* (2007):

[59] ICSID Case No ARB/06/5, Award, 15 April 2009, paras 113, 144.

[60] ICSID Case No ARB/07/27, Decision on Jurisdiction, 10 June 2010.

[61] *cf* CN Brower, M Ottolenghi and P Prows, 'The Saga of CMS: *Res Judicata*, Precedent and the Legitimacy of ICSID Arbitration' in C Binder, U Kriebaum, A Reinisch and S Wittich (eds), *International Investment Law for the 21st Century. Essays in Honour of C Schreuer* (Oxford: OUP, 2009) 843 ff.

[62] *cf* Schill (2009) 293–321.

> The Tribunal considers that it is not bound by previous decisions. At the same time, it is of the opinion that it must pay due consideration to earlier decisions of international tribunals (. . .) It has a duty to adopt solutions established in a series of consistent cases
>
> (. . .) It also believes that, subject to the specifics of a given treaty and of the circumstances of the actual case, it has a duty to seek to contribute to the harmonious development of international investment law and thereby meet the legitimate expectations of the community of States and investors towards certainty of the rule of law.[63]

Arbitrators are also increasingly aware of the 'public law dimensions' of commercial and investment arbitration and act no longer only as agents of the parties to the dispute, but also with due regard to the interests of the community of states participating in the network of BITs. The judicial discussion of precedents, judicial balancing of public and private interests and rights, the admission of amicus curiae briefs and the provision for appellate procedures in recent BITs (eg, by Canada and the United States) illustrate the increasing 'judicialization' of investment law based on a de facto system of judicial precedents.[64] Just as the ICJ, the WTO Appellate Body and European courts have interpreted commercial and environmental treaty language in 'dynamic, evolutionary' ways to take into account current realities[65], also investor–state arbitral tribunals increasingly engage in 'evolutionary interpretation' balancing public and private interests, economic, social and environmental dimensions of 'development' and civil, political, economic and social human rights and corresponding government obligations. International law provides for only few legal hierarchies ranking treaty rules (eg, in Article 103 UN Charter) and general international law rules (such as *jus cogens*). As 'new generation BITs' increasingly reaffirm states' rights to regulate and protect public interests, principle-oriented judicial reasoning and 'balancing' justifying judicial solutions of legal problems and of related disputes become increasingly important. In the *Iron Rhine Railway (Belgium v Netherland)* arbitration, the tribunal referred to UN resolutions on 'sustainable development' and the need for reconciling economic and environmental development:

> Today, both international and EC law require the integration of appropriate environmental measures in the design and implementation of economic development activities. . . . Environmental law and the law on development stand not as alternatives but as mutually reinforcing, integral concepts, which require that where development may cause significant harm to the environment there is a duty to prevent, or at least mitigate, such harm.[66]

The increasing references in investment adjudication to trade law, environmental law and human rights acknowledge the need for reconciling the diverse, specialized legal

[63] *Saipem v Bangladesh*, Decision on Jurisdiction, 21 March 2007, para 67.

[64] *cf* A Stone Sweet, 'Investor–State Arbitration: Proportionality's New Frontier' (2010) 4 *Law & Ethics of Human Rights* Art 4.

[65] *cf* the recent ICJ Judgment (13 July 2009), *Dispute Regarding Navigational and Related Rights (Costa Rica v Nicaragua)*, para 64: '(T)here are situations in which the parties' intent upon conclusion of the treaty was, or may be presumed to have been, to give the terms used – or some of them – a meaning or content capable of evolving, not one fixed once and for all, so as to make allowance for, among other things, developments in international law'. Hence, 'the notion of "commerce" does not have the same meaning today as it did in the mid-nineteenth century: it is the present meaning which must be accepted for purposes of applying the treaty' (paras 67, 70). In the judgment in *Gabcikovo-Nagymaros Project (Hungary v Slovakia)*, the ICJ referred to the development of new environmental norms and standards: 'Such new norms have to be taken into consideration, and such new standards given proper weight, not only when States contemplate new activities but also when continuing with activities begun in the past', as 'the Treaty is not static, and is open to adapt to the emerging norms of international law' ([1997] ICJ Rep 77, paras 140, 112).

[66] Permanent Court of Arbitration, Award, 24 May 2005, para 59.

regimes, dispute resolution mechanisms and related 'jurisdictional overlaps'.[67] As the jurisdiction of ICSID arbitration is limited 'to any legal dispute arising directly out of an investment' (Article 25 ICSID Convention), investment tribunals have declined competence to examine alleged human rights violations by detention and expulsion of foreign investors,[68] or counterclaims by the host state of alleged tax fraud by the investor.[69] Yet, according to Article 42 ICSID Convention, the

> (t)ribunal shall decide a dispute in accordance with such rules of law as may be agreed by the parties. In the absence of such agreement, the Tribunal shall apply the law of the Contracting State Party to the dispute (including its rules on the conflict of laws) and such rules of international law as may be applicable.

Hence, ICSID tribunals have emphasized that a limited jurisdiction must not imply a limited scope of the applicable law:

> [T]he Bilateral Investment Treaty is not a self-contained closed legal system limited to provide for substantive material rules of direct applicability, but is has to be envisaged within a wider judicial context in which rules from other sources are integrated through implied incorporation methods or by direct reference to certain supplementary rules, whether of international law character or of domestic law nature.[70]

Most ICSID tribunals no longer perceive themselves as exclusively 'private dispute resolution service providers' referring only to arguments presented by the parties to the dispute, but acknowledge the 'public law dimensions' of investor–state disputes; they increasingly make also their own independent, legal assessments following the maxim of *jus novit curia*, according to which a court should – of its own motion – apply any rule of law relevant to the facts and to the dispute resolution, even if the applicable rule of law has not been explicitly pleaded (except for 'exception clauses' whose invocation remains within the discretion of the parties to the dispute).[71] The more tribunals admit the inherent conflicts between public and private interests, 'public law' and 'private law' perspectives in investment law, and competing interests also among capital-importing countries (eg, negotiating BITs in order to attract scarce foreign capital and know-how), the more adjudicators acknowledge the need for 'balancing' all public and private interests involved rather than defining the relevant 'epistemic community' in narrow commercial terms.[72] Hence, investment tribunals may challenge both private claims focusing one-sidedly on cosmopolitan investor rights as well as government claims that tribunals must always defer to government discretion and to intergovernmental interpretations

[67] On the frequent jurisdictional overlaps of economic disputes see: L Guglya, 'The Interplay of International Dispute Resolution Mechanisms: the Softwood Lumber Controversy' (2011) 2 *Journal of International Dispute Settlement* 175–207.

[68] *cf Biloune and Marine Drive Complex Ltd v Ghana*, UNCITRAL Award, 27 October 1989, 95 ILR 184. See also *Biwater Gauff Ltd v Tanzania*, ICSID Case No ARB/05/22, Award, 24 July 2008, where the tribunal did not elaborate on the human rights arguments presented in an *amicus curiae* submission.

[69] *cf Amco v Indonesia*, Decision on Jurisdiction, 10 May 1988, 1 ICSID Reports 543.

[70] *Asian Agricultural Products Ltd v Sri Lanka*, ICSID Case No ARB/87/3, Final Award, 27 June 1990, paras 20–21.

[71] On these two types of 'dispute-oriented tribunals' and 'legislator-oriented tribunals' see: OK Fouchald, 'Legal Reasoning of ICSID Tribunals: An Empirical Analysis' (2008) 19 *EJIL* 301–64.

[72] *cf* PM Haas, 'Introduction: Epistemic Communities and International Policy Coordination' (1992) 46 *International Organizations* 1 ff, who defined an epistemic community as 'a network of professionals with recognized expertise and competence in a particular domain and an authoritative claim to policy-relevant knowledge within that domain or issue-area'.

limiting the jurisdiction of tribunals even retroactively in pending investment disputes.[73] In *EDF Services v Romania* (2009), the arbitral tribunal rightly emphasized:

> The idea that legitimate expectations, and therefore FET, imply the stability of the legal and business framework, may not be correct if stated in an overly-broad and unqualified formulation. The FET might then mean the virtual freezing of the legal regulation of economic activities, in contrast with the State's normal regulatory power and the evolutionary character of economic life. Except where specific promises or representations are made by the State to the investor the latter may not rely on a bilateral investment treaty as a kind of insurance policy against the risk of any changes in the host State's legal and economic framework. Such expectation would be neither legitimate nor reasonable.[74]

Similarly, in *Saluka v Czech Republic* (2006), the tribunal held:

> No investor may reasonably expect that the circumstances prevailing at the time the investment is made remain totally unchanged. In order to determine whether frustration of the foreign investor's expectations was justified and reasonable, the host State's legitimate right subsequently to regulate domestic matters in the public interest must be taken into consideration as well.[75]

Yet, as discussed in chapters VI and VIII, the judicial balancing between public and private rights and interests may legitimately differ depending on the relevant constitutional context and 'principles of justice', for instance depending on whether democracy is legally defined in terms of 'parliamentary freedom' to regulate (as in many Anglo-Saxon democracies) or in terms of equal constitutional rights of citizens limiting governmental 'rule by law' (as in the constitutional and economic laws of many European democracies). The judicial balancing between public and private rights and the allocation of procedural burdens of proof may also be influenced by diverse judicial conceptions of investment law, for instance as *restraining public regulatory powers* for the benefit of cosmopolitan rights rather than as *serving exclusively public interests*.[76]

Table 23: Judicial 'proportionality balancing' of jurisdictional claims, 'development objectives' and individual rights promoting 'constitutionalization' of investment law

- Principles used by tribunals for resolving jurisdictional overlaps include, inter alia, '*lis pendens*', '*res judicata*', comity, '*forum non conveniens*', 'fork in the road preclusion' (*electa una via*), joinder or de facto consolidation of different claims, agreed settlement of disputes, voluntary waiver of the right to initiate proceedings, agreed designation of a specific *forum*, or withdrawal of consent to a certain dispute settlement mechanism.
- Principles used by tribunals for deciding whether a regulatory activity (eg, by a government-owned corporation) can be 'attributed' to the state (in terms of state responsibility) include, inter alia: formal authority to exercise public power; functional exercise of government power; private action under governmental control and instructions; agreed *lex specialis* rules (eg, 'umbrella clauses') in BITs; state failure to grant 'full protection and security' and prevent 'denial of justice'.

[73] See the 'Interpretive Note' issued by the NAFTA Federal Trade Commission on 31 July 2001 in order to limit the judicial articulation of stricter standards by NAFTA investment tribunals: 'The concepts of "fair and equitable treatment" and "full protection and security" do not require treatment in addition to or beyond that which is required by the customary international law minimum standard of treatment of aliens'.

[74] *EDF (Services) Ltd v Romania*, ICSID Case No ARB/05/13, Arbitral Award, 8 October 2009, para 217.

[75] *Saluka v Czech Republic*, UNCITRAL Partial Award, 17 March 2006, para 305.

[76] On these competing conceptions of 'public–private divides' see: A Mills, 'Antinomies of Public and Private at the Foundations of International Investment Law and Arbitration' (2011) 14 *JIEL* 469 ff, 500–02.

- On 'balancing' of competing 'development dimensions' see *Lemire v Ukraine* (2010): 'Economic development is an objective which must benefit all, primarily national citizens and companies, and secondarily foreign investors. Thus, the object and purpose of the Treaty is not to protect foreign investments *per se*, but as an aid to the development of the domestic economy. And local development requires that the preferential treatment of foreigners be balanced against the legitimate right of Ukraine to pass legislation and adopt measures for the protection of what as a sovereign it perceives to be its public interest'.
- Principles for examining 'indirect expropriation' include, inter alia: 'non-discriminatory treatment' and 'regulation for a public purpose, which is enacted in accordance with due process' without impairing 'specific commitments' by the government to the foreign investor; 'fair and equitable treatment' (FET); 'interference with the use of property which has the effect of depriving the owner, in whole or in significant part, of the use or reasonably-to-be-expected economic benefit of property even if not necessarily to the obvious benefit of the host State'; 'substantial deprivation' or permanent 'disappearance' of the economic value of the investor's property; legitimate public interests; 'fair balance' or 'proportionality balancing' of public and private interests involved.
- Even though most BITs do not refer to human rights, human rights are increasingly being raised in investment treaty lawsuits by host states, investors, third parties or judges in order to justify governmental restrictions or 'affirmative action policies', investment treaty breaches, protection of investor rights or interpretations of investment rules (eg, on FET, 'protection and security' obligations, a 'state of necessity', 'public order', 'just compensation') in conformity with human rights of third parties (such as rights of access to water, essential medicines and information, rights of indigenous people). Due to their different procedures, jurisdictions and applicable laws, investment and human rights tribunals risk resolving 'overlapping disputes' (eg, over property expropriations, denial of justice, due process claims, claims for moral damages arising out of government interferences into rights of investors) in different ways.

From a citizen perspective, the protection of 'cosmopolitan rights' and increasing regard for human rights obligations of governments render international investment law more developed compared with the prevailing 'Westphalian conceptions' of WTO law, notwithstanding the lack of explicit investor responsibilities and of explicit references to human rights in most BITs which could require investment arbitrators to make explicit findings on human rights obligations. The one-sided focus of BITs on protection of vaguely formulated investor rights has prompted some countries (like Bolivia and Venezuela) to withdraw from the ICSID Convention or (like Australia) to refrain from providing for investor–state arbitration in future international economic agreements. Other countries have responded by providing for 'general exceptions' and appellate review procedures in their 'new generation BITs' (like Canada and the United States) or by encouraging ICSID annulment proceedings to admit – as stated by the 2010 ICSID ad hoc committee annulling the award in *Sempra v Argentina* – 'that a manifest error of law may, in an exceptional situation, be of such egregious nature as to amount to a manifest excess of powers'.[77] The fact that judicial decisions and scholarly opinions have become

[77] According to this ICSID ad hoc Committee, the arbitration award amounted to a manifest excess of powers owing to the erroneous interpretation of the treaty-based emergency exception in terms of the customary law defence of necessity (as codified in Art 25 of the ILC Articles on State Responsibility) rather than in terms of Art XI of the underlying BIT (*cf* 'Latest Developments in Investor–State Dispute Settlement', note 54). Previous ICSID jurisprudence had excluded the erroneous application of the proper law as a valid reason for annulment, *cf* I Marboe, 'ICSID Annulment Decisions: Three Generations Revisited' in Binder, Kriebaum, Reinisch and Wittich (eds) (n 61) 200–20; Sauvant (ed) (n 58).

the most frequently used interpretive arguments in ICSID jurisprudence illustrates the primary role of judges and jurisprudence in the 'recognition' and interpretation of the general principles and standards characteristic of modern investment law. Yet, the legitimacy of many investment tribunals continues to be undermined by the non-publication of many arbitral awards and the confidentiality and lack of transparency of many arbitral procedures. The ECJ's case law on the inconsistency of EU member states' BITs with EU law, and on the lack of standing of arbitral tribunals for requesting preliminary rulings from the ECJ, is influenced by this problematic role of arbitration in transnational lawmaking as well as by the fear that arbitrators may neglect or incorrectly apply EU law as relevant context for the settlement of commercial and investment disputes.[78]

Lessons from the transformation of international investment law?

The transformation of international investment law from a 'Westphalian' into a more 'cosmopolitan rule-of-law system' evolved since the 1960s in essentially five phases:

- Since the conclusion of the first BIT between Germany and Pakistan in 1959, the number of BITs has dynamically increased to now more than 2,800 agreements. Yet, the 'first generation BITs' did not yet provide for direct access of the foreign investor to independent international arbitration.
- The 1965 ICSID Convention, which entered into force already in 1966 (following 20 ratifications), offered a multilateral legal framework for institutionalized, transnational arbitration of investment disputes based on consent between the states and investors involved. The first ICSID disputes were based on investor-state contracts[79] or on national legislation providing for direct access of foreign investors to international arbitration.[80]
- Treaty-based investor-state arbitration was provided for only in the 'second generation BITs' concluded since about the 1970s. In view of its many advantages for private investors (eg in terms of direct access to independent international arbitration usually without prior exhaustion of local remedies, direct control of the procedures without dependence on 'diplomatic protection', availability of institutionalized ICSID procedures), most modern BITs provide for treaty-based investor-state arbitration.[81]
- In contrast to the less than 400 BITs concluded prior to 1989, the number of new BITs increased dramatically since the 1990s and approaches now 3,000 BITs or corresponding treaty provisions in free trade agreements (like NAFTA Chapter XI) and other sectorial agreements (like the Energy Charter Treaty which entered into force in 1998), including increasingly also BITs among LDCs.

[78] On the new EU investment policy competence under Art 207 TFEU, the relevant ECJ jurisprudence, the *amicus curiae* briefs submitted by the EU Commission in investor–state arbitration proceedings inside the EU, and the EU proposals for terminating intra-EU BITs among EU member states see: M Bungenberg, J Griebel and S Hindeland (eds), *International Investment Law and EU Law* (Heidelberg: Springer, 2011); N Lavranos, 'Member States' BITs: Lost in Transition?' (29 September 2011), available at: ssm.com/abstract=1935625.

[79] The first ICSID dispute based on an investor-state contract was *Holliday Inns v Morocco*, ICSID Case No ARB/72/1.

[80] The first ICSID dispute based on national legislation was *SPP v Egypt*, ICSID Case No ARB/84/3.

[81] The first ICSID dispute based on a BIT clause was *AAPL v Sri Lanka*, ICSID Report IV, at 250.

- Since the 1990s, also the number of treaty-based ICSID disputes, or investor-state disputes based on UNCITRAL or other commercial arbitration procedures, and the emergence of case-law referring to the today almost 400 known investor-state arbitral awards and related 'annulment decisions' or national court decisions as relevant precedents, increased dramatically.

Foreign direct investments offer obvious economic advantages (eg in terms of transfer of capital and know-how) to the host state justifying legal 'investment incentives' compensating for the less secure legal status and potential discrimination of foreigners in the domestic legal system of host states. The 'political economy' for the regulation of transnational movements of other natural and legal persons (like foreign workers, traders, portfolio investors, tourists, refugees) offers less incentives for host states to commit to multilevel guarantees of cosmopolitan and judicial remedies in transnational legal systems. Even most regional human rights courts offer individual access only after prior exhaustion of local judicial remedies. With only few exceptions (like the 'domain name dispute settlement arbitration' established in the context of the arbitration centre of the World Intellectual Property Organization, the 'preshipment inspection arbitration' established in the context of the WTO Agreement on Preshipment Inspection), 'cosmopolitan dispute settlement institutions' similar to institutionalized arbitration and its quasi-automatic enforceability in domestic legal systems (eg due to the ICSID Convention and, in case of commercial arbitration, the 1958 New York Convention on Recognition and Enforcement of Foreign Arbitral Awards) do not (yet) exist in most other fields of IEL. Nor are governments in most UN member states politically willing to submit to compulsory international jurisdiction for the protection of other cosmopolitan rights of citizens. Yet, this current reluctance of governments to limit their 'Westphalian privileges' (eg in terms of limited legal and judicial accountability vis-à-vis foreigners) by additional legal and judicial guarantees of cosmopolitan rights may change, for instance by recognition of individual legal and judicial remedies by international courts and the ever larger number of multilevel legal and judicial safeguards of cosmopolitan rights in regional economic integration agreements and human rights agreements.

3 'NETWORK GOVERNANCE', 'COMPENSATORY CONSTITUTIONALIZATION' AND THE EMERGING 'COMMON LAW OF ADJUDICATION' CAN LIMIT LEGAL FRAGMENTATION

Intergovernmental 'networks' among heads of governments (eg, meeting in the G20), trade ministers, finance minister, ministers for agriculture and development, environmental ministers, monetary authorities, competition authorities, food, health and environmental authorities, other regulatory agencies and also among courts have become one of the defining characteristics of multilevel economic governance.[82] They are supplemented by, and often closely interact with, complex 'corporate governance' and other private–public governance networks like the UN Global Compact promoting 'corporate social responsibility', the Forest and Marine Stewardship Councils promoting and certifying sustainable forestry and fishery, the Global Reporting Initiative promoting global

[82] *cf* AM Slaughter (2004) 36 ff; AM Slaughter, 'A Global Community of Courts' (2003) 44 *Harvard International Law Journal* 191 ff; D Terris, PR Romano and L Swigart, 'Toward a Community of International Judges' (2008) 30 *Loyola of Los Angeles International & Comparative Law Review* 419 ff.

standards for the reporting of business activities on consumer, environmental and social protection. Such private–public co-regulation increasingly influences multilevel economic and environmental rulemaking.[83] The interrelationships between these private and public, national and international governance networks are partly regulated and coordinated in the law of worldwide, regional and national economic organizations, for instance in the WTO Agreements on technical barriers to trade (TBT), sanitary and phytosanitary standards (SPS) and on preshipment inspection companies.[84] Many activities and rulemaking are, however, coordinated only ad hoc, for instance by requests from the G20 for certain 'crisis management' initiatives by the IMF, the Bank for International Settlements (BIS) and by the WTO to limit systemic risks of the financial and trade imbalances in 2009/2010. The overall coherence and predictability of this ever more complex, formal and informal 'multilevel economic governance' depends increasingly on multilevel rules and institutions promoting transnational rule of law. As discussed in chapter IV and in the preceding section 2, multilevel judicial protection of cosmopolitan rights in regional economic and human rights regimes (like the EU, the EEA and the ECHR) as well as in functional economic integration regimes (like international trade and investment law) have proven to be of crucial importance for protecting transnational rule of law on the basis of an emerging 'common law of adjudication' setting incentives for different jurisdictions to cooperate.

For instance, as illustrated by the more than 40 investor–state arbitration procedures and other investment disputes challenging Argentina's monetary, payments and financial restrictions during the 2001–02 Argentine financial crisis,[85] foreign investment disputes can be submitted to numerous alternative jurisdictions such as national courts; commercial arbitration (eg, based on UNCITRAL procedures); institutionalized investor–state arbitration based on ISCID procedures; regional economic or human rights courts; international courts (like the ICJ); international arbitration among states (eg, administered by the Permanent Court of Arbitration in The Hague); or specialized, intergovernmental dispute settlement proceedings (eg, administered by the WTO or the WIPO Arbitration Centre).[86] There are few formal structures and hierarchies regulating the interrelationships between such competing jurisdictions and their different procedures, applicable laws, judicial remedies and other reasons for potential divergence between such competing jurisdictions. Yet, national and international courts increasingly practice 'judicial comity' and cooperate in diverse ways in order to avoid mutually conflicting judgments resulting from 'forum shopping', 'rule shopping', parallel confidential arbitration proceedings, inadequate regard to precedents or lack of appellate review in investor–state arbitration. The increasing cross-references in the judgments of different jurisdictions justifying their responses to issues of procedures, treaty interpretation and judicial powers continue to develop a 'common law of international adjudication',[87] for instance regarding

[83] *cf* MC Cicirello, 'The Participation of NGOs in the International Regulatory Function' in A Constantinides and N Zaikos (eds), *The Diversity of International Law. Essays in Honour of Professor KK Koufa* (Leiden: Nijhoff, 2009) 71–82.

[84] *cf* the case studies in C Joerges and EU Petersmann (eds) (2006) chs 9–16.

[85] *cf* W Burke-White, 'The Argentine Financial Crisis: State Liability under BITs and the Legitimacy of the ICSID System' (2008) 3 *Asian Journal of WTO & International Health Law and Policy* 199–234; J Kurtz, 'Adjudging the Exceptional at International Investment Law: Security, Public Order and Financial Crisis' (2010) 59 *ICLQ* 325–71.

[86] For overviews of these alternative dispute settlement *forums* see: Dolzer and Schreuer (2008).

[87] *cf* C Brown, *A Common Law of International Adjudication* (Oxford: OUP, 2007).

- inherent procedural powers of courts (eg, to allow representation by private lawyers, allocate burden of proof, grant provisional measures with legally binding force, interpret and revise judgments, allow amicus curiae briefs and NGO access to hearings and documents, suspend proceedings pending the clarification by another court of a relevant legal issue);
- the remedial powers of courts (eg, based on customary international law rules of state responsibility);
- the emergence of an 'international judicial system' (eg, based on explicit 'judicial comity' and cross-references); and
- the judicial methods of treaty interpretation and 'judicial balancing' of private rights and public interests.[88]

The 'proliferation' of international courts and tribunals, their increasing cooperation and 'cross-fertilization'[89] reflect the increasing 'legalization' and 'judicialization' of international economic relations. As explained by Brown,[90] they are likely to continue for a number of reasons:

- International trade, investment and other economic and environmental agreements are increasingly based on common standards and principles of regulation, such as equal freedoms, non-discrimination, national treatment, protection of property rights, 'fair and equitable treatment', access to justice, rule of law and transparency of government restrictions.
- Similarly, the constitutive instruments of courts and applicable procedures reflect common principles of 'administration of justice' and promote similarities in their interpretation of rules and judicial 'administration of justice'.
- The jurisprudence of regional and worldwide economic courts is increasingly following precedents in order to promote legal coherence and predictability.
- International tribunals tend to apply the same customary methods of 'effective' and 'evolutional' treaty interpretation (as codified in the VCLT); they increasingly review whether legislative or administrative government measures have been transparent, 'suitable', necessary and proportionate means for realizing legitimate public interests.
- Even if the applicable treaty law often differs between jurisdictions, the 'application of customary rules and general principles of law harmonizes issues of procedures and remedies precisely because they are not derived from any specific dispute settlement regime'.[91]
- International courts often assert 'inherent powers' to the extent necessary for filling 'regulatory gaps' in their procedural rules and remedies, and justify their 'administration of justice' by referring to similar practices of other courts.
- Even though the limited mandates and legitimate functions of courts vary depending on their constitutive instruments and applicable legal systems, the common judicial tasks of settling disputes in accordance with the applicable law and administering justice promotes convergence in jurisprudence.

[88] For details see Brown (n 87) and N Lavranos, *Jurisdictional Competition. Selected Cases in International and European Law* (Groningen: Europea Law Publishing, 2009); Y Shany, *Regulating Jurisdictional Relations between National and International Courts* (Oxford: OUP, 2007).

[89] *cf* C Brown, 'The Cross-Fertilization of Principles Relating to Procedures and Remedies in the Jurisprudence of International Courts and Tribunals' (2008) 30 *Loyola of Los Angeles International and Comparative Law Review* 219–46.

[90] *cf* n 87.

[91] Brown (n 89) 233.

- The limited number of lawyers serving as international judges and representing complainants and defendants in international court proceedings favours common legal and judicial reasoning based on common procedural experiences and legal practices (eg, in the submissions and arguments of litigants).
- International courts with overlapping jurisdictions (such as the ICJ, the ITLOS and UNCLOS arbitration procedures) have found it necessary to offer similar procedural and legal remedies, for instance by emphasizing that provisional measures ordered by the ICJ are no less legally binding than provisional measures pursuant to Article 290:6 of the UNCLOS.[92]
- Common and mutually coherent judicial practices tend to be perceived positively by international courts as promoting the objective (eg, in Article 3 DSU) of legal 'security and predictability' in international dispute settlement.
- Even if trade jurisprudence (eg, in the GATT and WTO) and investment jurisprudence (eg, in the ICJ and ICSID) initially evolved without cooperation among these separate dispute settlement systems, international economic courts increasingly realize the common 'paradigmatic structures' of most trade and investment disputes, eg, in terms of: (1) pleaded rights to market access; (2) non-economic 'public interest justifications' of market restrictions or other market regulations; (3) judicial review of the transparent and non-discriminatory nature, 'necessity' and 'proportionality' of the restrictions concerned; and (4) independent and impartial, judicial administration of justice (eg, in allocating procedural burdens of proof and justifying judicial findings).

Multilevel judicial cooperation can promote 'compensatory constitutionalization' of multilevel economic governance

Due to the 'internationalization' of human rights and of constitutionalism, the authoritative decision-making processes constituting international law are today ever more influenced by democratic discourse, parliamentary control of foreign policy decisions and national and international 'courts of justice' committed to protecting human rights, rule of law and other 'principles of justice' in international economic cooperation between citizens. Chapters I to IV argued that the five kinds of rules that have historically proven to be necessary for democratic supply of *national public goods* – ie, constitutional, legislative, administrative, judicial and international rules and institutions – are similarly necessary for democratic supply of *international public goods*. As national democracies and their 'sovereign equality' are likely to remain foundational principles of international law, *international governance* on the basis of limited, delegated powers will inevitably remain different from *national governments*. If multilevel rulemaking, rule administration and judicial government functions are required for supplying *international* public goods no less than for supplying national public goods, then the 'rules of recognition' of international law must no longer focus one-sidedly on legal views expressed by diplomats and ministers of foreign affairs, especially if the 'human rights coherence' (*cf* Table 4) of intergovernmental rulemaking and the 'normative force' of power-oriented conceptions of '*opinio juris sive necessitatis*' are challenged in parliaments, civil society and jurisprudence. The changing 'rules of recognition' may justify

[92] ibid 236–37.

dynamic 'evolutionary interpretations' of IEL to limit abuses of power and protect cosmopolitan rights and 'public reason' more effectively.

The increasing 'constitutionalization' and 'judicialization' of IEL can be viewed as 'compensatory constitutionalism'[93] remedying constitutional failures inside national democracies, for instance regarding discriminatory, welfare-reducing border discrimination against foreign goods, services, persons and capital movements and the 'de-constitutionalizing effects' of intergovernmental power politics and economic and environmental globalization on democratic self-governance. International lawyers outside Europe[94] increasingly acknowledge that international law and institutions enabling, constraining and supplementing national policies and laws in order to better realize their international objectives may serve 'constitutional functions', for instance by

- creating governance institutions and allocating governance authority in order to enable and constrain collective supply of public goods;
- limiting governance authority on the basis of 'the principle of subsidiarity' to ensure that an international organization 'shall act only if and insofar as the objectives of the proposed action cannot be sufficiently achieved by the Member States, either at central level or at the regional and local level, but can rather, by reason of the scale or effects of the proposed action, be better achieved at Union level' (Article 5 TEU);
- prescribing legal supremacy of constitutional over legislative and administrative rules and, thereby, promoting legal stability of constitutionally entrenched rules compared with ordinary rulemaking;
- constraining political governance and supplementing national constitutionalism by multilevel fundamental rights;
- protecting rule of law by separation of powers and judicial protection of fundamental rights in transnational relations; and
- strengthening democratic and legal accountability of intergovernmental rulemaking to citizens, for instance by institutionalizing multilevel parliamentary review of multilevel economic governance.

The discussion (in chapter I, section 4) of the collective action problems in multilevel trade and environmental governance emphasized that the mutual coherence and effectiveness of market-based, international regimes (such as WTO law and carbon-emission trading in the context of the UNFCCC regime) cannot be secured without multilevel legal and judicial protection of legal predictability and certainty, with due respect for legitimate 'constitutional pluralism.' In the twenty-first century, the 'systemic nature' of IEL must be defined, legitimated and protected in conformity with the human rights obligations of UN member states as a constitutional condition for the legitimacy and democratic support of international economic regulation. The functional interrelationships between human rights and IEL are reciprocal: protection and promotion of human rights becomes ever more dependent on IEL as the most important instrument for promoting consumer welfare and mutually beneficial, peaceful cooperation across frontiers; conversely, IEL becomes ever more dependent on respect for human rights as a precondition for international rule of law and for reducing economic transaction costs by protect-

[93] *cf* A Peters, 'Compensatory Constitutionalism: The Function and Potential of Fundamental International Norms and Structures' (2006) 19 *Leiden Journal of International Law* 579 ff; Petersmann (1991) 210 ff.

[94] *cf* JL Dunoff and JP Trachtman, 'A Functionalist Approach to International Constitutionalization' in Dunoff and Trachtman (eds) (2009) 3, 9 ff, 18 ff.

ing producers, traders, investors and consumers in their worldwide division of labour. As recently emphasized by WTO Director-General Pascal Lamy, there are no inherent conflicts between the welfare objectives and liberty-based rule of law principles of WTO law and human rights:

> The opening of markets creates efficiency, stimulates growth and helps spur development, thereby contributing to the implementation of the fundamental human rights that are social and economic rights. One could almost claim that trade is human rights in practice! The reduction of trade barriers in agriculture, enhanced market access for agricultural products and the gradual decrease in subsidies provided by rich countries to their farmers, for example, all contribute to the same objective: the implementation of the right to food. . . . The primary vocation of the WTO is to regulate, not to deregulate trade as is often thought. By putting in place rules to regulate trade flows and remove trade distortions, the WTO aims to create a global level playing field, where fairness is the rule and where the rights of individual members are safeguarded. . . . For trade to act as a positive vector for the reinforcement of human rights, a coordinated international effort is needed. A coherent approach, which integrates trade and human rights policy goals, should be developed.[95]

The 'need for universal adherence to and implementation of the rule of law at both the national and international levels' is recognized in a few UN resolutions.[96] But neither the UN Charter nor other UN treaties constitute effective 'rule of law' systems[97] constitutionally restraining 'the rule of men' and their 'rule by law'.[98] In the UN Charter, all UN member states have reaffirmed – on behalf of 'We the peoples of the United Nations' – their 'faith in fundamental human rights, in the dignity and worth of the human person, in the equal rights of men and women and of nations large and small' so as 'to establish conditions under which justice and respect for the obligations arising from treaties and other sources of international law can be maintained' (Preamble). In the various UN human rights conventions, all UN member states have recognized 'the inherent dignity and . . . equal and inalienable rights of all members of the human family [as] the foundation of freedom, justice and peace in the world' (Preamble of the 1966 UN Covenant on Economic, Social and Cultural Rights). Yet, as long as UN human rights conventions do not provide for effective judicial remedies and only about one-third of UN member states have submitted to the compulsory jurisdiction of the ICJ and of other worldwide courts (such as the ITLOS), the UN objective 'to bring about by peaceful means, and in conformity with the principles of justice and international law, adjustment or settlement of international disputes' (Article 1 UN Charter) is not effectively secured. Hence, also constitutional democracies take the 'realist' view that governments should only aim at 'international rule of law',[99] but submit to 'rule of international law' only as long as international law rules

[95] P.Lamy, Speech of 13 January 2010 on 'Towards a Shared Responsibility and Greater Coherence: Human Rights, Trade and Macroeconomic Policy', available on the WTO website at: www.wto.org. See also: *cf* D Kinley (2009).

[96] The quotation is from paragraph 134 of UN General Assembly Resolution A/60/L.1, adopted during the 2005 World Summit meeting on 25 October 2005 (in the same paragraph, UN member states also 'reaffirm our commitment . . . to an international order based on the rule of law and international law, which is essential for peaceful coexistence and cooperation among States').

[97] On the ancient legal ideal of 'rule of law', and its dialectic development on the basis of constitutional rights and principles of justice restraining the instrumental 'governance by law', see Aristotle (1996), book III, para 16, at 1287 a-b.

[98] *cf* I Brownlie, *The Rule of Law in International Affairs* (Oxford: OUP, 1998) 214 ff.

[99] *cf* GJ Ikenberry and AM Slaughter, '*Forging A World of Liberty under Law. US National Security in the 21st Century*' Princeton Project Paper (September 2006).

remain consistent with the constitutional guarantees of human rights, democracy and justice in domestic jurisdictions.[100] Due to the diversity of domestic constitutional traditions, democratic preferences and international 'bargaining power' among states, national conceptions of 'international rule of law' continue to differ fundamentally among UN member states.

'Dynamic interpretation' of IEL in conformity with constitutional rights

The dynamic evolution of European economic integration law was to a large extent due to the 'dynamic interpretation methods' applied by European courts in their multilevel, judicial interpretation and enforcement of the EU and EEA guarantees for free movements of goods, services, persons, capital and related payments for the benefit of European citizens. This purposive, interpretive approach has been clearly spelt out by the ECJ:

> [E]very provision of Community law must be placed in its context and interpreted in the light of the provisions of Community law as a whole, regard being had to the objective thereof and to its state of evolution at the date on which the provision in question is to be applied.[101]

The judicial methods of interpreting European economic law reflect the customary rules of international treaty interpretation, according to which 'a treaty shall be interpreted in good faith in accordance with the ordinary meaning to be given to the terms of the treaty in their context and in the light of its object and purpose' (Article 31, paragraph 1). The 1969 VCLT was drafted at a time when human rights remained deeply contested and suppressed in many states. Hence, the diplomats negotiating the VCLT focused on international treaties among states and on their synallagmatic interrelationships of rights and duties among states. Although drafted as a general treaty applicable to all international treaty relationships among states, the VCLT 'contains many hidden assumptions that are not justified in respect of human rights treaties'[102] and which reflect neither the 'constitutional functions' of human rights treaties nor the 'internationalization of constitutional law principles' resulting from human rights law, limited delegation of powers and the hierarchical legal structures of the law of many international organizations.[103] The ECtHR has inferred from the individual rights of access to justice (*cf* Articles 6, 13 ECHR) and from the limitation clauses in many human rights guarantees (like Articles 8–10 ECHR providing for limitations 'necessary in a democratic society') the need for reviewing the 'necessity' and 'proportionality' of legislative and administrative restrictions of individual rights. Similarly, the ECJ, the EFTA Court and national courts in all 30 EEA countries engage in 'proportionality review' of multilevel economic and environmental restrictions and distortions.[104] This multilevel judicial review of the

[100] *cf* Petersmann, 'Human Rights, International Economic Law and "Constitutional Justice"' (2008) 19 *EJIL* 769, 780 ff.

[101] Case 283/81, *CILFIT* [1982] ECR 3415, para 20.

[102] *cf* M Scheinin, 'Impact on the Law of Treaties' in M Kamminga and M Scheinin (2009) 23 ff.

[103] *cf* EU Petersmann, 'Human Rights, Markets and Economic Welfare: Constitutional Functions of the Emerging UN Human Rights Constitution' in F Abbott, C Breining and T Cottier (eds) (2006) 29–67.

[104] *cf* TI Harbo, *The Function of Proportionality Analysis in European Law* (doctoral thesis defended in January 2011 at the European University Institute, Florence). Harbo compares proportionality analysis (PA) in EU law, EEA law, ECHR law and in those countries (like England and Norway) whose courts did not practice PA before EU/EEA membership. Harbo concludes that – even though application of PA is flexible and contex-

legality, 'suitability', 'necessity' and 'proportionality *stricto sensu*' of legislative and administrative restrictions has enabled new forms of 'public reason' legitimizing multilevel governance and judicial clarification of indeterminate European economic rules for the benefit of transnational rule of law and the constitutional rights of European citizens. If properly applied, both 'evolutionary interpretation' methods as well as judicial 'proportionality review' are fully consistent with the customary methods of textual, systemic, functional and 'constitutional' treaty interpretation as codified in the VCLT.

The VCLT's codification (in its Preamble and Article 31) of the customary law requirement of settling 'disputes concerning treaties, like other international disputes, . . . in conformity with the principles of justice and international law', including 'universal respect for, and observance of, human rights and fundamental freedoms for all', recalls the constitutional functions of courts to interpret and apply international law in conformity with principles of justice and *erga omnes* human rights obligations. For example, according to the ECtHR, 'the Court's obligation is to have regard to the special character of the Convention as a constitutional instrument of European public order for the protection of individual human beings and its role, as set out in Article 19 of the Convention, is to ensure the observance of the engagements undertaken by the Contracting Parties'.[105] Similarly, the EC Court and the EFTA Court emphasize their judicial function of protecting rule of international law with due regard to the rights of producers, investors, traders, consumers and other citizens against arbitrary interferences by governments and other abuses of public and private power. Just as the idea of 'rule of law' has always been related to justice,[106] so do human rights instruments emphasize 'that human rights should be protected by the rule of law' and by effective legal remedies for individuals.[107] As democratic pluralism often prompts parliaments and governments to respond to domestic or foreign political events by approving 'incompletely theorized agreements', courts of justice may have to defend 'principled constitutional interpretations' challenging opportunistic compromises favoured by political decision-makers without regard to the overall coherence of legal systems.

Similar to the rights-based conceptions of European economic law, the increasing focus on rule of international law, legal security, legal remedies and judicial protection of individual rights of private economic actors is becoming a defining element of international investment law, intellectual property law, regional economic integration law and of certain environmental agreements beyond Europe, reflecting a gradual 'paradigm shift' from state-centred to citizen-oriented conceptions of IEL. Individual producers, investors, traders and consumers have reasonable self-interests in insisting that IEL should be designed and interpreted, like domestic laws, for the benefit of citizens and their constitutional rights. The diplomatic focus on 'member-driven governance in the

tual – the similar application of PA by the ECJ, the EFTA Court and the ECtHR justifies referring to a common European conception of PA. European law recognizes 'proportionality' as a constitutional principle (*cf* Art 52 EU Charter of Fundamental Rights) promoting efficiency, predictability and legitimacy of decisions and 'rule of law'.

[105] ECtHR, Grand Chamber, *Bankovic and Others against Belgium and Others*, Inadmissibility Decision, 12 December 2001.

[106] On the ancient Greek concept of 'law as participation in the idea of justice', and the need to relate justice not only to the value of equality, see: CJ Friedrich, *The Philosophy of Law in Historical Perspective* (Chicago: Chicago University Press, 1963) chs II and XX.

[107] *cf* the Preamble of the Universal Declaration of Human Rights (1948) and F Francioni (ed), *Access to Justice* (Oxford: OUP, 2008).

WTO' and diplomatic self-interests (eg, in limiting judicial accountability of trade diplomats) explain why WTO members, WTO dispute settlement panels and the Appellate Body hardly ever refer to the customary law requirement of interpreting international treaties, and settling international disputes, 'in conformity with principles of justice' and human rights obligations of the countries concerned.[108] Similarly, foreign investors, host states and arbitrators in international investor–state arbitration all too often collude in avoiding the human rights dimensions of investor–state disputes over governmental restrictions of foreign investments.[109]

Who guards the guardians? Multilevel constitutional and judicial protection of individual rights beyond Europe?

As explained in chapters II and III, European integration law has successfully protected cosmopolitan rights due to its 'multilevel constitutionalism' based on

- multilevel constitutional guarantees of equal freedoms and inalienable human rights;
- legal primacy of EU law and of other international guarantees of equal freedoms and human rights (eg, in the ECHR) as 'integrating parts' of European integration law and domestic constitutional restraints;
- multilevel judicial protection of European constitutional law by national and international courts as 'exemplars of public reason' (Rawls) and the only independent branch of governance justifying its decisions by constitutional and legal reasoning alone;
- constitutional empowerment and judicial protection of citizens across frontiers as self-interested guardians of their constitutional rights to transnational rule of law; and
- the institution of 'communitarian' forms of multilevel governance driven by independent Community institutions with limited legislative, administrative and judicial powers.

The ideal of 'constitutional justice' is informed by the inalienable *jus cogens* and *erga omnes* core of human rights. Just as justice requires the judge to treat all the parties to the dispute equally and to administer justice, so do human rights require economic regulation promoting general consumer welfare with due respect for the equal rights of citizens. Today, almost all UN member states support multilevel governance for a mutually beneficial division of labour based on international agreements, transnational rule of law and its judicial protection, for example in the context of today more than 2800 BITs, more than 250 regional trade and investment agreements (like NAFTA) and, albeit to more limited degrees, in the law of the WTO and other worldwide agreements on international judicial cooperation (eg, under the 1958 UN Convention on Recognition and Enforcement of Foreign Arbitral Awards) and international judicial remedies (eg, pursuant to the 1965 ICSID Convention on the Settlement of Investment Disputes between States and Nationals of other States). Yet, the necessary strengthening of judicial review raises the constitutional question of 'who guards the guardians'? In European economic law, the treaties establishing the EC, the EU, the EEA and the ever larger number of EU

[108] *cf* EU Petersmann, 'Administration of Justice in the WTO: Did the WTO Appellate Body Commit "Grave Injustice"?' (2009) 8 *The Law & Practice of International Courts and Tribunals* 329–74.

[109] *cf* EU Petersmann, 'Introduction and Summary: "Administration of Justice" in International Investment Law and Adjudication' in Dupuy, Francioni and Petersmann (eds) (2009) 3–39.

free trade agreements with third countries have a long tradition of being based on common constitutional 'principles of freedom, democracy, respect for human rights, fundamental freedoms and rule of law' (Article 6, EU Nice Treaty), providing for parliamentary control and effective legal and judicial safeguards not only of sovereign rights of states, but also of individual rights of citizens. The EU Charter of Fundamental Rights bases the human rights approach to European economic law, and to the rights-based conception of the EC's international 'market freedoms' as fundamental freedoms of individuals to be protected by national and European courts, on 'the indivisible, universal values of human dignity, freedom, equality and solidarity' as well as 'on the principles of democracy and the rule of law'.[110] In European economic law, citizens, parliaments and courts are the ultimate guardians of rule of law and of its democratic legitimacy.

As explained in chapters III and IV, human rights law calls for recognizing individuals as legal subjects entitled to 'rule of law' and judicial remedies also in transnational economic cooperation beyond Europe. Yet, as discussed in chapter IV, section 1, judicial protection of 'rule of international law' for the benefit of citizens remains imperfect also inside the EU,[111] as illustrated by the ECJ's power-oriented refusal to review the legality of EU measures in light of the EU's international legal obligations under WTO law and under the UN Convention on the Law of the Sea.[112] The multilevel governance and constitutional as well as judicial protection of 'rule of law' and of democratic citizen rights inside the common market of the 30 EEA member states refutes the prevailing North American view that rule of law and democracy can be effective only inside nation states.[113] The frequent disregard for NAFTA law in the legislative, administrative and judicial practices of NAFTA countries confirms the European experience that the 'public good' of a rules-based, common market depends on multilevel judicial protection of rule of law not only in intergovernmental relations among states but, more importantly, also in transnational cooperation and transactions among citizens. The 'constitutional nationalism' and power-oriented foreign policies prevailing outside Europe unduly neglect this dependence of the collective supply of international public goods on multilevel judicial protection of international rule of law and on settling 'disputes concerning treaties, like other international disputes, . . . in conformity with the principles of justice and international law', including 'universal respect for, and observance of, human rights and fundamental freedoms for all' (VCLT, Preamble). As explained by Kantian legal theory (*cf* chapter III, sections 1 and 2), multilevel constitutional and judicial protection of equal constitutional rights offers not only the most effective answer to the questions of 'who guards the guardians' so as to ensure that IEL is interpreted in conformity with the

[110] The quotation is from the Preamble to the Charter of Fundamental Rights of the European Union, as adopted first in December 2000 and subsequently incorporated into EU law by the 2007 Lisbon Treaty; *cf* I Pernice, *The Treaty of Lisbon and Fundamental Rights* in S Griller and J Ziller (eds), *The Lisbon Treaty. EU Constitutionalism without a Constitutional Treaty?* (Heidelberg: Springer Verlag, 2008) 235 ff.

[111] *cf* L Lenaerts, 'The Rule of Law and the Coherence of the Judicial System of the European Union' 2007 44 *CMLR* 1625–59.

[112] On this politically motivated self-restraint in the case law of the ECJ see Mendez (n 38); on the various indirect methods of cooperation of the ECJ with WTO dispute settlement bodies (eg, by means of 'WTO consistent interpretations' of EU rules and principles) see: M Bronckers, 'From "Direct Effect" to "Muted Dialogue": Recent Developments in the European Court's Case Law on the WTO and Beyond' 2008 11 *JIEL* 885–98.

[113] On the diverse European conceptions of rights-based, cosmopolitan international economic law see: J Habermas, *The Divided West* (Cambridge: Polity Press, 2006) 115 ff; A von Bogdandy and S Della Valle, 'Universalism and Particularism as Paradigms of International Law' New York University School of Law International Law and Justice Working Paper 2008/3.

human rights of citizens; without international rule of law and its judicial protection on the basis of 'proportionality balancing' protecting 'rights-based public reason' for the benefit of citizens, the collective action problems in multilevel governance of interdependent public goods can hardly be solved for the benefit of citizens and of their constitutional rights.

4 THE 'DUAL NATURE' OF COSMOPOLITAN RIGHTS ENTAILS COMPETING 'ENFORCEMENT' – AND 'BALANCING-PARADIGMS': JUDICIAL PROTECTION OF ECONOMIC RIGHTS VERSUS HUMAN RIGHTS?

The preceding chapters have argued that human rights, the citizen-oriented functions of IEL, the need for transnational 'rule of law communities' in the global division of labour and multilevel governance of international public goods require overcoming the traditional dichotomy of rule of law at national and international levels. But it was also emphasized that 'rule of law' remains a contested and contextual concept. The universal recognition of human rights and the need for their protection by 'rule of law' call for a 'human rights approach' to IEL, as proposed by the UN High Commissioner for Human Rights, aimed at protecting 'human rights coherence' in IEL, transnational rule of law for the benefit of citizens and 'proportionality balancing' of rights and public interest legislation in IEL.[114] Extending such a 'constitutional concept' of transnational rule of law beyond European economic law is a challenge which is increasingly recognized in transnational economic adjudication, for instance by investor–state arbitral tribunals reviewing public interest restrictions enacted by host states of private investor rights protected in BITs.[115]

Reconciling state-centred and citizen-oriented interpretations of IEL requires stronger protection of constitutional rights by 'courts of justice'

The preceding discussion acknowledged the legal and political obstacles in interpreting, for instance, WTO commitments for promoting 'sustainable development' (WTO Preamble) and 'providing security and predictability to the multilateral trading system' (Article 3 DSU) as requiring recognition of citizens as legal subjects of WTO rights and obligations. The institutionalized discussion and approval of all WTO panel and appellate reports by WTO members meeting in the 'Dispute Settlement Body' (DSB) remains dominated by trade diplomats with strong self-interests in preventing the WTO legal and dispute settlement system from holding diplomats and governments accountable vis-à-

[114] *cf* EU Petersmann, 'The "Human Rights Approach" Advocated by the UN High Commissioner for Human Rights and by the ILO: Is it Relevant for WTO Law and Policy?' (2004) 7 *JIEL* 605–28. As discussed in chs II to IV, the constitutional requirement of clarifying and 'optimizing' constitutional rights and human rights in conformity with 'proportionality balancing' is also of systemic legal importance for the 'secondary rules' on recognizing, changing and adjudicating 'primary rules' in order to secure legitimacy of national and international law. Human and constitutional rights operate both as 'primary rules of conduct' and constitutional restraints of secondary 'rules of recognition' in national and international legal systems. In contrast to Kelsen's 'Grundnorm', which explained the hierarchical order of international and national law on the basis of a legal fiction, the human rights conception of law as evolving in response to 'struggles for human rights' offers a more realistic conception of modern legal systems.

[115] *cf* Stone Sweet (n 64); Dupuy, Francioni and Petersmann (eds) (2009).

vis citizens. Hence, most WTO diplomats are unlikely to support the view that – rather than interpreting the exclusive and compulsory jurisdiction of WTO dispute settlement bodies (Article 23 DSU) as preventing domestic courts from holding their own governments judicially accountable for violations of WTO law (as suggested by some EU and US trade lawyers)[116] – the human right of access to justice and the WTO guarantees of individual access to courts justify interpreting Article 23 DSU as an exclusive jurisdiction only for intergovernmental disputes; from the point of view of citizens involved in trade disputes with governments, the multilevel 'dispute settlement system of the WTO' should provide 'security and predictability to the multilateral trading system' (Article 3 DSU) also for citizens engaged in, and benefiting from international trade whenever they request domestic courts to interpret domestic trade rules in conformity with the WTO obligations ratified by parliaments. Just as European courts have justified citizen-oriented interpretations of the intergovernmental EC Treaty rules as constituting fundamental rights of EU citizens as legal subjects of European integration law, so do the human rights obligations of all WTO members offer arguments against power-oriented, intergovernmental definitions of 'state interests' without regard to general citizen interests in transnational rule of law. The increasing insistence by citizens and judges on transnational rule of law as a constitutional restraint on abuses of foreign policy powers can also be justified by a 'moral duty of justice . . . to help ensure that all persons have access to institutions that protect their basic rights'.[117] A rules-based trading system preventing and settling international economic disputes through domestic courts – rather than only through intergovernmental WTO dispute settlement proceedings and medieval 'trade wars' – would also contribute to 'democratic peace' in international relations, as illustrated by 65 years of 'democratic peace' among the 30 EEA member states.

The prevailing disregard – in state-centred WTO negotiations and WTO legal practices – for the human rights obligations of all WTO members reflects not only the limited jurisdiction of WTO bodies and the lack of expertise of trade diplomats regarding human rights; there is also concern by trade diplomats and economists that too many human rights advocates appear to be more interested in redistributing other people's welfare than in creating the legal conditions for empowering the poor to increase their own economic resources (eg, through more effective legal protection of open markets, non-discriminatory conditions of competition and international rule of law).[118] Economists and trade politicians fear a divisive 'politicization' of reciprocal trade liberalization and trade regulation by 'human rights fundamentalists' who all too often ignore the necessary economic foundation of constitutional democracies in consumer-driven trade, competition and a mutually welfare-increasing division of labour. Protection of human rights requires constitutional construction not only of citizen-driven 'political markets' (democracies), but also of consumer-driven 'social market economies' that

[116] *cf* R Bhala and K Kennedy, *World Trade Law* (Newark: Lexis Publishing, 1998) 43.

[117] See A Buchanan (2004) 27, 86. The author bases his book on such a 'natural duty of justice' and rejects the realist perception of international relations as anarchic struggles for power and military dominance (the Hobbesian war of all against all). Chapter VI discusses the controversial questions of how to define 'principles of justice' and legitimate tolerance in international law and international relations among liberal and non-liberal states, and to what extent principles of justice in constitutional democracies can and should be extended to international economic regulation. The main conclusion is that existing international human rights law already prescribes far more comprehensive protection of human rights than the minimalist protection suggested by Rawls in his proposals for *The Law of Peoples* (1999).

[118] *cf* EU Petersmann, 'Taking Human Dignity, Poverty and Empowerment of Individuals More Seriously: Rejoinder to Alston' (2002) 13 *EJIL* 845–51.

protect the economic as well as non-economic dimensions of human liberty and of non-discriminatory competition in conformity with the 'indivisibility' of the human rights of citizens. The unnecessary poverty of more than 1 billion people living on one dollar per day or less, and the continuing failure of UN and WTO member states to protect rule of law and global public goods effectively in so many UN member states as well as in transnational relations, confirm that these human rights dimensions and constitutional tasks of IEL continue to be unduly neglected by many governments.

The 'dual nature' of IEL may justify cosmopolitan interpretations

Chapters III and IV inferred from the 'dual nature' of human rights – as positive national and international law and moral entitlements – that, in the words of the UN General Assembly, '(e)veryone has the right, individually and in association with others, to develop and discuss new human rights ideas and principles and to advocate their acceptance'.[119] As cosmopolitan economic rights (like property rights and freedom of trade) can be derived from human rights, chapter IV argued for conceiving IEL as an instrument for protecting and promoting human rights and consumer welfare. Just as national constitutional courts inside the EU have made their judicial application and protection of European economic law conditional on 'human rights coherence',[120] European courts should specify positively their 'constitutional conditions' for applying international legal obligations of the EU for the benefit of EU citizens rather than denying – for political rather than legal reasons – judicial protection of legitimate reliance by EU citizens on the EU's constitutional obligation of 'strict observance of international law' (Article 3 TEU) as an integrating part of European law. With the incorporation of the EU Charter of Fundamental Rights into European constitutional law and the Lisbon Treaty's commitments to respect for international law, transnational rule of law in Europe goes far beyond merely formal conceptions of 'Rechtsstaat' and 'rule by law', as emphasized in the ECJ's *Kadi* judgment (*cf* Table 18 and related text). Judicial administration of justice and 'proportionality balancing' require more convincing 'constitutional justifications' of why the ECJ tolerates fundamental freedoms of EU citizens being limited by illegal and welfare-reducing EU restrictions in blatant disregard of the constitutionally limited mandate of EU institutions.

Judicial protection of individual rights in investor–state arbitration increasingly engages in 'proportionality review' of governmental restrictions and accepts amicus curiae submissions from non-governmental third parties in recognition of the fact that investor–state disputes often affect legitimate interests of third parties. The impact of human rights on the interpretation and development of IEL in worldwide economic organizations and international dispute settlement proceedings remains controversial. In Article 3 of the WTO Dispute Settlement Understanding (DSU), the 'Members recognize that it serves to preserve the rights and obligations of Members under the covered agreements, and to clarify the existing provisions of those agreements in accordance with customary rules of interpretation of public international law' (paragraph 2). There is broad

[119] UN Doc A/RES/53/144 (1998) on 'Declaration on the Right and Responsibility of Individuals, Groups and Organs of Society to Promote and Protect Universally Recognized Human Rights and Fundamental Freedoms', Art 7.

[120] *cf* the case law discussed in ch IV, section 3.

agreement today that the VCLT (notably Articles 31 and 32) codifies these customary methods of treaty interpretation and calls for *positive law approaches* aimed at clarifying the textual meaning of international rules ratified by states in conformity with the context of treaty rules, the declared treaty objectives and the intentions of states and past precedents.[121] Notwithstanding the numerous academic controversies about the appropriate methodologies for interpreting and understanding IEL,[122] the customary law requirement of interpreting international treaties 'in conformity with principles of justice' and human rights also calls for 'constitutional interpretations' and may justify normative 'advocacy approaches', for instance by clarifying the indeterminate 'object and purpose' of treaties in conformity with the human rights obligations of states in order to challenge illegitimate treaty practices. Similar to the ICJ's obiter dictum – 'whatever the legal reasoning of a court of justice, its decisions must by definition be just, and therefore in that sense equitable',[123] – WTO dispute settlement bodies may infer from the WTO Preamble's objectives (such as 'sustainable development') citizen-oriented functions of certain WTO rules. For example, the WTO obligation to 'preserve the basic principles and further the objectives underlying this multilateral trading system' (WTO Preamble) could be interpreted as referring not only to the more than 40 WTO provisions explicitly referring to 'principles' underlying the GATT (eg, Articles III, VIII, X, XIII, XX, XXXVI GATT), the General Agreement on Trade in Services (eg, Preamble and Article X GATS) and the Agreement on Trade-Related Intellectual Property Rights (eg, Articles 8 and 62 TRIPS); it may also be invoked as justifying application of customary law principles of procedural and substantive international law and other 'general principles of law' relevant for interpreting and applying WTO rules and 'administering justice' in WTO dispute settlement proceedings.[124] Obviously, citizen-oriented interpretations of state-centred rules may cause 'systemic frictions' and contestation that may gradually lead to recognition of new forms of 'public reason'.

The 'balancing' of economic and human rights and the legal ranking of WTO rules based on economic efficiency remain contested

The text and context of WTO law require *systematic approaches* to the clarification of the contextual and 'systemic dimensions' of what the WTO Agreement calls 'the basic principles and . . . objectives underlying this multilateral trading system' (Preamble) as well as the 'dispute settlement system' (Article 3 DSU) of the WTO. For instance, as the DSU does not explicitly regulate a number of procedural questions, WTO dispute settlement bodies have asserted inherent powers which they perceived as necessary for the

[121] *cf* I Van Damme, *Treaty Interpretation by the WTO Appellate Body* (Oxford: OUP, 2009).

[122] G Shaffer, 'A New Legal Realism: Method in International Economic Law Scholarship' in CB Picker, ID Bunn and DW Arner (eds), *International Economic Law. The State and Future of the Discipline* (Oxford: Hart Publishing, 2008) 29–42, distinguishes the following four legal methodologies in international economic law research: (1) doctrinal legal formalism and positivism; (2) normative advocacy approaches; (3) systemic theoretical approaches; and (4) empirical 'new legal realist approaches', acknowledging that 'there is no single "correct" approach to legal scholarship' (at 41) and positive, normative, systemic, functional and empirical approaches must complement each other. For an economic analysis of the whole structures of international law see: JP Trachtman (2008).

[123] *North Sea Continental Shelf*, Judgment [1969] ICJ Rep 48–49, para 88.

[124] *cf* AD Mitchell (2008).

peaceful settlement of disputes (such as judicial clarification of the admissibility of preliminary rulings, of opening WTO panel and Appellate Body meetings to the public and of accepting amicus curiae submissions by third parties, including non-governmental organizations). Many WTO rules, and their contextual and functional interpretations, are hardly comprehensible without understanding their underlying economic assumptions.[125] For example:

- The GATT legally ranks and regulates the various trade policy instruments according to their economic efficiency: non-discriminatory domestic regulations are allowed (eg, pursuant to Article III GATT) as they tend to be the most efficient policy instrument for correcting 'market failures' (eg, by means of competition law, social law and environmental law) and for providing 'public goods' (eg, by means of tax law); import tariffs are to be progressively liberalized by means of reciprocal tariff bindings (*cf* Articles II, XXVIII *bis* GATT) in view of the adverse effects of discriminatory tariffs on consumer welfare and on allocative efficiency; discriminatory non-tariff trade barriers are generally prohibited (eg, by Articles II, XI, XIII GATT) in view of their welfare-reducing and trade-distorting economic effects, subject to limited exceptions (eg, in Articles XVIII to XXI GATT).
- The GATT and WTO subsidy rules are based on the 'traffic light approach': export subsidies and import distorting domestic subsidies are prohibited (Article 3 Agreement on Subsidies) in view of their trade distorting effects; 'actionable subsidies' (Article 5) may be challenged depending on their 'adverse effects to the interests of other Members'; and 'non-actionable subsidies' (Article 8) are permitted and recognized as second best policy instruments for promoting public interests.

Empirical studies may be of crucial importance for evaluating the effectiveness of WTO rules and procedures[126] and for determining the facts in the context of result-oriented rules (eg, about 'injury' caused by increased imports justifying safeguard measures pursuant to Article XIX GATT). The GATT and WTO anti-dumping rules permit the unilateral imposition of anti-dumping duties in order to correct price distortions caused by introducing

> products of one country . . . into the commerce of another country at less than the normal value of the products . . . if it causes or threatens material injury to an established industry in the territory of a contracting party or materially retards the establishment of a domestic industry (Article VI:1 GATT).

The WTO Appellate Body case law on the legal inconsistency of 'zeroing practices' (in the calculation of 'dumping margins') with the 'fair comparison' requirement in WTO anti-dumping rules illustrates the frequent need of interpreting and clarifying indeterminate WTO rules in conformity with criteria of economic rationality, 'fairness' and due process

[125] On economic analysis of international trade law see: Petersmann (1991) ch IV and M Matsushita, 'A Review of some Appellate Decisions: Law, Policy and Economics in Dispute Settlement' in Y Taniguchi, A Yanovich and J Bohanes (eds) (2007) 282–93.

[126] For instance, Shaffer has demonstrated in numerous empirical studies that the success of WTO dispute settlement proceedings may depend on 'private–public partnerships' enabling the complaining WTO member to benefit from the knowledge and legal resources of the export industry adversely affected by the challenged trade restrictive measures; *cf* G Shaffer, 'Developing Country Use of the WTO Dispute Settlement System: Why it Matters, the Barriers Posed, and its Impact on Bargaining' in J Hartigan (ed), *Trade Disputes and the Dispute Settlement Understanding of the WTO: An Interdisciplinary Assessment* (Bingley: Emerald Group Publishing, 2009.

of law.[127] 'Economic approaches' to interpreting and applying economic rules also raise the question whether governments enjoy discretion for applying such rules (eg, on 'dumping') for political reasons even if the economic rationale (eg, of preventing 'predatory dumping' that risks undermining competition in the importing country) is not applicable.

The answers to interpretative questions of IEL are often influenced by the respective legal methodologies, 'struggles for rights' and policy perspectives applied. For instance, in the *EC-Tariff Preferences* case, the WTO Panel interpreted the term 'non-discriminatory' in the 'Enabling Clause' as requiring identical treatment for all less-developed WTO members; on appeal, the WTO Appellate Body overruled this formal interpretation by allowing also differential treatment of some developing countries provided the differential treatment was justified by special needs and was available to all eligible beneficiaries of the Generalized System of Preferences.[128] The regular, institutionalized discussion and approval of all WTO dispute settlement reports among WTO members meeting in the DSB reveal that the quasi-judicial clarification of WTO rules by WTO dispute settlement panels and the Appellate Body often remain contested among WTO members even if the DSB adopts the dispute settlement reports.[129] The longstanding WTO negotiations on clarification and progressive development of WTO dispute settlement procedures[130] confirm that proposals for the further strengthening of the WTO dispute settlement system vary depending on their 'state-centred' or 'citizen-centred' conceptions of the relevant WTO provisions for the settlement of international trade disputes (eg, by means of WTO consultations, panel proceedings, Appellate Body proceedings, arbitration procedures) and the WTO provisions on individual access to domestic courts.[131] For instance, state-centred conceptions of WTO rules argue for limiting the customary law rules on state responsibility in the WTO context and reject citizen-oriented proposals to apply the customary law remedies of reparation of injury and reimbursement of illegally levied duties in the context of WTO dispute settlement procedures.

[127] *cf*, eg, the *EC-Bed linen* case (WT/DS141/AB/R, para 55), adopted in March 2001. The Appellate Body's interpretation of the 'fair comparison' requirement, which was subsequently confirmed by the Appellate Body in five additional rulings, had been rejected by an earlier GATT panel report (*EC-Audio Cassettes*, ADP/136, 28 April 1995, not adopted) on the basis of the argument that 'if the existence and extent of dumping and the imposition of duties had been conducted on a transaction-to-transaction basis, the EC would have been entitled to impose a duty with respect to dumped transactions, where injury existed, irrespective of the prices at which other un-dumped transactions occurred' (para 356). The panel's narrow, textual interpretations of rules without regard to their underlying principles (such as the requirement of a 'fair comparison' in the inevitable aggregation and averaging of multiple price comparisons) was characteristic of many 'bureaucratic interpretations' of GATT 1947 and the 1979 Tokyo Round Agreements at the insistence of GATT diplomats and GATT officials who, even after the establishment of a GATT Legal Division in 1983, often continued to prevent GATT panellists from receiving independent legal advice. On the constitutional significance of the 'zeroing case law' of the WTO for promoting a legal obligation of panels to respect consistent WTO jurisprudence see: S Cho, 'Global Constitutional Lawmaking' (2010) 31 *University of Pennsylvania Journal of International Law* 621–78.

[128] *cf* WT/DS246AB/R (2004).

[129] For examples of 'judicial clarification', and its frequent contestation in discussions in the WTO Dispute Settlement Body, regarding the interpretation of the subsidy rules of the WTO Agreement on Agriculture, or the WTO jurisprudence concerning the admissibility of *amicus curiae* briefs, see: EU Petersmann, 'WTO Dispute Settlement Practice 1995–2005: Lessons from the Past and Future Challenges' in Taniguchi, Yanovich and Bohanes (eds) (2007) 38–97.

[130] *cf* the more than 50 proposals by WTO Members discussed in F Ortino and EU Petersmann (eds) (2004) chs 1 to 12.

[131] Examples include: Art X GATT, Art 13 of the WTO Anti-dumping Agreement, Art 11 of the WTO Agreement on Customs Valuation, Art 4 of the Agreement on Preshipment Inspection, Art 23 of the WTO Agreement on Subsidies, Art VI of the GATS, Arts 41–50, 59 of the TRIPS Agreement, Art XX of the Government Procurement Agreement and Art 2 of China's WTO Accession Protocol.

The citizen-driven competition, common market and environmental rules of the EU and EEA suggest that international market regulation can become not only more legitimate and more effective by engaging citizens and other market actors; citizen-driven regulatory systems can also set powerful incentives for decentralized enforcement (eg, of common market, competition and environmental rules) and judicial clarification of transnational rule of law.[132] Chapters I to IV argued that multilevel constitutional protection of human rights, rule of law and of other interdependent public goods require that – similar to the protection of labour rights protected in the 'Constitution' (*sic*) of the ILO, of the human right to health in the 'Constitution' (*sic*) of the WHO, of the right to education protected in the 'Constitution' (*sic*) of UNESCO and of the right to food protected in the laws and 'Constitution' (*sic*) of the FAO – regional and worldwide trade organizations should likewise interpret national and international guarantees of freedom, non-discrimination, rule of law and protection of other 'public interests' in mutually coherent ways for the benefit of citizens and their human rights. National and regional public goods (like rules-based common markets) can often be transformed into global public goods most effectively by extending rights-based, decentralized regulatory systems. For instance, the worldwide 'trading community' of producers, investors, traders and consumers engaging in a worldwide division of labour can maximize general consumer welfare only on the basis of more coherent, multilevel constitutional, competition, trade and other economic and environmental rules that may be enforced most effectively at decentralized level by means of multilevel judicial protection of transnational rule of law. The national and international courts involved may legitimately apply competing 'rule of law paradigms', 'enforcement paradigms' and 'judicial review standards' that can be coordinated in decentralized ways based on respect for legitimate 'constitutional pluralism'. The cooperation between competing, national and international jurisdictions for the settlement of disputes over intellectual property rights illustrates this need for protection of transnational rule of law even if the moral or utilitarian foundations of IEL rules remain contested.

Can intellectual property rights be justified by human rights?

Arguably, there are numerous interrelationships between the human right of authors to benefit from 'the protection of the moral and material interests resulting from any scientific, literary or artistic production of which he is the author' (Articles 27 UDHR, 15 ICESCR), the right of everyone to 'enjoy the benefits of scientific progress and its applications' (Article 15 ICESCR), the intellectual property rights protected in WIPO Conventions, the TRIPS Agreement and regional economic agreements[133] and their legal and judicial protection by regional human rights conventions and human rights courts, national courts and other human rights bodies.[134] The increasing 'forum shopping' in transnational disputes over intellectual property rights should not prompt WTO dispute

[132] *cf* J Scott (ed), *Envirionmental Protection. European Law and Governance* (Oxford: OUP, 2009).

[133] *cf* FM Abbott, 'WTO Dispute Settlement Practice relating to the TRIPS Agreement' in Ortino and Petersmann (eds) (2004) 421–54; LR Helfer, KJ Alter and MF Guerzovich, 'Islands of Effective International Adjudication: Constructing an Intellectual Property Rule of Law in the Andean Community' (2009) 103 *AJIL* 1–47.

[134] L Helfer, 'The New Innovation Frontier? Intellectual Property and the European Court of Human Rights' (2008) 49 *Harvard International Law Journal* 1–52.

settlement bodies and investment tribunals reviewing alleged violations of property rights to disregard the human rights and constitutional dimensions of such disputes. The UN Committee on Economic, Social and Cultural Rights, in its General Comment on Article 15 ICESCR, emphasized that – in reconciling protection of author rights with protection of all other human rights:

> [T]he private interests of authors should not be unduly favoured and the public interest in enjoying broad access to their productions should be given due consideration. States Parties should therefore ensure that their legal or other regimes for the protection of the moral and material interests resulting from one's scientific, literary or artistic productions constitute no impediment to their ability to comply with their core obligations in relation to the rights to food, health and education, as well as to take part in cultural life and to enjoy the benefits of scientific progress and its applications, or any other right enshrined in the Covenant. Ultimately, intellectual property is a social product and has a social function. [135]

This judicial task of interpreting intellectual property provisions in WIPO conventions, WTO agreements, investment agreements, free trade area and regional economic integration agreements in conformity with the human rights obligations of the countries concerned requires reviewing the often one-sided focus of investment, WIPO and WTO dispute settlement bodies on economic rules without adequate regard to the customary law requirement of interpreting treaties, and settling international disputes, 'in conformity with principles of justice' and the human rights obligations of states. Transnational rule of law without mutually conflicting judicial interpretations of fragmented legal regimes requires not only 'judicial comity' and judicial respect for legitimately diverse legal and judicial systems; it may also justify judicial clarification of legal duties to secure access to essential pharmaceuticals necessary for survival.[136]

Should courts of justice limit 'hegemonic IEL' by multilevel protection of rule of law in conformity with human rights?

Do state duties to protect human rights entail also judicial duties to interpret IEL for the benefit of citizens? As long as the United States and other world powers continue to use 'hegemonic international law'[137] as a tool for promoting 'national interests' as defined by governments in cooperation with powerful interest groups (eg, the pharmaceutical lobbies that strongly influenced the drafting of the TRIPS Agreement), there remains a strong risk that conceptions of 'rule of law' in one jurisdiction may not be shared in other jurisdictions. National legal and judicial doctrines accepted in one jurisdiction (eg, regarding 'judicial deference' vis-à-vis administrative regulation pursuant to the 'Chevron

[135] UN Committee on Economic, Social and Cultural Rights, *General Comment No 17 (2005), The right of everyone to benefit from the protection of the moral and material interests resulting from any scientific, literary or artistic production of which he or she is the author* (E/C.12/GC/17, 12 January 2006), para 35.

[136] *cf* WA Cann, 'On the Relationship between Intellectual Property Rights and the Need of Less-Developed Countries for Access to Pharmaceuticals: Creating a Legal Duty to Supply under a Theory of Progressive Global Constitutionalism' (2004) 25 *University of Pennsylvania Journal of International Economic Law* 755–944.

[137] *cf* former US Ambassador J Bolton, 'Is there Really "Law" in International Affairs?' (2000) 10 *Transnational Law and Contemporary Problems* 1 ff (stating that the absence of legitimately authoritative legal sources and democratic institutions make it impossible for international law to be legitimate law); D Vagts, 'Hegemonic International Law' (2002) 95 *AJIL* 843 ff.

doctrine' in US administrative law) may be inappropriate in other jurisdictions for the necessary 'balancing' of economic rules with non-economic public interests as defined by human rights and constitutional rights. For example, the requirement in Article 17.6(ii) of the WTO Agreement on Implementation of Article VI GATT 1994 of 'judicial deference' in case of 'more than one permissible interpretation' of anti-dumping rules by national administrations – which had been introduced into this Agreement at the insistence of the United States in order to make the 'Chevron doctrine' part of the WTO legal and judicial system – has so far prompted neither WTO dispute settlement panels nor the WTO Appellate Body to limit their judicial review standards in the large number of WTO disputes over anti-dumping measures.[138] Most national parliaments do not effectively scrutinize intergovernmental trade practices (like calculation and administration of anti-dumping duties) and administrative compliance with the 'principles' underlying WTO anti-dumping rules (such as 'a fair comparison . . . between the export price and the normal value'); hence, the different 'constitutional context' of the WTO legal system may justify strict judicial review rather than deference to the powerful 'anti-dumping lobbies' in the US Congress, notwithstanding the WTO Appellate Body's acknowledgment that the textual recognition of the possibility of 'more than one permissible interpretation' must be taken into account. Anglo-Saxon claims for prioritizing civil and political rights based on 'mature constitutional systems, for example in the United States, Canada and Australia',[139] run counter to different constitutional traditions in Europe and in other continents where national constitutions and courts (eg, in South Africa and India) tend to protect economic and social rights more comprehensively than in many Anglo-Saxon countries.[140] Disregard for economic, social and cultural human rights and constitutional rights may undermine the legitimacy of IEL, as illustrated by the jurisprudence of European courts referring to fundamental rights not only as a justification of *protecting* intellectual property (eg, as private property protected under Article 14 of the German Basic Law), but as requiring 'external limits on intellectual property'.[141]

The ECtHR, for instance, has recognized that the entitlement of 'every natural or legal person . . . to the peaceful enjoyment of his possessions' (Article 1 of Protocol 1 to the ECHR) also protects intellectual property rights, including applications to register patents, trademarks, copyrights and other economic interests in intangible knowledge goods.[142] In accordance with its jurisprudence recognizing positive obligations of states to protect human rights, the ECtHR has acknowledged positive obligations to protect private property, for instance by providing 'a legal system so that property rights can be

[138] On the 'Chevron doctrine' of judicial deference and its controversial relationship with the 'Charming Betsy doctrine' of consistent interpretation see: A Davies, 'Connecting or Compartmentalizing the WTO and United States Legal Systems? The Role of the Charming Betsy Canon' (2007) 10 *JIEL* 117–49.

[139] See DZ Cass (2005) 191, and my criticism of her Anglo-Saxon bias disregarding the different constitutional traditions in civil law countries in Asia, Europe and Latin-America, *cf* Joerges and Petersmann (eds) (2006) ch 1.

[140] Studies of IEL from a comparative constitutional perspective – as the contributions to M Hilf and EU Petersmann (eds) (1993) – remain rare and tend to be ignored by 'realist' international law specialists due to their power-oriented, nationalist conceptions of foreign trade laws, foreign policies and 'international hegemonic law' serving national interests of powerful states. The criticism by Anglo-Saxon human rights specialists (like Alston) of protecting 'economic liberties' as fundamental freedoms disregards the 'indivisible' nature of constitutional guarantees of human liberty in European constitutional law, which requires constitutional justification of governmental restrictions of liberties in the economy no less than in the polity.

[141] *cf* C Geiger, 'Fundamental Rights: A Safeguard for the Coherence of Intellectual Property Law?' (2004) 35 *International Review of Intellectual Property and Competition Law* 277, 278.

[142] *cf* Helfer (n 134).

enforced': states must 'afford judicial procedures which offer the necessary procedural guarantees and therefore enable the domestic courts and tribunals to adjudicate effectively and fairly any (property) disputes between private persons'.[143] The ECtHR reviews whether government interferences with property are 'provided by law', pursue 'a legitimate aim' in the 'public interest' and achieve 'a fair balance . . . between the demands of the general interest of the community and the requirement of the protection of the individual's fundamental rights' that presents 'a reasonable relationship of proportionality between the means employed'; but the Court grants states a 'margin of appreciation' because national legislatures may be better placed than the international judge to assess the necessity of regulations for securing public interests. In *Dima v Romania*, the ECtHR reaffirmed its 'limited power' to review national court findings interpreting national intellectual property legislation and found 'no appearance of arbitrariness' in the ruling of Romania's Supreme Court denying a copyright and author right of Dima.[144] In *Anheuser-Busch Inc v Portugal*, the ECtHR recognized that Article 1 also protects applications to register trademarks that were 'capable of possessing substantial financial value'; in its judicial review of whether the Portuguese administrative and judicial decisions denying registration of the trademark 'Budweiser' interfered with 'legitimate expectations' protected by Article 1, the ECtHR concluded that the Supreme Court's rejection of Anheuser-Busch's claim of priority was neither arbitrary nor manifestly unreasonable.[145] The judicial interpretation of Article 1 as requiring legal and judicial protection of 'rule of law' in the regulation of private property did not prevent the ECtHR from emphasizing that it could not 'take the place of the national courts, its role being rather to ensure that the decisions of those courts are not flawed by arbitrariness or otherwise manifestly unreasonable'.[146]

Such a 'rule of law paradigm', limiting the judicial review by the ECtHR to arbitrary or unreasonable application of national intellectual property legislation, appears to be appropriate also in view of the existence of special, national and international jurisdictions for enforcing the state's positive obligations to provide for legal, administrative and judicial protection of intellectual property. As these legal obligations are regulated in specific international WIPO, WTO, investment and economic integration agreements and in their domestic implementing legislation, it may be reasonable for human rights courts to leave it to such special jurisdictions provided in economic agreements (such as WIPO and WTO dispute settlement proceedings, ECJ and EFTA Court proceedings, national courts) to review challenges by intellectual property owners that domestic enforcement mechanisms and related 'judicial balancing' (eg, of the relationships between trademarks and geographical indications in the *Anheuser-Busch* dispute) offer inadequate remedies.[147] Yet, such judicial self-restraint may be less justified if human rights (such as the right to freedom of expression protected in Article 10 ECHR) may justify limitations of intellectual property rights, for instance invocation of private copyrights in order to prevent publication of legitimate photos of 'public figures' in the public

[143] For a discussion of this case law, see Helfer (n 134) 40 ff.

[144] *Dima v Romania*, App no 58472/00 (2005). Dima was recognized in a Romanian statute as the 'graphic designer' of Romania's state emblem and seal, but was neither paid for his work nor recognized as holder of a copyright or author right under Romanian law.

[145] *Anheuser-Busch v Portugal*, App no 73049/01, 45 EHRR 36 [846] (Grand Chamber 2007).

[146] ibid (fn 145) 851.

[147] *cf* Helfer (n 134) who explains the relative advantages of the 'rule of law paradigm' of the ECtHR compared with an 'enforcement paradigm' or 'intellectual property balancing paradigm'.

press; even if legislative restrictions of intellectual property rights may be justified in the public interest, they may require compensation (eg, pursuant to Article 1 Protocol 1 to the ECHR). Similarly, specialized economic courts might legitimately exercise self-restraint by relying on the jurisprudence of human rights courts as to whether human rights (like freedom of expression, freedom of the press and access to essential medicines) justify limitations of intellectual property rights.[148] The mutual coherence of economic law and human rights law requires 'judicial comity' among economic courts and human rights courts; but autonomous, overlapping jurisdictions must respect their common constitutional principles in their joint clarification and protection of legal coherence and transnational rule of law. Similar to the principle of 'complementarity' in the cooperation among national and international criminal courts pursuant to the 1998 Statute of the International Criminal Court,[149] regional human rights courts (like the ECtHR) can assist national and regional economic courts (like the ECJ) in clarifying the human rights dimensions of domestic economic legislation.

5 CONSTITUTIONAL PLURALISM REQUIRES MULTILEVEL JUDICIAL COOPERATION IN PROTECTING TRANSNATIONAL RULE OF LAW AND 'HUMAN RIGHTS COHERENCE'

The human rights commitments in the UN Charter as well as in the 'constitutions' (*sic*) establishing various UN Specialized Agencies – like the ILO Constitution committed to labour rights and 'freedom of expression and of association'; the WHO Constitution committed to 'fundamental rights of every human being' including 'enjoyment of the highest attainable standard of health'; the FAO Constitution aimed at 'ensuring humanity's freedom from hunger'; the UNESCO Constitution committed to 'the democratic principles of the dignity, equality and mutual respect of men' and 'the education of humanity for justice and liberty and peace' – reflected the postwar ambitions, as stated in the Preamble of the UN Charter, 'to establish conditions under which justice and respect for the obligations arising from treaties and other sources of international law can be maintained'. The same is true for the setting up of the International Court of Justice as 'the principal judicial organ of the United Nations' (Article 92 UN Charter). Yet, notwithstanding the recognition of 'duties to protect' the human rights of citizens and of corresponding limitations of 'state sovereignty' in favour of human rights conceptions of 'popular sovereignty' (as illustrated by the humanitarian interventions in Kosovo and Libya), UN institutions remain reluctant to intervene inside UN member states so as to protect human rights effectively vis-à-vis the often pervasive abuses of power inside many UN member states. UN law has so far failed to evolve into a 'constitution of the international community' capable of effective protection of human rights, democratic governance and international rule of law.[150] The limited acceptance of the ICJ's compulsory

[148] See, eg, the case law of the ECtHR that injunctions, based on the Austrian Copyright Act and prohibiting newspapers from publishing photographs of politicians or other individuals involved in matters of public interest, violated the right to freedom of expression; *Verlagsgruppse News GMBH v Austria*, App no 10520/02 (2006).

[149] *cf* W Burke-White, 'Proactive Complementarity: The International Criminal Court and National Courts in the Rome System of International Justice' (2008) 49 *Harvard International Law Journal* 53 ff.

[150] On the potential 'constitutional functions' of UN law for promoting human rights, rule of law and democratic governance see: B Fassbender (2009).

jurisdiction by only about one-third of UN member states also prevented the ICJ from evolving into an effective guardian of international rule of law. Both national legal systems (eg, the 'Charming Betsy' doctrine in US jurisprudence) as well as the customary rules of international treaty interpretation (eg, Article 31 VCLT) remain based on legal presumptions that national and international rules must be construed in conformity with all other legal obligations of states. But specialized national and international courts all too often neglect this 'consistent interpretation principle' and the customary law requirement of interpreting international law 'in conformity with principles of justice' and the human rights obligations of states.

There are many obstacles to the strengthening of principles of constitutional, representative, participatory and deliberative democracy in the policymaking of worldwide organizations like the UN and the WTO. As long as neither UN nor WTO law protect international rule of law for the benefit of citizens through compulsory adjudication and effective judicial remedies, citizens rightly criticize the often arbitrary, welfare-reducing violations of UN and WTO rules ratified by national parliaments as 'feudalistic relics' of past times. Even though all WTO ministerial conferences since 1999 have been accompanied by interparliamentary meetings of parliamentarians from the majority of WTO member states, formal establishment of consultative parliamentary bodies in worldwide organizations remains opposed by many governments, including constitutional democracies like the United States.[151] As the postwar attempts at promoting and protecting human rights and international rule of law by 'foundational UN constitutionalism' have failed, transnational rule of law and constitutional limitations of abuses of foreign policy powers must be pursued by citizens and courts 'bottom-up' through national and regional 'piecemeal reforms', as illustrated by the progressive transformation and 'constitutional reforms' of European economic law following the popular rejection of the 'foundational EU Treaty Constitution' of 2004 in the Dutch and French *referenda* of 2005. Arguably, the *Kadi* judgments (*cf* Table 18) and the insistence by the ECJ and the EU's General Court on 'human rights coherence' of international rules reflect general constitutional principles that should be applied by all domestic courts in their domestic application of international rules regardless of their diverse conceptions of human rights.

Domestic constitutionalism, administrative law and their limits

American proponents of GAL admit that their GAL proposals (eg, for judicial deference following the 'Chevron doctrine' in US administrative law) are influenced by US administrative law.[152] Yet, at the worldwide level of international economic regulation, the characteristic foundations of US administrative law – like constitutional democracy, effective

[151] *cf* E Mann, 'A Parliamentary Dimension to the WTO: More than Just a Vision?' in EU Petersmann (2005) 421–28. On involvement of parliamentarians and civil society in WTO discussions see also the contributions by Charnovitz, Hilf, Eeckhout, Petersmann and US Congressman Sawyer to E Baron Crespo (ed), *The Parliamentary Dimension of the WTO* (European Parliament Doc WTO/242, 2006); *WTO Policy Issues for Parliamentarians* (WTO 2001); *Regional Workshop for Parliamentarians on the Multilateral Trading System* (Commonwealth Parliamentary Association/WTO 2003); *For A Free, Just and Equitable Multilateral Trading System: Providing a Parliamentary Dimension* (Inter-Parliamentary Union 2001).

[152] *cf* R Stewart, 'US Administrative Law: A Model for Global Administrative Law?' (2005) 68 *Law & Contemporary Problems* 63 ff.

congressional and judicial control of limited delegation of administrative powers, competition law and other regulation of market failures as well as of government failures – hardly exist. In contrast to European administrative law, American conceptions of GAL also neglect economic and social human rights and their 'constitutional principles.' As illustrated by the *Kadi* case, international administrative law risks undermining rather than protecting human rights. The preceding sections concluded that democratic legitimacy, transnational rule of law and economic efficiency of multilevel governance in international economic cooperation among 193 UN member states and billions of citizens require more than administrative reforms. Transnational rule of law based on stronger legal and judicial protection of cosmopolitan rights requires 'bottom-up constitutional reforms', as illustrated by the multilevel cooperation among national and international courts across Europe interpreting and enforcing national, European and certain international legal obligations of states in mutually consistent ways for the benefit of citizens in conformity with the 'consistent interpretation principles' recognized in national and international legal systems.

Proposals to separate the intergovernmental and 'administrative' dimensions of IEL from their 'constitutional foundations' often claim that the 'input legitimacy' and 'output legitimacy' of multilevel governance (eg, in the WTO) and of GAL can be secured by domestic constitutionalism, for example by parliamentary delegation of only limited powers to international organizations, parliamentary review of whether international agreements deserve parliamentary ratification and parliamentary design and control of domestic implementing legislation.[153] Yet, empirical studies of parliamentary involvement in, and review of, intergovernmental rulemaking in worldwide organizations confirm that parliamentary delegation of powers, and parliamentary review of their intergovernmental exercise, often remain superficial and ineffective. Intergovernmental economic negotiations tend to be dominated by powerful producer interests and – once they have resulted in agreed 'package deals' elaborated in secretive negotiations in distant international organizations (like the 30,000 pages of the 1994 Uruguay Round Agreements) – can hardly be reopened and changed by any national parliament.[154] In

[153] *cf* former US Congressman and WTO Appellate Body member J Bacchus, 'A Few Thoughts on Legitimacy, Democracy and the WTO' in Petersmann (2005) 429, 435: 'the principal focus of efforts to improve the "legitimacy" of the WTO-based trading system by increasing the "democracy" in international trade policy-making should not be on creating any new international mechanism . . . Rather, the principal focus of those efforts should be on ensuring more "democratic governance" of national trade policy-making through more effective domestic mechanisms of "democratic governance" within the national governments of the individual states that are the Members of the WTO'. Similarly, former WTO Director-General M Moore, 'The Democratic Roots of the World Trade Organization' in PFJ Macrory, AE Appelton and MG Plummer (eds), *The WTO. Legal, Economic and Political Analysis*, vol I (Heidelberg: Springer Verlag, 2005) 39, 44 f: 'There is no meaningful "democratic deficit" in the WTO unless one takes the position that governments do not legitimately represent their citizens and their interests'; 'democratic accountability rests with governments and governments alone. If WTO negotiations are shrouded in too much secrecy, or if citizens are left in the dark, or if certain Ministers only listen to "big business" and national elites, then it is a failure of governments – and their obligation to represent all their citizens' interests – not a failure of the WTO'.

[154] The Uruguay Round Agreements have illustrated that – once the intergovernmental negotiations had led to international agreement – national parliaments in most WTO member countries 'rubber-stamped' the results without any concrete possibility for 'reopening' the negotiations; the German Parliament, for example, had not even received a complete German translation of the voluminous WTO texts when the parliament had to decide on the ratification of the WTO Agreement; *cf* the country studies in J Jackson and A Sykes (eds), *Implementing the Uruguay Round* (Oxford: Clarendon Press, 1997). Rulemaking and policymaking in the WTO continue to be not effectively controlled in most national parliaments (with the exception of, eg, the Swiss Parliament and the US Congress), *cf The Role of Parliaments in Scrutinising and Influencing Trade Policy – A Comparative Analysis*, European Parliament Study (PE 370-166v01-00) December 2005.

worldwide organizations with effective dispute settlement and enforcement systems (like the WTO), opting out of global regimes – or non-compliance with ratified international commitments – may offer no realistic policy alternatives in view of their prohibitive costs. At the request of trade politicians, domestic courts in most WTO member states – notwithstanding their frequent acknowledgment of the 'consistent interpretation requirement' of construing domestic rules in conformity with the international legal obligations of the country concerned – often avoid taking into account WTO rules and WTO dispute settlement rulings in the application of domestic trade laws.[155] Such politically motivated 'dualism' between international legal obligations and their domestic application further undermines the functional unity and effectiveness of IEL to the detriment of citizens who are treated as mere objects of international law rather than as legal subjects entitled to 'participatory democracy' and judicial protection of rule of law. Due to the 'rational ignorance' of most citizens vis-à-vis complex global governance problems and the 'information asymmetries' and 'discourse failures' preventing 'deliberative democracy' from operating as effective restraint on 'global governance failures', domestic constitutionalism offers only limited help in limiting multilevel economic governance failures. Outside constitutional democracies, administrative law can be a powerful tool of suppression and disregard of human rights, as illustrated by the administrative law traditions in communist countries and in corrupt 'failed states'.

Transnational rule of law, like welfare, depends on citizens defending their human rights and on judicial protection of common 'constitutional principles of justice'

Law, as Lon Fuller explained, orders social life not only by 'subjecting human conduct to the governance of rules';[156] in order to remain effective, law must also aim at establishing a *just* order and procedures for the *fair* resolution of disputes.[157] Chapters I to IV proceeded from the principle of 'responsible self-government' underlying modern economics and Rawls' theory of justice: welfare and rule of law depend on citizens establishing reasonable rules and institutions.

The three complementary 'international treaty constitutions' in postwar Europe – the EU Treaty as interpreted by the ECJ, the EEA Agreement as interpreted by the EFTA Court and the ECHR as interpreted by the ECtHR – evolved progressively in response to requests by citizens for 'constitutional treaty interpretations' by national and European

[155] *cf* JA Restani and I Bloom, 'Interpreting International Trade Statutes: Is the Charming Betsy Sinking?' (2001) 24 *Fordham International Law Journal* 1533. The ECJ has a long history of ignoring GATT and WTO rules at the request of political EC bodies which repeatedly misled the ECJ on the meaning of GATT/WTO rules and dispute settlement reports (eg, in Case 112/80, *Dürbeck* [1981] ECR 1095, the Commission misinformed the EC Court on an unpublished GATT dispute settlement finding against the EC, and the Court relied on this information without verifying the obviously wrong information submitted to the Court). The judicial denial of 'direct applicably' of GATT obligations does, however, not preclude indirect ways of interpreting domestic trade laws (eg, the EU's customs union rules based on Art XXIV GATT) in conformity with WTO rules and WTO dispute settlement rulings.

[156] Fuller (1969) 96.

[157] For Fuller's criticism of positivist conceptions of law see LL Fuller, 'Positivism and Fidelity to Law – A Reply to Professor Hart' (1958) 71 *Harvard Law Review* 630. As explained in chs II and III, the incorporation of 'inalienable' human rights 'deriving from respect for human dignity' into positive law has merged legal positivism and natural rights theories, notwithstanding the lack of consensus on how to interpret their interrelationships.

'courts of justice' interpreting international guarantees of freedom, non-discrimination and rule of law for the benefit of individual 'fundamental freedoms' and judicial protection of human rights and 'common constitutional principles'.[158] In the EU, the different layers of private and public, national and international rules were progressively integrated – through successive treaty amendments and judicial protection of individual rights – into a mutually coherent, legal and constitutional system 'founded on the principles of liberty, democracy, respect for human rights and fundamental freedoms, and the rule of law, principles which are common to the Member States' (Article 6 EU). In its 1986 judgment in *Les Verts*, the ECJ declared that

> the European Economic Community is a Community based on the rule of law, inasmuch as neither its Member States nor its institutions can avoid a review of the question whether the measures adopted by them are in conformity with the basic constitutional charter, the Treaty.[159]

The 2007 Lisbon Treaty emphasizes the establishment of 'an area of freedom, security and justice' based on 'the values of respect for human dignity, freedom, democracy, equality, the rule of law and respect for human rights' and 'justice' as foundational values of the EU (Preamble and Articles 2–3 TEU).

The citizen-driven interpretation and judicial enforcement of European competition, common market, environmental and constitutional rules has dramatically enhanced the problem-solving capacities of constitutional democracies throughout Europe. Welfare-reducing violations of international disciplines have remained frequent, however, in those areas where – as in the case of the fiscal and debt disciplines provided for in the EU's Growth and Stability Pact, or as regards the WTO obligations of the EU – EU citizens were denied legal and judicial remedies to challenge non-compliance with internationally agreed rules. The bail-out prohibition in Article 125 TFEU entailed that the bail-out agreements for Greece, Ireland and Portugal – and the establishment of the temporary European Financial Stability Facility in 2010 and of the permanent European Financial Stability Mechanism in 2012 – had to be approved and controlled by national parliaments. The five EU Regulations and additional EU Directive of November 2011 on strengthening economic governance in the European Monetary Union all aim explicitly at strengthening rule of law based on 'stronger national ownership of commonly agreed rules and policies'.[160] The criminal charges of negligence and judicial procedures against Iceland's former Prime Minister challenging his handling of the collapse (in 2009) of Iceland's top three banks, like the judicial review and sanction procedures provided for in the 2012 'Treaty on Stability, Coordination and Governance in the Economic and Monetary Union' signed by 25 EU member states in March 2012, illustrate the perceived need for making internationally agreed legal and economic disciplines inside domestic legal and policy systems more effective. In international monetary relations, for instance, the IMF Agreement provides that exchange contracts undermining IMF-consistent exchange control regulations 'shall be unenforceable in the territories of any member' (Article VIII:2);[161] in disputes over sovereign bonds, the standardized contractual clauses governing sovereign debt contracts likewise provide for the direct applicability of inter-

[158] *cf* Petersmann (n 100).
[159] Case 294/83, *Parti écologiste 'Les Verts' v European Parliament* [1986] ECR 1339, para 23.
[160] The quoted text appears in the Preambles of all five regulations, cf OJ EU L 306 of 23 November 2011.
[161] *cf* J Gold, *The Fund Agreement in the Courts*, vol 2 (Washington: IMF, 1982).

national law by national courts and investor–state arbitration, including the possibility of class actions by private individual bondholders.[162] Transnational rule of law does not prevent national courts from insisting that international financial stand-by agreements must be applied in conformity with social rights guaranteed by domestic constitutional law.[163] In the external trade and maritime relations with third countries, however, EU diplomats continue to insist that worldwide UN conventions (like UNCLOS), the WTO Agreement and also future free trade agreements concluded by the EU confer rights and obligations only on governments without limiting the 'freedom of manoeuvre'[164] of EU diplomats to violate the law. Arguably, the lack of effective legal and judicial remedies against the persistent violations of the EU's fiscal, debt and international trade disciplines undermine not only the legitimacy, but also the economic efficiency of EU law and policies to the detriment of EU citizens.

The 'constitutional approach to IEL' advocated in this study perceives the law of international organizations, intergovernmental rulemaking, GAL and multilevel judicial protection of rule of law – as in European economic integration – as mutually complementary methods of regulating, limiting and legitimizing multilevel governance of interdependent public goods for the benefit of citizens. As GAL advocates, it remains sceptical of comprehensive 'constitutional visions' for a 'fully justifiable global order' in view of the reality and legitimacy of 'constitutional pluralism' and the limited reasonableness of individuals with diverse worldviews. Yet, it also criticizes GAL conceptions neglecting the need for justifying and reviewing administrative regulation on the basis of common constitutional principles of justice. Citizens and diverse constitutional democracies are unlikely to ever agree on any comprehensive theory of justice in view of their legitimately different value preferences and often conflicting self-interests. Yet, human rights law, constitutional democracies and also UN law remain committed to 'establish justice' (Preamble US Constitution) and 'maintain international peace and security . . . in conformity with the principles of justice and international law' (Article 1 UN Charter). True, many worldwide economic agreements – such as the agreements establishing the IMF, GATT, the WTO, the World Bank Group, the International Civil Aviation Organization and International Maritime Organization – pursue economic objectives and practices without any reference to 'justice', human rights, democratic governance and rule of law. The VCLT confirms, however, 'that disputes concerning treaties, like other international disputes, should be settled by peaceful means and in conformity with the principles of justice and international law', including 'respect for, and observance of, human rights and fundamental freedoms for all' (Preamble). The proposals by the UN High Commissioner for Human Rights and by WTO Director-General Pascal Lamy for interpreting WTO rules in conformity with the human rights obligations of their member states[165] reflect this 'constitutional insight' that – as long as citizens, parliaments

[162] *cf G Beccara and others v the Argentine Republic*, Case No ARB/07/5 (filed in 2006).

[163] *cf* Latvian Constitutional Court, Judgment No 2009-43-01, 21 December 2009 (discussed in M Waibel, *Sovereign Debt before International Courts and Tribunals* (Cambridge: CUP, 2011).

[164] This term continues to be used by both the political EU institutions and the EU Court of Justice (eg, in Joined cases C-120 and C-121/06 P, FIAMM [2008] ECR I-6513, para 119) as the main justification for their disregard of legally binding WTO rules and WTO dispute settlement rulings.

[165] On the 'human rights approach' to IEL advocated by the UNHCHR, see ch VII section 4. The speeches by WTO Director-General Pascal Lamy on 'Globalization and Trade Opening Can Promote Human Rights' (5 June 2009) and 'Towards Shared Responsibility and Greater Coherence: Human Rights, Trade and Macroeconomic Policy' (13 January 2010) are published on the WTO website: www.wto.org.

and 'courts of justice' do not control more effectively intergovernmental power politics disregarding 'rule of law'[166] and 'human rights coherence' of IEL – collective supply of international public goods, like maximization of consumer welfare through a mutually beneficial world trading and financial system and prevention of climate change, cannot succeed.

Limitation of welfare-reducing trade mercantilism by cosmopolitan rights and transnational rule of law depends on 'struggles for justice'

The Dutch and French *referenda* rejecting the 2004 Draft Treaty on a European Constitution illustrate that – even among constitutional democracies in Europe – citizens with diverse democratic preferences and self-interests tend to disagree on comprehensive theories of justice and international 'foundational Constitutionalism'. Arguably, representative democracy finds its natural limits inside historically grown, national communities and, beyond national borders, musts be strengthened by participatory and deliberative forms of constitutionally limited, democratic self-governance. Proposals for *worldwide* 'treaty constitutions' will be distrusted even more by reasonable citizens. The international structures of the EC Treaty, the EEA Agreement and the ECHR were transformed only piecemeal into rights-based, constitutional structures driven by judicial interpretations protecting rights of citizens in national and European courts. The 2007 Lisbon Treaty has further constitutionally constrained majority politics by non-majoritarian governance institutions (like independent European supervisory and regulatory agencies) and by strengthening multilevel 'judicial governance' as guardian of 'rule of law'.[167] Also in the WTO, 'member-driven governance' is increasingly limited by the already more than 250 WTO panel, appellate and arbitral rulings on legally binding settlements of disputes and clarifications of indeterminate WTO rules.[168] Yet, human rights play only a marginal role in most international economic disputes, for example, in worldwide tribunals like the ICJ, WTO dispute settlement bodies, investor–state arbitration proceedings and also in the ECJ and EFTA Court. Whereas constitutional democracies accept that private and governmental 'rule by law' must be constitutionally and judicially restrained by 'rule of law', the legitimate functions of 'judicial governance' of international economic cooperation among citizens remain contested by many governments insisting on foreign policy discretion. Most diplomats and WTO judges (about 70 per cent of 'WTO panellists' continue to be former trade diplomats) are likely to agree with US Supreme Court Justice Oliver Wendell Holmes who – when he was greeted, on

[166] On the pursuit of 'order' rather than 'justice' in international relations see: R Foot, JL Gaddis and A Hurrel (eds), *Order and Justice in International Relations* (Oxford: OUP, 2003); J Thomson, *Justice and World Order* (London: Routledge, 1992).

[167] On 'judicial governance' see: M Shapiro and A Stone Sweet, *On Law, Politics and Judicialization* (Oxford: OUP, 2004) ch 4 (describing adjudication as a particular mode of governance, through which the legal structures of a legal community are continuously adapted to the needs and purposes of citizens and governments). The Lisbon Treaty considerably extends the jurisdiction of the ECJ compared with the previous Nice Treaty; *cf* Hinarejos (n 37).

[168] *cf* EU Petersmann, 'From "Member-Driven Governance" to Constitutionally Limited "Multilevel Trade Governance" in the WTO' in G Sacerdoti *et al* (eds), *The WTO at 10: The Role of Dispute Settlement* (Cambridge: CUP, 2006) 86–110.

his way to the court, by another lawyer: 'Do justice, Justice!' – replied: 'That's not my job; I have to apply the rules whether I like them or not'.[169]

WTO members, WTO lawyers and WTO dispute settlement bodies emphasize the limited terms of reference of WTO dispute settlement panels

> to examine, in the light of the relevant provisions in (. . . the covered agreement(s) cited by the parties to the dispute), the matter referred to the DSB . . . and to make such findings as will assist the DSB in making the recommendations or in giving the rulings provided for in that/those agreement(s) (Article 7 DSU).

The emphasis on the 'member-driven character' of intergovernmental organizations and the limited mandate of intergovernmental dispute settlement procedures prompt most governments to argue that WTO dispute settlement bodies have no mandate to follow the example of regional courts and human rights bodies to interpret international guarantees of freedom, non-discrimination, rule of law, 'public morals', 'public order' or 'human health' (eg, in Articles XX GATT, XIV GATS) not only in terms of intergovernmental rights and obligations among WTO members, but also as legal safeguards protecting rights of producers, investors, traders and consumers. This is especially so if, as in the US complaint challenging China's censorship restrictions of copyrighted information materials, the complainant deliberately avoids challenging the 'human rights coherence' of restrictions of individual rights.[170] As the EC and US legislation implementing the WTO Agreements explicitly enjoin domestic courts *not* to directly apply the WTO obligations vis-à-vis EC trade regulations and US federal trade law, most domestic courts in Europe and North America tend to ignore WTO rules and WTO dispute settlement rulings even if the 'reasonable period' for the domestic implementation of WTO dispute settlement rulings has expired.[171] As discussed in section 1, this separation of 'rule of law among states' from 'rule of law among private economic actors' undermines the legal effectiveness and democratic legitimacy of WTO law and of its dispute settlement system as 'a central element in providing security and predictability to the multilateral trading system' (Article 3 DSU).

[169] For a discussion of this dictum by Justice Holmes see: R Dworkin (2006) ch 1; T Sowell, *The Quest for Cosmic Justice* (New York: The Free Press, 1999) 169.

[170] *cf* the WTO Appellate Body report on *China – Publications and Audiovisual Products* (WT/DS363/AB/R), adopted 19 January 2010. Also in the consultations on the dispute between the Google Company and China over Chinese restrictions of internet services, the Chinese censorship was apparently not challenged on human rights grounds.

[171] See EU Petersmann, 'Multilevel Judicial Trade Governance without Justice? On the Role of Domestic Courts in the WTO Legal and Dispute Settlement System' in ME Janow (ed), *The WTO at 10: Governance, Dispute Settlement and Developing Countries* (New York: Juris Publishing, 2007) 959–86. See, eg, the judgment of 21 January 2005 (*Corus Staal*) by the US Court of Appeals for the Federal Circuit, available at: www.fedcir.gov/opinions/04-1107.pdf): '[WTO decisions are] not binding on the US, much less this court'. The US Supreme Court denied petition *for certiorari* on 9 January 2006 (available at www.supremecourtus.gov/docket/05-364.htm), notwithstanding an amicus curiae brief filed by the EC Commission supporting this petition ('We argue that the Federal Circuit went too far by construing the Uruguay Round Agreements Act to make considerations of compliance with international obligations completely irrelevant in construing a Department of Commerce anti-dumping determination, and further argue that the Department's "zeroing" methodology – held invalid by both a WTO Appellate Body and a NAFTA Bi-national Panel – is not entitled to *Chevron* deference because it would bring the United States into noncompliance with treaty obligations' (available at:'www.robbinsrussell.com/pdf/265.pdf).

Table 24: The ECJ's refusal to review EC restrictions on the basis of the EC's legal obligations under GATT/WTO law

Since its judgment in *International Fruit Company* (Case 21-24/72, ECR 1972, 1219), the ECJ has consistently denied – at the request of the EU Commission and EU Council – that individuals and EC member states can rely on the GATT obligations of the EC for contesting the legality of EC measures and for obtaining compensation (pursuant to Articles 235, 288 EC) for private damages caused by the EC's violation of international law, even if legally binding GATT (WTO) dispute settlement rulings had formally confirmed the illegality of the EC measures and the period for domestic implementation had expired. The Court recognized that the GATT obligations of the EC – like other international agreements concluded by the EC – form an 'integrating part' of the Community legal system with a legal rank inferior to the EC Treaty, but superior to acts of the EC institutions. The ECJ also enforced GATT obligations at the request of the EU Commission against EC member states (Case C-61/94 *Commission v Germany* [1996] ECR I-3989). The Court initially justified its refusal to review the legality of EC acts on the basis of GATT/WTO law by claiming that GATT rules were too imprecise, conditional and subject to safeguard clauses; that GATT's reciprocity principle prevented judicial application of GATT rules; and Article 22 DSU allowed mutually agreed compensation as a means of averting trade sanctions. This judicial reasoning was widely criticized for being inconsistent (1) with the precise and unconditional nature of most GATT/WTO obligations; (2) with the ECJ's enforcement of reciprocal free trade agreements with similar safeguard and dispute settlement provisions; (3) the legal irrelevance of Article 22 DSU for the WTO inconsistency of the trade restrictions; and (4) the limitation of the legal and judicial accountability of the EU institutions for violations of their international legal obligations undermining rule of law inside the EU. In response to this criticism, the ECJ conceded the political nature of its refusal to maintain rule of law: 'To review the legality of actions of the Community institutions in the light of (WTO) rules could lead to an unequal application of the WTO rules depriving the legislative or executive organs of the Community of the scope of manoeuvre enjoyed by their counterparts in the Community's trading partners' (Case C-149/96 *Portugal v Council* [1999] ECR I-8395, paragraphs 42–46). In a few judgments, the ECJ interpreted EC rules in conformity with the EC's WTO obligations. Yet, the exceptions acknowledged by the ECJ – 'it is only where the Community intends to implement a particular obligation assumed in the context of the WTO or where the Community measure refers expressly to specific provisions of the WTO agreements that the Court can review the legality of the conduct of the defendant institutions in the light of the WTO rules' (Case C-149/96 *Portugal v Council* [1999[ECR I-8395, paragraph 53) – have hardly ever led to application of GATT/WTO rules in the more than 60 disputes in the ECJ over GATT/WTO violations by the EC. The ECJ's similar refusal to review EC measures in light of the UN Law of the Sea Convention (Case C-308/06 *Intertanko* [2008] ECR I-4057) confirms that the judicial self-restraint by the ECJ to enforce EC obligations under worldwide treaties with separate jurisdictions for international dispute settlement is based on political rather than legal grounds. From a democratic citizen perspective, the ECJ should – rather than ignoring the EU's constitutional requirement of 'strict observance of international law' (Article 3 TEU) – limit its 'political question doctrine' to invocations of WTO and UNCLOS law where foreign complainants have direct or indirect access to WTO and UNCLOS dispute settlement procedures (eg, *not* in complaints by EU member states or EU citizens legitimately requesting the ECJ to protect them against adverse effects of arbitrary EU violations of international law).

Should WTO judges protect legal security also for the benefit of private traders?

Should international judges and governments apply international economic rules and related dispute settlement procedures without regard to justice, just as economists perceive trade law as a mere instrument for promoting economic welfare and for justifying trade protection for import-competing producers? Does the separation of the judicial power from the legislative and executive powers require that, as postulated by Montesquieu, decisions of courts must always conform to the exact letter of the law as understood by the legislator? Does the frequent emphasis by governments on the 'member-driven' character of WTO law, and the frequent recourse to the *Oxford English Dictionary* in the case law of WTO panels and the Appellate Body, confirm the view that, also in WTO law, judges must apply the positive law literally without regard to the normative question of whether the applicable rules lead to a just resolution of the dispute? Does justice also require respect for international law by *domestic* judges, for example by interpreting domestic laws in conformity with self-imposed international treaties approved by parliaments and legally binding on all state organs?

Most multilateral agreements, including the WTO Agreement, were elaborated without an official 'legislative history'. In order to reduce 'negotiation costs' and bridge diverse legislative intentions and preferences of individual countries and their negotiators, they often make use not only of 'constructive ambiguity' to reach agreement on general treaty provisions; international economic agreements also increasingly provide that disputes over the interpretation of treaty rights and obligations shall be decided by independent dispute settlement bodies. Delegating powers to interpret and clarify indeterminate treaty rules to international judicial bodies enhances legal security and reduces transaction costs; but it also refutes the medieval conception of judges as passive agents applying substantive rules, enacted by the lawmaker, to the particular circumstances of a dispute in predictable, secure and legitimate procedures. In the absence of a single 'international legislator' ensuring the overall coherence among the thousands of international agreements and 'secondary rules' adopted by international organizations, international courts must choose between many possible dictionary meanings in order to clarify the normative ambiguities underlying imprecise legal provisions, for instance by engaging in systematic 'balancing' of competing rights and obligations in the judicial examination of whether restrictions of individual rights 'are necessary in a democratic society in the interest of public safety, for the protection of public order, health or morals, or for the protection of the rights and freedoms of others'.[172] This increasing recourse – also in the case law of the WTO Appellate Body and in international investment arbitration – to judicial 'balancing' and 'principles' for justifying interpretive choices accords with modern constitutional theories of adjudication, such as Dworkin's 'adjudicative principle of integrity' requiring judges to regard law as expressing 'a coherent conception of justice and fairness':

> Law as integrity asks judges to assume, so far as this is possible, that the law is structured by a coherent set of principles about justice and fairness and procedural due process, and it asks

[172] Such 'necessity clauses' appear in numerous Articles of the ECHR and reflect similar 'necessity clauses' in EC law, WTO law, investment treaties and many other international treaties and national constitutions. According to the ECtHR, the individual rights of access to justice (Arts 6, 13 ECHR) and the limitation clauses of human rights require courts to 'balance' and optimize competing human rights.

> them to enforce these in the fresh cases that come before them, so that each person's situation is fair and just according to the same standards.[173]

In intergovernmental dispute settlement proceedings in worldwide organizations, state-centred conceptions of 'justice' and 'fairness' tend to prevail in interpreting IEL, for example in GATT dispute settlement findings on whether a subsidy has been 'applied in a manner which results in that contracting party having more than an equitable share of world export trade in that product' (Article XVI:3 GATT).[174] According to Article 3 of the WTO Dispute Settlement Understanding (DSU), the

> dispute settlement system of the WTO is a central element in providing security and predictability to the multilateral trading system. The Members recognize that it serves to preserve the rights and obligations of Members under the covered agreements, and to clarify the existing provisions of those agreements in accordance with the customary rules of interpretation of public international law (paragraph 2).

Does this reference to the 'rights and obligations of Members' exclude interpreting and applying WTO provisions (eg, on private access to domestic courts, protection of private 'trading rights' and intellectual property rights) as also protecting private rights and legitimate expectations of producers, investors, traders and consumers participating in international trade? The globalization of international markets and the human rights obligations of all UN member states entail that national and international judges are likely to be confronted increasingly with citizen-oriented claims for interpreting IEL rules 'in conformity with the principles of justice' and human rights (Preamble VCLT). The increasing participation, directly and indirectly (eg, through amicus curiae submissions), of individuals and non-governmental organizations in international economic disputes (eg, in European economic and human rights courts, WTO dispute settlement proceedings initiated by the EU and the United States at the request of private industries) promotes arguments that the human rights obligations of all UN member states require interpreting intergovernmental rules (eg, prohibitions of discrimination in GATT and WTO law, in ILO conventions, Articles 12 and 141 EC Treaty) and guarantees of due process of law no longer exclusively from the perspective of 'government interests'; as governments receive their legitimacy from protecting the rights of their citizens, intergovernmental rules for private trade should also protect private rights (eg, to invoke WTO guarantees of intellectual property rights, 'core labour rights' protected by ILO conventions, the EC Treaty's 'market freedoms') and private interests (eg, to submit amicus curiae communications to trade and investment tribunals, to open WTO panel and Appellate Body meetings to the public). In such judicial choices among state-centred versus citizen-oriented interpretations of international trade, investment and intellectual property rules, judicial answers may legitimately differ depending on the specific legal and constitutional context. Access to justice and 'deliberative democracy' require transparent, public discussions among citizens, their democratic representatives and 'courts of justice' justifying IEL rules for the benefit of citizens affected by the dispute concerned.

[173] R Dworkin, *Law's Empire* (Cambridge: Harvard University Press, 1986) 225, 243.

[174] *cf* the *GATT Analytical Index* (WTO 1995) recording the GATT dispute settlement practice relating to Art XVI:3, which focuses on macroeconomic trade shares rather than on microeconomic distortions of competition favouring subsidized products and producers.

Formal versus substantive 'principles of justice': constitutional interpretation as a requirement of customary international law

According to the WTO Appellate Body, the requirement, in Article 31 VCLT, that 'a Treaty shall be interpreted in good faith in accordance with the ordinary meaning to be given to the terms of the treaty in their context and in the light of its object and purpose', constitutes 'one holistic rule',[175] whose different elements (text, context, object and purpose) are often difficult to separate. The customary methods of treaty interpretation, as codified in the VCLT, prescribe not only formal legal principles for the interpretation of international treaties (like *pacta sunt servanda, lex specialis, lex posterior, lex superior*); the VCLT also requires 'that disputes concerning treaties, like other international disputes, should be settled by peaceful means and in conformity with the principles of justice and international law' (Preamble). The VCLT refers, inter alia, to

> principles of international law embodied in the Charter of the United Nations, such as the principles of the equal rights and self-determination of peoples, of the sovereign equality and independence of States, of non-interference in the domestic affairs of States, of the prohibition of the threat or use of force and of universal respect for, and observance of, human rights and fundamental freedoms for all' (Preamble).[176]

The globalization of economic, environmental, legal and technological cooperation and of human rights continues to promote new modes of legal and 'constitutional' reasoning (eg, on the human rights responsibilities of governments and NGOs) differing from the 'legal formalism' reflected in some of the 'conflict rules' in the VCLT.[177] For example, the application of biotechnologies to parts of the human body, animals, food and agriculture raises new legal questions (eg, regarding the legal status of human stem cells, embryos, the foetus) whose national and regional regulation may legitimately differ (eg, in Europe, the United States and LDCs); hence, international judges may exercise judicial deference in deciding related international economic[178] and human rights disputes.[179]

175 This term had already been used in the WTO Panel report on US-Section 301 (WT/DS152/R), para 7.22. The Appellate Body confirmed in *EC-Chicken Cuts*: 'Interpretation pursuant to the customary rules codified in Article 31 of the Vienna Convention is ultimately a holistic exercise that should not be mechanically subdivided into rigid components' (WT/DS269,286/AB/R, para 176, adopted in September 2005).

176 Arguably, this Preamble text refers not only to the preceding sub-paragraph on 'conditions under which justice and respect for the obligations arising from treaties can be maintained', but also to 'principles of justice and international law', in conformity with the recognition in numerous legal systems that human rights constitute not only individual rights, but also corresponding obligations of governments and 'principles of law' to be taken into account in legislation, administration, adjudication and international treaty interpretation pursuant to Art 31 VCLT.

177 On the 'formalism' of the general international law rules coordinating the fragmented bilateral, regional and worldwide treaty systems see M Koskenniemi, *Fragmentation of International Law: Difficulties Arising from the Diversification and Expansion of International Law*, UN document A/CN.4/L.682, 4 April 2006. On the moral and constitutional values underlying human rights law see, eg, CS Nino, *The Ethics of Human Rights* (Oxford: OUP, 1991); P Hayden (ed), *The Philosophy of Human Rights* (St Paul: Paragon House, 2001). D Beyleveld and R Brownsword, *Human Dignity in Bioethics and Biolaw* (Oxford: OUP, 2001); J Pauwelyn, T Cottier and E Bürgi (eds) (2005); Abbott, Breining and T Cottier (eds) (2006).

178 See EU Petersmann, 'The WTO Dispute over Genetically Modified Organisms: Interface Problems of International Trade Law, Environmental Law and Biotechnology Law' in F Francioni and T Scovazzi (eds), *Biotechnology and International Law* (Oxford: Hart Publishing, 2006) 173–200 (the 2006 WTO dispute settlement panel exercised 'judicial economy' vis-à-vis numerous disputed legal questions).

179 *cf* EU Petersmann, 'Biotechnology, Human Rights and International Economic Law' in F Francioni and T Scovazzi (eds), *Biotechnology and International Law* (Oxford: Hart Publishing, 2006). For example, the

Similar to the successful transformation of EC treaty law into citizen-oriented constitutional law focusing on legal protection of fundamental rights and citizen welfare, the increasing limitation of 'state sovereignty' by 'duties to protect' human rights and other 'common concerns' illustrates that the future legitimacy and effectiveness of UN law and IEL will depend on redefining their interstate foundation in conformity with the human rights obligations of all UN member countries. In many UN member states, governments remain the main violators of human rights and the main obstacle to mutually welfare-increasing cooperation among citizens across national frontiers. Hence, international legal safeguards are needed not only in relations among states, but also for the protection of citizens against their own governments and 'constitutional failures' inside states. The more justice is recognized as an agreed objective of national and international law, the more justice-related claims will be raised also in *international* rulemaking and dispute settlement proceedings, for instance in investor–state arbitration, regional courts and human rights bodies. The following chapter explains why the common 'constitutional core' of theories of justice – in spite of the legitimate diversity of conceptions of justice – can be defined in terms of basic human rights, which increasingly limit the power-oriented, positivist traditions and conceptions of international law. Respect for human dignity, equal basic liberties and social justice can be understood as the '*jus cogens* core' of UN human rights law, requiring also reconciliation of state sovereignty, popular sovereignty and 'individual sovereignty' in IEL by reinterpreting, wherever possible, state-centred international law rules for the benefit of citizens and their human rights.

The utilitarian logic of economists separating 'economic efficiency' from questions of equity, like the 'power-oriented realism' of state-centred diplomats, render legal discussions of judicial and justice-related questions difficult inside specialized economic regimes. Human rights activists claim that justice, as defined by human rights norms, requires far-reaching changes in IEL and institutions. As discussed in chapter VII, WTO members increasingly engage in discussions with UN human rights rapporteurs and challenge claims that human rights call for trade protectionism (eg, in favour of local farmers); but they disagree on any official response to the various reports by the UN High Commissioner for Human Rights on the human rights obligations of WTO members and the human rights deficits of WTO practices.[180] The diversity of governmental and judicial approaches to the interpretation and application of international economic rules confirms the need for more transparent, democratic discourse on the constitutional functions of IEL to protect equal freedoms and welfare-enhancing, peaceful cooperation – not only in intergovernmental relations, but also among private citizens and non-governmental organizations as the main driving forces of the international economy and of citizen-oriented reforms of international law. By challenging state-centred traditions and vested interests protected by the traditional 'international law among states', citizens

European Court of Human Rights, in its judgment of 8 July 2004 in *Case of Vo v France* (App no 53924/00), explicitly left open the controversial question whether Art 2 of the ECHR (right to life) also protects the human embryo and the foetus' right to life: 'it is neither desirable, nor even possible as matters stand, to answer in the abstract the question whether the unborn child is a person for the purposes of Article 2 of the Convention' (para 85).

[180] *cf* Petersmann (n 114) 605–28. Over the past years, meetings between UN human rights rapporteurs (eg, on the human rights to food and to health protection) and WTO diplomats have become more frequent. But WTO documents hardly ever refer to the human rights obligations of WTO members, notwithstanding increasing references to human rights in speeches by WTO Director-General Pascal Lamy.

may ultimately learn – through public discourse, struggles for justice and 'trials and errors' – how to defend their human rights and democratic self-government more effectively in international economic regulation against the ubiquitous abuses of foreign policy powers as well as of private economic power at home and abroad.

VI

Transnational Rule of Law Must be Justified by an 'Overlapping Consensus' on Principles of Justice

THE IDEA OF 'justice as a prerequisite to living a civic life, to living in community' (Plato) belongs to the oldest traditions of legal philosophy in Europe.[1] International courts, like the ICJ and investment tribunals, often refer to 'considerations of basic justice'[2] in order to decide procedural and substantive legal problems that are not specifically regulated in the applicable rules of law. Similarly, national courts often describe international arbitral awards as 'a decision of international justice whose validity must be ascertained with regard to the rules applicable in the country where its recognition and enforcement are sought'.[3] International courts and investment arbitral tribunals increasingly recognize that IEL can and must be construed in conformity with the human rights obligations of states.[4] Chapter V argued that the human rights obligations of all UN member states and the globalization of IEL on the basis of legitimate 'constitutional pluralism' require governments and courts of justice to protect transnational rule of law for the benefit of citizens rather than only in terms of 'rule of international law' protecting rights of governments. The interdependent national and international legal regimes have to be construed and mutually adjusted on the basis of common principles of justice and 'public reason' which can be justified and supported by citizens and courts as protecting legitimate expectations of citizens and governments in transnational rule of law. Yet, respect for legitimate 'constitutional pluralism' and for 'reasonable disagreement' also requires acknowledging that the diversity of private and public, economic, political, legal and constitutional conceptions of IEL is likely to persist due to competing conceptions of 'justice'. As illustrated by the cooperation among national and international courts in ever more fields of European integration law, the common search for an 'overlapping consensus' on transnational rule of law – especially transnational rule of IEL for the benefit of individuals limiting authoritarian claims of governments to disregard or overrule individual rights – will often remain contested and

[1] The citation from Plato's *Protagoras* is quoted from FJ Garcia (2003) 2.

[2] See, eg, the arbitral tribunal in *Suez Sociedad General de Aguas de Barcelona SA and Vivendi Universal SA v Argentina*: 'considerations of basic justice would lead tribunals to be guided by the basic judicial principle that "like cases should be decided alike", unless a strong reason exists to distinguish the current case from previous ones' (ICSID Case No ARB/03/19, Award, 3 August 2006, para 189).

[3] See the case law cited and discussed by E Gaillard, *Legal Theory of International Arbitration* (Leiden: Nijhoff Publishers, 2010) 63 f.

[4] See, eg, the UNCITRAL Arbitral Decision on Liability of 30 July 2010 in *AWG v Argentina* (ie, one of the more than 40 arbitration proceedings against Argentina's restrictions in response to its financial crisis in 2001) para 262: 'In the circumstances of these cases, Argentina's human rights obligations and its investment treaty obligations are not inconsistent, contradictory, or mutually exclusive'.

subject to political and 'judicial dialogues' clarifying transnational rule of law. This chapter discusses the diversity of theories of justice, the 'reasonable disagreement' on 'principles of justice' and the need to justify transnational rule of law for the benefit of citizens by an 'overlapping consensus' (Rawls) on 'universalizable' principles of law recognizing individuals as main actors, beneficiaries and primary subjects of IEL. The universal human rights obligations require treating sovereign states, governments and international organizations as constitutionally limited agents of citizens, whose legitimate authority depends – as explained in chapters II to V – on respect for human rights, democratic governance, legal and judicial accountability and transnational rule of law within the limits of legitimate 'constitutional pluralism'.

Chapters II to IV emphasized that law and governance – including IEL and multilevel economic governance – must be justified by political morality.[5] Morality and justice refer not only to the virtuous 'good life' (Plato) of individuals in their social relations to others, the reasonable justifiability of individual conduct and the non-violent resolution of conflicts among individuals on the basis of 'just rules' and fair procedures. Justice also refers to political morality, such as the 'right social and political order' and the justifiability of what the American philosopher John Rawls calls the 'basic structure' of societies, ie, the way in which 'the political constitution and the principal economic and social arrangements . . . distribute fundamental rights and duties and determine the division of advantages from social cooperation'.[6] According to Kantian philosophy, individuals as well as states have moral obligations to transform the lawless state of nature into a 'universal law of right' and 'conditions within which the will of one person can be reconciled with the will of another in accordance with a universal law of freedom'.[7] By regulating the opportunities of producers, investors, traders and consumers to increase their individual and social welfare through division of labour and trade, IEL inescapably involves questions of legal and judicial justice (eg, in the sense of just rules and fair procedures), distributive justice (eg, in the sense of principles justifying the distribution of economic gains) and corrective justice (eg, in the sense of determining and correcting improper gains). For instance, the 'near-death experience' (Stiglitz) of the 'casino capitalism' revealed by the 2008 financial crisis has been to 'market fundamentalism' (ie, the notion that unfettered markets, all by themselves, can ensure economic prosperity and growth) what the fall of the Berlin wall has been to communism. Yet, in spite of legislative and administrative remedies adopted at national and EU levels, the G20 summit meetings in 2010 failed to agree on adjusting the inadequate 'constitutional structures' and surveillance functions, lending functions, regulatory functions and social functions of the Bretton Woods institutions and of the Basel Committee on Banking Regulation and Supervisory Practices in order to avoid a repetition of the financial crises.[8] The global

[5] In his recent book *Justice for Hedgehogs* (Cambridge: Harvard University Press, 2011) R Dworkin distinguishes morality (as the standards governing how we ought to treat other people) and ethics (as the standards how we ought to live ourselves), but argues that living morally and living ethically are inseparable; what we achieve is less important than the manner in which we live our lives.

[6] J Rawls (1971) 7.

[7] I Kant, 'The Metaphysics of Morals' in Kant (1970) 133.

[8] *cf* JE Stiglitz (2010); HR Torres, 'Reforming the IMF – Why its Legitimacy is at Stake' (2007) 10 *JIEL* 443–60; FJ Garcia, 'Global Justice and the Bretton Woods Institutions' (2007) 10 *JIEL* 461–81. The Basel Committee, which has been described as an 'international club for banking regulators', has a more exclusive membership than the Bank for International Settlement, *cf* D Singh, 'The Role of the IMF and World Bank in Financial Sector Reform and Compliance' in W Shan, P Simons and D Singh (eds), *Redefining Sovereignty in International Economic Law* (Oxford: Hart Publishing, 2008) 331–62.

institutions and 'basic structures' of IEL, and their influence on the allocation and distribution of scarce resources in societies, continue to be widely perceived as unjust and inefficient, for instance in terms of failing to maximize general consumer welfare, prevent unnecessary poverty in LDCs and protect other global public goods. Civil, political, economic, social and cultural human rights need to be mutually reconciled, 'balanced' and 'optimized' depending on the diverse contexts of the diverse national and international legal systems. The international human rights dimensions of IEL need to be clarified through deliberative democracy and, if necessary, through citizen-driven remedies, adjudication and 'struggles for justice'.

OVERVIEW OF CHAPTER VI

Section 1 recalls that the legitimacy of, and democratic support by citizens for national and international governance systems depends on their justification in terms of principles of justice, such as legal and judicial protection of human rights, constitutional and cosmopolitan rights of citizens in their social cooperation. Section 2 gives an overview of the legitimate diversity of theories of justice, such as rights-based theories of justice, Rawls' constitutional theory of 'justice as fairness' and 'procedural justice', utilitarian, communitarian and merit-based theories of justice. Section 3 argues that in citizen-driven economic cooperation among producers, investors, traders and consumers living in some 200 sovereign states, the transnational legal and judicial protection of economic freedoms, property rights, rule of law and human rights depends on struggles by citizens and courts of justice for 'constitutional justice', 'distributive' and 'corrective justice' and for transnational rule of law. Citizens and UN member states remain unlikely to ever agree on comprehensive theories of 'social justice' in IEL, as illustrated by the US refusal to ratify the 1966 UN Covenant on Economic, Social and Cultural Rights (ICESCR). Yet, as explained in section 4, the human rights obligations of all UN member states reflect an 'overlapping consensus' on the need for justifying IEL in terms of equal fundamental freedoms, cosmopolitan rights and social justice. As recognized in UN human rights instruments and illustrated by the recent human rights revolutions in Arab countries, responsibility for a just national and international constitutional order satisfying the basic needs and protecting the human rights of all citizens lies with 'the peoples of the United Nations' and their citizens' willingness to defend their human rights and institutionalize 'public reason'.

1 JUSTICE AS CONSTITUTIONAL OBJECTIVE OF NATIONAL AND INTERNATIONAL LAW

According to John Rawls, 'justice is the first virtue of social institutions, as truth is of systems of thought'.[9] In both national as well as international legal systems, the agreed

[9] Rawls (1971) 3. This recognition that social institutions affecting basic human interests must pursue justice, should not be read to imply that obligations of justice depend on social cooperation and are limited to our cooperative interactions with others. The moral concept of justice as a virtue, independent from social institutions, goes back to Socrates. European and UN human rights law proceed from the Kantian imperative to respect each person's dignity, as a moral requirement grounded in the nature of persons and preceding institutionalized cooperation. A Buchanan (2004) derives from the Kantian 'moral equality principle' a

objectives and purposes of law inform the general conceptions of law,[10] notwithstanding the political reality of antagonistic economic, political and legal actors pursuing conflicting economic, political and legal objectives.[11] The UN Charter, the EU Treaty as well as numerous other international treaties (eg, on the International Criminal Court) and national constitutions (notably in 'transition countries' moving from authoritarian rule to constitutional democracy) refer to 'justice' as a central objective of international and national law and acknowledge the interrelationships between respect for human rights, democratic peace and justice.

In view of the human rights obligations of all UN member states and the customary law requirement of interpreting international law 'in conformity with principles of justice' and human rights, national and international legal systems in the twenty-first century – including IEL – have become constitutionally embedded into principles of morality, human rights and democratic constitutionalism, as discussed in chapters II to V. Yet, neither governments nor citizens agree on a comprehensive theory of justice for guiding individuals, governments, judges and international organizations in their search for an international legal order protecting human rights, democratic peace and economic welfare more effectively. In contrast to the search for truth in the natural sciences, law and jurisprudence (eg in the sense of the right application of the law on the basis of objective criteria) are less about 'truth' (eg in case of establishing legal facts) than – notably in case of normative decisions – about 'institutionalizing public reason' providing for 'reasonable procedures' of rule-making, rule-administration and rule-enforcement based on 'balanced judgments' (eg resulting from democratic discourse among free and equal citizens, representative parliamentary decision-making, judicial procedures administered by impartial and independent judges so as to secure 'rule of law', 'balancing' among competing human and constitutional rights based on principles of non-discrimination, necessity and proportionality). Arguably, reasonable judgments and justice (eg in the sense of reasonable justification) are the equivalent in normative social sciences to truth in the natural sciences.[12] Hence, reasonable people may disagree on how to define 'principles of

positive, moral duty to help ensure that all persons have access to national as well as international, just institutions protecting their basic human rights (at 86–88).

[10] *cf* P Capps (2009) 40 ff and ch 3 (arguing that international law is purposively orientated to the achievement of human dignity, and that interpretations of international law rules must be justified as being practically reasonable for protecting human dignity and human rights. Legal respect for the autonomy of others calls for separating legal reasoning from economic and political reasoning. Transparency and predictable, authoritative decision-making in the interests of justice require that the legal reasoning must be public in nature and acceptable as reasonable by all members of the legal community. Capps endorses the view adopted also in this study that Kant's legal and constitutional theory can be used to underpin a 'realistic utopia' for reinterpreting and redesigning modern international law, notwithstanding certain inconsistencies in Kant's work and the disagreement on its practical relevance for international law in the twenty-first century).

[11] *cf*, eg, EA Posner and AO Sykes, 'Economic Foundations of the Law of the Sea' (2010) 104 *AJIL* 569–96 (explaining the 'economic logic underlying UNCLOS' and the political disregard of 'poor nations' legitimate interests in equitable treatment').

[12] Cf R Alexy, 'The Reasonableness of Law' in G Bongiovanni, G Sartor and C Valantini (eds), *Reasonableness and Law* (Heidelberg: Springer Verlag, 2009) 5–15. TM Franck (1995) emphasizes that 'fairness is not "out there" to be discovered, it is a product of social context and history' that remains 'relative' and subject to the Rawlsian idea of 'an overlapping consensus' (at 16); 'the idea that principles of fairness and justice exist in an objective world "out there", needing only to be discovered by mankind, and of universally equal validity, has found diminishing support among moral philosophers in the modern world' (at 17). UN human rights instruments emphasize the interrelationships between respect for human rights, peace and justice not only inside states, but in international relations. For a discussion of this 'democratic peace hypothesis' see Buchanan (2004) 79.

justice'.[13] For instance, how should an international theory of justice based on human rights and their underlying moral principles be reconciled with communitarian values and the Hegelian claim that freedom is constituted by the state? Should human rights law be construed as 'constitutional contracts' among individuals, among representatives of different peoples or among states? Should international law be perceived as an instrument for advancing *national interests* as defined by governments, or for advancing transnational *community interests* as often claimed by international organizations and international 'courts of justice'? Should 'reasonable interpretations' of IEL in the twenty-first century be guided by ideal or non-ideal theories of justice?[14] Representatives of non-governmental organizations (eg, in the ILO, in UN human rights bodies) also emphasize the task of international rules to promote *group interests* (eg, of workers, indigenous people), functional interests (like protection of the environment and of economic efficiency) and *individual interests* (as protected by human rights). Such different perspectives may give rise to antagonistic conflicts among competing economic, political and legal actors,[15] for example whenever permanent members of the UN Security Council exercise their veto rights on strategic grounds of hegemonic state interests, or coastal states unilaterally extend their national fishery and economic zones at the expense of landlocked states, illustrating the use of international law as a policy instrument for advancing national interests at the expense of other states and of collective citizen interests.

From power-oriented to rights-based conceptions of 'constitutional justice as institutionalized protection of human rights'

Greek and Roman law and philosophy defined 'justice' in terms of *general principles* of procedural and substantive law (eg, justice as 'rule following', fair procedures, protection of liberty and equality of free citizens) as well as in terms of *specific principles* justifying distributive, corrective, reciprocal ('commutative') justice or equity in response to particular circumstances (eg, *suum cuique tribuere*).[16] From the peace treaties of Westphalia (1648) to the demise of the East–West divide (1989), *international law* theories focused on the sovereignty and consent of states and on the intergovernmental constitution of

[13] For an overview of the diverse theories of justice see also T Campbell, *Justice*, 2nd edn (London: McMillan, 2000); SC Kolm, *Modern Theories of Justice* (Cambridge: MIT Press, 1998).

[14] Whereas Rawls' *A Theory of Justice* (1971) for a constitutional democracy was based on ideal theory in a law abiding society, the Rawlsian theory of international justice underlying his *The Law of Peoples* (1999) – and its justification of tolerance towards non-democratic, but 'decent societies' – was influenced by non-ideal theories of justice. As discussed in chs II to V, respect for the reality of legitimate 'constitutional pluralism' requires acknowledging that appeals to rationality and reasonableness often do not resolve questions of social justice in practice. Also the Kantian legal theory of multilevel constitutionalism reflects European conceptions that differ from the legitimate constitutional traditions outside Europe.

[15] On the contextual nature of the legal dimensions of 'justice' (eg, 'transitional justice' in post-conflict situations) see the case studies in: KM Clarke and M Goodale (eds), *Mirrors of Justice. Law and Power in the Post-Cold War World* (Cambridge: CUP, 2010).

[16] See CJ Friedrich (1963) ch II, describing Plato's concept of justice as the 'good life' of individuals and the 'right order' of polities under the control of reason. In contrast to Plato's focus on general rules of universal justice, Aristotle focused more on rules of justice for particular circumstances justifying correction of injustices, reciprocal justice and distributive justice 'among those who have a share in the constitution', see: D Ross (ed), *The Nicomachean Ethics of Aristotle* (New York: OUP, 1959) book V, ch 2. Both Greek and Roman legal philosophy related justice more to the value of rationality and equality among citizens than to individual freedom as primary value.

functionally limited, international organizations and legal communities of states.[17] Today's recognition – in numerous worldwide and regional human rights conventions and other human rights instruments – of 'the inherent dignity and of the equal and inalienable rights of all members of the human family [as] the foundation of freedom, justice and peace in the world'[18] suggests that international law, public policy and 'justice' must be based on 'normative individualism', ie, that 'all human beings are born free and equal in dignity and rights', as recognized in the Universal Declaration of Human Rights (Article 1 UDHR) and in numerous other human rights instruments. Also in IEL, rules and policies derive their *input legitimacy* from respect for human rights, consumer-driven competition and citizen-driven democratic regulation of 'market failures' as well as of 'public goods'; *output-legitimacy*, for instance in terms of maximizing individual and social 'utilities', 'economic efficiency' and GDP, remains always imperfect and difficult to measure for all citizens.[19]

Arguably, the quasi-universal UN membership and the increasing number of *erga omnes* obligations and *jus cogens* rules based on UN law could enable a progressive transformation of the UN Charter into a constitution not only of the United Nations as a worldwide organization, but of the international community as a whole, with legally binding effects on all subjects of international law such as states, international organizations, peoples, minorities, non-governmental organizations (eg, in terms of 'social corporate responsibilities') and individuals.[20] *De lege ferenda*, the increasing number of UN Security Council actions vis-à-vis non-state entities (eg, in the course of the Yugoslav crisis) illustrate the normative need for stronger protection of human rights and other community values by means of UN law. *De lege lata*, however, there remains such a gap between the 'constitutional UN goals' and their practical disregard in UN power politics that most international lawyers consider it premature to present the power-oriented structures of UN law as a legitimate constitution of the global community – for instance, in view of its lack of effective protection of human rights and of international rule of law. As long as UN law fails to effectively protect human rights and citizen-driven open markets, the deliberate decision of WTO members to keep the WTO legal system outside the system of UN Specialized Agencies remains legitimate. Yet, the 'overlapping nature' of many international public goods entails that also WTO law cannot realize its statutory goals of 'sustainable development' without interpreting and developing WTO law in conformity with the legal obligations of all WTO members under UN law. Many

[17] On the legal constitution of the international society and its conception as a legal community in the publications of A Verdross, eg, *Die Verfassung der Völkerrechtsgemeinschaft* (Vienna: Springer, 1926), H Mosler, eg, *The International Society as a Legal Community* (Alphen aan den Rijn: Sijthoff, 1980), the 'New Haven School' and of an increasing number of contemporaneous international lawyers see B Fassbender (2009) ch 2.

[18] This text from the Preamble of the Universal Declaration on Human Rights has been subsequently included into most UN human rights conventions.

[19] The founding father of liberal economics, Adam Smith, justified his 'system of natural liberty' on considerations of both economic welfare and justice: 'Justice is the main pillar that upholds the whole edifice. If it is removed, the immense fabric of human society . . . must in a moment crumble into atoms' (A Smith, *The Theory of Moral Sentiments* (Oxford: Clarendon Press, 1759/1976) 167). On 'justice as efficiency' see: R Posner, *Economic Analysis of Law*, 2nd edn (Boston: Little Brown, 1977) 10: 'Efficiency means exploiting resources in such a way that "value" – human satisfaction as measured by aggregate consumer willingness to pay – is maximized'. For a criticism of utilitarian theories of justice, see: Campbell (n 13); Kolm (n 13).

[20] *cf* Fassbender (2009), who understands 'international constitutional law. . . as a sub-discipline of public international law' (at 173) rather than – as in this book – as a multilevel constitutional system. In ch 2, Fassbender gives a good overview of the 'Vienna school', 'New Haven school' and of the German 'international community school' advocating diverse constitutional conceptions of UN law.

national constitutions (like the German Basic Law of 1949) and treaty constitutions (like the 2007 Lisbon Treaty) rightly acknowledge that – in a globally integrated world – national and regional constitutions can no longer realize many constitutional objectives without 'strict observance and the development of international law, including respect for the principles of the United Nations Charter' (Article 3 TEU). The UN Charter, the Lisbon Treaty and many national constitutions further emphasize that international peace, security and respect for human rights can be secured only 'in conformity with the principles of justice and international law' (Article 1 UN Charter). The legitimate 'constituent power' in international law lies – as emphasized in the Preamble of the UN Charter – with 'the Peoples of the United Nations'. Will citizens, their people and governments learn, during the twenty-first century, to transform UN law into a more legitimate and more effective 'treaty constitution' not only of the UN as an organization with limited powers delegated by UN member states, but of the international community of 'UN citizens' and their existential need for legal protection of interdependent, (inter) national public goods?

De-fragmentation of IEL through rights-based interpretations

This study proceeds from the legal presumption that the universal recognition – in national constitutions (eg, Article 1 of the German Basic Law), the law of the European Union (eg, Article 1 of the EU Charter of Fundamental Rights), in regional as well as worldwide human rights conventions and other human rights instruments (eg, Article 1 UDHR) – of 'inalienable' and 'indivisible' human rights deriving from 'human dignity' requires interpreting national and international law as a functional unity for promoting individual and democratic self-development and satisfaction of basic social needs necessary for a life in dignity.[21] Contrary to the value relativism of allegedly 'post-modern' and 'critical legal studies', respect for human dignity as the source of inalienable human rights offers a national as well as international *jus cogens* foundation for reducing the fragmentation among more than 200 national legal systems and the more than 50,000 international treaties registered by the UN Secretariat. From the perspective of national democracies and the European Union as the sole 'international democracy' to date, constitutional democracy and the universal recognition of human rights offer the most convincing framework for a modern, cosmopolitan theory of justice that takes into account the legal and political need (as explained already by Immanuel Kant in his essay of 1795 on 'Perpetual Peace') to protect human rights not only through *national constitutional law* limiting abuses of domestic policy powers, but through *international* as well as *cosmopolitan constitutional restraints* protecting human rights across frontiers vis-à-vis foreign and international abuses of power.[22] The 'common constitutional principles' underlying national and international human rights law and IEL offer a flexible basis not only for interpreting international law (eg, its legal primacy over domestic law pursuant to Article 27 VCLT) in conformity with the human rights obligations of governments vis-à-vis citizens; the 'constitutional functions' of IEL for protecting mutually beneficial

[21] On the concept of human dignity see: D Kretzmer and E Klein (eds) (2002); EU Petersmann, 'Human Rights, Markets and Economic Welfare: Constitutional Functions of the Emerging UN Human Rights Constitution' in F Abbott, C Breining and T Cottier (eds) (2006) 29–67.

[22] *cf* ch III, sections 1 and 2.

economic cooperation among citizens also need to be clarified with due respect for the legitimate diversity of national and international human rights conceptions.[23]

Market competition as necessary complement of human rights

Freedom of expression and other fundamental freedoms inevitably entail communication among citizens ('opinion markets') not only in terms of 'deliberative democracy' in the polity and in law-creating processes (such as contracts and other rulemaking based on consent) but also in the economic activities of citizens. Supply and demand for scarce goods and services gives rise to citizen-driven economic markets driven by discourses about the valuation, scarcity and innovation of goods, services and production processes demanded by consumers. Theories of justice, human rights, constitutional rights and cosmopolitan rights[24] often neglect that citizen-driven markets are inevitable consequences of protection of human rights and offer citizens decentralized information and coordination mechanisms providing individuals with information (eg, on the relative scarcity of resources), goods and services necessary for the enjoyment of human rights. Yet, as emphasized by *ordo*-liberal economic theories since Adam Smith, markets are no 'gift of nature' but must be legally constructed to limit 'market failures' and provide 'collective public goods'.[25] The globalization of human rights requires not only national, international and cosmopolitan constitutional rules constituting and restraining *political markets* (eg, for the collective protection of public goods); mutually beneficial cooperation among citizens across frontiers also requires the legal constitution of transnational *economic markets* for private goods which – in order to promote consumer welfare efficiently – must be regulated by non-discriminatory rules (such as investment, trade, competition, consumer protection, environmental and social rules) enhancing individual capacity for self-development, limiting abuses of public and private power and coordinating the global division of labour among producers, investors, traders and consumers around the globe.

In today's globally integrated world, almost seven billion individuals and some 200 sovereign states compete for scarce goods, services and capital. Conflicts of interests are

[23] On the disagreement among courts on the often diverse and contextual conceptions of human dignity beyond a common minimum content (such as respect for the intrinsic worth of each human being, the status of individuals as autonomous legal subjects, the existence of the state for the individual rather than vice versa) see: C McCrudden, 'Human Dignity and Judicial Interpretation of Human Rights' (2008) 19 *EJIL* 655–724.

[24] 'Human rights' protect universal rights deriving from respect for human dignity. 'Constitutional rights' of citizens and cosmopolitan rights (eg, for protection of private property and other rights of participants in the global division of labour) often go beyond UN human rights law. As the 'human right to democratic governance' includes a right of citizens to define their respective national and international human rights through constitutional contracts and 'constitutional conventions' – like the two European Conventions which, in December 2000, adopted the European Charter of Fundamental Rights (Official Journal of the EC of 18 December 2000, C 364/1-21) and, in July 2003, the Draft Treaty establishing a Constitution for Europe (whose essential constitutional guarantees were subsequently included into the 2007 Lisbon Treaty on the EU) – human rights, constitutional rights of citizens and cosmopolitan rights inevitably overlap.

[25] For a criticism of the neglect in UN human rights law of freedom of profession, property rights and other economic liberties essential for reducing unnecessary poverty, and of the authoritarian perception (widespread especially among human rights specialists from Anglo-Saxon countries without constitutional protection of economic and social rights) of individuals as mere objects of economic government policies, see EU Petersmann, 'Taking Human Dignity, Poverty and Empowerment of Individuals More Seriously: Rejoinder to Alston' (2002) 13 *EJIL* 845–51. On the necessary 'legal constitution' of market competition for promoting consumer welfare see: EU Petersmann (1991) chs III, V and VII.

inevitable and ubiquitous. Just as national theories of justice focus on transforming the power-oriented 'state of nature' among rational egoists (*homo homini lupus est*) into a civil society based on just rules, so must the prevention and peaceful settlement of disputes in international relations among states, as well as in transnational relations among citizens with foreign governments, be a central objective of international law and theories of international justice. From a human rights perspective, 'international justice' refers, primarily, to human rights and democratic procedures that justify the allocation of governance powers, the protection of equal basic rights and the distribution of scarce resources necessary for personal self-development of individuals as morally and rationally autonomous, social human beings. The recognition, in all major UN human rights conventions[26] and UN human rights declarations, of 'human dignity' (eg, in the sense of reasonable autonomy, legal freedom, equality and social responsibility of individuals) and human liberty as moral sources and ultimate objectives of 'inalienable' human rights calls for constitutional protection of 'inalienable' human rights as '*jus cogens* core' of national and international constitutional law. Human rights must be the guiding principles for theories of justice also in IEL aimed at empowerment of individuals through protection of equal basic rights, non-discriminatory competition, satisfaction of basic individual needs and democratic self-government necessary for personal self-development in dignity.[27]

The legal implications of the universal recognition of human rights for theories of justice and for the interpretation of UN Charter obligations and of IEL remain contested.[28] More than one hundred international treaties and other human rights instruments now re-confirm and legally protect – through worldwide, regional and national human rights bodies – an 'inalienable core' of human rights.[29] Hence, as emphasized by the European Court of First Instance,[30] there is strong evidence that the core of many human rights listed in the UDHR of 1948 has evolved into constitutional obligations (*ius cogens*) of all UN member states and UN bodies under the UN Charter. UN human rights law permits UN member states to protect higher human rights standards at national and regional levels than at UN levels; it also provides for obligations to protect human rights

[26] See, eg, the 1966 Covenants on Civil and Political Rights (ICCPR), on Elimination of all Forms of Racial Discrimination (ICERD) and the ICESCR, the 1980 Convention on the Elimination of all Forms of Discrimination against Women (ICEDAW), the 1984 Convention against Torture (ICAT) and the 1989 Convention on the Rights of the Child (ICRC).

[27] On the 'indivisibility' of the various civil, political, economic and social dimensions of human liberty – both as a human right as well as the most important incentive and instrument for promoting human development and social welfare – see also: A Sen (2000). Sen fails, however, to identify the legal obstacles to realizing the goal of 'development as freedom'.

[28] The International Court of Justice has long since recognized that UN member states also have human rights obligations under the UN Charter: see, eg, the *Barcelona Traction* judgment ([1970] ICJ Rep 32) and the *Nicaragua* judgment ([1986] ICJ Rep 114). On the expanding scope of human rights obligations under the UN Charter and under general international law, and on the necessary reinterpretation of international law from the perspective of human rights see, eg, Buchanan (2004).

[29] eg, in the 1989 UN Convention on the Rights of the Child ratified by more than 190 states, all states parties recognized 'that the United Nations has, in the Universal Declaration of Human Rights and in the International Covenants on Human Rights, proclaimed and agreed that everyone is entitled to all the rights and freedoms set forth therein'. On UN human rights practices see, eg: Compilation of General Comments and General Recommendations Adopted by Human Rights Treaty Bodies, HRI/GEN/1/Rev.6, UN 2002; P Alston and J Crawford (eds), *The Future of UN Human Rights Treaty Monitoring* (Cambridge: CUP, 2000).

[30] See S Griller, 'International Law, Human Rights and the European Community's Autonomous Legal Order: Notes on the ECJ Decision in *Kadi*' (2008) 4 *European Constitutional Law Review* 528–53.

beyond national jurisdictions.[31] Contrary to Rawls' suggestion that 'international justice' should be based on equal freedoms of 'peoples' and international tolerance for 'decent states' that lack effective human rights protection,[32] UN human rights law offers a more appropriate constitutional basis for international and 'cosmopolitan justice' and for the necessary transformation of the UN Charter into a legitimate constitution for the collective supply of global public goods based on 'duties to protect' human rights and other agreed 'common concerns'.

2 THE LEGITIMATE DIVERSITY OF THEORIES OF JUSTICE REINFORCES THE ARGUMENT FOR A HUMAN RIGHT TO JUSTIFICATION

Justice is acknowledged as an objective of numerous international treaties and national constitutions. Yet, legal principles and procedures for realizing justice tend to be contextual; they frequently differ depending on the prevailing preferences of people and on the particular circumstances in different countries. As human rights are designed to protect individual and democratic diversity, many democratic constitutions and regional human rights treaties go beyond the minimum standards of universal UN human rights law. Especially in the field of IEL, national and international human rights instruments vary in their regulation and 'balancing' of economic rights (such as freedom of profession, the right to possess private property) and corresponding obligations of governments and intergovernmental organizations. Just as social, religious and political traditions influence the legal protection of civil and political rights, so may the availability of natural resources and economic traditions (like 'Islamic banking') influence protection of economic and social rights. Legal theories of justice differ considerably according to their underlying values and worldviews such as those associated with liberal, communitarian, republican or other constitutional premises. For example:

1. *Rights-based theories of justice* give constitutional priority to 'inalienable' human rights and constitutional limitation of government powers to protect the autonomy and independence of individuals who, as Kant explained, must be treated as ends in themselves and never merely as means for securing benefit to another. Anglo-American

[31] According to the UN General Assembly Resolution adopted by the 2005 World Summit on 'Responsibility of Protect', 'each individual state has the responsibility to protect its population from genocide, war crimes, ethnic cleansing and crimes against humanity'. The Resolution also provides that the international community bears the responsibility – within the framework of the UN – to help protect populations though diplomatic, humanitarian and other peaceful means; only when 'national authorities are manifestly failing to protect their population' against these four crimes and should peaceful means be inadequate, the UN Security Council may take collective action under Chapter VII of the UN Charter on a case-by-case basis and in cooperation with relevant regional organizations. On this 'three pillar approach' and legal obligations to protect rights beyond the national jurisdiction see: C Stahn, 'Responsibility to Protect: Political Rhetoric or Emerging Legal Norm?' (2007) 101 *AJIL* 99–120. See also the Report of the Commission on Human Security, *Human Security Now: Protecting and Empowering People* (New York: UN, 2003) which emphasizes that respecting human rights and promoting democratic principles are central to protection of security of peoples.

[32] See J Rawls (1999). For a criticism of the Rawlsian theory of 'international justice' from a moral perspective see: T Pogge, *Realizing Rawls* (Ithaca: Cornell University Press, 1989); T Pogge, 'The Incoherence between Rawls' Theories of Justice' (2004) 72 *Fordham Law Review* 1739. Pogge argues that the negative, moral duty not to harm other persons requires that support be withheld from international rules and institutions that cause avoidable poverty and violations of human rights. For my criticism of the Rawlsian theory as falling behind existing human rights law see: EU Petersmann, 'International Trade Law, Human Rights and Theories of Justice' in S Charnovitz et al (eds), *Law in the Service of Humanity. Essays in Honour of F Feliciano* (Cambridge: CUP, 2005) 44–57.

libertarians (such as John Locke, Robert Nozick) focus on liberty, individual choice and property rights ('justice in holdings'); other human rights and legitimate government powers tend to be conceived narrowly (ie, essentially limited to protection of private liberty, property rights and rule of law) without much regard for the distributive effects of liberty rights and acquired property rights.[33] Constitutional law in the EU and in many European countries (for instance, France, Germany and Switzerland) protects personal self-development by complementing general liberty and property rights not only by civil and political, but also by economic and social rights, subject to democratic legislation that is constitutionally required to protect and mutually balance human rights in non-discriminatory, necessary and proportionate ways.[34]

2. Rawls' constitutional theory of '*justice as fairness*' and '*procedural justice*'[35] proceeds from the exercise of rational choice by individuals (deliberating in a fictitious 'original position' behind a 'veil of uncertainty') to define the basic rights and liberties of free and equal citizens in a constitutional democracy. According to Rawls' 'welfare liberalism', reasonable citizens would give priority to maximum equal liberty as the 'first principle of justice', but would also recognize the 'principle of fair equality of opportunity' and a 'difference principle' within a system of equal basic rights.[36] The 'secondary principles of social justice' are asserted as rationally necessary for defining 'the appropriate distribution of the benefits and burdens of social co-operation'[37] to reduce the arbitrary effects of the distribution of 'natural primary goods' (like individual health and intelligence, natural resources inside countries) and promote a just distribution of 'social primary goods' (like constitutional rights, income and wealth).

[33] John Locke justified property rights as moral entitlements to the fruits of one's labour provided the valuable good (or the added value of the good) was produced without violating the rights and basic needs of others; see the 'Essay Concerning the True Origin, Extent and End of Civil Government' in J Locke, *Two Treatises of Government* (Cambridge: CUP, 1689/1960) paras 27–41, where Locke assumes that, in a state of nature without money, persons must limit their unilateral appropriations to a proportional share so that 'enough, and as good' for others is left. Locke's labour theory as the moral justification of just property acquisition raises numerous problems (*cf* JW Harris, *Property and Justice* (Oxford: OUP, 1996)).-According to R Nozick (1974), 'justice in holdings is historical' and depends on whether the acquisition, transfer and distribution of the property rights were lawful according to the rules in effect at the time (at 152), not on 'who ends up with what' (at 154). Accordingly, Nozick divides 'justice in holdings' into justice in the original acquisition of holdings, justice in the transfer of holdings and rectification of injustice in holdings; distributive justice means 'simply that a distribution is just if everyone is entitled to the holdings they possess under the distribution' (at 151), even if the distribution of resources has been distorted by inequalities and prevents self-development of individuals and satisfaction of their basic needs.

[34] Art 6 EU named liberty as the first principle on which the EU was founded, prior to 'respect for human rights and fundamental freedoms, and the rule of law'. The EU Charter of Fundamental Rights, as incorporated into EU law by the 2007 Lisbon Treaty, protects the 'right to liberty and security of person' in addition to numerous specific liberty rights, including freedom to choose an occupation and engage in work, freedom to conduct a business, and the right to property. On individual liberty and fundamental freedoms as founding principles of EU constitutional law see: A von Bogdandy, 'Constitutional Principles', and T Kingreen, 'Fundamental Freedoms' in A von Bogdandy and J Bast (eds) (2006) 3 ff, 549 ff. On the constitutional protection of a general right to liberty in Art 2 of the German Basic Law see: R Alexy (2002) ch 7. Anglo-Saxon common law countries, while protecting specific liberties, tend to offer less constitutional protection to general and economic liberty rights such as freedom of profession and trade. In German and EU law, constitutional protection of 'market freedoms' subjects all governmental restrictions of individual liberty to the need of constitutional justification.

[35] Rawls (1971) 85.

[36] Even though 'each person is to have an equal right to the most extensive total system of equal basic liberties compatible with a similar system of liberty for all' (Rawls (1971) 250), Rawls' concept of maximum equal liberty is narrower than Kant's moral categorical imperative and was even further limited – in view of the 'burdens of judgment' and 'reasonable disagreement' – in Rawls (1993) 54 ff, 99 ff.

[37] Rawls (1971) 4.

As national welfare, according to Rawls, depends more on a country's social institutions than on its natural resources, each people can agree on social and constitutional arrangements that provide its citizens with the natural and social goods essential for satisfying basic needs.[38] In view of the often non-democratic traditions (notably in 'failed states') and different social preferences and ambitions of people and their national governments, Rawls declines to apply his 'difference principle' for justice among individuals inside democracies to international relations among states, and accepts only moral obligations to assist foreigners.[39] This limited Rawlsian conception of international justice is inconsistent with the universal recognition of human rights, which entails moral and legal obligations of individuals and their governments not only vis-à-vis national citizens at home, but also *vis-à-vis* foreigners abroad.[40] Some theorists justify an 'international difference principle' also by the fact that the distribution of natural territorial resources among states is no less 'morally arbitrary' than the distribution of natural human talents inside states.[41]

3. *Utilitarian theories of justice* justify individual liberty and equal opportunities for exchange and competition among individuals not in deontological terms of equal freedoms or constitutional contracts, but as result-oriented mechanisms satisfying individual preferences and promoting 'welfare' (eg, in the sense of the greatest happiness of the greatest number). Yet, some economists (like Hayek) doubt whether market-driven distributions of goods and income can maximize not only utility and efficiency, but 'justice'; arguably, only individual conduct can be 'unjust', not market-mechanisms (eg, market prices, competition).[42]
4. *Communitarian theories of justice* regard all values as embedded in a particular social culture. Rather than individual freedom, they emphasize 'participatory', 'representative' and 'deliberative democracy' and other democratic procedures for determining social and political community values, as illustrated by the socialist maxim (eg, in

[38] See Rawls (1999) 37–38, 106–20: 'the crucial element in how a country fares is its political culture – its members' political and civic virtues – and not the level of its resources' (at 117). For a criticism of Rawls' 'purely domestic poverty hypothesis' (based on the widespread economic belief that 'countries shape their own destiny') and of Rawls' support only for moral obligations of international assistance, see: T Pogge (2003). According to Pogge, the world trading system and the more advantaged citizens of the affluent countries could easily eradicate the avoidable, life-threatening poverty from the world and must be held morally responsible for 'harming the global poor', including many of the millions of deaths each year resulting from poverty-related diseases.

[39] For a criticism of this Rawlsian position see Pogge (nn 32 and 38); F Teson (1998) ch IV.

[40] On transboundary human rights obligations of governments, non-governmental organizations and individuals see, eg, A Clapham, *Human Rights Obligations of Non-State Actors* (Oxford: OUP, 2006); P Alston (ed), *Non-State Actors and Human Rights* (Oxford: OUP, 2005).

[41] Garcia (2003) 134. Yet, even if it is true that objections to justice of a domestic system of 'natural liberty' apply with equal force to the morally arbitrary reality of international inequalities of natural resources, the normative basis of an international 'difference principle' can be based more convincingly on human rights and individual needs than on economic resource endowments that depend also on the domestic economic system.

[42] See FA Hayek, *The Mirage of Social Justice* (London: McMillan, 1976). Nozick (1974) pt II, argues that a person's 'holdings' are just if they result from legitimate actions in accordance with agreed rules of ownership, transfer and rectification of illegitimate transfers. The consequences of unequal, initial distribution of wealth and human capacities are disregarded. For a criticism of the economists' proclivity to look at outcomes rather than at rules and to separate 'efficiency' from 'equity' see: G Brennan and J Buchanan, *The Reason of Rules. Constitutional Political Economy* (Cambridge: Harvard University Press, 1985); VJ Vanberg, *The Constitution of Markets* (London: Routledge, 2001). Other authors like O O'Neill, *Bounds of Justice* (Cambridge: CUP, 2000) 282–84, welcome that utilitarianism counts each person's preferences equally and, hence, should be sensitive to the persisting poverty problems in the world economy (even though macroeconomic calculations often fail to prioritize individual preferences according to human needs and often disregard harmful externalities beyond developed countries' borders).

Article 6 of China's Constitution of 1982): 'from each according to his ability, to each according to his work'. A national communitarian concept of economic justice may object to international trade liberalization, for example, if the domestic 'winners' benefiting from trade gains do not compensate the domestic 'losers' bearing the adjustment costs.[43] Others argue in favour of communitarian theories of international justice based on the reality of inequality in the international division of labour,[44] the arbitrary impact of international borders on the distribution of natural resources and the emergence of an international 'legal community'. Regardless of whether trans-boundary moral and legal obligations of assistance are justified on utilitarian, liberal or communitarian grounds, theories of justice also differ regarding the choice of redistributive policy instruments. For example, they may reach different answers to the questions of whether a Rawlsian 'difference principle' can justify preferential market access for less-developed countries;[45] or whether an equal 'level playing field' in international economic relations should be promoted primarily through financial transfers and investment promotion for the benefit of poor countries.[46]

5. *Merit-based theories of justice* combine notions of equality, desert and 'corrective justice' (eg, punishment and compensation for injuries) in order to 'give everyone his or her due'. Justice requires treating individuals as rational agents responsible for their actions, and merits reward or punishment for conduct. Many economists, for example, argue that social and economic inequalities among developed and less-developed countries are *not* the result of inherent differences in their natural endowments (ie, an arbitrary distribution of natural primary goods in terms of Rawls' theory of justice); rather, 'rich countries are rich because their citizens produce more per head, not because they have secured privileged access to 'the planet's goods', or to its resources.'[47]

The diversity of moral, legal, economic and political theories of justice illustrates how transnational relations and multilevel governance in the international legal order have become more complex than many theories admit. International law continues to be based on state-centred rules protecting 'sovereign equality' of states (Article 2 UN Charter); yet, already the UN Charter has recognized that *normative legitimacy* (in con-

[43] Aristotle already argued that justice as a virtue applies only to people who 'have a share in the constitution' (n 16). By contrast, cosmopolitan moral theories argue that the 'categorical imperative' to respect 'just rules' is founded on respect for the human dignity of all persons, regardless of national boundaries and of the citizen status of individuals.

[44] See, eg, Garcia (2003) who argues that 'the socioeconomic predicate underlying the need for a domestic theory of justice (social cooperation yielding new benefits and burdens) is present in international economic relations', just as 'the problem of inequality in natural endowments is as present internationally among states as it is domestically between individuals, and leads in a similar fashion to inequalities in the distribution of resulting social goods such as wealth, knowledge and power. For these reasons, this book argues that the international problem of inequality should be treated in the same manner as the domestic problem, and with similar results, despite Rawls' own reluctance to do so' (at 119).

[45] This is the view of Garcia (2003) 120 ff.

[46] See, eg, EB Kapstein, *Economic Justice in an Unfair World* (Princeton: Princeton University Press, 2006) chs 3, 5 and 6. Also Pogge (2003) and many others argue in favour of global resource taxes (such as the 'Tobin tax') for addressing distributive international inequalities. Garcia (2003) (at 145) argues that, whereas the WTO is capable of realizing 'distributive justice' by means of differential treatment of LDCs, there are no international institutions capable of collecting and redistributing international taxes.

[47] D Henderson, *The Role of Business in Modern World: Progress, Pressures and Prospects for the Market Economy* (London: Institute of Economic Affairs, 2004) 83. See also: D Palmeter, 'A Note on the Ethics of Free Trade' (2005) 4 *World Trade Review* 448–67.

trast to factual legitimacy deriving from tradition, charisma or power) depends on 'We the Peoples of the United Nations' (Preamble UN Charter) and on respect for the human rights of individuals as the ultimate sources of values and units of moral concerns.[48] Universal recognition of human rights proceeds from agreed, moral and legal values such as respect for human dignity, equal human worth, individual and democratic self-government and access to courts. These legal entitlements of every human being, independent of the benevolence of governments, go far beyond the moral principles and 'global ethics' common to the various religions and moral philosophies around the world.[49] Justice has become a matter of multilevel protection of 'inalienable' human rights and constitutional empowerment and protection of individual and democratic self-development.[50]

Justice in terms of equal human rights is legally defined ever more comprehensively (eg, in the EU Charter of Fundamental Rights). The 'inalienable core' of human rights can no longer be lawfully taken away by governments, as confirmed in the jurisprudence of national and European courts on the constitutional nature of national, European and UN human rights guarantees and in the General Comments of the UN Human Rights Committee on the limited rights of states to suspend their human rights obligations under UN law unilaterally.[51] Beyond the 'self-evident' rights of life, liberty and property recognized in constitutional democracies and also in the UDHR, the major unresolved problems of national as well as 'international justice' relate to democratic, economic and social human rights and corresponding 'duties to protect', including the right of 'everyone . . . to a social and international order in which the rights and freedoms set forth in this Declaration can be fully realized' (Article 28 UDHR). Inside states, Rawlsian justice in the sense of 'the way in which the major social institutions distribute fundamental rights and duties and determine the division of advantages from social cooperation',[52] and democratic legislation defining, balancing and implementing human rights and constitutional rights, legitimately differs between countries. The legitimate diversity of theories of justice reinforces the argument for a human right to justification of all government restrictions of equal freedoms and other human rights; for without such

[48] As morality and justice are based on normative individualism, it remains controversial to what extent people and states can be viewed as subjects of moral rights and obligations (eg, to the extent that governments act as moral and democratic agents for the individual citizens of a state).

[49] On the 'global ethic' common to all world religions see, eg: H Küng, *A Global Ethic for Global Politics and Economics* (London: SCM Press, 1998); H Küng and H Schmidt (eds), *A Global Ethic and Global Responsibilities: Two Declarations* (London: SCM Press, 1998); The Global Ethic Foundation, *World Religions, Universal Peace, Global Ethic* (Tübingen: The Global Ethic Foundation, 2002).

[50] On 'justice as human rights' see Campbell (n 13) 53–54. On American conceptions of fundamental rights as legal and judicial 'trumps' see R Dworkin (1977); on the different European conception of fundamental rights as constitutional 'balancing principles' for optimizing constitutional rights see Alexy (2002). Contrary to the claim by Fukuyama that democracy and market capitalism herald the 'end of history', non-democratic governance structures persist in many countries as well as in many international markets. UN human rights law neglects freedom of profession, property rights and other constitutional conditions for increasing economic welfare through international division of labour; notably in many less-developed countries, it has failed to effectively empower the poor vis-à-vis their exploitation by governing elites; *cf* D Acemoglu and JA Robinson, *Economic Origins of Dictatorship and Democracy* (Cambridge: CUP, 2005).

[51] See, eg, Human Rights Committee, General Comment No 26: '5. The Committee is therefore firmly of the view that international law does not permit a State which has ratified or acceded or succeeded to the Covenant to denounce it or withdraw from it'. On the contested role of *jus cogens* see: E Wyler and A Papaux, 'The Search for Universal Justice' in RSJ Macdonald and DM Johnston (eds), *Towards World Constitutionalism. Issues in the Legal Ordering of the World Community* (The Hague: Martinus Nijhoff, 2005) 273, 290 ff.

[52] Rawls (1971) 7.

justification, individual access to justice and 'public reason' cannot be effectively protected.

3 JUSTICE REQUIRES LIBERAL AND RIGHTS-BASED IEL: STRUGGLES FOR 'CONSTITUTIONAL' AND 'CORRECTIVE JUSTICE'

There is broad agreement today – not only among economists, lawyers and political philosophers, but among the governments representing the 155 WTO member countries and other customs territories cooperating in the WTO (like the EU, Hong Kong, Macau, Taiwan) – that the basic principle of freedom of trade can be justified by all 'liberal' (ie, liberty-based) theories of justice, such as

- utilitarian theories defining justice in terms of maximum satisfaction of individual preferences and consumer welfare;
- libertarian theories focusing on protection of individual liberty and property rights;
- egalitarian concepts defining justice more broadly in terms of equal human rights and democratic consent; or
- international theories of justice based on sovereign equality and effective empowerment of states to increase their national welfare through liberal trade.

In competitive markets, voluntary international trade would not take place if it were not perceived as mutually beneficial by the parties to the trade transaction. Many principles of liberal IEL such as non-discriminatory market access, sovereign rights to restrict 'injurious imports' and protect non-economic 'public interests', government obligations to correct 'market failures' (such as 'information asymmetries' facilitating abuses of market power), preferential treatment of private and public actors in less-developed economies and international adjudication for the peaceful settlement of international economic disputes are justifiable on grounds of human rights, democratic constitutionalism, distributive justice and corrective justice. As a result of the universal recognition of human rights and the globalization of market economies, international economic discrimination against foreigners is subject to increasing legal restraints. From the procedural perspective of 'justice as peaceful conflict resolution',[53] it is justifiable and 'just' that ever more international trade, investment and economic integration agreements provide not only for peaceful *dispute settlement* by independent (quasi)judicial bodies, but also for *dispute prevention* through non-discriminatory competition, investment and trade rules and individual judicial remedies in domestic courts.

Struggles for 'constitutional justice' in IEL

Peaceful cooperation to increase the production and availability of resources for personal self-development depends on rules and their perception as just, for example, in the sense of justifying a rules-based, mutually beneficial division of labour. Since the democratic

[53] See, eg: S Hampshire, *Justice is Conflict* (Princeton: Princeton University Press, 2001); EU Petersmann, 'Justice as Conflict Resolution: Proliferation, Fragmentation and Decentralization of Dispute Settlement in International Trade Law' (2006) 27 *University of Pennsylvania Journal of International Economic Law* 273–366.

revolutions in America and France in the eighteenth century, there have been increasing calls for designing national and international law as instruments for constitutional protection of individual rights and justice: 'Justice is the end of government. It is the end of civil society. It ever has been and will be pursued until it is obtained, or until liberty be lost in the pursuit'.[54]

Early natural rights theorists focused on a limited number of specific rights, such as rights to life, liberty, property and happiness. Kant, rejecting Hobbes' power-oriented view of sovereignty, criticized international lawyers for disregarding the need for more comprehensive, constitutional limitations of state powers – not only inside states, but in international relations between states as well as in transnational relations of citizens with foreign powers. Kant combined the concepts of human reason, freedom and equality into the 'moral imperative' that human beings, as 'ends in themselves', must be treated as legal subjects of more broadly defined, equal liberty rights as constitutional restraints on abuses of power. Kant hoped that man's selfish tendencies (his 'unsocial sociability') would 'become in the long run the cause of a law-governed social order', enabling man to solve also 'the greatest problem for the human species (. . .) attaining a civil society which can administer justice universally'.[55]

Up until the Second World War, international law's justification of colonialism and imperialism meant that the related acquisition and distribution of 'social primary goods' – such as 'rights and liberties, powers and opportunities, income and wealth'[56] – could not be justified in terms of liberal theories of justice. The UN Charter aims at establishing 'conditions under which justice and respect for the obligations arising from treaties and other sources of international law can be maintained' (Preamble); the UN shall also 'bring about by peaceful means, and in conformity with the principles of justice and international law, adjustment or settlement of international disputes or situations which might lead to a breach of the peace' (Article 1). While committing all UN member states to 'universal respect for, and observance of, human rights and fundamental freedoms for all without distinction as to race, sex, language or religion', including 'respect for the principle of equal rights and self-determination of people' (Article 55), the UN Charter does not define these human rights obligations and 'principles of justice' (Article 1) more specifically. In fields like decolonization, humanitarian law, human rights, judicial dispute settlement, development assistance and environmental protection, the UN has contributed to far-reaching structural changes of international law, promoting greater 'justice' in international and social relations for the benefit of citizens and their individual rights. Yet, the UN obviously failed in realizing its objective to establish a 'New International Economic Order' promoting 'social justice'.[57]

The evolution of economic law in Europe radically changed with the EC Treaty and the increasing democratic pressures for rights-based 'constitutional approaches' to European integration law. The legal transformation of the worldwide trading system – notably through the replacement of the power-oriented GATT 1947 and the 1979 Tokyo

[54] A Hamilton and J Madison, *The Federalist Papers* (Washington, 1788/1961) ch 51.

[55] I Kant, 'Idea for a Universal History with a Cosmopolitan Purpose' in Kant (1970) 44–45.

[56] *cf* Rawls (1971) 62.

[57] See EU Petersmann, 'Charter of Economic Rights and Duties of States' in R Bernhardt (ed), *Encyclopedia of Public International Law*, vol I (Heidelberg: Springer, 1992) 561–66; EU Petersmann, 'The New International Economic Order: Principles, Politics and International Law' in Macdonald and Johnston (eds), *The International Law and Policy of Human Welfare* (The Hague: Martinus Nijhoff, 1978) 449–69.

Round Agreements by the 1994 Agreement establishing the WTO – succeeded in introducing a worldwide legal and compulsory dispute settlement system outside the UN framework.[58] As discussed in chapter VII, in the context of the 'Doha Development Round' negotiations in the WTO, justice-related claims for 'sustainable development' and more 'equitable' rules (eg, for agricultural subsidies, trade in cotton, textiles, bananas, protection of bio-genetic resources, trade facilitation for poor countries) are increasingly raised by governments and non-governmental organizations in the context of both WTO *negotiations* as well as WTO *dispute settlement* proceedings.[59] For example, in response to the WTO Appellate Body report on India's challenge to the EC's trade preferences for LDCs with anti-drugs programmes, the EC explicitly linked its new Generalized System of Tariff Preferences (GSP) to respect for UN human rights conventions and to the social standards in conventions of the International Labour Organization (ILO).[60] The WTO Appellate Body case law on the inconsistency of the 'zeroing methodology' in the calculation of anti-dumping duties with the WTO legal requirement of a 'fair price comparison', as well as the Appellate Body's insistence that WTO dispute settlement panels must interpret WTO rules with due respect for legal precedents approved by WTO members, has been welcomed by lawyers as an overdue 'constitutional turn' in WTO dispute settlement jurisprudence.[61] On the worldwide level (eg, of UN law and WTO law), regional level (eg, in the context of more than 250 regional trade arrangements), as well as on bilateral and national levels (eg, in the context of bilateral investment treaties), one-sidedly state-centred conceptions of justice are increasingly contested by cosmopolitan and constitutional conceptions of IEL. Yet, WTO members have not formally responded to the proposals by the UN High Commissioner for Human Rights for a human rights approach to international trade; they also continue to insist that the WTO should remain outside the system of UN Specialized Agencies limited to membership of sovereign states (in contrast to the WTO membership also of other customs territories and international organizations like the EU). As many GATT/WTO rules (eg on cotton, textiles and agricultural trade) were drafted in response to protectionist pressures from producer interests rather than 'principles of justice', many WTO members increasingly resort to regional trade agreements as economically sub-optimal, but politically more justifiable instruments of trade regulation.

Struggles for 'corrective justice' in IEL

The rational egoism and limited altruism of individuals, and the scarcity of resources in relation to almost unlimited demand, render conflicts of interest – among individuals (eg, the seller offering a high price, the buyer demanding a low price) as well as between

[58] *cf* EU Petersmann, 'The Transformation of the World Trading System through the 1994 Agreement Establishing the World Trade Organization' (1995) 6 *EJIL* 161–221.

[59] *cf* EU Petersmann (ed), *Developing Countries in the Doha Round. WTO Decision-making Procedures and Negotiations on Trade in Agriculture and Services* (Florence: Robert Schuman Centre, 2005).

[60] *cf* WTO Appellate Body Report, *EC – Tariff Preferences*, WT/DS246/AB/R, adopted 20 April 2004 (paras 163–64). Council Regulation 980/2005 of 27 June 2005 on the EC's new GSP scheme for 2006–2015 ([2005] OJ L169/1) was explicitly designed to reflect 'the integral nature of the concept of sustainable development' as defined by the Appellate Body, *cf* J Harrison, 'Incentives for Development: The EC's Generalized System of Preferences, India's WTO Challenge and Reform' (2005) 42 *CMLR* 1663.

[61] *cf* S Cho, 'Global Constitutional Lawmaking' (2009–10) 31 *University of Pennsylvania Journal of International Law* 621.

governments (eg, in exporting and importing countries) – inevitable in economic relations. As explained in chapter VIII, the approaches by governments, courts and individuals to the interpretation, application and 'balancing' of international economic rules with human rights and other fields of international law differ considerably. The more human rights and other concepts of political morality (like justice, equity, sustainable development) become integral parts of positive international law, the more legal and judicial conceptions of justice are being invoked by governmental and non-governmental actors for justifying new ways of making, interpreting and enforcing international law. For instance, the interpretation of the EC Treaty's common market rules as 'fundamental freedoms' was enforced by the EC Court at the request of EC citizens supported by the EC Commission against the resistance by national governments in EC member states. Similarly, incorporation of human rights into EC law was requested by EC citizens, national and EC courts and the European Parliament long before national governments finally agreed to incorporate explicit human rights obligations into the EU Treaty (eg, Article 6). The GATT commitments to 'equitable' market shares (*cf* Articles XVI, XXXVI GATT) and to non-reciprocal and preferential treatment of LDCs (*cf* Part IV of GATT, the 'Enabling Clause' adopted in 1979) were likewise progressively clarified in GATT and WTO dispute settlement proceedings and subsequent agreements implementing such general 'principles of justice' by means of more precise trade rules (eg, prohibiting export subsidies).[62]

Up until 1983, the GATT Secretariat had no 'Legal Office' and prided itself on its 'pragmatism' and avoidance of 'legalism'. This 'power politics in disguise' facilitated the widespread legal discrimination against cotton, textiles, agricultural and steel exports from less-developed countries, at the request of protectionist interest groups in developed countries. My appointment, in 1981, as the first legal officer ever employed by the GATT was a response to the increasing criticism of GATT's legally incoherent 'diplomat's jurisprudence' (Hudec), as illustrated by the frequent disregard of the customary methods of treaty interpretation in GATT dispute settlement proceedings prior to the establishment of a GATT Office of Legal Affairs in 1983 and by the political vetoing of the adoption of GATT dispute settlement reports.[63] The 1994 WTO 'Dispute Settlement Understanding' (DSU) brought about a definitive shift away from GATT's power-oriented trade diplomacy towards a global rule of law system with compulsory worldwide jurisdiction for the quasi-judicial settlement of trade disputes by means of panel, appellate and arbitration proceedings interpreting, applying and enforcing WTO rules on the basis of the 'customary rules of interpretation of public international law' (Article 3 DSU). Yet, many WTO governments and WTO dispute settlement panels insist on narrow interpretations of the limited mandate of WTO bodies; they are reluctant to deal in the WTO with trade-related human rights problems, competition, investment, social and environmental problems. As discussed in chapter V, they also induce domestic courts to refrain from holding governments legally and judicially accountable for their welfare-reducing violations of WTO obligations, thereby undermining rule of law, democratic governance and legitimate expectations of citizens. Such diverse perceptions of WTO rules reflect the divisions in legal theory between the idealist, Kantian view that law,

[62] See EU Petersmann, 'Strategic Use of WTO Dispute Settlement Proceedings for Advancing WTO Negotiations on Agriculture' in EU Petersmann (2005) 127–46.

[63] *cf* EU Petersmann (1997).

politics and morality should not conflict with one another; and the 'realist' and utilitarian claims that morality must not be mixed up with positive law, nor interfere with the defence of borders, the distinction of friend from foe,[64] and the use of 'efficient' policy instruments.

Struggles for reciprocal 'commutative justice' and 'equity' in IEL

Apart from 'distributive justice' and 'corrective justice', the additional Aristotelian distinctions between reciprocal 'commutative justice' and 'equity' – as different 'spheres of justice' – are well reflected in many IEL agreements. GATT/WTO law, for instance, prohibits the use of subsidies 'which results in that contracting party having more than an equitable share of world export trade in that product' (Article XVI:3 GATT); it promotes 'measures designed to attain stable, equitable and remunerative prices' for certain primary products (*cf* Article XXXVI:4 GATT); and the admissibility of 'non-violation complaints' (*eg*, pursuant to GATT Article XXIII:1(b)) is aimed at maintaining the agreed 'balance of reciprocal concessions' if unilateral, albeit lawful measures (like production subsidies) 'nullify or impair tariff benefits' that are protected under reciprocal tariff commitments under GATT/WTO law. Yet, just as the term 'commutative justice' has remained contested and is often avoided in favour of more specific principles of contract law (eg, in the GATT jurisprudence on 'nullification or impairment of treaty benefits'), GATT/WTO dispute settlement proceedings based on 'non-violation complaints' and GATT/WTO dispute settlement rulings based on principles of 'equity' have remained rare.[65] In international maritime disputes (eg about the 'equitable' delimitation of national territorial seas and 'exclusive economic zones') and investment disputes over 'fair and equitable treatment' of foreign investors, by contrast, international economic courts and arbitral tribunals often justify their dispute settlement findings on grounds of principles of equity.[66]

Struggles for 'rule of law' depend on the perceived legitimacy of the rules concerned

International legal theory suggests that *compliance* with international rules depends no less on the perceived legitimacy of the international rules[67] than on governments' rational cost/benefit analyses[68] and 'internalization'[69] of international rules in domestic

[64] *cf* C Schmitt, *Uber die drei Arten des rechtswissenschaftlichen Denkens* (Berlin: Dunker Humbolt, 1934); J Goldsmith and E Posner (2005).

[65] On 'non-violation complaints' in GATT/WTO law *cf* Petersmann (1997), ch 4. On the different 'spheres of justice' in European economic law see: HW Micklitz, *The Many Concepts of Social Justice in European Private Law* (Cheltenham : E Elgar, 2011), Part II on 'Corrective, Commutative, Procedural and Social Justice'.

[66] On the FET standard as part of general international law and investment law, and the related case-law, see : I Tudor, *The Fair and Equitable Treatment Standard in the International Law of Foreign Investment* (Oxford: OUP, 2008).

[67] *cf* T Franck, *The Power of Legitimacy Amongst Nations* (Oxford: OUP, 1990) who identifies (at 24) the following four major factors for assessing a rule's legitimacy: its determinacy, rulemaking process, conceptual coherence and conformity with the hierarchical rule system.

[68] *cf* L Henkin, *How Nations Behave*, 2nd edn (New York: Columbia University Press, 1979) who asserts that, for reasons of cost/benefit analysis, 'almost all nations observe almost all principles of international law and almost all of their obligations almost all of the time' (at 47). This appears to be true also for most WTO rules.

[69] *cf* HH Koh, 'Why do Nations Obey International Law?' (1997) 106 *Yale Law Journal* 2628, 2646.

laws and policy-making processes. These assumptions are consistent with those of political scientists, according to whom political processes tend to be determined not only by actors' relative power and interests (.eg, in individual and collective utility maximization), but also by rules, institutions and ideas, including political struggles for 'justice'.[70] From the perspective of citizens and democracies, foreign policies and international organizations can be understood as a 'fourth branch of governance' for the collective supply of international public goods which – like domestic rulemaking, administration and adjudication for the collective supply of national public goods – must be evaluated in terms of its contribution to the protection of human rights of citizens.[71] Constitutional democracy requires the subjection of foreign policies, including their collective exercise in international organizations, to constitutional safeguards similar to those delimiting the use of domestic powers. Theories of justice must focus on the just treatment of *individuals* (rather than states) as the ultimate units of moral concern. Just as the ECtHR emphasizes the need for an 'evolutionary interpretation' of the ECHR as a 'living instrument which must be interpreted in the light of present-day conditions',[72] so must IEL be construed with due regard to the human rights obligations of all UN member states and to the common concerns of humankind. The EC Court and the ECtHR rightly emphasize that human rights constitutionally restrain the limited powers of *intergovernmental* organizations in Europe, which must respect the fundamental rights guarantees in the ECHR as a 'constitutional instrument of European public order'.[73] In a series of recent judgments, the European Court of First Instance and the ECJ similarly emphasized that the powers of UN and EC bodies remain limited by human rights.[74]

As predicted by Kant's theory of history, the human struggles for human rights, constitutionalism and international trade have led to increasingly comprehensive legal guarantees of individual freedoms in national, regional and worldwide legal instruments. Yet, as illustrated by the 'market failures' and 'regulatory failures' leading to the global financial crisis in 2008, the rational egoism and limited reasonableness of individuals make it uncertain whether global human rights and an efficient global market integration law

[70] See, eg, J Goldstein and RO Keohane (eds), *Ideas and Foreign Policy* (Ithaca: Cornell University Press, 1993).

[71] See EU Petersmann, 'Constitutionalism and International Organizations' (1996) 17 *Northwestern Journal of International Law & Business* 398, 415 *et seq*.

[72] See *Tyrer v the United Kingdom*, Judgment (1978) Series A no 26, 15–16, § 31, and subsequent case law.

[73] On the ECJ jurisprudence asserting that respect for fundamental rights is a 'condition of the legality of Community acts', see the ECJ Opinion 2/92 concerning accession by the EC to the ECHR, ECR 1996 I-1759; Case C-84/95, *Bosphorus* [1996] ECR I-3953. On the constitutional functions of the ECHR see the judgment of the ECtHR of 30 June 2005 (*Bosphorus v Ireland*) which confirmed, inter alia, 'that a Contracting Party is responsible under Article 1 of the Convention for all acts and omissions of its organs regardless of whether the act or omission in question was a consequence of domestic law or of the necessity to comply with international legal obligations' (para 153).

[74] On the broad interpretation of UN human rights as international *ius cogens* and constitutional limitation of intergovernmental powers see the EC Court of First Instance in Cases T-315/01 (*Kadi v Council and Commission)* and T-306/01 (*Yusuf v Council and Commission*), Judgments (21 September 2005) in (2005) *CMLR* 1334. On appeal, in joined cases C-402/05P and C-415/05P, *Kadi* and *Al Barakaat International Foundation v Council of the EU and Commission of the EC* (*cf* Table 18), the ECJ emphasized that 'the constitutional principles of the EC Treaty . . . include the principle that all Community acts must respect fundamental rights, that respect constituting a condition of their lawfulness which it is for the Court to review in the framework of the complete system of legal remedies established by the Treaty' (para 285). According to the ECJ, EC measures implementing UN Security Council sanctions must remain in conformity with primary EC law and the ECHR. The ECJ rejected the previous finding by the Court of First Instance that the primacy of UN law (based on Art 103 UN Charter) could entail immunity from judicial review of implementing measures inside the EC.

can be effectively protected in the twenty-first century. Mankind is still far away from the Kantian ideal of universal just rules protecting maximum equal freedom of individuals, constitutional republics, mutually beneficial international trade and democratic peace. The constitutional insight underlying UN human rights law and IEL – ie, that international law, fundamental freedoms and other constitutional safeguards may be necessary for protecting citizens against their own governments – continues to be resisted by many rulers and their legal advisors. Just as it is better to light a candle than to curse the darkness, so do the calls by the UN High Commissioner for Human Rights for a 'human rights approach' to IEL deserve support in spite of the reality of intergovernmental power politics in many areas of international relations.

4 THREE BASIC PRINCIPLES OF 'SOCIAL JUSTICE' IN IEL: 'TAKING HUMAN DIGNITY, POVERTY AND EMPOWERMENT OF INDIVIDUALS MORE SERIOUSLY'

UN proposals – since the 1970s – for a 'New International Economic Order' were discredited by the UN's neglect for the UN Charter obligations to protect human rights. The emergence – since the mid-1990s – of a rules-based world trading system committed to freedom of trade and 'sustainable development' like the increasing number of investment protection rules and investor–state arbitration remedies based on BITs, contributed to increasing calls for citizen-oriented reforms of IEL and stronger judicial protection of transnational rule of law and 'social justice' in international trade, investment and environmental agreements.[75] The comprehensive constitutional protection of economic and social rights in European integration law, like the innovative protection of 'dignity rights', liberty rights, equality rights, solidarity rights, citizen rights and rights to justice in the EU Charter of Fundamental Rights, challenge Anglo-Saxon traditions of prioritizing civil and political human rights without constitutional protection of economic and social rights. Separating civil, political, economic, social and cultural human rights – as in some UN human rights conventions – risks undermining not only the 'indivisibility' and 'interdependence' of human rights and the need for comprehensive 'constitutional empowerment' of individuals in accordance with their individual value choices (eg, for economic and professional independence);[76] without constitutional protection of economic liberty (like freedom of profession), property rights, equal opportunities and open markets, citizens may also lack adequate constitutional safeguards and incentives for reducing the scarcity of resources through mutually beneficial division of labour.

[75] See: T Cottier, J Pauwelyn and E Bürgi (eds) (2005) and my contribution on: 'Human Rights and International Trade Law: Defining and Connecting the two Fields' (at 29–94); PM Dupuy, F Francioni and EU Petersmann (eds) (2009). On the political controversies over whether, and how, human rights are relevant for designing WTO agreements see, eg, the *Report of the UN Special Rapporteur on the Right to Food*, O De Schutter, on his *Mission to the WTO* (25 June 2008), document A/HRC/10/5/Add.2 of 4 February 2009. *Bridges Weekly Trade News Digest* of 8 July 2009 reported that, during the meeting of the UN Rapporteur with WTO delegates on 2 July 2009, 'delegates roundly criticized the Rapporteur for defending protectionist policies and not sufficiently condemning developed country trade barriers and subsidies'.

[76] *cf* EU Petersmann, 'On "Indivisibility" of Human Rights' (2003) 14 *EJIL* 381–85. Since the 1993 Vienna Declaration of the World Conference on Human Rights (*cf* para 5: 'All human rights are universal, indivisible, and interdependent and interrelated'), the 'indivisibility' of human rights has become recognized in ever more regional documents (like the Preamble of the EU Charter of Fundamental Rights) and UN instruments (eg, UN General Assembly Res 63/116 of 10 December 2008 confirming the commitment of all UN member states 'towards the full realization of all human rights for all, which are universal, indivisible, interrelated, interdependent and mutually reinforcing').

The need for constitutional empowerment of citizens in their international division of labour

A number of reports by the UN High Commissioner for Human Rights call for a 'human rights approach' to the interpretation, application and progressive development of IEL, for instance by interpreting the law of international economic organizations in conformity with the human rights obligations of states and by strengthening 'corporate social responsibility' of companies and other non-governmental organizations.[77] The 1998 Declaration by the 182 member states of the ILO on 'Fundamental Principles and Rights at Work', the focus on trade-facilitation and capacity-building in LDCs in the 2001 'Doha Declaration' and 'Development Round' negotiations among WTO Members, and the 2008 ILO Declaration on 'Social Justice for a Fair Globalization' reflect these increasing civil society pressures for strengthening 'principles of justice' in modern IEL. Also human rights lawyers have become more willing to explore the economic dimensions of human rights law with due regard to IEL: UN human rights law should no longer focus one-sidely on redistributing scarce resources to the needy and poor, but also on empowering individuals to increase their resources through division of labour. Diplomats and economic lawyers increasingly admit that reducing the unnecessary poverty of more than one billion of people living on one dollar or less per day requires far-reaching changes in IEL and in domestic legal systems of many LDCs.

This need for 'taking human dignity, poverty and empowerment of individuals more seriously'[78] has also contributed to the acceptance by WTO dispute settlement bodies and investor–state tribunals of amicus curiae briefs from NGOs addressing civil society concerns about adverse social effects of IEL.[79] The citizen-oriented 'judicialization' and progressive 'constitutionalization' of European and IEL have led to an increasing number of international dispute settlement bodies with compulsory jurisdiction for the settlement of international economic disputes. The increasing judicial accountability of governments for their often protectionist and welfare-reducing violations of international trade and investment rules refutes the view of many diplomats that lack of rule of law in multilevel economic governance – such as the widespread disregard by domestic and European courts for WTO law – is an inevitable fact of life.

Does 'reasonable disagreement' exclude an 'overlapping international consensus' on principles of justice in IEL justifying transnational rule of law?

Administration of justice by independent courts through fair procedures, reasoned interpretation, clarification and enforcement of legal principles and rules has been among the oldest paradigms of 'constitutional justice' in domestic legal systems. International commercial law, as one of the oldest branches of international law, has evolved in response to

[77] See ch IV section 2, ch VII, section 4 and EU Petersmann, 'The "Human Rights Approach" Advocated by the UN High Commissioner for Human Rights and by the ILO: Is it Relevant for WTO Law and Policy?' (2004) 7 *JIEL* 605–28; J Harrison, *The Human Rights Impact of the World Trade Organization* (Oxford: Hart Publishing, 2007).

[78] On the 'Alston/Petersmann' debate in (2002) *EJIL* see: Petersmann (n 25).

[79] *cf* J Harrison, 'Human Rights Arguments in *Amicus Curiae* Submissions: Promoting Social Justice?' in Dupuy, Francioni and Petersmann (eds) (2009) 396–421.

the decentralized information, coordination and sanctioning mechanisms of market competition by promoting mutually beneficial cooperation without requiring citizens and governments to relinquish their diverse conceptions of social justice. Yet, the legal insecurity related with transnational trade has prompted traders and governments since ancient times to reduce transaction costs by particular legal remedies (eg, the *praetor peregrinus* in Roman law) and judicial remedies (like commercial arbitration based on privately agreed *lex mercatoria* protected by public authorities). The dynamically evolving jurisprudence of international economic courts has progressively strengthened judicial review of border discrimination and of other welfare-reducing, governmental or private restrictions of competition and of mutually beneficial economic cooperation, notably by strengthening individual rights of 'access to justice'.[80] The principles of 'procedural justice' underlying investor–state arbitration and international economic adjudication are increasingly contested, for example if confidentiality and party autonomy governing commercial arbitration and WTO dispute settlement proceedings risk neglecting adversely affected third parties and public interests. There are also concerns that rule-following and 'formal equality' (eg, of foreign investors and home states) may not ensure 'substantive justice' in the settlement of investment disputes unless arbitrators and courts take more seriously their customary law obligation of settling disputes in conformity with human rights obligations of governments and other 'principles of justice' calling for judicial 'balancing' of all private and public interests affected by the dispute. As in domestic jurisdictions, the constitutional task of judges to apply the law and settle disputes in conformity with 'principles of justice' may require review of whether judicial reasoning in IEL – for example, regarding contract claims and 'contractual justice' in investor–state disputes, treaty claims and 'reciprocal justice' in WTO disputes – remains compatible with redistributive principles of case-specific equity, 'social justice' and 'corrective justice'.[81]

Legal and judicial protection and clarification of constitutional freedoms, human rights and rule of law has become the common foundation of constitutional democracies. Chapter III argued that, from a cosmopolitan Kantian constitutional perspective, the international division of labour among free citizens requires constitutional protection of cosmopolitan freedoms as integral part of the 'first principle of justice' of constitutional democracies whose welfare depends on multilevel governance of interdependent public goods. It was further argued that the universal recognition of 'indivisible' civil, political, economic, social and cultural human rights reflects a cosmopolitan 'difference principle' as 'second principle of justice' which, contrary to Rawls' theory of justice, includes cosmopolitan rights and duties also across national boundaries vis-à-vis foreigners. In order to institutionalize these principles of justice and 'cosmopolitan public reason' in multilevel governance, Chapters III to V endorsed the Kantian theory of multilevel constitutionalism and Rawls' explanation that the stability of democratic self-governance depends on constitutional, legislative, administrative and judicial institutionalization of public reason and judicial protection of individual rights. Arguably, these three complementary principles of justice also underlie UN human rights law and modern IEL and can be reconciled with respect for legitimate constitutional pluralism:

[80] *cf* F Francioni (ed) (2007).

[81] *cf* EU Petersmann, 'Introduction and Summary: "Administration of Justice" in International Investment Law and Adjudication?' in Dupuy, Francioni and Petersmann (eds) (2009) ch 1.

- First, equal freedoms of citizens as 'first principle of justice', subject to legal and judicial 'balancing' with all other human rights, must be constitutionally protected for the reasons explained by philosophers from Kant and Rawls to Sen (*cf* section A below). The 'indivisibility' of human rights requires recognizing that, for many people, economic and social freedoms are of no less existential importance for empowering individuals to realize their private and public autonomy and reasonableness through mutually beneficial cooperation than civil and political freedoms. Ever more democratic constitutions as well as the UN Charter are committed to 'promoting and encouraging respect for human rights and for fundamental freedoms for all' (Article 1).
- Secondly, for the reasons explained by Rawls, a 'difference principle' as 'second principle of justice' requires empowering and protecting poor people to effectively develop their human capacities and enjoy their human rights (section B below). Fair procedures for democratic rulemaking, administration and judicial governance must protect 'social justice' and equitable settlement of disputes, as reflected in procedural human rights (eg, of access to justice) as well as in economic, social and cultural rights.
- Thirdly, even though reasonable people may disagree on the extent to which the first and second principles of justice must be protected and 'balanced' inside and beyond states in international law, human rights require multilevel constitutional protection of cosmopolitan rights and duties across national frontiers to protect international public goods against both 'market failures' as well as 'governance failures' in all human interactions, at home and abroad (section C).

As explained by Rawls in conformity with modern economic theory, rights-based empowerment of citizens for individual and democratic self-governance will normally enable each people and democratic state to satisfy the essential needs of their citizens. Yet, contrary to Rawls' minimal conception of 'international justice', modern human rights law also includes cosmopolitan rights and 'duties to protect' citizens abroad against gross violations of human rights (eg, in 'failed states').[82] The legitimate diversity of principles underlying constitutional law, human rights law, economic, labour and social law protects democratic 'margins of appreciation' to decide on how individuals, democratic governance institutions and 'courts of justice' may reasonably interpret, reconcile and implement the diverse 'principles of justice' in conformity with the 'public reason' and democratic preferences prevailing in diverse jurisdictions.

A Equal Fundamental Freedoms as First Principle of Justice: Just Trade is Liberal Trade Subject to Protection of Human Rights and Rule of Law

After centuries of constitutional struggles, the liberal claim in Article 1 of the French Declaration of the Rights of Man and the Citizen of 1789 ('All men are born and remain free and equal in their rights') as well as in Article 1 UDHR ('All human beings are born free and equal in dignity and rights') has become part of the universal human rights obligations of all UN member states. Chapters II to IV inferred from this universal recognition of an 'inalienable core' of human rights that respect for human dignity and human liberty – as a 'constitutional contract' based on a *jus cogens* core limiting all government

[82] It remains contested to what extent the transnational 'duties to protect' and 'duties to prevent' under UN human rights law go beyond the UN Security Council resolutions on 'responsibility tp protect' people against humanitarian atrocities of their own governments, cf L Feinstein and AM Slaughter, 'Duty to Prevent' (2004) 83 *Foreign Affairs* 136–50.

powers and the state-centred structures of public international law – require recognition of individuals and of democratically governed peoples as legal subjects and ultimate values of international law.[83] Even though national and international human rights instruments define human rights in diverse ways, there is an 'overlapping consensus' concerning a core of inalienable, indivisible and peremptory human rights, such as rights to life, respect for human dignity and liberty, freedom from torture and slavery, rights not to be discriminated against and to judicial protection necessary for the enjoyment of other rights.[84] Such 'inalienable' core human rights no longer depend on 'contractarian thought-experiments';[85] they have become part of positive, national as well as international constitutional law and *jus cogens* which may neither be suspended nor subordinated to other rights nor be limited by reservations.[86]

Diverse conceptions of equal liberty rights

Views on the scope of constitutional protection of human liberty legitimately differ in national and regional legal systems and international treaty regimes. For example, while French, German and European constitutional laws protect economic liberties as 'fundamental freedoms' subject to democratic regulation, constitutional laws in Anglo-Saxon countries tend to protect 'market freedoms' through *objective*, legal and institutional limitations of government powers (eg, in the 'commerce clause' in Article I, section 8 of the US Constitution) and as residual de facto liberties of common market legislation rather than as *individual rights*.[87] The case law of European courts protecting the common market freedoms of EU and EEA law as fundamental rights of European 'market citizens' has prompted EU member states to accept corresponding constitutional guarantees in the EU Charter of Fundamental Rights.[88]

[83] On the controversial *jus cogens* core of 'inalienable' human rights and the *erga omnes* character of human rights obligations see: O De Schutter, 'The Status of Human Rights in International Law' in C Krause and M Scheinin (2009) 39 ff.

[84] See the recent jurisprudence of the EC Court of First Instance (n 74) defining more broadly 'the mandatory provisions concerning the universal protection of human rights, from which neither the Member States nor the bodies of the United Nations may derogate because they constitute intransgressible principles of international customary law' (Case T-306/01, *Yusuf*, para 282 ff). Also the International Court of Justice has recently (eg, in *Congo v Rwanda*) confirmed the expanding scope of peremptory norms of international law which can neither be suspended nor limited by treaty reservations; *cf* SRS Bedi, *The Development of Human Rights Law by the Judges of the ICJ* (Oxford: Hart Publishing, 2007).

[85] Such as the two 'original positions' used by Rawls for modelling negotiations on a national constitutional contract among parties representing citizens inside a state (Rawls (1971) ch III), and negotiations on an international constitutional contract among parties representing 'liberal' or 'decent peoples' which, according to Rawls, must be based on tolerance vis-à-vis non-liberal societies and cannot impose a liberal, cosmopolitan vision of 'global justice for all persons' (*cf* Rawls (1999) ch 3). Pogge (2003) 246 f, 252) and others (like C Beitz, *Political Theory and International Relations* (Princeton: Princeton University Press, 1979) 150 f) rightly criticize Rawls' 'statism' and argue for a 'cosmopolitan original position': rational representatives of people and of cosmopolitan citizens would also apply the 'difference principle' to the international redistribution of resources; international social inequalities are, therefore, justifiable only if they satisfy the difference principle (ie, they are unjust unless they work for the benefit of the least advantaged). The universal recognition of human rights offers a positive law justification of 'cosmopolitan justice'.

[86] See General Comments No 24 and 26 of the UN Human Rights Committee (n 29). Similar to human rights theories, constitutionalism and the universal recognition of *jus cogens* emphasize the need for higher-level 'constitutional rules' limiting post-constitutional 'lower-level law' and government powers.

[87] For comparative studies of European, American and other constitutional systems see: M Hilf and EU Petersmann (eds) (1993).

[88] *cf* NN Shuibhne, 'The Resilience of EU Market Citizenship' (2010) 47 *CMLR* 1597–628.

The French Declaration on the Rights of Man and the Citizen (1789) defined liberty in terms of maximum equal freedom:

> Liberty is the power to do anything which does not harm another; hence the only limits to the exercise of each man's natural rights are those which secure to other members of society the enjoyment of the same rights. These limits may be fixed only by statute law (Article 4).

Similar constitutional guarantees of equal individual freedom subject to democratic legislation are recognized in many constitutional democracies, and also in international human rights law, either in terms of individual rights to maximum equal freedom (eg, Article 2:1 German Basic Law) or in terms of a constitutional requirement, often unwritten (eg, in the constitutional law of the United States and some other Anglo-Saxon countries), of a legislative basis for restrictions of freedom and other human rights (*cf* Article 29 UDHR).[89] Respect for maximum equal 'liberties to be' is of existential importance for personal self-development in dignity. As explained in Kant's moral theory of the 'categorical imperative'[90], as well as in Rawls' theory of justice,[91] the 'inalienable' and 'indivisible' core of human liberty rights constitutes the first principle of justice, without prejudice to legitimately diverse definitions of specific liberty rights and of their mutual balancing in national, regional and worldwide human rights instruments. Legal equality also protects equal freedoms to be different and to decide autonomously which dimensions of civil, political, economic, social and cultural liberties an individual values most.

'Liberties to be' and 'liberties to have and acquire'

The core of *existential equal liberties* is recognized as 'inalienable'. *Market freedoms* (such as freedoms to produce, invest, import and export as protected by IEL) and 'process freedoms' also serve instrumental objectives[92] that require democratic regulation balancing human rights and private and public interests, for example in order to protect social human rights, basic social needs (distributive justice) and adequate resources for individual self-development of one's human 'capacities' (eg, by means of education) in dignity.[93] Hence, 'liberties to be' must be distinguished from *instrumental freedoms* (eg,

[89] See, eg: FL Morrison and RE Hudec, 'Judicial Protection of Individual Rights under the Foreign Trade Laws of the US' in Hilf and Petersmann (eds) (1993) 92; CB Macpherson, *The Life and Times of Liberal Democracy* (Oxford: OUP, 1977) 7.

[90] On Kant's moral 'categorical imperatives' for acting in accordance with universal laws ('Act only in accordance with that maxim through which you can at the same time will that it become a universal law'), for respecting human dignity by treating humanity as an end in itself ('So act that you use humanity, whether in your own person or that of another, always at the same time as an end, never merely as a means') and for respecting individual autonomy ('the idea of the will of every rational being as a will giving universal law') and individual rights ('Any action is right if it can coexist with everyone's freedom according to a universal law') and on Kant's theory of the antagonistic human nature promoting market competition and national and international constitutional guarantees of equal freedoms see, eg, AW Wood, *Kant's Ethical Thought* (Princeton: Princeton University Press, 1999). Kantian legal theory gives priority to a legal duty of states to ensure conditions of maximum law-governed freedom over moral 'duties of benevolence' to provide for the needs of citizens (*cf* AD Rosen, *Kant's Theory of Justice* (Ithaca: Cornell University Press, 1993) 217; P Guyer, *Kant on Freedom, Law and Happiness* (Cambridge: CUP, 2000) 264 *et seq*.

[91] See, eg, Rawls (1971) ch II.

[92] On human freedom as foundational value, ultimate objective and most important instrument for human development see: Sen (2000). On 'process freedoms' see: Kolm (n 13) 13.

[93] *cf The Principle of Respect for Human Dignity* (Strasbourg: Council of Europe, 1999). On diverse judicial interpretations of 'human dignity' as foundational source of human rights see: McCrudden (n 23). Most

'liberties to have', produce, acquire, sell or consume) that may have a price rather than 'dignity' (in Kant's terms). Yet, also economic liberties (such as free choice of one's profession) and property rights have 'inalienable cores' as existential pre-requisites for autonomous, personal self-development. Respect for human dignity requires treating human beings as ends and legal subjects rather than as mere objects of regulation or private means to securing benefits for other persons. Just as citizens are recognized as holders of individual rights in all fields of constitutional democracies, so should individuals also be recognized as legal subjects and 'democratic principals' in the law of international economic organizations.[94] In contrast to Anglo-American constitutional theories which conceptualize narrowly human rights to liberty (eg, in terms of basic personal freedom of bodily movement and democratic liberties),[95] EU law recognizes individual producers, investors, traders, consumers and 'EU citizens' as legal subjects in most fields of European integration law. Citizens are entitled to legal and judicial protection of their 'market freedoms' across national frontiers as 'fundamental rights' to be protected by national and EC courts,[96] subject to national and EC powers to reconcile competing liberty rights and protect other 'public interests.'

Maximum equal liberties or equal essential liberties?

Constitutional rights to broadly defined freedoms are recognized in national constitutions of EU member states as well as in European constitutional law. For instance, in Article 1 of the German Basic Law of 1949, '[t]he German people . . . acknowledge inviolable and inalienable human rights as the basis of every community, of peace and of justice in the world' (paragraph 2). The 'basic rights shall bind the legislature, the executive, and the judiciary as directly applicable law' (paragraph 3). Maximum equal freedoms are recognized as individual rights and objective constitutional principle in Article 2: 'Every person shall have the right to free development of his personality insofar as he does not violate the rights of others or offend against the constitutional order or the moral law' (paragraph 1). This constitutional right to general freedom of action is construed and legally protected broadly by the German Constitutional Court and includes, as discussed in chapter III, sections 2 and 3, both 'negative freedoms' as well as 'positive freedoms' of individuals. Arguably, one major advantage of such a broad constitutional guarantee of individual freedom of action is to protect procedural 'rights to justification', to judicial

courts have avoided legal definitions of the concept of 'human dignity' (such as whether human dignity should be understood as an 'intrinsic value' inherent to personhood or as an 'extrinsic value' dependent on merit or achievement). The German Federal Constitutional Court has adopted the Kantian 'object formula': 'it contradicts human dignity to turn man into an object within the state' (BVerfGE vol 27, 1 at 6). On the judicial protection of maximum equal freedoms also in terms of economic liberty rights by the German Constitutional Court see, eg, C Starck, 'Constitutional Definition and Protection of Rights and Freedoms' in C Starck (ed), *Rights, Institutions and Impact of International Law according to the German Basic Law* (Baden-Baden: Nomos, 1987) 20–46.

[94] According to the German Constitutional Court (BVerfGE vol 27, 1 at 6), the 'maxim "man must always be an end in itself" applies without limitation for all areas of law; for the dignity of a human being as a person, which cannot be lost, exists precisely in the fact that he continues to be recognized as an autonomous personality'. *cf* D Ullrich, 'Concurring Visions: Human Dignity in the Canadian Charter of Rights and Freedoms and the Basic Law of the Federal Republic of Germany' (2003) 3 *Global Jurist Frontiers* 1–103.

[95] *cf* Campbell (n 13) 56–59.

[96] *cf* C Barnard, *The Substantive Law of the EU: The Four Freedoms* (Oxford: OUP, 2007).

remedies (*cf* Article 19 of the German Basic Law) and 'deliberative democracy' whenever governments restrict individual freedoms. According to the EU Treaty (Article 2 TEU) and the Charter of Fundamental Rights of the EU, 'the Union is founded on the indivisible, universal values of human dignity, freedom, equality and solidarity' (Preamble of the EU Charter); these principles are protected by specific dignity rights (Chapter I), liberty rights (Chapter II), equality rights (Chapter III), solidarity rights (Chapter IV), citizen rights (Chapter V) and access to justice guarantees (Chapter VI of the EU Charter of Fundamental Rights). From the point of view of liberal economic and constitutional theories, the legal protection of liberal trade through 'fundamental market freedoms' among the 27 EU member states, as well as in their external free trade agreements with other European countries, can be seen as a requirement of justice,[97] notwithstanding the constitutional need to regulate and balance such freedoms to engage in mutually beneficial market transactions with all other fundamental rights of citizens. Founding economic freedoms on human rights requires governments to justify economic restrictions in constitutional terms and promotes, thereby, human rights to justification and 'deliberative democracy'.

B Constitutional Protection of Social Justice as Second Principle of Justice: Just Trade Requires Fair Procedures and Protection of Social Rights

According to Kant, the reciprocal recognition of individual freedom constitutes the origin of all other just rules of law.[98] Kant perceived social justice as a moral virtue rather than as a constitutional principle and legal obligation. Rawls' *Theory of Justice* emphasizes the need for protecting equal liberties as 'first principle of justice' before 'social and economic inequalities are to be arranged so that they are both (a) to the greatest benefit of the least advantaged and (b) attached to offices and positions open to all under conditions of fair equality of opportunity'.[99] This 'difference principle' for the distribution of 'social primary goods' (ie, goods 'that every rational man is presumed to want') inside constitutional democracies is rationally chosen by individuals in the 'original position' as a 'second principle of justice' in order to limit social and economic inequalities (which inevitably result from the unequal distribution of human capacities and other natural resources) and provide the least well-off group (through what Rawls calls the 'transfer branch' of government) with the resources necessary for their personal self-development.

[97] See Garcia (2003) 103 ff and Petersmann (1991) 400 ff, for an explanation of why liberal and non-discriminatory trade rules can serve 'constitutional functions' for promoting 'utilitarian justice' (eg, in the sense of protecting individual preferences for lower prices, greater consumer choice, more stable and competitive employment opportunities, enhanced productivity and competition, technological innovation), 'libertarian justice' (eg, in the sense of protecting freedom, individual choice and property rights across frontiers) as well as 'egalitarian justice' (eg, in the sense of protecting equal freedoms, non-discriminatory conditions of competition, preferential treatment of less-developed countries, fair procedures for protecting other fundamental rights and public interests). Arguably, liberal international trade rules correspond to the two Rawlsian 'principles of justice' by promoting 'an equal right to the most extensive basic liberty compatible with a similar liberty for others' (Rawls (1971) 60–61) and non-reciprocal, preferential treatment of exporters from less-developed countries (eg, pursuant to Part IV GATT, the 'Enabling Clause' of WTO law and the numerous 'special and differential treatment clauses' in WTO Agreements).

[98] 'Freedom [in the sense of independence from the coercive will of another], in so far as it can coexist with the freedom of everyone else in accordance with a universal law, is the sole human right belonging to every man by virtue of his humanity', Kant (n 7) 136. All other legal principles (like equality, procedural justice, multilevel constitutionalism) presuppose legal freedom of action.

[99] Rawls (1971) 63.

The two Rawlsian principles of justice are supplemented by two 'priority rules':[100] the 'priority of liberty' requires that liberty can be restricted only for the sake of liberty; and the 'priority of justice over efficiency and welfare' requires that fair opportunity is prior to the difference principle, and the latter is prior to efficiency and welfare maximization. Arguably, the recognition of 'indivisible' civil, political, economic, social and cultural human rights in European and UN human rights law goes beyond Rawlsian conceptions of social justice by acknowledging the need for legal empowerment of all individuals to live a life in human dignity and 'social security' (eg, as protected by economic and social human rights, labour rights and constitutional rights). Notwithstanding due respect for reasonable disagreement on the precise scope of such social protection, the underlying distributive and participatory rights reflect a second, basic principle of 'social justice', on which the fairness and legitimacy of all rule-making processes depends.[101]

The diversity of rights-based, procedural and outcome-oriented theories of justice and of European versus North American or Asian conceptions of economic regulation illustrates, like the controversies inside the EU over protection of social rights at EU levels and national levels,[102] the continuing disagreement among citizens and their democratic representatives on how 'social justice' should be protected inside constitutional democracies as well as in transnational relations. The Bretton Woods and WTO Agreements – notably their protection of 'sovereign rights' to adopt non-discriminatory economic regulation and restrict international trade to the extent necessary for non-economic public interest regulation – reflect the Rawlsian view that the available economic and 'social resources' of a people (eg, in terms of its human capital) for protecting social rights depend on national rules and institutions and differ depending on the respective national legal, social and democratic cultures.[103]

Social justice as procedural justice inside well-ordered states and 'access justice' beyond states?

From the perspective of *procedural justice* (like Rawls' theory of justice), there are no independent criteria for the right result: 'instead there is a correct or fair procedure such that the outcome is likewise correct or fair, whatever it is, provided that the procedure has been properly followed'.[104] Rawls' justification of his refusal to extend his 'difference principle' for justice inside constitutional democracies to international economic inequality among nations and to poverty in foreign countries – ie, 'that there is no society anywhere in the world – except for marginal cases [the footnote mentions 'arctic eskimos'] – with resources so scarce that it could not, were it reasonably and rationally organized and governed, become well-ordered[105] – seems to be consistent with economic

[100] ibid 302 f.

[101] Similar to Sen's view that freedom is both constitutive of one's humanity and of instrumental importance for personal self-development, social justice can be justified as being both of existential importance for social self-development and for promoting social peace; *cf* R Wilkinson and K Pickett, *The Spirit Level* (London: Penguin, 2009).

[102] *cf* Micklitz (n 65) and U Neergaard, R Nielsen and L Roseberry (eds), *Integrating Welfare Functions into EU Law. From Rome to Lisbon* (Copenhagen: DJOF, 2009).

[103] See n 38 and related text.

[104] Rawls (1971) 86.

[105] Rawls (1999) 108. 'I believe that the causes of the wealth of a people and the forms it takes lie in their political culture and in the religious, philosophical, and moral traditions that support the basic structure of

theory and empirical evidence. Insufficient 'democratic responsibility' of citizens for defending their human rights against unnecessary poverty inflicted by abuses of government powers explains why so many people in LDCs remain unnecessarily poor and why people in developed countries are reluctant to grant cosmopolitan development assistance to rulers in 'failed states'. Yet, the more almost all aspects of contemporary life are influenced by international relations and by respect for human rights, the less convincing become introverted theories of justice focusing one-sidedly on nation states without extending justice and protection of human rights to transnational relations adversely affecting poor people. In European law, the 'welfare state' protecting 'social justice' for the benefit of workers and consumers through private law, labour, social and consumer legislation has been complemented by ever more EU guarantees of 'access justice' protecting effective access to the common market, for instance by anti-discrimination laws and the 'Europeanisation' of consumer protection of 'EU market citizens'.[106] The universal recognition of human rights goes likewise beyond the Rawlsian conception of an international *Law of Peoples* and entails cosmopolitan legal duties of all states not only inside their national jurisdictions, but also for protecting and promoting human rights in their external relations with poor people and non-democratic rulers in other countries. As explained by cosmopolitan and human rights advocates, human rights entail cosmopolitan legal duties beyond nation states to assist poor people in other countries to cope with the adjustment costs of global problems (such as climate change), the harmful 'external effects' of foreign policies on poor countries and with grave violations of human rights inflicted, or not prevented, by non-democratic governments.[107]

The need for fairness of international rules and institutions

Voluntary compliance with agreed rules depends on whether procedures for the making, interpretation, administration and enforcement of rules are perceived as fair. In his study, *Fairness in International Law and Institutions*, Thomas Franck distinguishes procedural fairness and distributive justice as two aspects of the concept of fairness. He describes an 'overlapping consensus' in the international legal community on an increasing number of international legal procedures, substantive rules and institutions responding to international fairness concerns;[108] the latter often vary depending on the international legal conceptions of procedural justice and on whether international law is perceived as a law among states, law among peoples, or – as in this study – also as a cosmopolitan law of

their political and social institutions, as well as in the industriousness and cooperative talents of its members, all supported by their political virtues'. 'Historical examples seem to indicate that resource-poor countries may do very well (eg, Japan), while resource-rich countries may have serious difficulties (eg, Argentina). The crucial elements that make the difference are the political culture, the political virtues and civic society of the country, its members' probity and industriousness, their capacity for innovation and much else' (Rawls (1999) mentions population control).

[106] *cf* Micklitz (n 65), according to whom 'access justice contains two elements : first, breaking down the barriers which limit participation and access , and second, strengthening the position of consumers and workers with a view to enforcing their rights' (37).

[107] See the literature mentioned in n 40 and D Kinley (2009); G Brock, *Global Justice. A Cosmopolitan Account* (Oxford: OUP, 2009).

[108] See Franck (1995).

individuals.[109] Many rules of IEL are shaped by their underlying conceptions of fairness and distributive justice. For example:

- Robert Nozick's libertarian 'entitlement theory', according to which 'a distribution is just if everyone is entitled to the holdings they possess under the distribution',[110] underlies many property rights claims by foreign investors in international investment arbitration requesting protection of their investments and compensation for the taking of their property titles.
- The Rawlsian 'maximin principle' for preferential treatment of the least advantaged underlies redistributive claims and corresponding government obligations inside countries and regional communities depending on their respective constitutional and human rights law, economic and social legislation (eg, for 'transitional justice' in 'economies in transition') and available resources.[111]
- As the economic efficiency and fairness of market competition depend on equal freedoms (opportunities) and non-discriminatory conditions of competition, competition rules prohibiting anti-competitive agreements (like cartels) and abuses of market power, and protecting 'consumer welfare' against other competitive distortions and 'market failures', are necessary components of 'social market economies' (as emphasized in Table 3 and the related text).[112] The lack of effective competition rules in WTO law, like the selfish preferences of trade politicians applying WTO agreements as 'intergovernmental Hobbesian bargains' (eg, granting rights only to governments without legal and judicial accountability vis-à-vis domestic citizens), illustrate that modern IEL outside Europe often fails to protect consumer welfare and 'social justice' effectively.
- 'Transnational justice' based on democratic constitutions and human rights must be distinguished from redistributive rights and duties among states ('international justice').[113] As the distribution of natural resources between states is no less arbitrary than the distribution of 'primary natural resources' among individuals inside states, Rawls' acceptance of distributive and social rights and obligations inside states – but only of moral obligations internationally (ie, of better-off societies to aid 'burdened societies', limited only by international human rights to assistance for subsistence) – reflects a communitarian position inconsistent with social human rights. If the Rawlsian 'difference principle' – according to which inequalities in the access to, or the distribution of, 'social primary goods' must be justifiable as being advantageous for the least fortunate groups in society – is applied to transnational relations, it may justify claims by needy individuals and groups within LDCs for economic assistance, access to wealthy markets in rich countries and related adjustments of IEL.[114]

[109] See D Held, 'Law of States, Law of Peoples: Three Models of Sovereignty' (2002) 8 *Legal Theory* 1–44 according to whom 'cosmopolitanism can be taken as the moral and political outlook that offers the best prospects of overcoming the problems and limits of classic and liberal sovereignty' (at 24).

[110] Nozick (1974) 151.

[111] On the 'maximin principle' see Rawls (1971) 152–57, according to whom rational individuals would choose principles of justice guaranteeing them the maximum social primary goods possible if they happen to be born with the minimum distribution of natural primary goods. J Mandle, *Global Justice* (Cambridge: Polity, 2006) rightly emphasizes that government obligations to protect human rights may legitimately differentiate between domestic citizens and foreigners.

[112] On the changing 'welfare functions' of EU law see: Neergaard, Nielsen and Roseberry (eds) (n 102).

[113] On this distinction see Buchanan (2004) 191 ff.

[114] For a discussion of these complex questions see Rawls (1971) who affirms moral duties of international assistance but recognizes only an international human right to resources for subsistence because: (i) states

Cosmopolitan procedural and substantive rights to social justice?

Cosmopolitan conceptions of social justice offer a large variety of views on how the 'global commonwealth of citizens' could collectively provide international public goods more effectively, for example by establishing a 'cosmopolitan democracy'[115] protecting democratic participation of citizens across borders, providing for parliamentary assemblies inside existing worldwide organizations,[116] promoting transnational 'deliberative democracy' to correct the prevailing 'discourse failures' regarding international 'public goods'[117] and regulating the conditions for humanitarian interventions aimed at protecting citizens against gross human rights violations by their own governments.[118] The protection of many human rights (eg, to non-discrimination, participation in democratic elections) continues to dynamically evolve over time. From the perspective of *rights-based theories of justice*, modern human rights law goes far beyond the 'natural rights' derived from respect for human dignity in classical social contract theories from Locke to Kant. Yet, as illustrated by the lack of effective judicial remedies of individuals in the law of most worldwide organizations, there is no worldwide agreement on how to render human rights to 'social justice' more effective in transnational cooperation among citizens.

Most UN human rights conventions do not offer effective legal and judicial remedies to individuals at home and abroad and neglect the constitutional task of 'economic welfare creation'. There is also no agreement on how to effectively protect 'freedom from hunger', or 'access to water', as enforceable human rights beyond national jurisdictions, nor on 'who owes what to the very poor'.[119] The 1986 UN Declaration on the Right to Development focused on advancing a system of international duties that might give better effect to existing socio-economic rights, yet without clarifying the controversial legal relationships between 'rights to development' and corresponding obligations of individuals, peoples and states inside domestic jurisdictions as well as in relation to poor people

are economically self-sufficient (ie, well-ordered states can produce all the goods its citizens need); (ii) states are distributionally autonomous (ie, they can regulate the distribution of goods among their citizens); and (iii) international tolerance may prohibit the imposition of foreign standards of transnational justice. Garcia (2003) 148 ff, and Buchanan (2004) 191 ff, rightly endorse more comprehensive international redistributive rights because they serve the same human interests as other human rights (such as 'negative rights' and 'subsistence rights'). Justice requires limits on economic and social inequalities that impede the self-development of poor and disadvantaged people, as well as more demanding, international justificatory standards for the severe inequalities and persistent injustices in so many countries. For an application of theories of justice to the WTO Doha Round negotiations see: Petersmann (2005) eg, the contribution by Ambassador F Ismail from South Africa.

[115] D Archibugi, *The Global Commonwealth of Citizens: Toward Cosmopolitan Democracy* (Princeton: Princeton University Press, 2008).

[116] *cf* A Kuper, *Democracy Beyond Borders. Justice and Representation in Global Institutions* (Oxford: OUP, 2004); see also the various contributions on the lack of parliamentary control of international organizations and the proposals for creating a WTO parliamentary assembly in: Petersmann (2005).

[117] *cf* G Pincione and F Teson, *Rational Choice and Democratic Deliberation: A Theory of Discourse Failure* (Cambridge: CUP, 2006).

[118] See n 31. On the need for supplementing 'procedural democracy' by judicial protection of substantive rights: C Brettschneider, *Democratic Rights: The Substance of Self-Government* (Princeton: Princeton University Press, 2007).

[119] *cf* TW Pogge (ed), *Freedom from Poverty as a Human Right: Who Owes What to the Very Poor* (Oxford: OUP, 2007).

abroad.[120] The Declaration criticizes the international economic order (eg, its failure to offer LDCs an environment conducive to overcome unnecessary poverty) without refuting the Rawlsian insight that domestic disorder and inadequate legal systems inside many LDCs are more important obstacles to poverty reduction than international rules (eg, on discrimination of cotton, textiles and other exports from LDCs). As discussed below, the progressive development of fundamental labour rights and 'core labour standards' through successive ILO Declarations adopted by the 'tripartite' ILO bodies (including governments, worker representatives and employer representatives) – such as the 1944 'Philadelphia Declaration', the 1998 'Declaration on Fundamental Principles and Rights at Work' and the 2008 ILO 'Declaration on Social Justice for a Fair Globalization' – offers a successful example of 'tripartite, global social dialogues' promoting progressive development of legal obligations to respect and protect global labour standards.

Outcome-oriented theories of social justice?

Outcome-oriented theories of justice argue that rights and 'constitutional contracts' constituting 'free, equal and independent people' (Locke) are good only to the extent that they actually enhance human capacities to live a life in dignity. The diverse 'capabilities approaches' proposed by economists (like Sen) and political philosophers (like Nussbaum) complement – rather than contradict – contractarian justifications of social justice and the Rawlsian idea of 'overlapping consensus', for example by clarifying 'that the capabilities approach is one *species* of a human rights approach', and the 'political principles involving capability are (partial) articulations of the notion of a life with human dignity'.[121] Not only may the democratic specifications (eg, in the EU Charter of Fundamental Rights) of human rights and constitutional rights deriving from human dignity and from the 'inviolability' of persons (as moral equals with unequal resources) legitimately differ among different democratic communities; the 'lists of central human capabilities' identified by philosophers,[122] like judicial determinations of social human entitlements required by respect for human dignity,[123] also vary often legitimately among jurisdictions depending on their democratic preferences and conceptions of individual responsibilities.

Inevitable disagreement on 'international social justice'

Many theories of justice (eg, of Kant and Rawls) consider international obligations of assistance to be moral rather than legal obligations, for example in view of

[120] *cf* BA Andreassen and SP Marks (eds), *Development as a Human Right: Legal, Political and Economic Dimensions* (Cambridge: Harvard School of Public Health, 2006); ME Salomon, *Global Responsibility for Human Rights: World Poverty and the Development of International Law* (Oxford: OUP, 2007); SP Marks (ed), *Implementing the Right to Development: The Role of International Law* (Geneva: Friedrich Ebert Stiftung, 2008).

[121] *cf* MC Nussbaum (2006) 5–7.

[122] *cf* the 'list of ten capabilities as central requirements of a life with dignity' proposed by Nussbaum (2006) 75–78, 392 ff.

[123] *cf* the comparative survey of national and international jurisprudence in: BG Ramcharan (2005).

- the disagreement on principles for 'social benevolence';
- the Rawlsian argument that well-ordered national societies can and should be capable of satisfying the essential needs of their citizens; or
- the acknowledgment – in numerous international agreements – of the 'subsidiarity' and legitimate diversity of national social policies, as reflected in the 'exception clauses' in bilateral, regional and worldwide agreements (like Article XX GATT) protecting sovereign rights to give priority to non-economic value preferences inside states over economic market freedoms.

Modern human rights law and IEL also include positive law obligations of protecting human rights, labour rights and 'sustainable development' beyond state borders. Yet, the diverse conceptions of state sovereignty, popular sovereignty and 'individual sovereignty' in donor and recipient countries often lead to disagreement on principles of 'international social justice' unless citizens and their representative governments can agree on specific international treaty obligations for the benefit of specific beneficiaries. This frequent lack of consensus on how to protect social justice more effectively in international and transnational relations underlines the task of IEL to establish legal conditions and incentives for wealth creation through mutually beneficial division of labour among countries and citizens with diverse conceptions for a good life and social justice. Justice based proposals for changing international economic rules (eg, in the WTO) focus increasingly on capacity building and 'trade facilitation' in LDCs by enhancing legal conditions for mutually beneficial trade. For example, WTO ambassador Faizel Ismail from South Africa identified, on the basis of Sen's conception of development as a 'process of expanding human freedom', types of 'unfreedom' in WTO law that must be removed to integrate a genuine development dimension into WTO rules and into the Doha Round negotiations; for instance:

- Removal of market access barriers that deny LDCs the export opportunities and productivity gains which markets offer.
- Capacity building through trade facilitation and more effective 'special and differential treatment' of LDCs.
- More transparent and more inclusive WTO negotiations helping LDCs to effectively voice and defend their interests.[124]

Dynamic evolution of international development law and social law

As discussed in chapter VIII, UN human rights law, ILO conventions, financial assistance provided by international lending institutions, international trade law and international commodity agreements, the UN Convention on the Law of the Sea and environmental conventions protecting the 'common heritage of mankind' include, to varying degrees, provisions recognizing demands for redistributive justice or transnational protection of social human rights. Modern international law goes far beyond the Rawlsian concept of 'distributive justice inside states' and 'international charity among states'.[125] Yet, the failures of so many international commodity agreements to stabilize 'fair commodity

[124] *cf* Petersmann (n 59) 16 ff.

[125] For an overview of the various areas of international law influenced by considerations of distributive justice, see Franck (1995).

prices', the persistence of extreme poverty (eg, of more than one billion people living on one dollar or less per day), and the absence of effective guarantees of human rights and democratic governance in many UN member states as well as in the law of most worldwide organizations, illustrate that international law fails to protect distributive justice effectively. Even if legitimacy and justice are defined more pragmatically – *not* in terms of effective protection of human rights, but in terms of dispute prevention and dispute settlement through just rules and fair procedures – the fact remains that only few international organizations outside Europe provide for compulsory jurisdiction for settling international disputes with due respect for equal liberties and human rights under the rule of law.

The less extensive ratification of the UN Convention on Economic, Social and Cultural Rights (ICESCR) (compared with the UN Convention on Civil and Political Rights) illustrates the relatively weaker consensus among states on distributive justice than on formal equality (eg, in terms of protection of equal civil and political human rights) in national and international relations. National laws implementing international economic, social and labour rights legitimately differ also among constitutional democracies. The 1998 ILO Declaration on Fundamental Principles and Rights at Work and its Follow-Up, like the 2008 ILO Declaration on Social Justice for a Fair Globalization as well as numerous other UN resolutions (eg, of the 2005 UN World Summit), recognize universal principles and legal obligations of all UN member states to protect core labour rights[126] and 'decent work'[127] based on the declared conviction 'that in a world of growing

[126] *cf* ILO, *Declaration on Fundamental Principles and Rights at Work and its Follow-Up* (Geneva: ILO, 1998) in which the International Labour Conference declares in section 2 'that all members, even if they have not ratified the Conventions in question, have an obligation, arising from the very fact of membership in the Organization, to respect, to promote and to realize, in good faith and in accordance with the constitution, the principles concerning the fundamental rights which are the subject of those Conventions, namely:

(a) freedom of association and the effective recognition of the right to collective bargaining;
(b) the elimination of all forms of forced or compulsory labour;
(c) the effective abolition of child labor; and
(d) the elimination of discrimination in respect of employment and occupation.'

[127] *cf* ILO, *Declaration on Social Justice and a Fair Globalization* (Geneva: ILO, 2008), which defines 'the four strategic objectives' of the ILO's 'Decent Work Agenda' and of 'the ILO's constitutional mandate' as follows:

'(i) promoting employment by creating a sustainable institutional and economic environment in which
- individuals can develop and update the necessary capacities and skills they need to enable them to be productively occupied for their personal fulfillment and the common well-being;
- all enterprises, public or private, are sustainable to enable growth and the generation of greater employment and income opportunities and prospects for all; and
- societies can achieve their goals of economic development, good living standards and social progress;

(ii) developing and enhancing measures of social protection – social security and labour protection – which are sustainable and adapted to national circumstances, including:
- the extension of social security to all, including measures to provide basic income to all in need of such protection, and adapting its scope and coverage to meet the new needs and uncertainties generated by the rapidity of technological, societal, demographic and economic changes;
- healthy and safe working conditions; and
- policies in regard to wages and earnings, hours and other conditions of work, designed to ensure a just share of the fruits of progress to all and a minimum living wage to all employed and in need of such protection;

(iii) promoting social dialogue and tripartism as the most appropriate methods for . . .
(iv) respecting, promoting and realizing the fundamental principles and rights at work, which are of particular significance, as both rights and enabling conditions that are necessary for the full realization of all of the strategic objectives, noting:

interdependence and complexity and the internationalization of production: the fundamental values of freedom, human dignity, social justice, security and non-discrimination are essential for sustainable economic and social development and efficiency'; 'social dialogue and the practice of "tripartism" between governments and the representative organizations of workers and employers within and across borders are now more relevant to achieving solutions and to building up social cohesion and the rule of law through, among other means, international labour standards'; 'the importance of the employment relationship should be recognized as a means of providing legal protection to workers'; and 'productive, profitable and sustainable enterprises, together with a strong social economy and a viable public sector, are critical to sustainable economic development and employment opportunities'.[128]

Many UN human rights specialists continue to focus primarily on redistributing scarce resources for the benefit of the poor without sufficient regard to legal protection of constitutional and economic rights (like freedom of profession) as preconditions and incentives for empowering individuals to increase scarce resources through mutually beneficial division of labour. Empowering people to earn their own living offers long-term alternatives to unnecessary poverty that are more consistent with the demands of respect for human dignity and autonomy than long-term redistributive assistance to the unemployed.[129] Arguably, the basic objectives of national and international labour law are improperly defined in terms of 'protecting social justice against markets' and preventing a 'race to the bottom' by rational states trapped in a 'prisoner's dilemma game'.[130] Also human rights and citizen-driven markets must be recognized as complementary instruments that – by empowering individuals to increase their individual and social welfare through voluntary cooperation – enable people to live a life in dignity.[131]

As it is the *national* 'basic structure of political and social institutions' which determines whether a people prospers or not, the scope of extraterritorial obligations of promoting and protecting economic and social human rights abroad – for instance, in the context of trade, agricultural, investment and humanitarian policies towards poor people in LDCs – is likely to remain controversial. Also the methodologies of related 'human rights impact assessments' – for instance, of the EU's protectionist common agricultural policies (eg, in case of displacement of local products in LDCs by subsidized imports from the EU) – remain controversial. Power-oriented structures of the *international* legal and economic order influence the distribution of opportunities, income and resources among individuals, people and states in often discriminatory ways, for example in case of collusion among corrupt rulers and TNCs in LDCs to the detriment of local citizens,

- that freedom of association and the effective recognition of the right to collective bargaining are particularly important to enable the attainment of the four strategic objectives; and
- that the violation of fundamental principles and rights at work cannot be invoked or otherwise used as a legitimate comparative advantage and that labour standards should not be used for protectionist trade purposes'.

128 ILO Declaration 2008 (n 127) at 7–8. On the aim of this Declaration to strengthen labor rights vis-à-vis trade liberalization, see: F Maupain, 'New Foundation or New Façade? The ILO and the 2008 Declaration on Social Justice for a Fair Globalization' (2009) 20 *EJIL* 823–52.

129 This insight is illustrated by the saying : Give a poor person a fish, and you will feed him for a day. Teach a poor person to fish, and you can free him from hunger for a lifetime.

130 *cf* BA Langille, 'What is International Labour Law For?' 3(1) (2009) *Law and Ethics of Human Rights.*

131 See my criticism of authoritarian human rights conceptions that disregard the decentralized 'information, coordination and empowering functions' of citizen-driven markets for satisfying consumer demand and enabling citizens to engage in voluntary division of labour in: Petersmann (n 25).

or trade protectionism discriminating against cotton, textiles and agricultural imports from LDCs. The approval of some of these international legal structures (such as the successive international textiles agreements since 1961) by the adversely affected LDCs themselves resulted all too often from power politics. The focus on 'capacity building', 'trade facilitation' and additional market access opportunities for LDCs in the WTO's Doha Round negotiations confirms that international procedural, distributive and corrective justice requires international negotiations on agreed rules and procedures redressing existing inequalities by means of precise legal remedies and institutions that must remain democratically accountable and respect human rights.

C The 'Kantian Imperative' of Multilevel Constitutional Protection of a Just Cosmopolitan Order based on 'Consistent Interpretations' of Rule of Law

The inadequate evolution of global IEL in response to global interdependence reinforces the importance of the 'Kantian moral imperative' (described in chapter III, section 1) to protect human rights in all human interactions at national, transnational and international levels by constitutional safeguards protecting transnational rule of law on the basis of mutually consistent interpretations and principles of justice. Even in common law countries like Britain, Australia and the United States, rule of law is increasingly conceived in terms of 'constitutional justice' rather than as a purely procedural ideal, ie common law doctrines of 'legislative supremacy' are qualified by a 'counterbalancing judicial sovereignty' so as to protect constitutional rights (eg, of procedural fairness and equality), human rights and rule of law.[132] Arguably, the 'constitutional coherence' pursued by the 'Kantian imperative' of multilevel constitutional guarantees of equal freedoms complements the 'consistent interpretation requirements' recognized in national and international legal systems: just as national legal systems must be interpreted in conformity with the international legal obligations of the country concerned, international treaties must be construed in conformity with all other international legal obligations and constitutional principles of justice, as recognized in the VCLT.[133] According to Rawls, once citizens have agreed on reciprocal protection of equal freedoms and other principles of justice (as, eg, in the 1776 US Declaration of Independence), the next constitutional task is 'to choose a constitution and a legislature to enact laws . . ., all in accordance with the principles of justice initially agreed upon'.[134] All modern constitutions recognize that international law and participation in international organizations are of constitutional importance for securing collective supply of international public goods demanded by citizens. Yet, as criticized in chapters IV to VI, the current IEL system protects neither transnational rule of law for the benefit of citizens nor a just international economic and constitutional order based on coherent principles of justice.

Chapter V argued that both human rights and IEL – as preconditions for 'freedom, justice and peace in the world' – cannot become effective unless they protect transnational 'rule of law' for the benefit of citizens as a constitutional restraint on (inter) governmental 'rule by law' . Chapter VI explained why transnational rule of law – also in the worldwide division of labour – must be constitutionally justified by an 'overlapping

[132] *cf* TRS Allan, *Constitutional Justice. A Liberal Theory of the Rule of Law* (Oxford: OUP, 2003).
[133] On the 'consistent interpretation principle' see: A Nollkaemper, *National Courts and the International Rule of Law* (Oxford: OUP, 2011) 139–65.
[134] Rawls (1971) 13.

consensus' on principles of justice among citizens and states with often conflicting self-interests. The legitimacy of protecting economic freedoms through international treaty rules derives from their existential objective of protecting the private autonomy of citizens to enhance their welfare through mutually beneficial division of labour. Economists and lawyers have long emphasized that the effectiveness and synergies of private and public, national and international liberal trade and economic rules can be mutually strengthened and reinforced (following the 'plywood principle') if precise and unconditional *international law* guarantees of individual freedom (such as the EU customs union rules based on Article XXIV GATT) are interpreted not only as intergovernmental limitations of state powers, but also as directly applicable *individual freedoms* which citizens should be entitled to invoke and enforce in domestic courts.[135] Yet, trade politicians and their legal advocates – also inside the EU – assert discretionary trade policy powers and 'freedom of manoeuvre' to violate international law by presenting WTO agreements as 'intergovernmental Hobbesian bargains' that provide for no procedural remedies and rights of citizens against violations of WTO obligations by their own governments. Chapters III to V argued that such authoritarian conceptions of international law – treating citizens as mere objects rather than democratic subjects of international law and of the international division of labour – run counter to the human rights imperative of treating citizens as ultimate values and legal subjects entitled not only to equal freedoms, transnational rule of law and mutually beneficial trade across frontiers; as 'democratic principals' and ultimate sources of legal and economic values, citizens must also be empowered to hold government agents accountable for respecting their limited mandates to promote citizen welfare and rule of law. As explained in Kantian legal theory more than 200 years ago, equal freedoms of citizens under the rule of law cannot remain effective without multilevel constitutional and judicial restraints of public and private abuses of power in all human interactions inside states, beyond states as well as in intergovernmental relations.[136]

Why do citizens and people fail to protect a just international economic and constitutional order?

From a human rights perspective, all political power – including international rulemaking and multilevel economic governance in international organizations – must be democratically constituted, exercised and controlled and respond to demands of justice as defined by human rights. National and international human rights recognize (eg, in Article 29 UDHR) the need for democratic rulemaking and for constitutional rules protecting, implementing and balancing human rights.[137] Virtually all democracies have

[135] *cf* EU Petersmann, 'Application of GATT by the Court of Justice of the EC' (1983) 20 *C MLR* 397–437.

[136] *cf* ch III, sections 1 and 2.

[137] On the emerging 'human right to democratic governance' see, eg: TM Franck, 'The Emerging Right to Democratic Governance' (1992) *AJIL* 46–91; GH Fox and BR Roth (eds), *Democratic Governance and International Law* (Oxford: OUP, 2000); E Stein, 'International Integration and Democracy: No Love at First Sight' (2001) *AJIL* 489–532. On the possibilities of 'democratizing' existing international legal regimes see: S Wheatley, 'A Democratic Rule of International Law' (2011) 22 *EJIL* 549–70. On the reasons why constitutional democracy tends to promote 'democratic peace' and accountability for abuses of foreign policy powers see: PK Huth and TL Allee, *The Democratic Peace and Territorial Conflict in the 20th Century* (Oxford: OUP, 2002).

adopted constitutions based on the insight that democracy can remain democratically legitimate and sustainable over time only as 'constitutional democracy' empowering citizens as 'democratic principals' and constitutionally restraining the limited powers delegated to governance 'agents'. European constitutional law reflects the similar experience that economic markets, no less than *political markets*, are unlikely to promote general consumer welfare without constitutional guarantees of equal freedoms, non-discriminatory competition and democratic governance enabling citizens to assume their democratic responsibilities and challenge abuses of public and private power.[138] All democracies apply 'constitutional safeguards' for reviewing international treaty obligations prior to their incorporation into domestic legal systems, such as constitutional requirements of parliamentary ratification of international treaties and of their implementation through democratic legislation.[139] Democratic self-government – of the people, by the people and for the people – presupposes not only that citizens must govern themselves according to just rules and democratic decisions that implement agreed constitutional rules and protect citizens' constitutional rights.[140] As explained by Rawls, democracy also entails the primary responsibility of people to maintain a just constitutional order enabling satisfaction of all basic human needs. Why have citizens and people failed, so far, to protect their human right (as proclaimed in Article 28 UDHR) to a just international economic and constitutional order?

Chapters II to VI have argued that – just as all conflicts start inside the human mind – the necessary limitation of intergovernmental power politics and of Westphalian conceptions of 'international law among sovereign states' must be based on reasonable self-commitments to multilevel constitutional protection of equal human rights with due respect for 'constitutional pluralism' and 'reasonable disagreement' among citizens. As UN human rights and ILO law often only prescribe minimum standards, many national and regional constitutional rights in democracies go far beyond UN law. Also regional economic integration agreements among WTO members tend to go far beyond general WTO disciplines and often differ among each other. For example, whereas EU and EEA member states accept free movement of persons inside the EU and in the EEA, the US Congress opposes free movement of persons within the North American Free Trade Agreement (NAFTA).[141] Depending on their diverse constitutional and human rights traditions, regional economic integration agreements also regulate *individual rights* (eg, of a 'negative', 'positive', procedural or participatory nature) and the 'constitutional functions' of human rights as *objective principles* of constitutional order in diverse ways.[142] In Europe, the ECtHR has emphasized that human rights treaties now form part of an objective 'constitutional order' based no longer exclusively on states, but on individuals as legal subjects of modern international law.[143] Whereas Article 6 TEU recognizes the fundamental rights guarantees of the ECHR as 'general principles of the Union's law'

[138] On the EC's 'economic constitution', and the need for constitutional protection of market freedoms across frontiers, see, eg, EU Petersmann, 'Human Rights and International Trade Law: Defining and Connecting the Two Fields' in Cottier, Pauwelyn and Bürgi (eds) (2005) 29, 49 ff.

[139] See the comparative studies in J Jackson and A Sykes (eds), *Implementing the Uruguay Round* (Oxford: Clarendon Press, 1997).

[140] On the diverse concepts of constitutional self-government see: CL Eisgruber, *Constitutional Self-Government* (Cambridge: Harvard University Press, 2001).

[141] *cf* JP Trachtman (2009) ch VII.

[142] On these various 'individual' and 'objective' functions of human rights see, eg, Alexy (2002) ch 3.

[143] *cf* ECtHR, *Loizidou v Turkey*, Judgment, 23 March 1995 (Preliminary Objections), para.75.

and prescribes accession of the EU to the ECHR, the regional human rights conventions in Africa, the Americas and Arab countries have so far hardly influenced the regional economic agreements in these regions. Outside Europe, the promise of UN human rights – that 'everyone is entitled to a social and international order in which the rights and freedoms . . . can be fully realized'[144] – remains a cosmopolitan dream. Even if the expanding *jus cogens* core of human rights, and its multilevel legal and judicial protection through national, regional and UN human rights law, may be viewed as an emerging 'UN human rights constitution',[145] the intergovernmental structures of UN law fail to protect human rights effectively. As enjoyment of most human rights depends on production and distribution of scarce goods and services whose availability, quality and accessibility can be increased through international trade, IEL and its legal protection of a mutually beneficial division of labour are of existential importance for protecting human rights. Yet, even though UN human rights instruments rightly emphasize that 'democracy, development and respect for human rights and fundamental freedoms are interdependent and mutually reinforcing',[146] UN law fails to offer an appropriate legal framework for a just international economic and constitutional order. Hence, it is justifiable that the WTO remains outside the system of UN Specialized Agencies and enables membership not only of states, but also of autonomous customs unions (like Hong Kong, Macau and Taiwan) and international economic unions (like the EU).

Widespread poverty and human rights violations – notably outside the 31 market-based democracies cooperating in the Organization for Economic Cooperation and Development – also confirm that WTO law, like UN law, fails to protect consumer welfare and human rights effectively. The negative economic and social impacts of the increasing number of financial, food, energy, climate change and poverty crises require 'rethinking poverty reduction strategies'.[147] Similar to the 'human rights conditionality' of membership in the EU as well as in other European organizations (like the Council of Europe), UN law and IEL outside Europe must promote a new 'cosmopolitan public reason' in order to protect consumer welfare and human rights more effectively. Chapter VII discusses in more detail the far-reaching constitutional reforms necessary for transforming WTO law in a more legitimate and more efficient legal framework for protecting consumer welfare and human rights. Chapter VIII discusses why the judge often remains the ultimate guardian not only of justice in concrete disputes, but also of the 'constitutional unity' of international law and of the never-ending human pursuit for justice also in IEL.[148]

[144] Art 28 of the UDHR. See also UN General Assembly Declaration 41/128, 4 December 1986, on the 'Right to Development'.

[145] *cf* Petersmann (n 21).

[146] Para 8 of the 1993 Vienna Declaration adopted by the UN World Conference on Human Rights, reproduced in: *The UN and Human Rights 1945-1995* (New York: UN, 1995) 247.

[147] *Rethinking Poverty: Report on the World Social Situation 2010* (New York: UN, 2010).

[148] *cf* EU Petersmann, 'Multilevel Judicial Governance as Guardian of the Constitutional Unity of International Economic Law' 30 (2008) *Loyola of Los Angeles International & Comparative Law Review* 101–52.

VII

The Need for Constitutional Reforms of the Law of International Organizations: The Example of the World Trading System

CHAPTERS I TO IV explained why the international monetary, trading, financial, development, legal and environmental systems should be perceived as interdependent public goods whose effectiveness, coherence and legitimacy depend – as explained by Rawls – on a four-stage sequence of constitutional, legislative, administrative and judicial 'institutionalization of public reason'. It was further argued that, from the perspective of citizens, the necessary participation of states in international economic organizations can be perceived as a 'fourth branch of governance' which, like all other branches of government, must remain subject to constitutional, legislative, administrative and judicial restraints to protect rights of citizens in the global division of labour and limit abuses of regulatory powers. Multilevel economic governance is likely to realize its task of limiting market failures (Table 3) as well as governance failures only to the extent it remains justifiable in terms of 'common constitutional principles' protecting 'human rights coherence' (Table 4), 'democratic constitutionalism' (Table 5) and respect for 'multilevel constitutional pluralism' (Table 6). In order to regulate the 'collective action problems' and horizontal as well as vertical interdependencies among national and international, interdependent public goods in more legitimate, coherent and more effective ways, the five different conceptions of IEL need to be integrated into a 'layered', multilevel legal order (Table 7) deriving its legitimacy from protection of human rights, consumer welfare and transnational rule of law for the benefit of citizens rather than only in terms of rights of governments and majority politics. National and international lawmakers, administrative agencies, courts and citizens must cooperate in the necessary 'constitutionalization' and coordination of interdependent, national and international legal systems with due respect for legitimate 'legal pluralism' and 'reasonable disagreement' among citizens and governments with often conflicting self-interests.

Inside federal and regional constitutional systems, private freedom to choose the law governing commercial transactions and corporations may be sufficiently regulated by 'conflicts of law', company law, constitutional restraints, competition laws and 'regulatory competition' in order to avoid harmful external effects of the 'market for law'.[1] In

[1] *cf* EA O'Hara and LE Ribstein, *The Law Market* (Oxford: OUP, 2009), according to whom private persons will select the law applicable to their private relationships in the same way that consumers select products fitting their individual needs best. The regulatory challenge is 'to foster the beneficial aspects of the law market with enforcement of choice-of-law clauses while simultaneously protecting states' ability to impose reasonable regulation' (at 16). In his book review: JP Trachtman (2010) 104 *AJIL* 140 ff, Trachtman has convincingly explained why – contrary to the views of O'Hara and Ribstein (eg, at 224) – this 'contract approach' relying on

international economic relations, however, the 'regulatory gaps' in IEL (eg, in terms of inadequate regulation of private and public defaults, securities, antitrust, consumer protection and other public interest legislation) and the insufficient constitutional protection of human rights and labour rights illustrates that private 'law markets' and 'regulatory competition' risk undermining important public interests. Chapter V emphasized that – the more individual and democratic self-governance depend on transnational rule of law regulating economic, environmental, technological, legal and political globalization – the more national and international jurisdictions must cooperate. But, as explained in chapter VI, legitimate transnational rule of law may be different from intergovernmental 'international law among states' if the latter fails to remain justifiable in terms of principles of justice, such as access to justice as a right to public democratic and judicial justification of restrictions of human rights, constitutional rights and cosmopolitan rights and to legal and judicial remedies against public and private abuses of power.[2]

As legal regulation and protection of *international* public goods must build on *national* and *regional* public goods and their multilevel governance, chapters I to VI emphasized the need for 'constitutionalizing' IEL by multilevel legal and judicial protection of constitutional and cosmopolitan rights of citizens to set decentralized incentives for 'struggles for rights', 'private–public partnerships' and judicial remedies defending transnational rule of law for the benefit of citizens. The more global interdependence transforms national constitutions into 'partial constitutions'[3] that cannot unilaterally protect human rights in transnational relations nor ensure the collective supply of 'international public goods', the stronger becomes the need for examining how international law and international organizations can be transformed to address the pervasive 'collective action problems' at transnational levels more effectively, such as the 'jurisdiction gaps', the 'participation gaps', the 'incentive gaps', the 'rule of law gap', the 'prisoner dilemmas' impeding the supply of international public goods and the increasing democratic insistence on devolving decision-making powers to the lowest possible level close to citizens ('subsidiarity') in order to promote private autonomy, democratic legitimacy, economic efficiency and legal accountability.

OVERVIEW OF CHAPTER VII

Section 1 gives a historical overview of the change from 'instrumental' to 'constitutional conceptions' of multilevel economic regulation and of the corresponding 'three globalizations of legal thought'. Section 2 discusses 'constitutional economics' and its recommendations for legal reforms of the law of international organizations. Section 3 explores the implications of rights-based constitutionalism and cosmopolitanism for redesigning the law of international trade organizations. Section 4 explains why the 'human rights approaches to international economic regulation', as recommended by the UN High

'regulatory competition' and national regulation cannot convincingly be extended to the 'international law market' and international regulatory jurisdiction.

[2] *cf* M Kumm, 'The Idea of Socratic Contestation and the Right to Justification: The Point of Rights-Based Proportionality Review' (2010) 4(2) *Law & Ethics of Human Rights*: 'The real question is not whether judicial review is democratically legitimate, but how judicial institutions ought to be structured to best serve their democracy-enhancing and rights-protecting purpose'.

[3] *cf* EU Petersmann (1991) 354 ff; R Uerpmann-Wittzack, 'The Constitutional Role of Multilateral Treaty Systems' in A von Bogdandy and J Bast (eds) (2006) 145 ff.

Commissioner for Human Rights as well as by the ILO, have so far hardly influenced WTO law and WTO practices. Section 5 discusses the legal and political consequences of the failure to conclude the Doha Development Round negotiations since 2001; while the WTO will remain the worldwide legal and institutional framework for trade policy coordination, surveillance of domestic policies and dispute settlement in international trade, its regulatory functions (eg, for trade liberalization and market regulation) are likely to shift to more decentralized regional and bilateral fora – in conformity with the 'subsidiarity principle' – before worldwide consensus on the necessary WTO reforms may become possible.

1 FROM INSTRUMENTAL TO CONSTITUTIONAL CONCEPTIONS OF MULTILEVEL ECONOMIC REGULATION: DEVELOPMENT AS FREEDOM AND PROTECTION OF HUMAN RIGHTS

Economic and political markets emerge wherever personal autonomy and diversity of individual capacities and preferences of citizens (eg, in their roles as investors, producers, traders, consumers) are respected and legally protected by rules. The complex interrelationships between law, the economy and political institutions continue to be viewed differently from economic perspectives (such as mercantilism during the seventeenth century, liberalism from the eighteenth century, economic constitutionalism in the post-war twentieth century), legal, political and social perspectives.[4] Individual welfare can scarcely be inferred from statistics on national income of GDP (measuring the value of an economy's total output without regard to distribution of income and pollution of the environment). Nor do poverty reduction and 'individual development' automatically 'trickle down' from macroeconomic growth and development.

Three stages of thought in modern international trade theory and policies

The evolution of post-mercantilist economic and trade theory is usually classified into the following three stages:

1. From the eighteenth century up until the First World War, the economic theories of Adam Smith and David Ricardo on the gains from trade resulting from 'absolute' and 'comparative advantages' justified the case for free trade as a special case of the argument for consumer-driven market competition.
2. Since the beginning of the twentieth century up until the 1960s, in parallel with the ever more state interventions aimed at correcting 'market failures' and promoting 'social welfare', more and more arguments for 'import substitution' and other qualifications to economic laissez-faire and complete free trade were developed.
3. In the third stage of economic thought, 'the link between the case for free trade and the case for laissez-faire has been broken' on the basis of the economic theories of 'optimal intervention' (as developed by James Meade, HG Johnson and WM Corden): Even if there may be many economic and political reasons for government interven-

[4] *cf* Petersmann (1991) and DM Trubek, 'Max Weber on Law and the Rise of Capitalism' (1972) 2 *Wisconsin Law Review* 720–53.

tions correcting 'domestic distortions' and providing collective 'public goods', *non-discriminatory* regulatory measures (such as competition laws limiting restrictive business practices, environmental laws limiting harmful 'externalities', consumer protection laws limiting 'information asymmetries' and protecting consumer welfare, social laws protecting social justice) are almost always more efficient 'optimal policy instruments' than trade restrictions and other border discrimination with their welfare-reducing distortions of competition and arbitrary income redistribution for the benefit of 'rent-seeking' interest groups.[5]

This economic 'ranking' of alternative policy instruments underlies the corresponding legal ranking of economic policy instruments in modern trade and economic law: GATT and WTO law, for example, protect national sovereignty over non-discriminatory regulation for economic as well as non-economic public interests (*cf* Articles III and XX GATT) and production subsidies (*cf* Article III:8 and XVI.1 GATT). They limit discriminatory tariffs and non-tariff trade barriers (*cf* Articles II, XI ff GATT) subject to broadly defined 'safeguard clauses' and 'general exceptions' (eg, in Articles XIX–XXI GATT) acknowledging sovereign rights to unilateral trade restrictions for non-economic policy purposes.[6] GATT regulates the substitutability of trade and monetary policy instruments (*cf* Articles XII–XV) without limiting national sovereignty over domestic fiscal and social policy instruments and international capital movements. While trade liberalization focuses on promoting competition, productivity, economic growth and new jobs in the export sector, the need for complementary domestic regulation (like social adjustment assistance) is reflected in the numerous GATT/WTO rules on safeguard measures and 'exceptions' for public interest regulation. However, as discussed in chapter V, section 4, the legal ranking of trade policy instruments in WTO law pursuant to their economic efficiency remains contested, for instance regarding the consistency of certain TRIPS provisions with human rights of access to essential medicines.

The corresponding 'three globalizations of legal thought'

Adam Smith's *Inquiry into the Nature and Causes of the Wealth of Nations* (1776) identified the liberal laws and institutions of England – notably its legal guarantees of economic freedom, property rights and legal security for investors, producers, traders and consumers – as one of the major sources of its citizen-driven market competition and economic welfare. The diverse experiences of LDCs with promoting economic development seem to confirm not only Smith's basic hypothesis that governments usually cannot directly produce economic wealth, but only a framework of rules that may encourage or impede the creation of wealth by investors, producers and traders. The increasing number of resource-poor countries that became rich through international division of labour (like Chile, Hong Kong, Taiwan, Singapore, Switzerland) also seems to corroborate the economic theorem that 'the division of labour is limited by the extent of the market' (Smith); if the international division of labour is appropriately regulated, it can be mutually beneficial as explained by Ricardo's 'law of comparative advantage'. Laws and institutions for the correction of 'market failures' (like cartelization criticized

[5] *cf* WM Corden, *Trade Policy and Economic Welfare* (Oxford: Clarendon Press, 1974).
[6] *cf* Petersmann (1991) 57 ff, 221 ff.

by Smith) and of 'governance failures' (like discriminatory trade barriers criticized by Ricardo) are legal preconditions for protecting consumer welfare and promoting consumer-driven market competition and mutually beneficial exchanges (eg, of scarce goods, services and capital).

Economists tend to focus on two basic governance mechanisms, whose different structures and dynamics require careful coordination:[7] hierarchical organizations (such as firms, states, international organizations) and decentralized market competition (eg, price competition as spontaneous information, allocation, coordination and sanctioning mechanisms forcing suppliers to become sensitive to preferences of consumers). Organizations pursue agreed objectives through hierarchical rules, decision-making procedures and institutions that differ fundamentally from market mechanisms for the decentralized coordination of international movements of goods, services and capital among billions of self-interested individuals. Markets are characterized by rivalry among autonomous actors and the ubiquity of 'market failures'. Due to their inherent antagonism and the tensions between *global* economic integration and *national* polities, global market competition without adequate competition, environmental, social and other market regulations gives rise to increasingly complex 'market governance problems', such as collective action problems regarding interdependent public goods and transnational externalities that cannot be unilaterally 'internalized' by national policies.

Smith emphasized that efficient market competition is no gift of nature but depends on rules and government interventions constituting open markets, defining rights and obligations of market actors, correcting market failures and supplying public goods. Since the invention of modern economics by Smith, the dialectic evolution of legal approaches to the regulation of the economy may be subdivided into three phases:[8]

1. *Classical liberalism* (eg, during the second half of the nineteenth century) focused on the evolution of 'common law societies' and, in civil law countries, the creation of private law systems protecting private autonomy on the basis of equal freedoms, property rights, rule of law, a market economy and monetary stability (gold or silver standards) within nation states, whose foreign policies remained power-oriented (eg, colonialism, reciprocal trade agreements).
2. The emergence of the *'social state'* during the first half of the twentieth century aimed at protecting social welfare, group rights, social rights and social justice through ever more government interventions into the economy as well as into the polity at national and international levels (ILO 1919, Bretton Woods institutions 1944, GATT 1947, Havana Charter 1948), for instance by increasingly active use of administrative law for regulating the economy and the polity.
3. *Constitutional liberalism* (eg, since the postwar creation of ever more constitutional democracies cooperating in the framework of the EU, EEA and the WTO) aims at reconciling 'economic liberalism' and 'social welfare states' within multilevel governance systems committed to constitutional 'checks and balances' (eg, by national and international adjudication based on 'rule of law') and transnational 'social market economies.' International development organizations (like the World Bank and

[7] *cf* FA Hayek, *Law, Legislation and Liberty*, vol 1 (London: Routledge, 1973) 46. On the frequent neglect by economists of judicial decision-making see section 3 and ch VIII.

[8] *cf* D Kennedy, 'Three Globalizations of Law and Legal Thought: 1850–2000' in DM Trubek and A Santos (eds) (2006) 19–73.

regional development banks) engage ever more in systematic efforts to reform national legal, judicial and welfare systems as preconditions for the efficient functioning and social acceptability of market economies.[9]

Yet, the role of law as a constitutive part of 'human development', the limited capacities of governments to correct 'market failures' and supply 'public goods' and the necessary combination of a 'limiting constitution' (eg, limiting abuses of public and private power) with an 'enabling constitution' (eg, constituting institutions for collective supply of public goods) – not only at national levels but also based on international law and institutions with 'constitutional functions' for complementing domestic constitutional rules by collective supply of international public goods – remain contested within and among societies due to the legitimately diverse preferences of individuals and social communities. The perspectives of law, economics, political science and social theory on 'law and development' differ depending on the diverse legal institutions and historical experiences of countries with creating and regulating national market economies. For example, 'common law' countries with (unwritten) constitutions prioritizing civil and political over economic and social rights often rely more on 'common law freedoms' and market competition compared with 'civil law countries' with constitutional protection also of economic and social rights, for instance in the common market governed by EU and EEA law. The economic emergency experiences in post-colonial developing countries in Africa, Asia and Latin America (eg, during the Latin American sovereign debt crises in the 1980s, the Asian financial crisis in the 1990s), like the devastating experience with 'market-shock therapy' in post-communist Russia, illustrated the limits of 'efficient market assumptions' and the need for appropriate regulation focusing not only on economic growth, but also on poverty alleviation and 'development as freedom'[10] enhancing people's capabilities and enabling individuals to lead the life they have reason to value.

Constitutional economics,[11] as discussed in section 2, has convincingly criticized the 'constitutional ignorance' of neoclassical welfare economics and trade theory, for instance their often unrealistic assumptions of perfect knowledge and perfect competition, factor mobility at zero transaction costs, 'optimal' government corrections of market failures and authoritarian definitions of 'social welfare functions' by aggregating diverse individual preferences. Like public choice theory, constitutional economics asserts that – just as democracies are not sustainable over time without 'constitutional democracy' – market economies cannot maximize consumer welfare without respect for human rights (normative individualism) and 'economic constitutions' protecting consumer-driven, non-discriminatory competition, citizen rights and social justice against the inherent tendencies of self-interested competitors and governments to distort

[9] *cf* A Santos, 'The World Bank's Uses of the "Rule of Law" Promise in Economic Development' in Trubek and Santos (eds) (2006) 253–300.

[10] *cf* Nobel Prize economist Amartya Sen (2000) who convincingly argues that law, democracy and freedom – both as a constitutional right and as the most important instrument (incentive) for promoting human welfare – must be included in the very definition of development as 'human freedom' to develop one's 'human capacities' autonomously.

[11] cf RB McKenzie, *Constitutional Economics* (Lexington: Lexington Books, 1984); DR Lee and RB McKenzie, *Regulating Government. A Preface to Constitutional Economics* (Lexington: Lexington Books, 1987); J Buchanan, 'Constitutional Economics' in J Eatwell, M Milgate and P Newman (eds), *The New Palgrave Dictionary of Economics and the Law* (New York: WW Norton, 1987).

competition by abuses of private and public power.[12] Inside constitutional democracies, there tends to be broad agreement among economists and constitutional lawyers that trade and trade law are mere *instruments* for promoting individual and social welfare as defined in national constitutions. Yet, there exists no corresponding consensus for answering the question: what are *international trade* and *international trade law* for? Should competition and trade policies aim at promoting national consumer welfare, 'total national welfare' (as defined by government discretion and powerful producer interests), 'international welfare' or empowerment of individuals to increase their welfare through trade in a rules-based trading system?

From welfare economics to *ordo*-liberalism: consumer welfare requires a rights-based legal order protecting non-discriminatory conditions of competition

Economists refer to markets as geographical spaces of competition between goods and services, in which the market forces of demand and supply have a tendency to bring about equilibrium prices. Neo-classical welfare economics often assumes perfect competition and omniscient, omnipotent and benevolent governments maximizing social welfare through optimal interventions (eg, strategic trade policy). Even if market failures are admitted (eg, in case of abuses of market power, external effects, asymmetries in information, non-supply of public goods like social justice), welfare economists often ignore the legal preconditions of efficient competition and the authoritarian premises of their assumptions, for instance if 'economic welfare' is defined as 'total welfare' (rather than general consumer welfare) with discretionary rights of the rulers to redistribute income among domestic citizens by legally limiting the rights of consumers for the benefit of powerful producer lobbies. The destruction of trillions of US dollars of private savings due to the international financial crisis of 2008, and the arbitrary income redistribution resulting from governmental bailouts of bankrupt, yet systemically important banking and car industries 'privatizing profits and socializing losses', illustrate how under-regulated market competition may lead to socially unreasonable results.

Modern 'law and economics' literature[13] and 'institutional economics'[14] examine the manifold interrelationships between legal rules and economic welfare, for instance the contribution of contract law, corporate law and property rights to the efficient functioning of markets and reduction of transaction costs; or of liability rules, individual access to courts, litigation rules and law enforcement procedures as legal incentives for decentralized 'internalization of external effects' and spontaneous protection of market participants against other market failures. They emphasize that what are traded in markets are not physical resources but *legal rights* to have, use, or transfer scarce resources. *Ordo*-liberalism[15] focuses on the interdependence of economic, legal and political orders, and of related (economic, political and legal) theories about social order, in order to better protect competitive markets by means of coherent legal protection of the 'constituent

[12] VJ Vanberg (2001); EU Petersmann, 'Constitutionalism and the Regulation of International Markets' in LY Yueh (ed), *The Law and Economics of Globalization* (Cheltenham: Edward Elgar, 2009) 49–92.

[13] See, eg, L Kaplow and S Shavell, 'Economic Analysis of Law' NBER Working Paper No 6960 (1999).

[14] See, eg, DC North, *Institutions, Institutional Change and Economic Performance* (Cambridge: CUP, 1990); World Development Report 2002: *Building Institutions for Markets* (New York: OUP, 2002).

[15] See eg, VJ Vanberg, 'Freiburg School of Law and Economics' in P Newman (ed), *The New Palgrave Dictionary of Economics and the Law*, vol 2 (New York: WW Norton, 1998) 172–79.

principles' and 'regulative principles' without which undistorted competition cannot unfold and general consumer welfare cannot be effectively protected.[16] Whereas welfare economics proceeds from competition within a given set of rules, *ordo*-liberal economists also review the legal and political rules according to which economic and political 'games of competition' must be played in order to promote general consumer welfare rather than particular, mutually conflicting producer interests (eg, in protecting rents at the expense of consumer welfare).[17] Central themes of *ordo*-liberal economists and lawyers are the search not only for an economically efficient legal and political order, but for a socially just market economy: which welfare-increasing *choices among the basic legal rules* of the game may enable more efficient *choices within rules* without endangering the social consensus necessary for economic and democratic liberalization processes? The *ordo*-liberal approach attempted to translate the philosophy of the classical economists into the language of the law in order to define and create the legal framework necessary for decentralized coordination of individual supply and demand through a properly functioning price system and undistorted competition. Yet, the *ordo*-liberal focus on the need for *non-discriminatory* trade and competition rules remained confronted with the diverging political and constitutional traditions of discrimination, such as national sovereignty to maintain discriminatory border restrictions and 'parliamentary discretion' to regulate different economic sectors in response to different producer lobbies so as to maintain political majorities.

From public choice theory to constitutional economics: promotion of general citizen welfare requires a rights-based constitutional order

Empirical evidence shows that there is often a wide discrepancy between economic theories (eg, on maximizing consumer welfare, 'productive efficiency' and 'allocative efficiency') and the reality of economic policies. Public choice theory[18] questions whether government institutions have the power, information and motivation for correcting the manifold market imperfections, for instance because individuals are likely to pursue their self-interests in 'political markets' no less than in economic markets. Hence, government regulations are often 'captured' by rent-seeking interests in redistributing income for the benefit of the regulated industries in exchange for political support of the regulators.[19] In response to such 'public choice' concerns, modern *constitutional economics* emphasizes the need for limiting and regulating government powers (eg, monetary, taxing, spending and regulatory powers) through agreed constitutional rules in order to constrain legislative, administrative and other government failures by designing a 'constitution of liberty' that maximizes general citizen welfare.[20] Likewise, constitutional approaches to economic regulation emphasize that the economic welfare of the 'private law society'

[16] *cf* eg, Petersmann (1991) 63–68.

[17] The game metaphor was used by FA Hayek (1960) 229, in order to emphasize the dependence of competition on rules and the unpredictability of particular outcomes of competition.

[18] *cf* J Buchanan and RD Tollison (eds), *The Theory of Public Choice II* (Ann Arbor: Michigan University Press, 1984).

[19] On the redistributive nature and 'politicization' of government regulations of the economy, and the inseparable unity of the economy and the polity see, eg, Lee and McKenzie (n 11).

[20] See, eg: McKenzie (n 11); Buchanan (n 11). For a recent survey of the literature see, eg, Vanberg (nn 12 and 15).

(Böhm) – and also private law as the 'science of liberty' (von Savigny) – depend on constitutional controls of private and public power and on constitutional rights which, as in the EU's common market law and in EU competition law, empower individuals to defend their market freedoms and non-discriminatory competition (as citizen-driven coordination and discovery processes) in national and international courts.

Constitutional economists emphasize not only (like *institutional economists*) the functional dependence of efficient market competition on liberty rights (eg, freedom of profession, freedom of contract, freedom of consumer choice), property rights (eg, in savings, investments and traded goods), non-discriminatory market access rights (eg, as in EC law), and on legal security (eg, *pacta sunt servanda*, due process of law, access to courts) as legal preconditions for efficient agreements on market transactions and reduction of transaction costs. They also argue that people can realize mutual gains not only from voluntary contracts in economic markets, but also from *constitutional contracts* in political markets enabling citizens to escape from prisoners' dilemmas. Constitutional theories of justice (from Kant to Rawls) explain why rational citizens should protect their basic liberties and other human rights through long-term constitutional rules limiting post-constitutional legislative, administrative and other decision-making processes by 'constitutional principles of justice', which – according to Kant – should also protect peaceful cooperation among citizens *across* national frontiers.[21] Only *general* citizen interests (eg, in equal human rights) and *general* consumer interests (eg, in non-discriminatory competition), but not protectionist self-interests of producers are in the rational self-interest of *all* citizens. Hence, reasonable consumers would not consent to special interest rules that tend to be neither efficient nor in the rational long-term interests of consumers. Yet, citizens have only rarely the opportunity to engage in such 'constitutional choices' of the long-term rules constituting competition; and in the rare examples of popular constitutional *referenda*, as in the popular Dutch and French referenda on the 2004 Treaty Establishing a Constitution for Europe, there is no effective 'Rawlsian veil of uncertainty': the individual voting patterns are likely to be influenced by individual calculations of the future individual benefits and costs (eg, as winners or losers in competition, as taxpayers financing protection rents and legal guarantees of social justice, as beneficiaries of special privileges).

Interrelationships between 'constitutional democracy' and 'social market economies': people are the real wealth of a nation

Constitutional economics concludes that both political markets (democracy) and economic markets are confronted with the same basic constitutional problem, ie, how markets can be constrained by agreed legal rules to be responsive to general citizen interests. Just as voluntarily agreed market transactions and non-discriminatory market competition can promote general consumer welfare, so can mutually agreed constitutional rules and democratic procedures promote general citizen welfare. Constitutional economists have elaborated additional techniques facilitating 'rational choices' and agreement on 'social contracts' necessary for protecting consumer sovereignty and citizen sovereignty, such as negotiations 'behind a veil of uncertainty' and 'competition among jurisdictions'

[21] *cf* chs III and VI.

enhancing the capacity of democratic governments to serve the common interests of their constituents by limiting the scope for rent seeking.[22] By placing constitutional liberties and other agreed core values beyond the power of majoritarian politics, and by protecting a decentralized 'private law society' enabling voluntary cooperation, constitutional citizen rights and open markets facilitate individual consent to the basic constitutional rules. The constitutional recognition of the 'indivisibility' of human rights reflects the economic recognition of the remarkable empirical connections and mutually reinforcing character of economic, legal and political freedoms.[23] Such constitutional perceptions of economic law are in line with the empirical evidence in many OECD countries that high constitutional, labour and social standards can reinforce rather than undermine successful trade performance and capital inflows.[24]

If 'people are the real wealth of a nation', national development cannot be measured simply by national income per capita alone but must also take into account life expectancy, literacy and other non-monetary measurement standards of individual well-being and substantive freedoms to live the life individuals have reason to value.[25] The objective of development 'should be to create an enabling environment for people to enjoy long, healthy and creative lives'.[26] While macroeconomic income and growth policies and open, dynamic markets remain vital for creating jobs and individual salaries, the 'lack of a significant correlation between economic growth and improvements in health and education'[27] confirms that human welfare does not automatically 'trickle down' to all citizens unless 'market failures' and collective supply of 'public goods' are properly regulated. Even if – contrary to Rawls' assertion that reasonable people can agree on what constitutes a just society and its constitutive rules and institutions – an international 'overlapping consensus' on 'distributive justice' should be impossible in view of legitimate differences in reasonable people's outlooks, people can agree that some states of affairs are better and less unjust than others.[28]

The high decision-making costs of consensus requirements make democratic majority decisions inevitable. As majority decisions are replete with opportunities for special interests to exploit the rest of the population, majoritarian democracy remains sustainable only as *constitutional democracy* limiting abuses of majority decisions, for example, by means of equal human rights and other constitutional guarantees for institutional 'checks and balances' and non-discriminatory open markets. Economic integration law, such as the EU and WTO guarantees of economic freedoms limiting discriminatory border restrictions and discriminatory internal restrictions, has increasingly assumed 'constitutional functions' for limiting constitutional failures at national levels, for instance by

[22] *cf* VJ Vanberg, 'Globalization, Democracy and Citizens' Sovereignty: Can Competition among Governments Enhance Democracy?' (2000) 11 *Constitutional Political Economy* 87–112.

[23] Sen (2000) 6, 11: 'Freedoms of different kinds can strengthen one another'.

[24] *cf* OECD, *Trade, Employment and Labour Standards* (Paris: OECD, 1996) 111–12.

[25] This was the central thesis of the first *Human Development Report 1990* (New York: UNDP, 1990), which defined human development as a process of 'enlarging people's choices', emphasizing the freedom to be healthy, to be educated and to enjoy a decent standard of living. But it also acknowledged that human well-being encompassed a broader range of capabilities, including political freedoms and human rights.

[26] *Human Development Report 2010* (New York: UNDP, 2010) 1. The report reaffirms a broad definition of 'human development (as) the expansion of people's freedoms to live long, healthy and creative lives; to advance other goals they have reason to value; and to engage actively in shaping development equitably and sustainably on a shared planet. People are both the beneficiaries and the drivers of human development, as individuals and in groups' (at 2).

[27] ibid 5.

[28] This point is emphasized in Sen's recent book: A Sen (2009).

protecting equal individual market freedoms inside the EU (for free movements of goods, services, persons, freedom of establishment, capital movements and related payments) against welfare-reducing, discriminatory border restrictions. Constitutional rights are not only necessary inside democracies for protecting citizens vis-à-vis abuses of power by their own governments. They are no less necessary in transnational relations for limiting the perennial abuses of foreign policy powers and of intergovernmental collusion in restricting mutually beneficial economic cooperation among free citizens across national frontiers.

The need for functionally limited 'multilevel constitutionalism' protecting non-discriminatory conditions of competition and human rights across frontiers

Most citizens, politicians, lawyers and governments outside Europe continue to favor 'constitutional nationalism' in view of the power-oriented nature of international relations. Hence, international economic relations and IEL continue to be shaped in many 'strategic areas' by border discrimination and state-centered power politics (eg, on reciprocal market access for agricultural goods, state subsidies for air planes, export restrictions for energy resources and 'rare earth metals') rather than by citizen-driven market competition and non-discriminatory protection of equal rights of citizens. Likewise, most theories of justice (eg, by Rawls) focus on social justice *inside* constitutional democracies rather than on 'transitional justice' in the anarchic *international* relations. It is mainly among the 30 EEA member states and the 47 member states of the ECHR that functionally limited, non-discriminatory guarantees of European constitutional law are increasingly limiting abuses of national government powers and other 'constitutional failures' inside nation states, such as their welfare-reducing border discrimination and failures to protect transnational rule of law for the benefit of citizens. Since the Constitutions (*sic*) establishing the ILO and UN Specialized Agencies committed to the promotion of human rights (like the WHO, FAO, UNESCO 'Constitutions'), there are also an increasing number of international 'constitutional rules' legally committing governments to respect for human rights and constituting international rulemaking, executive and judicial governance mechanisms protecting mutually beneficial cooperation among citizens across frontiers. Multilateral trade negotiations in the WTO, for instance, are no longer only 'member-driven' by states; they are also influenced by the expertise and advice of the WTO Secretariat, the already more than 250 dispute settlement reports of WTO dispute settlement bodies interpreting and progressively developing WTO rules, by regional actors (like the EU), the regular interparliamentary meetings during WTO ministerial conferences, and by ever more non-governmental organizations, such as companies, non-governmental standard setting organizations, trade unions and civil society associations. The 'constitutional role' of international organizations for creating a more efficient world economy, their ever more comprehensive 'multilevel economic governance',[29] multilevel enforcement of international rules and multilevel adjudication of transnational disputes[30] also require multilevel 'constitutional' (with a small 'c') conceptions of economic governance by means of IEL.

[29] *cf* C Joerges and EU Petersmann (eds) (2006); A Follesdal, RA Wessel and J Wouters (eds) (2008).

[30] *cf* A van Hoek, T Hol, O Jansen, P Rijpkema and R Widdrshoven (eds), *Multilevel Governance in Enforcement and Adjudication* (Groeningen: Intersentia, 2006).

The increasing move from 'negative integration' (focusing on reciprocal liberalization of discriminatory border barriers) to 'positive integration' (focusing on harmonization of laws and policy integration) in the EU and WTO illustrates the functional need and political pressures to reduce the adjustment costs of market integration through policy coordination and 'legal integration' aimed at reducing transaction costs and discriminatory market access barriers, and at promoting regulatory competition and social justice. Most multilevel governance problems – such as multilevel rulemaking and rule implementation – cannot be solved by transferring the constitutional methods applied inside constitutional democracies to the international level of functionally limited international organizations. Some organizations – like the World Bank, the OECD and the EU Commission – have committed themselves to 'principles of good governance' (such as transparency, democratic participation, accountability, effectiveness, coherence) to legitimize their international governance and integration law.[31] Yet, such functional and technocratic justifications have been criticized as being insufficient for protecting human rights and constitutional democracy from being undermined through abuses of power, such as intergovernmental collusion in international organizations far away from citizens and from parliamentary control.[32] UN human rights bodies and the ILO have endorsed civil society calls for developing human rights approaches to the interpretation and application of IEL, taking into account the human rights obligations of all UN member states under the UN Charter as well as under general international law to respect, protect and fulfil human rights at home and abroad.

The proposals for interpreting IEL in conformity with the human rights obligations of states reflects the emphasis by many economists, since Adam Smith, that economic efficiency requires rule of law and respect for justice (*ubi commercium, ibi* jus).[33] Consumer-driven markets, human rights and citizen-driven 'constitutional democracies' proceed from similar value premises such as

- values can be derived only from the individual and his consent (normative individualism);
- individual autonomy (human dignity) must therefore be respected and protected; and
- the proper functioning of economic as well as political market competition resulting from legal protection of equal freedoms depends on an 'enabling constitution', a 'limiting constitution' and complementary, functionally limited 'multilevel governance constitutions' protecting non-discriminatory conditions of competition and promoting personal self-development.

The financial crisis that began in 2008 has confirmed that the information, coordination and 'sanctioning functions' of market mechanisms – based on decentralized dialogues among citizens about the value, production and distribution of scarce goods and services – can operate as indispensable, yet imperfect constraints on abuses of public

[31] See, eg: World Bank (ed), *Governance and Human Rights* (Washington: World Bank, 1995); OECD (ed), *Participatory Development and Good Governance* (Paris: OECD, 1995); European Commission, *Governance in Europe* – A White Book (Brussels: EU, 2001).

[32] *cf* C Radaelli, *Technocracy in the EU* (Harlow: Addison Longman, 1999); C Joerges, Y Mény and J Weiler (eds), *Symposium: Mountain or Molehill? A Critical Appraisal of the Commission White Paper on Governance* (Florence: Robert Schuman Centre, 2002).

[33] According to Adam Smith, 'Justice is the main pillar that upholds the whole edifice. If it is removed, the immense fabric of human society . . . must in a moment crumble into atoms', A Smith, *The Theory of Moral Sentiments* (Oxford: Clarendon Press, 1759/1976) 167.

powers (like fiscal, regulatory and administrative irresponsibility in Greece) and private power (like financial and legal irresponsibility in Irish banks). An increasing number of empirical studies confirm that the economic welfare of most countries, and the consumer welfare of their citizens, are related to their constitutional guarantees of freedom, property rights and of decentralized dialogues about 'supply and demand':[34] 'individual rights are a cause of prosperity'.[35] Since economic welfare can be increased by 'successful struggle for rights of which the right to property is the most fundamental',[36] 'almost all of the countries that have enjoyed good economic performance across generations are countries that have stable democratic governments.[37]

This focus of constitutional economics on empowerment of individuals is in line with the long-standing emphasis by many economists – from Smith via Hayek to Nobel prize winning economist *Amartya Sen* – that market economies and economic welfare are mere instruments for enabling and promoting individual freedom as the ultimate goal of economic life and the most efficient means of realizing general welfare.[38] 'Economic considerations are merely those by which we reconcile and adjust our different purposes, none of which, in the last resort, are economic (except those of the miser or the man for whom making money has become an end in itself)'.[39] As discussed in chapters V and VI, modern theories of justice increasingly postulate that 'basic equal freedoms' as 'first principle of justice', and constitutional 'difference principles' as 'secondary principles of justice' justifying preferential treatment of disadvantaged individuals whose personal self-development requires social assistance, should be applied not only inside nation states (as postulated by Rawls), but also in 'international democracies' (like the EU) and for the benefit of poor people and their human rights in third countries. International human rights law reflects these principles of justice by providing only for minimum standards respecting popular self-determination of how a society, depending on its resources and democratic preferences, chooses to constitutionally protect 'negative freedom' (eg, from arbitrary government interference),'positive freedom' (eg, in terms of real individual capacity to live the life one has reason to value) and cosmopolitan rights in the national polity and transnational economy. The variety of catalogues of human, constitutional and cosmopolitan rights in the constitutions and regional human rights conventions of democracies offer empirical evidence for this reality of legitimate constitutional pluralism.

[34] See, eg, the annual reports on 'Economic Freedom in the World' published by the Fraser Institute in Vancouver, which emphasize the empirical correlation between economic freedom, economic welfare, relatively higher average income of poor people and, with a few exceptions (such as Hong Kong), political freedom.

[35] M Olson, *Power and Prosperity* (New York: Basic Books, 2000) 43.

[36] See R Pipes, *Property and Freedom* (New York: Knopf, 1999) 291.

[37] Olson (n 35) 187.

[38] A Sen (2002) eg, ch 17 on 'markets and freedoms' conceptualizes freedom similar to the budget of a utility-maximizing individual: The more individual freedom, the larger is individual welfare. Such constitutional definitions of 'Pareto-efficiency' complement the moral and legal Kantian 'categorical imperative' of maximizing equal freedoms of individuals in national, transnational and international relations. On legal protection of 'market freedoms' in national and European constitutional law, see: EU Petersmann, 'Human Rights and International Trade Law: Defining and Connecting the Two Fields' in F Abbott, C Breining and T Cottier (eds) (2006) 29–94.

[39] Hayek (n 7) 35.

2 CONSTITUTIONAL ECONOMICS, HUMAN RIGHTS AND CONSTITUTIONAL PLURALISM: A NEW RESEARCH AGENDA FOR REDESIGNING THE LAW OF INTERNATIONAL ORGANIZATIONS

Constitutional democracies recognize 'inalienable' human rights as the birthright of every human being deriving from respect for human dignity, personal autonomy and reasonable responsibility for one's basic needs and personal self-development. The rational pursuit of individual self-development and progressive 'self-liberation' from dependence on others (eg, family assistance, social assistance) depends, inter alia, on economic freedoms (such as freedom of profession, freedom of contract, property rights) as legal preconditions for producing goods, services and income that can be exchanged for other goods and services necessary for individual survival and social cooperation among free citizens. This moral and constitutional foundation of modern human rights law is not inconsistent with economic theories explaining the historical bottom-up struggles of citizens for human rights (eg, in the English, American and French Revolutions during the seventeenth and eighteenth centuries) as rational responses to market failures and to government failures so as to internalize external effects of arbitrary governmental restraints of economic and political competition. Just as economics emphasizes that the legitimacy of economic markets derives from satisfying general consumer interests (rather than protectionist self-interests of producers), so do human rights emphasize that the democratic legitimacy of political markets derives from serving general citizen interests as defined by human rights (rather than the self-interests of political entrepreneurs). Hence, consumers in economic markets, like citizens in political markets, have rational self-interests in defining more precisely the 'enabling constitution' needed for promoting efficient supply of private and public goods meeting the individual and democratic demand of free citizens; the 'limiting constitution' needed for protecting equal freedoms and non-discriminatory competition against abuses of power; and supplementary, functionally limited 'multilevel governance constitutions' for collective supply of interdependent public goods.

The numerous parallels and interrelationships between the voluntary exchange paradigms ('consumer sovereignty') of market theories, the constitutional contract paradigm ('citizen sovereignty') of democratic theories and modern conceptions of inalienable human rights ('personal autonomy') and 'constitutional pluralism' continue to give rise to increasing research on the similar value premises, similar constitutional problems and complementary functions of human rights and non-discriminatory market competition.[40] As social traditions, democratic preferences and national constitutions legitimately differ among countries, international law must respect this 'constitutional pluralism', including the sovereign right of constitutional democracies to disregard, for legitimate constitutional reasons, international law obligations subject to the 'secondary' international law rules on state responsibility. As discussed in chapters III to V, European courts interpret the intergovernmental EU Treaty guarantees of free movements of goods, services, persons, capital and payments as 'fundamental individual freedoms' of EU citizens and 'balance' and delimit the EU's market freedoms with civil, political and social human

[40] *cf*, eg: EU Petersmann, 'Human Rights in International Economic Law in the 21st Century' (2001) 4 *JIEL* 3 ff; J Harrison (2007); H Hestermeyer (2007); W Benedek, K de Freyter and F Marella (eds) (2008). On the diverse conceptions of 'constitutional pluralism' see ch II, sections 3 and 4.

rights and constitutional rights as protected by national constitutions and by the ECtHR.[41] The ECtHR has, likewise, recognized that citizens must be constitutionally protected by fundamental rights not only in their *individual* economic activities (eg, as owners and sellers of private property rights), but also in their *collective*, private economic activities (eg, in economic companies and trade unions) producing and consuming scarce resources.[42]

Chapter V concluded with my long-standing argument that the 1969 Vienna Convention on the Law of Treaties requires not only textual, systemic and functional, but also 'constitutional interpretation' of international treaties 'in conformity with the principles of justice and international law', including 'universal respect for, and observance of, human rights and fundamental freedoms for all' (Preamble VCLT). Hence, also UN human rights bodies, other worldwide organizations and international courts increasingly recall that –- as also explained by modern theories of justice (as discussed in Chapter VI) and by 'constitutional economics' (as discussed in Section 128) –- IEL and market freedoms (eg, as protected by the WTO legal and dispute settlement system) must remain consistent with universal human rights obligations of UN member states and with their democratically agreed, constitutional principles of justice.

Principles of justice are consistent with 'constitutional economics'

Chapter VI argued that the core 'principles of justice' underlying human rights and constitutional democracies – like constitutional protection of equal freedoms (as 'first principle of justice'), differential treatment protecting the poor (as 'second principle of justice') and transnational rule of law protecting cosmopolitan rights across frontiers (as a 'third principle of justice') – are consistent with economic proposals for prioritizing macroeconomic growth and open markets (eg, in order to promote jobs, income and innovation). Governmental resources for social policies aimed at satisfying the basic needs of all (eg, in terms of education and health protection also of poor people who do

[41] The scope of judicial protection of the EC Treaty's economic freedoms dynamically evolved in response to their judicial balancing with non-economic rights and national sovereignty, as illustrated by the explicit revision by the ECJ of its judicial interpretation of Arts 28ff EC Treaty in 1993 (judgments in the *Keck/Mithouard* cases) which limited the scope of these prohibitions of quantitative trade restrictions to product-related measures (ie, no longer covering non-discriminatory national sales modalities). The EU's 'market freedoms' have been increasingly construed as liberty rights protecting market access and prohibiting disproportionate national restrictions (eg, for goods) rather than only as rights to non-discriminatory treatment across frontiers (eg, for access of workers to national social systems, freedom of investments subject to non-discriminatory, national regulations). The limited EU competences for social law and policies have made the reconciliation of the common market freedoms with labour and social rights particularly controversial in EC rulemaking (such as the EC's Posted Worker Directive 96/71/EC) as well as in the case law of the ECJ (such as in the *Viking* Case C-438/05 [2007] ECR I-10779, concerning strike actions against the re-flagging of a Finnish ship in order to replace its crew with Estonians, and the *Laval* Case C-341/05 [2007] ECR I-11767, concerning strike actions by Swedish construction workers against building services by a Latvian construction company).

[42] *cf* M Emberland (2006). Some provisions of the ECHR also explicitly protect rights of 'legal persons' (eg, Art 10 ECHR: freedom of expression, Art 1 of Protocol 1: private possessions and property rights) and complaints 'from any person' (Art 34 ECHR). Yet, the ECtHR has construed many rights protected by the ECHR (such as Art 6: right to a fair trial, Art 8: right to protection of one's home, Art 11: freedom of assembly, Art 13: right to effective remedies, Art 41: right to request compensation for non-material damage), as well as corresponding obligations of governments (eg, under Art 1 to secure the fundamental rights 'to everyone within their jurisdiction', including economic actors and companies from outside Europe), as also protecting rights of companies.

not sufficiently benefit from wealth creation through economic growth) depend on income generated by economic growth. Yet, growth policies must protect general consumer welfare through correction of 'market failures' by means of competition, environmental, social and liberal trade legislation. As illustrated by the unnecessary poverty in India, constitutional commitments to protecting human rights may not be enough to prevent child malnutrition, female illiteracy and many other social ills unless economic growth generates sufficient financial resources for targeted social programmes supplementing the favourable effects of economic growth policies on poverty alleviation (for instance by pulling the poor up into gainful employment and providing revenues for financing social assistance programmes). Hence, constitutional protection of human rights must be complemented by 'market-creating policies'. Correcting market failures as well as governance failures requires financial resources that have to be generated through open markets, legal security and democratic institutions that continue to be lacking in many less-developed UN member states (notably in Africa).

Overcoming 'collective action problems' in worldwide organizations requires institutional reforms: the example of the WTO

The fact that – 10 years after the launching of the DDR negotiations in 2001 – the 153 WTO members have not reached agreement even on the 'modalities' for multilateral liberalization of trade in goods and services illustrates the 'collective action problems' of 'member-driven', consensus-based trade negotiations among 153 developed and less-developed WTO members without collective leadership for identifying and defending their common, collective self-interests. In line with the policy proposals from 'constitutional economics', 'ordo-liberalism' and from 'public choice economics' for protecting general citizen interests by legal and institutional restraints on special group interests, the GATT and WTO Directors-General have commissioned or supported a large number of advisory reports recommending institutional reforms of the GATT/WTO trading system. For instance:

- The 1985 'Leutwiler Report' on 'Trade Policies for a Better Future: Proposals for Action'[43] focused on making trade policies, GATT negotiations and 'protection costs' more transparent, for example by institutionalized GATT surveillance of trade policies, publication of 'protection balance sheets' demonstrating the social costs of trade protection and by more transparent and more rules-based GATT dispute settlement procedures. The WTO 'Trade Policy Review Mechanism' and the WTO dispute settlement system transformed some of these policy recommendations into WTO law.
- The 1989 'Long Report' on 'Public Scrutiny of Protection: Domestic Policy Transparency and Trade Liberalization'[44] recommended further limiting the 'inherent biases' in domestic policymaking processes favouring protectionism by additional *domestic* transparency requirements and government institutions (following the model of Australia's 'Industries Assistance Commission') limiting the scope for 'rent-seeking' and 'regulatory capture' at domestic policy levels.

[43] Reproduced in: A Dunkel (ed), *Trade Policies for a Better Future: The Leutwiler Report, GATT and the Uruguay Round* (Dordrecht: Nijhoff, 1987) 9–70.

[44] O Long (ed), *Public Scrutiny of Protection: Domestic Policy Transparency and Trade Liberalization* (London: Trade Policy Research Centre, 1989).

- The 2005 'Sutherland Report' on 'The Future of the WTO: Addressing Institutional Challenges in the New Millennium'[45] recommended, inter alia, strengthening the roles of the Director-General and of the WTO Secretariat; to establish a senior officials 'consultative body', facilitate WTO majority decisions by a critical mass, promote dialogue with civil society and improve WTO review and WTO disciplines concerning the spread of preferential trade agreements.
- The 2007 'First Warwick Commission Report' on 'The Multilateral Trade Regime: Which Way Forward?'[46] recommended, inter alia, additional reforms of WTO decision-making (by use of a 'critical mass approach') and of dispute settlement procedures (eg, by promoting transparency through admission of amicus curiae briefs).
- A 'discussion draft' published in November 2009[47] promoted further discussions of WTO reforms by offering a 'mapping study' compiling a useful sampling of the numerous proposals and political statements on reforms of the WTO and global trade governance put forward by WTO member states, WTO institutions, other international organizations, academics and stakeholders since 1995.
- In their Interim Report on 'The Doha Round: Setting a Deadline, Defining a Final Deal' of 12 January 2011, the former WTO Director-General Peter Sutherland and Professor Jagdish Bhagwati, describe the failure to conclude the Doha Round negotiations since 2001 as 'a failure of global leadership in some quarters that is difficult to comprehend for various reasons':
  - The market access commitments on offer would provide a global economic stimulus of more than 600 billion dollars in new trade annually;
  - The legal binding of currently applied market access would act as an insurance policy against potential reintroduction of lawful tariffs that could destroy up to 900 billion dollars in trade;
  - Reform of farm trade and conclusion of the Doha Round negotiations would enable the WTO membership to deal with the new trade policy agenda *inside* the WTO rather than in ever more bilateral and regional agreements *outside* the WTO;
  - The Doha Round agreements would offer special advantages for LLDCs as illustrated by the 'duty free, quota free' trade liberalization for the 49 least-developed countries, their complete exclusion from any new obligations except binding their tariff schedules at current levels (the 'Round for Free'), the various forms of 'flexibilities' for developing countries and the 'trade creation' expected from the Agreement on Trade Facilitation worth more than 300 billion US dollars.[48]

Some of the proposed institutional reforms have been realized through decisions of WTO bodies (eg, reforms of the periodical 'trade policy reviews' of WTO members, the

[45] *The Future of the WTO: Addressing Institutional Challenges in the New Millennium* (Geneva: WTO, 2005).

[46] *The Multilateral Trade Regime: Which Way Forward* (Coventry: University of Warwick, 2007).

[47] C Deere-Birkbeck and C Monagle (eds), *Strengthening Multilateralism: A Mapping of Proposals on WTO Reform and Global Trade Governance* (Geneva/Oxford: International Centre for Trade and Sustainable Development, 2009).

[48] J Bhagwati et al (eds), *High Level Experts Group – Interim Report January 2011* (2011); the final Report was published in May 2011: *World Trade and the Doha Round. Final Report of the High-Level Trade Experts Group*. The most recent draft consolidated negotiating text of the *Agreement on Trade Facilitation* is reproduced in WTO document TN/TF/W/165/Rev.6 of 22 December 2010; its economic importance for developing countries is explained in: G McLinden et al (eds), *Border Management Modernization* (Washington: World Bank, 2011).

establishment of a new Regional Trade Agreements Committee with new review procedures, admission of amicus curiae briefs and opening of hearings to the public by WTO dispute settlement bodies) and of the WTO Director-General (eg, on the now annual WTO Public Fora with civil society representatives, stronger WTO collaboration with trade-related UN Specialized Agencies). But most WTO diplomats remain unwilling to challenge the GATT/WTO mantras of 'member-driven governance' and consensus-based negotiations, for instance

- by strengthening the powers of initiative and surveillance of the WTO Director-General and of the WTO Secretariat;
- by setting up a WTO Executive Council composed of trade ministers, to be assisted by a WTO Committee on legal and institutional affairs with a mandate to recommend further institutional reforms; and
- to strengthen the 'constitutional checks and balances' inside the WTO legal system by promoting stronger parliamentary control, multilevel judicial enforceability of certain agreed 'WTO freedoms' and 'WTO prohibitions of discrimination' and by further strengthening 'private–public partnerships' in implementing WTO rules (eg, by inviting civil society NGOs to participate in the WTO's Trade Policy Reviews of all WTO members).

The G20 group of major economies has recently initiated overdue institutional reforms of the IMF like increased quotas and voting powers for emerging economies like China, and provision for additional IMF lending resources in order to better respond to the financial crisis. There remains a regrettable lack of leadership – not only by the United States, but also by newly emerging economies like China and India – for concluding the Doha Round negotiations and for reforming the political WTO decision-making processes. The authoritarian treatment of citizens as mere objects of WTO law, the imbalances between the efficient settlements of the already more than 400 WTO dispute settlement proceedings and the inefficacy of the WTO decision-making and rulemaking system and the ever larger number of bilateral and regional trade agreements concluded outside the WTO risk undermining the legitimacy, effectiveness and efficiency of the world trading system.

The need for 'institutional guardians' of 'global public goods' and 'club goods' vis-à-vis national interest group politics

A review of the economic, political and legal theories of international trade cooperation shows that 'motivations for cooperating in the trade field vary enormously among the parties involved. This means that if cooperative efforts are to succeed and bargains are to endure, negotiating packages must contain enough for everyone'.[49] WTO rules provide a framework for the pursuit of

- *national* policy objectives such as promoting domestic competition, consumer welfare and domestic legal reforms through WTO negotiations and WTO legal obligations;

[49] P Lamy, Foreword to the *World Trade Report 2007* (Geneva: WTO, 2007) iv. Chapter II of this WTO report gives an excellent overview of the diverse economic, political and legal rationales of why countries participate in the WTO.

- the collective supply of *international public goods* like an efficient world trading system and rule of international law beneficial for all countries; as well as for
- '*WTO club goods*' like reciprocal market access commitments, WTO dispute settlement proceedings limited to WTO members, or free trade areas pursuant to Articles XXIV GATT and V GATS.

Individual WTO member governments tend to focus on *national interests*, including accommodation of domestic interest groups whose political support may be necessary for majority politics. The lack of an institutional guardian mandated to defend the *collective interests* of all WTO members – similar to the task of the EU Commission for initiating decision-making in the EU and for guarding the 'Community interests' – vis-à-vis national and group interests remains the major political weakness of WTO decision-making procedures. Such institutional 'guardian powers' must be complemented by constitutional rules specifying and protecting the collective interests and providing policy instruments for facilitating consensus building, including financial resources for 'capacity building' ('aid for trade') and 'trade facilitation' enabling governments to comply with WTO obligations and exploit new trading opportunities. Regrettably, the WTO lacks adequate rules and institutions protecting global public goods and international 'club goods',[50] such as

- an adequate WTO mandate empowering the WTO Director-General and the WTO Secretariat to initiate rulemaking and exercise leadership for defending the common interests of all WTO members (eg, in promoting rule of law and general consumer welfare through trade liberalization) vis-à-vis powerful competing group interests (such as agricultural, cotton and industrial lobbies benefiting from restrictions on competing exports from LDCs);
- more precise legal definition in WTO law of the collective self-interests of WTO members, for instance by adequate WTO competition rules protecting general consumer welfare, limiting restrictive business practices and empowering citizens to challenge anticompetitive practices and violations of WTO rules;
- delegation of limited WTO rulemaking functions – apart from market access commitments which will continue to require reciprocal bargaining at international and domestic levels – to different regulatory procedures (such as 'Plurilateral Trade Agreements' in terms of Annex 4 to the WTO Agreement) and majoritarian decision-making, subject to 'opt-outs' for non-consenting WTO members;
- the establishment of a Ministerial Executive Council with limited membership and powers of supervision, initiation of rulemaking and 'consensus building';
- a standing Committee on legal and institutional affairs which could assist the WTO General Council by keeping the evolution of the WTO legal and dispute settlement system under regular review and promoting 'authoritative interpretations' of WTO rules by WTO members;
- a parliamentary WTO body which could assist domestic members of parliaments to receive first-hand information on WTO politics, hold WTO bodies politically accountable and promote civil society support for a mutually beneficial world trading system;[51]

[50] *cf* DP Steger (ed), *Redesigning the World Trade Organization for the 21st Century* (Ottawa: W Laurier University Press, 2010).

[51] On the lack of effective parliamentary control of WTO politics inside most WTO member countries (with the exception of the US Congress and the Swiss Parliament) as well as in the EC, see E Baron Crespo (ed), *The*

- more comprehensive technical and financial assistance programs helping less-developed WTO members to comply with WTO rules and benefit from the WTO trading system;
- multilevel judicial protection of transnational rule of law, which could be promoted by a WTO commitment to interpreting domestic trade rules in conformity with WTO obligations (as required by the 'consistent interpretation principle' already recognized in national and international legal systems) and by offering domestic courts an advisory procedure for requesting non-binding legal opinions (eg, by an independent WTO Advocate-General) on the interpretation of WTO rules.

The Bretton Woods institutions were designed during the 1940s for the postwar era dominated by the hegemonic leadership of the United States, the 'Cold War' with communist countries and the gradual phasing out of colonial policies. At the beginning of the twenty-first century, the IMF, the World Bank Group and the WTO are confronted with fundamentally different regulatory challenges. The law of international organizations and their often still 'Westphalian paradim' of authoritarian regulation needs fundamental constitutional reforms in order to enable citizens and governments to protect human rights and other international public goods more effectively.

3 COSMOPOLITAN CONSTITUTIONALISM VERSUS 'STATIST' AND COMMUNITARIAN CONCEPTIONS OF THE LAW OF INTERNATIONAL TRADE ORGANIZATIONS

Most international trade agreements protect access to foreign markets and 'freedoms of trade' subject to exceptions reserving sovereign rights to protect non-economic community interests. Legal and judicial interpretations of these interrelationships between, eg, GATT/WTO guarantees of freedom, non-discrimination, rule of law and sovereign rights of WTO members to protect non-economic public interests tends to be influenced by legal conceptions of the 'rules of recognition' underlying national and international legal systems and of the interrelationships between 'inalienable' human rights, popular rights to self-determination, and the 'sovereign equality of states' (Article 2 UN Charter). For instance, conceptions of international law as being founded on the consent of states – and of national law as being founded on Constitutions adopted by 'We the People' – tend to embrace a dualist paradigm limiting 'Constitutionalism' (with a 'big C') to national constitutional systems. Chapters II to VI, by contrast, argued for cosmopolitan conceptions of national and modern international legal systems as deriving both their legitimacy from respect for human rights, democracy and rule of law, thereby conceiving national and international constitutionalism as a functional unity (multilevel small c constitutionalism) for protecting the human rights of citizens across frontiers. The competing conceptions reflect different interpretations of the interrelationships between the

Parliamentary Dimension of the WTO (Strasbourg: European Parliament, 2006) as well as the comparative study: *The Role of Parliaments in Scrutinising and Influencing Trade Policy. A Comparative Analysis prepared for the European Parliament* (Strasbourg: European Parliament document 370-166v01-00) December 2005). M Krajewski, 'Legitimizing Global Economic Governance through Transnational Parliamentarization: The Parliamentary Dimensions of the WTO and the World Bank' University of Bremen Working Paper 136/2010 also concludes that the contribution of transnational parliamentarization to 'democratic global governance should not be measured on the basis of their formal decision-making power but with regard to their role as *fora* for transnational discourses and on their potential to empower national parliamentarians' (at 31 ff).

UN Charter principles of 'state sovereignty', 'popular sovereignty' and human rights ('individual sovereignty') as well as of the 'rules of recognition' of national and international legal systems. As discussed in Chapters II to VI, the more national Constitutions become 'partial constitutions' that can protect many human and constitutional rights of citizens in a globally integrated world only in cooperation with international law and international institutions as a 'fourth branch of governance', the more it becomes necessary to analyse the interrelationships between national and international legal systems and human rights from the perspective of multilevel 'cosmopolitan constitutionalism' limiting 'state sovereignty' and 'rules of recognition' by cosmopolitan principles of human rights, democratic constitutionalism and transnational rule of law.[52]

The universal recognition of human rights and of additional cosmopolitan rights (like individual trading rights, property rights, labour rights, access to justice) limits the vast foreign policy powers and regulatory discretion which governments and diplomats often enjoy in worldwide organizations; the rights also provide legal rules and principles for parliamentary, judicial and civil society control of the exercise of foreign policy powers (eg, to discriminate against foreigners). The normative principles underlying cosmopolitan rights (like individualism, universality, non-discrimination, judicial remedies) constrain the often asymmetrical, political influence of concentrated, 'rent-seeking' producer interests – compared with dispersed, less informed consumer interests – in GATT/WTO negotiations (eg, on anti-dumping rules, subsidies, intellectual property rights) that are often one-sidedly influenced by producer lobbies to the detriment of general consumer welfare. The US Reciprocal Trade Agreements Act of 1934 fundamentally changed trade policymaking in the United States by delegating limited powers to the executive branch for the negotiation of reciprocal trade agreements and their congressional 'fast-track approval'.[53] This 'legislative self-restraint' was justifiable on political and economic grounds, such as transparency and fairness arguments for balancing 'rights to protection' of import-competing producers by 'rights to import' of those who benefit from trade liberalization; giving export interests a strong voice in the political struggle against discriminatory market access barriers can offset protectionist pressures from import-

[52] This 'clash of constitutional paradigms', and the need for reconceptualizing 'sovereignty' and 'big C Constitutionalism', are explained in greater detail by M Kumm, 'The Cosmopolitan Turn in Constitutionalism' in JL Dunoff and JP Trachtman (2009) 258–324. On the 'Kantian revolution' replacing the statist paradigm of Constitutionalism by a cosmopolitan paradigm of multilevel constitutionalism integrating national and international law in order to better protect human rights and other international public goods, and on why cosmopolitan interpretations of IEL and of the modern 'rules of recognition' are more appropriate for limiting collective action problems in IEL than statist paradigms, see ch III. Kant's and Kumm's conceptions of cosmopolitan constitutionalism concur that national Constitutionalism has to be evaluated in the broader context of 'how it relates to the wider international community of which it is an integral part' and to the need for 'cosmopolitan public reason' rather than only in terms of the will of 'We the People' (*cf* Kumm at 268). Both national and international legal systems are reconceived as 'reflecting a common commitment to basic constitutional principles' (Kumm at 271).

[53] *cf* K Dam, 'Cordell Hull, the Reciprocal Trade Agreement Act and the WTO' in EU Petersmann (2005) 83–98, who describes how Secretary of State Cordell Hull designed this Act as a means of breaking 'the logrolling dynamics' of the protectionist Smoot-Hawley tariff legislation of 1930 by giving export industries an equal voice with import-competing industries in trade policymaking. Dam explains why the 'Hull principles' of reciprocity and non-discrimination are harder to apply to sectoral services negotiations than to cross-sectoral tariff liberalization commitments. Yet, as the US Executive no longer benefits from such authorizing legislation, the 'Cordell Hull principles' of advance authorization, international trade negotiations out of the public eye, reciprocal international trade agreements, and their more or less automatic approval and domestic implementation by Congress no longer apply to the WTO Doha Round negotiations and no longer restrain protectionist interests inside the US Congress.

competing producers. Since powerful trade union representatives and producer lobbies in the US Congress have prevented renewal of fast-track authority for concluding future Doha Round Agreements, the lack of leadership and the mercantilist stance of the United States in the Doha Round negotiations on reciprocal market access commitments are widely blamed for the failure to conclude the Doha Round after ten years of negotiations.[54]

The lack of WTO provisions protecting consumer welfare and enabling citizens to invoke and enforce precise and unconditional WTO guarantees in domestic courts reflects the 'mercantilist bias' of WTO rules and policies. As long as few import-competing producers threatened by trade competition can influence domestic trade policymaking so much more strongly (eg, by election campaign financing) than the many consumers and exporters benefiting from trade liberalization, Cordell Hull's insights on the 'constitutional failures' of trade policymaking and on the need for offsetting the political influence of import-competing firms remain of crucial importance for promoting consumer welfare, rule of law and peaceful international cooperation through liberal trade. Can 'constitutional' and 'cosmopolitan' reforms of the law of international trade organizations limit protectionist abuses of the corporatist 'government/producer partnership' dominating multilevel trade negotiations in the WTO?

Chapters I to IV argued that – from the perspective of citizens – international organizations with rulemaking, administrative and judicial powers for multilevel governance of interdependent public goods must be subjected to more effective constitutional restraints based on common constitutional principles and restraints to secure that diplomats and governments regulate economic markets for the benefit of citizens and their constitutional rights rather than only in terms of rights of the rulers. Just as mutually beneficial common markets inside constitutional democracies and the European common market are regulated by rights-based market, competition, environmental and constitutional rules, so should the law of worldwide economic organizations offer citizens effective legal and judicial remedies against discretionary, welfare-reducing government restrictions of mutually beneficial economic cooperation among citizens. Chapters II to IV argued that 'constitutionalism'[55] should protect human, constitutional and cosmopolitan rights of citizens across national frontiers for the benefit of functionally limited 'international communities' of citizens providing public goods, including the 'global trading community' of producers, investors, traders and consumers participating in the worldwide division of labour governed by WTO law. If international organizations are perceived as an ever more important 'fourth branch of governance' for the multilevel governance of 'international public goods' in a globally interdependent world where individual lives of citizens are increasingly affected by globalization, then the need for constitutionalizing multilevel economic governance derives primarily from protection of human rights and domestic constitutionalism. The customary rules of treaty interpretation confirm that international agreements have to be interpreted and applied in conformity with the human rights obligations of their member states as the ultimate source

[54] *cf* EU Petersmann, 'The Future of the WTO: From Authoritarian "Mercantilism" to Multilevel Governance for the Benefit of Citizens?' (2011) 6 *Asian Journal of WTO & International Health Law and Policy* 45–79.

[55] The term 'constitutionalism' was defined in ch II by the commitment of a political community to constitutional rules and principles governing the collective supply of national or international 'public goods' for the benefit of citizens, and by the related beliefs ('public reason') associated with the idea of 'constitutionally limited governance' under the rule of law protecting all citizens and their cosmopolitan rights with due respect for 'constitutional pluralism'.

of the legitimacy of governments. Do Pascal Lamy's proposals for reforming WTO governance by 'WTO cosmopolitics'[56] – moving 'from the world of Hobbes to the world of Kant' – offer a politically realistic strategy for improving multilevel trade governance?

Cosmopolitan reforms of IEL based on human rights and 'WTO cosmopolitics'?

Chapters III and IV argued that, in the twenty-first century, governments, states, international law and international organizations receive their legitimacy from promoting human, constitutional and cosmopolitan rights of citizens. Chapter IV, section 4 emphasized that – just as UN human rights instruments derive *human rights* from respect for human dignity, and democratic constitutions derive *constitutional rights* of citizens from respect for human rights – IEL and *cosmopolitan economic rights* can be derived from, and must remain consistent with human rights. For instance, 'trading rights' and individual rights of access to domestic courts (as protected in WTO law), investor rights and judicial remedies (as protected in BITs), 'market freedoms' and social 'access rights' (as protected in EU and EEA law), intellectual property rights (as protected in WTO and WIPO conventions), labour rights (as protected in ILO conventions) and other rights of citizens engaged in mutually beneficial cooperation across frontiers can be legitimized by reference to underlying cosmopolitan principles of justice. Chapter III argued that – for the reasons explained in Kant's theory of multilevel constitutional protection of equal human freedoms – multilevel governance for the collective supply of 'international public goods' must be constituted and constitutionally limited by 'multilevel constitutionalism' protecting citizens and their constitutional rights (including economic freedoms) by means of multilevel judicial protection of individual rights and constitutional restraints on abuses of private and public, national and international governance powers. Yet, chapter IV also emphasized that respect for 'constitutional pluralism' requires respecting legitimately diverse democratic legislation and constitutional interpretations of human rights. As governments often resist and contest the implications of human rights and constitutional rights for legal, administrative and judicial protection of economic rights, the transformation of intergovernmental 'Hobbesian bargains' into cosmopolitan rights and judicial remedies may be possible only at national and regional levels in response to 'struggles for justice' by citizens and courts of justice.

In 1969, John H Jackson remarked that even though the GATT had 'an immense impact on the individual citizen, there is presently no *direct* relationship between GATT and such private persons'.[57] In his remarks concluding a series of conferences comparing the diverse regulatory approaches in major constitutional democracies regarding liberalization and regulation of trade, Jackson emphasized in 1992 that – in view of the US scepticism vis-à-vis international law and the political reluctance outside Europe to protect international trade liberalization through constitutional rules – the task of more effective legal protection of the international public good of a liberal trading system had to focus realistically on strengthening the incorporation of liberal international trade rules into *domestic* legal systems and on setting incentives for domestic citizens, parlia-

[56] For a discussion of Pascal Lamy's speeches on 'cosmopolitics' see: S Charnovitz, 'The WTO and Cosmopolitics' in Petersmann (2005) 437 ff; P Lamy, 'Europe and the Future of Economic Governance' (2004) 42 *Journal of Common Market Studies* 5–21.

[57] JH Jackson, *World Trade and the Law of GATT* (Indianapolis: Bobbs-Merrill, 1969) 187.

ments and courts to support and enforce the treaty rules.[58] In a speech in early 2001, the EU Trade Commissioner and later WTO Director-General Pascal Lamy argued similarly for 'cosmopolitics' involving civil society and NGOs as 'social intermediaries' and 'cosmopolitan constituencies' in multilevel regulation and protection of international public goods.[59] As the supranational principles of EU law (like 'legal primacy', 'direct effect', 'direct applicability' of precise and unconditional EU guarantees in domestic legal systems) are neither politically realistic nor desirable in worldwide institutions, my publications have argued long since that cosmopolitan reforms of IEL depend on 'linking' international guarantees of freedom, non-discrimination, rule of law and social justice to the interpretation of corresponding domestic law guarantees based on the 'consistent interpretation principle' recognized in national and international legal systems. Mutually consistent conceptions of multilevel economic rules are also pursued in numerous initiatives for more comprehensive forms of multilevel trade governance, as illustrated by

- the ever closer cooperation among the WTO and other international organizations pursuant to Article V:1 WTO Agreement;
- the annual public symposia organized by the WTO in cooperation with NGOs pursuant to Article V:2 WTO Agreement;
- the regular meetings of parliamentarians during WTO ministerial conferences;
- the enormous increase in transparency of WTO documents, WTO negotiations and WTO dispute settlement proceedings (eg, due to public meetings of dispute settlement bodies, admission of amicus curiae briefs, de-restriction and publication of all adopted dispute settlement reports and almost all other WTO documents); and
- the participation of the WTO Director-General in G20 meetings and other global governance bodies.

Yet, while economics has become global, politics and political identities tend to remain local. The relationships between globalization, global governance, 'global law' (eg, in terms of legal harmonization) and cosmopolitanism remain deeply contested among WTO members and inside national communities. The 'flexibilities' of worldwide agreements (eg, for protecting national 'public order', 'public morals' and other non-economic 'public interests') entail that global cosmopolitan values (like human rights) and corresponding 'global civic responsibilities' (eg, vis-à-vis migrant workers) continue to be regulated and protected in diverse ways in national and local legal systems. During the ten years of Doha Round negotiations, WTO members presented only few proposals for incorporating WTO rules more effectively into domestic legal and judicial systems.

The 'cosmopolitan paradox': perennial tensions between liberal individualism and communitarian citizenships

Ancient Stoic cosmopolitanism sought to contextualize the central role of the local *polis* in Greek political philosophy in the larger world of the *cosmos* so that all human beings could live together in reasonable harmony. The Kantian conception of a 'cosmopolitan right' of 'world citizens' (*Weltbürger*) was linked to the idea of advancing 'the public use

[58] J Jackson, 'National Constitutions, Transnational Economic Policy and International Economic Law: Some Summary Reflections' in M Hilf and EU Petersmann (eds) (1993) 569–76.

[59] See n 56.

of reason'[60] by participation in a cosmopolitan society, including the right to present oneself in other political communities and engage in peaceful dialogue and international trade. The basic principles underlying modern 'cosmopolitanism'[61] are similar to those of human rights:

- respect for equal worth and dignity of individuals as the ultimate units of moral concern;
- human freedom to reason and act self-consciously;
- personal responsibility and accountability for one's self-determination;
- voluntary consent as principle legitimating private coordination and political governance;
- inclusive public decision-making procedures affording all affected members of a community equal opportunities of participation;
- avoidance of serious harm; and
- sustainable use of the world's resources.

Human rights, constitutional law and modern IEL continue to supplant 'moral cosmopolitanism' (challenging the moral significance of local and national boundaries) by legal cosmopolitanism aimed at reconciling state sovereignty, popular sovereignty and cosmopolitan rights protecting competing identities (eg, 'individual sovereignty'), 'human capacities' and responsibilities of citizens in a globally integrating world. Paradoxically, the increasing recognition of cosmopolitan values (eg, in UN human rights law) and of the need for 'enabling, constraining and supplemental constitutionalization'[62] of multilevel governance may *increase* (rather than decrease) the scope for 'reasonable disagreement' in domestic politics – even in constitutional democracies like the United States where, as explained by Dworkin, there is pervasive disagreement among conservatives and democrats on human rights and democracy.[63] This 'cosmopolitan paradox' – ie, that democratic agreement is necessary for rule of law and self-government, yet remains inevitably limited by 'reasonable disagreement' among rational citizens and their representative institutions[64] – requires respect for 'constitutional pluralism' and for the 'normalcy and morality of conflicts' (Besson) in the interpretation and development of 'primary rules of conduct' and 'secondary rules' of IEL for adapting rules to changing circumstances and resolving disputes about the existence or validity of norms.[65] Yet, in contrast to Hegelian

[60] *cf* I Kant (1970) 41–53, 54–60, 105–08.

[61] *cf* D Held, 'Principles of Cosmopolitan Order' in G Brock and H Brighouse (eds), *The Political Philosophy of Cosmopolitanism* (Oxford: OUP, 2005) 10–27.

[62] *cf* JL Dunoff and JP Trachtman, 'A Functional Approach to International Constitutionalization' in JL Dunoff and JP Trachtman (eds) (2009) 3, 9 ff.

[63] *cf* R Dworkin, *Is Democracy Possible Here?* (Princeton: Princeton University Press, 2006). Dworkin's proposal – ie, to base constitutionalism on two basic principles of human dignity (ie, first, that each human life is intrinsically and equally valuable and secondly, that each person has an inalienable personal responsibility for realizing her unique potential and human values in her own life) – illustrates how limited reasonable constitutional consensus on substantive justice might be even inside one of the most stable constitutional democracies.

[64] On the normalcy and morality of conflicts, and the 'paradox of reasonable disagreement' (ie, rule of law as a necessary response to disagreement and conflicts of interests depends on legal respect for reasonable disagreement and on dialogue and cooperation among legal institutions), see also: S Besson (2005); EU Petersmann, 'Justice as Conflict Resolution: Proliferation, Fragmentation and Decentralization of Dispute Settlement in International Trade Law' (2006) 27 *University of Pennsylvania Journal of International Economic Law* 273–366.

[65] Chs I and II defined IEL by using Hart's definition of a legal system as a complex union of 'primary rules' (conferring rights and duties on individuals and people regulating their behaviour) and 'secondary rules' that 'specify the ways in which the primary rules may be conclusively ascertained, introduced, eliminated, varied, and the fact of their violation conclusively determined' (*cf* Hart (1994) 94). Such 'secondary rules' usually

glorification of 'nations' and 'states' as the 'absolute power on earth' justifying 'the sacrifice of personal actuality' and 'absolute obedience, renunciation of personal opinions and reasoning, in fact complete absence of mind',[66] cosmopolitanism challenges nationalism as a potential threat to multinational and 'multicultural citizenship' (as in the case of 'EU citizenship')[67] and to cosmopolitan support for multilevel governance of interdependent public goods.[68] Cosmopolitan loyalty for transnational rule of law and for multilevel governance of the worldwide division of labour requires multiple loyalties inside and beyond nation states[69] and reconciliation of the perennial tensions between cosmopolitan individualism and communitarian citizenships.

Inside states, many individuals and social groups challenge 'liberal individualism' as the normative basis of constitutionalism and economic regulation on communitarian grounds: individual self-development can hardly be understood without taking into account its family and social context such as the respective education, religious and political systems; every individual is born into some society and 'socialized' by its particular customs and traditions. Communitarian conceptions risk being undermined by both 'liberal individualism', delegation of ever more governance powers to transnational institutions as well as by legal protection of cosmopolitan rights (eg, to practise foreign religious and authoritarian family traditions alien to local communities in host countries of migrant workers). Communitarian conceptions of democracy may cherish foreign policy discretion to discriminate against foreigners. Hence, cosmopolitan proposals for compensating inadequate parliamentary control of IEL by stronger rights-based constitutionalism (eg, by 'participatory democratic rights', multilevel judicial protection of transnational rule of law) often clash with powerful community ideologies.

Political philosophy acknowledges for more than 2400 years (eg, since the works of Plato and Aristotle) the interrelationships between different types of citizenship, people and political institutions. Inside families and local communities, communitarian conceptions of trust, love and of virtues of citizenship often supplant liberal individualist concerns for justice. The 'market freedoms' and citizenship rights of European citizens under European law, like the procedural and substantive 'investor rights' under international investment law protecting foreign investors against discriminatory restrictions in host states, illustrate that IEL proceeds from a liberal understanding of 'market citizens' that differs from the communitarian conceptions of political citizens inside national constitutional democracies. In international economic markets, producers, investors, traders

assert a higher 'constitutional rank' in order to ensure 'social peace' by enabling a community to resolve governance problems and collective action problems peacefully in response to changing circumstances.

[66] GWF Hegel, *The Philosophy of Right*, trans Knox (Oxford: Clarendon Press, 1952) 211–12, paras 328, 331.

[67] W Kymlicka, *Multicultural Citizenship* (Oxford: Clarendon Press, 1995).

[68] On the lack of 'voice' as a major cause for lack of loyalty and desire for secession ('exit') see: AO Hirschman, *Exit, Voice and Loyalty – Responses to Decline in Firms, Organizations and States* (Cambridge: Harvard University Press, 1970).

[69] JA Rabkin, *Law without Nations? Why Constitutional Government Requires Sovereign States* (Cambridge: Harvard University Press, 2005) argues that only a sovereign state can reliably protect human rights and constitutional democracy. The 2009 Lisbon Treaty protects the 'national identities' (Art 4) and sovereign rights of member states (eg, to withdraw from the EU pursuant to Art 50 TEU) and focuses on a 'Community' of different states and 'peoples'. 'Citizenship of the Union shall be additional to and not replace national citizenship' (Art 9 TEU). The idea of a European federal state is ever less supported by political parties, citizens and governments inside the EU.

and consumers are primarily perceived as competitors with competing self-interests (eg, the seller requesting a high price, the consumer offering a low price). The adoption of national and international competition rules by more than 90 WTO member states today reflects the increasing insight that markets will protect general consumer welfare only if conflicts of interests are reconciled through non-discriminatory, common market and competition rules limiting abuses of public and private power. The financial crisis which began in 2008 illustrates that, without proper international financial market regulation, restrictive business practices and selfish abuses of market power (eg, by 'insider trading' and other financial practices exploiting 'information asymmetries' to the detriment of consumers) remain perennial regulatory challenges even inside constitutional democracies with competition laws.

Chapters II to VI argued that rights-based 'economic constitutionalism' offers citizens the most effective remedies for holding governments accountable for their limited mandates and abuses of discretionary international economic regulation. In the global division of labour based on transnational market competition, legal and judicial protection of equal freedoms and non-discriminatory conditions of competition should not be distorted by welfare-reducing border discrimination and xenophobic discrimination of foreign competitors. Each polity may 'balance' civil, political, economic, social and cosmopolitan rights and promote 'public reason' in legitimately diverse ways. Also 'affirmative action' for LDCs in international trade regulation – eg, by means of 'trade facilitation', capacity building and non-reciprocal tariff preferences enabling industries in LDCs to actually benefit from additional market opportunities – is justifiable on grounds of non-discriminatory conditions of competition and inclusive decision-making The fact that intergovernmental rulemaking all too often distorts competition for the benefit of 'rent-seeking' interest groups (like producers of bananas, cotton, milk, textiles, steel, cars, airplanes, energy, banking and telecommunication services) illustrates that competing struggles for legal and judicial empowerment of individuals in IEL, and for stronger constitutional protection of community interests, will remain a perennial challenge of IEL. In view of the ubiquity of 'market failures', rational participants in under-regulated, international market competition have good reasons to perceive themselves as being more separate from another than inside families, private social networks and national communities based on trust. As, without effective protection of human rights, foreign investments and international services trade (eg, by migrant workers) risk being impeded by discrimination of 'foreigners' in the polity of host countries, cosmopolitan rights protecting 'liberal individualism' (eg, in the sense of pursuing one's own advancement and the happiness of one's family) and promoting social integration are necessary legal foundations for the global division of labour. Just as foreign investors may have good reasons to trust more in independent, international regulatory and dispute settlement bodies (eg, transnational investor–state arbitration under ICSID procedures) than in submitting investor–state disputes to the national jurisdictions in host states, so do migrant workers often need protection by cosmopolitan rights and labour law conventions against discriminatory abuses in host countries.

EU citizenship and 'market citizenship' in European economic law as models for cosmopolitan citizenship in IEL?

The judicial protection of individual 'market freedoms', fundamental rights and citizen rights in EU law reflects a strong commitment to 'liberal individualism'[70] and cosmopolitan economic law. But the comprehensive, regulatory EU powers also reveal communitarian confidence of the 'EU citizenry' in comprehensive EU market regulation – even in fields (like the EC Directives on tobacco advertising and tobacco products adopted on the legal basis of Article 95 EC) where risk and health regulation in the common market remains contested by citizens as well as in the ECJ jurisprudence.[71] The ECJ judgments extending EU citizenship rights (eg, of migrant family members) to non-discriminatory access to national social benefits in host states (eg, access to universities and related scholarships) illustrates the increasing judicial protection of 'national solidarity without nationality' aimed at promoting free movement and non-discriminatory treatment of EU and EEA citizens across the common market.[72] Beyond EU and EEA law and their unique historical context (eg, due to the periodic European wars), such comprehensive legislative and judicial 'communitarian protection of cosmopolitan rights' remains hardly conceivable yet in regional economic agreements outside Europe.

The increasing emancipation of EU citizenship rights from the exercise of common market freedoms reflects the political objectives of European integration law:[73] fundamental rights and EU citizenship are of crucial political importance for promoting citizen support for EU law and a sense of European identity and transnational 'community'. Worldwide economic organizations, by contrast, pursue primarily economic objectives for resolving transnational governance problems (such as harmful externalities of nationalist policies) through cooperation among nation states and citizens belonging to different national peoples. Compulsory transnational dispute settlement systems can be justified as examples of 'non-majoritarian politics' committing states to constitutional protection of general citizen interests that should no longer depend on the vicissitudes of majority politics and national interest group politics; but, as emphasized by Majone,[74] supranational problem-solving may neither be justifiable nor politically acceptable for redistributive issues of social policies. Hence, only the procedural and some of the economic rights of EU citizens – rather than their social and political 'community

[70] A Somek, *Individualism: An Essay on the Authority of the European Union* (Oxford: OUP, 2008) defines liberal individualism as the 'belief that what matters to life is personal advancement and the happiness of those to whom one feels personally attached' (at 2); 'a conception of citizenship that emphasizes difference, but avoids any encounter with it in the public realm' (at 159). Chapter III supported Kantian legal theory and Jhering's legal theory of 'struggles for rights', which perceive 'life of the law as a struggle', and 'the struggle for his rights as a duty of the person whose rights have been violated' as well as a 'duty to society' (*cf* R Jhering, *The Struggle for Law* (Chicago: Callaghan, 1915) chs II to IV). As explained by Rawls, the welfare of citizens also depends on their struggles for institutionalizing human rights and 'public reason'.

[71] Somek (n 70) contrasts the relatively homogenous democracy inside the EU (where EU citizens support EU risk and health regulation even though the interests of the almost 500 million EU citizens cannot be fully represented by the European Parliament) with the insistence on 'subsidiarity' and diversity in more pluralistic democracies contesting such delegation of regulatory powers and 'paternalistic risk regulation'.

[72] *cf* HW Micklitz, 'Judicial Activism of the European Court of Justice and the Development of the European Social Model in Anti-Discrimination and Consumer Law' in U Neergaard, R Nielsen and L Roseberry (eds), *The Role of Courts in Developing a European Social Model* (Copenhagen: DJOF, 2010) 25–62.

[73] *cf* NN Shuibhne, 'The Resilience of EU Market Citizenship' (2010) 47 *CMLR* 1597–628.

[74] *cf* G Majone, 'Europe's Democracy Deficit: A Question of Standards' (1998) 4 *European Law Journal* 5–28.

rights'[75] – may be politically acceptable inspirations for designing a cosmopolitan IEL. The opposition by most states to GATS commitment for free movement of workers and to protecting the social rights of migrant workers by ILO conventions, like their opposition to free movement of persons in regional common markets and free trade areas outside Europe (such as NAFTA), confirm that EU citizenship rights go far beyond what most states are willing to accept as cosmopolitan economic rights in worldwide economic integration law. Also adjudication in the WTO and in most regional economic agreements remains intergovernmental in contrast to judicial protection of EU citizenship rights by the ECJ, whose judicial protection of equal rights of EU citizens aims also at protecting trust and loyalty of citizens vis-à-vis others 'with whom we share our political space'[76] and our 'duties of justice'.[77]

'Cosmopolitan democracy' in the WTO? Cosmopolitan functions of the WTO?

From a human rights perspective, citizens constitute not only 'peoples' and democratic states but – through demand and supply – also transnational markets and – through the intermediary of their elected representatives – intergovernmental organizations as a necessary 'fourth branch of governance' for the collective supply of international public goods. Democratic control by citizens and by national parliaments of intergovernmental rulemaking in distant, worldwide organisations remains far more difficult than in domestic political processes.[78] For example, national parliaments and civil society groups often complain of the 'information asymmetries' resulting from intergovernmental rulemaking by bureaucratic networks in non-transparent, intergovernmental organisations without effective parliamentary participation and democratic control by public opinion and civil society. Also standard-setting and other decision-making in non-governmental organizations are often insufficiently 'inclusive' due to lack of participatory or consultative rights of adversely affected third parties. Such democratic concerns increase if intergovernmental negotiations (eg, in the WTO) are strongly influenced by powerful interest groups (eg, agricultural, textile and steel lobbies); take place behind closed doors without adequate 'deliberative democracy'; do not refer to human rights in the international negotiations and balancing processes; and may lead to comprehensive 'package deals' (like the 1994 WTO Agreement) which can hardly be re-opened at the request of a single national parliament, or at the request of a few WTO members in the consensus-based WTO decision-making processes, once the international negotiations have been closed.

[75] *cf* AJ Menendez, 'European Citizenship after *Martinez Sala* and *Baumbast*: Has European Law become more Human but less Social? in M Maduro and L Azoulai (eds), *The Past and Future of EU Law* (Oxford: Hart Publishing, 2010) 363 ff, who describes the ECJ judgments in *Martinez Sala* and *Baumbast* as 'unleashing the emancipatory potential of European law', 'redrawing the economic and political boundaries of the old continent' and 'making the Community right-holder a civic and solidaristic political citizen and not a mere solitary and egotistic market actor'.

[76] Somek (n 70) 235–36.

[77] *cf* J Rawls (1971) 336 (referring to 'assurance games' among 'contingent compliers' motivated by a duty of justice to 'comply with fair practices that exist and apply to them when they believe that the relevant others likewise do their part').

[78] See the comparative study of the control of trade policies by 11 parliaments in: *The Role of Parliaments in Scrutinising and Influencing Trade Policy* (n 51) (the study suggests that, with the exception of the Swiss Parliament and US Congress, most parliaments do not appear to control trade policy and WTO rulemaking effectively). On the few formal parliamentary bodies in international organizations and on informal inter-parliamentary networks for reviewing certain other international organizations (like the World Bank) see Krajewski (n 51).

At international levels – far away from the local communities in which citizens live and cooperate, and far away also from national parliaments – intergovernmental rules and procedures inevitably suffer from 'democratic deficits' compared with local and national democratic processes and constitutionally limited, parliamentary decision-making. In contrast to the parliamentary bodies of regional organizations (eg, in the EU and the Council of Europe) and a few inter-regional organizations (eg, in NATO), hardly any worldwide organization provides for parliamentary participation and parliamentary control through worldwide parliamentary bodies. As most citizens and parliamentarians focus on local and national politics and even the European Parliament cannot ensure equal representation of all EU citizens, the democratic legitimacy of worldwide organizations must derive from the consent of national parliaments and cosmopolitan rights supported by citizens rather than from utopian proposals for 'world parliaments'. It remains an important task to strengthen the democratic accountability of multilevel governance through participatory citizen rights, parliamentary rights and judicial remedies against abuses of foreign policy powers. UN human rights instruments recognize that human rights need to be protected and mutually balanced through democratic legislation, and that 'everyone has the right to take part in the government of his country, directly or through freely chosen representatives' (Article 21:1 UDHR); yet, these and other core guarantees of a 'human right to democratic governance'[79] focus on *national* rather than *international* governance. The recognition in UN human rights instruments of a human right 'to a social and international order in which the rights and freedoms set forth in this Declaration can be fully realised' (Article 28 UDHR), justify cosmopolitan conceptions of IEL as illustrated by the EU Treaty commitments to respect for equal rights of 'EU citizens' (Article 9 TEU), 'representative parliamentary democracy' at national and European levels (Articles 10 and 12 TEU) and 'participatory democracy' (Article 11 TEU). Yet, proposals for multilevel parliamentary control of UN institutions continue being resisted by many governments. It is to be welcomed that – in the WTO – national parliaments and the European Parliament have taken the initiative of convening interparliamentary meetings in the context of all WTO ministerial conferences since the WTO Ministerial Conference of 1999 in order to secure better first-hand information of national parliamentarians on WTO negotiations (eg, from the WTO Director-General and WTO ambassadors) and convey parliamentary concerns. Yet, as representative parliamentary governance at worldwide levels and proposals for 'UN citizenship' or 'WTO citizenship' remain politically unrealistic, 'cosmopolitan democracy' must rely on national parliamentary control of multilevel governance and on cosmopolitan rights empowering citizens and civil society to engage in 'participatory self-governance' and 'deliberative democracy' across frontiers by exercising their cosmopolitan rights and defending transnational rule of law against 'Westphalian power politics'.

Cosmopolitan rights as countervailing empowerment and protection of citizens against abuses of regulatory powers

The legitimacy of international organizations depends no less on respect for, and promotion of, human rights than the legitimacy of national governance institutions. As

[79] See the discussion in ch VI, section 4, fn 137 and related text.

international organizations have no mandate to disregard or violate the human rights obligations of states, WTO Director-General Pascal Lamy rightly acknowledged what has also been previously emphasized by the UN High Commissioner for Human Rights and by civil society organizations like the International Law Association: WTO law must be construed in conformity with the human rights obligations of WTO members; if applied and progressively developed in conformity with human rights, WTO law can significantly contribute to promoting consumer welfare and rule of law protecting citizen rights.[80] Such 'human rights approaches' to interpreting and developing IEL, as they are applied in European economic law long since, concord with the constitutional and 'New Haven' approaches to international law supported in this study: legal rules and governmental organizations, including international law and intergovernmental organizations, derive their legitimacy from their instrumental function of protecting the constitutional rights of citizen and their democratic participation in transnational decision-making processes.[81] The protection of property rights in international investment treaties can be perceived as an example of compensating the inferior legal and democratic status of foreigners in host states by procedural and substantive legal guarantees of a higher legal rank in order to counter potential asymmetries in government decisions restricting foreign property. By protecting principles of 'fair and equitable treatment', 'full protection and security', access to justice, fair procedures, national treatment, most-favoured-nation treatment and free transferability of funds, and by mandating international arbitral and investment courts to settle investor–state disputes with due regard to 'principles of justice' and human rights (including protection of property rights against arbitrary discrimination or expropriation), international investment treaties and dispute settlement procedures have contributed to rule of law, peaceful settlement of disputes and equal protection of cosmopolitan rights in the worldwide division of labour.[82]

The more individuals have rights and duties under international human rights law, humanitarian, economic and social law, the more it becomes anachronistic for trade diplomats to alienate and exclude citizens – as the main actors in the international economy and 'democratic owners' of representative governance institutions – from participating in multilevel economic regulation and international dispute settlement. As discussed in the preceding section 2, 'constitutional economics' likewise argues for empowering self-interested citizens by individual rights and obligations as the most effective incentive for promoting not only 'transnational rule of law', but mutually beneficial cooperation among citizens and the decentralized limitation of 'market failures', in economic mar-

[80] *cf* Pascal Lamy, *Globalization and Trade Opening Can Promote Human Rights*, speech delivered on 5 June 2009 at the University of Geneva. On 'human rights approaches' to IEL, see section 4. On the recognition and promotion of human rights by international organizations, see: Report of the Office of the High Commissioner for Human Rights on 'Interdependence between democracy and human rights' E/CN.4/2004/54 (17 February 2004). On the various ILA Resolutions on international trade law, human rights and rule of law see: Petersmann, 'International Trade Law, Human Rights and the Customary International Law Rules on Treaty Interpretation', in Joseph, Kinley and Waincymer (2009), 69–90.

[81] *cf* ch II and R Higgins, 'Conceptual Thinking about the Individual in International Law' (1978) 24 *New York Law School Review* 11–29; WM Reisman, 'A Judge's Judge: Justice Florentino P Feliciano's Philosophy of the Judicial Function' in S Charnovitz, D Steger and P van den Bossche (eds), *Law in the Service of Human Dignity* (Cambridge: CUP, 2005) 3–10.

[82] *cf* PM Dupuy, F Francioni and EU Petersmann (eds) (2009).

kets no less than in political markets.[83] As virtually all WTO member states have adopted national constitutions and international obligations committing their respective governments to legal and judicial protection of rule of law in international trade, national and international trade courts should cooperate in interpreting national and international trade rules in mutually coherent ways for the benefit of citizens engaged in international trade. Such legal and judicial protection of transnational rule of law is in line with the emphasis by economists – from Smith to Hayek and Sen – that market economies and economic welfare are mere *instruments* for enabling and promoting individual freedom as the ultimate goal of economic life and the most efficient means of realizing general welfare. WTO Members should recognize for the world trading system what the World Bank has long since recognized for its development assistance: 'Sustainable development is impossible without human rights', just as 'advancement of an interconnected set of human rights is impossible without development'[84] and without a mutually beneficial world trading system protecting individual rights to produce, invest, trade and consume on the basis of rule of law and respect for human rights. An efficient world trading system requires multilevel legal and judicial protection of the 'constitutional functions' of international trade law guarantees of freedom, non-discrimination, rule of law and national sovereignty (eg, over domestic regulation and protection of non-economic public interests).

For instance, the WTO guarantees of freedom, non-discrimination and judicial protection of rule of law – by protecting access to national and international dispute settlement bodies and the right of every WTO member to challenge trade restrictions under the WTO dispute settlement system without having to prove damages or another 'legal interest'[85] – aim at protecting also, albeit only indirectly, freedom of trade and equal liberties of producers, traders and consumers. These 'constitutional functions' support claims that international guarantees of human right and economic freedoms should be interpreted not only as *intergovernmental rights*; they also justify legal and judicial protection of *private freedoms* by interpreting domestic constitutional rights to liberty in conformity with 'strict observance of international law' (Article 3 Lisbon TEU) for the benefit of citizens. Such interpretations of constitutional rights to freedom in conformity with self-imposed *international* guarantees of freedom (such as GATT's customs union rules as incorporated into the EU Treaty and enforced by European courts also at the request of individual complainants) reflect citizen-oriented, constitutional conceptions of 'indivisible liberty' and 'rule of law' that should also be protected in the transnational cooperation among citizens in conformity with international trade agreements ratified by domestic parliaments.[86]

[83] Institutional economists also claim that open-access societies reinforce democracy, *cf* North (n 14) and his recent NBER Working Paper 'A Conceptual Framework for Interpreting Recorded Human History' (2006).

[84] *Development and Human Rights. The Role of the World Bank* (Washington: World Bank, 1998) 2.

[85] In the WTO dispute over EC import restrictions on bananas, the EC claimed that the United States had no 'legal right or interest' to sue as it did not export any bananas (Panel Report, *EC – Bananas III*, WT/DS27/R/USA, para II.21). The Appellate Body confirmed the finding by the Panel that the DSU did not require a 'legal interest to sue' (Appellate Body Report, *EC – Bananas III*, WT/DS27/AB/R, para 132). As violations of WTO rules are presumed to 'nullify' treaty benefits (eg, reasonable expectations of non-discriminatory conditions of trade competition), complainants are also not legally required to prove damages, *cf* EU Petersmann (1997) 142 ff.

[86] Such 'constitutional interpretations' of international 'market freedoms' tend to be rejected by Anglo-Saxon lawyers from countries without constitutional protection of economic and social rights, such as Australian lawyers Alston and Cass who have imputed to me the absurd views 'that the WTO agreements

What kinds of cosmopolitan rights vis-à-vis multilevel economic governance?

The 2008 Report of the UN Commission on *Legal Empowerment of the Poor*, like the 2009 Report of the Eminent Persons Panel on 'Protecting Dignity: An Agenda for Human Rights', emphasize that strengthening legal and judicial remedies for promoting rule of law and human rights are indispensable for reinforcing national capacities to combat poverty and enhance social welfare: bridging the 'gap between the high aspirations of human rights and its sobering realities on the ground, between human rights law and its implementation, between the lofty rhetoric of governments and their lack of political will to keep their promises is . . . the major challenge of our time'.[87] European economic law illustrates that – the more trade and economic policy powers are delegated to international organizations – the stronger becomes the need for cosmopolitan rights protecting citizens, their 'market freedoms' and mutually beneficial, economic cooperation against welfare-reducing restrictions and distortions by multilevel governance institutions. The more regional and worldwide governance institutions operate far away from adversely affected citizens and national parliaments, the less effective *procedural* citizen rights for democratic participation, representation and control at national levels risk becoming; hence, the decreasing effectiveness of 'procedural' and 'communitarian democracy' at national levels must be compensated by stronger cosmopolitan rights also in relation to transnational governance institutions. If, as argued in this study, cosmopolitan economic rights are derived from human rights and from constitutional 'principles of justice' (like maximum equal freedoms in IEL subject to democratic legislation protecting and balancing all human and constitutional rights), then cosmopolitan rights must be interpreted as limitations on all governance institutions and abuses of all public and private power.

UN law and the customary 'international law among sovereign states' did not provide for individual rights of access to justice in international tribunals. It is only on the basis of reciprocal international treaties that – for example, in human rights law, trade law, investment law, environmental law, regional economic integration law and the law of the sea – individual rights of access to national and international courts have become progressively recognized in response to requests from citizens, notwithstanding authoritarian resistance by governments interested in limiting their legal and judicial accountability with respect to citizens.[88] Notably, in the field of bilateral and regional investment trea-

consist of a series of human rights' (DZ Cass (2005) at 146); that WTO law prescribes 'direct effect' (Cass, at 147 f); and that my support for a 'human rights approach to international trade' is 'fixated on only one category of human rights, namely individual economic rights' (at 172). Such polemics ignores that my arguments for protecting freedom of trade are based on constitutional rights to liberty (eg, in German and EU law) and on constitutional obligations to respect 'strict observance of international law' (Art 3 TEU). My proposal to interpret – inside the EU – the 'human right to liberty' (eg, in Art 6 of the EU Charter of Fundamental Rights, Art 3 UDHR) more broadly than it is done in Anglo-Saxon countries follows from my Kantian definition of the 'first principle of justice' so as to avoid the widespread disregard (eg, in UN human rights law) for constitutional protection of freedom of profession and other economic freedoms necessary for individual autonomy. Contrary to Alston and Cass, I have never argued for a specific 'human right to free trade' as such specific human rights run counter to the 'indivisibility' of human rights and to the necessary balancing of liberty rights with all other human rights and constitutional rights.

[87] *Protecting Dignity: An Agenda for Human Rights: Progress Report* (Bern: Swiss Confederation, 2009) 1; Commission on Legal Empowerment of the Poor, *Making the Law Work for Everyone: Report of the Commission on Legal Empowerment of the Poor*, vol I (Geneva: UN, 2008).

[88] *cf* F Francioni (ed) (2007).

ties and of investment arbitration, the right of access to justice has shifted from individual access to national courts, and diplomatic protection of individual rights by means of interstate claims, to investor–state arbitration offering private actors direct access to international arbitral tribunals; their arbitral awards can be enforced in national courts all over the world pursuant to the rules of the 1958 New York Convention on Mutual Recognition and Enforcement of Arbitral Awards, without the traditional need for the interposition of the home state of the investor by means of diplomatic protection.[89] This paradigm shift reflects, albeit imperfectly, the increasing recognition of individuals as legal subjects and right holders in IEL. In human rights law, direct access of individuals to regional human rights courts remains more limited, for instance by requirements of prior exhaustion of local remedies and the more limited number of countries accepting compulsory jurisdiction of regional human rights courts for individual complaints.

Chapters III to V argued that – even though the human rights obligations of all UN member states entail cosmopolitan rights of citizens – rendering human and cosmopolitan rights more effective depends on extending bottom-up constitutional, legislative, administrative and judicial safeguards institutionalizing 'public cosmopolitan reason' and multilevel constitutional protection to all human interactions at national, transnational and international levels. Sections 2 and 3 extended this argument to IEL: even though the law of international economic organizations requires member states to protect economic freedoms, non-discriminatory conditions of competition, monetary and legal stability, private property rights and rules-based settlement of disputes for the benefit of citizens and their international economic transactions, the transformation of these rights and obligations of states into cosmopolitan rights empowering citizens depends on more effective domestic rules and institutions implementing and protecting IEL and transnational rule of law for the benefit of citizens. Due to the mercantilist reciprocity principle underlying IEL, such domestic legal reforms are likely to be accepted by governments only on the basis of reciprocal international commitments. Moreover, as confirmed by comparative legal and institutional analyses, legislative and administrative implementation of, for example, international GATT, WTO and human rights obligations tends to vary among domestic legal systems. For instance, in contrast to European legal traditions of interpreting copyrights and other 'authors rights' as being based on human personality rights, many countries perceive and protect intellectual property rights as purely 'utilitarian rights' and legal instruments of economic policy. Similarly, the 'trading rights' and individual 'access to judicial remedies' protected by some WTO agreements (like the WTO Protocol on the Accession of China, the WTO agreements on Preshipment Inspection and Government Procurement) are considered by many WTO governments as economic rights rather than as 'fundamental freedoms' and 'access to justice' as in European law. The EU Charter of Fundamental Rights' legal distinctions between general and specific dignity rights (Title I), liberty rights (Title II), equality rights (Title III), solidarity rights (Title IV), citizen rights (Title V) and 'rights to justice' (Title VI) implement the human rights obligations of all EU member states in innovative ways different from the distinctions among civil, political, economic, social and cultural rights in UN human rights conventions.[90]

[89] *cf* F Francioni, 'Access to Justice, Denial of Justice and International Investment Law' in Dupuy, Francioni and Petersmann (eds) (2009) ch 3.

[90] The Charter, first proclaimed by the European Parliament, the EU Commission and the EU Council in December 2000 (Official Journal of the EC, C 364/1-22 of 18 December 2000) became part of EU constitutional law as a result of the entry into force of the Lisbon Treaty in December 2009.

As it was to be expected from the perspective of rights-based constitutional theory, European integration law has proven to be most successful in those areas where individual citizens and national courts could directly enforce EU and EEA free trade, common market and competition rules, fundamental freedoms and human rights vis-à-vis national governments and EU institutions. Vice versa, those areas of European law where EU citizens and national courts were prevented from directly enforcing the legal obligations of the EU and EU governments (like the EU's WTO obligations, the EU's legal disciplines for national budgetary and fiscal policies, the EU's prohibition of 'bailouts'), 'rent-seeking pressures' to violate rule of law so as to redistribute income (eg, for import-competing farmers and traders, bankrupt banks and industries, insolvent EU member states) have often prevailed to the detriment of consumer welfare. Due to pressures from the political EU organs and the judicial self-restraint by the ECJ, there has been only one judgment by the EC Court since 1958 establishing a violation by the EU of its international legal obligations,[91] compared with more than 40 GATT and WTO dispute settlement findings of violations of GATT and WTO obligations by the EU and EU member states. The legal advocates of the EU Commission justify the frequent violations of WTO guarantees of freedom – even if EU violations of WTO rules had been formally established in legally binding WTO dispute settlement rulings and the 'reasonable period of time' for implementing such rulings had long expired – by power-oriented, Machiavellian arguments that judicial protection by the ECJ of the EU citizens' reliance on respect for the rule of international law would be 'naïve'.[92] The self-interests of EU institutions in avoiding legal and judicial accountability in respect of EU citizens for protectionist violations of WTO law and of corresponding freedoms of citizens prevail over the general citizen interest in rule of law in transnational economic cooperation.

In the field of the EU's common foreign and security policy, legal and judicial remedies are even more limited inside the EU[93] as well as in worldwide governance institutions. Yet, the more discretionary foreign policy powers are abused (eg, for imposing 'smart economic sanctions' against alleged terrorists without due process of law, restrictions on imports of bananas from Latin America in favour of former colonies in Africa in violation of GATT obligations), the more limitation of the judicial task of protecting the EU's 'strict observance of international law' (Article 3 TEU) risks undermining rule of

[91] Case T-115/94, *Opel Austria* [1997] CMLR 733.

[92] This term was used by PJ Kuijper, 'WTO Law in the European Court of Justice' (2005) 42 *CMLR* 1313–41. At the request of the political EU institutions, the ECJ has refrained from reviewing the legality of EU acts in the light of GATT law for more than 30 years, even if the EU violations had been formally established in legally binding GATT and WTO dispute settlement rulings and the 'reasonable period' for implementing WTO dispute settlement rulings had expired. Notwithstanding the longstanding EC jurisprudence that GATT and WTO obligations form an 'integral part of the Community legal system' binding on all EU institutions and judicially enforceable vis-à-vis EU member states, the Court consistently denies EU citizens as well as EU member states rights to directly invoke GATT and WTO rules (*cf* Cases C-120/06 P and C-121/06 P, *FIAMM*, Judgment, 9 September 2008) and the Law of the Sea Convention in domestic courts (*cf* Case C-308/06, *Intertanko*, Judgment, 3 June 2008). The ECJ's arguments against 'direct applicability' rely on obvious misinterpretations of WTO rules (eg, in Case T-69/00, *FIAMM* [2005] ECR II-5393: 'applicants are wrong in inferring from Articles 21 and 22 of the DSU an obligation on the WTO Member to comply, within a specified period, with the recommendations and rulings of the WTO bodies') as well as on political arguments (like lack of international reciprocity, need to protect the 'scope of manoeuvre' of the political EU bodies) that had been rejected as legally irrelevant by the ECJ in its *Kupferberg* judgment (Case 104/81 [1982[ECR 3659). The EU legal services welcome this judicial self-restraint and that 'the *Nakajima* doctrine has never really been applied' (Kuijper, at 1340).

[93] *cf* P Eeckhout, *Does Europe's Constitution Stop at the Water's Edge? Law and Policy in the EU's External Relations* (Leuven: Europa Publishing, 2005) 20: 'In CFSP matters there is both a democratic and judicial deficit'.

law to the detriment of EU citizens.[94] Without rule of law and respect for international treaty obligations ratified by parliaments, democracy becomes illusionary in the EU's multilevel economic governance. The politically motivated refusal of the ECJ to review EU violations of reciprocal international obligations amounts to a 'political question doctrine' that leaves EU member states and EU citizens without judicial remedies against arbitrary violations of the rule of law by EU institutions. Limiting such 'protectionist collusion' among EU institutions would require agreements on stronger judicial remedies which governments are willing to accept so far only in limited areas of regional human rights and economic agreements and bilateral investment treaties. Without such international agreements, international courts remain reluctant to invoke the customary law obligation of interpreting law, and settling international disputes, 'in conformity with principles of justice' and human rights for strengthening cosmopolitan, judicial remedies of citizens against violations of international treaty obligations.

4 THE 'HUMAN RIGHTS APPROACH' TO IEL ADVOCATED BY THE UNHCHR, THE ILO AND FAO: FOOD SECURITY AND 'FREEDOM FROM HUNGER'

All WTO Members have obligations under international treaty law (eg, the UN Charter, UN and regional human rights conventions) as well as under general international law, including customary law as well as 'general principles of law', to respect, protect and promote human rights. There is also increasing agreement that the UN, UN Specialized Agencies and other international organizations have to respect the human rights obligations of their member states even if the constitutive agreements – as in the case of the UN Charter and most UN Specialized Agencies – do not explicitly require the organization to respect, protect or fulfil human rights. States remain the principal duty bearers under international human rights law, but they cannot avoid their human rights responsibilities by transferring governance functions to international organizations.[95] In view of the customary law requirement of interpreting international treaties in conformity with the human rights obligations of their member states (*cf* Article 31 VCLT), treaty obligations – such as to promote 'sustainable development' (Preamble WTO Agreement) – may need to be construed in conformity with human rights instruments such as the 1986 UN Declaration on the 'Right to Development'[96] which defined development in terms of enjoyment of human rights:

- 'The right to development is an inalienable human right by virtue of which every human person and all peoples are entitled to participate in, contribute to, and enjoy economic, social, cultural and political development, in which all human rights and fundamental freedoms can be fully realized' (Article 1).
- 'The human person is the central subject of development and should be the active participant and beneficiary of the right to development' (Article 2).

[94] See Tables 18 and 24 and related text. The EU's legal advocates (like Kuijper, (n 92)) claim that the ECJ should focus on the WTO's 'law in action' (as defined by EU politicians) rather than on WTO 'law in the books' (eg, at 1332–34).

[95] This basic principle is also reflected in the International Law Commission's Draft Articles on the Responsibility of International Organizations, UN Doc A/63/10 (2008) eg, in Arts 25–30.

[96] See: *The United Nations and Human Rights 1945–1995* (New York: UN, 1995) 322–24.

- 'All human rights and fundamental freedoms are indivisible and interdependent; equal attention and urgent consideration should be given to the implementation, promotion and protection of civil, political, economic, social and cultural rights' (Article 6:2).
- 'States should take steps to eliminate obstacles to development resulting from failure to observe civil and political rights, as well as economic, social and cultural rights' (Article 6:3).

Yet, in cases of international economic organizations without a specific human rights mandate, there are longstanding traditions by diplomats, economists and civil servants of focusing on the specific economic objectives rather than perceiving the economic objectives as *means* for promoting human rights objectives. In the World Bank, for instance, the official acknowledgment of the human rights dimensions of the Bank's financial and development activities[97] has not prevented the 'marginality of human rights' in most of the operational activities of the Bank, in part also due to the statutory requirement of 'only economic considerations' in the financial decision-making of the Bank (Article IV) without 'regard to political or other non-economic considerations' (Article III, section 5,b of the World Bank Agreement).[98] Also in the development operations of the UN, the human rights objectives of UN operational assistance often remain marginal notwithstanding the official recognition by the 2005 World Summit that human rights, development, peace and security are the three basic 'pillars' of the UN system and justify 'mainstreaming' of human rights throughout the UN system.[99] In the IMF and the WTO, the governing bodies have so far avoided explicit recognition of human rights obligations in view of the lack of any references to human rights in their constitutive agreements and the widespread disagreement among their member states on the scope and relevance of human rights obligations under general international law (eg, *jus cogens* obligations of international organizations) for designing monetary and trade policies. Even though, according to Article 103 UN Charter, the human rights obligations under the Charter may prevail over other international obligations and international organizations, like states, cannot invoke their internal laws to justify non-compliance with international obligations,[100] WTO members have hardly ever invoked human rights obligations in WTO dispute settlement proceedings as justification for contested trade restrictions. As legal systems are social constructs, many IMF and WTO diplomats continue to insist that human rights are not part of the IMF and WTO legal systems.

The fulfilment of most human rights (eg, to life, food, health, education) depends on access to scarce goods and services such as drinking water, sanitation, affordable medicines, health and educational services. Also enjoyment of civil and political human rights (eg, personal freedom, rule of law, access to justice, democratic self-government) requires economic resources, for instance for financing democratic and law enforcement institutions. The widespread, yet unnecessary poverty, health problems and legal insecurity among the more than one billion people living on one dollar a day or less bear witness to

[97] *cf Development and Human Rights: The Role of the World Bank* (Washington: World Bank, 1998); *Human Rights and Development* (Washington: World Bank 2006).

[98] *cf* GA Sarfaty, 'Why Culture Matters in International Institutions: The Marginality of Human Rights at the World Bank' (2009) 103 *AJIL* 647–83, according to whom the internal controversies about the scope of the Bank's human rights obligations and other 'bureaucratic obstacles have been more critical in impeding internal efforts' at a human rights approach than the restrictions in the Articles of Agreement.

[99] *cf* M Darrow and L Arbour, 'The Pillar of Glass: Human Rights in the Development Operations of the United Nations' (2009) 103 *AJIL* 446–501.

[100] *cf* the ILC Draft Article 35:1 on the Responsibility of International Organizations (n 95).

the fact that many UN member states and UN law have so far failed to realize the UN objective of 'universal respect for, and observance of, human rights and fundamental freedoms for all' and 'creation of conditions of stability and well-being which are necessary for peaceful and friendly relations among nations' (Article 55 UN Charter). Even though international trade is essential for increasing the availability and quality of scarce resources, UN human rights bodies have, until a few years ago, neglected international trade law or, as in a report for the UN Commission on Human Rights of 2001, discredited the WTO as 'a veritable nightmare' for developing countries and women.[101]

Human rights dimensions of WTO Law: the reports by the UN High Commissioner for Human Rights

In response to the widespread criticism of the anti-market bias of such 'nightmare reports', the UN High Commissioner for Human Rights (UNHCHR) has published more differentiated reports[102] analyzing human rights dimensions of the WTO Agreements on Trade-Related Intellectual Property Rights (TRIPS), the Agreement on Agriculture, the General Agreement on Trade in Services (GATS), safeguard measures under WTO law, international investment agreements, non-discrimination in the context of globalization and on the impact of trade rules on the right of everyone to the enjoyment of the highest attainable standard of physical and mental health. The reports acknowledge the virtues of specialization but call for a 'human rights approach to trade' which

'(i) sets the promotion and protection of human rights as objectives of trade liberalization, not exceptions;
(ii) examines the effect of trade liberalization on individuals and seeks to devise trade law and policy to take into account the rights of all individuals, in particular vulnerable individuals and groups;
(iii) emphasizes the role of the State in the process of liberalization – not only as negotiators of trade law and setters of trade policy, but also as the primary duty bearer of human rights;
(iv) seeks consistency between the progressive liberalization of trade and the progressive realization of human rights;
(v) requires a constant examination of the impact of trade liberalization on the enjoyment of human rights;
(vi) promotes international cooperation for the realization of human rights and freedoms in the context of trade liberalization'.

The UNHCHR emphasizes that, because every WTO Member has ratified one or more UN human rights conventions and also has human rights obligations under general

[101] *Globalization and its impact on the full enjoyment of human rights*, ECOSOC document E/CN.4/Sub.2/2000/12 (15 June 2000), para 15. Apart from a reference to patents and their possibly adverse effects on pharmaceutical prices (depending on the competition, patent and social laws of the countries concerned), the report nowhere identifies conflicts between WTO rules and human rights.

[102] For a discussion of these reports see: EU Petersmann, 'The Human Rights Approach Advocated by the UN High Commissioner for Human Rights and by the ILO: Is it Relevant for WTO Law and Policy?' (2004) 7 *JIEL* 605–28; Harrison (2007). On the human rights dimensions of WTO law, see also: R Howse and R Teitel, *Beyond the Divide: The Covenant on Economic, Social and Cultural Rights and the WTO* (Geneva: Friedrich Ebert Stiftung, 2007); P Hilpold, 'WTO Law and Human Rights: Bringing Together Two Autopoietic Orders' *Law* (2011) 10(2) *Chinese Journal of International* 323–72; A Chapman and S Russell (eds), *Core Obligations: Building a Framework for Economic, Social and Cultural Rights* (Antwerpen: Intersentia, 2002).

international law, human rights may be 'relevant context' for the interpretation and application of WTO rules. According to the UNHCHR, the required human rights approach to international trade must recognize as 'entitlements the basic needs necessary to lead a life in dignity and ensure their protection in the processes of economic liberalization'; these entitlements cannot be 'left subject to the whims of the market'. The UNHCHR differentiates between obligations to respect human rights (eg, by refraining from interfering in the enjoyment of such rights), to protect human rights (eg, by preventing violations of such rights by third parties) and to fulfil human rights (eg, by taking appropriate legislative, administrative, budgetary, judicial and other measures towards the full realization of such rights). As recourse to trade sanctions for promoting respect for human rights abroad can aggravate the problems of the people concerned by adverse trade effects, the UNHCHR reports emphasize both potential synergies as well as potential conflicts between human rights and trade rules in the context of trade liberalization, trade restrictions and other trade regulation.

Because enjoyment of human rights depends on availability, accessibility, acceptability and quality of traded goods and services, the relevance of WTO rules for the collective supply of public goods (like access to low-priced goods and services), for limitations of 'market failures' (eg, inadequate supply of public goods like essential medicines for poor people) and for protection and fulfilment of human rights is acknowledged and discussed. The reports underline that what are referred to – in numerous WTO provisions – as *rights* of WTO Members to regulate, may be *duties* to regulate under human rights law (eg, to protect and fulfil human rights of access to water, food, essential medicines, basic health care and education services at affordable prices). The UNHCHR suggests, inter alia,

- to recognize the promotion of human rights as an objective of the WTO;
- to encourage interpretations of WTO rules that are compatible with international human rights as progressively clarified eg, in the 'General Comments' adopted by UN human rights bodies;
- to carry out 'human rights assessments' of WTO rules; and
- to strengthen intergovernmental protection of human rights so that trade rules and policies promote the human rights and basic needs of all.

Avoidance of human rights arguments in WTO dispute settlement practices

As WTO bodies and trade diplomats have neither legal expertise in human rights nor common views on the human rights dimensions of WTO law, human rights are hardly ever mentioned in WTO negotiations and WTO dispute settlement proceedings. WTO law and its Dispute Settlement Understanding regulate 'the dispute settlement system of the WTO' (Article 3 DSU) as a multilevel system with compulsory jurisdiction for (quasi) judicial settlement of disputes at intergovernmental and domestic levels. As the WTO dispute settlement system 'serves to preserve the rights and obligations of Members under the covered agreements, and to clarify the existing provisions of those agreements in accordance with customary rules of interpretation of public international law' (Article 3 DSU), the customary rules of treaty interpretation codified in the VCLT apply: 'disputes concerning treaties, like other international disputes, should be settled by peaceful means and in conformity with the principles of justice and international law', including 'universal respect for, and observance of, human rights and fundamental freedoms for all' (Preamble VCLT). Yet, hardly any of the more than 250 WTO dispute settlement reports has referred to human rights. Most *domestic courts*, for example in the EU and in the United States, tend to ignore WTO obligations and WTO dispute settlement rulings in their adjudication of transnational trade disputes.

This neglect by WTO dispute settlement bodies of the human rights obligations of WTO members, like the frequent neglect by domestic courts for constitutional requirements of interpreting domestic law in conformity with the international law obligations of the countries concerned (including WTO dispute settlement rulings), leads to citizens lacking effective judicial remedies against violations by governments of their WTO obligations. As discussed in chapter V, the artificial separation of rule of law at international and domestic levels runs counter not only to citizen-oriented conceptions of rule of law and of rules-based, democratic governance; it also undermines the WTO objective of 'providing security and predictability to the multilateral trading system' (Article 3 DSU) as well as its underlying economic objective of reducing transaction costs. For, the *economic value* of investments, trade transactions and consumer welfare risks being reduced if producers, investors, traders and consumers can no longer rely on legal security. Since Adam Smith's explanation of the *Wealth of Nations* as being dependent on the respective laws and institutions, lack of rule of law is widely recognized as one of the principal causes of corruption and waste of scarce resources. The Latin American economist de Soto, for example, explains much of the economic poverty in Latin America as caused by inadequate protection of property rights, which operates as a disincentive for borrowing, investments and enjoyment of human rights.[103] The WTO's one-sided focus on intellectual property rights and 'rights to trade' protected in the 2001 WTO Protocol on the Accession of China, and its neglect of other *individual* rights, reflect the 'Westphalian focus' of 'member-driven WTO governance' on rights and obligations of governments rather than on legal empowerment and legal protection of private producers, investors, traders and consumers.

As every WTO Member has accepted obligations under international law to protect and promote human rights, citizens are entitled to evaluate the WTO system – like any domestic legal and political system – from the perspective of human rights. It seems unlikely that the intergovernmental WTO Councils will respond to the UN proposals to adopt a 'human rights approach to trade', notwithstanding WTO Director-General Pascal Lamy's courageous acknowledgment that trade liberalization and human rights consistent interpretations of WTO rules will enhance the interests and welfare of citizens.[104] In view of the insertion of human rights clauses into ever more preferential trade agreements among WTO Members, it may only be a matter of time until WTO dispute settlement bodies are asked by complainants or defendants to interpret WTO rules with due regard to the human rights obligations of the WTO Members concerned. Such human rights clauses have rarely been invoked so far; arguably, they call for *non-discriminatory* regulations (eg, of health risks, supply of public services) rather than for trade restrictions if the latter reduce consumer welfare by arbitrarily discriminating in favour of domestic producers. The case law of European courts confirms not only that concerns

[103] *cf* H de Soto, *The Mystery of Capital: Why Capitalism Triumphs in the West and Fails Everywhere Else* (London: Black Swan, 2002).
[104] *cf* Lamy (n 80).

of trade diplomats – that human rights arguments may render trade rules and trade disputes unpredictable – are unwarranted; the customary methods of treaty interpretation also enable interpreting trade rules (eg, WTO law) in conformity with the human rights obligations of states without requiring 'a rigid concept of hierarchy of norms nor new substantive obligations to be imposed on states'.[105] As discussed in chapters II to V, there have only been a few disputes over the past 50 years where the ECJ was asked to review alleged inconsistencies of trade restrictions with human rights; not a single ECJ judgment seems to have concluded that the respective trade rules could not be interpreted and applied in conformity with the human rights obligations under national constitutions and European constitutional law. The universal recognition of human rights further illustrates that every modern legal system rests on rules as well as on general principles promoting the overall coherence of rules. In examining the potential impact of human rights as 'relevant context' for interpreting WTO rules, WTO dispute settlement bodies should distinguish the following three different kinds of trade regulations[106] :

1. International trade measures for *promotion of human rights abroad* must respect the 'sovereign equality of states', the legitimate diversity of their national human rights laws and the often harmful effects of trade restrictions on citizen welfare and the enjoyment of human rights. The increasing recourse to UN human rights law as 'objective standard' for differentiating trade preferences for LDCs may entail future WTO disputes on whether such trade differentiation can be justified in terms of human rights.
2. WTO disputes over import restrictions for *protection of human rights at home* – for instance, over the EC's import restrictions on hormone-fed beef, asbestos and the US restrictions on gambling services – illustrate that WTO rules grant importing countries broad regulatory discretion regarding restrictions of imported goods with potential risks for human welfare and human rights. As UN human rights conventions prescribe minimum standards that do not prevent WTO members from accepting higher human rights standards in regional and national human rights laws, the WTO-consistency of import restrictions designed to protect the human rights of domestic citizens may be legitimately influenced by arguments based on *regional* and *national* human rights rather than only UN human rights law. WTO law recognizes that 'public morality' and 'public order' may legitimately vary from one community to the other.[107] Hence, WTO dispute settlement bodies have to respect the legitimate 'margin of appreciation' of national authorities to define 'public morality', 'public order' and human rights in conformity with national and regional democratic preferences.
3. *Non-discriminatory WTO rules* regulating intellectual property rights, technical and health standards, competition, environmental and investment rules and public services, like the proposed WTO rules on trade facilitation and on a WTO register for private geographical indications, may give rise to legal challenges whether such WTO rules are themselves consistent with human and constitutional rights. WTO rules and

[105] B Choudhury et al, 'A Call for a WTO Ministerial Decision on Trade and Human Rights' in T Cottier and P Delimatsis (eds), *The Prospects of International Trade Regulation. From Fragmentation to Coherence* (Cambridge: CUP, 2011) 323–58. A WTO Declaration on Trade and Human Rights was already proposed by EU Petersmann, 'Human Rights and International Trade Law' in T Cottier J Pauwelyn and E Bürgi (eds) (2005) 29 ff, 71, and is also discussed by Hilpold (n 102) sections 45–48.

[106] For a detailed explanation see: EU Petersmann, 'WTO Dispute Settlement Practice 1995–2005: Lessons from the Past and Future Challenges' in Y Taniguchi, A Yanovich and J Bohanes (eds) (2007) 38–94.

[107] See, eg, the footnote to GATS Art XIV(a) which states: 'The public order exception may be invoked only where a genuine and sufficiently serious threat is posed to one of the fundamental interests of society'.

WTO dispute settlement proceedings should respect the legitimate diversity of 'balancing principles' which national and international courts apply in examining whether the regulation of economic freedoms and other economic rights are consistent with human rights. These balancing principles may legitimately differ, for instance depending on whether WTO obligations protect *private rights* of market participants (such as 'rights to trade', procedural rights, property rights and judicial remedies) or government obligations to protect human rights and related public interests (like protection of health and the environment).

The 1998 ILO Declaration on Fundamental Principles and Rights at Work: the expanding scope of an 'inalienable core' of basic rights

Human rights are increasingly acknowledged today in national constitutions as well as in the law of worldwide organizations (like the UN, the FAO, WHO, UNESCO) and regional economic integration agreements (like the TEU, the 2000 Cotonou Agreement, the 2001 Quebec Ministerial Declaration on a Free Trade Area of the Americas) as international *erga omnes* obligations of states with an 'inalienable' and 'indivisible' *jus cogens* core. The 1996 WTO Declaration on core labour standards helped to reach consensus in the International Labour Organization (ILO) to adopt, on 18 June 1998, the Declaration on Fundamental Principles and Rights at Work which recognizes

> that all Members, even if they have not ratified the Conventions in question, have an obligation, arising from the very fact of membership in the Organization, to respect, to promote and to realize, in good faith and in accordance with the Constitution, the principles concerning the fundamental rights which are the subject of those Conventions, namely: (a) freedom of association and the effective recognition of the right to collective bargaining; (b) the elimination of all forms of forced or compulsory labor; (c) the effective abolition of child labor; and (d) the elimination of discrimination in respect of employment and occupation.[108]

The ILO Declaration and other modern human rights instruments[109] confirm that – in addition to the longstanding prohibitions of genocide, slavery, apartheid and torture – there is an increasing core of additional human rights which must be respected as *erga omnes* obligations. Since the end of the Cold War, the international *jus cogens* core of human rights continues to expand, as recognized by international courts,[110] notwithstanding divergent views on the precise scope and definition of such 'inalienable human rights'.[111] Even though UN human rights law fails to provide for effective international

[108] ILO, *Declaration on Fundamental Principles and Rights at Work* (Geneva: ILO 1998) 7.

[109] eg, the 1989 UN Convention on the Rights of the Child (ratified by more than 190 states) and the 1993 Vienna Declaration of the UN World Conference on Human Rights, in which more than 170 UN member states recognized that 'the universal nature of (human) rights and freedoms is beyond question' (para 1).

[110] See the broad interpretation of UN human rights as international *jus cogens*, and as constitutional limitation of intergovernmental powers also of UN bodies, by the EC Court of First Instance in Cases T-315/01 (*Kadi v Council and Commission)* and T-306/01 (*Yusuf v Council and Commission*) Judgments, 21 September 2005 [2005] CMLR 1334.

[111] *cf* JH Knox, 'Horizontal Human Rights Law' (2008) 102 *AJIL* 1–47; S Gardbaum, 'Human Rights as International Constitutional Rights' (2008) 19 *EJIL* 749–68, discussing arguments that human rights law is evolving into constitutional law also at international level, characterized by a higher legal rank (eg, of *jus cogens* obligations) and by entrenchment against ordinary methods of legal amendment or repeal by national legal acts (eg, in view of the fact that UN human rights conventions include no provisions on termination or withdrawal, and the UN Human Rights Committee declared in its General Comment 26 of 1997 that a state may not withdraw from the ICCPR).

enforcement mechanisms, the multilevel human rights guarantees evolve into a worldwide 'constitutional public order' limiting all governance powers by *erga omnes* obligations to protect individual rights and interpret international and national laws as a functional unity for promoting and protecting 'human self-development' as defined by human rights. Chapters II to V discussed how national and international courts use legal 'balancing principles' (like non-discrimination, suitability, necessity and proportionality tests) for reconciling economic and non-economic rights and governmental limitations, with due respect for the 'margin of appreciation' which national legislatures may enjoy in their domestic protection and promotion of human rights. Just as views on the interpretation of government obligations to respect, protect and fulfil human rights may legitimately differ among countries, there are also diverging views on whether, and to what extent, international organizations should not only *respect* human rights, but *protect* and *fulfil* human rights. Yet, such differences of view over the interpretation and legal protection of human rights do not change the fact that citizens have become subjects of international law and should no longer be treated by trade diplomats as mere objects of their intergovernmental rulemaking and economic management.

Liberal trade rules, like human rights, should focus on human self-development

Chapters II to VI argued that – in contrast to the often accidental distribution of 'natural primary goods' (like natural resources, individual human capacities and diseases) – constitutional law and human rights law should aim at a fair distribution of 'social primary goods' by means of equal constitutional rights and social 'difference principles' empowering individuals to develop their human resources in order to live the life they have reason to value. The reports by the UNHCHR emphasize potential synergies between trade rules and human rights: 'trade liberalization is generally a positive contributor to poverty alleviation – it allows people to exploit their productive potential, assists economic growth, curtails arbitrary policy interventions and helps to insulate against shocks'.[112] Also intellectual property rights may act as incentives for innovation in the pharmaceutical industry and for the transfer of technology to less-developed countries. Yet, the UNHCHR also recalls potential conflicts between 'existential' human rights and 'instrumental' WTO rules (such as on protection of intellectual property rights and investor rights), for example if trade protection increases prices so that food, seeds or pharmaceutical products are no longer accessible for poor people. According to the High Commissioner, the needed 'human rights assessments' of trade rules and trade policies must focus on the rights and basic needs of vulnerable individuals and of the most disadvantaged communities whose human rights risk being adversely affected most in the process of trade liberalization. For example, the increasing number of plant breeders' rights and patents on seeds – by restricting or prohibiting the re-use and exchange of seeds – may have negative effects on rural livelihoods, food supply, cultural practices and the enjoyment of human rights (eg, of access to adequate and affordable food, rights to protection of health and an adequate standard of living) in rural areas of poor countries.[113]

[112] UN Doc E/CN.4/2002/54, para 33.

[113] *cf Seeds of Hunger: Intellectual Property Rights on Seeds and the Human Rights Response* (Geneva: 3d, 2009).

Nowhere within the macroeconomic objectives and state-centred rules of WTO law is there reference to human rights. The High Commissioner, therefore, emphasizes the need for using WTO rules (eg, for preferential treatment of LDCs), WTO safeguard clauses and WTO 'exceptions' for actively promoting mutually coherent interpretations of WTO law and human rights in order to enhance 'human development.' The UNHCHR criticizes the lack of guidance and of monitoring mechanisms in WTO law for ensuring that human rights are taken into account.[114] The reports do not, however, identify concrete conflicts between human rights and WTO law. In view of the citizen-oriented functions of WTO rules for enabling citizens to increase their welfare through mutually beneficial trade transactions, for enhancing the domestic use of non-discriminatory policy instruments and for protecting the priority of non-economic values (as reflected in the numerous 'public interest clauses' in WTO law), conflicts between the flexible WTO rules and human rights appear unlikely on the level of international principles. The WTO 'waivers' and formal amendment of Article 31(f) of the TRIPS Agreement illustrate that – if any such conflicts should arise (eg, in order to protect human rights to health by granting compulsory licences for the production of generic medicines) – WTO members have been willing to use the existing safeguard clauses in WTO law for avoiding any such legal conflicts.[115] Just as, in March 2012, the EU Commission requested an advisory opinion from the ECJ on whether the controversial Anti-Counterfeiting Agreement of December 2011 is consistent with EU law and human rights, it remains likely that also WTO dispute settlement bodies will be requested to review whether compulsory licences granted by WTO members for essential medicines (like the first ever compulsory licence granted under India's 1970 Patent Act in March 2012 for Bayer's patented anti-cancer drug Sorafenib) are consistent with WTO law as construed in conformity with the human rights obligations of WTO members (eg, the human right of access to essential medicines).

Even if the WTO objective of 'sustainable development' and the numerous WTO 'exceptions' appear to offer enough policy space for taking into account human rights obligations of WTO Members, WTO law in no way ensures that human rights obligations are actually taken into account in the legislative and administrative implementation of WTO rules inside states and in their judicial protection by international and domestic courts. The longstanding preference of WTO diplomats and WTO judges for avoiding human rights discourse in WTO bodies is unlikely to change. More than 35 WTO Members (including the United States) have not ratified the UN Covenant on Economic, Social and Cultural Rights. In view of the narrow limitation of the 'terms of reference' of WTO dispute settlement bodies to the 'covered WTO agreements', it remains controversial in WTO law whether – in WTO dispute settlement proceedings – the parties to the dispute may invoke human rights law not only as relevant context for interpreting WTO rules, but directly for justifying departures from their WTO obligations (eg, in the case of US trade sanctions in response to human rights violations in Myanmar). In the US complaint against Chinese censorship restrictions denying protection of copyrights, the United States did not invoke any human rights arguments challenging politically motivated censorship.[116] The 2001 WTO Declaration on the TRIPS Agreement and

[114] *cf Report of the High Commissioner for Human Rights on Implementation of Economic, Social and Cultural Rights* of 8 June 2009 (E/2009/90).

[115] For a discussion of these legal adaptations of WTO rules see: Hestermeyer (2007) 255 ff.

[116] *cf* the WTO panel report adopted in March 2009, WT/DS362/R. Similarly, in Google's dispute over Chinese restrictions of internet access to censored information, human rights arguments don't seem to have been raised.

Public Health, the 2003 WTO 'waiver' from Article 31(f) of the TRIPS Agreement in order to facilitate the use of compulsory licensing by LDCs with insufficient or no pharmaceutical manufacturing capacity (used for the first time in September 2008 for shipping generic medicines from Canada to treat HIV/AIDS patients in Rwanda) and the formal amendment of the TRIPS Agreement decided on 6 December 2005 suggest that WTO rules and WTO practices are flexible enough to ensure their consistency with the human rights obligations of all WTO members.[117] In order to avoid potential conflicts between intellectual property rights and human rights (eg, to health, food and education), it is important not only that WTO dispute settlement bodies acknowledge their legal obligation to construe WTO rules in conformity with the human rights obligations of WTO members; in view of the role of governments in building stronger healthcare systems, stronger commitments by WTO member governments will also be important for realizing the right to health.[118]

The World Food Convention, WTO rules and the human right to food

According to the FAO, approximately 1.2 billion people worldwide live in food insecurity, of which at least 60 per cent are living in sub-Saharan Africa or South Asia.[119] The right to adequate food is recognized in Article 25 of the UDHR and Article 11 of the 1966 ICESCR as part of the right of everyone 'to a standard of living adequate for the health and well-being of himself and of his family'. It has been gradually reinforced in the international food security context, beginning with the adoption of the Rome Declaration on World Food Security at the World Food Summit in 1996 when FAO members placed food security at the heart of the organization's work. According to the contemporaneous World Food Summit Action Plan, food security exists 'when all people at all times, have physical and economic access to sufficient, safe and nutritious food to meet their dietary needs and food preferences for an active and healthy life'. In 1999, General Comment No 12 of the Committee on Economic, Social and Cultural Rights on the 'Right to Adequate Food' confirmed that 'the right to adequate food is realized when every . . . [individual], alone or in community with others, has physical and economic access at all times to adequate food or means for its procurement'. It signifies that states are under a duty *to respect* existing access to adequate food for their populations; they should therefore abstain from adopting measures that prevent such access. They have an obligation *to protect*, which means they must ensure that individuals and business enterprises involved in commercial agricultural production should not deprive individuals of their right to adequate food supplies. Finally, governments have a duty *to fulfil*, ie, *to facilitate* people's access to food, including the utilisation of resources essential to the production of food and, where necessary, to ensure the livelihoods of their people by providing food directly, ie, by means of food aid.[120]

[117] *cf* Hestermeyer (2007) 255 ff; D Ovett, 'Making Trade Policies More Accountable and Human-Rights Consistent: A NGO Perspective of Using Human Rights Instruments in the Case of Access to Medicines' in Benedek, de Freyter and Marella (eds) (2008) 170 ff.

[118] *cf* A Clapham and M Robinson (eds), *Realizing the Right to Health* (Zürich: Rüffer & Rub, 2009).

[119] *The State of Food Insecurity in the World: Economic Crises –Impacts and Lessons Learned* (Rome: UN Food and Agriculture Organization, 2009).

[120] For a discussion of the relevant human rights instruments and WTO rules on market access, domestic support (eg, for public stockholding for food security purposes), export restrictions, reduction of export subsi-

The FAO Voluntary Guidelines on the Progressive Realization of the Right to Adequate Food in the Context of National Food Security, which were adopted in 2004, build upon General Comment No 12 in making a rights-based approach to food security essential to FAO food policy. The Guidelines are being operationalised by means of right to food impact assessments (Guideline 17) with monitoring efforts coordinated by the FAO. The High Level Task Force on the Global Food Security Crisis, which was established by the UN Secretary-General in 2008 in response to the sharp spike in global food prices, has produced a Comprehensive Framework for Action supported by all the major UN and other organizations, including the WTO, that are in some way involved with food security. Its three-fold aims are to take immediate steps to increase food supplies through, inter alia, emergency food assistance, to strengthen food and nutrition security in the long term by, inter alia, improving international food markets and to strengthen the global information and monitoring system on food security. The UN Special Rapporteur on the Right to Food, Olivier De Schutter, has recommended stronger integration of food security issues, arising from the right to food, in trade policies, intellectual property regimes, competition laws and the regulatory framework governing supply chains in the agrifood sector in order to better protect the most vulnerable and the food insecure as a result of the global food security crisis. Yet, the Rapporteur's call for protectionist restrictions of trade in agriculture have provoked strong criticism from WTO members and the WTO Director-General.[121]

The definition of food security in the WTO context focuses narrowly on adequate supply of imported food into members' territories without any reference to a rights based approach. WTO members of the Cairns Group of agricultural exporting countries support liberalization and the elimination of trade distortions arising from agricultural support mechanisms. However, the removal of agricultural subsidies and resulting price rises on world markets could aggravate food insecurity still further in LDCs which rely on imports of subsidized grains and oil seeds from developed country members. By prohibiting quantitative export restrictions and promoting the 'binding' of tariffs (possibly including export duties), WTO rules also tend to promote supply of basic foodstuffs for LDCs and net-food importing developing countries, yet without securing effective access to food by poor people. WTO rules include a set of disciplines that specifically address issues of food security, which are contained in the 1994 Marrakesh Ministerial Decision on 'Measures Concerning the Possible Negative Effects of the Reform Programme on Least-Developed and Net-Food Importing Developing Countries' ('NFIDC Decision'). The NFIDC Decision anticipates the problem that the WTO agricultural reform programme could lead to many least-developed and net-food importing developing countries experiencing 'negative effects in terms of the availability of adequate supplies of basic foodstuffs from external sources on reasonable terms and conditions, including short-term difficulties in financing normal levels of commercial imports of basic

dies and net-food-importing developing countries see: C Breining-Kaufmann, 'The Right to Food and Trade in Agriculture' in Cottier, Pauwelyn and Bürgi (eds) (2005) 341–81.

[121] Cf. the 2011 report by O de Schutter, UN Human Rights Council's Special Rapporteur on the Right to Food, on *The WTO and the Post-Global Food Crisis Agenda: Putting Food Security First in the International Food System* (published on the website of the UN Office for the High Commissioner for Human Rights) and the criticism of its protectionist recommendations in an open letter by WTO Director-General P.Lamy posted on the WTO website on 14 December 2011 (referring also to written comments by the WTO Secretariat on an earlier draft of the report). See also: C Häberli and B Karapinar (eds), *Food Crisis and the WTO: World Trade Forum* (Cambridge: CUP, 2010).

foodstuffs' (paragraph 2). A series of specific measures, which WTO Member governments have agreed on in order to operationalise the NFIDC Decision, concern food aid, technical and financial assistance; differential treatment within the framework of any agreement on agricultural export credits; and access to the resources of international financial institutions. Monitoring of the NFIDC Decision is undertaken by the WTO Committee on Agriculture on an annual basis, with input from the main agencies involved in its implementation, ie, the International Grains Council, the IMF, the World Food Programme and the World Bank.

On food aid, the NFIDC Decision urges close cooperation with the Committee on Food Aid, established under the FAO Food Aid Convention 1999 as extended. Under this FAO Convention, all food aid to LDCs is provided in the form of grants. Additionally, the NFDIC Decision calls on WTO Members to give greater consideration to requests for technical and financial assistance to these countries in order to improve their agricultural productivity and infrastructure. The African Development Bank, the European Investment Bank, the FAO and the World Bank have all responded, with the IMF renewing its commitment to provide assistance to developing countries in order to cope with balance of payments shortfalls arising from multilateral trade liberalization. In the NFIDC Decision, ministers have also agreed to ensure that any agreement on export credits would include appropriate provisions on differential treatment for LDCs and NFIDCs (paragraph 4). According to a WTO Secretariat Note prepared for the WTO Committee on Agriculture,[122] the most important food commodity for LDCs and NFIDCs in terms of imports is wheat. In terms of the actual monitoring of the ability of LDCs and NFIDCs to finance their food imports, including cereals such as wheat, the Committee places significant reliance on the Inter-agency panel of financial and commodity experts, which includes the FAO, the International Grains Council, IMF and UNCTAD. The continuing effects of the agricultural reform process, including the rising food prices and food price volatility, on NFIDCs are part of the regular review process envisaged by the NFIDC Decision (paragraph 6) and have prompted the World Bank to establish a rapid response Food Security Fund for the poorest countries. As emphasized by World Bank President Robert Zoellick in contrast to the UN human rights rapporteur, 'the answer to food price volatility is not to prosecute or block markets, but to use them better'.[123] The mutual adjustment and coordinated administration of FAO, WTO, financial and human rights provisions on food security illustrate that a 'human rights approach' to trade regulation may not necessitate incorporation of explicit human rights guarantees into WTO law. As stated by the UN Special Rapporteur on the right to food, De Schutter, in his press release dated 23 December 2010 on his mission to China: 'The right to food depends on people having incomes that allow them to purchase food'. As 'the shrinking of arable land represents a major threat to the ability of China to maintain its current self-sufficiency in grain', and 'climate change will cause agricultural productivity to drop by 5 to 10 per cent by 2030 in the absence of mitigation actions',[124] an open world trading system guaranteeing access to food will be of ever greater importance.

[122] Implementation of the Decision on Measures Concerning the Possible Negative Effects of the Reform Programme on Least-Developed and Net Food-Importing Developing Countries, Note by the Secretariat, Revision, G/AG/W/Rev.12 (4 November 2009) 13.

[123] *cf* n 121 and R Zoellick, 'Free markets can still feed the world' *Financial Times* (6 January 2011) 11.

[124] *cf* www2.ohchr.org/English/issues/food/index.htm.

5 THE FAILURE TO CONCLUDE THE 'DOHA DEVELOPMENT ROUND' (DDR) NEGOTIATIONS AND THE FUTURE OF THE WORLD TRADING SYSTEM

Since LDCs became the majority of GATT contracting parties in the 1960s, they have insisted in all 'GATT Rounds' of multilateral trade negotiations on their 'special and differential treatment' as being 'essential to further the development of the economies of the less-developed countries' (Article XXXVI GATT). As the existing 'legal flexibilities' of GATT 1947 – for instance, for 'infant industry protection' and balance-of-payments restrictions of LDCs under Article XVIII GATT, non-reciprocal tariff liberalization and international 'commodity agreements' pursuant to Article XXXVI:8 GATT – were considered to be insufficient, the 1979 GATT Understanding on Special and Differential Treatment of LDCs ('Enabling Clause') provided an explicit legal basis for additional preferential treatment, notably by means of the GSP and preferential trade agreements among LDCs. The economic paradigm underlying the request by LDCs for 'legal flexibility' (eg, the idea of industrialization via import substitution) prompted most less-developed GATT contracting parties to refrain from ratifying the 1979 Tokyo Round Agreements on technical and other non-tariff barriers to trade. Yet, during the 1990s, legal exemptions of LDCs from GATT and WTO legal disciplines were increasingly recognized as being often politically, economically and legally counterproductive. The Uruguay Round Agreements were concluded as a 'single undertaking' (*cf* Article II WTO Agreement); only the 'Plurilateral Trade Agreements' in Annex 4 do not create rights or obligations for WTO members that have not accepted these agreements.

The WTO Agreement on Textiles and Clothing enabled the progressive liberalization and termination, by 1 January 2005, of the longstanding quantitative trade restrictions in the clothing and textiles sector, where LDCs had become highly competitive exporters. The 'domestic support commitments' and 'export subsidy commitments' under the WTO Agreement on Agriculture continue, however, to legalize vast trade-distorting subsidies granted by developed countries to the detriment of competing agricultural exports from LDCs. Many less-developed WTO members perceive the WTO Agreements on Agriculture, Textiles and TRIPS as evidence that WTO rules favour one-sidedly powerful trade interests in developed countries without adequate regard to the different trade interests of LDCs in limiting trade-distorting subsidies more evenly,[125] improving market access for competitive exports from LDCs and designing intellectual property protection with more regard for their development needs (eg, regarding protection of their 'traditional knowledge' and 'geographical indications', their need for transfer of technology and production of generic medicines). The focus of the DDR negotiations on 'development' was understood by LDCs as a collective effort at 'rebalancing' WTO rules for the benefit of the majority of LDCs; yet, the United States, for instance, perceived the focus on 'development' as requiring additional, welfare-increasing trade liberalization and reciprocal WTO commitments from LDCs. One important political lesson from the TRIPS Agreement has been that – in view of the mercantilist logic underlying reciprocity-based GATT/WTO negotiations – WTO Agreements introducing 'cross-issue linkages to overcome existing distributional conflicts' are 'likely to emerge when the interests

[125] R Rosa Cedro and B Furtado Vieira, 'John Rawls' Justice as Fairness and the WTO: A Critical Analysis on the Initial Position of the Multilateral Agricultural Negotiations' (2010) 3(2) *The Law and Development Review*.

of powerful states align and when concentrated interest groups within those states actively support cooperation'.[126] The past eight GATT Rounds on reciprocal trade liberalization had enabled governments to overcome the protectionist pressures from rent-seeking domestic producer interests at home by inducing export interests in additional market opportunities to support the conclusion of GATT agreements. Yet, the one-sided focus of the DDR on interests of LDCs and the unwillingness of the BRICS (Brazil, Russia, India, China, South Africa) to offer *new* market access liberalization going beyond their 'legal binding' of their unilaterally liberalized 'applied tariffs' had the consequence that producers in developed countries offered much less support for concluding the DDR negotiations.

Limitation of the DDR Agenda in 2003/2004

The 2001 WTO Ministerial Declaration launching the 'Doha Round' of multilateral trade negotiations in the WTO listed more than 20 different objectives of the negotiations, including the elaboration of multilateral competition, investment and environmental rules aimed at limiting market failures as well as governance failures distorting the world trading system. The Declaration noted not only that the 'multilateral trading system embodied in the World Trade Organization has contributed significantly to economic growth, development and employment throughout the past fifty years' (paragraph 1); it also emphasized that 'international trade can play a major role in the promotion of economic development and the alleviation of poverty' (paragraph 2).[127] WTO members place the 'needs and interests' of LDCs 'at the heart of the Work Programme adopted in this Declaration' (paragraph 2) and commit themselves

> to continue to make positive efforts designed to ensure that developing countries, and especially the least developed among them, secure a share in the growth of world trade commensurate with the needs of their economic development. In this context, enhanced market access, balanced rules, and well targeted, sustainably financed technical assistance and capacity-building programmes have important roles to play (paragraph 2).

More specific trade and development objectives include, inter alia, the 'objective of duty-free, quota-free market access for products originating from least-developed countries' (paragraph 42); an 'Integrated Framework for Trade-Related Technical Assistance to Least-Developed Countries' (paragraph 43); more effective 'special and differential treatment' of LDCs (paragraph 44); as well as a work programme for the 'fuller integration of small, vulnerable economies into the multilateral trading system' (paragraph 35). At the 2003 WTO Ministerial Conference at Cancun, some of these ambitious objectives (such as trade-related competition, investment and additional government procurement rules) were abandoned in response to objections from LDCs.[128] The WTO General Council Decision of 1 August 2004 'rededicates and recommits Members to fulfilling the development dimension of the Doha Development Agenda' and provided that, apart from trade facilitation, the other 'Singapore issues' (ie, trade-related competition rules,

[126] The quotations are from A Bradford, 'When the WTO Works, and How it Fails' (2010) 51 *Virginia Journal of International Law* 1, 51.

[127] *cf The Doha Declaration* (Geneva: WTO, 2002) 2.

[128] *cf* EU Petersmann (ed), *Developing Countries in the Doha Round. WTO Decision-making Procedures and Negotiations on Trade in Agriculture and Services* (Florence: Robert Schuman Centre, 2005).

investment rules, transparency in government procurement) will no longer form part of the Work Programme and Doha Round negotiations.[129] This limitation of the agenda responded to long-standing concerns expressed by many LDCs that both WTO law and the Agenda were not adequately reflecting the development priorities of LDCs (eg, concerning market access for agricultural exports from LDCs, limitation of domestic subsidies and export subsidies distorting agricultural trade).[130] Yet, the lack of WTO competition rules and of transparency in government procurement practices impedes consumer welfare especially in LDCs and undermined the credibility of governments in LDCs without adequate competition and government procurement laws.

The Doha Round negotiations from 2001 until 2011 demonstrated the limits of the WTO's capacity to regulate market failures as well as governance failures by consensus-based negotiations on new trade, competition, investment, government procurement, environmental rules and trade facilitation. The ambitious 'Doha Development Agenda' approved at the 2001 Doha Ministerial Conference – including also provisions for additional market access opportunities for exports from LDCs, a new Trade Facilitation Agreement and new forms of special and differential treatment of LDCs based no longer only on exceptions, but also on 'graduated implementation' of WTO rules with due regard to their different levels of competitiveness[131] – generated excessive expectations. The focus on 'development' and on a 'Round for free for LLDCs' prompted various groups of LDCs to resist reciprocal trade liberalization and additional market regulation. The prioritization of negotiating agreements on agriculture and NAMA (= non-agricultural market access) delayed negotiations on liberalization in services trade, which represents 50 to 70 per cent of the GDP of WTO members; sector-specific, legal liberalization and regulation of services trade are further complicated by the lack of an across-the-board 'liberalization formula' (as used for liberalization of trade in goods).[132] In view of many years of unilateral and preferential trade liberalization preceding and during the Doha Round, the trade liberalization negotiations may only result in legally 'binding' existing trade liberalization rather than delivering 'new additional market access'. The 2011 'Bhagwati/Sutherland High Level Expert Group Report'[133] demonstrated that concluding the DDR in 2011 could offer more welfare gains than in previous GATT/WTO Rounds. Yet, notably the United States, Brazil, China, India and too many other WTO members gave in to protectionist pressures at home and refused to make the necessary compromises.

The failure to conclude the DDR negotiations in 2011

At the WTO General Council meeting in February 2010, Director-General Pascal Lamy reported that – although some technical progress continued to be made in the Doha

[129] For an overview of these negotiations on the 'Singapore issues' see: Petersmann (2005).

[130] For economic, legal and political criticism of the WTO system from the perspective of LDCs see the various contributions to: Yong-Shik Lee (ed), *Economic Development Through World Trade. A Developing World Perspective* (Alphen aan den Rijn: Kluwer, 2008).

[131] *cf* T Cottier, 'From Progressive Liberalization to Progressive Regulation in WTO Law' (2006) 9 *JIEL* 779–821.

[132] PA Messerlin, 'The Doha Round' in A Lukauskas, RM Steren and G Zanini (eds), *Handbook of Trade Policy for Development* (Oxford: OUP, 2011); F Ismail, *Reforming the WTO: Developing Countries in the Doha Round* (Geneva: CUTS International and Friedrich Ebert Stiftung, 2009).

[133] See n 48.

Round negotiations across the negotiating agenda – gaps remained due to the lack of the necessary political will to make the liberalization commitments enabling a successful conclusion of the negotiations. The WTO's week-long 'stocktaking' of the Doha Round negotiations in March 2010 ended without a breakthrough on the three most controversial issues of agriculture, industrial market access and services; while the United States claims more concessions especially from Brazil, China and India, developing countries criticize notably the United States for being unwilling to make concessions. Even though the seventh WTO Ministerial Conference in December 2009 had called for concluding the negotiations in 2010, the continued lack of 'fast-track authority' from the US Congress and the US midterm elections in November 2010 contributed to the fact that the G20 summit meeting in June 2010 did not even refer to conclusion of the Doha Round negotiations before the end of 2010 as a realistic option. A *Financial Times* editorial of 30 December 2010 concluded that 2010 was 'A bad year for global governance – The world did not rise above short-term crisis policies'.

As the negotiations aim at a 'single undertaking' that must be approved by consensus of all WTO members, the dissatisfaction of important WTO members and domestic interest groups with the negotiating proposals continued to prevent agreement in 2011. For example:

- Proposals by the richer LDCs (such as Brazil, China and India) to leave their applied, average tariff rates for agricultural goods essentially unchanged (at about 13.5 per cent), to reduce tariff rates for manufactured goods only slightly (from 6.4 per cent to 5.6 per cent) and to insist on 'safeguard clauses' authorizing unilateral adjustments of their agricultural import tariffs by a margin of about 30 per cent were criticized by some developed countries as offering insufficient new market access and inadequate legal security.[134]
- Proposals by developed countries to limit their agricultural subsidies (such as US subsidies for cotton) and to further open their markets (eg, for EC imports of bananas) were criticized by LDCs as offering too few export opportunities (eg, for agricultural exports and services from LDCs) with too little protection against trade-distorting subsidies.
- The proposals for 'rule-making' (eg, additional legal disciplines on anti-dumping measures, subsidies, geographical indications) remain contested by vested interests.
- The market access commitments, national treatment commitments and additional commitments under the General Agreement on Trade in Services (GATS) are widely perceived as inadequate.
- The international food, financial and climate change crises have lead to new regulatory problems (eg, export restrictions introduced in response to the food and energy crises, inadequate regulation of financial services, risk of WTO-inconsistent carbon taxes and 'border tax adjustments' in the context of a 'Kyoto II' Protocol to the UN Framework Convention for Climate Change) that raised doubts about the adequacy of the DDR Agenda and may have to be addressed in the WTO.
- The contraction of world trade caused by the financial crisis prompted some countries to increase tariffs in order to cope with adjustment problems, thus illustrating the

[134] These and the following figures are taken from: A Mattoo and A Subramaniam, 'From Doha to the Next Bretton Woods. A New Multilateral Trade Agenda' (January/February 2009) *Foreign Affairs* 15 ff.

importance of legally binding 'applied tariff ceilings' in order to prevent countries from raising their tariffs to their often much higher 'legally bound tariffs'.[135]

- The lack of a non-plenary WTO Executive Council for initiating reforms and 'consensus-building', the lack of a clear mandate of the WTO Director-General and WTO Secretariat for defending the common interests of all WTO members and the inadequate use of 'plurilateral agreements' (Article II:3 WTO Agreement) in WTO practice aggravate the collective action problems in the plenary WTO bodies and negotiating groups for the collective supply of 'WTO club goods' (such as collective rulemaking and trade liberalization among WTO members) or 'global public goods' (eg, a rules-based world trading system benefiting all countries). As 'member-driven governance' by WTO members tends to focus on the pursuit of national or group interests, the WTO Secretariat was much less involved in the DDR negotiations compared with the previous Uruguay Round negotiations.

At an informal Trade Negotiations Committee meeting in July 2011, WTO Director-General Pascal Lamy confirmed that there was 'consensus that the full DDA package would not be possible by the end of the year'; he further sensed a 'collective assessment that the LDC-Plus package as we framed it in May is not taking shape as we would have wished'; some WTO members felt 'that the LDC component alone would not address their constituency requirements and that there had to be a "plus" element in addition to the LDC part of the package'. Lamy criticized 'the paralysis in the negotiation function of the WTO, whether it is on market access or on the rule-making'.[136] The WTO's World Trade Report 2011 offered empirical evidence for the fact that trade liberalization and rulemaking was increasingly shifting to the almost 300 preferential trade agreements concluded by WTO members, entailing additional market segmentation due to discriminatory trade preferences and divergent market regulations.[137] Without reforms of the deficiencies in the WTO legal framework (as discussed in section 2) and renewed efforts at multilateralizing preferential arrangements, consensus-based WTO negotiations are unlikely to meet the regulatory challenges of the world trading system in the twenty-first century. The two most significant outcomes of the eighth WTO Ministerial Conference in December 2011 were the admission of four new WTO members (Russia, Montenegro and the two Pacific islands Vanuatu and Samoa) and the agreement by 42 WTO members on a new plurilateral Government Procurement Agreement improving the disciplines for this key sector of the economy and expanding the market access coverage valued at between 80 and 100 billion dollars a year. The inability of WTO members to conclude their DDR negotiations and to deliver a new round of trade liberalization raises doubts about the ability of the WTO to meet the regulatory challenges of the twenty-first century.

[135] Recent estimates suggest that, if WTO members were to raise their applied tariffs to their currently legally bound ceilings, applied tariffs would double, leading to a decrease in world economic welfare of $500 billion.

[136] Quoted from: *WTO News* (26 July 2011).

[137] World Trade Report 2011: *PTAs and the WTO: From Coexistence to Coherence* (Geneva: WTO, July 2011). The Report examines the continuing proliferation of preferential trade agreements, the decreasing importance of tariff preferences, the increasing regulation of 'deeper integration', and the impact of these developments on the WTO.

Competing regional and bilateral trade liberalization and regulation as inevitable 'second-best policy'

The de facto 'shelving' of the DDR negotiations by the 2011 WTO Ministerial Conference left open whether WTO members might compromise on a more limited package of negotiating issues beneficial for all WTO members. In view of the United States' insistence on additional market access commitments, WTO negotiators are more likely to focus on sub-optimal preferential and plurilateral trade agreements (eg, on liberalization of trade in services). Just as consensus on the 1994 WTO Agreement was politically possible only after many years of prioritizing regional free trade and plurilateral trade agreements (like the 1979 Tokyo Round Agreements ratified only by limited numbers of GATT contracting parties), the collective action problems impeding conclusion of the Doha Round negotiations are likely to be overcome only after circumventing the cumbersome WTO negotiating procedures (eg, the 'single undertaking' and 'consensus' rules where anyone can block a deal) and limited mandate of the DDR negotiations (eg, the exclusion of competition and investment rules). Even the proposals for preferential treatment of LDCs (like 'duty free, quota free' preferences for LLDCs, 'trade facilitation') remain contested also by LDCs and vested interests complaining of 'preference erosion' and of inadequate 'export capacities' for benefiting from 'trade facilitation' (which would also increase import competition in LDCs). Even declaring the Doha Round negotiations 'dead' would not avoid that the regulatory challenges of the Doha Round, the lack of trust among WTO negotiators, and domestic opposition will continue to impede future WTO negotiations and rulemaking in the WTO. The coordination, surveillance and dispute settlement functions of the WTO are likely to remain of crucial importance for the world trading system. Its liberalization and regulatory functions, however, risk shifting to regional and plurilateral trade negotiations outside the WTO.

The in excess of 70 regional trade agreements (RTAs) concluded by WTO members since 2003 illustrate that RTAs are increasingly perceived as alternative fora for 'competitive trade liberalization' and trade regulation outside the framework of the consensus-based WTO negotiations, especially in case of the 'new generation' of 'deep economic integration agreements' negotiated by the EU as illustrated by the 2010 free trade agreement between the EU and Korea. Bilateral and regional trade liberalization are sub-optimal alternatives[138] to non-discriminatory liberalization; but they offer quicker welfare gains and 'deeper' legal harmonization of domestic market regulations. By putting pressure on third WTO members to participate in multilateral trade liberalization, RTAs may reduce collective action problems in the WTO, for instance by setting incentives for integrating and 'multilateralizing RTAs' inside the WTO system.[139] RTAs enable like-minded countries to realize trade liberalization and trade regulation, and to reach bilateral or plurilateral agreement on 'special and differential treatment' of LDCs, without opposition from third WTO members. Yet, there are also clear limits to what can be

[138] On the importance of always considering one's 'Best Alternative to a Negotiated Agreement' (= BATNA) see: R Fisher, *Getting to Yes. Negotiating Agreement without Giving In* (London: Random House Books, 1999). On the political dimensions of many RTAs (including the 'diminished giant syndrome' prompting the EU and United States to use their diminished economic power outside the WTO) see also EU Petersmann, 'The WTO and Regional Trade Agreements as Competing *Fora* for Trade Liberalization and Trade Regulation' in L Bartels and F Ortino (eds) (2006) 281–312.

[139] *cf* R Baldwin and P Low (eds), *Multilateralizing Regionalism* (Cambridge: CUP, 2009).

achieved in RTAs compared with worldwide WTO negotiations. For example, certain reforms of non-tariff barriers (like anti-dumping regulations and agricultural subsidies) may be politically acceptable only as parts of global WTO agreements.

The initiatives for transforming RTAs into, for instance, an ASEAN Community, a Southern African Community, Andean, Central and South American Economic Communities reflect the European experience that mutual agreement on regional trade liberalization and economic integration may depend on embedding the 'economic bargains' into a broader constitutional framework of 'just rules', 'fair procedures', 'integration law' and 'community institutions' supported by domestic citizens, business, governments and non-governmental constituencies as being mutually beneficial not only for producers and export industries, but also for consumers and non-economic citizen-interests (like rule of law and peaceful cooperation among neighbouring countries in Africa, Asia and Latin America). Compared with multilateral negotiations among 153 WTO members with diverse and often conflicting trade policy objectives, RTAs enable agreements among limited 'coalitions of the willing' and the setting-up of institutions helping to reach politically and socially acceptable compromises (eg, facilitated by means of financial compensation and 'capacity building') for the collective supply of regional 'public goods.' The transformation of national into global public goods (like an open world trading system) passes often inevitably through regional and inter-regional public goods, such as the EU free trade agreements with non-European African, Caribbean and Pacific countries, Chile, Korea and Mexico. The more the failure of the DDR negotiations shifts trade liberalization and trade regulation to bilateral and regional agreements, the more 'multilateralizing' and legally consolidating bilateral and regional market liberalization and regulation will become a future task of the WTO.

Risks of 'regulatory capture' of WTO rulemaking and the need for 'trade facilitation' in LDCs

'Capture theories' present international rules and organizations like the WTO as institutions designed to help governments to resist domestic pressures for welfare-reducing trade protection in order to promote national as well as international public goods more effectively. Yet, the lack of WTO rules protecting non-discriminatory conditions of competition and consumer welfare, like the GATT/WTO rules justifying welfare-reducing trade restrictions and trade distortions to the detriment of exports from LDCs (eg, of textiles, clothing and agricultural products), illustrate that GATT/WTO rules themselves have been drafted ('captured') for the benefit of powerful producer interests in developed countries and of democratically unaccountable rulers.[140] From the point of view of citizens benefiting from an open world trading system, the intergovernmental WTO rules and institutions fail to protect the general citizen interests in maximizing consumer welfare through open markets and non-discriminatory conditions of competition. Idealists view the WTO as an instrument for promoting economic welfare through trade and efficient use of policy instruments. Realists counter that GATT and WTO rules and negotiations are no less used for justifying trade protection, trade discrimination and the

[140] *cf* D Zang, 'Divided by Common Language: "Capture" Theories in GATT/WTO and the Communicative Impasse' (2010) 32 *Hastings International & Comparative Law Review* 423, 470 ff.

redistribution of income for the benefit of rent-seeking interest groups by means of power politics (eg, 'voluntary export restrictions' imposed by developed countries). The lack of economic rationality of many WTO rules on import protection (eg, by means of discriminatory anti-dumping measures) and agricultural export subsidies illustrates the ambivalence of the economic functions and political exceptions of GATT/WTO rules, as reflected also in the mercantilist terminology of some WTO rules (eg, on 'tariff concessions'). The disregard for WTO legal disciplines on subsidies during the 2008/2009 financial crisis (eg, in the case of automobile subsidies) confirms the statement by WTO Director-General Pascal Lamy: 'if the rules are not perceived as serving national interests at the same time as promoting international cooperation, adherence will prove no less elusive than the holy grail'.[141]

The reciprocity principle underlying the WTO objective of 'reciprocal and mutually advantageous arrangements directed to the substantial reduction of tariffs and other barriers to trade' (Preamble WTO Agreement) is based more on political than on economic rationales. In the Doha Round negotiations, realists blame the lack of reciprocity (eg, between the EU offer for 'agricultural access' to the EU market, the US offer for limiting trade-distorting US subsidies for agricultural producers, the offers by LDCs for access of industrial goods and services to their respective markets) as the major stumbling block preventing a 'grand bargain'. Yet, economists counter that the 'balance of concessions' may exist only in the eyes of the negotiators. The strong economic growth in China and India promoted by unilateral trade liberalization over the past years offers empirical evidence that the alleged 'reciprocity advantages' may be smaller than the gains from unilateral liberalization and the opportunity costs of delaying conclusion of the Doha negotiations by more years. Some objectives in the Preamble of the WTO Agreement – such as recognition of the 'need for positive efforts designed to ensure that developing countries, and especially the least developed among them, secure a share in the growth in international trade commensurate with the needs of their economic development' – reflect principles of distributive justice and solidarity underlying the DDR negotiations on 'trade facilitation' and 'aid for trade'. Many economists emphasize that trade liberalization by developed countries opening additional export opportunities for LDCs would offer much more economic gains than the decreasing financial assistance from developed countries.

Discretionary domestic trade policymaking processes (eg, on the imposition of anti-dumping duties and other import protection) tend to be dominated by producer interests and bureaucratic and political self-interests (eg, in limiting judicial accountability of trade politicians) rather than by general citizen interests in promoting consumer welfare and citizen rights. The treatment of citizens as marginal objects of non-transparent 'benevolent trade governance' alienates citizens and justifies their widespread, democratic distrust vis-à-vis intergovernmental power politics in the WTO. Due to political pressures from governments, domestic courts in most WTO member countries – and also in constitutional democracies like the United States and the EU – all too often disregard WTO dispute settlement rulings and WTO obligations of the governments concerned, thereby further undermining rule of law and domestic consumer welfare.

[141] P Lamy, Foreword to the *World Trade Report 2006: Exploring the Links between Subsidies, Trade and the WTO* (Geneva: WTO, 2006) v. The report analyzes the differing views among WTO members as to whether the WTO subsidy rules are tight enough to prevent unwarranted trade distortions, or accommodating enough to allow governments to pursue economic and non-economic policy objectives which they consider to be important.

The WTO exceptions for free trade areas and customs unions – by requiring reciprocal liberalization of trade restrictions 'with respect to substantially all the trade in products originating in such territories' (Article XXIV:8 GATT) – protect consumer welfare more comprehensively than power-oriented, producer-driven GATT/WTO negotiations on reciprocal trade liberalization and trade regulation. The experience of rights-based European economic law confirms that – unless trade policy discretion is legally limited by rights of citizens and their multilevel judicial protection – governments risk giving in to protectionist pressures from powerful interest groups. The phasing out of the International Textiles Agreement in 2004, the July 2004 WTO Framework Agreement on the liberalization of cotton trade and the elimination of US cotton subsidies and the 'Enhanced Integrated Framework' of IMF, World Bank and WTO financial and technical assistance for LDCs ('aid for trade') illustrate successful struggles of LDCs for adjusting WTO rules to their special development needs, for example by insisting on more effective WTO legal disciplines on market distortions by developed countries and on additional WTO commitments for 'trade facilitation' and 'aid for trade'.[142] At the second 'Global Review of Aid for Trade' conference held in July 2009 at the WTO, WTO members committed several billions of dollars to 'aid for trade' programmes. LDCs lacking human, institutional and production capacities need such development assistance in order to

- realize the benefits from trade liberalization by regulating domestic markets;
- improve their infrastructures and competitiveness;
- enhance their ability to meet standards in developed export markets;
- improve their institutional capacity to engage in trade negotiations;
- make use of WTO legal and dispute settlement remedies; and
- better implement their WTO obligations inside their own economies.[143]

LDCs reliant on only a few imports and exports may also require adjustment assistance to cope with trade-related adjustment problems (eg, in order to redeploy labour from import-competing sectors to export sectors in response to price changes, to respond to 'preference erosion', or to limit higher food costs in net-food importing LDCs if developed countries reduce their subsidies for agricultural exports).

Hence, 'aid for trade' is increasingly recognized as an essential component of 'development' and of 'special and differential treatment', linking trade commitments in the multilateral trading system with the domestic capacity of poor countries to meet them and to develop their regional economic cooperation.[144] The various trade facilitation and

[142] For an overview see: GP Sampson and WB Chambers (eds), *Developing Countries and the WTO. Policy Approaches* (New York: United Nations University Press, 2008); D Njinkeu and H Cameron (eds), *Aid for Trade and Development* (Cambridge: CUP, 2008); *Aid for Trade. Evolution of a Timely Initiative* (Geneva: AITIC, 2009); *Aid for Trade at a Glance: 2009* (Geneva: WTO/OECD, 2009); *Unlocking Global Opportunities. The Aid for Trade Program of the World Bank Group* (Washington: World Bank, 2009).

[143] The Negotiating Group on Trade Facilitation has prepared a comprehensive *Draft Consolidated Negotiating Text* for a new WTO Agreement on Trade Facilitation (TN/TF/W/165/Rev.6, 22 December 2010) aimed at facilitating domestic implementation of WTO obligations under Arts III, V, VIII and X GATT (eg, regarding prior publication of trade regulations, impartiality, non-discrimination and transparency of fees, charges and formalities connected with importation and exportation, release and clearance of goods by customs administrations, freedom of transit).

[144] For 13 case studies illustrating the vastly different trade-development-poverty reduction linkages in LDCs with different economic resources and 'supply capacities' see: MA Razzaque and S Raihan (eds), *Trade-Development-Poverty Linkages: Reflections from Selected Asian and Sub-Saharan African Countries*, 2 vols (Jaipur: CUTS, 2008).

'aid for trade' programmes, which coordinate (eg, through the 'Enhanced Integrated Framework') the trade-related, financial and technical assistance of the WTO, IMF, World Bank and of other UN institutions and special trust funds, have rightly abandoned 'the same size fits all philosophy' in favour of country specific capacity-building assistance (eg, for promoting private sector capacity to produce and trade, trade-related infrastructures for domestic implementation of WTO obligations, and regional trade developments).[145]

A 'human rights approach' to the Doha Round Agreements lacks political support

The presentations in the WTO by the UN human rights rapporteurs on the human right to health (Paul Hunt) and the human right to food (Olivier De Schutter) of their respective reports on the impact of these human rights on the world trading system have led to controversial discussions among WTO members on whether WTO rules (eg, on safeguard measures, agricultural subsidies, intellectual property rights and compulsory licences) are flexible enough to protect and promote human health and food security in less-developed WTO members.[146] The adoption by WTO Members of 'waivers' and of an amendment of the TRIPS Agreement in order to facilitate compulsory licensing by LDCs (eg, of intellectual property rights for generic pharmaceuticals and seeds),[147] like the 'L'Aquila Food Security Initiative' approved by the Group of Eight industrialized countries on 10 July 2009 in order to complement international food aid by financial support for agricultural production and related investments for 'food security' in LDCs,[148] illustrate how human rights concerns about food security and health security may influence the international trading system (eg, WTO rules and practices on protection of intellectual property rights and on agricultural trade liberalization). The ratification of the 2005 Protocol Amending the TRIPS Agreement, which was designed to provide an expeditious solution to the difficulties that WTO members with insufficient or no manufacturing capacities in the pharmaceutical sector could face in making effective use of compulsory licensing under the TRIPS Agreement, so far by only about 30 WTO members confirms, however, the previous experience under GATT 1947 that formal amendments of worldwide treaties risk never entering into force.[149] Yet, as the WTO waiver for compulsory licences continues until the entry into force of the Amendment Protocol,

[145] *cf* WTO Aid for Trade Task Force, *Recommendations of the Task Force on Trade for Aid*, WT/AFT/1 (27 July 2006).

[146] See n 121 above and, eg, UN Doc A/HRC/10/5/Add.2 (4 February 2009) (Report of the Special Rapporteur on the right to food, Olivier de Schutter: *Mission to the WTO*), which was presented by de Schutter to the WTO Committee on Agriculture on 2 July 2009; E/CN.4/2004/49/Add.1 (1 March 2004) (Report of Special Rapporteur P Hunt on the Rights of Everyone to the Enjoyment of the Highest Attainable Standard of Physical and Mental Health: *Mission to the WTO*).

[147] *cf* FM Abbott, 'The WTO Medicines Decision: World Pharmaceutical Trade and the Protection of Public Health' (2005) 99 *AJIL* 317ff; Hestermeyer (2007) 255 ff.

[148] *cf* R Johnson, *Food Security: The Role of Agricultural Trade* (Washington: International Policy Council, 2009) who argues that successful agricultural trade liberalization requires a shared vision of a global food system that ensures food security, food safety and sustainability.

[149] *cf* M Kennedy, 'When will the Protocol Amending the TRIPS Agreement Enter into Force?' (2010) 13 *JIEL* 459–73. Entry into force of the Protocol requires ratification by two-thirds of the 153 WTO members. One reason for the limited number of acceptances is due to the ratification by the EU without additional ratifications by the 27 EU member states, which remain autonomous WTO members.

neither the disagreement among WTO members on the human rights dimensions of WTO rules nor the little interest shown by LDCs in ratifying the Amendment Protocol (Rwanda remained the only sub-Saharan African country having ratified the Protocol by 2010) offer evidence for the claim (raised ever less frequently by human right advocates) that WTO rules are not flexible enough for respecting, protecting and fulfilling human rights in the trade policies of WTO members.

The central premise of constitutional theory – ie, that constitutional principles and restraints are necessary for limiting abuses of legislative, administrative, judicial and also private power – also holds true for intergovernmental politics in international organizations that are not effectively controlled by parliaments, courts, 'deliberative democracy', participatory democracy, constitutional restraints and human rights. The state-centred, intergovernmental focus of international law and international organizations on *intergovernmental* rights and foreign policy discretion reflects a medieval neglect for citizen rights and consumer welfare, which are not adequately protected in the governmental distribution of 'protection rents' in response to domestic, political pressures. The legitimacy of the WTO is further challenged by the fact that, from the perspective of Rawlsian principles of justice emphasizing the *domestic* causes of unnecessary poverty and the comparative advantages of a 'transfer branch' of governments as the most efficient social policy instrument, LDC claims for preferential treatment in the WTO often fail to demonstrate that governments maintaining sub-optimal trade and market restrictions are actually committed to maximizing the human development of their citizens. Development and human rights bodies – such as the UN Human Rights Council, the UN Committee on Economic, Social and Cultural Rights, or the UN Committee on the Rights of the Child – rightly call for 'human rights assessments' and democratic review of national trade policy measures on the basis of human rights standards like transparency, accountability, participation, non-discrimination and access to essential resources and social protection necessary for a life in dignity. Such promotion of 'deliberative democracy' could contribute to limiting welfare-reducing trade restrictions and to using alternative, more efficient policy instruments and development-oriented reforms of WTO rules.

The consensus practices in WTO decision-making and WTO amendment procedures make it unlikely that WTO members will ever agree on including human rights clauses into future WTO agreements or on refocusing the WTO Trade Policy Review Mechanism on country specific linkages of trade liberalization, development and trade-related adjustment problems with due regard to poverty reduction and human rights. Many WTO diplomats, notably from non-democratic countries, have self-interests in defining the WTO objective of 'sustainable development' without reference to human rights. The Doha Development Agenda and the proposed Trade Facilitation Agreement offer opportunities for linking WTO rules to financial and technical assistance (eg, by the World Bank Group) in order to help LDCs in their domestic implementation of WTO obligations and render trade liberalization agreements more effective instruments for promoting consumer welfare. The human right to democratic self-government would benefit from governments publicly explaining to their citizens the contribution of their trade and economic policies to promotion of human welfare and human rights. Yet, worldwide economic organizations like the WTO must respect the reality that their member states continue to have diverse conceptions of human rights, democratic self-governance and 'sustainable development'.

The need for clarifying 'principles of justice' case-by-case as relevant legal context for interpreting WTO rules

Failure of the DDR negotiations on further improvements of the WTO dispute settlement system remains unlikely to adversely affect the WTO dispute settlement rules and procedures. As illustrated by the WTO Appellate Body findings on the illegality of 'zeroing practices' in the calculation of anti-dumping duties based on 'fair price comparisons' and on the legal 'precedent effects' of established WTO Appellate Body jurisprudence,[150] the WTO jurisprudence has also begun clarifying 'principles of justice' and fairness that may be of contextual importance for interpreting WTO rules requiring fair procedures, due process of law and respect for legal 'predictability' (*cf* Article 3 DSU) and 'equity' (*cf* Article XVI:3 GATT). There is ample evidence that trade liberalization may not only *promote* human rights by enhancing the available quantity, quality and diversity of goods and services, competition and the efficient use of scarce resources. Trade policy decisions may also *adversely affect* access to essential medicines, to education materials, social security (eg, of children and poor farmers), the traditional livelihoods of indigenous people, or the protection of the environment and of scarce, natural resources. Yet, WTO members only rarely invoke 'principles of justice' in WTO dispute settlement proceedings, perhaps also in order to avoid counterclaims that governments calling for distributive justice in the WTO should prove their own commitment to justice as defined by human rights.

As trade liberalization tends to be beneficial for poor countries no less than for rich countries, a general exemption of LDCs from the WTO's reciprocity principle could impede their economic development. Non-reciprocity should depend on the country-specific adjustment problems, adjustment capabilities and development needs in the respective LDCs. As the UN defines the 50 LLDCs by their low GDP, by their 'human resource weakness' and 'economic vulnerability', the 32 WTO Members with LLDC status may need exemption from reciprocal liberalization commitments, as it has been agreed in the Doha Round offers for 'duty free, quota free' trade preferences for LLDCs. The EU justified an additional offer of a 'Round for Free' (ie, non-reciprocal, duty free and quota free market access) for 58 LDCs from Africa, the Caribbean and the Pacific on similar grounds (eg, their 'small, weak and vulnerable economies'). The 'upper income developing countries' cooperating in the 'Geneva G20' group have made their market access commitments subject to various conditions aimed at enhancing their adjustment capabilities, such as additional export opportunities in agriculture, protection of food security and rural development in LDCs, and liberalization of international movements of natural services suppliers. Since more than 70 per cent of poor people in LDCs live in rural areas, LDCs legitimately insist that their farmers must be protected against the trade distortions caused by the high agricultural protectionism in developed countries and their subsidized exports of surplus products.

Many of the 'small, weak and vulnerable' WTO members cooperating in the 'G90' group emphasize the need for SDT for dealing with their special development challenges, such as preference erosion, dependence on commodities and food imports, rural development, food security and supply side limitations. Increasing their export capabilities

[150] See the analysis of this Appellate Body jurisprudence by: S Cho, 'Global Constitutional Lawmaking' (2010) 31 *University of Pennsylvania Journal of International Law* 621–78.

through 'aid for trade' and non-reciprocal liberalization of import barriers (eg, for cotton) in developed countries has been recognized as a crucial component of a future 'Doha bargain'.[151] The 2001 Doha Declaration further recognizes that 'technical cooperation and capacity building are core elements of the development dimension of the multilateral trading system'; 'sustainably financed technical assistance and capacity building programs have important roles to play'.[152] The WTO General Council's 'Framework Agreement' of July 2004 called more specifically for 'developing countries and in particular least developed countries to be provided with enhanced Trade-Related Technical Assistance and capacity building to increase their effective participation in the negotiations, to facilitate their implementation of WTO rules and to enable them to adjust and diversify their economies'.[153] Yet, many of the 88 proposals by LDCs for making SDT provisions in the WTO Agreements more 'precise, mandatory and operational' have remained controversial because their focus on 'policy space' left their contribution to promotion of human development, human rights and welfare-increasing trade for the benefit of citizens in LDCs doubtful.

'Corrective justice' calls for empowering and protecting LDCs and their citizens in the WTO Dispute Settlement System

The GATT 1947 was likened to a 'bicycle' driven by bi-level trade negotiations at national and intergovernmental levels and risking to topple down if negotiators allowed import-competing producers to block reciprocal trade liberalization. In GATT's dispute settlement system, power politics and asymmetries in 'legal resources' often favoured developed compared with less-developed countries; the latter often also lacked the legal expertise for using GATT law and dispute settlement procedures strategically.[154] The 'legalization' and ever more frequent use of the compulsory WTO dispute settlement system transformed the 'GATT 1947 bicycle' into a 'WTO tricycle' that is increasingly 'wheeled' by the WTO dispute settlement rulings clarifying and progressively developing WTO rights and obligations. LLDCs have so far rarely participated in WTO dispute settlement proceedings due to their limited WTO commitments and their weak institutional capacities to self-enforce their WTO rights through WTO legal, dispute settlement and retaliation procedures.[155] LDCs, by contrast, have – over the past years – become the main users of the WTO dispute settlement system challenging trade restrictions and trade distortions not only by developed, but also by other less-developed WTO members. In 2010, for example, the majority of WTO disputes initiated were brought by LDCs. Notably in the area of agricultural subsidies (such as EC subsidies for sugar, US subsidies for cotton), LDCs have successfully used the WTO dispute settlement system not only for enforcing their rights; their successful WTO complaints also improved their bargaining position in the Doha Round negotiations by clarifying the illegality of

[151] *cf ABC of Aid for Trade* (Jaipur: Cuts, 2007).

[152] WT/MIN801)/DEC/W/1, paras 2, 38.

[153] WT/L/579 (2004).

[154] *cf* Petersmann (1997) 66 ff.

[155] *cf* CP Bown, *Self-Enforcing Trade. Developing Countries and WTO Dispute Settlement* (Washington: Brookings Institution Press, 2009). Bangladesh has remained the sole LLDC having brought a complaint under the DSU so far, which was settled by consultations.

the trade-distorting subsidies concerned.[156] Since the inception of the WTO, almost 50 per cent of panellists have come from LDCs. Case studies demonstrate that the factual, political and legal help from non-governmental organizations inside LDCs (like domestic industry associations assisting in the collection of relevant information, provision of legal resources and political support by export industries), from international NGOs (like Oxfam, the International Centre for Trade and Sustainable Development) and from the Advisory Centre on WTO Law at Geneva has been of crucial importance assisting LDCs in winning WTO disputes even against the most powerful WTO members like the United States and the EU.[157]

As described in chapter V, protection of human rights and rule of law depend on procedural guarantees of 'access to justice' in terms of both access to courts and to effective legal remedies, including legal aid for the needy. The contribution of WTO law to 'sustainable development' in LDCs also depends, inter alia, on effective access of LDCs to the WTO legal and dispute settlement procedures for protecting 'rule of law', undertaking more actively WTO commitments helping LDCs to liberalize and regulate their domestic economies and for participating in the progressive clarification of contested WTO rights and obligations through WTO negotiations and dispute settlement procedures.[158] WTO law promotes access to justice by providing for two different kinds of special and differential treatment of LDCs:

1. Provisions specifying how generally applicable principles should be implemented in cases involving LDCs (eg, WTO provisions on composition of dispute settlement panels, determination of a 'reasonable period' for implementing dispute settlement findings) and WTO provisions compensating the lack of financial and legal resources of LDCs in WTO dispute settlement proceedings (eg, Article 27.2 DSU, the Advisory Centre for WTO Law), have proven effective and need to be further extended.
2. Procedural privileges exclusively available for LDCs only (*cf* Articles 3.12, 21.2, 21.7 and 8 DSU) have, however, been invoked only reluctantly and with limited success.[159]

Effective use of the WTO dispute settlement system by LDCs is closely linked to effective legal and judicial remedies at national levels, as illustrated by the private rights to initiate WTO dispute settlement proceedings pursuant to section 301 of the US Trade Act and the corresponding EC Trade Barriers Regulation, which have enhanced 'private–public partnerships' and available 'legal resources' in WTO litigation.[160] Some LDCs, like Brazil, have successfully enhanced their collaboration with private industries in jointly pursuing WTO dispute settlement proceedings challenging illegal market access barriers

[156] See: EU Petersmann, 'Strategic Use of WTO Dispute Settlement Proceedings for Advancing WTO Negotiations on Agriculture' in Petersmann (2005) 127–46.

[157] *cf* GC Shaffer and R Meléndez-Ortiz (eds), *Dispute Settlement at the WTO. The Developing Country Experience* (Cambridge: CUP, 2010); Advisory Centre on WTO Law, 2010 Report on Operations (Geneva 2011). See also the speech by WTO Director-General Pascal Lamy, 4 October 2011, on *The ACWL at Ten – Looking back, looking forward* (accessible on the WTO website at: www.wto.org).

[158] On 'legal assistance' for LDCs in the WTO dispute settlement system see, for instance, the annual reports of the Advisory Centre on WTO Law (eg, n 157).

[159] See: F Roessler, 'Special and Differential Treatment of Developing Countries under the WTO Dispute Settlement System' in F Ortino and EU Petersmann (eds) (2004) 87 ff.

[160] *cf* CT Garcia Molyneux, *Domestic Structures and International Trade. The Unfair Trade Instruments of the United States and the European Union* (Oxford: Hart Publishing, 2001); G Shaffer, *Defending Interests: Public–Private Partnerships in WTO Litigation* (Washington: Brookings Institution Press, 2003).

and trade-distorting subsidies in developed WTO members.[161] Proposals for introducing special WTO remedies for LDCs (such as financial damages and attorney's fee awards) remain controversial. The still limited number of LDCs actively using the dispute settlement panel, appellate and arbitration procedures of the WTO illustrates the need for additional financial, technical and legal assistance and 'capacity building' for the benefit of LDCs, which often lack a citizen-driven, transparent rule of law system limiting domestic and foreign power politics. The numerous proposals in the DDR negotiations for further improvements of the WTO's dispute settlement procedures have so far not led to agreement on major reforms.[162] Yet, the increasing recourse by LDCs to the WTO dispute settlement system reflects the insight that the effectiveness of the rights of LDCs under WTO law often depends on their judicial enforcement and clarification.

Need for reforming the 'single undertaking' requirement for WTO negotiations

The 1948 Havana Charter for an International Trade Organization never became effective since, following its rejection by the US Congress, other countries lost interest in joining the Agreement without the United States. The tariff liberalization resulting from the eight GATT Rounds of multilateral trade negotiations was implemented through Tariff Protocols providing for the entry into force of GATT 'schedules of concessions' on mutually agreed terms different from GATT amendment procedures, requiring a two-thirds majority decision only in case of Accession Protocols (Article XXXIII GATT). The 1964 and 1979 agreements on non-tariff barriers resulting from the Kennedy and Tokyo Rounds were concluded as self-standing agreements and entered into force only for the limited number of GATT contracting parties that ratified these agreements. The 1994 Uruguay Round Agreements were concluded as a 'single undertaking' and, following a decision taken by all GATT Contracting Parties in December 1994, entered into force for 'original members' either on 1 January 1995 or on the thirtieth day following their acceptance during 1995–96 (*cf* Articles XI, XIV WTO Agreement); for subsequently acceding countries and customs territories, the date of entry into force of the WTO Agreement was specified in their respective Accession Protocols (Article XII WTO Agreement). The decision to terminate GATT 1947 by the end of 1995 entailed a quasi-universal WTO membership of 153 WTO members (January 2012) covering about 95 per cent of world trade and conducting accession negotiations with more than 25 third countries. The 2001 Doha Ministerial Declaration provides that 'the conduct, conclusion and entry into force of the outcome of negotiations shall be treated as parts of a single undertaking'; but the Declaration postponed the decision on the adoption and implementation of future Doha Round Agreements until after the results of the negotiations in all areas have been established.[163] WTO members neither agree on replacing the WTO Agreement by new Doha Round Agreements (following the 'single undertaking approach' applied at the end of the Uruguay Round Agreements) nor on how to prevent

[161] *cf* Shaffer and Meléndenz-Ortiz (n 157) and G Shaffer, 'Developing Country Use of the WTO Dispute Settlement System: Why it Matters, the Barriers Posed, and its Impact on Bargaining' in J Hartigan (ed), *Trade Disputes and the Dispute Settlement Understanding of the WTO: An Interdisciplinary Assessment* (Bingley: Emerald Group Publishing, 2009).

[162] For a survey and analysis of these proposals, see Ortino and Petersmann (eds) (2004) chs 1 to 12.

[163] *Doha Declaration* (n 127) para 47.

that implementation of future Doha Agreements through WTO amendment procedures entails many years of delays, two classes of WTO membership and 'free-riding' by those WTO members which, following entry into force of the WTO amendments on ratification by two-thirds of the 153 WTO members, may prefer invoking and benefiting from the WTO non-discrimination commitments without ratifying the Doha Round Agreements.[164]

The GATT and WTO amendment procedures are cumbersome and time-consuming. As amendments of certain GATT and WTO provisions require unanimous acceptance by all members, a previous Protocol amending Part I of GATT 1947 was abandoned after 10 years because one GATT contracting party was unable to obtain parliamentary approval.[165] The last GATT amendment of 1965 adding Part IV on 'Trade and Development' to GATT 1947 achieved unanimous acceptance only in 1979. The 2005 WTO Protocol amending Article 31 of the TRIPS Agreement had been ratified, by the end of 2010, by only 31 out of 153 WTO members. As many future Doha Round Agreements are aimed at amending and supplementing numerous WTO agreements, the two-thirds requirements for amendments pursuant to Article X WTO Agreement – and the required 'three-fourths majority' for excluding 'any Member which has not accepted it within a period specified by the Ministerial Conference' (Article X:3) – appear to be unavoidable to the extent that Doha Round results cannot be given legal effect through modification of GATT and GATS schedules, a new Agreement replacing the existing WTO by a new 'WTO II', or by decisions of the WTO Ministerial Conference. For instance, if the 'negotiation phase' of the Doha Round could ever be successfully concluded with a consensus decision to proceed to the 'implementation phase' aimed at elaborating and signing a single DDR Protocol implementing the Doha Round Agreements to be ratified by national parliaments, the WTO members having ratified the Doha Agreements could insist on receiving a temporary 'WTO waiver' from their WTO most-favoured-nation commitments vis-à-vis those WTO members that fail ratifying the 'single DDR Agreement' and thereby also undermine the 'single WTO undertaking'. Obtaining the 'three-fourths' majority necessary for such a temporary waiver could be facilitated by granting longer transition periods to the least-developed WTO members, who have already been exempted from tariff reduction commitments in the Doha Round; the scope of such a 'waiver' could be limited to trade relations among those WTO members who could be reasonably expected to implement the 'single undertaking' by an agreed date. An alternative option could be implementing (part of the) DDR Agreements by means of temporary 'Plurilateral Agreements' (Annex 4 WTO Agreement) pending the procedures for formal amendments of the other WTO Agreements.[166] Rather than leaving entry into force of the Doha Round Agreements to the 'two-thirds' requirement with its risk of unpredictable delays, WTO members could also condition the entry into force of the Doha Round Agreements by additional 'critical mass provisions', target dates and other 'decisions' (eg, by the WTO Ministerial Conference pursuant to Article IV:1 WTO Agreement) to ensure overall reciprocity of their final bargain.

[164] *cf* M Kennedy, 'Two Single Undertakings – Can the WTO Successfully Implement the Results of a Round?' (2011) 14 *JIEL* 77–120.

[165] GATT BISD 15S/65.

[166] *cf* H Nottage and T Sebastian, 'Giving Legal Effect to the Results of WTO Trade Negotiations: An Analysis of the Methods of Changing WTO Law' (2006) 9 *JIEL* 989–1016.

As amendments of WTO rules usually apply only to those WTO members that have ratified the amendment, integrating future Doha Round Agreements into WTO law – even if done by a single 'protocol amendment' – will inevitably transform the WTO legal and institutional system by creating not only additional categories of WTO members with diverse legal rights and corresponding obligations; implementing the Doha Agreements may also require institutional amendments, for instance regarding amendments of WTO dispute settlement procedures and their application to new Doha Round Agreements like the Trade Facilitation Agreement that will not be applicable to any WTO member until it accepted it. Even more so than the 1994 WTO Agreement, a future Doha Round Implementation Protocol risks remaining an 'incomplete agreement' delegating the future clarification of numerous legal controversies to the WTO dispute settlement bodies whenever the political WTO bodies fail to adopt 'authoritative interpretations' (*cf* Article IX:2 WTO Agreement) or other agreed clarifications of WTO rules. The likely increase in recourse to WTO dispute settlement proceedings would increase the importance of further clarifying the 'legal-political equilibrium' among the political and judicial dimensions of the WTO legal and dispute settlement system. Just as European economic courts, similar to national courts in constitutional democracies, operate as parts of a 'four-stage process' (Rawls) of constitutional, legislative, administrative and judicial rule clarification reflecting different perspectives of 'public reason', WTO members and WTO dispute settlement bodies will have to further clarify the 'basic principles and objectives underlying this multilateral trading system' (WTO Preamble) in order to justify – notably in respect of domestic citizens – their often divergent interpretations and progressive clarification and development of WTO rules. This difficult task of multilevel judicial rule clarification and dispute settlement is explored in the concluding chapter. As in many national and regional jurisdictions, views about the appropriate 'institutional balance' between the legislative, executive and judicial organs remain contested also in the WTO and have been discussed in a number of WTO dispute settlement reports like India-Quantitative Restrictions,[167] Turkey-Textiles[168] and US-Poultry (China).[169]

[167] *cf* WT/DS90/AB/R, adopted September 1999.
[168] *cf* WT/DS34/AB/R, adopted November 1999.
[169] *cf* WT/DS392/R, adopted October 2010.

VIII

From 'Constitutional Nationalism' to Multilevel Judicial Protection of Cosmopolitan Rights in IEL

OVER THE PAST centuries, claims to supreme political and legal power over people (sovereignty) by rulers (eg, the Pope, emperors, monarchs, colonial powers) and states have become increasingly contested. The 'Westphalian' system of international law among sovereign states – based on *internal sovereignty* (as defined by constitutional law) and *external sovereignty* (as defined by state-centred international law) – was power-oriented and lacked democratic legitimacy, as illustrated by colonialism and imperial wars. Also the UN Charter and UN institutions (eg, the Security Council) remain based on power-oriented structures lacking input legitimacy (eg, in terms of respect for human rights and democracy) as well as output legitimacy (eg, in terms of reduction of unnecessary poverty). Even though proclaimed on behalf of 'We the Peoples of the United Nations determined . . . to reaffirm faith in fundamental human rights' (Preamble UN Charter), the intergovernmental structures of UN law have failed to effectively protect human rights in many UN member states, thereby undermining the democratic legitimacy and overall effectiveness of UN law.

Virtually all national constitutions subject the incorporation of international rules into their respective domestic legal system to constitutional safeguards, like parliamentary ratification of treaties and 'later-in-time rules' protecting the sovereign right of parliaments to override the domestic law effects of international treaties by later legislation. Following the postwar recognition of human rights and other 'principles of justice' as integral parts of national and international legal systems, national and international courts throughout Europe have interpreted international guarantees of freedom, non-discrimination and rule of law for the benefit of citizens even if the international rules were addressed to states without explicitly providing for cosmopolitan rights:

> [T]he fact that certain provisions of the Treaty are formally addressed to the Member States does not prevent rights from being conferred at the same time on any individual who has an interest in compliance with the obligations thus laid down (see Case 43/75 *Defrenne v Sabena* [1976] ECR 455, par. 31). Such consideration must, *a fortiori*, be applicable to Article 48 of the Treaty, which . . . is designed to ensure that there is no discrimination on the labour market.[1]

This multilevel, judicial clarification of international rules in conformity with constitutional principles of justice was accepted by citizens, parliaments and governments as a

[1] *cf* Case C-281/98, *Angonese* [2000] ECR I-4139.

justified, integral part of the constitutional 'four-stage sequence'[2] of progressive development and clarification of constitutional guarantees and 'public reason' through rule-making, rule application and judicial protection of individual rights for the benefit of citizens. The progressive 'constitutionalization' of European economic law through multilevel constitutional principles, rules, institutions and procedures emphasized that the legitimacy and effectiveness of European economic law – as an instrument for promoting consumer welfare and fundamental freedoms of domestic citizens – depend on its consistency with the multilevel human rights obligations and other constitutional obligations of governments as well as on multilevel judicial protection of rule of law for the benefit of citizens, with due respect for the legitimate diversity of constitutional democracies. Chapters I to VII argued that the human rights obligations of UN member states and the existential importance of the citizen-driven, global division of labour for individual and democratic self-development call for progressively extending 'multilevel cosmopolitan constitutionalism' so as to protect legitimate 'struggles for justice' and cosmopolitan rights beyond states.

OVERVIEW OF CHAPTER VIII

This chapter illustrates why multilevel judicial protection of cosmopolitan rights of producers, investors, traders and consumers in the international division of labour is essential for 'constitutionalizing' IEL and protecting human rights more effectively. As explained in the Introduction, human and cosmopolitan rights promote and protect reasonable autonomy of individuals as well as democratic and judicial 'public reason' necessary for institutionalizing 'just rules' and reasonable institutions as preconditions for rule of law and welfare. Cosmopolitan rights, democracy and rule of law limit state sovereignty and popular sovereignty by 'cosmopolitan constitutionalism' necessary for providing international 'aggregate public goods'; they can also be perceived as 'intermediate public goods' beneficial for all citizens, just as judgments by independent 'courts of justice' aimed at settling disputes peacefully and clarifying and protecting 'rule of law' and 'principles of justice' can be perceived as 'single best effort public goods'. Section 1 recalls why – in citizen-driven international economic relations – the constitutional principles of 'state sovereignty' and 'popular sovereignty' are increasingly interpreted in favour of 'individual sovereignty' and cosmopolitan rights limiting the 'rules of recognition' by empowering citizens to protect themselves more effectively against the ubiquitous 'governance failures' and 'market failures' distorting international competition. Section 2 discusses how judicial protection of cosmopolitan rights, 'participatory' and 'deliberative democracy' can limit intergovernmental power politics and compensate the decreasing effectiveness of parliamentary, democratic control of global economic governance. Sections 3 and 4 illustrate how courts throughout Europe – and increasingly also in international trade and investment adjudication beyond Europe – review the 'suitability', 'necessity' and 'proportionality' of government restrictions of economic rights and clarify indeterminate IEL rules with due regard to the interests of adversely affected citizens. Sections 5 and 6 conclude that 'multilevel judicial governance' can act as the

[2] On the explanation of the 'four-stage sequence' as 'part of a moral theory' of justice which may also guide constitutional bodies in their interpretation of constitutional and legislative rules, see: J Rawls (1971) 195 ff.

most independent, impartial 'guardian' of cosmopolitan rights and of the 'constitutional unity' of IEL; for, in contrast to political majority decisions, courts of justice must justify their judicial interpretations and enforcement of economic rules in terms of constitutional principles of justice and protection of human rights.

1 LIMITATION OF STATE SOVEREIGNTY BY CONSTITUTIONAL, POPULAR AND 'INDIVIDUAL SOVEREIGNTY' IN IEL REQUIRES PROTECTION OF COSMOPOLITAN RIGHTS

The claims by rulers to supreme ordering power ('political sovereignty') must be distinguished from democratic constitutional law as the legitimate legal source of sovereign powers ('constitutional sovereignty'), as well as from 'democratic sovereignty' and 'individual sovereignty' in the sense of the actual capacity of self-government by a democratic polity and individual citizens. Modern globalization is characterized by increasing economic, political, legal and other limitations of political sovereignty and by reallocation of government powers to 'We the people' (eg, in former communist countries), indigenous people, international organizations and individual human beings as legal subjects of 'inalienable' human rights. This dynamic transformation of the relevant 'interpretive community' for recognizing and developing international law continues to progressively limit the 'sovereign equality' of UN member states as one of the constitutional principles of the UN Charter (Article 2) by the 'right to self-determination of peoples' – as universally recognized in the UN Charter (eg, Articles 1, 73) and in the UN human rights covenants of 1966 (Article 1) – as well as by the universal recognition, in numerous UN human rights instruments, of 'the inherent dignity and of the equal and inalienable rights of all members of the human family [as] the foundation of freedom, justice and peace in the world' (Preamble of the 1966 UN ICESCR). Human rights, like democratic constitutions, proceed from the two premises that (1) human rights are not granted, but only recognized by governments; and (2) citizens constitute governments with limited powers that must be exercised for the protection of the human rights and public interests of their citizens.[3] The UN Human Rights Committee has rightly emphasized (eg, in its General Comments 24 and 26 on the UN Covenant on Civil and Political Rights) that even if human rights treaties are concluded among states, unilateral reservations and denunciations may be legally invalid and cannot take away 'inalienable' human rights of citizens,[4] just as democratic governments may lack powers to unilaterally abrogate constitutional rights of their citizens. In constitutional democracies and international legal systems with compulsory judicial review, legal interpretation and judicial protection of individual freedoms and rule of law are no longer 'Westphalian monopolies' of rulers and their diplomats. The universal recognition of human rights, including 'access to justice', provides for common constitutional principles connecting and coordinating national and international legal systems and judicial procedures for peaceful conflict resolution

[3] These constitutional premises prompted me to argue long since (eg, in EU Petersmann, 1991) that precise and unconditional, intergovernmental guarantees of freedom, non-discrimination and rule of law (eg, in GATT Arts II, III, XI:1) can serve 'constitutional functions' for enlarging corresponding, constitutional freedoms, other rights of citizens and 'rule of law' in mutually beneficial, international economic cooperation among citizens across discriminatory state boundaries.

[4] cf Compilation of General Comments and General Recommendations by Human Rights Treaty Bodies, UN Doc HRI/GEN/1, Rev.7 (2004).

based on judicial clarification of 'principles of justice' with due respect for 'constitutional pluralism'.

Human rights call for limiting state sovereignty by multilevel 'cosmopolitan constitutionalism' protecting cosmopolitan rights

Rawls' *Theory of Justice* explains why – in constitutional democracies – constitutional, legislative, administrative and judicial principles, rules and procedures should be interpreted and clarified from the point of view of reasonable citizens deliberating behind a 'veil of uncertainty'. Chapters II to VI of this book inferred from the universal recognition of 'inalienable rights' of all citizens a constitutional duty of 'courts of justice' to consider interpreting IEL and its 'rules of recognition' from similar constitutional and cosmopolitan perspectives. Chapters V and VI explained why the recognition of individuals and of people as 'primary subjects' also of international law entails a revival of the ancient constitutional ideal of *rule of law* as a constitutional restraint on the *rule by men* and their *rule by law*. In a globally interdependent world economy increasingly limited by transnational and 'global law', individual and democratic self-governance remains illusionary if compliance with agreed constitutional rules, democratic legislation and international agreements ratified by parliaments is not protected by governments and courts beyond state borders. The more the welfare of citizens depends on international law and on peaceful international cooperation, the more it becomes necessary to protect cosmopolitan rights and 'the sovereignty of the law'[5] also in international economic cooperation among citizens beyond Europe. The multilevel legal and judicial protection of transnational 'rule of law' in European human rights, economic and international investment law confirms that multilevel judicial protection of human rights and economic rights as constitutional foundation of self-governance of citizens in citizen-driven, political and economic markets is justifiable by the same 'cosmopolitan principles of justice', like respect for individual autonomy and responsibility.

Chapters II to V argued that human rights require the legal construction of an international 'social market economy' that must be legitimized and 'embedded' by new forms of participatory 'cosmopolitan democracy': the more remotely regional and worldwide governance institutions operate from citizens, the less effective *procedural* citizen rights for democratic participation, representation and parliamentary control risk becoming. This decreasing effectiveness of representative democracy beyond states must be compensated by *substantive*, cosmopolitan rights, and by their judicial protection through interrelated networks of national and international courts of justice, protecting transnational rule of law for the benefit of citizens. Similar to national administrative laws deriving democratic legitimacy and effectiveness from being instruments of democratic constitutionalism, so depend the democratic legitimacy and effectiveness of the emerging 'global administrative law' (eg, as applied in the operational work of global organizations) on protecting human rights and cosmopolitan interests of citizens. Constitutional approaches require that the interpretation and progressive development of IEL by political, administrative and judicial governance institutions remain democratically accountable and justifiable by 'public reason' and 'principles of justice'. For instance, respect for individual and

[5] *cf* FG Jacobs (2007).

democratic freedom entails diversity and regulatory competition – among individuals as well as among private and public, national, regional and worldwide organizations with diverse memberships. This legal diversity and non-discriminatory conditions of competition must be protected by competition rules and other 'cosmopolitan principles', including human rights, 'participatory' as well as 'deliberative democracy' so as to promote inclusive, coherent decision-making based on 'subsidiarity', avoidance of serious harm, satisfaction of basic human needs, the 'consistent interpretation principle' recognized in national and international legal systems and other 'constitutional principles'.

Chapters III and IV inferred from UN human rights law – for example, from the recognition that '(e)veryone has the right to recognition everywhere as a person before the law' (Article 6 UDHR), including the right 'to a social and international order in which the rights and freedoms set forth in this Declaration can be fully realized' (Article 28) – that respect for human dignity, liberty and other human rights – ie, *normative individualism* limiting state sovereignty, 'the will of the people' (Article 21 UDHR) and their 'right of self-determination' (Article 1 of the 1966 UN human rights covenants) – calls for cosmopolitan empowerment and protection of individuals in the international regulation of the division of labour. The universal recognition in UN human rights law – that '(a)ll human beings are born free and equal in dignity and rights' and 'endowed with reason and conscience' (Article 1 UDHR) – lends support to the view that economic cooperation among citizens and its legal regulation must also be based on respect for 'individual sovereignty' (eg, in the sense of moral, personal and legal autonomy), responsibility and on enabling individuals to fully develop their unique, human capacities.[6] Human dignity as a moral 'right to have rights' requires individuals to be treated as legal subjects rather than as mere objects of authoritarian government policies, especially in multilevel regulation of mutually beneficial, transnational economic cooperation among citizens. The authoritarian, state-centred practices of treating citizens as mere objects even in those fields of international law which regulate mutually beneficial private cooperation across frontiers (such as WTO law), need to be challenged in light of the human rights objective of empowering citizens and protecting human rights across national borders. From a human rights perspective, the legitimacy of intergovernmental organizations (such as the WTO) depends less on 'output legitimacy' (eg, in terms of promoting economic growth through progressive, albeit limited trade liberalization since 1948) than on 'input legitimacy' in terms of respect for human rights, fundamental freedoms, democratic procedures and rule of law for the benefit of all citizens. The human rights obligations of UN member states are relevant context for interpreting the law of international organizations even if the diplomatic drafters of that law pragmatically avoided references to the universal human rights obligations of all governance institutions. Just as democratic polities must be legally constituted by human rights and by a political constitution protecting all citizens equally, so must the international division of labour and international organizations for the collective supply of 'international public goods' be legally constituted through functionally limited 'treaty constitutions'[7] with legislative, administrative

[6] On 'individual sovereignty' see also UN Secretary-General Kofi Annan, 'Two Concepts of Sovereignty' *The Economist* (18 September 1999) and EU Petersmann, 'From State Sovereignty to the Sovereignty of Citizens in the International Relations Law of the EU?' in N Walker (ed), *Sovereignty in Transition* (Oxford: Hart Publishing, 2003) 145–66.

[7] For an explanation of the notion of national 'economic constitutions' and international 'treaty constitutions' see ch II, section 3 and Petersmann (1991) 61 ff, 210 ff.

and judicial functions protecting rule of law in transnational cooperation among citizens based on respect for human rights and social justice.

This last chapter focuses on the complex processes of 'weighing and balancing' of competing rights of individuals and corresponding obligations of governments in order to promote transnational rule of law in conformity with the legitimate diversity of 'constitutional pluralism'. As explained in chapters II to IV, the 'transformation power' of economic constitutionalism and its contribution to the necessary 'civilization' of IEL depends on 'struggles for human rights' and for cosmopolitan conceptions of IEL. The increasing complexity of 'global economic governance' makes mutually consistent forms of decentralized self-governance and 'participatory democracy' increasingly important. The basic principles of rights-based, consumer-driven competition and citizen-driven 'constitutional democracies' must be extended to multilevel governance of international markets. The difference between American and European approaches lies *not* in the European recourse to 'normative', 'soft' and 'civilian power' (which are likewise used in US foreign policies). European citizens and parliaments are more willing to limit 'constitutional nationalism' and 'popular sovereignty' by *multilevel constitutional restraints* on multilevel economic governance. The Washington model of 'congressional interest group politics' focuses, by contrast, on advancing *national* interests through intergovernmental power politics as defined by parliamentary and political majorities in response to domestic lobbying pressures. Multilevel legal and judicial protection of transnational 'rule of law' on the basis of cosmopolitan rights – as it is increasingly accepted throughout Europe as a constitutional constraint of intergovernmental rulemaking based on political majority decisions of national parliaments and their democratic constituencies – requires legislative, administrative and judicial justification and 'balancing' of cosmopolitan civil, political, economic, social and cultural rights. Such rights-based and citizen-driven processes also promote 'public reason' and its continuous review through 'participatory' and 'deliberative democracy'.

Synergies between human rights and cosmopolitan economic integration law

The Westphalian system of international law among sovereign states conceived international law as reciprocal limitations on state power aimed at protecting international order rather than human rights and justice. Proposals for international arbitration, adjudication and rule of law among states received broader support in international state practice only following the public criticism and legal limitations of Westphalian power politics after the First and Second World Wars .[8] Also the state-centred UN legal system protects neither human rights nor democratic peace effectively. Politicians – also in constitutional democracies like the United States and the EU – like to present compliance with international law as a policy choice depending on their political 'cost- benefit calculations' rather than on 'rule of international law' and its authoritarian culture of legal

[8] cf M Pomerance, The United States and the World Court as a 'Supreme Court of the Nations': Dreams, Illusions and Disillusion (Dordrecht: Kluwer, 1996). A de Tocqueville, Democracy in America, vol 1 (New York: A Knopf, 1945) criticized during the nineteenth century that '(i)n the nations of Europe, the courts of justice are called upon to try only the controversies of private individuals; but the Supreme Court of the United States summons sovereign powers to its bar' (at 151).

formalism.[9] The frequent lack of legal, judicial and democratic accountability for opportunistic violations of IEL (eg, in case of discriminatory import protection and export subsidies for producers in the EU and the United States) is portrayed by many politicians and special interest groups as politically beneficial, for example in terms of helping politicians in gaining political support from domestic constituencies by redistributing income from 'rationally ignorant consumers' to politically influential 'rent-seeking' producer interests.

The universal recognition and institutionalization of human rights and free trade areas protecting economic freedoms and 'access to justice' beyond state borders increasingly limit state sovereignty by new forms of 'cosmopolitan law'.[10] Access by third countries to regional human rights and economic organizations in Europe and in the Americas has become subject to increasing 'human rights conditionality', notwithstanding the persistence of 'US exceptionalism' as illustrated by the US refusal to ratify many UN human rights conventions and submit to the jurisdiction of international human rights courts and international criminal courts.[11] If law is perceived from a cosmopolitan perspective as a struggle for individual constitutional rights and human rights to be protected by rule of law, the multilevel legal and judicial protection of human rights and economic freedoms reflects an increasing recognition of the constitutional insight that 'there can be no adequate institutionalization of equal rights and duties without a corresponding institutionalization of national and transnational forms of public debate, democratic participation, and accountability.'[12] As discussed in chapter V, European Courts interpret and enforce the fundamental rights guarantees of the ECHR as a 'constitutional instrument of European public order' not only against *national* implementation of rules adopted by international organizations;[13] European courts also invoke human rights law as constitutional restraints on multilevel governance in the UN and European institutions.[14] The emerging 'multilevel human rights constitution' based on national, regional and worldwide guarantees of human rights, constitutional rights, democratic self-determination of peoples and their multilevel judicial protection by national and international courts, confirms the cosmopolitan claim that, also in multilevel regulation of transnational economic cooperation among citizens, the 'people' and their democratic 'sovereignty' are legally

[9] *cf* JL Goldsmith and EA Posner (2005).

[10] *cf* P Eleftheriadis, 'Cosmopolitan Law' (2003) 2 *European Law Journal* 241–63; P Eleftheriadis, 'The European Constitution and Cosmopolitan Ideals' (2001) 1 *The Columbia Journal of European Law* 21 ff.

[11] See, eg: M Ignatieff, *American Exceptionalism and Human Rights* (Princeton: Princeton Yniversity Press, 2005); J Rubenfeld, 'The Two World Orders' in G Nolte (ed), *European and US Constitutionalism* (Cambridge: CUP, 2005) 280–96; C Stahn, 'Responsibility to Protect: Political Rhetoric or Emerging Legal Norm?' (2007) 101 *AJIL* 99–120.

[12] D Held, 'Principles of Cosmopolitan Order' in G Brock and H Brighouse (eds), *The Political Philosophy of Cosmopolitanism* (Oxford: OUP, 2005) 10–27, 18.

[13] On the long-standing ECJ jurisprudence that respect for fundamental rights is a 'condition of the legality of Community acts', see: ECJ Opinion 2/92 on accession by the EC to the ECHR [1996] ECR I-1759; Case C-84/95, *Bosphorus* [1996] ECR I-3953. On the constitutional functions of the ECHR see the judgment of the ECtHR of 30 June 2005 (App no 6422/2002, *Bosphorus v Ireland*) which confirmed, inter alia, 'that a Contracting Party is responsible under Article 1 of the Convention for all acts and omissions of its organs regardless of whether the act or omission in question was a consequence of domestic law or of the necessity to comply with international legal obligations' (para 153).

[14] See the broad interpretation of UN human rights as international *jus cogens* and constitutional limitation of intergovernmental powers by the EC Court of First Instance in Cases T-315/01 (*Kadi v Council and Commission*) and T-306/01 (*Yusuf v Council and Commission*) Judgments (21 September 2005) [2005] CMLR, 1334. For detailed analysis of the related case law of the ECJ see Table 18 and G de Burca, 'The European Court of Justice and the International Legal Order after Kadi' Jean Monnet Working Paper 01/2009.

constituted, and constitutionally limited, by multilevel constitutional and cosmopolitan guarantees and their protection by courts of justice.

The conception of multilevel economic regulation as deriving its legitimacy from respect for human rights, democratic self-government and 'rule of law' may influence the interpretation, development and 'judicial balancing' of IEL rules,[15] for instance by also protecting citizens in transnational economic cooperation as subjects of international law and of human rights, 'market rights' and social rights. Just as decolonization and political democracy resulted from struggles for the liberation of suppressed people, so will the needed democratization of the power-oriented IEL system not come about without bottom-up struggles for the defence of cosmopolitan human rights against power politics, including border discrimination reducing consumer welfare by impeding mutually beneficial division of labour among citizens across frontiers. The UN High Commissioner for Human Rights has, as discussed in chapter VII, section 4, called for a human rights approach to international trade and investment law.[16] Similarly, WTO Director-General Pascal Lamy has called for 'cosmopolitics', 'cosmopolitan constituencies' and for promoting synergies between human rights and IEL in support of global public goods such as a liberal trading system. The regular interparliamentary meetings at WTO ministerial conferences since 1989, like the annual public fora of WTO diplomats with civil society organizations, reflect increasing recognition of 'cosmopolitan dimensions' of WTO law and of the democratic need for justifying multilevel trade governance in relation to civil society.

The 'intergovernmental power politics' and 'producer biases' characteristic of WTO negotiations are easier to overcome in RTAs

Today's global discourse on how to integrate economic, social, labour and environmental rights more effectively into international law and organizations remains contested not only by diplomats, but also in civil society[17]. UN human rights law – due to its inadequate protection of economic liberties (like freedom of profession, private property, open markets, freedom of trade), rule of law, democratic self-governance and other legal preconditions for a welfare-enhancing division of labour – fails to effectively empower citizens to overcome poverty by increasing the supply of goods and services demanded by consumers through mutually beneficial economic cooperation.[18] Nor have the UN Conference on Trade and Development (UNCTAD) or other UN institutions exercised leadership for a liberal (ie, liberty-based) international trade order committed to the protection of human rights. As illustrated by the non-ratification of the Inter-American Convention on Human Rights by Canada and the United States and the lack of references

[15] See EU Petersmann, 'Constitutionalism and WTO Law – From a State-Centred Approach towards a Human Rights Approach in International Economic Law' in DLM Kennedy and JD Southwick (eds), *The Political Economy of International Trade Law* (Cambridge: CUP, 2002) 32–67.

[16] See ch VII, section 4.

[17] *cf*, eg: M Risse, 'A Right to Work? A Right to Leisure? Labor Rights as Human Rights' (2009) 1 *Law & Ethics of Human Rights*, and the critical Comment by T Pogge (2009) 3 *Law & Ethics of Human Rights*; RP Hiskes, *The Human Right to a Green Future. Environmental Rights and Intergenerational Justice* (Cambridge: CUP, 2009); M Langford (ed), *Social Rights Jurisprudence. Emerging Trends in International and Comparative Law* (Cambridge: CUP, 2009).

[18] See the criticism of UN human rights law and policies by EU Petersmann, 'Human Rights and International Trade Law – Defining and Connecting the Two Fields' in T Cottier, J Pauwelyn and E Bürgi (eds) (2005) 29–94.

by NAFTA dispute settlement bodies to human rights, numerous UN member states oppose rendering human rights and judicial remedies more effective in IEL.[19]

The worldwide liberalization and regulation of welfare-reducing trade barriers continues to be based on WTO law and on the more than 250 regional trade agreements (RTAs) pursuant to GATT Article XXIV and GATS Article V.[20] Clarification of the interrelationships between UN law, WTO law and human rights is essentially left to the WTO dispute settlement system, to its institutionalized surveillance by the WTO membership (eg, in the WTO Dispute Settlement Body) and to RTAs that regulate the interrelationships between economic law and human rights in diverse ways (eg, in EU law, EEA law, NAFTA law and RTAs among LDCs). The 'member-driven' character of the WTO entails that WTO rules and policies tend to be 'producer-driven' for the benefit of powerful 'rent-seeking interest groups' (such as textiles, agricultural and steel lobbies, periodically elected trade politicians) to the detriment of general consumer welfare and citizen rights; these 'producer biases' of many WTO rules (eg, regarding anti-dumping and other safeguard measures, agricultural subsidies) also impede the successful conclusion of the WTO 'Development Round' by offering incentives for import-competing producers to resist proposals for non-discriminatory market access and additional development opportunities for less-developed WTO member countries. Trade liberalization and the regulation of trade-related citizen concerns and public interests continue to be easier in RTAs than in consensus-based WTO negotiations among governments, whose power-oriented trade policies remain inadequately controlled by parliaments, citizens and domestic courts.[21]

2 THE NEED FOR COMPENSATING THE 'CONSTITUTIONAL DEFICIT' IN MULTILEVEL ECONOMIC GOVERNANCE BY JUDICIAL PROTECTION OF COSMOPOLITAN RIGHTS

The modern globalization of the economy, the environment, of human rights and the ever greater interdependence of citizens in their worldwide division of labour are transforming the intergovernmental 'society of states' into a cosmopolitan community with complex layers and networks of private and public, national and international governance and legal regulation. As members of national parliaments depend on domestic political support and democratic elections tend to focus on 'domestic policy issues' rather than on 'global economic regulation', national parliaments are ever less controlling intergovernmental negotiations in regional and worldwide organizations on hundreds of different, often non-transparent and highly complex 'regulatory problems', like

[19] Some of the objections from LDCs are discussed in B Chimni, 'The Sen Conception of Development and Contemporary International Law Discourse: Some Parallels' (2008) 1 *The Law and Development Review*. On the need for agricultural trade reform in order to promote 'food security' see R Johnson, *Food Security: The Role of Agricultural Trade* (Washington: International Policy Council, 2009). The report by the UN Special Rapporteur on the Right to Food, O de Schutter, on his *Mission to the WTO* (UN Doc A/HRC/10/5/Add.2 (4 February 2009) and its proposals that the human right to food should justify production subsidies for, and import restrictions of, agricultural products, were criticized by many agricultural exporting countries during the discussion of the report in the WTO Committee on Agriculture on 2 July 2009 (*cf Bridges Weekly Trade News Digest*, 8 July 2009).

[20] *cf* L Bartels and F Ortino (eds) (2006).

[21] *cf* EU Petersmann, 'The WTO and Regional Trade Agreements as Competing Fora for Trade Liberalization and Trade Regulation' in Bartels and Ortino (eds) (2006) 281–312.

the illegality of agricultural, aircraft and other subsidies and anti-dumping duties challenged in WTO dispute settlement proceedings, in the ECJ or EFTA Court. As discussed in chapters II and III, the inevitable limits of 'representative democracy' and of 'parliamentary control' of intergovernmental rulemaking and administrative practices in international organizations must be compensated by stronger 'participatory democracy' and judicial remedies for individuals adversely affected by international economic regulation.

Constitutional nationalism must be complemented by functionally limited, multilevel constitutionalism

The progressive transformation of intergovernmental treaty rules into constitutional and judicial guarantees of individual rights in European integration law resulted from successful, legal challenges by citizens in national and European courts of discriminatory government restrictions and other welfare-reducing abuses of foreign policy powers. In Europe, these struggles for individual freedom and 'rule of international law' for the benefit of citizens have led to legal and judicial protection of 'new fundamental rights' (as codified in the EU Charter of Fundamental Rights) and 'constitutional principles' of EU law, as codified in Part I of the 2004 Treaty Establishing a Constitution for Europe and partly incorporated into the 2007 Lisbon Treaty on the European Union.[22] EU member states and EU courts continue to adapt European economic law to the 'rights revolution', to particular circumstances (such as the autonomy of Greenland and of Northern Cyprus inside the EU), and to the diverse forms of legal and economic association and partial integration of third countries (like the EEA members states, Switzerland and Turkey) into the EU's common market. The EU Treaty's core value premises – such as 'liberty, democracy, respect for human rights and fundamental freedoms, and rule of law' (Articles 6 EU, 2 TEU) – have gradually evolved into a non-derogable hard core of European constitutional law accepted by all 47 member states of the Council of Europe. The coherence, justice and legal effectiveness of the rule of law and judicial system of the EU rest on 'the interlocking system of jurisdiction of the Community courts and the national courts which is cemented together by the principle of upholding the "rule of law" in the Union legal order'.[23] In the EU's external relations as well as in RTAs outside Europe such as NAFTA and MERCOSUR, individual 'market freedoms' for international movements of goods, services, persons, capital and related payments – as they are legally and judicially protected inside the EU by means of legal primacy of EU law, its direct effect inside domestic laws, direct judicial applicability in national and European courts – are often rejected as inconsistent with the different traditions of 'popular sovereignty' and 'constitutional nationalism' outside Europe. In the EU's external relations, constitutionalism and cosmopolitanism remain limited, as illustrated by the long-standing claims of the EU Commission and EU Council that European courts should not hold the political EU institutions legally and judicially accountable in relation to EU citizens and EU member states for violations of the EU's international

[22] On the development of 'principles of European constitutional law' see: A von Bogdandy and J Bast (eds) (2006).

[23] K Lenaerts, 'The Rule of Law and the Coherence of the Judicial System of the European Union' (2007) 44 *CMLR* 1625, 1659.

legal obligations under GATT, WTO law and other multilateral agreements like the Law of the Sea Convention.[24]

There is broad agreement inside constitutional democracies that popular sovereignty and democratic nation states remain preconditions for legitimate transnational governance.[25] Yet, the rights-based, cosmopolitan European constitutionalism differs fundamentally from the constitutional nationalism in most democracies outside Europe.[26] For example, in contrast to the US focus on *national* constitutionalism and hegemonic, power-oriented foreign policies,[27] EU law remains constitutionally committed to 'the strict observance and the development of international law, including respect for the principles of the United Nations Charter' (Article 3 TEU). Even though the US Declaration of Independence prioritized 'inalienable rights' and the US Constitution confirms the federal insight that sovereignty is divisible, American lawyers remain reluctant to conceive self-imposed, international legal constraints on legislative and executive powers as functionally limited, constitutional limitations of foreign policy discretion for the benefit of general citizen interests, for instance because international rules 'do not establish the power they restrain and cannot be understood as emanations of a *pouvoir constituant*'.[28]

Constitutional functions of cosmopolitan interpretations of IEL and of its 'rules of recognition'

From the point of view of 'cosmopolitan constitutionalism', by contrast, the legitimacy of all governance powers must be justified by human rights, constitutional democracy

[24] See the power-oriented justifications by members of the EU legal services of their lack of judicial accountability for EU violations of WTO law (eg, PJ Kuijper, 'WTO Law in the European Court of Justice' (2005) 42 *CMLR* 1313–41, who criticizes the rule-oriented 'Kupferberg jurisprudence' of the ECJ as politically 'naïve', at 1320); Kuijper claims (at 1334) that 'it is difficult to point out one specific moment at which it can be established beyond doubt that WTO rules have been breached, even after a decision of a panel or report of the Appellate Body', and 'that it is rarely or never possible to speak of a sufficiently serious breach of WTO law' by the political EC institutions justifying the EC's non-contractual liability for damages pursuant to Art 288 EC Treaty. Such power-oriented claims for 'legal immunity' of EU rulers for violations of international law lack constitutional justification vis-à-vis adversely affected EU citizens. On recent developments in the European courts' case law refusing judicial enforcement of the EC's international legal obligations under WTO law and the Law of the Sea Convention see M Bronckers, 'From "Direct Effect" to "Muted Dialogue": Recent Developments in the European Court's Case Law on the WTO and Beyond' (2008) 11 *JIEL* 885–98.

[25] cf JA Rabkin, *Law without Nations? Why Constitutional Government Requires Sovereign States* (Cambridge: Harvard University Press, 2005).

[26] For some Anglo-Saxon communitarian lawyers, even the EU cannot be properly described as 'constitutionalized' until it embodies a European polity and *demos* legitimizing its community (*cf* J Weiler, *The Constitution of Europe* (Oxford: OUP, 1999)). Other Anglo-Saxon lawyers challenge the recognition of 'market freedoms' in European constitutional law on the ground that neither individual economic freedom nor other economic rights are 'a matter considered essential to constitutionalisation in the received tradition' of 'mature constitutional systems, for example in the United States, Canada and Australia' (DZ Cass (2005) 168, 176, 191). For a criticism of 'constitutional nationalism' see: EU Petersmann, 'Introduction and Summary' in C Joerges and EU Petersmann (eds) (2006) xxi–xxxviii.

[27] On the US penchant for imperial, unilateral foreign policies, notwithstanding US leadership in promoting multilateral legal disciplines for other countries after the First and Second World Wars, see: I Daalder and J Lindsay, *America Unbound: The Bush Revolution in Foreign Policy* (Washington: Brookings Institution Press, 2004). On the often sceptical US attitude vis-à-vis international law, see: JF Murphy, *The United States and the Rule of Law in International Affairs* (Cambridge: CUP, 2004); Goldsmith and Posner (2005).

[28] *cf* A von Bogdandy, 'Constitutionalism in International Law: Comment on a Proposal from Germany' (2006) 47 *Harvard International Law Journal* 223–42, 240.

and transnational rule of law rather than only in terms of majority politics (eg, US 'later in time legislation' violating international law). Chapter II, sections 2 and 3 recalled that worldwide agreements establishing international organizations are sometimes explicitly called 'constitutions' (eg, establishing the ILO, WHO, UNESCO, FAO) in view of their functionally limited delegation of rulemaking, administrative and dispute settlement powers subject to multilevel legal restraints. The interpretation of such functionally limited 'treaty constitutions', and of their international guarantees of private freedoms and rule of law, may justify 'constitutional' and 'dynamic-evolutionary interpretations' different from those of more 'static interpretation' of international treaties among states.[29] For instance, the customary rules of international treaty interpretation and WTO jurisprudence admit that the 'contractual' dimensions of WTO law may require different interpretative approaches (eg, for interpreting GATT and GATS schedules of reciprocal market access commitments, WTO 'non-violation complaints' aimed at maintaining the 'balance' of reciprocal tariff commitments) than their 'constitutional' dimensions (eg, in case of judicial clarification of the inherent powers of WTO dispute settlement bodies and of the powers of WTO members under WTO exceptions protecting 'public morals', 'public order' and other non-economic 'public interests'). The universal recognition of human rights entails 'constitutional principles' and *jus cogens* rules that may require rights-based interpretations going beyond the original meaning of treaty terms at the time of the conclusion of treaties like GATT 1947, which was negotiated in 1946–47 among just 23 governments. Thus, universal recognition of 'inalienable' human rights (eg, of access to essential medicines, food and education) may justify not only broad interpretations of the 'public interest exceptions' in international economic agreements and related limitations of economic freedoms and property rights, such as limitations of patents for pharmaceuticals by compulsory licensing for 'generic medicines', or limitations of market access commitments by domestic subsidies for food and education services. As the 'rules of recognition' of international law (as codified in Article 38 of the ICJ Statute) must be interpreted in conformity with the universal recognition of human rights, the latter also entail that the legally relevant 'interpretive community' for determining *opinio juris* in IEL is no longer limited to diplomats; it includes also parliaments, courts, civil society and 'public reason' as protected by domestic constitutional rules. As a consequence of this changing constitutional context, intergovernmental conferences of diplomats (eg, in UN institutions, the WTO Council) can no longer legitimately claim exclusive jurisdiction for determining the rights of citizens in IEL.

Transnational protection of cosmopolitan economic rights requires judicial remedies

The independent and impartial judge, enforcing 'due process of law' by listening to both parties of the dispute and administering justice, is the oldest paradigm of law and justice. The judicial task of impartial settlement of disputes 'in conformity with principles of justice' limits the 'rule by men', and their 'rule by law', so as to protect 'rule of law' for the benefit of citizens and their equal constitutional rights. WTO members tend to construe the limitation of the jurisdiction of WTO dispute settlement bodies to 'the covered

[29] On the problems of 'constitutional interpretation' see JE Alvarez, *International Organizations as Law-Makers* (New York: OUP, 2005) ch 2.

agreements' (Article 7 DSU) narrowly as permitting only legal claims and defences based on WTO rules. International lawyers and WTO dispute settlement bodies emphasize, however, that the customary methods of treaty interpretation require interpreting WTO rules as part of the international legal system in conformity with general international law rules unless WTO law has excluded recourse to other rules of international law.[30] WTO dispute settlement practice continues to identify an increasing number of general principles of law, for example, on inherent powers of courts, burden of proof, good faith, abuse of rights, due process of law, legal security and more specific treaty principles for the mutual balancing of rights and obligations under WTO law, for example, principles of legal precedent, transparency, non-discrimination, necessity and proportionality.[31] Some of these principles, for example, on burden of proof are applied as general principles of law, whereas others such as the non-discrimination and necessity principles of WTO law appear to be construed as WTO-specific 'principles underlying this multilateral trading system', as they have been explicitly acknowledged in the Preamble and in other provisions of the WTO Agreement.

The perspective of *international* judges with limited jurisdiction may differ fundamentally from that of investor–state arbitral tribunals and *domestic* judges confronted with arguments by citizens that domestic laws should be interpreted and applied in conformity with the international legal obligations of the government concerned. In the EU and in some other WTO members, the domestic constitutional perspective has occasionally prompted national judges and EU judges to interpret domestic trade rules such as the customs union rules in the EC Treaty as protecting private rights even if the respective trade rules were drafted as intergovernmental rights and obligations and implemented corresponding GATT/WTO obligations (eg, the EC customs union rules implementing the obligations of EC member states under GATT Article XXIV). Similarly, investor–state arbitral tribunals increasingly acknowledge investor rights deriving from BITs; both international treaty claims and contract claims of foreign investors, like the sovereign rights of host states to regulate and restrict foreign investments, must be interpreted with due regard to the 'public' and private interests of adversely affected third parties.[32] From the European perspective of a common market without a common state and with only limited EU competences, the 'empowering functions' of liberal trade and investment rules for the benefit of EU citizens, and their incorporation as an 'integral part of the Community legal system' in order to limit abuses of discretionary policy powers,

[30] See J Pauwelyn (2003) 37–38. According to Pauwelyn, 'it is for the party claiming that a treaty has "contracted out" of general international law to prove it' (at 213). Many WTO members and WTO lawyers proceed from the contrary presumption that the limitation of the jurisdiction of WTO dispute settlement bodies to 'the covered agreements' entail an agreed presumption in favour of exhaustive WTO regulation and confirms that '(i)n international law, every tribunal is a self-contained system (unless otherwise provided)', as stated by the International Criminal Tribunal for Yugoslavia in its *Tadic* judgment (1996) 32 *International Legal Materials* 35, para 11. For an explanation of this narrow perception of the WTO as – in principle – a self-contained legal regime see, eg, J Neumann, *Die Koordination des WTO-Rechts mit anderen völkerrechtichen Ordnungen: Konflikte des materiellen Rechts und Konkurrenzen der Streibeilegung* (Berlin: Dunker & Humblot, 2002).

[31] On general principles of international law as part of the WTO legal system, and the need for a principle-oriented WTO jurisprudence balancing WTO rights, WTO obligations as well as the numerous WTO exceptions protecting policy autonomy for non-economic regulation, see EU Petersmann, 'WTO Dispute Settlement Practice 1995–2005: Lessons from the Past and Future Problems' in Y Taniguchi, A Yanovich and J Bohanes (eds) (2007) 38–97; AD Mitchell (2008), who focuses on principles of good faith, due process, proportionality and special and differential treatment.

[32] *cf* PM Dupuy F Francioni and EU Petersmann (eds) (2009).

may justify 'constitutional interpretations' of complementary national, EU and WTO economic rules as a functional unity for the benefit of citizens. As GATT and WTO rules tend to be more precise and unconditional than many common market rules of the EU Treaty, the constitutional rights of EU citizens argue against limiting the legal and judicial accountability of EU bodies for their frequent violations of WTO obligations to the detriment of EU consumers and rule of law.[33]

Yet, such cosmopolitan judicial interpretations of intergovernmental economic rules may not be permissible for the international WTO judge who must interpret WTO rules 'in accordance with customary rules of interpretation of public international law', as prescribed in Article 3 DSU.[34] The WTO panel report on sections 301–10 of the US Trade Act emphasized, for example, that '(n)either the GATT nor the WTO has so far been interpreted by GATT/WTO institutions as a legal order producing direct effect', ie, creating rights and obligations not only for WTO member states, but direct individual rights for traders, producers and consumers.[35] Even though the WTO Agreement protects the discretion of each WTO member as to how WTO obligations are legally and judicially implemented inside domestic legal systems (*cf* Article XVI WTO Agreement, Article 19 DSU), WTO dispute settlement rulings may limit the regulatory discretion of national legislatures. The WTO panel report on Mexico's measures affecting telecommunications services, for instance, concluded that private price-fixing practices remained 'anti-competitive practices' prohibited under Mexico's obligations under the General Agreement on Trade in Services (GATS) even if Mexican legislation required such uniform pricing practices.[36] Due to different jurisdictions, applicable laws and judicial competences, 'constitutional interpretations' of national and international courts may differ depending on their diverse constitutional constraints. 'Constitutionalization' by means of jurisprudence must respect constitutional limits which may not apply to 'constitutionalization' by legislative and intergovernmental rulemaking. As the WTO guarantees of freedom, non-discrimination and rule of international law limit trade policy discretion far beyond the autonomous guarantees of free trade in the domestic laws of most states, the legitimacy of WTO jurisprudence derives not only from 'legal formalism',[37] but also from protecting individual freedom, non-discriminatory conditions of competition and rule of law across national frontiers for the benefit of welfare-increasing cooperation among citizens.

[33] See EU Petersmann, 'Can the EU's Disregard for "Strict Observance of International Law" (Article 3 TEU) be Constitutionally Justified?' in I Govaere, M Bronckers and R Quick (eds) (2011).

[34] On the 'constitutional limits' of WTO jurisprudence see the various contributions in T Cottier and P Mavroidis (eds) (2003) 43–90.

[35] See: United States – Sections 301–10 of the Trade Act of 1974, panel report adopted on 27 January 2000, WT/DS152/R, para 7.72. The Panel makes the following important reservation: 'The fact that WTO institutions have not to date construed any obligations as producing direct effect does not necessarily preclude that, in the legal system of any given member state, following internal constitutional principles, some obligations will be found to give rights to individuals. Our statement of fact does not prejudge any decisions by national courts on this issue'.

[36] Mexico – Measures Affecting Telecommunications Services, Panel Report (WT/DS204/R, 2 April 2004) adopted June 2004, paras 7.244–245.

[37] S Picciotto, 'The WTO's Appellate Body: Legal Formalism as a Legitimation of Global Governance' (2005) 18 *Governance: An International Journal of Policy, Administration and Institutions* 477 ff.

Cosmopolitan conflict resolution in IEL requires multilevel judicial cooperation in protecting transnational rule of law

In contrast to the 'Westphalian focus' on conflicts among national interests (eg, in territorial border disputes), IEL focuses on the collective protection of international public goods and common reasonable self-interests of citizens. Most conflicts in international trade (eg, in the WTO) do *not* involve conflicts among national interests, but conflicts among producer interests (eg, to exclude competitors from domestic markets) to the detriment of consumer interests inside states. Since the 1950s there have only been three judgments by the ECJ adjudicating international disputes among EU member states; the very limited number of judicial 'infringement proceedings' among the 27 EU member states illustrates that judicial interpretations of international economic rules as individual rights can de-politicize, decentralize and transform international economic disputes among states into private complaints by economic actors requesting independent judicial review of governmental restrictions by national and international courts of justice. The fragmented, decentralized nature of international economic relations among 200 sovereign states makes normative conflicts between national, bilateral, regional and worldwide rules inevitable. Customary international law (eg, as codified in the VCLT) offers not only *formal* legal principles for preventing and resolving such conflicts (eg, on the basis of *lex specialis*, *lex posterior*, rules on successive *inter-se* agreements, *ius cogens*, *erga omnes* obligations). The VCLT also provides (eg, in its Preamble and Article 31) for *substantive* requirements of interpreting international law 'in conformity with principles of justice' and human rights. Cosmopolitan constitutionalism justifies legal presumptions that national and international courts should cooperate in interpreting IEL in mutually consistent ways protecting transnational rule of law for the benefit of citizens and their cosmopolitan rights, including their human right to a rules-based international order protecting mutually beneficial cooperation among citizens across frontiers (*cf* Article 28 UDHR). As discussed below (section 4), constitutional, human rights and economic courts increasingly recognize legal duties to settle disputes with due regard to other judicial precedents and relevant 'public international law applicable to the protection of the rights' (as explicitly stipulated in Article 35 of the South African Constitution of 1996).

Just as constitutional democracies evolve in response to independent judicial interpretations of rules in the light of constitutional rights and principles of justice, so does the necessary adaptation of the 'international law among states' to the constitutional rights of citizens depend also on judicial procedures offering citizens opportunities for voicing, defending and enforcing cosmopolitan rights in transnational cooperation among citizens. The more consensus-based, worldwide negotiations fail to reach agreement on welfare-increasing regulation of 'governance failures', the more does the increasing number of bilateral, regional and plurilateral trade, investment and environmental agreements outside the WTO provide for decentralized 'bottom up reforms' of IEL. As illustrated by European law, multilevel cooperation among national, regional and worldwide dispute settlement bodies in adapting IEL to the cosmopolitan rights of citizens can operate as a powerful driving force for protecting human rights and transnational rule of law. The lack of adequate international legal disciplines for risk management in international financial markets illustrates that regulatory and judicial experiences in one sector of the world economy (eg, regarding WTO rules for risk assessment and risk management in international trade of foodstuffs and environmental goods) may offer lessons for other, less-developed sectors of international economic regulation such as 'poisonous bank assets', toxic financial instruments and financial insolvencies of 'banks that are too big to fail'.[38]

GATT/WTO rules differ from most other areas of international law insofar as they legally guarantee freedom, non-discrimination and rule of law for the benefit of private economic actors far beyond the autonomous guarantees in national and regional trade laws authorizing border discrimination. For example, multilevel human rights law tends to be based on a 'subsidiary logic': UN and regional human rights conventions often prescribe only *minimum standards* recognizing that many states protect and promote human rights by higher standards and more effective institutions in their respective national laws.[39] Many areas of IEL, by contrast, limit welfare-reducing border restrictions and border discrimination in national laws by committing countries to *higher international guarantees* of freedom, non-discrimination and rule of law in transnational relations. 'Cosmopolitan interpretations' protecting economic freedoms of citizens may be justifiable especially regarding international treaties constituting and limiting multilevel governance as a necessary precondition for the collective supply of global public goods (like a liberal, rules-based world trading system) that cannot be secured through power-oriented border discrimination and foreign policies focusing only on *national* interests. From a rights-based constitutional perspective, IEL rules (eg, the WTO objective of 'sustainable development') should be interpreted as *instruments* for protecting human rights and welfare-increasing, cosmopolitan cooperation among individuals and peoples, just as economists (from Adam Smith to Amartya Sen) perceive market economies and economic growth as *instruments* for enabling and promoting individual freedom as the ultimate goal of economic life and the most efficient means of realizing human welfare.[40] The inherent tendencies of freedom and competition to destroy themselves (*cf* Tables 3 and 4 on the *paradox of freedom*) require 'cosmopolitan restraints' on, and judicial review of, abuses of public and private regulatory powers in order to secure rule of law in international relations (eg, by means of the multilevel WTO dispute settlement system), open markets (eg, by means of WTO guarantees of non-discriminatory conditions of competition), respect for human rights and social justice (as reflected and protected in the numerous WTO safeguard clauses and 'exceptions' from WTO rules).[41] Cosmopolitanism offers criteria for mutually coherent, rights-based interpretations of the law of economic organizations in order to contain abuses of power in multilevel governance and protect individual rights and citizen interests more effectively. Similar to the constitutional empowerment of citizens and courts inside

[38] *cf* T Cottier, 'Challenges Ahead in International Economic Law' (2009) 12 *JIEL* 3–15.

[39] *cf* R Bernhardt, 'International Protection of Human Rights: Universalism and Regionalism' in S Yee and JY Morin (eds), *Multiculturalism and International Law* (Groningen: Europa Publishing, 2009) 467–76.

[40] On 'development as freedom' and substantive 'opportunity to achieve' see: A Sen (2002) ch 17 on 'markets and freedoms'; EU Petersmann (ed), *Developing Countries in the Doha Round. WTO Decision-making Procedures and Negotiations on Trade in Agriculture and Services* (Florence: Robert Schuman Centre, 2005) 3–18. See also, FA Hayek (1960) 35: 'Economic considerations are merely those by which we reconcile and adjust our different purposes, none of which, in the last resort, are economic (except those of the miser or the man for whom making money has become an end in itself').

[41] The various 'domestic policy functions', 'foreign policy functions', 'enabling, constraining and supplemental constitutional functions' of WTO guarantees of freedom, non-discrimination, rule of law and reciprocal liberalization were discussed in chs II and VII.

federal states to challenge discriminatory market access barriers imposed at cantonal (state) levels, non-discriminatory conditions of competition in the worldwide division of labour require cosmopolitan legal and judicial remedies against welfare-reducing, discriminatory market access barriers.

Alternative 'Institutional Choices' for Protecting Cosmopolitan Rights

All constitutional democracies rely essentially on constitutional, legislative, administrative, judicial and international rules and institutions as the five major policy instruments for protecting individual and democratic self-development. Which institutional reforms of IEL are necessary for protecting cosmopolitan rights more effectively in IEL? Delegation theories and principal-agent theories are used by social scientists to explain why, and how, citizens and other actors ('principals') delegate limited powers to institutions ('agents') in order to promote common interests subject to legal restraints aimed at limiting abuses of powers (eg, due to self-interests of the agents and information-asymmetries favouring 'stakeholder power' rather than 'shareholder power'). Principals are initially controlling the delegation of powers to take legally-binding decisions (eg, by legislators, administrations, courts, regulatory agencies, corporate governance bodies) and expect the benefits of delegation to outweigh the costs. Yet, the principal's ex post capacity to maintain effective control of the agent and limit the 'agency costs' is bound to diminish over time for a number of reasons.[42] Depending on the scope of the delegated powers, limited agency powers (eg, of regulatory agencies with limited mandates controlled by parliaments) may be distinguished from more expansive, open-ended 'fiduciary powers', such as those of constitutional courts as 'trustee courts' with expansive, constitutional mandates.[43]

One major objective of protecting cosmopolitan rights is to empower citizens – as the 'democratic principals' – to exercise control over their agents based on legal and judicial remedies against the ubiquitous abuses of delegated powers to regulate international economic transactions. As discussed in chapter VII, constitutional economics explains why long-term constitutional rules of a higher legal rank are important for limiting rule-making, administrative and judicial powers for the benefit of citizens and of their constitutional rights.[44] Economic analysis of law and 'public choice theories' examine the comparative costs and benefits of 'institutional choices' between alternative decision-making processes such as decentralized markets, majoritarian political processes and non-majoritarian decision-making by independent regulatory agencies and 'courts of justice'. Comparative institutional analysis completes the economic analysis of law and public policies by comparing and evaluating the imperfect decision-making alternatives.[45]

[42] *cf* M Thatcher and A Stone Sweet, 'Theory and Practice of Delegation to Non-Majoritarian Institutions' (2002) 25 *Western European Politics* 4 ff.

[43] *cf* G Majone, 'Two Logics of Delegation: Agency and Fiduciary Relations in EU Governance' (2001) 2 *European Union Politics* 103 ff; A Stone Sweet and F Grisel, 'Transnational Investment Arbitration: From Delegation to Constitutionalization?' in Dupuy, Francioni and Petersmann (eds) (2009) ch 6.

[44] *cf* G Brennan and JM Buchanan (1985).

[45] cf N Komesar *Imperfect Alternatives: Choosing Institutions in Law, Economics and Public Choice* (Chicago: Chicago University Press, 1994); D North, *Institutions, Institutional Change and Economic Performance* (Cambridge: CUP, 1990).

In today's globally integrated world economy, national foreign policy discretion to regulate international economic transactions by means of thousands of nationally or internationally agreed tariffs, non-tariff trade barriers, subsidies and taxes on thousands of different goods, services and transnational investments can no longer be effectively controlled by national parliaments. The lack of 'fast-track legislation' by the US Congress enabling the US President to conclude the DDR negotiations and the UN negotiations on prevention of climate change illustrates the frequent 'political capture' and incapacity of national parliaments to protect general citizen interests in collective supply of global public goods. Compared with traditionally power-oriented approaches to the regulation of international trade (eg, in the context of GATT 1947), of foreign investments (eg, by means of 'diplomatic protection', government support of anti-competitive business practices of TNCs by capital-exporting countries) and in most UN institutions, multilateral treaty systems with compulsory judicial settlement of disputes – like EU law, the EEA and WTO treaties – have been more successful in protecting mutually beneficial, transnational economic cooperation, rule of law and citizen-oriented 'constitutional interpretations' of IEL. Just as the success of the EU and EEA dispute settlement systems is due to their comprehensive remedies for individual citizens and to the close cooperation among national and international courts, so has the WTO dispute settlement system proven to be most successful in those cases where governments and private plaintiffs cooperated in 'private–public partnerships' jointly pursuing their legal claims.[46] In addition to preventing and adjudicating specific disputes, national and international courts, and their multilevel cooperation, also clarify disputed interpretations of rules, principles and incomplete agreements and contribute to the progressive adjustment and development of international legal systems governing economic and social cooperation among citizens across national frontiers.

'Participatory cosmopolitan democracy' and 'subsidiarity' as incentives for reforming IEL

In intergovernmental organizations for multilevel governance of international public goods, the influence of popular, parliamentary, deliberative and representative democracy on the law and policies of intergovernmental rulemaking, administration and adjudication – usually far away from individual citizens and their parliamentary representatives – remains inevitably limited.[47] Respect for human rights, individual and democratic self-government and social justice require more transparent, participatory and deliberative forms of transnational 'cosmopolitan democracy' so that citizens can better comprehend, influence and scrutinize multilevel governance and promote 'cosmopolitan public reason' as justification of citizen-oriented reforms of IEL.[48] Popular sovereignty and

[46] *cf* the reasons and empirical evidence in the studies by Bown, Petersmann, Shaffer and Meléndez-Ortiz, Garcia Molyneux and Shaffer cited in ch VII (fns 154–61).

[47] In its judgment of 30 June 2009 on whether ratification of the 2007 Lisbon Treaty was consistent with the guarantees of democratic governance in the German Basic Law, the German Constitutional Court noted that the European Parliament continues to represent member states rather than the will of a single European people; the Parliament does not constitute an effective control of EU executive power due to the lack of a parliamentary majority supporting EU governance and the lack of a parliamentary opposition (*cf* Table 13 and related text).

[48] See J Habermas (1996) 315–28, arguing that democratic self-government requires that only those rules can claim democratic legitimacy which can meet with the assent of all rational citizens in a discursive process equally open to all possibly affected persons. Public discourse and collaborative reasoning will enhance

human rights call for decentralized, citizen-driven governance based on principles of 'subsidiarity', ie, economic governance powers should be transferred from local and national to international levels 'only if and insofar as the objectives of the proposed action cannot be sufficiently achieved by the Member States, either at central or at regional and local level, but can rather, by reason of the scale or effects of the proposed action, be better achieved at the Union level'.[49] The purely intergovernmental structures of the WTO and of many other international organizations do not adequately empower, inform and include citizens and their parliamentary representatives in collective decision-making procedures to ensure 'cosmopolitics' for the benefit of all citizens and their individual and democratic self-determination. Cosmopolitanism requires decentralizing decision-making and promoting mutually beneficial cooperation across frontiers based on

- equal individual rights (subject to legitimate democratic diversity) to enhance the real capacity of informed, individual and democratic self-determination and 'participatory democracy';
- stronger, institutionalized accountability mechanisms for the consequences of individual and social actions (eg, corporate social responsibility for respecting human rights in corporate activities);
- inclusive decision-making procedures taking account of each person's equal rights, arguments and interests as closely as possible to the citizens concerned;
- legal protection of 'exit options' and alternative choices at subsidiary levels of decision-making (eg, RTAs as alternatives to consensus-based WTO agreements);
- the avoidance of serious harm by preferential use of scarce resources for satisfying the most urgent, basic human needs; and
- effective legal and judicial protection of transnational rule of law for the benefit of citizens.[50]

Human rights require a cosmopolitan market economy aimed at social justice

As discussed in chapter VI, designing the global division of labour on the basis of the three 'principles of justice' underlying 'cosmopolitan constitutionalism' – *ie* equal human freedoms, differential treatment of the poor, and multilevel protection of transnational rule of law for the benefit of citizens so as protect international 'aggregate public goods' – requires an international market economy based on cosmopolitan rights. Legal protection of individual freedoms and of other human rights entails competition

problem-solving and mutual learning. See also EU Petersmann, 'European and International Constitutional Law: Time for Promoting Cosmopolitan Democracy in the WTO' in G de Búrca and J Scott (eds), *The EU and the WTO* (Oxford: Hart Publishing, 2001) 81–110.

[49] This definition of the 'subsidiarity principle' in Art 5 TEU reflects its constitutional function to protect individual liberty by limiting and decentralizing collective governance powers, whose legitimacy derives from protecting individual liberty and human rights. The subsidiarity principle is in conformity with the Kantian legal theory of 'cosmopolitan (con)federalism', which aims at multilevel constitutional guarantees of individual, national and transnational freedoms under the rule of law as legal preconditions for 'democratic peace' among individuals as well as among republican states. The economic 'sufficiency criterion' (state action alone is insufficient for realizing the objective), 'benefit criterion' (common action must bring added value), 'optimal level criterion' (action taken close to the citizen is presumed to be more efficient) and 'autonomy criterion' (the action should protect individual autonomy) are justifiable also on legal and political grounds.

[50] For similar lists of 'constitutive', 'legitimating' and 'prioritizing cosmopolitan principles' see Held (n 12).

and markets coordinating consumer demand for, and supply of, scarce goods and services in the economy (eg, price competition among private producers) as well as in the polity (eg, political competition among competing political parties in periodical elections of representative governments for the collective supply of 'public goods'). Yet, as discussed in chapters I to III, the rational egoism, limited social reasonableness of human beings and their pervasive competition for scarce resources give rise to 'market failures' (*cf* Table 3) as well as 'governance failures' like selfish abuses of public governance powers by periodically elected politicians in exchange for political support from 'rent-seeking' interest groups (*cf* Tables 1 and 4). Hence, as discussed in chapter VII, non-discriminatory markets and efficient market competition – in the economy no less than in the polity – are no gifts of nature, but legal constructs depending on legal rules and institutions constituting and limiting private 'freedoms to have' (such as property rights in material means of production, means of exchange, intellectual property in immaterial inventions and other ideas), 'freedoms to acquire and sell' (such as freedom of contract, effective access to food and essential medicines) and 'freedoms to compete' (such as freedom of profession and trade). Maintaining non-discriminatory and efficient competition, and keeping international markets open and legally predictable, require numerous additional 'constituent principles' such as

- independent monetary authorities protecting monetary stability;
- financial authorities protecting financial stability and the efficient functioning of financial markets;
- contract law, legal liability rules and judicial remedies protecting rule of law in international market transactions among citizens; and
- 'regulative principles' – like competition rules, separation of powers and other constitutional 'checks and balances'– that legitimately differ among countries and their diverse legal, economic and political systems depending on their historical experiences, democratic preferences and respective resources.

Contrary to the views of the American legal philosopher John Rawls and to the US practice of refusing ratification of UN covenants protecting economic, social and cultural rights, individual rights to distributive and social justice and corresponding government obligations have become increasingly recognized not only *inside* constitutional democracies, but also in international law and transnational relations, albeit subject to limitations and conditionality.[51] For instance, the emerging 'Geneva consensus' (Lamy) in the Doha Round negotiations acknowledges that market access commitments by LDCs may need to be complemented by international adjustment and capacity-building assistance in order to avoid serious harm, promote social acceptability of trade competition and help meet the adjustment costs and human rights obligations in less-developed countries.[52] There is also increasing recognition that 'the well-being of the world depends

[51] For a criticism of the 'Washington Consensus' see: N Serra and JE Stiglitz (eds), *The Washington Consensus Reconsidered. Towards A New Global Governance* (Oxford: OUP, 2008). The Washington consensus focused on (1) fiscal policy discipline; (2) tax reform; (3) competitive exchange rates; (4) trade liberalization; (5) redirection of public subsidies toward non-discriminatory public services like primary education and health services; (6) privatization of state enterprises; (7) liberalization of inward foreign direct investments; (8) market-oriented interest rates; (9) deregulation; and (10) legal protection of property rights.

[52] *cf* GP Sampson and WB Chambers (eds), *Developing Countries and the WTO: Policy Approaches* (New York: United Nations University Press, 2008).

on the establishment of a stronger rule of law at the international level'.[53] If 'the primary subject of justice' is defined in the Rawlsian way as 'the basic structure of society, or more exactly, the way in which the major social institutions distribute fundamental rights and duties and determine the division of advantages from social cooperation',[54] then justice and respect for human rights require a cosmopolitan 'social market economy' aimed at protecting not only general *economic interests* of citizens (such as consumer welfare, non-discriminatory conditions of competition), but also *non-economic social interests* of citizens as defined by human rights, including labour rights, social rights and rights to 'sustainable development' without life-threatening climate change. As discussed in the following sections, the historical experience in regional human rights and economic integration agreements suggests that such a cosmopolitan IEL aiming at more equal protection of 'social primary goods' and of a 'social market economy' depends on multilevel judicial protection of cosmopolitan rights and transnational rule of law based on 'proportionality balancing' promoting 'cosmopolitan public reason' in IEL.

3 'PROPORTIONALITY BALANCING' AS 'RATIONALITY' AND 'REASONABLENESS TESTS': THE EXAMPLE OF RIGHTS-BASED ADJUDICATION IN EUROPEAN ECONOMIC LAW

The rights-based economic integration law in Europe and, to a lesser degree, in the North American Free Trade Agreement (eg, in Chapter XI NAFTA) confirms that – in a globally interdependent world composed of some 200 nation states – constitutional democracy cannot remain effective unless local and national constitutional rights and institutions are supplemented by transnational constitutional guarantees protecting rule of law, individual rights and mutually beneficial cooperation of free citizens across frontiers. Proposals for reciprocal constitutional restraints on *foreign policy powers* for the protection of cosmopolitan rights across frontiers aim at *strengthening* democracies by multilevel constitutional restraints enabling citizens, civil society, parliaments and governments to cooperate more effectively in the collective supply of international public goods. Just as European economic integration law has been of crucial importance for extending multilevel constitutionalism to all 47 member states of the Council of Europe based on common constitutional principles, so can multilevel judicial protection of human and cosmopolitan rights contribute to transforming IEL beyond Europe into a more legitimate, transnational rule of law system. Arguably, the judicial methodology applied by European courts in interpreting IEL for the benefit of citizens – ie, interpreting international economic rules with due regard to 'fundamental rights (as) an integral part of the general principles of law' and to the 'constitutional traditions common to the member states' within 'the framework of the structure and objectives of the Community'[55] – can be justified also in other parts of international trade and investment adjudication beyond Europe like BITs explicitly committed to protection of individual rights.

[53] JE Stiglitz, 'The Future of Global Governance' in Serra and Stiglitz (eds) (n 51) 309 ff, 313.

[54] *cf* Rawls (1971) 7.

[55] *cf* Case 11/70, *Internationale Handelsgesellschaft* [1970] ECR 1125, para 4; Case 4/73, *Nold* [1974] ECR 491, para 13.

'Proportionality balancing' as the 'ultimate rule of law' in Europe?

Inside constitutional democracies and regional integration law, the legal protection of civil, political, economic, social and cultural rights legitimately differs depending on the diverse constitutional traditions, development experiences and priorities of the countries concerned. On the worldwide level, the acceptance of the 1966 UN Covenant on Economic, Social and Cultural Rights (ICESCR) by some 160 countries has – in the words of the chairperson of the UN Committee on Economic, Social and Cultural Rights – so far failed to change the widely held perception of 'violations of ESC rights . . . as inevitabilities, as a "normal" state of affairs in an unfair world where goods, resources and power are divided in a grossly inequitable manner'.[56] UN Secretary-General Kofi Annan himself admitted that the intergovernmental structures of UN law do not effectively empower individuals to protect themselves against abuses of government powers and to create the economic resources needed for the enjoyment of human rights; the UN legal system is widely perceived as 'unjust, discriminatory and irresponsible' because it has failed to effectively respond to the three global challenges to the United Nations – 'an unjust world economy, world disorder and widespread contempt for human rights and the rule of law'.[57] As long as neither governments nor parliaments in UN member states are insisting on cosmopolitan reforms of UN law, the historical experience of European integration suggests that cosmopolitan reforms of IEL will come about, if at all, only in response to 'struggles for human rights' by citizens and their legal protection by national and international courts of justice.

Since the entry into force, as an integral part of EU constitutional law, of the EU Charter of Fundamental Rights on 1 December 2009 and the Lisbon Treaty's requirement of EU membership in the ECHR, European economic law is committed to more comprehensive legal and judicial protection of civil, political, economic, social and cultural human rights and constitutional rights of 500 million EU citizens than the law of any other international organization or constitutional democracy. The international, judicial and increasingly constitutional transformation of European economic law since the 1960s enabled a 'rights revolution' in national and European courts across Europe[58] that remains unique in granting effective legal, judicial and constitutional remedies empowering individuals against national rulers and intergovernmental organizations. Worldwide economic and human rights agreements, by contrast, either do not directly protect individual freedoms (eg, of profession, private property, open markets, freedom of trade, freedom of association) and other legal preconditions for empowering individuals to create the economic welfare needed for the enjoyment of human rights or offer only inadequate remedies (eg, for international labour rights protected by ILO conventions). UN human rights bodies have neither powers to prevent or effectively sanction the widespread violations of human rights in many UN member states, nor powers to effectively protect mutually beneficial economic cooperation among citizens in the worldwide division of labour. Most UN agencies and the WTO pursue authoritarian strategies based on 'governmental *fiat*' rather than rights-based development strategies. Since

[56] VB Dandan, 'Foreword' in S Leckie and A Gallagher (eds), *Economic, Social and Cultural Rights. A Legal Resource Guide* (Philadelphia: University of Philadelphia Press, 2006) ix.

[57] The speech of Kofi Annan is reproduced in UN Doc GA/105000 (19 September 2006).

[58] cf MOE Lasser and JG Clarke, Judicial Transformations. The Rights Revolution in the Courts of Europe (Oxford: OUP, 2009).

(inter)governmental power politics remains the main threat to the protection of human rights, empowerment of individuals to use legal and judicial remedies for securing their economic and social rights must be anchored in *national* constitutions, UN human rights law and in judicial protection of cosmopolitan interpretations of IEL rules so that they offer citizens more effective legal remedies in their transnational economic transactions.

Clarification of the constitutional foundation of human rights and cosmopolitan rights is the necessary first step in challenging the persistent neglect of economic and social rights by many governments and international organizations. Even inside Europe, the interaction between constitutional law and human rights legitimately differs between countries and among the regional organizations in Europe. The elaboration of the European Charter of Fundamental Rights and the 2007 Lisbon TEU confirm that social and intergovernmental agreement on multilevel constitutional safeguards of human rights depends on clarifying the underlying value premises, such as the need to reconcile state sovereignty, popular sovereignty and individual sovereignty through multilevel constitutional protection of fundamental rights. Also functionally limited initiatives for extending an international 'social market economy' beyond EU law (eg, based on the EEA Agreement), and for constitutionally limiting and legitimizing multilevel governance through cosmopolitan institutions (like the increasing 'interparliamentary' cooperation and civil society participation inside the WTO, the tripartite governance structures of the ILO), require clarification of the 'constitutional principles' underlying modern IEL. In the process of European economic integration, the clarification of the constitutional foundations of European economic law was initiated by national and European 'courts of justice' in their successful cooperation offering European citizens effective judicial remedies against violations of their constitutional rights, human rights, economic and social rights. Based on constitutional guarantees and fundamental rights of access to justice (eg, in Articles 6, 13 ECHR), almost all national and international European courts now review the 'constitutionality' of alleged conflicts between individual and public interests, for instance in case of governmental or EU restrictions of fundamental freedoms and other constitutional rights, on the basis of 'proportionality balancing' as the best judicial standard of reviewing legislative and administrative restrictions. As a result, the national and European judiciaries have progressively strengthened their constitutional powers and influence on interpreting and progressively developing European economic and constitutional law. The increase in 'multilevel judicial governance' has become accepted by parliaments and citizens throughout Europe as supplementary 'constitutional checks' and compensation for the waning influence of national parliaments on intergovernmental rulemaking.

According to David Beatty, the constitutional idea of a 'government by law and not by men' has become transformed in European constitutional law (eg, governing the EU, the EEA, the ECHR and the domestic implementation of these treaty regimes) by judicial proportionality review – commonly broken down into three distinct 'suitability' (rationality), 'necessity' (efficiency) and 'proportionality' *stricto sensu* (reasonableness) tests of the legality of legislative and administrative restrictions – securing a more substantial version of the rule of law for the benefit of citizens and their constitutional rights.[59] Review of whether a restriction is 'suitable' and 'necessary' for realizing specific public policy interests focuses on the rationality and efficiency between the means and the end.

[59] DM Beatty (2004).

The *proportionality stricto sensu* test reviews the reasonableness of the governmental balancing of competing values and rights of citizens. In contrast to Dworkin's claim that – in 'hard cases' involving conflicts between constitutional rights and other public interests under the US Constitution – human rights should 'trump' public policies, 'proportionality balancing' by European courts tends to perceive constitutional rights and public policies as possibly both reflecting constitutional principles subject to weighting in order to promote their mutual coherence and 'optimization' case-by-case. By double-checking legislative and administrative 'balancing' and clarifying 'public reason', judicial proportionality review of governmental restrictions of fundamental rights contributes to 'participatory' and 'deliberative democracy' across frontiers as a necessary compensation of the deficits of national parliamentary democracy in a globally integrating world.

Progressive clarification of cosmopolitan rights in European economic law

The expanding legal protection of fundamental rights in EU law in response to their judicial protection by national and European courts illustrates how judicial cooperation among national and international courts has succeeded in transforming European economic law for the benefit of citizens. The multilevel judicial protection differs depending on whether courts review restrictions by EU institutions, by EU member states, intergovernmental organizations (including UN Security Council decisions), non-governmental organizations (eg, trade unions exercising their right to strike in order to prevent companies from exercising their 'market freedoms' under EC law) and individuals (eg, demonstrators blocking imports or transit of goods protected by EC 'market freedoms'). The ECJ and national courts started interpreting and protecting the EC Treaty's guarantees of free movements of goods, services, persons, capital and related payments as individual 'fundamental freedoms' in the early 1960s.[60] The EC case law on protection of human rights and other, common constitutional rights of EC citizens evolved only later in essentially six 'phases'[61]:

1. In the supranational, but functionally limited European Coal and Steel Community, the Court held that it lacked competence to examine whether an ECSC decision amounted to an infringement of fundamental rights as recognized in the constitution of a member state.[62]
2. Since its *Stauder* judgment of 1969, the ECJ has declared in a series of judgments that fundamental rights form part of the general principles of Community law binding the member states and EC institutions, and that the ECJ ensures their observance.[63]
3. Since 1975, the increasingly extensive case law of the ECJ explicitly refers to the ECHR and protects more and more human rights and fundamental freedoms in a wide array of Community law areas, including civil, political, economic, social and labour rights, drawing inspiration 'from the constitutional traditions common to the Member States and from the guidelines supplied by international treaties for the

[60] cf C Barnard, The Substantive Law of the EU: The Four Freedoms (Oxford: OUP, 2007).

[61] *cf* ch III, section 4 and ch IV, section 3 and A Rosas, 'Fundamental Rights in the Luxembourg and Strasbourg Courts' in C Baudenbacher, P Tresselt and T Orlygsson (eds), *The EFTA Court. Ten Years On* (Oxford: Hart Publishing, 2005) 163, 169.

[62] Case 1/58, *Storck v High Authority* [1959] ECR 43.

[63] Case 29/69, *Stauder v City of Ulm* [1969] ECR 419; Case 11/70, *Internationale Handelsgesellschaft* [1970] ECR 1125.

protection of human rights on which the Member States have collaborated or of which they are signatories'.[64]

4. Since 1989, the ECHR has been characterized by the ECJ as having 'special significance' for the interpretation and development of EU law[65] in view of the fact that the ECHR is the only international human rights convention mentioned in Article 6 EU.
5. In the 1990s, the ECJ began to refer to individual judgments of the ECtHR[66] and has clarified that – in reconciling economic freedoms guaranteed by EC law with human rights guarantees of the ECHR that admit restrictions – all interests involved have to be weighed 'having regard to all circumstances of the case in order to determine whether a fair balance was struck between those interests', without giving priority to the economic freedoms of the EC Treaty at the expense of other fundamental rights.[67] The ECJ has also been willing to adjust its case law to new developments in the case law of the ECtHR,[68] and to differentiate – as in the case law of the ECtHR – between judicial review of EC measures,[69] state measures[70] and private restrictions of economic freedoms in the light of fundamental rights.[71]
6. In a series of judgments, the Court of First Instance protected human rights also against EC measures implementing UN Security Council sanctions against alleged terrorists. Yet, in the appeal against the *Kadi* judgment by the Court of First Instance[72] that the Community Courts should assess the listing and sanctioning of terrorists by the UN Security Council only in the light of UN human rights guarantees of a *jus cogens* nature, both Advocate-General Poiares Maduro and the ECJ convincingly argued that – in accordance with the long-standing ECJ findings that 'measures which are incompatible with the observance of human rights . . . are not acceptable in the Community'[73] – it is up to the Community Courts to protect European human rights also vis-à-vis European measures implementing UN Security Council sanctions.[74]

'Proportionality balancing' as cosmopolitan reasonableness remains contextual

As discussed in the following section, ever more national and international jurisdictions within and also beyond Europe recognize that protecting competing human rights as

[64] See, eg, Opinion 2/1994 on the ECHR, [1996] ECR I-1759, para 33.

[65] Joined Cases 46/87 and 222/88, *Hoechst* [1989] ECR 2859, para 13.

[66] *cf* Case 13/94, *P v S* ECR [1996] I-2143, para 16.

[67] *cf* Case C-112/00, *Schmidberger* [2003] ECR I-5659. The judicial balancing by the ECJ refutes the claim that the ECJ gives priority to economic freedoms at the expense of other human rights.

[68] In Case C-94/00, *Roquette Frères* [2002] ECR I-9011, para 29, for example, the ECJ referred explicitly to new case law of the ECtHR on the protection of the right to privacy of commercial enterprises in order to explain why – despite having suggested the opposite in the ECJ's earlier judgment in *Hoechst* – such enterprises may benefit from Art 8 ECHR.

[69] *cf*, eg, the ECJ cases listed above (nn 65 and 68).

[70] *cf*, eg, the *Omega* case C-36/02 [2004] ECR I-9609, in which the ECJ acknowledged that the restriction of market freedoms could be necessary for the protection of human dignity despite the fact that the German conception of protecting human dignity as a human right was not shared by all other EC member states.

[71] In Case C-438/05, *Viking Line* [2007] ECR I-10779, the ECJ confirmed that trade unions – in exercising their social rights to strike (eg, in order to prevent relocation of the shipping line Viking to another EC member state) – are legally bound by the EC's common market freedoms that have to be reconciled and 'balanced' with social and labour rights.

[72] Case T-315/01 [2005] ECR II-3649.

[73] Case C-112/00 (n 67), para 73.

[74] Case C-402/05 *Kadi*, Opinion (16 January 2008) and Judgment (3 September 2008) (*cf* Table 18).

well as other constitutional principles and legislative goals requires 'balancing' and demanding all governance institutions to explain how the simultaneous protection and promotion of all constitutional rights and corresponding government obligations can be 'optimized' under limited resources.[75] In the practice of national and international courts within and beyond Europe, the 'proportionality principle' has evolved as the preferred method for reconciling conflicting rights and obligations, or other conflicting private and public interests.[76] The common purpose of judicial 'proportionality review' of legislative and administrative restrictions of fundamental rights can be seen in promoting a higher degree and more transparency of 'public reason' in multilevel regulation and governmental restrictions of fundamental rights, for instance by limiting welfare-reducing border discrimination and protecting adversely affected interests abroad. The three successive tests focus on different dimensions of 'public reason':

1. The *suitability test* requires examining whether the governmental restriction of an individual right is a suitable means for realizing the declared public policy objective.
2. The *necessity test* requires a rational assessment of whether the allegedly infringing measure is the least restrictive measure necessary for achieving the proposed goal (eg, in the sense that there is no less restrictive, alternative measures reasonably available).
3. The *proportionality requirement stricto sensu* involves a reasonableness review of whether a restriction, even if suitable and necessary, imposes an excessive burden on the individual or otherwise limits competing constitutional principles in disproportionate ways.

The application by national courts and European courts of 'proportionality balancing' as a 'general principle of law' (*cf* Article 5 TEU) remains highly contextual. For example, the judicial reasoning may differ depending on the state or EC measures involved, the private rights or private interests affected, or the constitutional context concerned. Hence, in the particular context of 'parliamentary sovereignty' in the United Kingdom, thc British courts have traditionally applied a more limited '*Wednesbury reasonableness*' test; and particular administrative law contexts (eg, exercise of police powers in emergency situations), the 'complexity' of relevant factual assessments, the 'margin of appreciation'[77], or normative discretion of the government authorities often influence the scope of judicial balancing. The ECJ has been criticized for applying a laxer 'manifest error' or 'manifestly inappropriate test' in its judicial review of whether discretionary *EU measures* are 'manifestly inappropriate having regard to the objective which the competent institution is seeking to pursue',[78] compared with the 'least restrictive alternative test' and 'proportionality *stricto sensu* test' applied in its judicial review of whether *state measures* comply with EU law.

[75] *cf* R Alexy (2002) 66–67 and section 4.

[76] See, eg, N Emiliou, The Principle of Proportionality in European Law: A Comparative Study (Dordrecht: Kluwer, 1996).

[77] cf Y Arai-Takahashi, The Margin of Appreciation Doctrine and the Principle of Proportionality in the Jurisprudence of the European Court of Human Rights (Antwerpen: Intersentia, 2002).

[78] Case C-331/88, *Fedesa and others* [1990] ECR I-4023, para 14. Whenever the Community legislature exercises discretion involving political, economic or social choices requiring complex assessments, the ECJ applies the following limited standard of judicial review: 'In reviewing the legality of the exercises of such discretion, the Court must confine itself to examining whether that exercise discloses manifest error or constitutes a misuse of powers or a clear disregard of the limits of its discretion' (eg, C-122/00, *Omega Air and others* [2002] ECR I-2569, para 64; Case T-180/00, *Astipesca v Commission* [2002] ECR II-3985, para 79).

The relative intensity of judicial review may also be influenced by the applicable procedural law such as rights of the defence, rights of access to the file, the right to be heard, the duty to state reasons, the right to judicial protection, and rules on burden of proof. Particular factual circumstances of individual cases may justify recourse to particular principles of distributive, corrective, reciprocal justice or 'equity' as part of the judicial balancing (eg, precautionary principles in case of risk assessment and risk management). For example, in a dispute over private claims that the failure of the British government to provide compensation for fish destroyed pursuant to an EC Directive infringed the right to property, the ECJ emphasized that 'fundamental rights are not absolute rights but must be considered in relation to their social function'; as the destruction was necessary for safeguarding health from diseased fish stock, the absence of compensation did not constitute 'a disproportionate and intolerable interference impairing the very substance of the right to property'.[79] In its judicial review of whether an EC Regulation freezing the financial assets of an alleged terrorist pursuant to an UN Security Council Resolution amounted to an 'arbitrary and disproportionate' interference with the applicant's property, the ECJ referred to the case law of the ECtHR and examined 'whether a fair balance has been struck between the demands of the public interest and the interests of the individuals concerned', notably in the sense of 'a reasonable relationship of proportionality between the means employed and the aim sought to be realized'.[80] The rights of EU citizens to freely move and reside within the territory of EU member states without discrimination have prompted the ECJ to protect equal access to national university scholarships of 'students who have demonstrated a certain degree of integration into the society of that State', thereby taking into account particular circumstances justifying non-discriminatory treatment notwithstanding the *national* competence of EU member states for organizing their respective education and scholarship systems.[81]

'Proportionality balancing' among competing fundamental rights in the EU

The interrelationships between procedural justice and substantive justice legitimately differ among constitutional democracies[82], notably if – as in the *Defrenne* case – constitutional guarantees of freedom and non-discrimination (Article 141 EC Treaty) are also extended to relations among private parties.[83] They are particularly difficult to resolve by international courts with limited jurisdictions, for example if – as in the *Viking* and *Laval* cases in the ECJ – social rights to collective action by trade unions (as protected by national and European constitutional law in the EU) collide with the exercise of individual economic freedoms guaranteed by the EU Treaty.[84] In both cases, the ECJ rightly emphasized the complementarity of the EC's economic constitution and its social dimension:

[79] Cases C-20 and 64/00, *Booker Acquaculture Ltd* [2003] ECR I-7411, para 68.

[80] Joined Cases C-402/05P and C-415/05P, para 360 (Table 18).

[81] See, eg, Case C-209/03, *Bidar* [2005] ECR I-2119.

[82] cf MD Bayles, Procedural Justice. Allocating to Individuals (The Hague: Kluwer, 1990).

[83] Case 43/75, *Defrenne v Sabena* [1976] ECR 455.

[84] For a thorough analysis of the *Viking* case (n 71) concerning collective strike actions aimed at preventing the re-flagging of a vessel from Finland to Estonia, as well as of the *Laval* case (Case C-341/05, *Laval un Partneri* [2007] ECR-I 11767) concerning a Swedish trade union trying – by means of collective action – to force a Latvian producer of services to sign a collective agreement with it when performing construction services in Sweden, see: L Azoulay, 'The Court of Justice and the Social Market Economy: The Emergence of an Ideal and the Conditions for its Realization' (2008) 45 *CMLR* 1335–56.

> Since the Community has . . . not only an economic but also a social purpose, the rights under the provisions of the EC Treaty on the free movement of goods, persons, services and capital must be balanced against the objectives pursued by social policy, which include, as is clear from the first paragraph of Article 136 EC, *inter alia*, improved living and working conditions, so as to make possible their harmonization while improvement is being maintained, proper social protection and dialogue between management and labour.[85]

As the right of workers and their trade unions to negotiate and resort to collective actions is explicitly acknowledged in EU law (eg, in Article 28 of the Charter of Fundamental Rights), the ECJ recognized it as a 'fundamental right which forms an integral part of the general principles of Community law'. In *Laval*, the Court inferred from the incomplete harmonization of mandatory rules of social protection in EC Directive 96/71 on the posting of workers that it was up to the member states to reconcile their social protection measures with the free movement guarantees of the EC Treaty. In *Viking*, the ECJ itself emphasized the limits under EC law on the powers of trade unions to prevent companies from exercising their fundamental freedoms of establishment and of providing services in another member state. Yet, contrary to its judgment in *Albany* where 'certain restrictions of competition . . . inherent in collective agreements between organizations representing employers and workers' were exempted from the scope of EC competition rules,[86] the Court rejected a similar 'hierarchical solution' of the dispute in *Viking* and submitted the objectives and proportionality of the strike actions to strict judicial review.

Table 25: Judicial 'proportionality balancing' of common market freedoms and labour rights in the ECJ's *Laval* judgment of December 2007

In its preliminary ruling in the Laval Case 341/05 ([2007]ECR I-11767), the ECJ held, inter alia: 'Although the right to take collective action must . . . be recognized as a fundamental right which forms an integral part of the general principles of Community law the observance of which the Court ensures, the exercise of that right . . . is to be protected in accordance with Community law and national law and practices' (paragraph 91). '(T)he right of trade unions of a Member State to take collective action by which undertakings established in other Member States may be forced to sign the collective agreement for the building sector . . . constitutes a restriction on the freedom to provide services within the meaning of Article 49 EC' (paragraph 99). 'However, collective action . . . cannot be justified in the light of the public interest objective . . . where the negotiations on pay, which that action seeks to require an undertaking established in another Member State to enter into, form part of a national context characterized by a lack of provisions, of any kind, which are sufficiently precise and accessible that they do not render it impossible or excessively difficult in practice for such an undertaking to determine the obligations with which it is required to comply as regards minimum pay' (paragraph 110). 'Article 49 and Directive 96/71 are to be interpreted as precluding a trade union, in a Member State in which the terms and conditions of employment covering the matters referred to in Article 3(1), first subparagraph, (a) to (g) of that Directive are contained in legislative provisions, save for minimum rates of pay, from attempting, by means of collective action in the form of a blockade of sites such as that at issue in the main proceedings, to force a provider of services established in another Member State to enter into negotiations with it on the rates of pay for posted workers and to sign a collective agreement the terms of which lay down, as

[85] *Viking* (n 71), para 79; Case 341/05, *Laval* (n 84), para 105.
[86] Case C-67/96, *Albany* [1999] ECR I-5751.

regards some of those matters, more favourable conditions than those resulting from the relevant legislative provisions, while other terms relate to matters not referred to in Article 3 of the Directive' (paragraph 111). The judicial 'balancing' of freedom of services (Article 49 EC) for temporarily posted workers from other EC member states with the freedom of trade unions in the host state to negotiate collective agreements was, thus, essentially based on the lack of legal clarity in the Swedish legislation implementing the EC Directive regarding the applicable minimum wages for posted workers.

4 'PROPORTIONALITY BALANCING' IN TRADE AND INVESTMENT ADJUDICATION BEYOND EUROPE

Judicial 'proportionality review' and the distinction between rules and principles as mutually exclusive sub-categories of legal norms, as elaborated notably by Alexy[87] building on the earlier work of Dworkin,[88] are increasingly acknowledged beyond Europe in the jurisprudence of national and international courts.

Rules and principles as distinct sub-categories of legal norms

Rules are applied in an 'all or nothing fashion': within their scope of application, rules determine the outcome of a case without need for addressing other legal considerations. Conflicts among rules are resolved through determining their respective scope of application, for example if a general rule is excluded by a specific rule operating as an exception. Principles, by contrast, prescribe more general values that are applied in a 'more-or-less fashion' through a process of weighing and balancing that also takes into account competing principles in order to optimize their simultaneous realization. Conflicts among principles are resolved by favouring the principle that has more argumentative weight in the specific case, while simultaneously optimizing other applicable principles as far as legally and factually possible. As principles pertain to the legal order as a whole, there are no conflicts between a rule (with a specific scope of application) and a principle, which may partially overlap with specific rules. This seems to be especially true for constitutional rights and many human rights norms, whose scope of application as a rule/right must often be determined by taking into account and 'weighing' the 'core principles' (such as respect for human dignity and other 'inviolable cores' of human rights) underlying competing constitutional and human rights.[89]

The adoption of national, written constitutions by almost all UN member states (with the exception of Burma, Israel, New Zealand and the United Kingdom) and the universal recognition of human rights have led not only to universal recognition of constitutional rights and principles as integral parts of positive, national and international law. The 'rights revolution' has also promoted a 'pull of balancing' and 'proportionality analysis as a decision-making procedure' in the constitutional and judicial systems of

[87] See Alexy (2002) and R Alexy, *Theorie der Grundrechte* (München: Beck, 1985).

[88] R Dworkin (1977).

[89] Habermas (1996) 254–59, has criticized Alexy's 'law of balancing' for optimizing fundamental rights by warning against the risk of 'outweighing' of constitutional rights by other constitutional principles (eg, security), thus destroying the 'firewall' between rules and principles and sacrificing individual rights. On Alexy's response see his postscript (2002), at 388 ff.

ever more countries beyond Europe.[90] Avoiding 'categorical interpretations' by deciding disputes through weighing and balancing, with due regard to the particular circumstances of each case and of each jurisdiction, has the political advantage of demonstrating to the political branches of governance as well as to civil society that courts and their jurisprudence remain open to reasonable arguments. As human rights also protect individual and democratic diversity and may be legitimately promoted in diverse ways inside diverse national and regional legal systems (eg, depending on democratic preferences and available resources), judicial proportionality balancing promotes 'public learning' and 'deliberative democracy' by engaging citizens, civil society and all governance bodies in collective discussion on 'optimizing' constitutional principles and protecting competing human rights. The legislative, administrative and judicial balancing of constitutional principles remains open for subsequent adaptation and correction in future cases. In universal jurisdictions like the WTO where all WTO dispute settlement reports are examined, discussed and finally approved and enforced by the WTO membership assembled in the WTO Dispute Settlement Body, the 'institutionalized dialogue' between the legislative and the judicial branches on the interpretation of WTO rules and principles supports a dynamic evolution of WTO rulemaking and adjudication and illustrates the political advantages and legal limits of principle-oriented 'judicial governance'.

'Necessity' review in GATT adjudication as a rationality test

The transformation of dispute settlement by political 'GATT working parties' into third-party adjudication through independent 'GATT panels' emerged pragmatically in GATT dispute settlement practices during the 1950s. 'Necessity balancing' likewise emerged in GATT dispute settlement practices during the 1980s. This followed the establishment of a GATT Legal Office in 1983, the increasing appointment of lawyers as dispute settlement panellists, the newly emerging tradition of independent legal advice from GATT's Legal Office in panel deliberations and the increasing recourse in panel reports to the customary methods of international treaty interpretation and the case law of other international courts.[91] As the consensus practice in GATT 1947 enabled governments to prevent adoption of panel reports and undesired 'legal precedents' resulting from judicial rule clarification and rule following, the jurisprudence under GATT 1947 did not raise the political concerns about 'judicial rulemaking' which has become characteristic of WTO legal and dispute settlement practices. Notwithstanding frequent criticism of GATT dispute settlement reports during their discussion and review in GATT Council meetings, the progressive 'judicialization' of GATT dispute settlement

[90] *cf* A Stone Sweet and J Mathews, 'Proportionality Balancing and Global Constitutionalism' 47 (2008) *Columbia Journal of Transnational Law* 73 ff, according to whom 'virtually every effective system of constitutional justice in the world, with the partial exception of the United States, ha(s) embraced the main tenets of PA' (= proportionality analysis). The analytical structure of proportionality analysis contrasts with categorical, rule-based approaches seeking to dispense with balancing once the scope of the rights has been determined. See also: T Hirschl, *Towards Juristocracy: The Origins and Consequences of the New Constitutionalism* (Oxford: OUP, 2004) and Beatty (2004), who presents proportionality as a principle of constitutional justice that deserves universal acceptance as a 'neutral principle'. On the different 'strict scrutiny' approaches (examining whether the law in question is 'narrowly tailored to achieve a compelling governmental interest') and judicial reluctance towards proportionality analysis in US courts, and the 'Wednesbury deference doctrine' in British courts, see: D Halberstam, 'Desperately Seeking Europe: On Comparative Methodology and the Conception of Rights' (2007) 5 *International Journal of Constitutional Law* 166 ff.

[91] *cf* EU Petersmann (1997) ch 2.

practices was increasingly welcomed by GATT contracting parties because it enabled transforming bilateral, power-oriented trade conflicts into third party adjudication based on independent and impartial rule-clarifications that rendered GATT rules more predictable. The dispute settlement rulings tended to become legal precedents whose principled legal rationale could become applicable to all GATT contracting parties over time, thereby reducing transactions costs and enhancing legal security in international trade.

The 'general exceptions' in GATT Article XX became the main focus of judicial balancing of the economic market access commitments of GATT contracting parties with their sovereign rights to protect non-economic public interests. Pursuant to paragraphs (b) and (d) of Article XX, for instance, 'nothing in this Agreement shall be construed to prevent the adoption or enforcement by any contracting party of measures' . . . '(b) necessary to protect human, animal or plant life or health', or '(d) necessary to secure compliance with laws or regulations which are not inconsistent with the provisions of this Agreement, including those relating to customs enforcement, the enforcement of monopolies operated under paragraph 4 of Article II and Article XVII, the protection of patents, trade marks and copyrights, and the prevention of deceptive practices'. In the 1988 EC complaint against section 337 of the US Tariff Act of 1930 challenging discriminatory treatment of foreign products in case of patent infringement litigation in the United States, the US invoked Article XX(d) GATT as a justification and argued that the requirement of 'necessity' 'did not impose an obligation to use the least trade restrictive measure that could be envisaged; this would invite continuous disputes regarding measures that the CONTRACTING PARTIES had clearly intended to exempt from the obligations of the General Agreement'.[92] This reference to a deferential standard of judicial review similar to the 'rational basis standard' as applied in administrative judicial review by US courts was rejected by the EC which advocated interpreting the 'necessity' requirement in conformity with the 'least restrictive alternative test' applied in European courts. The Panel, including Pierre Pescatore who had previously served for more than 20 years as a judge in the EC Court of Justice, interpreted the necessity requirement in conformity with the following two least-restrictive alternative tests:

> [A] contracting party cannot justify a measure inconsistent with another GATT provision as 'necessary' in terms of Article XX(d) if an alternative measure which it could reasonably be expected to employ and which is not inconsistent with other GATT provisions is available to it. By the same token, in cases where a measure consistent with other GATT provisions is not reasonably available, a contracting party is bound to use, among the measures reasonably available to it, that which entails the least degree of inconsistency with other GATT provisions.[93]

This 'necessity' test was subsequently applied in numerous other GATT dispute settlement reports, prompting GATT panels to explain in great detail why, for example, discriminatory import restrictions of imported cigarettes in Thailand could not be justified as 'necessary' health protection measures under GATT Article XX (b) because 'a non-discriminatory regulation . . . coupled with a ban on unhealthy substances, would be an alternative consistent with the GATT'.[94] Such 'necessity review' was based on rational

[92] GATT Panel Report, *United States – Section 337 of the Tariff Act of 1930*, BISD 36S (1989), 345, para 3.59.

[93] ibid, para 5.26.

[94] GATT Panel Report, *Thailand – Restrictions on Importation of and Internal Taxes on Cigarettes*, BISD 37S (1990) 200, paras 72–81. The GATT dispute settlement practice regarding Art XX is listed in: *Guide to GATT Law and Practice*, vol 1 (Geneva: WTO 1995) 563 ff.

means-ends arguments. As GATT Articles III and XX protect national sovereignty to pursue non-economic policy objectives, GATT dispute settlement panels focused on conflicts of trade rules and hardly ever engaged in 'proportionality balancing *stricto sensu*', ie, challenging non-trade values underlying non-discriminatory internal regulations or border restrictions. GATT dispute settlement reports insisted that non-economic principles (like the 'polluter pays principle' in international environmental law and politics) could not override specific GATT rules.[95] The weak institutional structures, politicized dispute settlement procedures and consensus practices under GATT 1947 limited independent, judicial balancing of economic and non-economic values and of individual versus public interests. The systemic 'ordering functions' of constitutional principles and human rights for international trade law, for instance for determining the relative 'weight' of GATT principles and their systemic interrelationships within the broader international legal system, were hardly ever explored in GATT dispute settlement reports.

From 'necessity' to 'proportionality review' in WTO adjudication

The WTO Agreements and notably, compared with GATT 1947, their more differentiated procedural and substantive requirements for (phyto)sanitary measures and technical regulations and strict standards of judicial review (as set out in Articles 11 and 17 of the DSU) prompted WTO dispute settlement bodies to further clarify the judicial review standards and refine the 'necessity' and balancing requirements. In *EC-Hormones*, the Appellate Body declared the proper standards of review to be an 'objective assessment of the matter' as stated in Article 11 DSU, thereby rejecting both '*de novo* review' (in which a panel would always substitute its factual findings for those of the national authorities) as well as a total deference standard as inappropriate for the WTO dispute settlement system.[96] A report by a WTO Appellate Body division chaired by Claus-Dieter Ehlermann (a former Director-General of the EU Commission's Legal Service) later specified that

> determination of whether a measure . . . is 'necessary' . . . involves in every case a process of weighing and balancing a series of factors (that) include the contribution made by the compliance measure to the enforcement of the law or regulation at issue, the importance of the common interests or values protected by that law or regulation, and the accompanying impact of the law or regulation on imports or exports[97]:
>
> . . . the reach of the word 'necessary' is not limited to that which is 'indispensable' or 'of absolute necessity' or 'inevitable'. Measures which are indispensable or of absolute necessity or inevitable

[95] *cf* GATT Panel Report, *US Taxes on Petroleum* (adopted June 1987), BISD 34th Supplement, at 83 ff. The legal argument was based on the political nature of the 'polluter pays principle' rather than on the legal rule that, in case of conflicts between general principles and specific rules in international law, the specific rules will generally prevail.

[96] Appellate Body Report, *EC-Measures Concerning Meat and Meat Products*, WT/DS48/AB/R (adopted February 1998), para 117. The intensity of judicial review set forth in Art 11 DSU relates to the process of fact-finding (eg, lack of powers of panels to re-do the original investigation and substitute their findings for those of domestic authorities), the conclusions to be drawn from factual evidence (eg, power of panels to review whether domestic decision-making processes provided for a 'reasoned and adequate explanation' of their determinations and to review whether 'certain elements of evidence should be accorded more weight than other elements') and the full review of law and of the WTO consistency of domestic measures, *cf* M Oesch, *Standards of Review in WTO Dispute Resolution* (Oxford: OUP, 2003).

[97] Appellate Body Report, *Korea – Measures Affecting Imports of Fresh, Chilled and Frozen Beef*, WT/DS161/AB/R (10 January 2001), paras 161–66.

> to secure compliance certainly fulfil the requirements of Article XX(d). But other measures, too, may fall within the ambit of this exception. As used in Article XX(d), the term 'necessary' refers in our view to a range of degrees of necessity. At one end of this continuum lies 'necessary' understood as 'indispensable'; at the other is 'necessary' taken to mean as 'making a contribution to'. We consider that a 'necessary' measure is, in this continuum, located significantly closer to the pole of 'indispensable' than to the opposite pole of simply 'making a contribution to'.[98]

In the complaint by Antigua against US restrictions of imports of gambling services, the WTO Appellate Body applied a similarly flexible interpretation of the 'necessity' requirement to the interpretation of Article XIV on 'general exceptions' from the General Agreement on Trade in Services (GATS):

> [A]n alternative measure may be found not to be 'reasonably available', however, where it is merely theoretical in nature, for instance, when the responding Member is not capable of taking it, or where the measure imposes an undue burden on that Member, such as prohibitive costs or substantial technical difficulties. Moreover, a 'reasonably available' alternative measure must be a measure that would preserve for the responding Member its right to achieve its desired level of protection with respect to the objective pursued under paragraph (a) of Article XIV.[99]

The WTO Agreements on Sanitary and Phytosanitary Measures (SPS) and Technical Barriers to Trade (TBT) set out additional procedural as well as substantive requirements (such as risk-assessment procedures, requirements of 'sufficient scientific evidence' and 'scientific justification') for the 'necessity' and legal justifiability under WTO law of trade-restrictive (phyto)sanitary measures and technical regulations, with presumptions of legal WTO consistency if the measures conform with relevant 'international standards' of other international organizations (like the Codex Alimentarius Commission of the FAO, the UN's International Plant Protection Convention, or technical standards approved by the non-governmental International Standardizing Organization). By linking WTO rules and procedures to the use of standards and values of other international legal regimes, such positive obligations for domestic regulation render proportionality balancing at national and WTO levels more complex. For example, the positive normative standards in the SPS and TBT Agreements go beyond the principles of non-discrimination and 'necessity' in GATT law as well as in the customs union rules of EC law and US constitutional law by also providing for weighing and balancing regarding the legitimacy of the policy objectives pursued.[100] Hence, the 'necessity' and 'proportionality tests' for rulemaking and adjudication may differ in WTO law depending on the applicable WTO agreements concerned and individual circumstances at stake. The balancing of competing rights, principles, non-economic values and private and public interests will remain a central challenge to rulemaking and adjudication in the WTO legal system for many years to come and will be increasingly influenced also by comparative law experiences in trade-related fields of national and international law. As WTO law does not explicitly prescribe and define proportionality balancing, judicial 'optimization' of competing values – notably 'proportionality *stricto sensu* balancing' between competing value principles – is likely to remain contested inside the WTO, just as it

[98] Ibid, para 161.

[99] Appellate Body Report, *United States Measures Affecting the Cross-Border Supply of Gambling and Betting Services*, WT/DS285/AB/R (adopted April 2005), para 308. On 'proportionality balancing' in the case law of the WTO Appellate Body see: Mitchell (2008) 177–236.

[100] *cf* M Andenas and S Zleptnig, 'Proportionality: WTO Law in Comparative Perspective' (2007) 42 *Texas International Law Journal* 371, 423 ff.

remains contested inside constitutional democracies and in regional economic community law. Yet, *judicial* review and case-by-case clarification through structured weighing and balancing of competing interests and values of the legal rationality and reasonableness of *legislative*, *administrative* and *intergovernmental* 'balancing', are of constitutional importance for the gradual emergence of 'public reason' in parliamentary, executive and judicial governance of international economic relations.

Towards proportionality balancing in international investment adjudication

The more than 2800 BITs are based on common general principles (eg, for 'fair and equitable treatment', 'full protection and security', access to justice, due process of law, national treatment, most-favoured-nation treatment). Their judicial interpretation, clarification and progressive development are characteristic for the dynamic evolution of international investment law on the basis of BITs, regional and worldwide economic agreements (such as the World Bank Convention establishing ICSID) and more than 300 investor–state arbitration awards published over the past years.[101] The limited number of only six investment disputes in the ICJ, and the ICJ's rejection of half of these complaints for lack of jurisdiction,[102] reflect the procedural and substantive disadvantages of intergovernmental investment disputes in the ICJ compared with alternative investor–state arbitration pursuant to ICSID or UNCITRAL procedures. For instance, the customary law requirements of prior exhaustion of local remedies and the political uncertainties of diplomatic protection for private investors and TNCs registered in many countries result in transaction costs in ICJ proceedings which foreign investors prefer to avoid by submitting disputes directly to investor–state arbitration procedures that tend to be quicker, more flexible, less costly and more confidential than intergovernmental ICJ disputes. By giving private investors directly enforceable rights to challenge governmental investment restrictions in ad hoc arbitration leading to awards that are enforceable in many countries of the world, international investment law offers private citizens legal and judicial remedies that tend to be more effective than in most other areas of international law, including human rights law and international trade law. Similarly, certain intellectual property conventions concluded in the World Intellectual Property Organization (WIPO), the 1994 WTO Agreement on TRIPS and their legal implementation in domestic laws (by means of EC Directives and national legislation protecting private access to domestic courts), offer private owners of intellectual property rights effective legal and judicial remedies in domestic courts, European courts and WIPO arbitration.[103] As the term 'investment dispute' tends to be interpreted broadly in the context of BITs, intellectual property holders may also invoke ICSID arbitration challenging foreign governmental restrictions of intellectual property rights.

[101] *cf* R Dolzer and C Schreuer (2008). All investment arbitral awards cited are electronically available (eg, at: ita.law.uvic.ca/).

[102] *cf* A Newcombe and A Paradell, *Law and Practice of Investment Treaties* (Oxford: OUP, 2009) 35–39.

[103] *cf* CM Correa and AA Yusuf (eds), *Intellectual Property and International Trade: The TRIPS Agreement*, 2nd edn (Cambridge: CUP, 2008); G Tritton, *Intellectual Property Law in Europe*, 3rd edn (Oxford: OUP, 2008). By 2009, the WIPO Arbitration Centre had administered some 15,000 arbitral procedures on 'domain name disputes' and some 200 mediation and arbitration procedures on other intellectual property rights disputes.

Necessity and proportionality analyses are being increasingly applied in investment disputes, for example if investment tribunals balance the investor interests and the state interests in their judicial review of 'regulatory takings' or – as in the case of the altogether more than 40 ICSID disputes against Argentina challenging its restrictions taken in response to the financial crisis of 2001–02 – in their judicial review of the alleged 'necessity' of governmental restrictions of foreign property rights. Following decolonization, most investment disputes during the 1960s up until the 1980s related to 'direct expropriations' (ie, involving transfer of the title of ownership); their legality was examined by investment tribunals in the light of whether the expropriation was

- for a public purpose;
- non-discriminatory;
- in accordance with due process requirements; and
- whether compensation was paid or at least provided for.

Since the 1990s, most investment disputes relate to claims of 'indirect expropriation' and 'regulatory takings' where the conflicts between the regulatory interests of states and the investor interests in the protection of investments may require more differentiated, judicial review standards for delimiting non-compensable regulatory measures from 'indirect expropriation' requiring compensation (ie, in case of lawful expropriation) or damages (ie, in case of unlawful expropriation). The 'all or nothing' paradigm of international investment law, ie, its requirement of full indemnification of an expropriation (by means of compensation or damages) but no indemnification if there was no expropriation, is increasingly being criticized as offering too little flexibility for accommodating legitimate state interests and investor interests.[104] Investment tribunals continue to emphasize that 'regulatory actions and measures will not be initially excluded from the definition of expropriatory acts'.[105] Recent BITs and arbitration awards acknowledge, however, that 'except in rare circumstances, non-discriminatory regulatory actions by a Party that are designed and applied to protect legitimate public welfare objectives, such as public health, safety, and the environment, do not constitute indirect expropriation';[106] 'reasonable governmental regulation of this type cannot be achieved if any business that is adversely affected may seek compensation, and it is safe to say that customary international law recognizes this'.[107]

Courts continue to use diverse doctrines for delimiting lawful investment regulation from expropriatory 'regulatory takings'. The 'sole effects doctrine' focuses on 'the effect of depriving the owner, in whole or in significant part, of the use or reasonably-to-be expected economic benefit of property' for determining indirect expropriation.[108] A radical version of the 'police powers doctrine' excludes indirect expropriation and compensation whenever government interference based on 'police powers' met the 'public interest', 'non-discrimination' and 'due process' requirements. A more moderate 'police powers doctrine' determines 'indirect expropriation' by reviewing whether public policy measures 'are proportional to the public interest presumably protected thereby and to the protection legally

[104] *cf* U Kriebaum, 'Regulatory Takings: Balancing the Interests of the Investor and the State' (2007) 8 *Journal of World Investment & Trade* 717–44, with references to numerous investor–state arbitral awards.

[105] *Tecmed SA v United Mexican States*, Award, 29 May 2003, 10 ICSID Reports 119, para 122.

[106] Art 6.4(b) of the US Model BIT of 2004, reproduced in Dolzer and Schreuer (2009) 385 ff.

[107] *Feldman v Mexico*, Award, 16 December 2002, 7 ICSID Reports 341, para 103.

[108] *Metalclad Corp v United Mexican States*, Award, 30 August 2000, 5 ICSID Reports 212, para 103.

granted to investments'.[109] These various investment law doctrines are increasingly criticized for offering less flexibility for accommodating legitimate public and private interests than the alternative methods of property protection by the ECtHR, which acknowledges that even unjustified governmental interferences into property rights may not always require full compensation.[110] The main difference between the human rights approach and the investment law approach lies in the economic consequences of an expropriation: 'The proportionality test in the human rights system can lead to a situation where a property owner receives less compensation than the fair market value' and 'can achieve a more nuanced result by including the amount of compensation in its considerations'.[111] By balancing the conflicting public and private interests not only in determining 'expropriation', but also in the calculation of the amount of appropriate compensation, the legal and judicial suitability, necessity and proportionality tests applied in human rights law may better reconcile genuine public policy objectives and legitimate expectations of investors.

Judicial promotion of legal coherence in investor–state arbitration

Due to the lack of appellate review procedures for the more than 300 investor–state arbitral awards over the past years, investor–state arbitration has become criticized for the lack of coherence in the legal reasoning of arbitral tribunals if they decide on related investment disputes without coordination of simultaneous arbitral proceedings and without sufficient regard to the legal reasoning in other arbitral awards. For instance, among six awards (by 2010) regarding investor claims that certain restrictions adopted by Argentina during its financial crisis in 2001–02 were not 'necessary' to preserve public order and security in terms of Article XI of the US–Argentina BIT, two arbitral tribunals accepted Argentina's 'necessity' defence, but three rejected it.[112] The settlement of investment disputes in the ICJ is obviously governed by public international law, as in the ICJ judgment of 20 April 2010 concerning the 'Pulp Mills' dispute between Argentina and Uruguay. In commercial arbitration procedures focusing on contract claims rather than on treaty claims, judges increasingly acknowledge the public law dimensions of investment disputes and their social importance for broader citizen interests affected by foreign investments, for instance in case of government regulation so as to protect 'public order' in times of profound economic crises (eg, during Argentina's financial crisis in 2001) or to limit socially harmful investor practices (like 'gambling services'). Arguably, to the extent that commercial arbitrators have to apply and interpret BITs and other international public law provisions 'in conformity with principles of justice' and human rights as required by the customary methods of international treaty interpretation, commercial and ICSID arbitrators are not only 'agents' of the parties to the investment dispute, but of the broader legal community involved.[113] This is confirmed by Article V of the 1958 New York Convention on the Recognition and Enforcement of Foreign Arbitral

[109] *Tecmed* (n 105), para 122.
[110] See: Kriebaum (n 104).
[111] ibid.
[112] *cf* W Burke-White, 'The Argentine Financial Crisis: State Liability under BITs and the Legitimacy of the ICSID System' (2008) 3 *Asian Journal of WTO & Health Law and Policy* 199–234; A Stone Sweet, 'Investor–State Arbitration: Proportionality's New Frontier' (2010) 4 *Law & Ethics of Human Rights* 47–76.
[113] *cf* Stone Sweet (n 112) 59.

Awards, according to which the recognition and enforceability of arbitral awards depends on their consistency with 'public order' in the state of enforcement.

A decision of 25 September 2007 by an ICSID Annulment Committee strongly criticized the 2005 arbitral award in *CMS Gas Transmission Company v Argentina*, which had awarded compensation of $133.2 million to the investor and rejected Argentina's defence invoking an exception in a BIT provision authorizing the state party to take measures necessary for, inter alia, 'the maintenance of public order' or 'the protection of its own essential security interests'. The Annulment Committee found that the CMS Tribunal had made a 'manifest error of law' by mistakenly conflating the stringent customary law principles on 'necessity' in the protection of 'essential security interests' (as codified in Article 25 of the International Law Commission's Draft Articles on State Responsibility) with the terms of the BIT exception which Argentina had invoked when adopting its 'emergency law' in response to the Argentine financial crisis of 2001–02.[114] The Annulment Committee's report is not legally binding on the more than 20 other, currently pending, ICSID arbitration proceedings by foreign investors against Argentine measures in response to the financial crisis of 2001–02. Yet, the report is also likely to have persuasive effect on other ICSID arbitration proceedings and to influence the future interpretation of 'public order' exceptions in international trade, investment and regional integration agreements.[115] Even though ICSID tribunals may not be legally bound to follow the legal reasoning in previous investment disputes concerning similar legal issues, several recent ICSID arbitral awards acknowledge a 'duty' to take into account 'legal precedents' in order to 'meet the legitimate expectations of the community of States and investors towards certainty of the rule of law'.[116] Investor–state arbitral tribunals also increasingly resort to 'balancing' and 'proportionality' review of governmental restrictions of investor rights and protect third-party interests by admitting amicus curia briefs.[117] As argued by the German Constitutional Court in its *Görgülü* judgment, judicial duties to consider relevant international jurisprudence in the 'balancing' of multilevel human rights guarantees – like the judicial duties to take into account relevant judicial precedents as emphasized in international WTO and ICSID adjudication – may be based on legal presumptions of national and international legal systems about what the right interpretation of human, constitutional and economic rights requires.[118]

[114] *CMS Gas Transmission Company v Argentine Republic*, ICSID Case No ARB/01/8 (Annulment Proceeding), Decision of the Ad Hoc Committee, 25 September 2007. For a discussion see: J Kurtz, 'Adjudging the Exceptional at International Investment Law: Security, Public Order and Financial Crisis' (2010) 59 *ICLQ* 325–71.

[115] The treaty interpretation favoured by the Annulment Committee would leave greater room for national and judicial 'necessity tests' than in case of the application of the stringent customary standard (that the measure 'is the only way' to respond to the financial crisis) to the treaty exception. In *US-Gambling*, the WTO panel report (WT/DS285/R of November 2004) acknowledged that the 'public order' and 'public morals' exceptions in GATS Art XIV(a) reserve regulatory discretion to each WTO Member. The Appellate Body report (WT/DS285/AB/R, adopted in April 2005) upheld the Panel's finding that the US measures were designed 'to protect public morals or to maintain public order' within the meaning of Art XIV(a); but the Appellate Body reversed the Panel's finding that 'the United States had not shown that its measures were 'necessary' to do so because the Panel had erred in considering consultations with Antigua to constitute a 'reasonably available' alternative measure. The Appellate Body acknowledged that the United States had made a prima facie case showing of 'necessity' and Antigua had failed to identify any other alternative measures that might be 'reasonable available'.

[116] *cf* the case law discussed by Stone Sweet (n 112) 60–61, and D Di Pietro, 'The Use of Precedents in ICSID Arbitration: Regularity or Certainty?' (2007) 10 *International Arbitration Law Review* 96 ff.

[117] *cf* the case law cited by Stone Sweet (n 112) 61–75.

[118] *cf Görgülü v Germany* (2004) 2 BvR 1481/2004, eg, para 62 : 'As long as applicable methodological standards leave scope for interpretation and weighing of interests, German courts must give precedence to interpretation in accordance with the Convention' (*ie* the ECHR).

In an ICSID arbitration award against Argentina of 5 September 2008, the tribunal (chaired by WTO Appellate Body member Giorgio Sacerdoti) referred extensively – in its interpretation of whether Argentina's emergency measures in response to the financial crisis of 2001–02 had been 'necessary' for protecting 'public order' and 'essential security interests' pursuant to Article XI of the BIT – not only to the case law of other ICSID tribunals and of the Annulment Committee report of September 2007, but also to the relevant WTO jurisprudence and ICJ case law.[119] The tribunal agreed with previous findings by other ICSID tribunals that 'there is nothing in the context of customary international law or the object and purpose of the treaty that could on its own exclude major economic crises from the scope of Article XI'.[120] The tribunal held that:

- Argentina's economic crisis was covered by the terms of Article XI of the Argentina–US BIT;
- Argentina's invocation of Article XI was subject to judicial review rather than being 'self-judging'; and
- contrary to another finding in an ICSID award that 'the treaty thus becomes inseparable from the customary law standard insofar as the conditions for the operation of the state of necessity are concerned',[121] the treaty exception in Article XI BIT reflected the formulation of Article XX GATT and had to be examined separately from the customary law 'necessity exception'; hence, 'the Tribunal finds it more appropriate to refer to the GATT and WTO case law which has extensively dealt with the concept and requirements of necessity in the context of economic measures derogating to the obligations contained in GATT, rather than to refer to the requirement of necessity under customary international law'.[122]

In order to determine whether a measure which is not indispensable may nevertheless be 'necessary' in terms of Article XI of the BIT, the tribunal referred to the WTO panel report on 'Brazil – Measures Affecting Imports of Retreaded Tyres' and its following summary of the pertinent WTO case law:

> The necessity of a measure should be determined through 'a process of weighing and balancing of factors' which usually includes the assessment of the following three factors: the relative importance of the interests or values furthered by the challenged measures, the contribution of the measure to the realization of the ends pursued by it, and the restrictive impact of the measure on international commerce.[123]

Applying this judicial standard, the tribunal concluded that there was 'a genuine relationship of end and means' between the economic and financial situation of Argentina towards the end of 2001 and the financial and exchange restrictions at issue (such as the imposition of a bank freeze, the devaluation of the peso, the 'pesification' of the US dollar denominated contracts and deposits, the suspension of payments and rescheduling of government financial instruments held by the claimant). Based on the evidence adduced by the parties in these proceedings, the tribunal found 'that Argentina's conduct in the

[119] *Continental Casualty Company v Argentine Republic*, ICSID Case No ARB/03/9, Award, 5 September 2008, paras 164–95.

[120] *CMS* Award (n 114), para 359; *Continental Casualty Company* (*CCC*) Award (n 119), para 178.

[121] *Enron Corporation and Ponderosa Assets LP v Argentine Republic*, ICSID Case No ARB/01/3, Award, 22 May 2007, para 334.

[122] *CCC* Award (n 119), para 192.

[123] *Brazil-Tyres*, WT/DS332/R (adopted December 2007), para 7.104.

face of the economic and social crisis conformed, by and large, with the conditions required for derogating from its obligations under Article XI of the BIT as to the measures challenged in the present dispute'.[124] It was only with regard to Argentina's unilateral restructuring of certain treasury bills, that the tribunal rejected Argentina's defence of necessity based on Article XI BIT and found that this restructuring was in breach of Argentina's fair and equitable treatment obligation under Article II(2) of the BIT, entitling the claimant to indemnification for his loss by means of damages.

The *CCC* case, with its numerous references to other ICSID awards and to the case law of the ICJ, of WTO dispute settlement bodies as well as to the jurisprudence of national courts in Argentina relating to the constitutionality and legality of the governmental crisis measures, suggests that past criticism of the ad hoc nature and legal inconsistencies of confidential investor–state arbitral awards may no longer be justified. Most ICSID arbitral awards, annulment decisions and increasingly also decisions resulting from investor–state arbitration based on private commercial arbitration (eg, pursuant to UNCITRAL or ICC procedures) and the 1958 New York Convention on Recognition and Enforcement of Foreign Arbitral Awards are today published. There are increasing 'judicial dialogues' and 'judicial cooperation' among national, transnational and international courts in the field of trade and investment law and also beyond the highly developed cooperation among national and European courts in the field of European human rights law and economic law.[125] Proportionality balancing is an important tool in such multilevel 'judicial governance' for enhancing accountability, justification of governmental restrictions, related judicial remedies and for more coherent judicial reasoning on how to reconcile individual interests, state interests and Community interests. Whereas investor–state arbitration is typically about delimiting individual and state interests, ICJ and GATT/WTO jurisprudence usually deal with alleged conflicts among state interests. The case law of the ECJ and EFTA Court focuses often on delimitation of state interests and Community interests: 'Appraising the proportionality of national rules which pursue a legitimate aim under Community law involves weighing the national interest in attaining that aim against the Community interest in ensuring the free movement of goods'.[126] Proportionality balancing in domestic law, EU law, international law or transnational investor–state arbitration may accordingly vary depending on the respective legal context (individual versus state or Community interests, state versus Community interests) and constitutional context.[127]

[124] *CCC* Award (n 119), para 233.

[125] *cf* EU Petersmann, '"Constitutional Justice" Requires Judicial Cooperation and "Comity" in the Protection of "Rule of Law"' in F Fontanelli, G Martinico and P Carozza (eds) (2009) 1–19.

[126] Case C-169/91, *Stoke-on-Trent* [1992] ECR I-6625, 6658.

[127] eg, in the judicial review of the 'interstate commerce clause' in Art I, Sect 8, cl 3 of the US Constitution (providing that Congress shall have the power 'to regulate Commerce with foreign Nations, and among the several States, and with the Indian Tribes'), US courts tend to apply a 'strict necessity test' in their judicial review of discriminatory state regulation, but only a more deferential 'balancing approach' in their judicial review of non-discriminatory regulation, *cf* L Tribe, *American Constitutional Law*, 3rd edn (Foundation Press, 2000) 1051–55. On judicial review standards of US federal courts in their judicial review of US federal foreign trade laws see: FL Morrison and RE Hudec, 'Judicial Protection of Individual Rights under the Foreign Trade Laws of the United States' in M Hilf and EU Petersmann (eds) (1993) 91–133.

5 MULTILEVEL JUDICIAL GOVERNANCE AS GUARDIAN OF THE CONSTITUTIONAL UNITY OF IEL BASED ON 'COSMOPOLITAN REASON'

In his *Theory of Justice*,[128] Rawls used the idea of reasonableness for designing fair procedures that prompt reasonable citizens (as autonomous moral agents) to agree on basic equal freedoms and other principles of justice. In his later book, *Political Liberalism*, Rawls reframed his theory of justice as fairness by emphasizing the importance of the public use of reason for maintaining a stable, liberal society confronted with the problem of reasonable disagreement about individual conceptions for a good life and a just society. Public reason and 'deliberative democracy' require constitutional guarantees of basic equal rights, such as freedoms to participate as equals in public discourse and independent judicial protection of basic rights, as legal preconditions for public debate defining the conditions for a stable consensus on the principles of justice.[129] Chapters II to VII have argued that the universal recognition of human rights and the judicial task of settling disputes 'in conformity with principles of justice' and human rights (Preamble VCLT) call for democratic and judicial challenges of power-oriented 'intergovernmental reasoning' and of one-sidedly state-centred interpretations of 'rules of recognition' of the Westphalian system of 'international law among states' based on 'cosmopolitan public reason' recognizing the 'constitutional functions' of international law for protecting human rights and democratic self-government in a globally integrated world. In contrast to the Rawlsian conception of 'public reason' and to nationalist conceptions of (big C) Constitutions and democracy as legal frameworks for the self-government of 'We the People', 'cosmopolitan constitutionalism' justifies national and international legal authority by 'cosmopolitan principles of justice' (as discussed in chapter VI) like human rights and multilevel judicial protection of transnational rule of law for the benefit of citizens. Multilevel 'judicial governance', for example in the sense of judicial interpretation, clarification, application, enforcement and adaptation, by national and international courts of the often indeterminate, national and international rules governing the worldwide division of labour among citizens and states, is not only of strategic importance for transforming power-oriented, foreign economic policies into rules-based international economic cooperation based on 'rule of law'. Principle-oriented judicial interpretations and dispute settlements, with due regard to the human rights obligations of governments, also provide the most independent and impartial procedures for protecting the 'constitutional coherence' of the institutionally fragmented, international and domestic legal regimes governing international economic relations, for instance in terms of mutually consistent interpretations of legal rules and promotion of synergies.

[128] Rawls (1971).

[129] Whereas for Rawls, public reason is based on substantive principles that tend to be applied most consistently by supreme courts, Habermas' theory of 'deliberative democracy' focuses on the role of courts as guardians of the constitutional conditions of procedural legitimacy: 'if one understands the constitution as an interpretation and elaboration of a system of rights in which private and public autonomy are internally related (and must be simultaneously enhanced), then a rather bold constitutional adjudication is even required in cases that concern the implementation of democratic procedure and the deliberative form of political opinion- and will-formation', Habermas (1996) 279.

Constitutional and institutional choices: multilevel judicial rule clarification as 'exemplar of public reason' in IEL

The 'constitutional choice' of principles of justice and human rights continues to be based on national constitutions, human rights treaties, free trade agreements and transnational 'constitutional conventions' such as the 'European Conventions' which elaborated and adopted the EU Charter of Fundamental Rights of December 2000 (as incorporated into EU constitutional law by the 2007 Lisbon Treaty) and the 2003 Draft Constitution for Europe, whose principles have to a large extent also become part of European constitutional law due to their incorporation into the Lisbon Treaty. The 'institutional choices' among alternative decision-making processes in IEL – such as decentralized markets, private and public, national, transnational and intergovernmental rule making, the law of international organizations and multilevel governance procedures involving civil society – have been mainly entrusted to citizens, governments, parliaments and regulatory organizations at national and international levels of economic governance. According to Rawls, 'in a constitutional regime with judicial review, public reason is the reason of its supreme court'; it is of constitutional importance for the 'overlapping, constitutional consensus' necessary for a stable and just society among free, equal and rational citizens who tend to be deeply divided by conflicting moral, religious and philosophical doctrines.[130] The ECJ, the ECtHR and the EFTA Court successfully transformed the intergovernmental EC treaties and the ECHR into constitutional orders founded on respect for human rights. Their 'judicial constitutionalization' of intergovernmental treaty regimes for the benefit of citizens as legal subjects also of European law was accepted by citizens, national courts, parliaments and governments because the judicial 'European public reason' protected more effectively individual rights and European 'public goods' (like the EC's common market). The '*Solange* method' of cooperation among European courts 'as long as' ('solange' in German) constitutional rights are adequately protected, reflects an 'overlapping constitutional consensus' on the need for independent and impartial 'constitutional justice' in European law. The power-oriented rationality of governments interested in limiting their judicial accountability is also increasingly challenged in worldwide dispute settlement practices. Judicial interpretation of intergovernmental rules as protecting 'principles of justice' and individual rights may be justifiable notably in citizen-driven areas of IEL protecting mutually beneficial cooperation among citizens based on individual trading rights, investment rights, intellectual property rights, human rights of access to justice and other individual rights (eg to freedom of contract) and effective legal and judicial remedies. Multilevel economic, environmental and human rights governance can become more reasonable and more effective if national and international courts cooperate in protecting the rule of international law for the benefit of citizens with due regard for human rights and their constitutional concretization in national and international legal systems.

[130] J Rawls (1993) 231 ff.

From 'rationality' towards 'reasonableness review' in international economic adjudication

Most governments, economists and economic lawyers conceive IEL from a utilitarian perspective as an instrument for promoting economic efficiency and welfare rather than justice and equity. Most worldwide IEL treaties rank economic policy instruments according to their respective economic efficiency and reconcile economic and non-economic policy objectives based on the prevailing 'Hicks-Kaldor efficiency criterion': they promote trade and investment liberalization based on the economic assumption that the expected social benefits exceed the expected social costs, and that it remains to individual governments to decide whether to use 'safeguard clauses' and 'exception clauses' for compensating adversely affected domestic citizens and protecting non-economic public interests.[131] The 'necessity' and 'least restrictive alternative tests' in judicial proportionality balancing are based on 'rationality' in the instrumental sense of practical, cognitive optimality. The 'proportionality *stricto sensu*' test, by contrast, involves weighing and balancing of competing values which – in case of international dispute settlement and treaty interpretation pursuant to the customary methods of treaty interpretations – also require contextual and teleological interpretation of international law 'in conformity with principles of justice', including 'observance of human rights and fundamental freedoms for all' (Preamble VCLT). Taking into account human rights – such as peaceful enjoyment of private property – in the interpretation of international economic rules reflects 'reasonableness' as a subset of rational determinations that must also satisfy moral principles of justice – such as taking fairly into account the interests of others by treating each member of a polity with equal consideration and respect – and constitutional human rights standards – notably *jus cogens* rules and *erga omnes* obligations.[132]

The increasing recourse by national and international courts to 'proportionality balancing' in IEL should therefore not only be seen as an 'expansion of judicial power globally', 'exposing judges as lawmakers'.[133] More important is the constitutional legitimacy of proportionality balancing, deriving from its foundation in the universal recognition of human rights, including individual rights of access to justice and to impartial judicial remedies, and from its contribution to judicial protection of cosmopolitan 'public reason' and 'constitutional justice' in IEL.[134] Alternative approaches – such as

[131] For a discussion of the economic theory of 'optimal intervention', 'Hicks-Kaldor efficiency' (*ie* the criterion of the potential compensation of losers by winners) and other utilitarain assumptions underlying modern IEL see Petersmann (1991), Part IV on 'Economic Analysis of IEL'.

[132] *cf* G Sartor, 'A Sufficientist Approach to Reasonableness in Legal Decision-Making' EUI Law Department Working Paper 2009, 2: 'reasonableness requires the intersection of three requirements: sufficient rationality, sufficient morality and sufficient consonance' with the relevant context. Sartor explains why 'it is important to stress that rational problem-solving requires a connection between epistemic and practical reasoning' (at 6) and why, 'for reasonableness to be achieved, a sufficient level of rationality and morality is required, which is lower than cognitive and moral optimality' (at 38). Applying this reasonableness standard to complex legislative decision-making and proportionality balancing 'entails that constitutional review must leave the legislator a margin of epistemic and practical appreciation, even when the pursuit of constitutional values is at issue' (at 38).

[133] *cf* Stone Sweet and Mathews (n 90).

[134] *cf* EU Petersmann, 'Human Rights, International Economic Law and "Constitutional Justice"' (2008) 19 *EJIL* 769–98; M Kumm, 'Constitutional Rights as Principles: On the Structure and Domain of Constitutional Justice' (2004) 2 *International Journal of Constitutional Law* 574 ff.

'categorical' protection of individual rights as 'trumps', seeking to dispense with balancing by giving preference (eg, in US courts) to civil and political over economic and social rights, or unprincipled, authoritarian pronouncements by international judges without citizen-oriented reasoning (eg, in many panel proceedings under GATT 1947) – are becoming increasingly 'unreasonable' in IEL (eg, in the sense of unduly disregarding the relevant human rights context of modern IEL) in view of the commitments by all UN member states to protection of human rights and of legitimate, democratic diversity. Depending on the respective constitutional contexts, the more deferential, judicial application of 'Wednesbury reasonableness' in British courts,[135] like 'rational basis tests' in US courts and the only limited review of 'manifest error of appreciation' by EU institutions in European courts,[136] may remain justifiable. Political bodies also tend to welcome that international courts, including the ECJ, continue to be reluctant to engage in 'proportionality *stricto sensu*' review as, for example, in the ECJ's *Danish Bottles* case, where import restrictions on foreign beer and soft drink bottles were found to be 'disproportionately' restricting the EC's common market freedoms despite their judicial recognition as being 'necessary' for realizing the environmental policy objectives of Denmark.[137]

The 'suitability', 'necessity' and 'rationality' tests by constitutional and administrative courts protecting individual rights may be similar to the corresponding standards used in intergovernmental courts protecting rights and obligations of states. But their respective 'proportionality *stricto sensu*' and 'reasonableness' tests are bound to remain different due to their different contexts. Contextual interpretation of intergovernmental economic agreements with due regard to the human rights obligations of the parties to the dispute may reduce this 'gap' between rights-based and interstate proportionality balancing. Just as UN human rights law tends to be relatively more open-ended for legitimately diverse interpretations (eg, of economic and social rights) by national courts compared with *national* human rights and constitutional rules inside democracies, so do the 'interface provisions' in international trade and investment agreements (eg, Article XX GATT providing for unilateral rights to limit market access commitments by national restrictions protecting non-economic values) protect national 'margins of appreciation' regarding the relative 'weighing and balancing' of economic and non-economic values (eg, in case of national measures necessary for protecting 'public morals' and 'public order' pursuant to GATT Article XX,a and GATS Article XIV, a). Judicial 'optimization' of competing values in worldwide jurisdictions must remain more deferential than judicial 'optimization' of constitutional rights in national constitutional courts. Yet, also more deferential 'proportionality balancing' in WTO dispute settlement bodies and in other worldwide jurisdictions for the settlement of disputes among states (eg, in case of judicial delimitation of maritime boundaries based on principles of equity in the ICJ)

[135] *Associated Provincial Picture Houses v Wednesbury Corporation* [1948] 1 KB 223. Under this traditional 'Wednesbury' test in English law a decision can be challenged 'if it is so unreasonable that no reasonable public body could have made it' (*cf* Andenas and Zleptnig (n 100) 385). Due to EU law and the Human Rights Act of 1998, English courts are increasingly applying 'proportionality balancing' in areas of English law implementing EU law and the ECHR. See also M Kumm, 'Political Liberalism and the Structure of Rights: On the Place and Limits of the Proportionality Requirement' in G Pavlakos (ed), *Law, Rights, Discourse: The Legal Philosophy of Robert Alexy* (Oxford: Hart Publishing, 2007) 131 ff.

[136] See n 78 and related text. On the American 'rational basis' and 'strict scrutiny' standards of judicial review see: Stone Sweet and Mathews (n 90).

[137] For a comparative analysis of this *Danish Bottles* case and other ECJ, GATT and WTO dispute settlement jurisprudence on trade-related environmental measures see: EU Petersmann, (1995) ch II.

contributes to rationalizing, legitimizing and justifying third party adjudication in ways promoting its political acceptance by the parties to the dispute.[138]

Proportionality review and 'constitutional justice' as constitutional requirements in European economic law

In Europe, three different ways of judicial transformation of intergovernmental treaties into objective constitutional orders – ie, the judicial 'constitutionalization' of the intergovernmental EC Treaty and of the ECHR, and to a lesser extent of the European Economic Area (EEA) Agreement – succeeded because multilevel judicial protection of citizen rights vis-à-vis abuses of governance powers was accepted by citizens, national courts and parliaments as legitimate.[139] Arguably, the European '*Solange* method' of judicial cooperation 'as long as' other courts respect constitutional principles of justice should be supported by citizens, judges, civil society and their democratic representatives also in judicial cooperation with worldwide courts and dispute settlement bodies – notwithstanding the political opposition by rulers and diplomats in non-democratic UN member states. The universal recognition of citizens as subjects of human rights and modern international law entails that cosmopolitan conceptions of IEL are a precondition for maintaining an 'overlapping consensus' on rule of law not only inside constitutional democracies, but also in mutually beneficial, international economic cooperation among citizens. Hence, there is a need for a constitutional theory of adjudication in IEL protecting individual rights and mutually beneficial cooperation among citizens across national frontiers.[140] Just as 'public reason' among some 500 million EU citizens is no longer dominated just by the reasoning of their 27 national governments, so do human rights require national and international courts to interpret the state-centred structures of IEL in conformity with universal human rights and their underlying 'cosmopolitan public reason' requiring legal and judicial protection of individual rights, rule of law and of general consumer welfare in international civil society cooperation.

Similar to national constitutions and national regulatory agencies (such as competition, environmental and health regulators) for the collective supply of *national public goods* and constitutional protection of the rights of citizens, so also international trade and economic organizations for the collective supply of *international public goods* cannot realize their objectives without legal protection of the rights of citizens in their diverse roles as producers, investors, traders, competitors and consumers in transnational relations and democratic owners of all governance institutions. Judicial 'proportionality balancing' in the narrow sense of weighing among competing economic and non-economic values can hardly remain effective unless citizens have equal rights to participate in judicial procedures and the judicial 'balancing' of competing citizen interests is finally accepted as persuasive by citizens affected by the rules and politically supported

[138] On the necessity of 'trustee courts' helping contracting states – eg, by specifying 'appropriate argumentation frameworks' such as proportionality balancing – to resolve disputes resulting from the indeterminacy and inevitably incomplete nature of international agreements see: Stone Sweet and Mathews (n 90).

[139] *cf* EU Petersmann, 'Multilevel Judicial Governance as Guardian of the Constitutional Unity of International Economic Law' (2008/2009) 30 *Loyola International and Comparative Law Review* 101–52.

[140] *cf* EU Petersmann, 'Constitutional Theories of International Economic Adjudication and Investment Arbitration' in Dupuy, Francioni and Petersmann (eds) (2009) ch 8.

by parliaments as being justified in democratic societies. As the constitutional legitimacy of multilevel, national as well as international judicial justification and protection of the 'necessity' and 'proportionality' of governmental restrictions of individual freedoms and other citizen rights derives ultimately from respect for human rights and 'deliberative democracy', German courts have emphasized that 'the principle of proportionality possesses constitutional status', and failure to strike a proper balance between competing rights or other constitutional values violates 'objective constitutional law'.[141] Similarly, the ECJ interprets 'the principle of proportionality (as) one of the general principles of Community law' prohibiting unnecessary or disproportionate governmental restrictions of the freedoms and other fundamental rights of EU citizens.[142] Likewise, the ECtHR and national courts in the 47 member states of the ECHR subject almost every human right protected in the ECHR to judicial balancing.[143]

'Constitutional justice' in international trade and investment law beyond Europe?

If WTO dispute settlement bodies and other international economic courts followed the example of European courts and interpret IEL – as required by the customary methods of treaty interpretation – 'in conformity with the principles of justice' and the human rights obligations of the states concerned, multilevel 'judicial governance' in IEL could act as 'guardian of the constitutional unity' of IEL. The case law of WTO dispute settlement bodies interpreting WTO dispute settlement rules as admitting public meetings of WTO panels and the WTO Appellate Body,[144] like the admission by WTO dispute settlement bodies and investor–state arbitral tribunals of amicus curiae submissions,[145] reflect an increasing willingness of international courts to protect legitimate citizen interests in international economic adjudication and, thereby, also in intergovernmental rulemaking and economic regulation affecting citizens.

Yet, the 'vertical' as well as 'horizontal', judicial cooperation between national and European courts remains much more developed than judicial cooperation in other fields of international law. Most national and regional trade courts continue to disregard the WTO obligations of governments in domestic dispute settlement proceedings about international trade restrictions – for example, in the more than 50 decisions of national and European courts over EC import restrictions on bananas, whose inconsistencies with GATT/WTO law had been formally established in a dozen of GATT and WTO dispute settlement rulings since 1993;[146] also the Brazilian courts and regional MERCOSUR arbitration concerning Brazilian import restrictions on retreaded tyres adopted judgments without regard to GATT/WTO law, as formally established in WTO dispute settlement

[141] Bundesverfassungsgericht, Judgment, 15 December 1965 (BVerfGE 19, 342, 348 f).

[142] *cf*, eg, Case 265/87, *Schraeder* [1989] ECR 2237.

[143] *cf* H Keller and A Stone Sweet (eds), *A Europe of Rights: The Impact of the ECHR on National Legal Systems* (Oxford: OUP, 2008).

[144] *cf* L Ehring, 'Public Access to Dispute Settlement Hearings in the WTO' (2008) 11 *JIEL* 1021 ff, and notably the Appellate Body report adopted in November 2008 on *US-Continued Suspension of Obligations in the EC-Hormones Dispute* (WT/DS320/AB/R), eg, its procedural ruling of 10 July 2008 allowing public observation of the oral hearings in the Appellate Body (Annex IV of the report).

[145] *cf* J Harrison, 'Human Rights Arguments in *Amicus Curiae* Submissions: Promoting Social Justice?' in Dupuy, Francioni and Petersmann (eds) (2009) ch 18.

[146] *cf* Table 19 and JC Cascante and GG Sander, *Der Streit um die EG-Bananenmarktordnung. The EC Banana Organization Dispute* (Tuebingen: Mohr, 1999).

rulings.[147] Most governments remain eager to avoid legal and judicial accountability in domestic courts for their own violations of the rule of international law in international economic relations, to the detriment of the interests of their domestic citizens in rule of law. As long as governments, parliaments and domestic courts neglect their legal obligations that – as stated already in the 1948 Universal Declaration of Human Rights – 'human rights should be protected by the rule of law' also in 'relations between nations' (Preamble UDHR), rule of international law – and the right of 'everyone . . . to a social and international order in which the rights and freedoms set forth in this Declaration can be fully realized' (Article 28 UDHR) – cannot be effectively protected in international economic relations.

6 COSMOPOLITAN IEL DEPENDS ON DEMOCRATIC 'STRUGGLES FOR HUMAN RIGHTS'

The international economic order after the Second World War was initiated and designed by the executive branch of the US government and provided for US veto powers in the Bretton Woods institutions, in the UN Security Council as well as in the consensus practices of GATT 1947. Yet, as illustrated by the refusal of the US Congress to ratify the 1948 Havana Charter for an International Trade Organization and by the congressional interest group politics insisting on adapting IEL to American interests, there is a hegemonic tradition in the US Congress and in US courts to avoid submitting US foreign policies to international judicial protection of rule of international law. Due to their 'constitutional nationalism', many 'realist' Anglo-Saxon lawyers and politicians – and notably the industry lobbies dominating economic decision-making in the US Congress – claim that international organizations risk undermining parliamentary and majoritarian democracy; hence, the rulemaking, administrative and judicial powers of international organizations like the WTO should not be 'constitutionalized'.[148] The European openness to international law is criticized as a democratic deficiency by some US lawyers who praise the US' unilateralism and resistance against international influences as living up to the ideal of democratic self-determination: the postwar US support for internationalism and multilateralism was 'for the rest of the world, not for us', even though the United States' commitment to internationalism in economic affairs is recognized as serving US interests.[149] The widespread criticism by American, Australian and Canadian lawyers (like Alston, Cass and Howse) of proposals for limiting multilevel governance by 'multilevel constitutional restraints' reflects not only process-based and communitarian, Anglo-Saxon conceptions of parliamentary democracy and 'majoritarian economic governance' that define human rights to liberty and the legitimate judicial protection of

[147] *cf* N Lavranos and N Vielliard, 'Competing Jurisdictions between MERCOSUR and WTO' (2008) 7 *The Law and Practice of International Courts and Tribunals* 205–34; F Morosini, 'The MERCOSUR and WTO Retreaded Tires Dispute: Rehabilitating Regulatory Competition in International Trade and Environmental Regulation' SIEL Working Paper No 42/2008.

[148] See Cass (2005), notably pt III of her book ('Against Constitutionalization') where Cass claims that the 'WTO undermines decisions of democratically authorized national constituencies' (at 212). Yet, notwithstanding seven chapters favouring *national* over *multilevel* constitutionalism, her ch 8 concludes that 'trading democracy, not merely trading constitutionalization, should be the key to WTO constitutionalization in this century' (at 242). Cass admits in her concluding chapter that her 'received account' of Anglo-Saxon constitutionalism has 'been revealed as neither descriptively adequate nor normatively appealing' (at 240).

[149] *cf* Rubenfeld (n 11) 283, 293.

economic freedoms narrowly and disregard the 'collective action problems' in the supply of 'global public goods'; Anglo-Saxon conceptions of 'procedural democracy' and 'constitutional nationalism' also neglect the collective action problems and related governance problems of international 'aggregate public goods'. Many rulers in LDCs (eg, in Asia) – even if they criticize the North American focus on civil and political rather than economic and social human rights and argue in favour of development-oriented reforms of international law – likewise emphasize the classical international law principle of state sovereignty in order to limit their legal and judicial accountability in IEL and human right law.

In Europe, by contrast, the usually weak participation of the more than 350 million EU voters in the periodical elections of the now 736 members of the European Parliament reflect the widespread perception of citizens that – beyond nation states – parliamentary democracy all too often failed to respect and protect general citizen interests effectively. Most European citizens do not even know their representative in the European Parliament, and members of the European Parliament all too often pursue narrow self-interests (eg, of their local constituencies), thus confirming that parliamentary democracy beyond national polities often remains an ideal.[150] The increasingly comprehensive, multilevel guarantees – for example, in the EU Charter of Fundamental Rights as well as in the jurisprudence of national and European courts – of dignity rights, liberty rights, equality rights, solidarity rights, citizen rights and 'rights to justice' reflect the insight that democracy in its literal meaning (ie, 'rule of the people') must be constituted, limited and protected in transnational relations more effectively. Rights-based, cosmopolitan constitutionalism empowers citizens beyond national borders; it can thereby complement parliamentary majority politics at European levels far away from citizens, with its inevitable problems of unequal representation (eg, of more than one million EU citizens by each German member of the European Parliament compared with a few thousand citizens represented by parliamentarians from Luxembourg). Rights-based litigation offers more comprehensive 'due process guarantees' for reconciling the reality of human antagonism and diverse national traditions (eg, regarding conceptions for realizing a 'social market economy') than parliamentary majority decisions that are frequently 'captured' by organized interest groups (eg, due to the 'rational ignorance' of most EU voters vis-à-vis decision-making in the European Parliament). By conferring on EU citizens unique transnational constitutional rights, 'market freedoms' and judicial remedies, the European common market law and 'area of freedom and justice' (Articles 67 ff TFEU) are constitutionally more restrained than democratic governance of national economic markets in national democracies (like the United States). The proposition of this book – ie, to empower and protect producers, workers, investors, traders, consumers and other 'market citizens' by cosmopolitan rights and multilevel constitutional restraints also in their worldwide division of labour – could promote transnational rule of law, participatory democracy and a more 'self-enforcing, cosmopolitan IEL' in international relations beyond Europe.

[150] *cf* G Sartori, *The Theory of Democracy Revisited. Part One: The Contemporary Debate* (Chatham: Chatham House Publisher, 1987) 7: 'democracy is a high-flown name for something that does not exist'.

Multilevel constitutional protection of cosmopolitan rights as a 'transformation policy' and 'struggle for human rights'

More than 2400 years of historical experiences with republicanism confirm that rights-based constitutionalism offers the most effective safeguards for empowering citizens and protecting their common 'public interests'. The main difference between US and European approaches to multilevel governance lies in the postwar European preference for *multilevel constitutional restraints* on multilevel economic governance; the United States continues hegemonic, Westphalian state-centred approaches to international law based on 'constitutional nationalism'. The US and European approaches compete in worldwide treaty negotiations as illustrated by the US rejection of many UN human rights conventions, ILO conventions, the UN Convention on the International Criminal Court, the UNESCO Convention on Cultural Diversity and of many environmental conventions (like the UN Biodiversity Convention and the Kyoto Protocol); they also compete in resorting to regionalism, bilateralism and unilateralism as policy alternatives whenever the collective action problems prevent governments from supplying international public goods through worldwide agreements. It remains to be seen to what extent the human rights revolutions in Tunisia, Egypt and Libya in 2011 will influence multilevel economic and human rights regulation in Africa.

Europeans are more inclined to infer from the European integration experience that multilevel governance requires rule of law and rights-based, multilevel constitutionalism for adjusting and preserving individual and democratic self-government in an interdependent world. At the regional level, the EU has succeeded in using its normative and economic 'power of attraction' for extending its multilevel constitutionalism to 27 EU member states as well as to ever more third countries associated with the EU.[151] The progressive extension of the EU's rights-based free trade rules and human rights commitments to almost 100 additional countries in Europe, the Mediterranean, Africa and Latin America continues to promote peaceful transformations of power-oriented into rules-based politics – based on EU accession, association, free trade and cooperation agreements rather than on unilateral 'power' of the EU to make other countries do what they would not otherwise do.[152] With regard to countries outside Europe, the EU's cooperation agreements (eg, with Russia and the African, Caribbean and Pacific countries) and 'human rights conditionality[153] have been less successful in promoting multilevel constitutionalism and competition law enforced by independent competition authorities. The in excess of 200 RTAs concluded in the Americas, Africa and Asia are often dominated by national interests of 'regional hegemons' such as the US in North America, Argentina and Brazil in MERCOSUR, South Africa in the Southern African integration agreements, China and India in Asia; hence, they usually avoid multilevel constitutionalism such as supranational regulatory agencies and international courts with compulsory jurisdiction

[151] cf M Telò, Europe: A Civilian Power? European Union, Global Governance, World Order (Basingstoke: Palgrave MacMillan, 2006).

[152] *cf* H Sjursen, 'What Kind of Power?' (2006) 13 *Journal of European Public Policy* 169–81.

[153] Since the 1990s, it became official EU policy to include 'human rights clauses' in all new trade and cooperation agreements with third countries, *cf* L Bartels, *Human Rights Conditionality in the European Union's International Agreements* (Oxford: OUP, 2005).

for protecting rule of law.[154] 'Continental hegemons' (like Brazil, China, India, Russia, South Africa) favour the state-centred foreign policy approaches of the US rather than Europe's multilevel constitutionalism. The future legal and constitutional structures of IEL beyond Europe remain uncertain. The history of constitutionalism and of European economic law, as illustrated also by the European banking and sovereign debt crises and related 'rule of law crisis', suggests that the necessary 'constitutionalization' of IEL depends on 'struggles for human rights' by citizens, civil society, parliaments and courts against the never-ending abuses of private and public power by self-interested rulers and rent-seeking interest-groups. The independence, impartiality and 'due process' procedures of national and international courts render multilevel judicial remedies the most principle-oriented 'constitutional safeguard' for interpreting, clarifying and enforcing international agreements 'in conformity within principles of justice' and human rights, as required by the customary methods of treaty interpretation codified in the VCLT.

Just as the EU remains democratically legitimate only as a legal community with limited powers constitutionally restrained by 'strict observance of international law' (Article 3 Lisbon TEU), the democratic legitimacy of IEL depends on constitutional reforms promoting respect for human rights and common 'principles of justice'. Americans tend to view international courts as a potential threat to national democracy and American hegemony and insist on narrow interpretations of their jurisdictions. Europeans tend to be less concerned about 'counter-majoritarian difficulties' and hegemony in the multilevel constitutional context of the EU where 'judicial governance' by the ECJ and by the ECtHR has protected European citizens against welfare-reducing, nationalist discriminations. European integration has prompted European to realize that

- more and more objectives of national constitutions (such as international peace and protection of the environment) can no longer be achieved in a globally interdependent world without multilevel governance and multilevel constitutionalism promoting the collective supply of international public goods with due respect for international law;
- in order to remain legitimate and effective, multilevel governance – such as intergovernmental rulemaking, administration and judicial governance in Europe and also in worldwide institutions – must respect and protect human rights and remain democratically accountable within multilevel constitutional restraints. European integration illustrates that international law and international organisations for the collective supply of international public goods can also *enlarge* citizen rights, *enhance* the legitimacy of multilevel governance, *limit* abuses of multilevel governance and *facilitate* parliamentary accountability of foreign policies beyond what is possible through national constitutionalism;
- human rights and democratic self-government require redesigning 'constitutional sovereignty' in a manner reconciling state sovereignty, popular sovereignty and individual sovereignty based on respect for human dignity, human rights and transnational rule of law. From the point of view of the more than one billion people living in conditions of extreme poverty (eg, without adequate access to food, health, education, shelter,

[154] Yet, also in Africa and in the Americas, an increasing number of RTAs explicitly refer to human rights as an objective or fundamental principle of economic integration, or implicitly limit membership to countries committed to protection of human rights; *cf* the contributions by SF Musungu, 'International Trade and Human Rights in Africa: A Comment on Conceptual Linkages', and by FJ Garcia, 'Integrating Trade and Human Rights in the Americas' in F Abbott, C Breining and T Cottier (eds) (2006) chs 15 and 16.

clothing, water and justice), and from the point of view of the four billion people who are not effectively protected by rule of law,[155] the existing forms of worldwide governance and constitutional nationalism remain highly ineffective in terms of inadequate protection and promotion of universal human rights, rule of law, democratic peace and a healthy environment.

[155] Commission on Legal Empowerment of the Poor, Making the Law Work for Everyone: Report of the Commission on Legal Empowerment of the Poor, vol I (UN, 2008).

Conclusions and Research Agenda for IEL in the Twenty-First Century

Caminante, no hay camino. Se hace camino al andar.
(Traveller, there is no path. The path is made by walking).

ACCORDING TO MARK Twain, 'when the US Congress is in session, no one's life, liberty or property is safe'. For instance, following the American civil war, the US Congress acquiesced in the continuing racial discrimination until US courts began protecting the human and constitutional rights of black US citizens more effectively following the Second World War. Even though the parliamentary 'empowerment legislation' (Ermächtigungsgesetz) leading to the dictatorial Nazi regime and to the end of Germany's Weimar Republic in the 1930s remains an exception in the history of democracies, this study proceeded from the premise that the universal recognition of human rights by all UN member states and protection of international public goods require 'constitutional' rather than merely procedural conceptions of democracy. As national constitutions have become 'partial constitutions' that cannot protect most international public goods unilaterally without international cooperation based on international law and international organizations, the study endorsed the 'Kantian imperative' of protecting equal human freedoms, constitutional democracy and transnational rule of law based on 'cosmopolitan constitutionalism' at national and international levels. The book also emphasized the empirical fact and normative claim that – both in national as well as international legal regimes – protection of human rights and of other interdependent 'aggregate public goods' has been possible only within constitutional frameworks institutionalizing 'public reason' and 'principles of justice'. Yet, as human rights also protect individual and democratic diversity, constitutional democracies and cosmopolitan, transnational legal regimes legitimately differ from each other. Therefore, depending on the constitutionally agreed 'principles of justice' and democratic preferences of people, human rights and the legitimate reality of 'constitutional pluralism' protect many diverse paths to collective protection of national and international public goods.

This book has focused on European economic law and worldwide monetary, trade and investment law in view of the dearth of substantive 'principles of justice' governing the lending practices of international banks, financial regulation and global environmental governance. The nationalist interventions in response to the financial crisis which started in 2008 illustrate this lack of international agreement on how international capital markets, 'sovereign debts', sovereign wealth funds and financial services by international banks, hedge funds and credit rating agencies should be regulated by IEL and be institutionally supervised. Arguably, the inherent instability of electronically connected, global financial markets driven by profit-maximizing investors and speculators elude 'public reason' and effective control by the Bretton Woods institutions, the Bank for International Settlements (BIS) and the Financial Stability Board. Since 2008, the international coordination among national banks and reserve boards in the BIS and other organizations in the field (like the Financial Stability Forum, the International Accounting Standards Board) remained slow in initiating reforms of international financial regulation. Also at the national level, the 'Dodd–Frank' financial sector reform Bill – signed into law in July 2010 by US President Obama – addressed many regulatory problems only in vague terms (like capital requirements of international banks) and delegated their regulation to multiple agencies like the new Financial Stability Oversight Council. Similarly, the EU is in the process of adopting and implementing a series of EU regulations setting up new EU financial and supervisory bodies and stronger multilevel monetary, financial and 'economic governance' processes in order to govern more effectively the European financial, monetary and 'sovereign debt' crises since 2008. The financial crises at national, European and worldwide levels were facilitated by negligent regulation and supervision of private and public, selfish financial practices (eg, of mortgage lenders, fraudulous 'Ponzi schemes' by investment funds, excessive bonuses inducing excessive risk-taking by 'banks that are too big to fail', systemic violations of the EU's monetary, debt and fiscal disciplines by Greece's monetary and banking authorities) and by deep-seated 'moral hazards' (eg, of Greek governments and citizens accumulating more than 330 billion Euros of foreign debt and living at the expense of foreign lenders). As the ubiquitous conflicts of interests, 'market failures' and 'governance failures' originate inside the minds of individuals, the future of international economic and environmental regulation and poverty reduction remain uncertain and require institutionalizing a new 'cosmopolitan public reason' limiting and justifying multilevel economic regulation by stronger protection of human rights and other cosmopolitan rights empowering citizens to 'struggle for justice'.

As this study evolved into a much longer manuscript than initially envisaged, the following conclusions – structured around the fifteen research questions listed in the Introduction – offer only brief summaries of my answers discussed in the eight chapters of this book. By identifying additional research questions, the conclusions will, hopefully, contribute to promoting a more interdisciplinary research agenda for the necessary reforms of IEL.

1 How should IEL, its 'systemic' nature, legitimate objectives, 'primary' and 'secondary rules' and principles be defined? Does IEL constitute a 'legal system' for multilevel economic governance?

The evolution of the international economic order into a 'layered legal system' raises questions (discussed in Chapters I and II) as to the relationships between the different private and public, national, regional and worldwide levels of legal regulation of international movements of goods, services, persons, capital and related payments. Inside the EU's common market, national governments were forced – by citizens, parliaments and courts – to integrate the different layers of private and public, national and intergovernmental economic law into a mutually coherent constitutional system 'founded on the principles of liberty, democracy, respect for human rights and fundamental freedoms, and the rule of law, principles which are common to the Member States' (Article 6 EU).

As in constitutional democracies, 'governance' in European institutions is perceived as a multilevel process of rulemaking, administration and adjudication for the benefit of citizens and their human rights. In contrast to this citizen-oriented focus of European economic law, the Bretton Woods and WTO Agreements treat citizens and non-governmental organizations as mere objects of monetary, financial and trade governance, without individual rights to hold their own governments accountable for their frequent disregard of consumer welfare and violations of international treaties, such as WTO rules ratified by parliaments for the benefit of citizens. As long as citizens have no effective legal and judicial remedies against such violations of IEL by their own governments, bureaucratic self-interests and protectionist collusion – also among EU institutions, as illustrated by the ECJ's refusal to review violations of WTO obligations by the EU Commission and EU Council even if such violations of rule of law have been formally established by legally binding WTO dispute settlement rulings – all too often prevail. Citizens rightly challenge the democratic legitimacy of this 'feudalist exclusion' of citizen rights and the intergovernmental neglect of transnational rule of law, consumer welfare and other general citizen interests in international trade and financial regulation.

Chapter I distinguished five conceptions of IEL, which define the 'primary rules' and 'secondary rules' of transnational economic regulation from different public and private, national and international perspectives. In view of the increasing role of private actors and public–private partnerships in the collective supply of international public goods, it was argued that only an 'integrated methodology' combining the five different conceptions can offer more effective solutions for dealing with the five major 'collective action problems' impeding collective supply of 'aggregate efforts public goods'. The more national and international public goods, due to 'globalization', interact horizontally as well as vertically, the more IEL must take into account these legal, economic and political interdependencies through mutually consistent interpretations of the various interacting legal regimes. The global 'shift of power' (eg, in favour of the 'BRICS') tends to further weaken effective democratic control of multilevel economic governance by national parliaments and citizens. Notably outside Europe and North America, IEL often fails to effectively protect human rights, consumer welfare and democratic self-governance. Chapter II argued for a 'paradigm change' in favour of enhancing citizen-driven 'input legitimacy' of IEL by strengthening legal and judicial protection of human rights, constitutional and cosmopolitan rights of citizens as main actors, beneficiaries, sources of value and 'democratic owners' of IEL. The political premises (eg, the 'New Haven approach'), moral premises (eg, Kantian cosmopolitan legal theory) and constitutional premises (eg, constitutional pluralism, Rawls' theory of justice and 'cosmopolitan constitutionalism') of the proposed 'constitutionalization' and cosmopolitan conception of multilevel economic regulation were explained. As many multilateral economic agreements (like the WTO Agreement) explicitly recognize the 'systemic nature' of IEL (eg, the interrelationships of trade and monetary rules) and customary international law requires interpreting IEL in conformity with the human rights obligations of all UN member states, Rawls' constitutional theory of the 'four-stage sequence' of legitimate constitutional, legislative, administrative and judicial protection of public goods and of 'public reason' was considered as a useful template also for constitutional reforms of IEL and for multilevel protection of cosmopolitan rights.

The 'supranational' EU law and the much more deferential EEA law offer two diverse examples for multilevel 'constitutional protection' of cosmopolitan rights in IEL for the benefit of citizens. Yet, as illustrated by the financial crises in the EU as well as in Iceland, EU and EEA law continue to evolve as imperfect 'social experiments' revealing more and more market failures as well as multilevel governance failures. The law of some worldwide organizations (like the WTO) has hierarchical structures asserting legal supremacy not only vis-à-vis domestic laws (*cf* Article XVI:4 WTO Agreement); there are also vertical legal hierarchies and constitutional 'checks and balances' among the institutions and different levels of primary and secondary law of international organizations (*cf* Articles IX, XVI:3 WTO Agreement). WTO law increasingly limits regional agreements (*cf* Articles XXIV GATT, V GATS), bilateral agreements (*cf* Article 11 of the WTO Safeguards Agreement, the WTO Agreement on Textiles and Clothing) and national unilateralism through multilateral legal and institutional restraints (eg, in Articles 16, 17 and 23 DSU); such IEL guarantees of economic freedoms, non-discriminatory conditions of competition, rule of law and welfare-increasing cooperation among producers, investors, traders and consumers across national frontiers can serve 'constitutional functions' for contesting and reforming welfare-reducing border discrimination in national legal systems. As explained in chapter IV, clarification of the legal interrelationships between WTO law and the law of other worldwide organizations, and also between human rights law and IEL, requires 'legal balancing' (eg, between civil, political, economic and social freedoms) rather than reliance on legal hierarchies (eg, in the rare cases of conflicts between *jus cogens* rules and economic rules). Viewed from the perspective of 'principles of justice' (as discussed in chapter VI) and the related human rights to public justification and judicial review of welfare-reducing government restrictions of economic freedoms, 'human rights approaches' to IEL and judicial remedies tend to enhance 'participatory' and 'deliberative democracy' and 'public reason' in IEL: 'Having a legal remedy that allows for the contestation of acts by public authorities before an impartial and independent court and demanding its justification in terms of public reason is as basic a commitment of liberal democracy as the right to vote'.[1]

2 Does IEL need to be justified by theories of justice? Is the prevailing conception of IEL as 'public international law among states' consistent with the human rights obligations of UN member states? Do human rights require a cosmopolitan conception of IEL (as, for example, in the common market regulations of the EU and the EEA) in order to protect human rights and consumer welfare more effectively?

The legal methodology used in this book proceeds from the insight that – in contrast to the search for truth in the natural sciences – law is less about 'truth' (eg in case of establishing legal facts) than, notably in case of normative arguments, about 'institutionalizing public reason' providing for 'reasonable procedures' of rule-making, rule-administration and rule-enforcement based on 'balanced judgments' (eg resulting from democratic discourse among free and equal citizens, judicial procedures administered by impartial and independent judges so as to secure 'rule of law', 'balancing' among competing human and constitutional rights based on principles of non-discrimination, necessity and proportionality). Arguably, reasonable judgments and justice (eg in the sense of reasonable justification) are the equivalent in normative social sciences to truth in the natural sciences.

[1] M Kumm, 'The Idea of Socratic Contestation and the Right to Justification: The Point of Rights-Based Proportionality Review' (2010) 4(2) *Law & Ethics of Human Rights* Art 1.

Like all other legal and governance institutions, IEL needs justification not only in terms of 'utilitarian output legitimacy', but also in terms of the inalienable human rights of citizens and the corresponding obligations of UN member states. In contrast to the jurisprudence of the ECtHR clarifying the positive obligations of states under the ECHR to protect and fulfil human rights,[2] the human rights obligations of UN member states under UN human rights law to respect, protect and fulfil human rights in the field of IEL remain much more contested. Similar to the statement by the ECJ in its landmark *Internationale Handelsgesellschaft* judgment of 1970 that the protection of human rights in European economic law 'whilst inspired by the constitutional traditions common to the Member states, must be ensured within the framework of the structure and objectives of the Community',[3] the multilevel human rights obligations of states must be concretized in IEL with due regard to international human rights agreements, the particular structures and objectives of IEL and the constitutional principles common to human rights law and IEL. Chapter I inferred from the unnecessary poverty of more than one billion people, from the disregard for human rights and rule of law in so many UN member states as well as from the welfare-reducing governance crises in the international trading, financial and environmental systems that 'Westphalian conceptions' of IEL fail to effectively respect, protect and fulfil human rights and transnational rule of law. Since the human rights revolutions and Adam Smith's critique of market failures (like private cartel agreements) and governance failures (like colonialism) in the mercantilist 'private law' and 'common law societies' during the eighteenth century, IEL continues to dynamically evolve in response to unilateral reforms (like the abolition of the British Corn Laws in 1846), bilaterally agreed reforms (like the European system of bilateral free trade agreements following the Cobden–Chevallier trade agreement of 1860 between France and the United Kingdom) and multilaterally agreed reforms (like the Bretton Woods Agreements of 1944, GATT 1947 and the now almost 300 RTAs), as described in chapters I and II.

Chapter III interpreted the progressively universal recognition of human rights, including cosmopolitan economic rights to be protected by rule of law, in the sense of Kant's dialectic theory of history as reflecting a gradual 'enlightenment'[4] of individuals asserting their rights in national and international legal systems, including 'positive freedom of choice' in constituting their identities vis-à-vis inherited forms of socialization such as traditions of gender and racial discrimination, abuses of corporate power, religious dogmas and nationalist discrimination against foreigners. The 'human rights revolution' requires that – in the twenty-first century – all political power, law and governance must be justified vis-à-vis citizens and 'civil society' in terms of human rights and democratic governance.[5] The normative foundation of UN human rights law and of IEL in the

[2] *cf* D Xenos, *The Positive Obligations of the State under the European Convention on Human Rights* (London: Routledge, 2011).

[3] Case 11/70 [1970] ECR 1125, para 4.

[4] According to Kant (1970), 'enlightenment is man's emergence from his self-incurred immaturity. . . . The motto of enlightenment is therefore: *Sapere aude*! Have courage to use your own understanding' (at 54). On modern self-empowerment see: TM Franck, *The Empowered Self. Law and Society in the Age of Individualism* (Oxford: OUP, 1999).

[5] As discussed in ch VII, the modern distinction between civil society, political society and the state as three distinct, yet closely interrelated spheres of social interactions and of 'ethical life' among persons remains controversial depending on how one conceives of the individual, families, economic and other associations and of their roles in the larger society. In contrast to the hierarchical powers and enforcement mechanisms of the state, civil society is more influenced by deliberation and communicative learning processes (eg, for social conflict

twenty-first century was interpreted in conformity with the Kantian 'cosmopolitan constitutionalism' and 'categorical imperative' that morality and 'public reason' require not only respect for human dignity and equal human rights as constitutional restraints of national and international rulemaking, administration and adjudication. Modern human rights law also calls for a normative conception, and more comprehensive legal regulation and protection by means of cosmopolitan rights, of the 'civilized international society' of producers, traders, investors, consumers and other citizens cooperating in the worldwide division of labour: just as a liberal civil society and democracy depend on each other, so must democratic regulation of the worldwide division of labour for the benefit of all citizens and of their human rights empower, respect and legally protect individuals in their mutually beneficial international cooperation as an ever more important dimension of individual and social self-determination in transnational communities of self-governing citizens. The lack of a 'global *demos*' and the antagonistic competition between '*homini economici*' do not prevent cosmopolitan and communitarian 'human rights conceptions' of interdependent 'public goods' regimes governed by IEL. Markets and IEL can fulfil their 'public good functions' only if they are justifiable by principles of justice and supported ('embedded') by societies.

As explained in chapters II to IV, the European experiences with economic law prior to, and following the Second World War justify the critique of inadequate legal and judicial remedies in UN human rights, economic and environmental conventions: empowering market participants by means of legal rights and judicial remedies to challenge abuses of power (such as restrictive business practices, 'externalization' of environmental pollution) offers decentralized, market-based instruments for enforcing market and environmental regulation by self-interested citizens that tend to be more effective in promoting constitutional and democratic values than merely intergovernmental regimes.[6] Chapter III also used Kantian legal theory justifying multilevel, legal and judicial protection of cosmopolitan rights as being necessary not only on moral and constitutional grounds, but as the most 'realist' approach to limiting abuses of public and private power by 'countervailing rights', such as judicial remedies of producers, investors, traders, consumers and other self-interested citizens benefitting from the global division of labour against arbitrary, governmental violations of IEL. As economic rights need to be reconciled and 'balanced' with human, constitutional and all other rights of citizens, governments and courts of justice must justify their legal decisions by coherent theories of justice respecting the legitimate reality of 'constitutional pluralism'. Chapter III argued for a 'fourth concept of cosmopolitan liberty' protecting 'human capabilities' and 'sustainable development' by limiting the numerous 'protection biases' in power-oriented 'member-driven economic governance' (eg, in the WTO) in order to better protect human rights and consumer welfare. IEL will always remain composed of diverse, private and public, national and international legal systems. The mutual coherence of these subsystems requires taking more seriously the 'consistent interpretation' requirement of national and international legal systems so as to protect transnational rule of law with due respect for human rights and other constitutional 'principles of justice'.

resolution) among free individuals with diverse preferences (eg, on the desirable degree of their 'socialization' with others).

[6] *cf* BA Ackerman and RB Stewart, 'Reforming Environmental Law: The Democratic Case for Market Incentives' (1988) *Columbia Journal of Environmental Law* 13.

3 Is the 'constitutionalization' of IEL by means of multilevel regulation and limitation of abuses of economic power the logical continuation of postwar decolonization of international economic relations? Why did governments fail after the First World War, but succeeded after the Second World War, to reconstruct a liberal international economic order? Why has international trade law evolved since 1948 so much more successfully compared with international monetary, financial, investment and environmental law?

Similar to decolonization, the rights-based 'constitutionalization' of IEL aims to protect cosmopolitan rights against welfare-reducing abuses of public and private power. After the Second World War, in contrast to the regulatory failures of the League of Nations following the First World War, the hegemonic leadership of the United States for preparing and adopting the UN Charter, the Bretton Woods Agreements and GATT 1947 enabled the 'political postwar miracle' of a successful, legal and institutional reconstruction of a mutually coherent, multilateral trading system based on complex interactions between national, bilateral, regional and worldwide monetary and trade liberalization and regulation.

Chapter II described the main challenge of international law in the twenty-first century in terms of the 'Kantian constitutional imperative' and the need for collective learning through 'Socratic contestation': equal freedoms as the 'first principle of justice' require multilevel constitutional protection against abuses of power in all human interactions at national, international and transnational levels, subject to democratic legislation and judicial 'balancing' reconciling competing civil, political, economic, social and cultural human and constitutional rights and fundamental freedoms. Kant understood freedom in the sense of external autonomy of action (based on internal freedom limited by morality) and emphasized the mutual synergies of global public goods like liberal, rules-based trade and international peace. The universal recognition of civil, political, economic and social human rights can be understood as also protecting 'positive freedom' in the sense of individual access to essential 'natural goods' (like water and food) and 'social goods' (like access to education, essential medicines, equal constitutional rights) necessary for human self-development. This study emphasized the function of human rights and constitutional democracy to also protect individual and communitarian diversity so as to respect the human experience of 'plurality and difference'.[7] In IEL, respect for 'reasonable disagreement', cosmopolitan rights and other 'principles of justice' based on 'common but differentiated responsibilities' – such as principles of 'equity', 'precaution', 'good faith', the 'polluter pays principle' and the prohibition of causing transboundary harm – is necessary for overcoming 'collective action problems' inhibiting collective supply of global public goods like 'sustainable development'. The failures of the consensus-based Doha Round negotiations (as discussed in chapter VII) illustrate that – in contrast to *regional, communitarian regulation* of transnational movements of goods, services, persons and capital limiting discriminatory border restrictions and other *nationalist* distortions of competition inside common markets – *worldwide market regulation* must remain more deferential vis-à-vis diverse, yet legitimate democratic legislation at national and regional levels.

[7] *cf* H Arendt, *The Human Condition* (Chicago: Chicago University Press, 1958) 18 f. On protection of human diversity by means of human rights see, eg, S Caney and P Jones (eds), *Human Rights and Global Diversity* (London: Frank Cass, 2001).

Chapter IV explained why the 'disorder among fragmented legal systems' can be transformed into mutually coherent 'legal pluralism' if the legal sub-systems are interpreted and developed in conformity with the human rights obligations of all UN member states and with due respect for legitimate 'constitutional pluralism'. The 'dual nature' of human rights as positive law and 'moral rights to have legal rights and judicial remedies' entails not only reasonable disagreement on how human rights should be protected in diverse national and international legal systems; it also legitimizes civil society struggles for more effective protection of human and constitutional rights in IEL. Not only *national constitutions*, but also functionally limited '*treaty constitutions*' establishing international organizations for the collective supply of international public goods involve institutional choices (eg, among legislative, administrative, judicial and individual decision-making processes at local, state, federal and transnational levels) whose distributional implications remain inevitably contested (eg, regarding judicial protection of individual rights against abuses of power). The success of many UN Specialized Agencies also depended on citizens insisting on competitive supply of international public goods (like postal, telephone and other communication services), resisting protectionist pressures (like shipping and air transport cartels) and claiming rights of access (eg, to essential food, medicines and education). The relative success of the GATT/WTO legal and trading system was due, inter alia, to its use of legal principles, standards, rules and institutions that had been successfully tested in bilateral and regional trade agreements for many decades and protect mutually beneficial trade transactions with due respect for national sovereignty to regulate domestic economies (eg, by non-discriminatory rules in conformity with GATT Article III) and restrict trade if necessary for protecting non-economic policy objectives (eg, pursuant to Article XX, XXI GATT).

During the 1930s, the breakdown of the international monetary and financial system rendered a multilateral trading system impossible. The postwar Bretton Woods Agreements and GATT 1947 succeeded in establishing a legal and institutional framework for a mutually coherent evolution of the multilateral monetary, trading and financial systems during the second half of the twentieth century. The unilateral termination of the par value system by the United States in August 1971 led to a certain 'legal disintegration' in international monetary and financial regulation. For instance, the amendment of Article IV of the IMF Agreement in 1978 left all IMF member countries three alternative policy choices for 'orderly exchange arrangements': (1) by pegging the value of the national currency to the currency of another member or to the Fund's Special Drawing Rights; (2) through cooperative arrangements with other members (like regional monetary systems); or (3) by means of any other exchange arrangements (including floating exchange rates) subject to the prohibition of manipulation of exchange rates (like competitive devaluations). The more the major currencies floated against each other or joined the European Monetary System, the more the IMF surveillance functions pursuant to Article IV became limited to LDCs requesting balance-of-payments assistance from the IMF.[8] Since the beginning of the twenty-first century, the ever greater role and foreign currency reserves of newly industrializing countries (like the BRICS) have led to ever stronger demands for adjusting the outdated quota, voting and governance system of the IMF (eg, providing EU member states with seven directors on the IMF executive

[8] *cf* AF Lowenfeld, 'The International Monetary System: A Look Back over Seven Decades' (2010) 13 *JIEL* 575–95.

board, compared with only one for the United States and 12 for the 161 less-developed IMF member states). The criticism by many LDCs of the 'conditionality' of the IMF's financial assistance (eg, based on the 'Washington consensus' that 'crony capitalism', corruption and weak regulation had been major causes of the financial crises in Asia and Russia during the 1990s) prompted ever more LDCs to refrain from requesting financial assistance from the IMF. The recent involvement of the IMF in the financing of the public debts of Greece and Ireland – in spite of the absence of exchange rate problems of these eurozone member countries – raises legal doubts regarding the limited mandate in the IMF Agreement. In spite of more and more claims for adjusting the IMF Agreement to the changing world economy and to new 'fundamental disequilibria' in international monetary relations (eg, due to China's currency interventions keeping the value of the Chinese 'renminbi' artificially low and China's foreign exchange surpluses artificially high), there is no agreement yet on a new 'Bretton Woods II Agreement' adjusting IMF rules and IMF regulatory functions to regulate, for example, national currency manipulations, financial market supervision and restrictions of short-term, speculative capital flows more effectively. International investment regulation remains even more dominated by national, bilateral and regional regulation without agreement on how past attempts at negotiating worldwide investment rules (eg, in the OECD and WTO) could be pursued more successfully.

4 What are the main causes and origins of the current financial, environmental and poverty crises? Are the related failures of IEL the inevitable fate of humanity in view of the 'rational egoism' of individuals and the ubiquitous 'market failures' and 'governance failures'?

This study perceived law as an instrument for institutionalizing 'public reason' and realizing agreed policy goals. It agreed essentially with Rawls' 'domestic poverty hypothesis', ie, that the economic and social welfare of almost all states depends essentially on their domestic rules and institutions rather than on the morally arbitrary distribution of natural resources among countries. Yet, the capacity of all countries to increase the welfare of their domestic people through international trade depends on legal protection of the 'constitutional functions' of IEL for empowering citizens and people to engage in a mutually beneficial division of labour. In contrast to Rawls' disregard for transnational legal duties of assistance, the human rights obligations of all UN member states also entail cosmopolitan legal duties to respect, protect and fulfil human rights not only vis-à-vis domestic citizens; citizens and governments also have legal duties to protect human rights vis-à-vis foreign governments and international organizations and to cooperate in collective supply of international public goods. Yet, the scope and modalities of such international 'duties to protect' human rights and the basic needs of all human beings remain controversial. As discussed in chapter I, the international economic and environmental crises reflect the lack of agreement on how to regulate the collective action problems of interdependent public goods. In view of the scarcity of resources, the inevitable 'public choices' among competing public goods often remain contested. In contrast to the 1930s, it was largely due to the existing multilateral monetary and trade agreements that the American and European responses to the financial crises and 'great recession' since 2008 focused on domestic regulation of financial markets rather than – as in the 1930s and in 1971 – on sub-optimal, discriminatory border restrictions for imports of goods, services and capital. The WTO rules and institutions helped to resist protectionist pressures. The more economics and environmental problems are becoming global and politics rests local, the stronger is the need for 'bottom-up constitutionalism' correcting domestic governance failures and coordinating multilevel economic governance of interdependent public goods through international rules and institutions aimed at limiting – as discussed in Table 8 and in the related text – the 'protection biases' in 'political markets' for multilevel economic governance. The basic conclusion of this study is that the obvious 'governance failures' in the international trading, financial, environmental and transnational legal systems are not an inevitable fate of humanity, but the result of inadequate rules, institutions and nationalist, power-oriented 'public reason'.

Chapter II endorsed Kantian multilevel constitutionalism as a legal precondition for protecting equal freedoms, rule of law, 'democratic peace' and cosmopolitan rights beyond states. Kantian legal theory infers from the inevitable antagonism among free individuals the necessity of a decentralized, international order protecting the legitimate diversity of individuals and of democracies through human rights and other, multilevel constitutional safeguards.[9] By constraining discretionary state powers in ways that protect equal freedoms of cosmopolitan citizens in transnational cooperation, multilevel legal protection of voluntary economic cooperation and of human rights enhances the legitimacy of state powers by limiting their abuses and ability to exercise arbitrary domination. This need for multilevel legal protection of the Kantian ideals of respect for human dignity, 'normative individualism', diversity and transnational rule of law is also increasingly emphasized as a major objective of multilevel human rights and IEL, for example in the WTO negotiations on 'special safeguard mechanisms' protecting small farmers in LDCs and ensuring effective access to essential medicines, or in recent proposals to replace the arbitrary 'one dollar a day' definition of poverty by a 'rights-based poverty definition'.[10] While Kant explained man's 'unsocial sociability' ('*ungesellige Geselligkeit*') and the human antagonism as resulting from conflicts between rational egoism and limited reasonableness in the minds of all human beings,[11] modern psychoanalysis also emphasizes the anarchical, unruly 'animal nature' of human beings and our often 'repressed, unconscious rationality' (as revealed by 'Freudian slips').[12]

As explained in chapters IV to VII, 'human rights coherence', popular self-determination and transnational rule of law for the benefit of citizens must remain 'constitutional foundations' of democratically legitimate IEL. Just as human rights con-

[9] Even though the three treaty articles proposed by Kant for an international (con)federation among free states protecting 'perpetual peace' through cosmopolitan guarantees of equal freedoms and rule of law are very abstract, they aim at protecting individual freedom and responsibility, human diversity and 'subsidiarity' in the exercise of democratic self-regulation, *cf* EU Petersmann, 'How to Constitutionalize International Law and Foreign Policy for the Benefit of Civil Society?' (1999) 20 *Michigan Journal of International Law* 1–30. On individual liberty as constitutional foundation of EU law and 'legitimacy through subsidiarity', see: F Ronge, *Legitimität durch Subsidiarität – Der Beitrag des Subsidiaritätsprinzips zur Legitimation einer überstaatlichen politischen Ordnung in Europa* (Baden-Baden: Nomos, 1998). Ronge rightly emphasizes (at 128) that citizens no longer consider 'indirect legitimization' of European law by means of parliamentary treaty ratification as sufficient.

[10] D Woodward, 'How Poor is Poor? Towards a Rights-based Poverty Line (2010) available at: www.neweconomics.org/publications/how-poor-is-poor.

[11] *cf* J Rawls (1993) 48 ff, who distinguishes between the reasonable and the rational as a variation of the Kantian distinction between categorical and hypothetical imperatives.

[12] On interferences, resistance (*Widerstand*) and repression (*Verdrängung*) of individual compromises between conscious and unconscious rationalities see: S Freud, *Introductory Lectures on Psychoanalysis*, trans J Strachey (London: Hogarth Press, 1966) 42 ff.

ventions restrict regulatory powers of states by requirements that restrictions must be 'prescribed by law and . . . necessary in a democratic society in the interests of national security or public safety, for the prevention of disorder or crime, for the protection of health or morals or for the protection of the rights and freedoms of others' (Article 11, paragraph 2 ECHR), so do many IEL rules serve 'constitutional functions' for protecting basic principles of constitutionalism in domestic economic regulation. For instance:

- The 'national treatment clauses' (eg, in Article III GATT), 'general exceptions' and numerous 'safeguard clauses' in worldwide economic treaties (eg, Articles XVII–XXI GATT) protect the sovereign rights of all countries to unilaterally regulate their domestic economies, polities and 'public interests', thereby limiting both abuses of national policy powers (such as welfare-reducing, arbitrary discrimination against foreigners) as well as abuses of international regulation disregarding legitimate national 'margins of appreciation' in protecting national interests (such as 'public morals' and 'public order'). By requiring public justification and non-discriminatory application of import restrictions, the various 'safeguard clauses' promote transparency and 'public reason', for instance based on transparent deliberation of the trade-offs of costly trade restrictions for the protection of non-trade values.
- WTO dispute settlement bodies may enhance 'constitutional democracy' by enforcing democratically approved WTO obligations to protect 'constitutional principles' of liberty, non-discrimination and rule of law in international trade vis-à-vis majoritarian interest group politics. Yet, WTO bodies must practise deference in the interpretation of the non-economic values underlying WTO safeguard clauses; 'institutional sensitivity' towards democratically accountable jurisdictions outside the WTO is especially important whenever trade rules cannot be interpreted as protecting a 'win-win deal' beneficial for all reasonable citizens and may adversely affect non-economic values.[13]
- If a major purpose of constitutional democracy is to promote collective decisions by political institutions 'whose structure, composition and practices treat all members of the community, as individuals, with equal respect and concern',[14] then global governance institutions can and should promote 'deliberative democracy' and transparent, participatory and 'inclusive decision-making' on questions of social justice, for instance by providing independent 'cost/benefit analyses' (eg, in the context of the WTO's Trade Policy Review Mechanisms) helping citizens and civil society groups to resist one-sided interest group pressures exploiting 'information asymmetries' and 'power asymmetries' in trade policy decision-making processes.

[13] *cf* R Howse and K Nicolaidis, 'Legitimacy and Global Governance: Why Constitutionalizing the WTO is a Step too Far' in RB Porter et al (eds), *Efficiency, Equity, Legitimacy, The Multilateral Trading System at the Millenium* (Cambridge: Harvard University Press, 2001) 227 ff. The authors misunderstand 'global subsidiarity' and 'constitutionalization' as mutually exclusive rather than as mutually reinforcing, as illustrated by their misrepresentation of my publications as proposing transformation of the WTO into a 'federal constitution' rather than a 'cosmopolitan constitution' protecting 'subsidiarity'. On the 'constitutional functions' of national and international adjudication for protecting 'constitutional democracy' see: EU Petersmann, 'Judging Judges: From "Principal-Agent Theory" to "Constitutional Justice" in Multilevel Judicial Governance of Economic Cooperation among Citizens' (2008) 11 *JIEL* 827–84. For a criticism of majoritarian conceptions of democracy see: R Dworkin, *Freedom's Law* (Cambridge: Harvard University Press, 1996).

[14] Dworkin (n 13) 17.

5 Does multilevel governance of interdependent national, regional and worldwide public goods require a multilevel constitutional theory? Are cosmopolitan rights and transnational rule of law necessary for regulating the 'collective action problems' in the decentralized supply of interdependent 'aggregate efforts public goods'?

Since the ancient democracy of Athens during the fifth century BC, constitutionalism – ie, the self-commitment of reasonable individuals to constitutional long-term rules of a higher legal rank as an integral part of diverse 'mixed constitutions' based on ideas of separation of powers[15] – and constitutional respect for human autonomy in confronting the 'human dilemma' (such as the inevitable, internal and external conflicts of individuals caused by their rational egoism, limited reasonableness, emotions and 'animal instincts') continue to evolve through historical learning processes of 'trial and error'. Both constitutionalism and human rights can be likened to the Promethean promise of enabling human beings to overcome their human predicament[16] – provided they use the Promethean tools reasonably. The tragic fates of Prometheus and Sisyphus are reminders of the often tragic, human struggles to resist abuses of power. Chapters II and III inferred from the Kantian 'categorical imperative' that multilevel protection of human rights – also in the international division of labour – cannot remain effective without multilevel constitutional safeguards of equal freedoms for mutually beneficial cooperation among citizens. The long-standing failures of the 'international law among states' to protect human rights, democratic self-governance, poverty reduction and other 'international public goods' confirm the need for additional constitutional safeguards not only inside democracies, but also in the international regulation of transnational and international economic cooperation of citizens and people. This necessary 'constitutionalization' of IEL requires, as discussed in chapters I to V, constitutional theories on how to integrate the diverse private and public, national, regional and worldwide legal regimes and institutions into more coherent, multilevel governance systems respecting human rights, constitutional rights and legitimately different modes of democratic governance. Without mutually coherent 'integration law', the multilevel regulation of human rights, constitutional rights, governance institutions and IEL for the collective supply of international 'public goods' risks failing to overcome the collective action problems impeding the supply of interdependent, national and international 'aggregate efforts public goods'.

Chapters III and IV explained why the necessary 'civilization' and 'constitutionalization' of IEL require constitutional and cosmopolitan restraints of public and private power and 'human rights coherence' of multilevel economic regulation (*cf* Tables 3–6 and related texts). IEL should be conceived as a 'layered, multilevel legal order' (*cf* Table 7) based on respect for legitimate 'constitutional pluralism' as a framework for multilevel rulemaking, rule administration and judicial rule clarification and peaceful settlement of disputes for the benefit of citizens and their constitutional rights. As long as national constitutions and parliaments focus on *state interests* without subjecting foreign policy powers to more effective constitutional restraints, coherent theories for collective governance of interdependent 'aggregate public goods' are easier to derive from 'cosmopolitan constitutionalism' limiting intergovernmental organizations and *national foreign*

[15] *cf* A Riklin, *Machtteilung. Geschichte der Mischverfassung* (Darmstadt: Wissenschaftliche Buchgesellschaft, 2006).

[16] *cf* Arendt (n 7), who defines the 'human condition' in terms of 'labor, work and collective action'.

policies dominated by domestic interest-group politics by democratic and judicial safeguards of cosmopolitan rights.

'Conflicts law approaches' focusing on international private law techniques for determining whether rules of another legal order deserve recognition, GAL approaches and 'constitutional approaches' to IEL share the view that the current failures of IEL require a reframing of the interstate paradigm of international law to a more pluralistic and cosmopolitan framework. They disagree about whether the divisions and differences in regimes, interests and values are too wide and deep to support, at this point a constitutionalist paradigm for global governance.[17] The different responses to the global governance problems are often due to the different perspectives of private lawyers, constitutional, administrative and international lawyers. Lawyers from common law countries with nationalist constitutional traditions rejecting rights-based, international 'treaty constitutions' deliberately use administrative law terms rather than constitutional terms – even if the agreements constituting international organizations like the ILO, UNESCO, WHO and FAO have been explicitly designed as 'constitutions' (*sic*). European lawyers tend to emphasize the reality and normative legitimacy of multilevel 'constitutional pluralism' – also inside the EU, whose diverse national and regional constitutional sub-systems bear witness to its 'Leitmotiv' of 'unity in diversity' (as emphasized in the 2004 draft 'Treaty establishing a Constitution for Europe'). Anglo-Saxon common lawyers often misunderstand proposals for 'constitutionalizing international law' as utopian insistence on 'foundational Constitutionalism' pursuing a 'single design or order', or as a hegemonic European project aimed at compensating Europe's comparative lack of 'hard power' by additional 'legal power' based on European conceptions of 'global constitutionalism'.[18] As the diverse private law, constitutional law, administrative law and international law conceptions describe and assess the 'globalization' of IEL from different perspectives, it appears inappropriate to present GAL and 'constitutionalist conceptions' of the law of international organizations as 'alternatives'. Nor are GAL conceptions of international organizations as 'administrative agencies' without constitutional constraints a correct description of legal reality. The legal analyses of GAL would benefit from acknowledging the diverse legal contexts of national and international administrative rules and of their judicial review, which renders clarification of their respective legal status as customary law or general principles of law more difficult.

Multilevel constitutional approaches insist on the need for a coherent architecture and legitimation of the different local, national, regional and worldwide layers of governance and legal regulation. In contrast to the incremental reforms of IEL pursued by 'conflicts law' and GAL approaches, *Cottier* uses the image of a 'five storey house' in order to demonstrate the need for integrating the different 'partial conceptions' of IEL under a common roof based on a common foundation.[19] The image of a 'multilevel constitutional

[17] *cf* EU Petersmann, 'The Future of International Economic Law: A Research Agenda' in C Joerges and EU Petersmann (eds) (2011) 533–75.

[18] On European conceptions of the diverse private and public, national and international legal sub-systems of European and global governance as a mutually supportive, functional unity to be interpreted in the light of human rights and other 'constitutional contracts' of citizens see: A von Bogdandy, P Dann and M Goldmann, 'Developing the Publicness of Public International Law: Towards a Legal Framework for Global Governance Activities' (2008) 9 *German Law Journal* 1375 ff. On the increasing acknowledgment also by US lawyers of 'enabling constitutionalization', 'constraining constitutionalization' and 'supplemental constitutionalization' by means of 'international constitutional norms' see: JL Dunoff and JP Trachtman (eds) (2009) 10 ff.

[19] T Cottier, 'Towards a Five Storey House' in Joerges and Petersmann (eds) (2011) 495–532.

house' not only describes the existing realities of multilevel governance in the twenty-first century more precisely than the Westphalian notion of 'national sovereignty'. It also offers a more coherent normative conception of multilevel economic governance and of its 'constitutional foundations'. Like the 'conflicts law' approach, multilevel constitutional approaches perceive conflicting interests and legitimate disagreements as pervasive characteristics of national and international societies and their legal systems. Even though the higher degree of shared community values inside constitutional democracies might enable a higher degree of majority decisions in constitutional, legislative, administrative and judicial rulemaking at national levels, the large number of internal conflicts confirms that peace always remains at risk also at home. As the effectiveness of and voluntary compliance with rules depends on their perceived legitimacy and on competing rights and interests, the maintenance of agreement on common principles and rules must be promoted through procedural fairness, human rights protection, equal conditions of competition and balancing of competing interests on all levels of the 'constitutional house'. Nationalist, parochial balancing of interests (as illustrated by discrimination against foreign bank creditors during Iceland's bank defaults in 2009) risks lacking both legitimacy and effectiveness, for instance if its harmful external effects are challenged by third countries as violating IEL and justifying international sanctions.

Cottier defines the 'main constitutional function' of WTO law in terms of 'shaping predictable and stable framework conditions for domestic trade regulation, assuring agreed levels of market access, non-discrimination and fair conditions of competition'. He identifies a number of constitutional principles that 'can be globally shared and form the common core of global twenty-first century constitutionalism': rule of law; human rights; non-discrimination; mutual support; 'equal legitimacy of storeys'; 'appropriate structure-substance pairings'; appropriate allocation of powers; representation and voice; vertical and horizontal checks and balances; shared sovereignty; hierarchies of storeys based on fundamental values rather than formal ranking; effective decision-making and dispute resolution. Such multilevel 'constitutional principles' offer a coherent constitutional framework of potentially shared values while leaving ample room for divergence and cultural difference.[20] Chapters IV to VI explained how UN human rights law recognizes the need for multilevel constitutional protection of human rights and of transnational rule of law in the worldwide division of labour based on 'principles of justice' and individual access to courts of justice. National and international jurisdictions have legal duties to protect transnational rule of law for the benefit of citizens and their human rights by means of mutually 'consistent interpretations', 'judicial comity' and 'judicial balancing' of competing human rights, constitutional and cosmopolitan rights and jurisdictional claims.

6 How are the major theoretical approaches in international relations theories and international law related to each other? Do the legitimacy and effectiveness of IEL require an 'overlapping consensus' on principles of justice justifying international economic regulation and legitimizing IEL? Can the 'fragmented' private and public, national and international legal sub-systems of IEL be coordinated without recourse to some coherent theory of 'multilevel constitutional pluralism'?

Chapter I discussed 'realism', 'institutionalism', 'liberalism', 'rational choice' theories and 'constructivism' as the prevailing theories underlying multilevel economic governance.

[20] ibid.

While some approaches (like realism, institutionalism, functionalism) analyse international relations from the perspective of states and national power, other approaches focus on explaining the rational choices of individuals, groups and government institutions. Many 'realist' claims (eg that political morality does not reach beyond national legal systems) are empirically inconsistent with the increasing impact of international law (eg human rights law), international regulatory agencies (eg multilevel monetary and competition authorities in the EU), multilevel adjudication or 'human rights revolutions' on transnational relations; 'realist neglect' of international law all too often reflects ignorance or 'capture' of regulators by powerful lobbies benefitting from interest group politics at the expense of 'rationally ignorant consumers'. Economic analysis of law, by contrast, may be important not only for explaining 'economic structures' of private and public law but also for interpreting legal rules based on principles of economics. Also political theories of justice and other legal philosophies may be of direct, normative relevance for the interpretation of rules and the legal design of institutions, for instance by justifying inherent powers of 'courts of justice', justifying respect for 'reasonable disagreement' among citizens and polities, and explaining the ubiquity of conflicts of interests not only in terms of rational self-interests of the *homo economicus* but also in view of conflicts inside human minds (eg between sentiments, 'animal spirits', rationality and limited reasonableness).

Legal systems like IEL were analysed as a union of 'primary rules of conduct' and 'secondary rules' of recognition, change and adjudication that dynamically interact with changing *legal practices* by private and public legal actors, who often justify legal claims and interpretations of rules by invoking *legal principles*.[21] It was emphasized that, due to the 'dual nature' of modern legal systems based on human rights and 'principles of justice', the normative dimensions of positive law calling for justification of legal principles and rules constantly interact with social and legal practices and 'struggles for justice and rights'. 'Constitutional pluralism' requires respecting the reality of 'methodological pluralism' in the interpretation and development of IEL and the resultant plurality of conceptions of IEL, for instance as (1) public international law (eg the Bretton Woods Agreements), (2) 'global administrative law' (eg the legal practices of UN Specialized Agencies and the WTO), (3) 'conflicts law' (eg international commercial law and arbitration), (4) multilevel constitutional regulation (eg rights-based European economic law and adjudication) or (5) multilevel economic regulation of the economy (eg NAFTA law) within the limits of national, democratic constitutionalism. The conceptions of IEL differ because economic regulation and 'rule of law' tend to be justified in diverse ways, for instance on grounds of national or individual utility (eg 'national interests', public goods, welfare); state consent and 'sovereignty' (eg to adopt national legislation violating IEL); democratic or individual consent (eg to 'regulatory takings' of property rights); 'public choice' (eg majority and interest group politics); principles of 'good governance', human rights and other constitutional values (like private and public autonomy of arbitral tribunals). As the universal human rights obligations of all UN member states require interpreting international law, and settling related disputes, 'in conformity with the principles of justice' and human rights (as codified in the Preamble and Article 31 of the VCLT), 'cosmopolitan constitutionalism' was used as the most coherent legal method

[21] This constant interaction between 'law as a legal order' and 'law as legal practices' is emphasized by 'critical legal positivism', according to which law and its legal changes should be examined on (1) the surface level of positive law, (2) the legal culture, and (3) the deep structures of law; cf K Tuori, *Critical Legal Positivism* (Aldershot, 2002).

for justifying and coordinating national and IEL systems. Similar to Rawls' theory of a 'four-stage sequence' for legitimate constitutional, legislative, administrative and judicial governance protecting constitutional rights and 'public reason', human rights likewise call for 'constitutional pluralism' as a flexible framework for regulating and institutionalizing IEL on the basis of an 'overlapping consensus' among governments and citizens with diverse conceptions of justice and morality.

The Bretton Woods institutions, the WTO and UN Specialized Agencies are based not only on 'realist', institutional, liberal and 'constructivist' political, economic and legal theories. Their underlying principles of limited delegation of powers, separation of policy instruments and common commitments by all their member states to respect for human rights and public goods also reflect basic principles of 'constitutionalism' limiting 'member-driven governance' and one-sided, diplomatic claims of 'Westphalian legal positivism' (eg, based on explicit government consent as the sole source of international legal obligations). The strategic role of individual access to courts of justice in regional human rights treaties and regional economic integration agreements illustrates the 'constitutional functions' of compulsory jurisdictions for protecting cosmopolitan rights, interpreting and clarifying 'incomplete international agreements' and for the peaceful settlement of transnational disputes. Like other legal systems, IEL remains a legal and social construct whose effectiveness, legitimacy and 'recognition' depend on political support of the common good (*res publica*) by citizens based on a shared 'public reason'. Just as IEL (eg, competition rules, GATT rules, WTO subsidy rules) cannot be understood without economic theory, so can the need for reforming the law of international economic organizations and international economic adjudication hardly be understood without constitutional and political theories of justice. For instance, the judicial cooperation among national and European courts is justified by the need for 'consistent interpretations' in protecting the fundamental rights of EU citizens: national judges conceive themselves not only as national courts enforcing national laws, but also as Community courts enforcing EU and ECHR obligations for the benefit of European citizens and their rules-based, transnational cooperation.

7 Are the experiences of 'constitutionalism' and 'constitutionalization' relevant for limiting 'market failures' and 'governance failures' in IEL? How should the ambiguous terms 'constitution', 'constitutionalism', 'constitutionalization' and 'constitutional pluralism' be defined in the context of IEL? Have state constitutions become 'partial constitutions' in a globally integrating world where individuals and national communities are ever more influenced by events originating abroad such as global markets, financial crises, health pandemics, terrorism and environmental pollution?

Similar to the differences and complementarities of realist, institutional, liberal and constructivist conceptions of international law, the different private and public, national and international conceptions of IEL prioritize different perspectives and values. Chapters VI to VIII explained the need for justifying IEL by an 'overlapping consensus' on principles of justice and common constitutional principles, rules and institutions limiting 'market failures' as well as 'governance failures. The more 'globalization' reduces the capacity of individual states to protect the human rights and common reasonable self-interests of citizens through *national law*, the more national constitutions evolve into 'partial constitutions' that must be complemented by functionally limited 'international treaty constitutions' for the collective supply of international public goods. The complex interactions between local, national, regional and global public goods and corresponding interactions among multilevel governance institutions can be justified and coordinated best on the basis of multilevel 'cosmopolitan constitutionalism' based on human rights, democratic self-governance and transnational rule of law for the benefit of citizens. Chapter III explained why – unless citizens struggle for legal and judicial protection of human rights and constitutional rights in IEL – the existing abuses of public and private governance powers and 'feudalist structures' in so many UN member states and intergovernmental organizations are likely to persist. Similar to the successful 'revolution' in international humanitarian law for the protection of individuals in times of war and vis-à-vis gross human rights violations by their own governments, worldwide IEL needs a 'human rights revolution' reinforcing legal and judicial protection of cosmopolitan rights following the successful example of the transnational 'rights revolution' in European law. The psychological and social 'pre-commitment theories' explaining the need for *national* constitutionalism ('legal hands-tying') are even more important for 'constitutionalizing' *transnational* governance powers so that state sovereignty, popular sovereignty and IEL remain consistent with 'individual sovereignty' based on human rights and democratic principles of 'subsidiarity'.

Chapters IV and VII used the examples of inadequate parliamentary and democratic control of intergovernmental rulemaking in the WTO as well as the rights-based European economic integration in support of the argument that human rights require 'constitutional' and 'cosmopolitan conceptions' of economic integration law in order to supply international public goods more effectively. The legitimate functions, regulatory problems, systemic nature and dynamic evolution of IEL should be normatively conceived, and coherently developed, in the broader context of the multilevel human rights obligations and common constitutional principles accepted by all UN member states. The proposed 'bottom-up multilevel constitutional approach' to multilevel economic regulation shares the 'realist premises' that (1) 'legalism' has no intrinsic value; (2) 'law cannot control behaviour unless legal institutions support it'; and (3) without legal institutions – 'legislatures, enforcers, courts – international law is unavoidably weak'.[22]

Yet, in contrast to the often arbitrary 'cost-benefit' justifications of 'utilitarian arguments' for 'efficient violations' of international law, constitutionalism argues for limiting 'rule by law' through constitutional safeguards of 'rule of law' across frontiers based on respect for human rights and the legitimate diversity of constitutional democracies. The 'conflicts law' and GAL approaches also aim at promoting transnational 'rule of law' through fair procedures. But their different private law and common law pedigrees avoid human rights and 'constitutional justice' as constitutional principles for IEL, for instance based on the political argument – supported also in this study – that domestic constitutionalism must remain the primary site for controlling problems of global governance and protecting human rights. Citizens have more trust in and democratic control over domestic governance institutions. Cosmopolitan constitutionalism offers the most legitimate and most effective strategy for limiting abuses of multilevel governance in IEL by multilevel protection of cosmopolitan rights, stronger democratic safeguards and transnational rule of law for the benefit of citizens.

European integration law illustrates how 'multilevel constitutional strategies' of empowering, limiting and complementing multilevel regulatory institutions can enhance

[22] EA Posner (2009) xiv.

individual and democratic self-governance and the problem-solving capacities of governments. Like national constitutions, international treaties constituting, limiting and complementing multilevel governance powers for the collective supply of international public goods differ enormously depending on their respective constituencies, regulatory problems and diverse criteria of 'input-legitimacy' and 'output-legitimacy'. As explained in chapters IV and VII, the less 'parliamentary democracy' can effectively represent and protect all affected interests in transnational regulatory bodies like the WTO, the stronger is the need for compensatory 'participatory democracy' and 'deliberative democracy' recognizing procedural as well as substantive cosmopolitan rights of all citizens affected by international economic regulation. Yet, rights-based conceptions of democratic self-governance remain contested from both libertarian and communitarian perspectives, notably by lawyers in common law countries denying the 'indivisibility' of human liberty rights and constitutional protection of economic liberties subject to legal 'balancing' with all other constitutional rights. Without 'countervailing cosmopolitan rights', the necessary strengthening of global institutions for the collective supply of global public goods risks reinforcing power asymmetries and historical privileges not only among countries (eg, in the UN Security Council and the Bretton Woods institutions), but also among non-governmental civil society organizations to the benefit of powerful, industrial lobbies.

8 Are the 'principles' underlying international monetary, trade, financial, investment and environmental law mutually coherent? Should economic courts interpret treaty rules by 'balancing' economic principles with human rights principles? Does the universal recognition of human rights influence the interpretation of the 'rules of recognition' of public international law as defined in Article 38 ICJ Statute? Why is it that citizens, NGOs, parliaments, governments, courts of justice and international organizations (like the EU) often have such different views about the appropriate interpretation of IEL rules?

The Bretton Woods Agreements, GATT, the WTO and other worldwide economic agreements protect equal freedoms (eg, of transnational trade and related payments), non-discriminatory treatment (eg, in terms of most-favoured-nation and national treatment), legal security (eg, in terms of tariff bindings, prohibition of discriminatory non-tariff trade barriers, exchange rate stability), transnational rule of law and national sovereignty (eg, over protection and non-discriminatory regulation of non-economic policy objectives) in conformity with corresponding principles governing economic regulation inside constitutional democracies (eg, freedom of trade, non-discriminatory conditions of competition and rule of law inside national markets). As explained in my 1991 monograph, by linking the national and international legal principles through 'consistent interpretations' and multilevel judicial protection for the benefit of individuals and their mutually beneficial economic cooperation across frontiers, certain IEL principles, rules and institutions can serve 'constitutional functions' for protecting and extending domestic constitutional principles in the transnational division of labour among citizens. The need for reconciling and 'balancing' economic principles and rules with all other constitutional principles is recognized in the customary law requirement of interpreting international law 'in conformity with the principles of justice' and human rights. Similarly, the 'consistent interpretation requirement' is also a part of national and international legal systems recognizing legal presumptions that national and international law should be interpreted in mutually coherent ways protecting transnational rule of law unless, eg, domestic parliaments deliberately decide to violate international law. Respect for legitimate 'constitutional pluralism' requires deference for the legitimately diverse conceptions in constitutional democracies of the interrelationships between constitutional, political, economic and judicial institutions, as illustrated by the diverse constitutional and judicial traditions of protecting and 'balancing' constitutional and economic rights in transnational economic relations (eg, in NAFTA, EU and EEA law, regional human rights treaties and human rights jurisprudence).

Chapters III to VI inferred from the universal human rights obligations of all UN member states the need for more effective constitutional restraints on abuses of economic governance powers by means of cosmopolitan and constitutional conceptions of IEL recognizing individuals as 'primary legal subjects', main actors, sources of value and 'democratic owners' of IEL. In the twenty-first century, Westphalian conceptions of 'international law among sovereign states' advocated by monarchs, diplomats, other rulers and their generals have lost democratic legitimacy in view of their failures to protect human rights and consumer welfare in international economic relations. The *opinio juris sive necessitates* of civil society, parliaments, courts of justice, UN human rights bodies and other independent international institutions are no less important for interpreting IEL, its 'rules of recognition' and 'public reason' than claims of diplomats and authoritarian rulers. As explained in chapters III and VII, the complex mix of private and public authorities governing international economic relations and coordinating a plurality of overlapping, private and public, national and international legal regimes must be embedded by public law and inclusive, 'public participation' as democratic conditions of legitimate authority: private autonomy and properly functioning markets must be constituted and legitimized by human rights and constitutional law, and vice versa (ie, constitutional rules derive their legitimacy from respect for private autonomy and equality of citizens). The judicial authority to interpret IEL rules in the light of human rights, other principles of justice and general principles of law entails that – as illustrated by numerous examples in chapters V and VIII – judges may have to weigh, balance and review, for example, power-oriented 'legal interpretations' advocated by government officials, political majority decisions adopted by legislatures, selfish private decisions by economic actors and community interests of civil society within the limits of constitutional rules, legislation and judicial procedures aimed at 'administering justice'. The principle-oriented, transparent reasoning of independent and impartial courts of justice – as guardians of justice and of 'public reason' subject to critique by public opinion – may assert more democratic legitimacy than political majority decisions and private decisions representing powerful interest groups.[23]

[23] *cf* A von Bogdandy and I Venzke, 'On the Democratic Legitimation of International Judicial Lawmaking' (2011) 12 *German Law Journal* 1341–70.

9 What is the legitimate role of 'courts of justice' in interpreting and clarifying IEL rules, principles, individual rights, market access commitments and 'public interest' regulation? Are courts of justice the only branch of government that has to justify its decisions – as independent 'exemplars of public reason' (Rawls) – on the basis of constitutional principles of justice?

Chapters I to IV explained why – even if state consent continues to be seen as the legitimatory basis of international law – human rights and the Rawlsian 'four-stage sequence' of constitutional, legislative, administrative and judicial 'institutionalization of constitutional principles of justice' provide an appropriate template for evaluating the democratic legitimacy and 'public reason' of IEL. Individual and democratic self-government remain illusionary if international economic treaties ratified by domestic parliaments for the benefit of citizens are not respected and protected by courts, especially if such treaties were designed to protect mutually beneficial cooperation among private economic actors. Hence, chapter V emphasized the judicial functions of national and international courts to protect transnational rule of law for the benefit of citizens in the worldwide division of labour. As discussed in the Introduction, judicial clarification of incomplete and contested legislation and treaty provisions can also be perceived as a public good (eg, a 'single best efforts public good') beneficial not only for the peaceful settlement of disputes among the plaintiff and the defendant, but also for the larger legal community and for maintaining the 'public reason' justifying a legal system.

The interactions among constitutional, legislative, administrative and judicial rule-making at transnational levels are much less controlled by national parliaments and civil society than inside constitutional democracies. As discussed in chapters V and VIII, national, regional and worldwide economic and human rights adjudication often has legal effects far beyond the settlement of individual disputes. Many legal philosophers define law by how courts of justice will identify, apply and enforce legal rules[24] and create and stabilize normative expectations.[25] From such a perspective, 'judicial development of the law' is – as acknowledged also by the German Constitutional Court – inevitably part of the competence of national and international courts.[26] The multilevel judicial interpretation and development of human rights law, trade, investment and economic integration law, as discussed in chapters V, VII and VIII, confirms the importance of judge-made law for adjusting multilevel economic and human rights law to new regulatory needs and to dynamically evolving 'public reason'. For instance, the precise legal meaning of the general principles, standards and exception clauses in international trade and investment agreements continues to dynamically evolve on the basis of ever more national, regional and worldwide trade and investment adjudication. Chapters V and VIII emphasized that 'multilevel judicial governance' goes far beyond the 'cognitive clarification' of the

[24] *cf* the famous definition of law by US Supreme Court judge OW Holmes, 'The Path of the Law' (1897) *Harvard Law Review* 457, 461: 'The prophecies of what the courts will do in fact, and nothing more pretentious, are what I mean by the law'.

[25] *cf* J Habermas (1996) 427, and the finding by the WTO Appellate Body that adopted appellate reports 'create legitimate expectations among WTO Members and, therefore, should be taken into account where they are relevant to any dispute' (*Japan – Taxes on Alcoholic Beverages*, WT/DS 8,10 and 11/AB/R of 4 October 1996, 14–15).

[26] Bundesverfassungsgericht, judgment of 6 July 2010 (2 BvR 2661/06): 'There is particular reason for further development of the law by judges where programmes are fleshed out, gaps are closed, contradictions of evaluation are resolved' (para 64). The Court also emphasizes the democratic boundaries of judicial lawmaking.

contested meaning of rules; it progressively develops legal systems through judicial choices, justifications and 'judicial dialogues' (eg, with legislative, administrative and other judicial branches of governments, private plaintiffs, civil society representatives intervening in judicial proceedings or submitting amici curiae briefs) legitimating judicial lawmaking, limiting abuses of power and strengthening public reason.[27]

Judicial lawmaking is today recognized as a common and inevitable feature of all legal systems. Chapters V and VIII followed Dworkin's view that independent and impartial judges must seek and justify the 'right answer' that is 'best fitting' the applicable legal rules and principles for the settlement of disputes in terms of both *procedural justice* (eg, protecting due process of law, transparency, publicness and 'voice' for all adversely affected interests) as well as *substantive justice* (eg, in terms of case-specific proportionality analyses 'balancing' specific economic with non-economic public interests). In contrast to the political branches of governance, neither the limited judicial mandate nor the reality of 'methodological pluralism' – for instance, combining textual, systemic and functional methods of treaty interpretation with due respect for applicable human rights and principles of justice – justify judicial *discretion* regarding the final judgment. Different courts may engage in different kinds of judicial reasoning, 'judicial comity' (eg, vis-à-vis other courts) and judicial self-restraint (eg, vis-à-vis political branches of governance) which may be justifiable or even required depending on the relevant legal and political context; but the judicial reasoning must remain committed to justice as part of a broader, constitutionally restrained 'public reason' and avoid 'denial of justice'. All constitutional institutions should justify their decisions in terms of principles of justice that remain comprehensible for ordinary citizens. The comparatively greater independence, impartiality, transparency and institutional specialization of judicial procedures – for example, in comparison with periodically elected political bodies and their frequent 'political compromises' based on majority decisions – may render courts of justice 'exemplars of public reason' (Rawls) in international economic disputes where the claimant and defendant often pursue more narrow national or private self-interests.

10 Does the potential 'tyranny of majority politics' require judicial protection of constitutional citizen rights also vis-à-vis intergovernmental economic regulation (eg, of bailouts of insolvent banks and governments)? Why are governments so often requesting courts to exercise judicial deference vis-à-vis requests by citizens for judicial review of intergovernmental restrictions of individual economic liberties and property rights (eg, in case of UN 'smart sanctions' against individuals without judicial remedies, EU trade restrictions in manifest violation of WTO and EU guarantees of freedom and non-discrimination)?

Human rights approaches and cosmopolitan approaches to IEL reject the categorical division of domestic and foreign politics that characterizes nationalist, 'realist' approaches to intergovernmental economic regulation. They take the individual as the

[27] On 'judicial law-making (as) a permanent feature of administration of justice in every society' see: H Lauterpacht, *The Development of International Law by the International Court of Justice* (London, 1958) 155). On the interactions between intergovernmental and judicial lawmaking in IEL and human rights law (eg, due to the intergovernmental supervision and enforcement of decisions by the ECtHR and WTO dispute settlement bodies) and on the functional as well as democratic legitimation of judicial lawmaking in IEL, see von Bogdandy and Venzke (n 23) as well as: A von Bogdandy and I Venzke, 'Beyond Dispute: International Judicial Institutions as Lawmakers' (2011) 12 *German Law Journal* 979–1003.

ultimate source of justification of all law and governance institutions and argue for protecting all individuals by inalienable human rights, constitutional and cosmopolitan rights in mutually beneficial economic cooperation among citizens across frontiers. In view of the functional specialization and limitation of international organizations, the dangers of interest group politics – and the need for constitutional limitations of abuses of power – tend to be greater in specialized international economic organizations than in domestic parliaments committed to protection and 'balancing' of all public and private interests. The more the 'functional logic' of economic rulemaking in worldwide organizations (such as the 1994 WTO Agreement with more than 25,000 pages of text) and dispute settlement bodies (eg, WTO dispute settlement rulings with sometimes more than 1000 pages) remains incomprehensible for ordinary citizens and eludes democratic control by the general public, the stronger becomes the need for constitutional constraints and parliamentary and judicial review protecting non-economic interests of citizens and 'public reason'.

There are thousands of judgments by constitutional courts, regional human rights courts, national and regional economic courts and investor–state arbitral awards illustrating the need for protecting constitutional rights, human rights and other cosmopolitan rights of citizens against abuses of national and international governance institutions. Furthermore, intergovernmental dispute settlement proceedings (eg, in the WTO and the ICJ) are often about private legal claims that 'trading rights', 'investor rights', intellectual property rights or other cosmopolitan rights (eg, of access to justice in domestic courts) have been violated by foreign governments. Even inside the EU, bureaucracies and governments all too often pursue narrow self-interests in exceeding their limited powers and claiming legal and judicial immunity against legitimate claims by citizens to protect transnational rule of law (eg, 'strict observance of international law' as prescribed by the EU's Lisbon Treaty) and effective judicial remedies for the benefit of citizens.

11 Why do many international economic courts refer so rarely to the customary law requirement (as codified in the Preamble of the VCLT) of interpreting international law and settling disputes over the interpretation of treaties 'in conformity with the principles of justice' and human rights? Why is this customary law requirement of 'constitutional treaty interpretation' so often ignored by GATT/WTO dispute settlement panels and investor–state arbitrators?

Prior to the establishment of a GATT Legal Office in 1983, most GATT dispute settlement panels were composed of diplomats and serviced by GATT officials without expertise in international law. Also many investor–state arbitration tribunals are composed of lawyers with expertise in private rather than public international law who interpret their legal mandates narrowly (eg, in terms of rendering commercial dispute settlement services to the two parties to the dispute and arbitration contract). The terms of reference of most regional and worldwide dispute settlement bodies set up by economic treaties are limited to the 'covered agreements' (*cf* Article 7 DSU) without explicit references to human rights and 'principles of justice'. As long as the economic actors involved in trade and investment disputes hardly ever refer to human rights and principles of justice, economic lawyers and judges likewise prefer to refrain from such references in view of the diverse traditions of interpreting human rights and principles of justice in the context of economic rules.

In intergovernmental relations, Westphalian conceptions of 'international law among sovereign states' tend to enlarge government powers and enable intergovernmental compromises (eg, EU majority decisions violating the WTO obligations of the EU to the detriment of European consumer welfare) without publicity and without legal and judicial accountability of governments vis-à-vis adversely affected private interests and parliaments (*cf* Tables 18 and 24 and related texts). Even though international courts increasingly assert inherent powers for administering 'due process of law' (procedural justice), judicial powers to decide cases *ex aequo et bono* require special authorization by the parties to the dispute (*cf* Article 38:2 ICJ Statute). Due to power-oriented disagreements over the interpretation of international law rules referring to standards of equity (eg, in Article XVI:3 GATT), 'fair price comparisons' (eg, in Article 2 of the WTO Agreement on Article VI GATT), 'public morals' (eg, in Article XX,a GATT) and 'public order' (eg, in Article XIV,a GATS), ad hoc dispute settlement panels and arbitral tribunals may find it easier to reach agreed dispute settlement findings without introducing controversial theories and principles of 'substantive justice' that may be shared neither by the parties to the dispute nor by appellate review bodies, 'annulment procedures' (eg, pursuant to Article 52 ICSID) or in national courts deciding on the recognition and enforcement of arbitral awards. The 'systemic interpretation' of economic agreements required by Article 31(3)(c) VCLT – ie, taking 'into account, together with the context: . . . any relevant rules of international law applicable in the relations between the parties' – may call for 'dynamic interpretation'[28] and exceed the limited expertise and self-interests of trade diplomats deciding on GATT/WTO disputes affecting citizens and non-economic concerns in many countries.

12 What are the legal interrelationships between multilevel human rights law, multilevel 'constitutional law' (eg, establishing international 'courts of justice') and multilevel economic guarantees (eg, in RTAs) of equal freedoms, non-discrimination and judicial protection of rule of law? Do multilevel human rights and multilevel economic guarantees of freedom, non-discrimination and rule of law rest on common 'principles of justice'? How can the 'functional unity' of IEL be defined, if it exists at all?

The discussion, in chapters V and VIII, of investor–state arbitral awards determining the legal boundary between 'public interest regulation' of states and the protection of foreign private property referred to the frequent tensions between democratic demands (eg, for revoking licences on grounds of environmental protection) and confidential investor–state contracts and related arbitration by private arbitrators. The chapters also mentioned the increasing legal calls for judicial restraint in investor–state disputes: 'the objective of international investment law should not be the super-protection of investment and property rights'.[29] Chapters IV, VI and VII explained why – as investor–state arbitration is also embedded into public national and international law – the answers to the above-mentioned questions depend on how lawyers and judges define the 'principles

[28] *cf* the ICJ's Advisory Opinion on *Legal Consequences for States of the Continued Presence of South Africa in Namibia* [1971] ICJ Rep 16, para 53: 'an international instrument must be interpreted and applied within the overall framework of the juridical system in force at the time of the interpretation'.

[29] *cf* S Montt, *State Liability in Investment Treaty Arbitration – Global Constitutional and Administrative Law in the BIT Generation* (Oxford: Hart Publishing, 2009) 21 f. Montt rightly concludes that the protection of investment 'does not deserve a priori to trump all other non-economic values' (at 346).

of justice' underlying national and international legal and judicial systems. For instance, if the human right to liberty is defined broadly – as suggested in chapters III and VI following Kantian and Rawlsian theories of justice recognizing maximum equal liberties as 'first principle of justice', subject to rule of law, democratic legislation and 'constitutional balancing' of civil, political, economic, social and cultural liberties – then judges may recognize a human right to justification of governmental restrictions on ground of public interests, and a corresponding procedural burden of proof of the government involved. If human rights to liberty are defined more narrowly, as in many constitutional traditions prioritizing civil and political over economic and social rights, then the necessary 'balancing' of human and constitutional liberties and economic rights may lead to different conclusions.[30] Likewise, in Anglo-Saxon democracies prioritizing parliamentary sovereignty over human rights – as in communist countries prioritizing political party monopolies over human rights – constitutional balancing is likely to differ from that in constitutional democracies prioritizing maximum equal liberties under the rule of law.

Chapter IV explained why multilevel human rights law rests on a logic different from multilevel economic guarantees of freedom, non-discrimination and transnational rule of law: UN human rights law tends to prescribe only 'minimum standards' which constitutional laws, legislation and courts of justice tend to protect more comprehensively in many national and regional legal systems. By contrast, GATT and WTO guarantees of freedom, non-discrimination and rule of law tend to go far beyond autonomous, more limited guarantees in national and regional legal systems with longstanding traditions of border discrimination against imports from third countries. With regard to *internal* regulation *inside* countries, also GATT/WTO rules prescribe only minimum standards for market liberalization and market regulation respecting the sovereign rights of countries to regulate their domestic economic, political and legal systems in legitimately diverse ways (eg, the economic and political relations inside China among the four Chinese customs territories with independent WTO memberships).

Economists often define the functional unity of economic regulation by the goal of maximizing consumer welfare through non-discriminatory conditions of undistorted competition. The underlying value premise of 'normative individualism' – ie, values have to be defined by individuals benefitting from equal freedoms and human rights – is similar to the 'first principle of justice' as defined in Kantian and Rawlsian theories of justice. Chapter VII emphasized that constitutional democracies and 'constitutional economics' rest on similar constitutional principles. This book's proposal to transform power-oriented Westphalian conceptions of IEL into cosmopolitan and constitutional conceptions focusing on cosmopolitan rights, democratic self-government and transnational rule of law aims at an 'overlapping consensus' based on human rights and respect for 'constitutional pluralism' as common constitutional foundations of IEL in the twenty-first century among countries with often diverse conceptions of justice, constitutional systems and economic policies.

[30] *cf* Montt, ibid, who argues that 'property confers only liability-rule protection but no property-rule protection, that is, it does not include the right to "just say no"' (at 182). According to Montt, lawful regulation should be distinguished from expropriation by the type of regulation: regulation aimed at preventing harm and/or public nuisance on grounds of pre-eminent public interests should not be compensable; regulations expressing 'changing policy preferences' should be compensated on grounds of distributive justice (*cf* at 271–81).

13 What are the constitutive building blocks of a 'highly competitive social market economy' (Article 3 TEU)? Can the citizen-oriented approach to European economic law serve as a model for citizen-oriented interpretations of international trade, investment and environmental law beyond Europe? Can the 'collective action problems' impeding global public goods be resolved without recourse to the 'constitutional methods' used for national and regional public goods? What kinds of WTO reforms would a 'constitutional approach to IEL require?

Chapters I and VII discussed the various kinds of market failures and governance failures undermining the efficient functioning of market competition as a decentralized information, coordination and sanctioning mechanism. As explained in chapter VII, *ordo*-liberalism, 'constitutional economics' and 'public choice theories' perceive efficient markets as socially embedded, legal constructs depending on rules and institutions limiting such market failures (eg, by competition, environmental and social regulation) as well as governance failures (eg, by constitutional rights and restraints, monetary legislation, administrative institutions and judicial review). The commitment to a 'highly competitive social market economy' in European economic integration law illustrates the interrelationships between multilevel, national and international market competition and market regulations. Also multilevel trade regulation in the WTO is confronted with transnational market failures (eg, private and public restraints and distortions of competition) as well as governance failures (eg, arbitrary violations of the rule of law) that require multilevel regulation and 'social embedding' respecting the human rights obligations of UN member states.

Chapter VII explained why consumer-driven markets, legal and institutional limitations of market failures and multilevel, legal protection of non-discriminatory conditions of competition are necessary complements of human rights in order to promote access of citizens to efficient supply of scarce goods and services that consumers demand in order to develop their human capacities and enjoy their human rights. More effective regulation of the 'collective action problems' impeding collective supply of international public goods requires stronger legal and judicial protection of human rights and cosmopolitan rights to empower citizens to challenge abuses of public and private power in the regulation of the international division of labour. As mentioned in the Introduction, Tunisia's human rights revolution triggered by the protest of the young street vendor Mohammed Bouazizi against arbitrary market restrictions offers an empirical, recent example of the potential of economic freedoms for overcoming economic, political and legal oppression by authoritarian rulers. Similar to the increasing number of national regulatory agencies (like competition, food safety and environmental agencies), also functionally limited international monetary, trade, development and other organizations can be conceived – and must be constitutionally controlled – as a 'fourth branch of governance' requiring multilevel legal regulation in order to promote effective supply of interdependent public goods. The complex interactions between national, bilateral, regional and worldwide international rules and institutions (as discussed in Table 7 and the related text) offer 'checks and balances' whenever regulatory failures at one level (eg, in the consensus-based Doha Round negotiations in the WTO) justify recourse to alternative levels of regulation (eg, in the ever larger number of RTAs and BITs concluded among WTO members). In view of the obvious failures of consensus-based WTO decision-making procedures to further liberalize and regulate world trade through transparent, efficient and legitimate procedures, Chapter VII made a number of proposals for reforming WTO decision-making procedures and for facilitating 'plurilateral' trade liberalization and regulation in the context of the WTO as well as in RTAs.

14 Can parliamentary democracy remain effective in a globally integrating world without stronger protection of deliberative, participatory and 'cosmopolitan democracy'? Should IEL be evaluated in terms of its contribution to protecting human rights? Is the EU Charter of Fundamental Rights and its distinction between dignity rights, liberty rights, equality rights, solidarity rights, citizen rights and rights to justice consistent with the different distinctions between civil, political, economic, social and cultural human rights in UN law?

Chapters IV to VI explained why individual and democratic self-government on the basis of equal human rights and multilevel constitutionalism cannot remain effective in the worldwide division of labour unless the fragmented national and international legal subsystems are interpreted and developed coherently so as to protect transnational rule of law for the benefit of citizens. Beyond nation states, parliamentary representation (eg, in the European Parliament) tends to be undermined by unequal voting rights (eg, privileging citizens in small EU member states over citizens in large EU member states) and inadequate communication among citizens and parliamentarians in distant institutions abroad (eg, each German MEP representing more than one million German citizens who tend to remain 'rationally ignorant' of the complex EU decision-making processes), especially if international governance institutions (eg, in the EU) assert powers to violate international treaties ratified by national parliaments for the benefit of citizens and refuse protecting rights of citizens to transnational rule of law. Chapter IV argued that multilevel economic governance of the worldwide division of labour – in order to remain democratically justifiable – requires complementing parliamentary democracy by stronger deliberative, participatory, cosmopolitan and constitutional democracy protecting transnational rule of law for the benefit of citizens. As democratic decision-making derives its values and justification from protecting equal constitutional rights and general consumer welfare, IEL also needs to be evaluated – as rightly emphasized by UN human rights bodies – in terms of its contribution to respecting, protecting and fulfilling human and constitutional rights.[31]

Chapter VIII discussed numerous national and international judgments reviewing the non-discriminatory and transparent nature, 'suitability', 'necessity' and 'proportionality *stricto sensu*' of governmental restrictions of economic freedoms and cosmopolitan rights. The 'institutionalization of public reason' through 'four-stage sequences' of constitutional, legislative, administrative and judicial rulemaking and rule clarification and protection of 'transnational rule of law' may legitimately differ among constitutional democracies and specialized international legal regimes. Hence, the separation of civil, political, economic, social and cultural human right in some UN human right conventions does not prevent the different constitutional safeguards of dignity rights, liberty rights, equality rights, solidarity rights, citizen rights and right to justice as provided in

[31] *cf Human Rights Impact Assessments for Trade and Investment Agreements,* Report of the Expert Seminar, Geneva : South Centre, 23 June 2010, and O De Schutter, UN Special Rapporteur on the Right to Food, *Draft Guiding Principles on Human Rights Impact Assessments of Trade and Investment Agreements* (Geneva: UN High Commissioner for Human Rights, 1 July 2011).

the EU Charter of Fundamental Rights. IEL and economic adjudication must respect legitimate 'constitutional pluralism' protecting constitutional rights to design and institutionalize national, regional and worldwide governance in legitimately diverse ways. In the twenty-first century, the democratic legitimation of international treaties and related adjudication no longer derives only from the consent of the state parties to the treaties and to judicial procedures; the respective consent by national parliaments and citizens and the 'constitutional functions' of international rules and adjudication to protect domestic constitutional rights of citizens and 'public reason' (eg, as revealed in public judicial proceedings and related arguments by all parties involved), may be more important for legitimizing IEL than the 'governmental *fiat*' by 'Westphalian rulers' pursuing intergovernmental power politics all too often for selfish domestic interests.

15 Do the 'principles of justice' underlying UN law enable governments to supply 'international public goods' effectively? Which 'constitutional principles' are important for limiting the collective action problems in supplying interdependent public goods?

This study has argued that – for the reasons explained by Rawls – citizens and UN member states are unlikely ever to agree on comprehensive theories of justice justifying IEL and international institutions. Even though the UN Charter and the human rights obligations of all UN member states include numerous 'principles of justice', citizens and governments reasonably disagree on the interpretation and legal 'institutionalization' of UN human rights law. For instance, while many Anglo-Saxon democracies prioritize civil and political human rights and some Asian countries (like China) prioritize economic and social rights, European constitutional law protects civil, political, economic and social rights as integral parts of 'integration law' requiring more comprehensive legislative and judicial 'balancing' at national and international levels. It was argued that the different forms of European economic integration law (eg, in the EU and in the EEA) illustrate that Rawlsian 'four-stage sequences' of constitutional, legislative, administrative and judicial protection of public goods supported by 'public reason' enable governments to protect more effectively international public goods like the rules-based common market and common competition, environmental, social and constitutional rules among EU and EEA member countries. Yet, the European and worldwide monetary and financial crises (as discussed in Table 1 and related texts) also illustrated that 'human rights coherence' of IEL (as discussed in Table 4 and chapter IV) remains a permanent challenge. National parliaments and national courts all too often fail to effectively protect the constitutional rights of citizens vis-à-vis intergovernmental rulemaking and transnational abuses of public and private power. Hence, chapters III and VII described citizen-driven 'struggles for rights', their multilevel judicial protection and transnational rule of law as the central 'constitutional challenges' of IEL in the twenty-first century. In contrast to 'particular justice' in interpersonal relations (eg, in the Aristotelian sense of 'virtue towards others') and political majority decisions, multilevel judicial governance has to be justified more comprehensively in terms of 'principles of justice' and 'public reason'; it is, as illustrated by numerous judicial case studies in chapters V and VIII, of central importance for 'constitutionalizing' and 'legitimating' IEL.

In order to transform the power-oriented 'Westphalian conceptions' of IEL into cosmopolitan and constitutional conceptions of IEL, the study proposed to reinterpret and redesign IEL by focusing on the human and constitutional rights of citizens, democratic self-governance based on transnational rule of law, and on consumer welfare as the major sources of legitimizing IEL. Parliaments and courts of justice should review and, if necessary and constitutionally permitted (eg, based on the 'consistent interpretation principle'), reinterpret or disregard intergovernmental rules so as to avoid violating human rights and other commonly agreed 'principles of justice'. More effective regulation of the collective action problems impeding collective supply of international public goods requires cosmopolitan conceptions of IEL empowering citizens by more effective legal and judicial remedies against market failures as well as governance failures in multilevel economic governance. Just as Article 6 EU named 'liberty' as the first principle on which 'the Union is founded,' the new Article 2 TEU of the 2007 Lisbon Treaty lists 'respect for human dignity' and 'freedom' before other foundational principles of the EU. Similar commitments to respect human dignity, liberty and other human rights are included in numerous UN, regional and national human rights instruments as constitutional foundations of international law; they can be interpreted, as proposed in chapter VI, in conformity with modern theories of justice (from Kant to Rawls) prioritizing equal individual freedoms as 'first principle of justice' deriving from respect for human dignity. Yet, the legitimate reality of 'constitutional pluralism' also requires respecting that many constitutional democracies interpret equal *constitutional liberties* in the light of *communitarian conceptions* of democratic self-governance that are different from cosmopolitan conceptions. Chapters III and VI argued for interpreting equality of *human rights* not only in terms of 'negative liberties', but also as 'positive rights' to ensure and develop one's human capacities (eg, by means of rights of access to food, water, essential medicines and other resources necessary for survival and basic needs). Depending on their respective value preferences, constitutional traditions and resources, democratic communities may regulate the relationships between human rights and constitutional rights, and between 'negative' and 'positive liberties', in legitimately diverse ways. European and US constitutionalism, for example, have very different traditions of interpreting the constitutional obligations of states and of regional organizations (like the EU and NAFTA) to not only respect, but also protect and promote economic, social and cultural human rights and citizen rights.[32] This legitimate diversity of 'constitutional pluralism' explains why 'multilevel economic governance' must remain subject to principles of 'subsidiarity' (eg, regarding national budgetary, fiscal and debt policies inside the EU) and must respect legitimate diversity of principles of justice. The current eurozone crisis illustrates the sometimes conflicting perspectives of economists, politicians and lawyers. For instance, claims by economists and politicians that monetary unions cannot function without fiscal unions neglect that the drafters of the EU provisions on monetary union were conscious of the existence of monetary unions (eg, based on gold and silver standards) without fiscal union;[33] from the Maastricht Treaty up to the launching of the

[32] *cf* D Grimm, 'The Protective Function of the State' in G Nolte (ed), *European and US Constitutionalism* (Strasbourg: Council of Europe, 2005) 119 ff. See also Xenos (n 2).

[33] *cf* J Kay, 'As Europe's élite is fighting reality and will lose' *Financial Times* (26 October 2011) 7: 'a common fiscal policy is not necessary for a successful monetary union. No such agreement existed under the gold standard. Nor does one exist now between the US and several countries – including China – which have pegged their exchange rate to the dollar. Nor is a common fiscal policy efficient for a successful monetary union. Neither the European Commission nor the German government can put tanks on the streets of Athens. . . . Financial markets are desperate to be bailed out, with the support of Tim Geithner, in his capacity as ambassador for US investment banks. The decisive action they all seek is not really a European solution at all. It is that the German government should write very large cheques – or underwrite very large borrowings'.

euro in 1999, the EU law provisions protecting national sovereignty over fiscal and budgetary policies – and conditioning membership in the eurozone on 'economic convergence', the limitation of national fiscal deficits to three per cent of GDP, and of total government debts to 60 per cent GDP – were frequently justified in EU member states in terms of constitutional principles of national sovereignty, subsidiarity and democracy. Defaulting on private and public debts entails violations of contractual and treaty obligations undermining not only monetary stability but also rule of law.

Sisyphus and the need for perennial struggles by citizens for protecting public goods

Similar to the rivalry in economic market competition, political markets and democracy remain characterized by conflicting interests and power asymmetries enabling abuses of public and private power and other 'market failures' as well as 'governance failures'. Supporters of unregulated markets and 'majoritarian democracy' are likely to criticize the main thesis of this study – ie, that international public goods (like an efficient worldwide division of labour respecting human rights) cannot be effectively supplied by intergovernmental power politics without multilevel constitutionalism and stronger protection of human rights – as being *anti*-democratic, similar to populist criticism of constitutional adjudication as anti-democratic limitation of majority politics. Yet, majority politics can undermine 'constitutional democracy', as illustrated by the majoritarian, parliamentary delegation – in Germany's Weimar Republic in 1933 – of 'emergency powers' to Hitler. This book criticizes that the prevailing, nationalist paradigms of democracy and 'realist power politics' fail to protect human rights and transnational rule of law in the global division of labour. Similar to Sisyphus' perennial struggles, the human capacity to protect interdependent public goods more effectively in the twenty-first century depends on additional 'human rights revolutions' empowering and protecting individuals through equal rights and fair opportunities. Since ancient times, justice tends to be defined in terms of equal rights, notwithstanding the frequent disagreement on how to define the essential characteristics justifying formally equal or substantially different treatment in the administration of justice. Individual and collective freedoms are not only preconditions of human self-development and indispensable incentives for social progress (eg, in terms of learning, development of human capacities and opportunities); they also risk destroying themselves through selfish abuses of power unless all governance powers are constitutionally restrained by obligations to respect and protect equal freedoms and human rights (as discussed in Tables 3 and 4 and the related text). The ingenuity of Ulysses (whom some myths describe as the son of Sisyphus in view of the mythical cleverness of both) explains why constitutional self-restraints ('tying one's hands to the mast'), including cosmopolitan rights of 'market citizens' (eg, under EU law and BIT's), offer the most democratic way out of this dilemma of constant human antagonism eluding effective parliamentary control. The fact that – in order to limit the inherent tendencies of economic and political markets to destroy themselves through abuses of power – more and more governments adopt national competition laws and democratic constitutions illustrates the human capacity to learn through 'trial and error' how to protect public goods and overcome the 'paradoxes of liberty', ie, that the effectiveness of individual and collective freedoms of citizens depends on their constitutional and judicial restraints.

Janus and the need for cosmopolitan protection of foreigners

As the 'sovereign equality of states' will remain a constitutional foundation of UN law, the related discrimination of foreigners inside national communities needs to be attenuated by human rights, cosmopolitan rights and international 'market freedoms' for mutually beneficial cooperation among citizens across frontiers. The related tensions between equal human rights, unequal distribution of resources inside and among human communities, territorial fragmentation of legal systems and multilevel governance of the globally integrated world economy will remain perennial challenges of IEL calling for coherent 'constitutional principles of justice'. The Roman god Janus – guarding the inside as well as the outside of doors – symbolizes this perennial challenge of reconciling diverse constitutional communities and cosmopolitan rights of foreigners and 'the others'. The Lisbon Treaty's requirements of non-discriminatory treatment of EU citizens (*cf* Articles 18 ff TFEU), and the EU's positive obligations 'to eliminate inequalities, and to promote equality, between men and women' (Article 8 TFEU) and 'combat discrimination' (Article 10 TFEU), aim at reconciling the outside with the inside in mutually beneficial ways. The ECJ continues to progressively extend the scope of the general and specific EC prohibitions (eg, in Article 12 EC) of 'discrimination on grounds of nationality' to ever more areas of EC law, far beyond the single market paradigm. The Lisbon Treaty, for example by transforming the 'equality rights' of the Charter of Fundamental Rights (Articles 20 ff) into positive EU law, defines the 'European identity' in uniquely egalitarian, cosmopolitan and rights-based ways. In conformity with Robert Schumann's famous Declaration of May 1950 that Europe 'will be built through concrete achievements which first create a *de facto* solidarity', the progressive realization of the egalitarian and redistributive dimensions of European integration has been accompanied by the development of a European civic identity, inducing citizens, governments and courts 'to extend civic solidarity beyond their respective national borders with the goal of achieving mutual inclusion'.[34]

Kantian multilevel constitutionalism as incentive for 'cosmopolitan public reason' and for protecting international public goods

As discussed in chapter III, Kant conceived multilevel constitutionalism as an incentive for individual and democratic 'enlightenment'[35] by encouraging citizens to engage in mutually beneficial, cosmopolitan cooperation, antagonistic 'struggles for their rights' and multilevel, constitutional protection of international peace. Chapter VII described the multilevel judicial protection of human rights, fundamental freedoms and social rights in the EU and EEA, and their progressive extension to all EU citizens across the EU, as the main reason for the democratic legitimacy, support by citizens and legal effectiveness of rights-based European economic law. Also inside the EU, the differentiation between private goods to be produced in private markets, and collective production of 'national public goods', regional 'club goods' and 'global public goods' remains

[34] On this need for developing a European identity see J Habermas, *The Divided West* (Cambridge: Polity, 2006) ch 6.

[35] See (n 4).

contested, as illustrated by the controversies over European regulation of 'sovereign debts' of eurozone member countries and of international migration into the EU of 'economic refugees' from African countries. In many areas like environmental policies and international adjudication, the EU has become the international leader for protecting international public goods. Yet, the popular referenda rejecting the 2004 Treaty establishing a Constitution for Europe, the Lisbon Treaty's shelving of the 'symbols of the Union' (as defined in Article I-8 of the 2004 Treaty Constitution), and its requirement to 'respect the equality of Member States before the Treaties as well as their national identities' and 'territorial integrity' (Article 4 TEU) reveal the political limits of multilevel constitutionalism: the EU integration project remains based on non-discriminatory competition (eg, in the single market) among citizens wishing to preserve diverse EU member states and distinct national peoples. Just as reconciliation of the cosmopolitan human rights principles of EU law with exclusive, national and EU citizenship principles will remain a constant constitutional challenge inside the EU (eg, in the detention of illegal immigrants, constitutional tolerance vis-à-vis Muslim minorities inside EU member states, recognition of non-territorial nationality claims by the Roma people and other minorities), so will reconciliation of universal human rights, national constitutions and exclusionary national and international discrimination remain a perennial challenge of IEL.[36]

The continued existence of 'failed UN member states' without effective governance (such as Afghanistan and Somalia), like the international economic and environmental crises discussed in chapter I, illustrate that – without additional struggles by citizens and 'human rights revolutions' – equal human rights and 'sustainable development' for all will remain a cosmopolitan dream in many countries. As explained in chapter VI, constitutional prioritization of equal freedoms as 'first principle of justice' for promoting 'development as freedom'[37] at national and transnational levels must be accompanied by social 'difference principles' justifying distributive social rights and equitable 'burden sharing' arrangements; this study emphasized that the 'first principle of justice' must be construed in conformity with the 'indivisibility' of human rights as also including 'positive, cosmopolitan freedoms' necessary for human self-development. Development assistance responding to basic human needs and 'capacity-building' may be necessary for poor countries joining the collective supply of global public goods (eg, capacity-building for LLDCs as a precondition for their effective participation in UN human rights conventions and for realizing the opportunities of WTO trade liberalization agreements). As the costs of inaction risk being much higher than the costs of preventive actions, the economic and political pressures for resolving the procedural and substantive 'collective action problems' impeding the supply of so many international public goods are bound to increase. The elaboration of more comprehensive legal theories and practices for multilevel regulation of international public goods is the most difficult challenge of international and constitutional legal systems in the twenty-first century. The needed

[36] *cf* the General Comment No 20 on 'Non-Discrimination in Economic, Social and Cultural Rights', adopted by the UN Committee on Economic, Social and Cultural Rights in May 2009, UN Doc E/C.12/GC/20 (10 June 2009).

[37] *cf* A Sen (2000), who emphasizes the mutually reinforcing synergies among five different types of 'instrumental freedoms'. B Chimni, 'The Sen Conception of Development and Contemporary International Law Discourse: Some Parallels' (2008) 1 *The Law and Development Review* criticizes Sen for not identifying the legal means for implementing his development conception. See also: N Schrijver, *The Evolution of Sustainable Development in International Law* (Leiden: Martinus Nijhoff, 2008); AM Alavi, *Legalization of Development in the WTO: Between Law and Politics* (Alphen aan den Rijn: Kluwer Law International, 2009).

reforms of the procedures, incentives, financing, substantive principles, multilevel institutions and regulatory instruments for the collective supply of international public goods will require 'multicountry, multilevel, and often multisector and multiactor processes'[38] that elude 'one size fits all models'. Just as there are many diverse kinds of 'global public goods' with diverse regulatory tasks, chapter I discussed many regulatory alternatives for providing public goods, for instance through international networks of regulatory agencies, joint intergovernmental production in the framework of multilateral organizations, or 'privatization' of the supply as in the case of the private Internet Corporation for Assigned Names and Numbers (ICANN) offering worldwide administration of website addresses under the supervision of the US government and in cooperation with WIPO.[39] Yet, this study also identified a number of 'constitutional principles' that appear essential for successful supply of interdependent public goods:

- Chapters II to VI argued that 'human rights coherence' and multilevel constitutional protection of cosmopolitan rights are indispensable constitutional foundations for IEL in the twenty-first century. Yet, as recalled by the introductory motto of the 2004 Treaty establishing a Constitution for Europe – 'united in diversity' (*e pluribus unum*), multilevel constitutionalism must remain based on respect for legitimate 'constitutional pluralism', the 'principle of subsidiarity', and the inevitably limited 'overlapping consensus' among rational citizens and governments with diverse value preferences and different constitutional and cultural traditions.
- The ever more dynamic development of IEL through judicial interpretations by national and international courts supports the view of Rawls that – 'in a constitutional regime with judicial review – public reason is the reason of its supreme court'; it is of constitutional importance for the 'overlapping, constitutional consensus' necessary for a stable and just society among free, equal and rational citizens who tend to be deeply divided by conflicting moral, religious and philosophical doctrines.[40] The increasing judicial protection of 'market freedoms', 'trading rights', 'investor rights', other private property rights, labour rights, human rights and cosmopolitan rights in IEL confirms the European experience that judicial 'common law approaches' focusing on protection of 'constitutional principles' common to different national legal systems are likely to be more successful than over-ambitious codification of 'treaty constitutions', as illustrated by the 2004 Treaty on a Constitution for Europe. Intergovernmental statements as in the Preamble to the EEA Agreement, according to which the 30 EEA member states are 'convinced of the important role that individuals will play in the European Economic Area through the exercise of the rights conferred on them by this Agreement and through the judicial defence of these rights'[41] like recognition of the EU law principles of 'legal primacy' and 'direct effect' of 'market freedoms' and 'citizen rights' will remain rare beyond Europe.[42] In view of the imperfections of UN law

[38] See: I Kaul et al (2003) 13.

[39] On the diverse forms of international cooperation for collectively supplying international public goods see: Kaul et al (2003) 11 ff. Also the national and international designs and composite nature ('building blocks') of global public goods (eg, as the sum of national public goods plus international cooperation) may be diverse.

[40] Rawls (1993) 231 ff.

[41] Agreement on the European Economic Area, 1994 OJ L/13.

[42] In the EFTA Court case E-9/97, *Sveinbjörnsdottir v Iceland*, [1998] EFTA Court Reports, 95, the EFTA Court 'notes that the provisions of the EEA Agreement are, to a great extent, intended for the benefit of individuals and economic operators throughout the European Economic Area. Therefore, the proper functioning of the EEA Agreement is dependent on those individuals and economic operators being able to rely on the

and IEL, countries rightly insist on their national sovereignty of regulating the 'domestic law effects' of international rights and obligations in diverse ways depending on their national constitutional traditions. Yet, China's commitment – in its 2001 Protocol on Accession to the WTO – to legal protection of individual trading rights, intellectual property rights and rights of access to domestic courts, like China's increasing participation in UN human rights instruments, illustrate that countries may recognize the benefits of using international law for domestic reforms strengthening rule of law and individual rights of their citizens.[43]

- Multilevel constitutionalism offers an endless variety of procedural, substantive and institutional methods of protecting individual rights in the international economic cooperation among citizens as well as among governments without recourse to supranational 'federal constructs', which reasonable citizens distrust. Just as a unitarian 'United States of Europe' has turned out to be neither politically feasible nor desirable, so has nationalist discourse ignoring the past 'governance failures' in European history become replaced by a cosmopolitan 'European public reason'. Also in European integration law, the emergence of 'cosmopolitan IEL' for the reciprocal opening of national markets, the regulation of 'market failures' and the collective supply of international public goods for the benefit of citizens remains embedded in national constitutional democracies with diverse constitutional traditions and identities. The legitimate diversity of international economic law principles of 'social justice' at national and international levels is an inevitable consequence of the legitimate diversity of multilevel protection of human rights and constitutional democracies. Just as European integration law evolved in response to the political pragmatism of Jean Monnet and other founding fathers of European integration favouring 'functionally limited regulation' of certain areas of economic integration (eg, beginning with the coal and steel sectors before launching a 'common market'), so will political and legal 'trial and error' and pragmatic renunciation of 'constitutional dogmatism' remain a *finalité* of IEL.
- Multilevel governance in distant international organizations and intergovernmental networks for the collective supply of international public goods risk always remaining contested in view of their inevitable complexity, informality, low visibility, lack of transparency and detachment from citizens, from national parliaments and local democratic discourses. Yet, they can enhance multilevel 'checks and balances' among national and international governance institutions, offer citizens and governments transnational remedies against adverse 'external effects' of foreign policy measures, and *increase* legal and judicial accountability and democratic participation of citizens

rights thus intended for their benefit. The Court concludes from the foregoing considerations that the EEA Agreement is an international treaty *sui generis* which contains a distinct legal order of its own'. Yet, in most EEA member countries, the judicial protection of individual rights derived from EEA law is based on domestic implementing legislation ('indirect effect') rather than directly on EEA law. On NAFTA jurisprudence see: JA Huerta-Goldman, 'Trade Remedies Disputes – Reciprocal Relationships between WTO and NAFTA Tribunals' in F Fontanelli, G Martinico and P Carozza (2009) 299–318.

[43] China signed the ICESCR on 27 October 1997 and ratified it on 27 March 2001, subject to a reservation with regard to trade union rights and the right to strike; it also signed the ICCPR on 5 October 1998 and continues to claim in its 2008 notification to the UN Human Rights Council that China 'is carrying out necessary legislative, judiciary and administrative reforms to create conditions for early ratification' (UN Doc A/HRC/WG.6/4/CHN/1, para 11). Yet, like the United States and other hegemonic countries, China emphasizes national sovereignty and seems to be reluctant to allow Chinese citizens to invoke international treaties in domestic courts.

on the basis of cosmopolitan human, economic, social and labour rights.[44] Giovanni Sartori, in his classic *Theory of Democracy Revisited*, criticized the term democracy as a misleading and pompous 'name for something that does not exist';[45] the existing national and international rules and institutions promoting democratic rights, democratic procedures, parliamentary, participatory and deliberative democracy fall inevitably short of the normative ideals of 'governance by discussion' and 'government of the people, by the people, and for the people'. Most citizens remain 'rationally ignorant' of most transnational governance problems, and 'elitist democracy' has been described as the worst system of governance with the exception of all the others. Yet, even if democratic accountability of worldwide institutions risks always remaining inadequate, the historical failures of all non-democratic governance alternatives make rights-based, democratic participation and individual self-governance at all levels of human affairs inconvertible, normative ideals.

- European law has proven that diverse forms of 'transnational constitutional democracy' are politically practical – provided the four normative premises of democratic and economic constitutionalism are respected also in multilevel economic governance beyond state borders: First, the value premise of normative individualism (ie, that governments can derive value only from the free and informed consent of the governed individuals) applies also to *transnational* governance and requires *international* markets protected by transnational rule of law no less than rules-based, national markets as decentralized information and coordination mechanisms, without which citizens and their governments can neither know nor efficiently satisfy individual preferences. Secondly, the diversity of individual preferences, the scarcity of resources and the inevitable ubiquity of conflicts – both *within* individuals (eg, between their rational egoism and limited social reasonableness) as well as *among* individuals (eg, in their rational pursuit of self-interests) – require constitutional and judicial restraints of the Hobbesian war of each against all in *transnational* relations no less than *inside* states. As respect for normative individualism makes consensus among citizens on the outcomes of economic and political competition impossible, human reasonableness requires non-discriminatory conditions of competition based on constitutional protection of a limited 'overlapping consensus' on constitutional rules of justice. Thirdly, as explained by constitutional economics,[46] international division of labour based on consumer-driven market competition (as the most efficient information, allocation and coordination mechanism for increasing individual and social productivity and consumer welfare) depends on constitutional guarantees of the 'constitutive principles' of market economies (like freedom of contract, private property, monetary stability, freedom of profession and other market freedoms), as well as of 'regulative principles' of market economies (like competition, environmental, labour and social rules), empowering citizens to engage in mutually beneficial market exchanges subject

[44] On increased pluralism and accountability advantages in multilevel governance (eg, due to emergence of transnational 'epistemic communities' of knowledge-based expert groups challenging nationalist discrimination) see: J Rosenau, 'Strong Demand, Huge Supply: Governance in an Emerging Epoch' in I Bache and M Flinders (eds), *Multi-level Governance* (Oxford: OUP, 2004) 31 ff.

[45] G Sartori, *The Theory of Democracy Revisited. Part One: The Contemporary Debate* (Chatham: Chatham House, 1987) 7. On criticism of principal-agent models of democratic accountability see also: R Dahl, *Democracy and its Critics* (New Haven: Yale University Press, 1991).

[46] *cf* ch VII, section 2.

to rules and governmental limitations of 'market failures'. The inadequate constitutional and legal protection of a mutually beneficial, international division of labour beyond Europe and other RTAs is a major reason for the unnecessary poverty and exploitation, by abuses of private as well as public power, of more than one billion people living in poor countries on one dollar or less per day. Fourthly, in view of the ubiquity of abuses of private and public power, 'enabling constitutions' must not only be complemented by 'limiting constitutions' constraining abuses of power by governmental and private actors; there is also a need for 're-embedding global economic liberalism' by stronger guarantees of human, social, labour and other cosmopolitan rights, which may be based on 'supplementary constitutional instruments' like regional human rights conventions. Just as democratic governance for the collective supply of *national* and *European* public goods has proven sustainable only in mutually agreed frameworks of multilevel constitutional restraints, so can non-discriminatory competition in *international* markets remain effective only to the extent that market actors and market regulators are constitutionally restrained from abusing their powers. *Transnational* constitutionalism – not only in Europe but also beyond – is necessary for reforming existing 'constitutional failures' and for enabling governments to collectively supply *international* public goods.

Bibliography of Repeatedly Quoted Books

F Abbott, C Breining and T Cottier (eds), *International Trade and Human Rights* (Ann Arbor: Michigan University Press, 2006).

R Alexy, *A Theory of Fundamental Rights* (Oxford: OUP, 2002).

Aristotle, *The Politics and the Constitution of Athens*, S Everson (ed) (Cambridge: CUP, 1996).

S Barrett, *Why Cooperate? The Incentive to Supply Global Public Goods* (Oxford: OUP, 2007).

L Bartels and F Ortino (eds), *Regional Trade Agreements and the WTO Legal System* (Oxford: OUP, 2006).

DM Beatty, *The Ultimate Rule of Law* (Oxford: OUP, 2004).

PHF Bekker, R Dolzer and M Waibel (eds), *Making Transnational Law Work in the Global Economy. Essays in Honour of D Vagts* (Cambridge: CUP, 2010).

W Benedek, K de Freyter and F Marella (eds), *Economic Globalisation and Human Rights* (Cambridge: CUP, 2008).

S Besson, *The Morality of Conflict. Reasonable Disagreement and the Law* (Oxford: Hart Publishing, 2005).

S Besson and J Tasioulas (eds), *The Philosophy of International Law* (Oxford: OUP, 2010).

F Biermann, P Pattberg and F Zelli (eds), *Global Climate Governance Beyond 2012* (Cambridge: CUP, 2010).

A von Bogdandy and J Bast (eds), *Principles of European Constitutional Law* (Oxford: Hart Publishing, 2006).

G Bongiovanni, G Sartor and C Valentini (eds), *Reasonableness and Law* (Heidelberg: Springer Verlag, 2009).

G Brennan and JM Buchanan, *The Reason of Rules. Constitutional Political Economy* (Cambridge: CUP, 1985).

A Buchanan, *Justice, Legitimacy and Self-Determination. Moral Foundations for International Law* (Oxford: OUP, 2004).

G de Búrca and J Scott (eds), *The EU and the WTO: Legal and Constitutional Issues* (Oxford: Hart Publishing, 2001).

P Capps, *Human Dignity and the Foundations of International Law* (Oxford: Hart Publishing, 2009).

DZ Cass, *The Constitutionalization of the WTO. Legitimacy, Democracy and Community in the International Trading System* (Oxford: OUP, 2005).

T Cottier and M Elsig (eds), *Governing the World Trade Organization. Past, Present and Beyond Doha* (Cambridge: CUP, 2011).

T Cottier and P Mavroidis (eds), *The Role of the Judge in International Trade Regulation. Experience and Lessons for the WTO* (Ann Arbor: Michigan University Press, 2003).

T Cottier, J Pauwelyn and E Bürgi (eds), *Human Rights and International Trade* (Oxford: OUP, 2005).

WJ Davey and JH Jackson (eds), *The Future of International Economic Law* (Oxford: OUP, 2008).

R Dolzer and C Schreuer, *Principles of International Investment Law* (Oxford: OUP, 2008).

JL Dunoff and JP Trachtman (eds), *Ruling the World? Constitutionalism, International Law and Global Governance* (Cambridge: CUP, 2009).

PM Dupuy, F Francioni and EU Petersmann (eds), *Human Rights in International Investment Law and Arbitration* (Oxford: OUP, 2009).

R Dworkin, *Taking Rights Seriously* (London: Duckworth, 1977).

R Dworkin, *Justice in Robes* (Cambridge: Harvard University Press, 2006).

M Emberland, *The Human Rights of Companies: Exploring the Structure of ECHR Protection* (Oxford: OUP, 2006).

B Fassbender, *The United Nations Charter as the Constitution of the International Community* (Leiden: Nijhoff Publishers, 2009).

A Follesdal, RA Wessel and J Wouters (eds), *Multilevel Regulation and the EU* (Leiden: Nijhoff, 2008).

F Fontanelli, G Martinico and P Carozza (eds), *Shaping Rule of Law through Dialogue. International and Supranational Expereiences* (Groningen: Europa Law Publishing, 2009).

R Forst, *Das Recht auf Rechtfertigung. Elemente einer konstruktivistischen Theorie der Gerechtigkeit* (Frankfurt: Suhrkamp Verlag, 2007).

TM Franck, *Fairness in International Law and Institutions* (Oxford: OUP, 1995).

F Francioni (ed), *Access to Justice as a Human Right* (Oxford: OUP, 2007).

CJ Friedrich, *The Philosophy of Law in Historical Perspective* (Chicago: Chicago University Press, 1963).

W Friedmann, *The Changing Structures of International Law* (London: Sweet & Maxwell, 1964).

LL Fuller, *The Morality of Law*, 2nd edn (New Haven: Yale University Press, 1969).

FJ Garcia, *Trade, Inequality and Justice: Toward a Liberal Theory of Just Trade* (New York: Transnational Publishers, 2003).

V Gauri and DM Brunks (eds), *Courting Social Justice. Judicial Enforcement of Social and Economic Rights in the Developing World* (Cambridge: CUP, 2008).

DJ Gerber, *Global Competition: Law, Markets and Globalization* (Oxford: OUP, 2010).

JL Goldsmith and EA Posner, *The Limits of International Law* (Oxford: OUP, 2005).

I Govaere, R Quick and M Bronckers (eds), *Trade and Competition Law in the EU and Beyond* (Cheltenham: Edward Elgar, 2011).

J Habermas, *Between Facts and Norms – Contributions to a Discourse Theory of Law and Democracy* (Cambridge: MIT Press, 1996).

J Harrison, *The Human Rights Impact of the WTO* (Oxford: Hart Publishing, 2007).

HLA Hart, *The Concept of Law*, 2nd edn (Oxford: OUP, 1994).

FA Hayek, *The Constitution of Liberty* (London: Routledge, 1960).

A Héritier and M Rhodes (eds), *New Modes of Governance in Europe. Governing in the Shadow of Hierarchy* (Basingstoke: Palgrave Macmillan, 2011).

H Hestermeyer, *Human Rights and the WTO. The Case of Patents and Access to Medicines* (Oxford: OUP, 2007).

M Hilf and EU Petersmann (eds), *National Constitutions and International Economic Law* (The Hague: Kluwer Publishers, 1993).

RE Howard-Hassmann and CE Welch (eds), *Economic Rights in Canada and the United States* (Philadelphia: University of Philadelphia Press, 2006).

GC Hufbauer, S Charnovitz and J Kim, *Global Warming and the World Trading System* (Washington: Institute for International Economics, 2009).

JH Jackson, *The World Trade Organisation: Constitution and Jurisprudence* (London: Royal Institute of International Affairs, 1998).

FG Jacobs, *The Sovereignty of Law. The European Way* (Cambridge: CUP, 2007).

C Joerges and EU Petersmann (eds), *Constitutionalism, Multilevel Trade Governance and Social Regulation* (Oxford: Hart Publishing, 2006).

—— (eds), *Constitutionalism, Multilevel Trade Governance and International Economic Law*, 2nd edn (Oxford: Hart Publishing, 2011).

S Joseph, D Kinley and J Waincymer (eds), *The WTO and Human Rights* (Cheltenham: Edward Elgar, 2009).

MT Kamminga and M Scheinin (eds), *The Impact of Human Rights Law on General International Law* (Oxford: OUP, 2009).

I Kant, *Political Writings*, H Reiss (ed) (Cambridge: CUP, 1970).
I Kaul, I Grunberg and MA Stern (eds), *Global Public Goods. International Cooperation in the 21st Century* (Oxford: OUP, 1999).
I Kaul et al (eds), *Providing Global Public Goods. Managing Globalization* (New York: OUP, 2003).
H Keller and A Stone Sweet (eds), *A Europe of Rights. The Impact of the ECHR on National Legal Systems* (Oxford: OUP, 2008).
H Kelsen, *The General Theory of Law and State* (Cambridge: Harvard University Press 1949).
——, *Principles of International Law* (New York: Rhinehart, 1952).
D Kinley, *Civilizing Globalization. Human Rights and the Global Economy* (Cambridge: CUP, 2009).
J Klabbers, A Peters and G Ulfstein, *The Constitutionalization of International Law* (Oxford: OUP, 2009).
NK Komesar, *Imperfect Alternatives: Choosing Institutions in Law, Economics and Public Policy* (Chicago: University of Chicago Press, 1994).
C Krause and M Scheinin (eds), *International Protection of Human Rights: A Textbook* (Turku: Abo Akademi University, 2009).
D Kretzmer and E Klein (eds), *The Concept of Human Dignity in Human Rights Discourse* (The Hague: Kluwer, 2002).
P Kunig, N Lau and W Meng (eds), *International Economic Law. Basic Documents*, 2nd edn (Berlin: W de Gruyter, 1993).
KE Maskus and JH Reichman (eds), *International Public Goods and Transfer of Technology Under a Globalized Intellectual Property Regime* (Cambridge: CUP, 2005).
AD Mitchell, *Legal Principles in WTO Disputes* (Cambridge: CUP, 2008).
J Morsink, *Inherent Human Rights. Philosophical Roots of the Universal Declaration* (Philadelphia: University of Philadelphia Press, 2009).
D Nicol, *The Constitutional Protection of Capitalism* (Oxford: Hart Publishing, 2010).
R Nickel (ed), *Conflict of Laws and Laws of Conflict in Europe and Beyond* (Antwerp: Intersentia, 2010).
R Nozick, *Anarchy, State and Utopia* (Oxford: Blackwell, 1974).
MC Nussbaum, *Frontiers of Justice. Disability, Nationality, Species Membership* (Cambridge: Harvard University Press, 2006).
M Olson, *The Logic of Collective Action: Public Goods and the Theory of Groups*, 2nd edn (Cambridge: Harvard University Press, 1971).
F Ortino and EU Petersmann (eds), *The WTO Dispute Settlement System 1995–2003* (The Hague: Kluwer Publisher, 2004).
G Palombella and N Walker (eds), *Relocating the Rule of Law* (Oxford: Hart Publishing, 2009).
J Paulsson, *Denial of Justice in International Law* (Cambridge: CUP, 2005).
J Pauwelyn, *Conflict of Norms in Public International Law: How WTO Law Relates to Other Rules of International Law* (Cambridge: CUP, 2003).
EU Petersmann, *Constitutional Functions and Constitutional Problems of International Economic Law. International and Domestic Foreign Trade Law and Foreign Trade Policy in the United States, the European Community and Switzerland* (Fribourg: Fribourg University Press and Oxford/San Francisco: Westview Press, 1991).
—— *International and European Trade and Environmental Law after the Uruguay Round* (The Hague: Kluwer, 1995).
—— *The GATT/WTO Dispute Settlement System. International Law, International Organizations and Dispute Settlement* (The Hague: Kluwer, 1997).
——(ed), *Reforming the World Trading System. Legitimacy, Efficiency and Democratic Governance* (Oxford: OUP, 2005).
EU Petersmann and M Pollack (eds), *Transatlantic Economic Disputes. The EU, the US and the WTO* (Oxford: OUP, 2003).

T Pogge, *World Poverty and Human Rights* (Cambridge: Polity Press, 2003).
EA Posner, *The Perils of Global Legalism* (Chicago: Chicago University Press, 2009).
AH Qureshi and AR Ziegler, *International Economic Law*, 2nd edn (London: Sweet & Maxwell, 2007).
BG Ramcharan (ed), *Judicial Protection of Economic, Social and Cultural Rights* (Leiden: Nijhoff, 2005).
J Rawls, *A Theory of Justice* (Oxford: OUP, 1971).
—— *Political Liberalism* (Cambridge: Harvard University Press, 1993).
——*A Theory of Justice*, revised edn (Cambridge: Harvard University Press, 1999).
——*The Law of Peoples* (Cambridge: Harvard University Press, 1999; cited: Rawls 1999).
—— *Justice as Fairness: A Restatement* (ed by E Kelly, New York: Columbia University Press, 2001)
J Raz, *The Authority of Law* (Oxford: Clarendon Press, 1979).
T Sandefur, *The Right to Earn a Living. Economic Freedom and the Law* (Washington: Cato Institute, 2010).
A Sen, *Development as Freedom* (New York: A Knopf, 2000).
——*Rationality and Freedom* (Cambridge: Harvard University Press, 2002).
——*The Idea of Justice* (Cambridge: Harvard University Press, 2009).
SW Schill, *The Multilateralization of International Investment Law* (Cambridge: CUP, 2009).
BH Siegan, *Economic Liberties and the Constitution* (Chicago: The Univerrsity of Chicago Press, 1980).
AM Slaughter, *A New World Order* (Princeton: Princeton University Press, 2004).
JE Stiglitz, *Freefall. America, Free Markets and the Sinking of the World Economy* (New York: WW Norton & Co, 2010).
Y Taniguchi, A Yanovich and J Bohanes (eds), *The WTO in the 21st Century: Dispute Settlement, Multilateral Negotiations, Regional Integration* (Cambridge: CUP, 2007).
F Teson, *A Philosophy of International Law* (Boulder: Westview Press, 1998).
JP Trachtman, *The Economic Structure of International Law* (Cambridge: Harvard University Press, 2008).
——*The International Law of Economic Migration. Toward the Fourth Freedom* (Kalamazoo: Upjohn Institute, 2009).
DM Trubek and A Santos (eds), *The New Law and Economic Development. A Critical Appraisal* (Cambridge: CUP, 2006).
VJ Vanberg, *The Constitution of Markets: Essays in Political Economy* (London: Routledge, 2001).
I van Damme, *Treaty Interpretation by the WTO Appellate Body* (Oxford: OUP, 2009).
N Walker (ed), *Sovereignty in Transition* (Oxford: Hart Publishing, 2003).
R Wolfrum (ed), *Max Planck Encyclopedia of Public International Law* (Oxford: OUP online edn, 2010).
S Wheatley, *The Democratic Legitimacy of International Law* (Oxford: Hart Publishing, 2010).
S Zamora and RA Brand (eds), *Basic Documents of International Economic Law*, vols I and II (Chicago: Commerce Clearing House, 1990).

Index

Introductory Note

References such as '138–9' indicate (not necessarily continuous) discussion of a topic across a range of pages. Wherever possible in the case of topics with many references, these have either been divided into sub-topics or only the most significant discussions of the topic are listed. Because the entire volume is about 'international economic law', the use of this term (and certain others occurring throughout the work) as an entry point has been restricted. Information will be found under the corresponding detailed topics.